Sign Language and Linguistic Universals

Sign languages are of great interest to linguists, because, although they are the product of the same brain, their physical transmission differs greatly from that of spoken languages. In this pioneering and original study, Wendy Sandler and Diane Lillo-Martin compare sign languages with spoken languages, in order to seek the universal properties they share. Drawing on general linguistic theory, they describe and analyze sign language structure, showing linguistic universals in the phonology, morphology, and syntax of sign language, while also revealing non-universal aspects of its structure that must be attributed to its physical transmission system. No prior background in sign language linguistics is assumed, and numerous pictures are provided to make descriptions of signs and facial expressions accessible to readers. Engaging and informative, *Sign Language and Linguistic Universals* will be invaluable to linguists, psychologists, and all those interested in sign languages, linguistic theory, and the universal properties of human languages.

WENDY SANDLER is Professor of Linguistics in the Department of English Language and Literature at the University of Haifa, Israel, and has been investigating the phonology and morphology of American Sign Language and Israeli Sign Language for almost twenty years. She has previously published *Phonological Representation of the Sign* (1989) and *Language in Space: A Window on Israeli Sign Language* (co-authored with Irit Meir, 2004).

DIANE LILLO-MARTIN is Professor and Head in the Department of Linguistics, University of Connecticut, and Senior Research Scientist at the Haskins Laboratories, with research interests in both the structure and acquisition of American Sign Language. She has previously published *Universal Grammar and American Sign Language: Setting the Null Argument Parameters* (1991) and *Linguistic Theory and Language Acquisition* (co-authored with Stephen Crain, 1999).

Sign Language and Linguistic Universals

WENDY SANDLER
DIANE LILLO-MARTIN

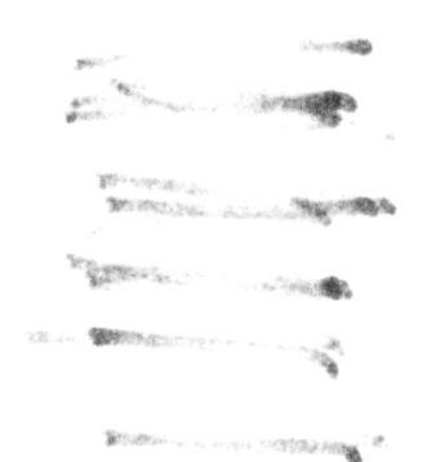

CAMBRIDGE
UNIVERSITY PRESS

CAMBRIDGE UNIVERSITY PRESS
Cambridge, New York, Melbourne, Madrid, Cape Town, Singapore, São Paulo

CAMBRIDGE UNIVERSITY PRESS
The Edinburgh Building, Cambridge CB2 2RU, UK

Published in the United States of America by Cambridge University Press, New York

www.cambridge.org
Information on this title: www.cambridge.org/9780521482486

First published 2006

Printed in the United Kingdom at the University Press, Cambridge

A catalogue record for this book is available from the British Library

ISBN-13 978-0-521-48248-6 hardback
ISBN-10 0-521-48248-8 hardback
ISBN-13 978-0-521-48395-7 paperback
ISBN-10 0-521-48395-6 paperback

We dedicate this book to our parents

Milton Sandler (1919–2005)	Clifford LeRoy Lillo
Bernice Sandler	Elizabeth Mae Lillo (1924–2004)

Contents

Preface

Natural sign languages are clearly very similar to natural spoken languages in many significant ways. Sign languages are conventional communication systems that arise spontaneously in all deaf communities. They are acquired during childhood through normal exposure without instruction. Sign languages effectively fulfill the same social and mental functions as spoken languages, and they can even be simultaneously interpreted into and from spoken languages in real time. These basic common characteristics lead to a compelling expectation: that natural languages in the two modalities will be similar to one another from a strictly linguistic point of view as well, in both content and organization.

But how similar are sign languages and spoken languages *really*? When we attempt to describe and analyze morphology, syntax, and phonology in sign language, are we wandering in the realm of metaphor? Or are we traveling in familiar territory? By "sign language phonology," for example, do we only mean that sign languages have a taxonomy of formational components? Or do we really mean they have a finite set of meaningless contrastive units that combine in constrained ways to form meaningful morphemes and words, and that the mental representations of these lexical items may differ predictably and discretely from their actual realization? The difference between the latter characterization and the former is the difference between metaphorical analogy with spoken language phonology and concrete comparison. More than that, the latter characterization describes a linguistic system and the former, well, almost anything.

We think that the way to address this question is to take linguistic theory seriously, as a theory about universal properties of human language, and to use it in the investigation of natural human languages in a different physical modality. It is this approach that we take in this book, as described in detail in Unit 1. The more rigorous the specific theory or subtheory appealed to in a particular analysis, the more convincing the cross-modality similarities that it reveals. And wherever this approach uncovers differences, it exposes the effects of the physical modality on each of the two natural language systems. The goal, then, is to appeal to general theories of linguistic structure to analyze the morphology, phonology, and syntax of sign languages, and in so doing, to arrive at a pool of properties that are truly universal. The results of that endeavor form the content of Units 2–4. Properties attributed to the modality of transmission are dealt with in Unit 5.

Throughout, we try to make the sign language phenomena and analyses clear and accessible, so that linguists can sink their teeth into them, whether or not they work in the same theoretical frameworks as those presented, and whether or not they have a sign language background. To the same end, the book is profusely illustrated with examples. We also try to avoid analyses that are overly theory-internal, in the hope that the accounts presented will be informative in their own right, and that the properties ascribed to sign language will be valid, regardless of the particular theoretical framework with which they are explored.

The field of sign language research is dynamic and prolific. Many phenomena have been described by different researchers from different points of view, but often without clarifying areas of convergence or divergence. Different models of various aspects of sign language structure abound as well. Even if it were possible to summarize all the work in the field, such an effort would be ill-advised, as it would likely leave the reader in a hopeless maze. Therefore, the book is not intended to be an exhaustive overview of the field, and much work has been left out.

The field has also been branching out and becoming specialized. There is a large and growing body of research in many areas such as psycholinguistics, acquisition, neurolinguistics, sociolinguistics, and bilingualism. Unfortunately, we were not able to include discussion of the many important and influential works in these areas. We have limited our discussion to studies which deal with the linguistic structure of sign language from the perspective of theoretical linguistics.

Our strategy has been twofold. First, we select phenomena that are important for understanding the structure of sign language and its relation to spoken language. Second, in accounting for those phenomena, we focus mainly on analyses that are (a) explanatory, (b) informed by general linguistic theory, and (c) part of more comprehensive sign language models. In this way, the same models are returned to at different points throughout the book, making it possible, we hope, for a coherent view of sign language linguistic structure to emerge, and for certain prominent models of that structure to be compared. We have attempted to include a fairly wide range of phenomena even though by necessity some works of relevance and interest have not been selected. This strategy is guided by our stated goal: to discover linguistic universals by viewing signed and spoken languages through the medium of linguistic theories that purport to capture such universals.

We are governed by the same strategy in selecting which sign languages to report on from among the ever growing list of sign languages being studied around the world. Our main focus is American Sign Language (ASL) because that language has been the subject of the most intensive theoretical research over the longest period of time so far. But theoretical research is on the rise in other places, and research on Israeli Sign Language (ISL), Sign Language of the Netherlands (SLN), Brazilian Sign Language (LSB), and other sign languages will also be reported.

Work on one sign language often reveals properties common to sign languages in general. There are two reasons for this. First, the modality appears to influence certain key aspects of the structure of these languages, though this does not mean that the structures so influenced necessarily fall outside the predictions of general linguistic theory (see Unit 5). Second, the field of sign language research is not very old, and for the most part we have not yet arrived at the level of detail that will ultimately distinguish grammars cross-sign-linguistically in a significant way. Therefore, at this point in the development of the field, analyses of specific sign languages shed light on the structure of languages in this modality more generally.

Another choice was to refrain from taking a position here on metatheoretical issues such as innateness and cognitive modularity. Such issues are, of course, of great importance, as they relate to the question of *why* there should be linguistic universals. However, our approach at this stage has been to contribute to the scientific discourse a detailed account of what we take those universals to be, and to separate them from characteristics that are widespread within each natural language modality, but not shared by the two.

We hope that this book will be read and used by linguists who are familiar with sign languages and those who are not. Because of the surface differences between sign and oral languages, and the concomitant differences in jargon and assumptions, too often researchers unfamiliar with sign languages find this field inaccessible or irrelevant. We believe it is highly relevant, and thus aim to make it accessible. Exposure to sign language linguistics can be like looking into a kaleidoscope. A multitude of colorful fragments fleetingly arranges itself into one pattern and then dissolves into another – with every slight turn of the barrel, another mysterious and alluring array presents itself. We hope that this volume will serve to make the patterns more clearly focused and less elusive, leading to an increase in research on sign languages that will benefit the study of theoretical linguistics and of language more generally.

This book was written over many years, sparked by a suggestion from Harry van der Hulst that there was a gap in the theoretical sign language literature that ought to be filled. We are grateful to Harry for encouraging us to fill it. The book was written by the two authors working together in Storrs and in Haifa, and by each going it alone, at home and during extended visits elsewhere. We are deeply indebted to many colleagues, friends, and family members for making it possible.

We extend our gratitude to Mark Aronoff, Željko Bošković, Diane Brentari, Laura Downing, Karen Emmorey, Richard Meier, and Carol Padden for taking the time to read large parts of the manuscript and to make thoughtful and detailed comments that were of immeasurable value to the final outcome. We are also grateful to John Kingston, Irit Meir, Carol Padden, Gunter Senft, and Rachel Sutton-Spence for discussions of data, specific concepts, and analyses. We applaud and thank Sarah Felber, who produced our index. There are others to whom the two authors wish to express gratitude individually.

WS spent 2001–2002, a critical year for book writing, on sabbatical, mostly at the University of Nijmegen, through the generosity of the Netherlands Organization for Scientific Research (NWO). I owe many thanks to colleagues on the sign language prosody project there: Onno Crasborn, Carlos Gussenhoven, Wim Emmerik, and Els van der Kooij. Thank you to Carlos Gussenhoven for being a most thoughtful and gracious host, and for teaching me a great deal about intonation and about all that I still must learn. Thanks also to researchers and students associated with the Language and Cognition Group and the Gesture Group at the Max Planck Institute for Psycholinguistics in Nijmegen, for their interest, support, and most helpful discussions, especially Nick Enfield, Marianne Gullberg, Satoro Kita, Stephen Levinson, Asli Ozürek, and Gunter Senft, and to Jennie Pyers and other members of the outstanding Sign Language Research Group that Dan Slobin organized there that year. The first two sabbatical months were spent at my alma mater, the University of Texas at Austin. Thanks to Richard Meier and his students for welcoming me to the lively sign language atmosphere at UT. I also wish to express my gratitude to my teacher Peter MacNeilage for discussions of sign language in the broader context during that period, and over the course of many years, discussions which have always been inspirational.

DLM would like to thank Željko Bošković, Deborah Chen Pichler, Gaurav Mathur, Karen Petronio, Ronice Quadros, Doreen Simons-Marques, and Sandra Wood for stimulating discussions about the structure of ASL and other sign languages which influenced portions of the text and the work on which it draws. I also extend appreciation to University of Connecticut graduate students attending my courses on the structure of ASL for their discussions and feedback on drafts of portions of the book.

As we acknowledge those with whom we have had stimulating and informative discussions, we want to single out for special mention two of our former students who have become close research colleagues. Irit Meir and Ronice Quadros worked with us first as students to be instructed and guided in the ways of theoretical linguistics. Over time, regular discussions in which the mentor leads the way became dialogues to which both teacher and student contribute. By now, our roles have morphed to that of collaborators, walking together on paths of search and discovery. Exploring the nature of a system like the grammar of sign languages is especially fruitful when ideas can be bounced off someone who shares the same background knowledge – particularly when that person is also able to tell us when an idea just isn't convincing. Thank you – *todos* – and *obrigado* for continuing to stimulate our fascination for sign linguistics.

Many thanks to Haifa research assistants Ofra Rosenstein and Svetlana Dachkovsky for their enthusiastic and capable help on this project, and to video technician Shai Davidi for always finding better and better techniques for producing the ISL pictures. We are deeply indebted to ISL research colleagues Meir Etedgi, Doron Levy, and Orna Levy who for many years have been deeply involved in the ISL research reported in this book, and who doubled as models for illustrations, together with Debi Menashe and Tali Mor. Special thanks to Carol Padden for modeling some of the ASL signs.

In Connecticut, gratitude goes to sign language research colleagues and sign models Laura Levesque, Brenda Schertz, Doreen Simons-Marques, and Sandra Wood. Invaluable technical assistance in preparing the book and the ASL illustrations was provided by Krystina Carver, Hayley Love, Angela Neff, and Serkan Şener. We also thank Ronice Quadros for providing LSB illustrations, and LSB sign model Gisele Rangel.

Financial support for the preparation of this book was provided in part by grants from the Israel Science Foundation (820/95 and 750/99–1) to Wendy Sandler, and from the US – Israel Binational Science Foundation (95–00310/2) to Wendy Sandler and Mark Aronoff. Support was also provided by a research grant from the National Institutes of Health to Diane Lillo-Martin, through Haskins Laboratories (NIDCD #00183), and by faculty grants from the University of Connecticut Research Foundation.

Our families have supported us with love, encouragement, patience, understanding, and humor through all the years that it took to produce this volume. Yoav and Hadar, and Steve, Stephanie, Amy, and Allan know how deeply grateful we are to them for helping us write this book, and we know that the best token of our appreciation is its completion!

Notation conventions

When we cite the work of others, we use their notation unless otherwise marked. Although this means that the notation used throughout the text is not uniform, we preferred to reproduce exactly the cited works rather than introduce our own interpretation of their notation.

Despite the variation found across sources, there are many conventions for sign language notation which are quite common. We provide here a summary of the conventions we have adopted. Other uses may include superscripts or subscripts where we keep the text on a single line; additional notational variants are described in the text.

SIGN	English glosses in small capital letters stand for signs with approximately the same meaning as the English word.
SIGN-SIGN	If more than one English word is required to gloss a single sign, the words are connected with hyphens.
S-I-G-N	Fingerspelling, representing each letter of a spelled-out English word by a different handshape, is indicated using hyphens.
#SIGN	Fingerspelled loan signs are represented with a preceding hatch mark.
SIGN^SIGN	Compounds are indicated with a caret between component signs.
______t	Non-manual markers are indicated by a solid line above the glosses for the signs they co-occur with. 't' indicates a topic non-manual; 'br' indicates brow raise; 'n' indicates a negative headshake; 'wh' indicates the WH-question non-manual; 'q' or 'y/n' indicates a yes/no question non-manual; 'hn' indicates head nod; 'mm' indicates the facial adverb 'with relaxed enjoyment'; 'th' indicates the facial adverb 'carelessly.'
SIGN[aspect]	When a sign is marked for an aspectual inflection, the name of that inflection is given in square brackets.

a-SIGN-b	Lower-case letters are used to indicate spatial locations. Nouns are marked with an index at the beginning of the gloss to indicate the locus with which they are associated. Verbs are marked with an index at the beginning to indicate the onset location, and/or at the end to indicate the endpoint location.
a-c-SIGN	Indices with a dash indicate a plural, in which the hand moves from locus 'a' to locus 'c.'
SIGN_i	Subscripts from the middle of the alphabet (or, in some cases, numbers) are used to indicate abstract coreference.
IX(loc)	Pointing signs, including pronouns, demonstratives, and locatives, are glossed IX (for 'index'). The object of the pointing is indicated in parentheses. Variants include PT ('point'), S/HE, THERE.
CL:C'x'	Classifiers are indicated using the abbreviation CL, followed by a symbol for the hand configuration used in the classifier, and a description of the meaning in single quotes.
*( )	An asterisk indicates an ungrammatical string. An asterisk outside parentheses indicates that the elements inside are obligatory. An asterisk inside the parentheses indicates that the elements inside are ungrammatical.
(she)	A pronoun will be included in parentheses if it is not given in the original language but is needed for a grammatical English translation.
(-them)	A pronoun within parentheses is marked with a hyphen if it is signified by verb agreement.

Unit 1

Introduction

1 One human language or two?

The study of language over the centuries has yielded a large inventory of concepts and categorizations that are commonly taken for granted. Consonants, vowels, syllables, morphemes, words, phrases, clauses, sentences, and at all levels, rules or constraints are accepted unquestioningly as the nuts and bolts of language. But how fundamental are these properties? In other words, are these and other ubiquitous properties of language genuine universals? That is the question that guides our enterprise.

We are compelled to ask this question by a deceptively simple discovery: natural human languages exist in a physical modality that is different from the one that has been studied for so many centuries – the modality of sign languages used by deaf people all over the world.

That these are natural languages in the same sense as spoken languages seems now to be beyond any doubt (see, among many others, Klima and Bellugi 1979, Wilbur 1979, Poizner, Klima, and Bellugi 1987, Lucas and Valli 1992, Sandler and Lillo-Martin 2001, Emmorey 2002). Sign languages arise spontaneously wherever deaf people have an opportunity to meet regularly. They are acquired by children raised in deaf families without instruction, and along a timetable that is similar to that of hearing children acquiring spoken language (overviews include Newport and Meier 1985, Lillo-Martin 1999a). Sign language appears as effortless and as user-friendly as its spoken counterpart. This impression of naturalness is reinforced by Bellugi and Fischer's (1972) discovery that transmission of a given proposition takes about the same time in both the manual–visual and the oral–aural modalities. They found that the general rate of transmission is the same, about one proposition every 1 to 2 seconds in both language modalities. When the signal is sped up, intelligibility breaks down in speech and in sign at the same point – at about two and a half to three times the normal rate (Fischer, Delhorne, and Reed 1999). As Emmorey (2002, p. 119) points out, this suggests "a modality independent upper limit for the ability to accelerate language processing." In sum, the way sign language is acquired and the ease and speed of its transmission strongly support the view that a single cognitive system underlies language in both modalities.

And, of course, sign languages are used for everything that spoken languages are – within the family circle, for social interaction, oratory, education, scientific exchange, introspection and dreaming, story-telling, theater, and poetry (Lane and Philip 1984, Padden and Humphries 1988, 2005). In short, whatever it is that humans are doing when they use spoken language, they are doing the same thing, in some significant sense, when they use sign language. Our goal here is to be more explicit about what is meant by "the same thing."

1.1 Separating the code from the mode: the role of linguistic theory

No serious approach to the study of sign language can be entirely atheoretical. One might adopt the hypothesis that sign language must be very much like spoken language, as it is the same human brain that is responsible for them both. An opposing hypothesis is that sign language is likely to be very different structurally from spoken language because of the different modality, despite the identity of species and function. Any of a number of variations on those two themes is imaginable. In order to investigate and categorize the system and its components, some kind of tool must be applied, and investigators will choose the tools that best fit their initial theory – anywhere along a continuum from a general cognitive model to a formal linguistic one.

Our choice is to use established models of linguistic structure and organization, and to push them as far as they will go in accounting for sign language – but, crucially, no farther. If spoken and signed languages are the product of the same cognitive system, we think it reasonable to start with the assumption that languages in the two modalities are likely to have structural and organizational similarities. If that is our hypothesis, then it makes sense to use similar tools – developed on the basis of centuries of cross-linguistic research – to study languages in the only other modality that is natural for humans. We want to know if there are language universals; we have tools for investigating this question; let's use them!

The majority of theoretical frameworks referred to in this book are generative. There are two reasons for this choice. The first is the philosophy behind this school of thought, which raises interesting challenges for sign language investigation. The second has to do with the rigorous investigative tools that have been developed in response to generative theories.

The motivating force behind the generative school of linguistics is the view that the commonalities among languages are more significant and more interesting than their differences. In a television series about this scientific paradigm,[1] its founder Noam Chomsky explains:

[1] *The Human Language, Part I.* A series by Gene Searchinger.

> As human beings, we are naturally interested in the differences among humans; we take the similarities among humans for granted. So, we're interested in the way humans look different from one another and [the way that] their faces are so different, and their sizes are so different, and the way they behave is so different, and so on. But from the point of view of, say, some Martian, we would all look alike. Just as from our point of view all frogs look alike. Now from the point of view of the frog, they look, I'm sure, very much different from one another, because they're interested in the differences among frogs. We just notice the overwhelming respects in which they're similar. If we can make the leap of the imagination that enables us to look at ourselves the way we look at other organisms, we will quickly discover that we're remarkably alike.

In the same program, Lila Gleitman makes clear that this leap of imagination pertains specifically to the study of language:

> In fact the existing differences among human languages has ... been called by Chomsky trivial ... trivial, compared with the differences between the human languages taken together and any other system of communication by other kinds of animals, by intelligent machines and the like – these are all vastly different from the set of human languages which by comparison are very, very much like each other.

Now, if Chomsky's Martian, noticing the remarkable similarities across human populations speaking different languages, were then to observe another group of earthlings signing to each other in sign language, would the Martian be struck by the same sensation of overwhelming similarity? The answer is no longer so obvious. In order to see things through the Martian's eyes, to try to determine the extent to which language in the two modalities that are natural to the species are alike, we adopt the research paradigm that is designed expressly to find universal properties of human language. Over the course of half a century of extremely intense scientific investigation, generative theory has developed and refined tools through which it has analyzed a large number of spoken languages. We are interested in learning what the same tools reveal in the study of sign language.

To the extent that sign languages are found to conform to the constructs and predictions of linguistic theory, we will have demonstrated that the models on which the predictions are based indeed reflect universal properties, that is, that any human language must conform to them. Where sign languages as a group fall outside such predictions, then the models will be revealed to be less than universal.

Insofar as differences in modality are implicated as the cause of such differences, this strategy will allow us to tease apart the linguistic code from the mode of its transmission. And where the mode does not seem to be to blame for differences in code, the finger must be pointed back at the theory, and revision must be considered in order to make the right predictions, universally. In both cases, sign language research is an instrument for refining both linguistic theory and broader theories of language as a cognitive system. There is also a third possibility, that linguistic theory makes the right predictions about sign languages but still misses generalizations. This more difficult issue is addressed below. Let us illustrate our approach, beginning with the word.

1.1.1 The word and its structure

Formulating a definition of the concept "word" is far from a simple task. Efforts to do so have resulted in theories that distinguish different aspects of "wordhood," such as the morphosyntactic or grammatical word, the lexeme (Matthews 1974), and the phonological word (see e.g., Hall and Kleinhenz 1999). All may overlap, but each can be shown to be distinct. The analyst of sign language words is confronted with similar issues, and similar distinctions emerge from investigating them.

Roughly speaking, it is useful to think of the sign as analogous to the word. Consider the American Sign Language (ASL) sign, ASK.[2] When this sign is inflected for agreement, e.g., first-person subject and non-first-person object (as shown in Figure 1.1a), or non-first-person object and first-person subject (Figure 1.1b), the sign has different forms, both of them different from the citation form of ASK. The signs in Figure 1.1 are two different morphosyntactic words as they have somewhat different forms (in each form, the hand moves along a different path in space) and different grammatical properties (First-person subject/third-person object, and third-person subject/first-person object, respectively). Yet the two signs are in some sense the same word, and can be characterized as belonging to the same lexeme, just as English *see* and *sees* both belong to the lexeme SEE. In addition to demonstrating that sign language words may systematically take different forms, this example reflects an additional phenomenon commonly found in spoken languages: the grammatical property of agreement is encoded by morphological changes in the form of the verb.

In sign language, as in spoken language, a distinction must also be made between the morphosyntactic word and the prosodic or phonological word. A word with a clitic, such as *Jill's* in *Jill's choosey*, constitutes a single stress group and therefore a single word phonologically, though it represents two morphosyntactic words, *Jill* and *is*. In Israeli Sign Language (ISL), a similar distinction occurs, also as a result of

[2] In the absence of a practical transcription system, we follow the convention in sign language linguistics and gloss signs with English words in upper-case letters. The numeral '1' stands for first person, and the letters 'a' and 'b' mark agreement with loci established in space to refer to the subject and object of the verb (cf. Chapter 3). See p. xx above for more detailed notation information.

a. 1-ASK-a b. b-ASK-1

Figure 1.1 Two inflected forms of the ASL lexeme ASK

a. SHOP b. IX 'there' c. SHOP-IX 'there'

Figure 1.2 Cliticization in ISL

cliticization, described in detail in Chapter 15. In this case, indexical locative forms cliticize to hosts. Indexing (glossed IX) is a device that plays a role in many aspects of the grammatical organization of sign languages, as we will see especially in Chapters 3, 20, and 21. It is manifested as pointing toward spatial locations or loci.

In Figure 1.2a, the citation form of the ISL sign SHOP is pictured. The deictic index IX 'there' is illustrated in Figure 1.2b. In the coalesced form, Figure 1.2, the dominant hand signs half of SHOP and makes a smooth transition into the deictic within a single path movement. Over the same time span, the non-dominant hand simply signs SHOP. As a result, what was originally two signs, each with its own movement, has become a cliticized form with a single movement. As we will see in Chapter 14, a single movement is considered by many researchers to define a syllable, and has been argued to be the optimal prosodic form of a word (Sandler 1999b, 1999c). At the same time, this process, together with the verb agreement process illustrated in Figure 1.1, reveals a property that is far more characteristic of sign languages than of spoken languages: simultaneity of structure. The different inflections of ASK are formed by simultaneously superimposing different directions of movement; the coalesced host and clitic take up a single syllable, whose bounds are simultaneously denoted by the other hand.

In these few simple examples, we have demonstrated some properties of sign language words that are far from trivial by appealing to general and theoretically interrelated linguistic principles. The concept "lexeme" unifies different forms of the same word; signs may be marked for inflection; prosodic structure plays a role in determining the form of words when they combine in sentences. None of these properties could have been assumed to exist in sign language a priori, nor are they likely to have been predicted by a general theory of cognition. All were revealed by using the tools of analysis provided by linguistic theory. Theories are statements of generalizations about language; if sign language instantiates these generalizations, we are more inclined to believe they are truly universal. The second unit of this book examines in detail these and many other morphological forms and processes that exist in sign languages, such as derivation, compounding, and allomorphy.

1.1.2 Sublexical units

Words of sign language are made up of still smaller elements – a finite set of discrete meaningless elements that recombine to create a potentially large lexicon. William Stokoe's (1960) discovery that a sign language has a phonemic level of structure was revolutionary. Not only was Stokoe's contribution socially revolutionary, showing plainly and publicly for the first time that deaf people command real languages like everybody else, it was also scientifically revolutionary, flinging sign language suddenly and dramatically into the arena of linguistic activity. From then on it would no longer be possible to claim, as even linguists of the stature of Leonard Bloomfield had done, that sign languages were primitive and transparent gesture systems (Bloomfield 1933, p. 39). If sign languages have such duality of patterning – that is, meaningless as well as meaningful components – then they could potentially manifest the same computational and communicative power as spoken languages. From the publication of Stokoe's (1960) *Sign Language Structure* on, the scientific community has had two kinds of natural human language to contend with.

Stokoe's investigation was both accessible and convincing because it exploited linguistic theory. Working within the structuralist phonemic tradition, he methodically demonstrated minimal pairs in ASL by substituting units within each of the three major formational categories that he posited: hand configuration, location, and movement. For example, the pair, TOUCH and SICK, shown in Figure 1.3, are minimally distinguished by different places of articulation. The handshape of the dominant, articulating hand is the same for both signs; the straight path movement to contact is also the same. The pair differs only in place specifications: [non-dominant hand] for TOUCH and [head] for SICK.

Structuralist theories of spoken language phonology – for this is the level of analysis at which Stokoe conducted his investigation – proved inadequate in accounting for the sound system of spoken languages, and this was the case for sign language phonological investigation as well.

a. TOUCH

b. SICK

Figure 1.3 Minimal pair in ASL, distinguished by place of articulation

Later researchers exploited generative theory, and interpreted the primitive units of the three sign language parameters as binary distinctive features (Sandler 1989, Corina 1993), showing as well that they are hierarchically organized. Let us look a bit closer at this example of the way that specific insights from spoken language phonological research were extended to sign language.

In spoken languages, models of the internal structure of phonological features have been proposed in which, for example, the place of articulation features are separated from laryngeal features such as voicing, and all of these from the feature [nasal] (Clements 1985, Sagey 1986, and many others). Clearly, each of these feature groups is separated by the physiology of the system: the place features are articulated in the oral cavity; features such as voicing, in the larynx, and nasality, by raising the velum.

The model that represents these features according to their articulatory class is explanatory because the same groups pattern together in rules of language. For example, in many languages, nasal consonants assimilate the place of articulation of a neighboring segment, whatever it is, without losing their nasal quality: *can* becomes [kæm] before *be* and [kæŋ] before *go*. Hierarchical models separate the nasal feature from other features on an articulatory basis, and group all oral place features together on the same basis. In this way, if the rule requires assimilation of the place feature class, all and only the features of this class will assimilate. In the case of [ŋ] resulting from the assimilation of the place features of [g] to the [n] segment, the rule will automatically assimilate both the [high] and [back] features responsible for velar consonants, while leaving the [nasal] specification unaffected.

Example (1) shows assimilation of place of articulation from [g] to the preceding [n]. The example, greatly oversimplified for clarity of exposition, shows assimilation by spreading the place class of the [g] segment to the [n] segment, and by disassociating the [n]'s original place specification. The "geometry" of the model captures the generalization that place features often behave as a class: any and all place features spread onto the nasal segment. The hierarchy is intended to be universal in predicting

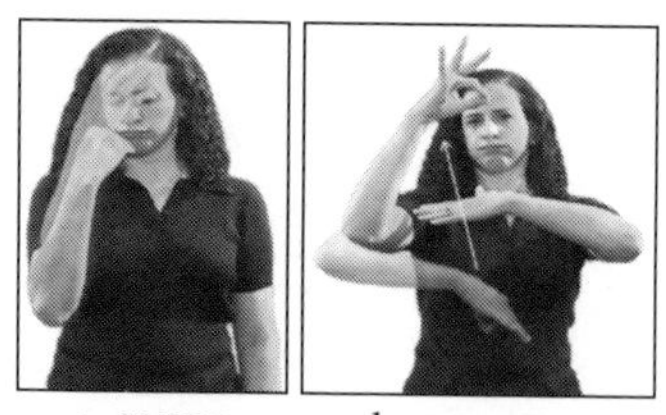

a. SLEEP b. SUNRISE

Figure 1.4 Components of a compound

which features are expected to behave as a class in any language. In principle, any terminal feature can spread alone, but spreading at any higher node must take along all subordinate features.

(1) Assimilation of place of articulation to a nasal consonant in a hierarchical model

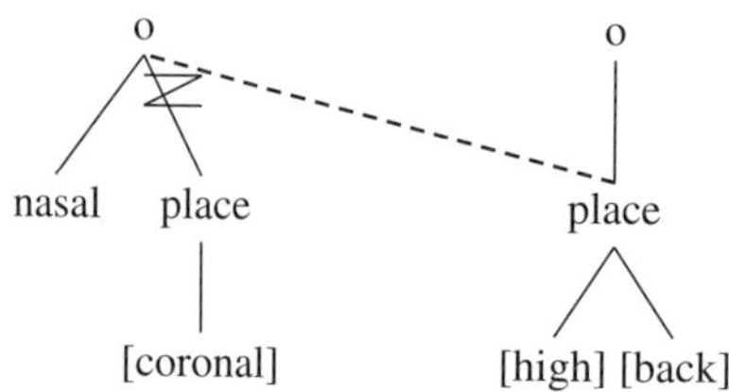

Hierarchical organization of features has been argued to exist in the Hand Configuration class of features in American Sign Language (Sandler 1987a, 1987b, Corina and Sagey 1989). As in the spoken language model, the features are assigned to classes according to articulatory criteria: the shape of the hand is determined by the fingers, and its orientation by the palm (Sandler 1987a, 1987b, 1989). On the basis of assimilation in compounds, it is further proposed that the handshape class dominates the orientation class. The relevant behavior is the following: orientation features may assimilate alone, but if handshape assimilates, orientation must necessarily assimilate as well. Figure 1.4 shows the individual words of the compound OVERSLEEP, which are SLEEP and SUNRISE. In SLEEP, the handshape is and the orientation is toward the signer. In SUNRISE, the handshape is and the orientation is toward the contralateral side of the body.

Partial assimilation – i.e., assimilation of palm orientation from the sign SUNRISE onto the first part of the compound, originally SLEEP – is shown in Figure 1.5. The hand for SLEEP has assimilated the contralateral orientation from SUNRISE; the model's palm is now pointing to her left rather than toward her face.

Figure 1.5 OVERSLEEP with orientation assimilation

These and other articulatory facts and the assimilatory behavior motivate the hand configuration hierarchy shown in (2). This process, partial assimilation of orientation only, and other details of the hand configuration category are explored and illustrated in Chapter 10.

(2) Hierarchical organization of hand configuration feature classes (Sandler 1989)

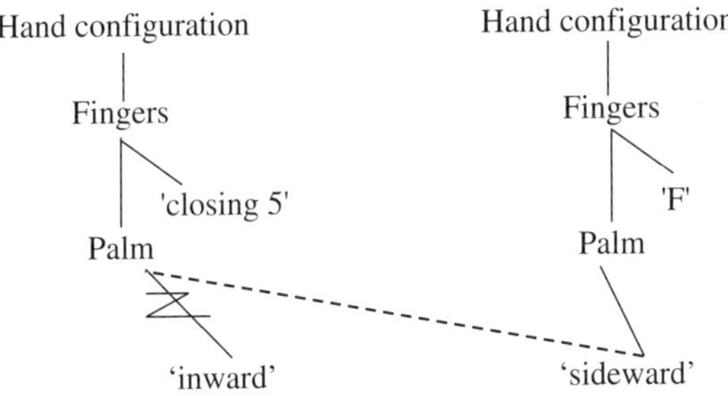

In addition to partial assimilation shown here, total assimilation of both handshape and orientation also occurs in compounds; that this is possible is predicted by the hierarchical model. The example shows how the tools developed for investigating universally viable models of spoken language uncover structural properties of sign language as well. In turn, hierarchical structure gains more credence as a phonological universal. In both spoken and signed languages, the particular hierarchy is determined by the physiology. The features and articulators, and their interorganization, are, of course, different in the two modalities.

1.1.3 The sentence

If sentences are composed of words, and words are signs as we have just described them, what are sign language sentences other than strings of signs? One of the foundational claims of generative syntax is that sentences are not simply strings of words, but are hierarchically structured in a rule-governed way. Is there reason to think that signed sentences are also hierarchically structured?

While some have argued against this idea, noting the variability of word order found in sign languages (Bouchard and Dubuisson 1995, Bouchard 1996), we think sign linguists have profited from pursuing the traditional view and applying precise notions of structure developed on the basis of spoken languages to the analysis of signed sentences. In this instance, theoretically informed models of syntactic structure have been able to more accurately define the contexts in which non-canonical orders are found.

Liddell (1980) expanded on an observation made by Fischer (1974) that when a sentence is signed with the object first (topicalized), an intonation break comes before the rest of the sentence. Liddell carefully studied the components of this intonation break, and proposed that a specific combination of brow raise, head tilt, and hold (holding all articulators in position) constituted a grammatical marker for topics. Example (3) shows that the topic, CAT, is marked with the non-manual marker for a topic (t), but not for the negative marker (n), which characterizes the rest of the sentence. The notation Liddell adopted is still in widespread use: the physical scope of a non-manual marker is shown with a line above the gloss of the constituent it characterizes, and an abbreviation of the relevant marker is printed above the right edge of the line, as in (3). Liddell argued that the physical scope of the non-manual marking and the linguistic scope of the structure it is hypothesized to manifest are one and the same. This idea has been adopted and extended by Neidle, Kegl, MacLaughlin, Bahan, and Lee (2000), but we will see alternatives in Units 3 and 4.

(3) ASL (Liddell 1980, p. 84)

___t __________n
CAT, DOG CHASE
'As for the cat, the dog didn't chase it.'

In addition to observing the non-manual marker that accompanies topics, Liddell made the case that a particular syntactic structure is involved. He proposed that topics occupy a hierarchically high position in the phrase structure, as schematized in (4). This proposal has the benefit of explaining both the position of topics and the extent of the non-manual marker. The negative marker 'n' extends only over its clause (S_1).

(4)

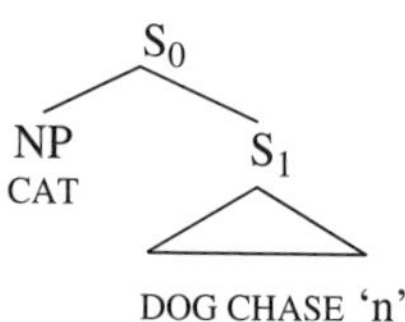

Liddell's analysis brings sign language squarely within the range of options found across spoken languages. Sentence-initial topic elements, separated from the rest of the sentence with an intonation break, are widespread. Languages do vary in the extent to which they make use of topic and other discourse-related phenomena in their sentence structure (see Chapter 22). But the use of syntactic structure – and operations to modify it – is a universal found across signed and spoken languages.

Another clear universal is the use of recursive structures in embedding. Language is non-finite, not only because there is no upper bound to the number of words possible, but also because there is no upper bound to the number of sentences possible. This is so because of recursion: it is always possible to embed a clause (or a noun phrase) under another matrix verb (or possessor), as the examples in (5) illustrate.

(5) a. George told a joke.
Sally said that George told a joke.
Mike thought that Sally said that George told a joke.
Kim hypothesized that Mike thought that Sally said that George told a joke.

b. the girl's dog
the girl's friend's dog
the girl's friend's cousin's dog
the girl's friend's cousin's roommate's dog

Do sign languages have this ubiquitous property of human language? Again, it may be surprising that some have claimed they do not (Thompson 1977). However, this claim too has been overridden by further studies which showed that not only do sign languages have embedding, but they follow both universal and language-particular constraints that distinguish embedded from non-embedded forms.

For example, Padden (1988 [1983]) showed that coordinate clauses in ASL adhere to the Coordinate Structure Constraint (Ross 1967). Although extraction out of an embedded clause is permitted, according to this universal constraint it is not possible to extract an element out of a conjoined clause. The permitted extraction and the constraint are illustrated schematically in (6)–(7).

(6) 

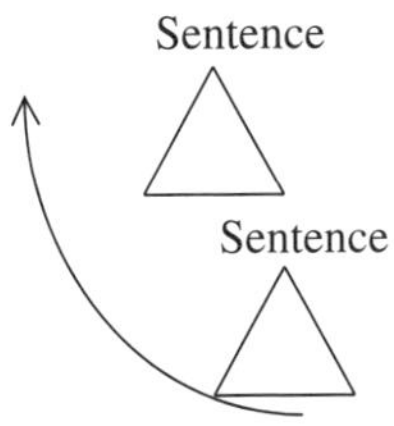

(7) *

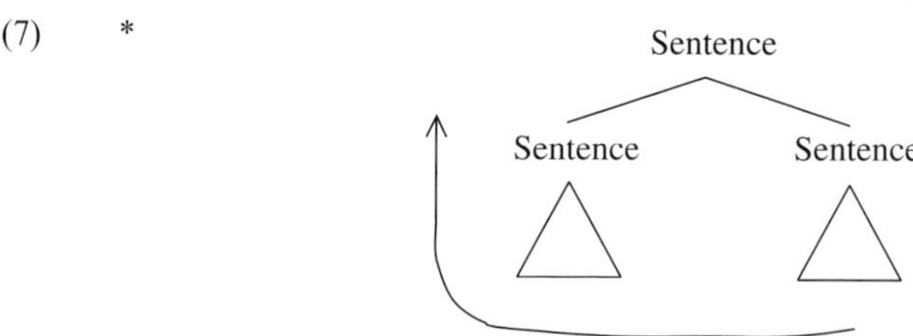

This constraint can be illustrated in English with the following examples. In (8a), the object has been extracted out of the embedded clause – corresponding to the structure in (6) – and the example is licit. However, when extraction takes place out of a conjoined clause, as in (8b), the result is ungrammaticality.

(8) a. √ That math test, Nicole told me Lee thought he passed.

b. * Baked beans, I think Uncle Bob really loves hamburgers but Aunt Mae detests.

As Padden showed, ASL conforms to this constraint, permitting a fronted topic related to an embedded clause, as in (9a), but not one related to a conjoined clause, as in (9b).

(9) ASL (Padden 1988 [1983], pp. 76–77)

a. √ $\overline{\text{EXERCISE CLASS}}^{\,t}$, $_1$INDEX HOPE SISTER SUCCEED PERSUADE MOTHER TAKE-UP.

'The exercise class, I hope my sister manages to persuade my mother to take (it).'

b. * $\overline{\text{FLOWER}}^{\,t}$, $_2$GIVE$_1$ MONEY, $_j$GIVE$_1$.

'Flowers, he gave me money but she gave me.'

These examples show that ASL does have embedding, that it distinguishes embedded clauses from conjoined clauses, and that it adheres to a universal constraint on recursive structures – strongly suggesting that these properties are true language universals.

Interestingly, the study of ASL syntax has also revealed something about the nature of cross-linguistic variation. It has been widely observed that in certain domains, the range of variation found across languages may be limited to a small number of choices. These options are captured by positing "parameters" which make available "settings" among which languages choose (Chomsky 1981, Chomsky and Lasnik 1993). In several cases, ASL seems to behave simultaneously like two different spoken language types. Later research has also observed the same phenomena in some spoken languages, though the tendency seems to be much stronger in sign languages.

As one example, languages vary in the ways that they may or may not permit various of the verb's arguments to be "null" – or not overtly expressed. Languages like Spanish and Italian, in which rich verbal morphology identifies the person and number of the subject, permit the subject to be left unexpressed, in examples like (10).

(10) Spanish
a. Hablo Español
(I-) speak Spanish
b. Hablamos Español
(we-) speak Spanish

We have already seen an example showing that ASL has rich verbal morphology (Figure 1.1). As might be expected, the subject and/or object of verbs like ASK, shown in the figure, may be left "null" in ASL, as the agreement morphology identifies the null argument (Lillo-Martin 1986a).

(11) a. 1-ASK-a
(I-) ask (-her/him).
b. b-ASK-1
(S/he-) asks (-me).

Importantly, not all verbs in ASL are like the example given, ASK. Many verbs do not modify their form to indicate subject or object (the so-called "plain" verbs). Do these verbs require their arguments to be overt, as in English?

As it happens, it is not only languages with rich verbal morphology which allow null arguments (subjects/objects). Languages like Japanese and Chinese – with *no* verbal agreement morphology – also allow the subject or object to be missing in the right discourse contexts, as in (12).

(12) Chinese (Huang 1984, p. 533)
Speaker A: Zhangsan kanjian Lisi le ma?
Zhangsan see Lisi ASP Q
'Did Zhangsan see Lisi?'
Speaker B:
a. *e* kanjian ta le.
[He] see he ASP
'(He) saw him.'
b. ta kanjian *e* le.
He see [he] ASP
'He saw (him).'
c. *e* kanjian *e* le.
[He] see [he] ASP
'(He) saw (him).'

With plain verbs, ASL turns out to be like Chinese: null arguments are allowed even without agreement, in the proper discourse context. An example is given in (13).

(13) ASL (Lillo-Martin 1986a, p. 421)
A. Did you eat my candy?
B. YES, EAT-UP.
'Yes, (I) ate (it) up.'

When it comes to null arguments, then, ASL allows two kinds: those identified by verbal agreement morphology, and those licensed by the discourse (Lillo-Martin 1986a). Indications are that other sign languages also work the same way (Quadros 1995). This analysis has been disputed (Bahan, Kegl, Lee, MacLaughlin, and Neidle 2000), but we will see support for this characterization of the facts in Chapter 21.

Most spoken languages do not have two kinds of null arguments – they may be like English, disallowing null arguments in general, or else choose between the Italian-type or the Chinese-type of null arguments (Jaeggli and Safir 1989). However, there are some examples of spoken languages which seem to behave similarly to ASL in having two kinds of null arguments (e.g., Warlpiri, Legate 2003).

In other ways as well, ASL allows multiple options: it has moved WH-phrases as well as WH-in situ (Lillo-Martin 1990) (see Chapter 23). It seems to have deteminers, but they are optional (MacLaughlin 1997) (see Chapter 20). An explanation for this tendency to "have it both ways" is still to be determined.

1.2 The mode and its implications for the study of language

One phenomenon that poses unique challenges for conventional phonological, morphological, and syntactic investigation is the classifier subsystem. These structures, named for the nominal classifiers represented as handshapes, seem to slip and slither through all the cracks. For example, in this system, Stokoe's phonological categories of Hand Configuration, Location, and Movement are not meaningless but meaning-bearing, and function as bound morphemes. By definition, then, each classifier construction is morphologically complex. Due to the propensity of sign languages to combine linguistic units simultaneously, a construction of this type may be extremely complex morphologically, yet be indistinguishable phonologically from a monosyllabic, monomorphemic word (Brentari 1995). Conversely, a construction built upon a single classifier can also span several intonational phrases and render a sequence of predicates (Aronoff, Meir, Padden, and Sandler 2003). Syntactically, classifiers are found in structures and subject to processes not otherwise used.

Figure 1.6 Excerpt from a classifier construction meaning, 'a person proceeds forward, dragging a dog squirming behind' (ASL)

Figure 1.6 shows an ASL classifier construction that means roughly 'a person proceeds forward, dragging a dog squirming behind.' Each handshape represents a different classifier: upright human (here, on the left hand) and animate being with legs (on the right hand). The expression does not take the form of a word, either phonologically or morphologically. Nor does it take the usual form of a sign language sentence. In fact, these forms are anomalous at every level of analysis. They are iconic, yet conventionalized, at once mimetic and linguistic. Researchers have turned to established theories here as well – theories of morphology, syntax, and prosody – in an effort to better comprehend these constructions. The result has been some success towards grasping the generalizations that can be made about the system, and at the same time an acknowledgment that some of its characteristics have so far eluded standard linguistic analysis (see Emmorey 2003 for recent papers on this topic). Is the mismatch due to modality? Is it to be ascribed to inadequacies in linguistic theory? We deal with classifier constructions from a linguistic point of view at some length in Chapters 5 and 20. In Chapter 25, we address modality issues that may partially explain these constructions and their behavior in sign languages.

Over the past several years, as research on more and more sign languages is published, a fascinating challenge to language theory has emerged: there is a common core of structures and processes that seems to be found, down to a level of detail that is quite intricate, in the description of sign language after sign language. Verb agreement and classifier constructions described briefly above are examples. Simultaneity of structure is another property found in all sign languages. While the structures and processes in question often fall within the bounds of more general theoretical predictions, we think that linguistic theory ought to be embarrassed when generalizations like these go uncaptured. We grapple with those challenges in the last unit of the book, attempting to evaluate the interaction of the linguistic code and the mode of expression.

The next three units of the book deal with the morphology, phonology and syntax of sign languages. At each level, a sizeable body of significant linguistic generalizations is found to characterize languages in both modalities; these generalizations can be said to be universal properties of language. Also at each level, certain sign language-specific properties are uncovered.

While the linguistic investigation pinpoints the properties of sign languages that are within its scientific domain, the last unit of the book brings together what is left over, the properties that are specific to sign language, such as the use of space to pick out referents, simultaneous instantiation of linguistic patterns, and the linguistic encoding of iconically motivated structure. There we attempt to reach a deeper understanding of so-called modality effects and their implications for the study of human language. Our examination of these effects prompts us to suggest that modality effects work both ways. It stands to reason that if the physical modality is responsible for certain aspects of sign language structure, such as simultaneity, then the converse property found in spoken language – in this case, linearity – must also be modality induced. Implications for future research follow from this view, as a comprehensive theory of language ought to be able to predict such generalizations of structure in a principled way.

Unit 2

Morphology

2 Morphology: introduction

At the very core of language is the word – the free-standing unit that unifies form and meaning. The word lists or lexicons of languages hold a vast number of words – an estimated 32,000 for adult speakers of English, for example. Many words are complex, consisting of more than one component that bears meaning and/or plays a grammatical role. The study of these complex word forms is the domain of morphology and the subject of this unit. In it, we will show that sign languages have a wide range of morphological processes, some fully productive, some idiosyncratic, all influenced by general linguistic organizing principles and most molded by modality-specific factors as well. In a sense that will become clear in the following sections, a lot of the "action" in sign language grammar takes place in the morphology.

Three observations suggest why sign language morphology may give us so much insight into the workings of the grammatical system. First, all natural sign languages have an iconic base. Indeed, it would be quite odd for a language in a manual–visual modality to avoid exploiting its ability to represent visual images and spatial relations iconically. Yet, despite the fact that they are often based on iconic images, the words of sign languages may be morphologically complex. In fact, the second noteworthy point is that there are many processes for making complex words in these languages. In some of these processes, the component parts of complex words are also relatively transparent. However, and this is the third point, universal principles of organization and structure that constrain spoken language morphology are active in sign language as well, despite their iconic base. So it seems that morphology is the most readily observable meeting place for the iconically motivated forms of sign language and linguistic structuring. For this reason, its study offers us a privileged vantage point from which to observe the linguistic system at work.

The exploration contained in this unit traverses the traditional word formation landscape of inflection, derivation, and compounding, and enters the somewhat wilder terrain of classifier constructions. A multifaceted interaction among three driving forces emerges from this sojourn: iconic motivation, lexicalization, and linguistic systematicity. Our goal in this unit is to arrive at a better understanding of each of these forces independently, and of the combined effect they have on sign language words.

3 Inflectional morphology

The sign language inflectional morphology of most interest is found on predicates.[1] The bulk of our discussion deals with the main types of predicate morphology: agreement (Section 3.1) and aspect (Section 3.2). A brief discussion of noun pluralization ends the chapter (Section 3.3).

3.1 Verb agreement

Agreement in natural languages can be described as a process whereby "a grammatical element X matches a grammatical element Y in property Z within some grammatical configuration" (Barlow and Ferguson 1988, p. 1). A prototypical example of agreement is that between a verb and its subject, such as the Swahili example given in (1).

(1) Swahili (Barlow and Ferguson 1988, p. 3)
Wa-toto wa-nakula nkate
CL2-child CL2-eat fish
'The children are eating fish.'

In the Swahili example, the subject is marked as animate plural with the class 2 marker *wa*, and the verb is similarly marked animate plural.

Studies of agreement in spoken languages have found various domains within which agreement is found, features with which elements agree, and conditions under which agreement is neutralized, mismatched, or otherwise variable. Some studies emphasize the morphological analyses of agreement processes, including examination of conditions for allomorphy, syncretism, etc. Others are more focused on the syntactic relationship between agreeing elements.

Traditionally, many analyses view the "controller" of agreement as a nominal expression, which has certain inherent features that are matched

[1] There is no gender- or case-marking morphology on nouns, except for possessive pronouns; number is optionally marked by reduplication on some nouns, and by number incorporation in others. See Section 3.3 on pluralization.

by the agreement "target" (cf. Lehmann 1988).[2] Thus, verbs agree with their subjects, not the other way around.

In sign languages, certain verbs are generally said to agree with both their subjects and their objects. The process is considered agreement because the verb is modified in its form depending on certain aspects of the form of the subject/object nominals. However, the system of verb agreement behaves rather differently from agreement in spoken languages – different enough as to raise the question of whether or not it should even be called agreement. There are also some typological differences between sign language agreement and spoken language agreement. However, as our description shows, the system has many morphological and syntactic properties of agreement, and we will follow the standard usage in calling it thus.

In this section, we will first describe the form of agreement in sign languages. Then, we will go over some issues concerning the properties of agreement and recent accounts of them. All of the proposals to be discussed in this chapter maintain the analysis of the system to be presented as "agreement." We will discuss problems with the "agreement" analysis, and several proposed solutions to these problems, in Unit 5.

3.1.1 Sign language verb agreement – basic description

In order to describe the verb agreement system of sign languages, it is first necessary to deal in some detail with what is often described as the linguistic use of space. In a signed discourse, the physical space surrounding the signer is used in two ways. As we have seen, signs are articulated in space, and the specified location or locations in space are themselves components of sign formation. In other words, location is simply one parameter which must be included in the lexical entry of a sign.

In addition to forming part of the lexical representation of signs, the space around the signer (including the signer) can be exploited referentially. To take the simplest example first, consider reference to first person (I/ me/ my/ myself). The physical location of the signer is the location used for signs which refer to first person. For example, the personal pronouns which refer to the signer are produced by pointing to oneself (making physical contact). The ASL sign I/ME is illustrated in Figure 3.1. The presence of an addressee or third person during a signed discourse also establishes a location which can be used for reference. In these cases, however, the signer does not actually make physical contact with the persons, but points toward them. A pronoun sign picking out a third-person referent who is present in the situation is illustrated in Figure 3.2. In such a case, it is said that a "locus" (not a physical

[2] "The noun(s) whose features are represented in the agreement marker(s) are called the controller(s) of agreement" (Janis 1995, p. 195).

I/ME (ASL)

Figure 3.1 First-person pronoun

a-IX(Mary) 'she' (ASL)

Figure 3.2 Pronoun picking out present referent

(geometrical) point, but an area of the signing space) is associated with a referent, and signs are directed at that locus.[3] When a signer refers to someone who is not physically present in the signed discourse, a locus must be associated with the referent. Roughly, the signer indicates that the interlocutors are to imagine that the referent is located in some area of the signing space, and this becomes the locus for the referent. This process is often called "nominal establishment" or "association of a nominal with a locus." Pronominal signs can then be directed with respect to this locus in the same way as for present referents. Which location the signer chooses may be influenced by an actual previous or potential location that a referent might occupy, or it might be arbitrary (although there are conventions for which locations are typically used, as discussed in Bahan and Petitto 1980).

[3] The notation for pronoun signs other than first person uses the following form: a-IX (Mary). Because of the importance of spatial loci for the grammar of ASL, we indicate them in sign glosses, using lower-case letters from the beginning of the alphabet (a,b,c, . . .). These indices refer to constant physical locations within an example or set of examples. For example, index 'a' can refer to a locus on the right side of the signer throughout one set of examples, while it might refer to a locus on the left side for another set. The actual physical location (right or left side) is in such cases irrelevant. What is important is the agreement between different uses of the same locus during a single discourse. To aid interpretation, we indicate the referent of the pronoun or the direction of the point in parentheses immediately following the gloss. The pronoun itself is glossed as IX, which stands for index, a term commonly used for pointing signs, which may be personal pronouns, locatives, and determiners. See p. xx above for a full description of notation used.

a-IX(right) 'she/he' (ASL)

Figure 3.3 Pronoun picking out non-present referent

A pronoun sign picking out a third-person referent who is not present in the situation is illustrated in Figure 3.3. We have focused on personal pronoun signs so far in our description of the linguistic use of space. Reflexive and possessive pronouns use the same locations, but different handshapes. For example, ASL uses the handshape for possessives and the handshape for reflexives, while ISL uses the handshape for possessives and the handshape (back of hand toward referent location) for reflexives. Although the shape of the hand used for different pronouns may vary from sign language to sign language, all signed languages reported on to date make similar use of space in their pronominal systems. See McBurney (2002) for a comprehensive review of pronominal systems across many sign languages, which is compared with the range of pronominal systems found in spoken languages.

The use of space for reference in sign languages permits them to use pronouns virtually unambiguously, since pronouns pick out particular referents rather than classes of referents. Compare this with first-person pronouns in spoken languages.[4] The first-person pronoun picks out the speaker, whoever the speaker may be in a particular discourse situation. Sign language pronouns other than first person also pick out particular referents, although who a point to the right picks out depends on the particular discourse situation. Furthermore, the lack of ambiguity is not absolute, since spatial locations used in signs can represent physical locations as well as referents. Thus, pointing to a locus may pick out a location (e.g., the doorway) or a referent (e.g., Mary standing in the doorway) in some contexts. However, sign language pronouns are distinctive in that they pick out particular referents, and not classes of potential referents, such as any relevant single female.[5]

While sign languages are unique in their ability to indicate an infinite number of spatial reference points, it should be noted that there are spoken languages which encode complex spatial distinctions, sometimes incorporating other sensory information as well. For example, in Yucatec

[4] We thank Richard Meier for bringing this comparison to our attention.

[5] Whether or not sign language pronouns are marked for grammatical categories, such as person, number, and gender, and other issues related to picking out referents will be discussed below and in much more detail in Unit 5.

a. 1-ASK-a 'I ask her'

b. a-ASK-b 'She asks him'

c. b-ASK-1 'He asks me'

Figure 3.4 Agreeing verb ASK (ASL)

Maya, there is a very large number of deictic forms. Hanks (1992) lists distinct forms meaning: 'here it is (tactual),' 'there it is (visual),' 'there it is (audible),' 'right here (immediate),' 'there (non-immediate),' 'out there (exlusive),' 'there (anaphoric),' '(in) here (inclusive),' 'this one (immediate),' 'that (one) (nonimmediate),' and 'the one,' among others.[6]

In sign languages, verb agreement follows pronouns in making use of referential loci in space.[7] A verb which agrees with both subject and object will generally make use of the referential space by using the locus for the subject as the beginning location of the verb, and the locus of the object as the ending point. In signing the verb, then, the hand moves from the locus of the subject to the locus of the object. In addition, the direction in which the hands are facing is also generally affected in agreeing forms: the verb faces its object. Three agreeing forms of the ASL verb ASK, a verb which changes both path and facing to mark agreement, are illustrated in Figure 3.4.[8] Other

[6] Thanks to Mark Aronoff for bringing up Mayan deictics in this context.

[7] The process described here has been called by various terms in the sign language literature. Fischer (1975) observed that verbs "cliticize" or "incorporate the location" of pronouns. Edge and Hermann (1977) describe certain verbs as "multidirectional" or "multiorientational." They say that such verbs incorporate their arguments, but they do not call the process agreement. Fischer and Gough (1978) described the processes of "directionality," "reversibility," and "locationality," and observed that they are in some ways analogous to person inflection; they also suggested that directionality "can be considered a process of incorporating a pronoun ... into a verb" (p. 26). Klima and Bellugi (1979) used the term "indexical inflection."

[8] Loci are indicated on verbs with lower-case letters from the beginning of the alphabet. An index preceding the verb gloss indicates a starting location and/or locus from which the hand faces away, while one after the verb gloss indicates the ending location/locus towards which the hand faces.

a. 1-TAKE-a 'I take her'

b. a-TAKE-b 'She takes him'

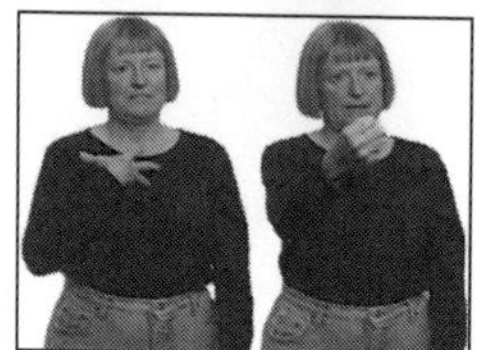

c. b-TAKE-1 'He takes me'

Figure 3.5 "Backwards" agreeing verb TAKE (ASL)

ASL verbs which change their facing as well as moving along a path from subject to object include BAWL-OUT, BLAME, INSULT, JOIN, and PAY. Verbs of ASL which do not change facing but do change path movement include HELP, INFORM, PHONE, and VISIT. ANALYZE, FEED, FORCE, PITY, and TEASE are among ASL verbs which change facing but not path.

A small set of "backwards" verbs moves in the opposite direction from regular verbs, starting at the location of the object and moving toward the location of the subject. Backwards verbs in ASL include COPY, EXTRACT, INVITE, MOOCH, STEAL, SUMMON, and TAKE. Like regular verbs, the facing may or may not change in backwards verbs, depending on the verb (e.g., INVITE does not change facing). Three agreeing forms of the backwards ASL verb TAKE, which changes both path and facing, are illustrated in Figure 3.5.

Pronouns and agreeing verbs can also be marked for number.[9] Multiple marking for verb agreement and pronouns uses an arcing movement. For example, a multiple personal pronoun uses the ☝ handshape directed at a location, moving in an arc. The multiple form of the third-person possessive pronoun is illustrated in Figure 3.6. This sweeping movement indicates a collective plural.[10] Verb agreement for object can

[9] In addition to the multiple form described here, there are also dual, exhaustive, and reciprocal forms. Klima and Bellugi (1979) describe a number of distributional aspect forms as well, which combine in complex ways we will not discuss here.

[10] A distributive plural uses a succession of points, distributed in space along the arc.

a:c-IX 'their' (ASL)

Figure 3.6 Possessive pronoun with multiple marking

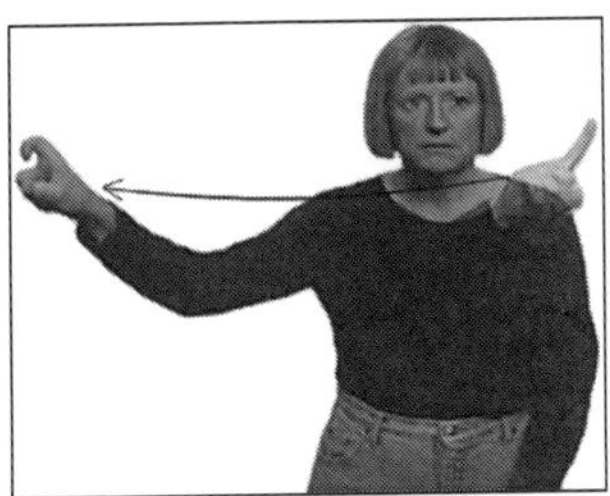

1-ASK-a:c 'I ask them' (ASL)

Figure 3.7 Verb with multiple object marking

also be marked as multiple with a sweeping, arcing movement. The verb ASK with first-person singular subject and third-person multiple object is illustrated in Figure 3.7. To summarize, agreement involves changing the direction of movement and/or facing of a sign to indicate the loci associated with the verb's arguments and their number. Whether this system involves agreement with the grammatical category of person or not is an issue of recent debate, which we will take up in Unit 5.

3.1.2 *Sign language verb agreement – additional complexities*

Morphologically, the verb agreement system of ASL is actually more complex than we have described so far. For one thing, not all verbs participate in the agreement system just described – only a relatively small set do. Verbs are traditionally divided into three main classes, following Padden (1988 [1983]): "agreeing" verbs,[11] which can take agreement morphology for referent arguments; "spatial" verbs, which agree with locative arguments or adjuncts; and "plain" verbs, which do not take any agreement morphology. The differences between these categories will be discussed further in Section 3.1.3.

The agreeing verbs can be further divided, and the system further constrained. The main class consists of those verbs which agree with

[11] Padden called them "inflecting" verbs, but since plain verbs may show inflection for aspect, the term now commonly used for verbs which mark person agreement is "agreeing."

a. a-ASK-1 + b-ASK-1

b. a,b-ASK-1

Figure 3.8 Non-singular subject agreement: 'the two of them ask me' (two variants, ASL)

subject and object. Verbs agree with their (subject and) "final" object, as it is called in the theory of Relational Grammar that Padden uses; descriptively, mono-transitives agree with their direct object, but ditransitives agree with their indirect object. Object agreement is obligatory, while subject agreement is optional (Meier 1981, 1982, 1987). Padden dubs the lack of subject agreement "Agreement Marker Omission." When the subject is not agreed with, a "neutral" location in the center of the signing space is used as the subject location. However, some verbs never modify their form for subject agreement, although they do obligatorily show object agreement.

Furthermore, there are restrictions on certain combinations of person and number agreement. For example, multiple marking is only found for object agreement, not subject agreement, in ASL. Subject agreement can be marked for dual or exhaustive plurals only, illustrated in Figure 3.8. Plural cannot be marked on both subject and object at the same time; when both subject and object are plural, the object is marked morphologically, but the plurality of the subject is marked in a different way (for example, through overt plural pronouns). Finally, many verbs do not have a regular form for first-person plurals. This whole system seems typologically very unusual, with unexpected classes of agreement patterns and optionality. Why do only certain verbs mark agreement? What determines the classes that do and do not mark agreement? Why are some verbs backwards? Why is subject agreement optional? Several recent studies investigate verb agreement patterns in signed languages and propose new analyses which reveal more regularity in the system. We turn next to the issue of how to correctly classify the various types of verbs.

3.1.3 Sign language verb agreement – accounting for verb classes

Padden (1988 [1983], 1990) shows that plain verbs, agreeing verbs, and spatial verbs must be distinguished morphosyntactically. We turn now to some of the distinguishing morphological and syntactic characteristics separating these three classes of verbs.

The primary characteristic of plain verbs is that they do not mark their subject or object arguments. It has been observed that many verbs that do not show agreement involve contact with the body. While it might be tempting to explain this group by appealing to a phonological constraint such as "body anchoring," however, Padden (1988 [1983]) points out that this does not suffice to predict all plain verbs, since there are some plain verbs which do not involve body contact.

Padden (1990) notices that some verbs which do not express agreement by path direction or by facing, such as WANT, can be signed in different locations in space, in a manner which seems like agreement.[12] However, Padden argues against an agreement analysis of these verbs for two reasons: (a) these plain verbs have an uninflected form which is optional, while agreeing verbs generally cannot appear in uninflected form; (b) since neither the path nor the facing of the hands is altered in the signing of plain verbs, the location in which they are signed may be ambiguous between the subject and the object, while agreeing verbs do not have such ambiguity. Padden's example of changes in the location for plain verbs like WANT is given in (2).

(2) ASL (Padden 1990, p. 121)

a. WOMAN $_{a}$WANT; MAN $_{b}$WANT
'The woman$_{i}$ is wanting and the man$_{j}$ is wanting, too.'
'The woman wants it$_{i}$, and the man wants it$_{j}$.'

b. WOMAN $_{a}$WANT $_{b}$WANT $_{c}$WANT[13]
'The women$_{i,j,k}$ are each wanting.'
'The woman wants this$_{i}$, that$_{j}$, and that one$_{k}$, too.'

[12] Note that these signs are produced in a single location, without the path movement or orientation change typical of agreeing verbs.

[13] Plural marking on nouns consists of reduplication of the sign in different locations in space or, if the sign is body anchored, by changing the position of the body for each reduplication. However, such marking is not obligatory and is not used in sentence (2b). Thus, the

As the translations of the examples in (2) show, each sentence is ambiguous between two interpretations: one (the first translation given for each) in which the locations of WANT refer to the subjects of the sentences, and one (the second translation) in which these locations refer to objects, although the context may disambiguate particular examples. Verbs like WANT are clearly not specified as agreeing with subject or object (or both), though they may be signed in the location of their subject or their object. BUILD, BUY, READ, and VOTE are other non-agreeing verbs which may be signed in particular locations.

Padden observes that nouns and adjectives may also be signed in a spatial location, like plain verbs such as WANT. Using criteria to distinguish inflectional affixes from clitics given by Zwicky and Pullum (1983), she argues that the location used in examples like (2) is a pronoun clitic, rather than a true agreement affix.[14]

That there is a difference between the use of spatial locations in "plain" and "agreeing" verbs seems clear. However, as plain verbs may utilize locations in space for reference, as may nouns and adjectives, a full analysis of the system of spatial "clitics" has yet to be undertaken.

We now turn to the third category of verbs, spatial verbs. Padden (1988 [1983]) distinguishes agreeing verbs from spatial verbs on several grounds. First, she shows that while agreeing verbs cannot begin in a locus which matches some referent other than the subject, spatial verbs often do so – matching instead the locus for the beginning location (or beginning of movement), as illustrated in (3).

(3) ASL (Padden 1988 [1983], p. 29)

ynq (over RIGHT)
$_2$INDEX $_i$COME$_1$ YESTERDAY, RIGHT?
'You came here yesterday, right?'

Second, Padden claims that agreeing verbs and spatial verbs behave differently with respect to the distinctiveness of variations in loci. With agreeing verbs, slight differences in location for subsequent reference to the same referent are not interpreted distinctively. With spatial verbs, however, such differences convey different meanings.[15] Padden gives the following examples in (4)–(5) to illustrate this difference.

The verb GIVE in (4) is an agreeing verb. As shown in Figure 3.9, the exhaustive form of GIVE may be signed with different specific locations, but both alternatives are simply considered variants of the exhaustive

sign WOMAN in (2b) can be interpreted as either singular or as plural, depending on whether different locations of WANT are interpreted as marking the object or the subject, respectively.

14 See Lillo-Martin (1986b) for an application of these criteria to the question of whether or not "agreement" is morphologically more like agreement or clitics.

15 Padden discusses this issue with respect to reciprocal and exhaustive forms; Janis (1992) extends it to all verb types.

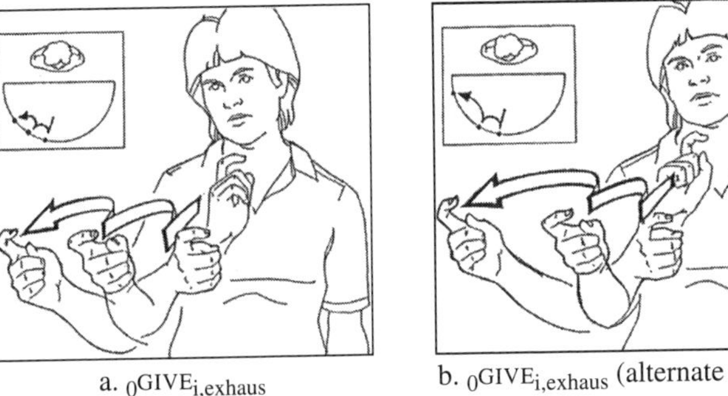

a. ${}_{0}$GIVE$_{i,exhaus}$ b. ${}_{0}$GIVE$_{i,exhaus}$ (alternate form)

Figure 3.9 Two forms of exhaustive with agreeing verb (reprinted with permission from Padden 1988 [1983])

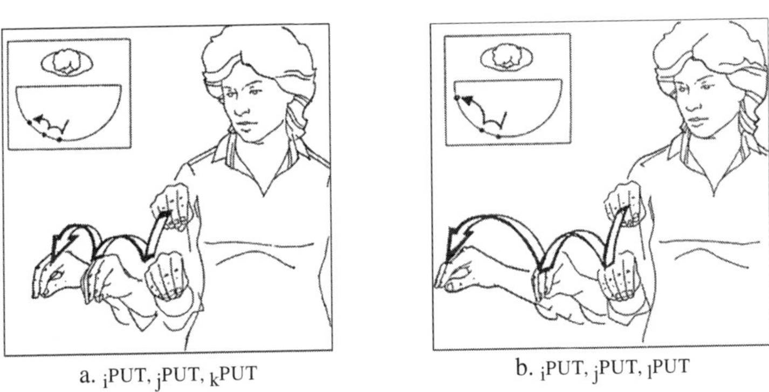

a. ${}_{i}$PUT, ${}_{j}$PUT, ${}_{k}$PUT   b. ${}_{i}$PUT, ${}_{j}$PUT, ${}_{l}$PUT

Figure 3.10 Two examples of spatial verbs (reprinted with permission from Padden 1988 [1983])

form – there is no difference in the interpretation between the forms in Figures 3.9a and 3.9b.

(4) ASL (Padden 1988 [1983], p. 36)

    ___________t
    a. 20 CHILDREN, ${}_{0}$GIVE$_{i,exhaus}$ BALLOON
    'I gave each of 20 children a balloon.'

In (5), PUT is a spatial verb. Figure 3.10 shows two variants of PUT very similar to the two variants of GIVE in Figure 3.9. However, the variants of PUT have different interpretations. As indicated by the translations in (5), the example in Figure 3.10a corresponds to a situation in which the candles are placed equidistant from one another, while the example in Figure 3.10b indicates that the candles were placed in a different arrangement.

(5) ASL (Padden 1988 [1983], p. 36)

a. CANDLE, $_1$INDEX $_i$PUT, $_j$PUT, $_k$PUT.
'I put three candles about equal distance from each other.'

b. CANDLE, $_1$INDEX $_i$PUT, $_j$PUT, $_l$PUT.
'I put one candle here, another one next to it and another way over there.'

These differences lead Padden to distinguish agreeing and spatial verbs as follows:[16]

> The phonetic representation of location in person agreement involves reference to vectors, not specific points. First-person agreement involves a vector located toward the upper center of the signer's body. Non-first-person agreement likewise involves general direction of movement away from the signer's body. Locative morphemes [those which are exploited by spatial verbs/WS/DLM], in contrast, access specific locations.
>
> (Padden 1990, p. 125)

All sign languages documented so far seem to have a tripartite division of verb types similar to the one that Padden proposes. While the existence of various verb types is clear, some researchers have challenged this sharp separation of verb classes (Engberg-Pedersen 1993).[17] In any case, while Padden's analysis lists which verbs belong to which class, it offers no explanation for the existence of the classes, nor any method of predicting class membership for any given verb. Others attempt to go beyond Padden's classification and explain the existence of different verb types in sign languages.

3.1.4 Determining agreement from nominal controllers

Janis (1992, 1995) provides the first major attempt to predict categories of agreeing forms. Rather than starting with the verb types, she examines the characteristics of the nominals with which verbs agree. For example, if a verb agrees with a locative, then the verb will display spatial agreement. In order to account for differences between verbs, Janis proposes a hierarchy of agreement controllers. The nominals most likely to control agreement are those which are highest in the hierarchy. This proposal takes after theories of spoken language agreement using similar hierarchies of potential agreement controllers (e.g., Givón 1976, Moravcsik 1988).

Janis' hierarchy of agreement controllers for ASL is based on case. Since the case a nominal will receive is based on aspects of the verb's semantics, her hierarchy is indirectly related to verbal semantics. Highest on the hierarchy

[16] Padden's use of the term non-first follows Meier's (1990) argument that pronouns in ASL distinguish only between first and non-first person, without a grammatical distinction between second and third person. We will adopt Meier's conclusion for the present, and discuss his argument in Unit 5.

[17] We will have more to say about spatial verbs in Chapter 6 below.

are locative nominals – those assigned locative case – which control locative agreement (spatial agreement in Padden's terms). For non-locative nominals, Janis' hierarchy stipulates that those with particular SRs (agent, experiencer when the verb is non-body-anchored, patient when animate, and recipient) may control agreement. Furthermore, nominals with certain grammatical roles (GRs) have priority in controlling agreement; specifically, indirect objects take precedence over direct objects, which take precedence over subjects. Finally, a subject cannot be the sole controller of agreement.

Janis argues that her analysis moves the agreement system of ASL closer to those found for spoken languages, in that the verbs which show agreement can be predicted on the basis of a hierarchy of controller features – such as GRs and SRs – features which are also employed by various spoken languages to determine agreement systems. However, she admits that the rankings offered for the controller features in ASL are typologically unusual; in particular, the rankings of locative over non-locative cases, and indirect objects over direct objects and subjects are not common.

These unusual rankings may just be a property of ASL which any analysis will have to deal with. In particular, the obligatoriness of object agreement with optional subject agreement seems to be an especially odd phenomenon. In spoken languages, if a language marks only one argument for agreement, it will be the subject and not the object. Janis' proposal also requires many stipulations and exceptions, and it cannot explain the class of "backwards" verbs. In an attempt to find a more unified and explanatory account of verb agreement, Meir (1998a, 1998b) approaches the issue with a proposal to account for backwards verbs based on aspects of their thematic structure. That analysis is then extended to an account for the distinction between plain, agreeing, and spatial verbs in a way that avoids the idiosyncrasy and stipulation of its predecessors.

3.1.5 Determining agreement based on the thematic structure of verbs

Let us begin by looking more closely at the intricacies of the problem. Recall that certain verbs appear to be morphologically backwards: they move from the locus associated with their object to the locus associated with their subject (see Figure 3.5). Friedman (1975) offers an account of backwards verbs: she argues that both regular and backwards agreement verbs are characterized by movement from the source NP, to the goal NP, rather than movement between subject and object. Padden (1988 [1983]) argues against the proposal by Friedman because, syntactically, regular and backwards verbs share certain properties which require reference to their subject and object. According to Padden's analysis, verbs must be lexically specified as "backwards."

One of Padden's arguments comes from the fact that with both regular and backwards verbs subject agreement is optional. For backwards verbs, this means that the verb may end at a neutral, central location, but it must begin directed toward a locus associated with its object. In addition, both regular and backwards verbs behave alike with respect to constraints such as her "Coreference Constraint on FORCE-type verbs." Matrix verbs such as FORCE take both a direct object NP and an embedded infinitival clause. The unexpressed subject of the embedded clause must be understood as coreferential with the matrix object according to this constraint. This is true whether the embedded verb is regular (6) or backwards (7).

(6) ASL (Padden 1988 [1983], p. 121)

a. ${}_{1}$INDEX ${}_{1}$FORCE${}_{2}$ ${}_{2}$GIVE${}_{1}$ MONEY.
'I'll force you to give me the money.'

b. *${}_{1}$INDEX ${}_{1}$FORCE${}_{2}$ ${}_{i}$GIVE${}_{2}$ MONEY.
'I'll force you that he would give you the money.'

(7) ASL (Padden 1988 [1983], p. 122)

a. ${}_{1}$URGE${}_{j}$ ${}_{i}$INVITE${}_{j}$ SISTER.
'I urged him to invite his sister.'

b. *${}_{1}$URGE${}_{j}$ ${}_{j}$INVITE${}_{i}$ SISTER.
'I urged him that she invite him.'

Padden argues, "an analysis of verb agreement which refers to the notion of 'subject' allows for the most general statement of the coreferentiality constraint for FORCE-type structures" (1988 [1983], p. 123). Although this constraint is a constraint on the verb's arguments, not on its agreement markers, it shows that the grammatical notions of subject and object are necessary; an analysis of the verb's arguments only in terms of notions such as source and goal would fail to express this kind of constraint without an extra rule.

Padden's account, then, captures the observation that grammatical roles such as subject and object are relevant to determining agreement in ASL. However, Friedman's observation that, semantically, backwards verbs have goal subjects and source objects just like regular agreeing verbs is missed by Padden's analysis.

Meir (1998a, 1998b, 2002) first observes that virtually the same class of verbs is backwards in ISL as in ASL. She proposes that the proper analysis of agreement in ISL (and presumably in ASL) is one which captures the relevance of both syntactic and semantic roles to the grammar. Furthermore, she notices that while the path of backwards verbs is from object to subject, they share with regular agreeing verbs the property of "facing" their objects. This means that the hand faces the spatial location of the object.[18] Her alternative is captured in the principles in (8).

[18] The property of facing is also noted elsewhere in the literature (under different names), e.g., in Friedman (1976), Fischer and Gough (1978). However, the systematic interaction of path direction, facing, and regular and backwards verbs was first reported and analyzed in Meir (1998a, 1998b).

(8) Principles of Sign Language Agreement Morphology (Meir 2002, p. 425)

a. The direction of the path movement of agreement verbs is from source to goal.
b. The facing of the hand(s) is towards the object of the verb (whichever of source or goal is not subject).

Meir's principles indicate that both GRs and SRs are relevant to agreement morphology. Thus, generalizations which apply to GRs may do so correctly; but the agreeing verb classes (regular, backwards) are still defined according to their semantic characteristics.

Meir's proposal goes yet a step further in characterizing the classes of verbs. She proposes that whether a verb is plain, agreeing, or spatial is determined by its thematic structure. Her theory relies on Jackendoff's (1990) model of Lexical Conceptual Structure (LCS), which employs hierarchically organized conceptual categories, such as Thing, Event, State, Action, and Path. The major conceptual categories can be further elaborated into more specific functions, taking another function or an argument as a complement, parallel to the syntactic X-bar schema.

In adopting Jackendoff's theory, Meir explains the particular relevance of the spatial grammatical relations that are so important in sign language grammar. She writes:

> Jackendoff adopts a "localistic" point of view, in that the basic major conceptual functions are those which encode spatial motion and location (e.g. PLACE, PATH, GO, STAY, ORIENT) (following Gruber 1976). These spatial conceptual categories are extended by abstraction to other semantic fields such as possession, ascription of properties, and temporal relations. That is, spatial relations are taken as the most basic semantic field.
>
> (Meir 1998a, pp. 28–29)

Meir (2002) proposes that agreeing and spatial verbs all contain a directional morpheme, glossed DIR, which denotes a path or trajectory a referent traverses. It is this morpheme which agrees with its source and goal. DIR as a bound morpheme fuses with roots of verbs of transfer, which make up the class of agreeing verbs. Thus, the Lexical Conceptual Structure (LCS) of such verbs will represent the movement (transfer) of a theme along a source-goal path, as illustrated in (9)–(10).

(9) (Meir 2002, pp. 434, 438)
DIR(ectional):[GO ([$]^{\gamma}$, [$_{\text{Path}}$ FROM[$]^{\alpha}$ TO[$]^{\beta}$)
DIR matches its complements in their R-loci

(10) The derived LCS of regular and backwards agreement verbs:

a. GIVE-type:
CAUSE ([α], [GO$_{\text{poss}}$ ([BOOK$]^{\gamma}$, [$_{\text{Path}}$ FROM[α] TO[β])]) AFF ([$]^{\alpha}$, [$]^{\beta}$)

b. TAKE-type:
CAUSE ([α], [GO$_{poss}$ ([BOOK]$^{\gamma}$, [$_{Path}$ FROM[β] TO[α])]) AFF ([ ]$^{\alpha}$, [ ]$^{\beta}$)

Certain properties of verbs of transfer help to account in a more parsimonious way for the apparently peculiar list of characteristics of agreement controllers posited by Janis (1992, 1995). For example, verbs of transfer must by definition select more than one argument (accounting for why agreement verbs are transitive, not intransitive). In addition, the subject and (dative) object of a verb of transfer are typically human or animate, or can be conceived of as such – that is, they must both be possible possessors. This takes care of the list of semantic roles which may be agreement controllers.

Meir also proposes that some candidate agreement verbs may not show agreement overtly for phonological reasons. In particular, if verbs are underlyingly specified for orientation, they may be agreeing verbs, but cannot mark facing; i.e., they are directional but not reversible verbs in the terminology of Fischer and Gough (1978). If both of the location segments of the verb are underlyingly specified, then the verb is reversible (marks facing) but not directional (won't mark path). And if both orientation and location are specified, then the verb will not mark agreement in any way. Verbs in ASL which would seem to fit the profile of verbs of transfer, such as BEG, FIRE, and FORGIVE, all seem to conform to the phonological restrictions suggested on the basis of ISL, and, as predicted, do not show overt agreement. Both languages also have verbs which fit the definition for agreeing verbs, but, because of a phonological specification for contact with part of the body on the first location, only show overt agreement with their objects, such as ISL ASK or ASL TELL.[19]

An interesting question is whether the restrictions on agreement are the same or different across sign languages. That there are many similar restrictions across sign languages is clear. Mathur (2000) compares agreeing verb forms across four sign languages – ASL, DGS (Deutsche Gebärdensprache, German Sign Language), AUSLAN (Australian Sign Language), and NS (Nihon Shuya, Japanese Sign Language). He proposes several phonetic constraints which affect potentially agreeing forms in all four languages. These constraints are offered as linguistic – not just articulatory – but phonetic. Whether sign languages have different constraints at the more abstract phonological level remains to be investigated.

Meir's proposal brings much greater explanation to the question of why sign language verb agreement has the apparently peculiar

[19] Note that there are different restrictions, depending on whether the verb is underlyingly specified for only the first location or both of them. In the former, a verb of transfer will show path agreement, but only with the object. In the latter, agreement is blocked altogether. These observations support models of sign language structure according to which such signs are characterized by a sequence of two locations (Liddell 1984b, Sandler 1989, Perlmutter 1992). They are less compatible with models positing direction features (e.g., Brentari 1990, 1998). See Chapters 9 and 13.

characteristics it has. However, there are some characteristics not (yet) explained by this approach. One is the fact that certain verbs which do mark agreement in some combinations of subject and object may fail to show agreement in other combinations. A related difficulty concerns the expression of number on agreeing verbs. We now turn to these issues, focusing exclusively on ASL.

3.1.6 Number agreement

As illustrated in Figure 3.7, verbs may agree with their objects in number. Agreement with a multiple object takes the form of a horizontal arcing movement at the end of the sign. Verbs may also agree with their subject or object for dual, taking the form of a single small, slightly displaced repetition of the movement; or for exhaustive, which employs several small, slightly displaced repetitions. These three number agreement forms are schematized in Figure 3.11. Optimally, any agreeing verb should be able to show any number inflection with any agreeing form. However, there are constraints on the combination of particular plural forms with particular agreeing forms. For example, Padden (1988 [1983]) notes that subjects cannot be marked with the multiple form. If the subject is multiple, it simply receives the singular form; its plurality is marked in another way (such as a separate pronoun sign with multiple marking). Furthermore, it is not possible for both subject and object to be marked plural. Again, if both the subject and object are plural, the verb is inflected only for plural object; the subject's plurality must be marked in a different way.

These constraints can simply be stated as part of the morphological process of agreement. However, Mathur (2000) and Rathmann and Mathur (2002) notice that there are further restrictions on the use of plural forms. For example, for many verbs the first-person object form cannot be marked for multiple, although multiple non-first marking is possible. Such verbs include *GIVE-us, *OFFER-us, and *FEED-us, which would require both flexion of the arm from the elbow and inward rotation from the shoulder; and *ANALYZE-us and *BAWL-OUT-us, which would require the non-dominant articulator to combine diagonal shoulder abduction with outward elbow rotation.

Mathur (2000) proposes that these constraints on plural forms are examples of more general phonetic constraints on the surface form of

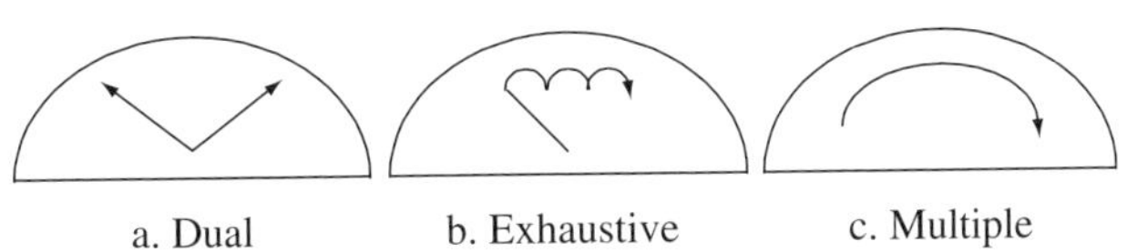

Figure 3.11 Three inflections for number, schematized

Figure 3.12 PICK-ON (ASL), citation form

agreeing verbs. We will present an example using the sign PICK-ON, which involves the dominant hand in a handshape tapping the non-dominant hand in a handshape (see Figure 3.12). For ease of discussion, the following descriptions will assume a right-dominant signer, as in the illustrations.

When PICK-ON is used with a first-person subject and the object is associated with a locus on the signer's right, the sign will move from an area close to the signer to the locus on the right as expected (illustrated in Figure 3.13a). Similarly, the verb with a first person object and a locus on the right as subject will take the expected form (illustrated in Figure 3.13b). However, if the subject is associated with a locus on the signer's left, and the object with the location on the right, the verb will not take the form of movement from the left to the right (for a right-handed signer), as illustrated in Figure 3.13c. This is because the phonological shape of this particular verb would require the left hand to be placed at the locus on the right, while the right arm crosses over the left and starts its movement at the locus on the left. Furthermore, the back of the right hand would need to be facing to the left, so that the front of the hand would be facing the object locus on the right. Such a form is not only physically awkward, but it presumably violates a phonetic constraint in the grammar.[20] Faced with such a situation, experienced but not novice signers will choose any of several alternatives, which might include changing hand dominance for this sign, or dropping the subject agreement and marking the object agreement only (perhaps using an overt pronoun for the subject). These two alternatives are illustrated in Figure 3.14. Thus, Mathur argues that phonetic constraints on articulation rule out certain agreeing forms, whether they combine with singular or plural arguments. If agreement

20 Rathmann and Mathur (1999) determined that the unacceptability of such forms was not simply due to articulatory difficulty by testing both experienced and novice signers on them. While novice signers (those with two years' experience or less) produce awkward forms, native signers reject them and replace them with alternative forms. This study does not say whether the relevant constraints are phonetic or phonological, but clearly they are part of the grammar.

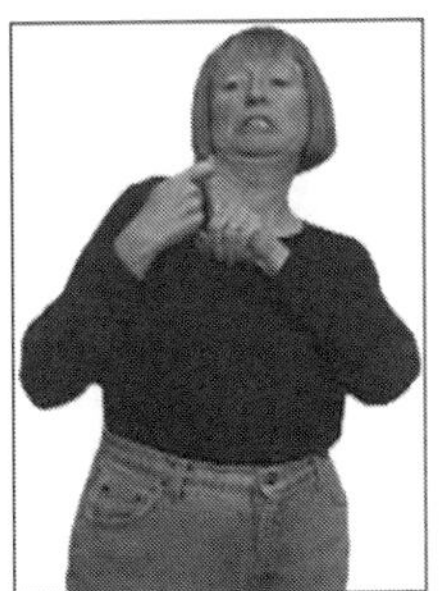

a. 1-PICK-ON-a(right) b. a(right)-PICK-ON-1

c. *b(left)-PICK-ON-a(right)

Figure 3.13 PICK-ON, three forms

a. b-PICK-ON-a (changed dominance)

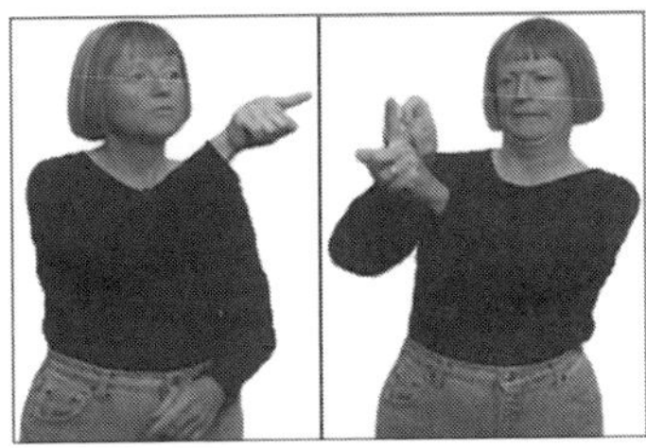

b. b(left)-PRON PICK-ON-a(right)

Figure 3.14 Alternatives to b(left)-PICK-ON-a(right) (ASL)

produces a form which violates the phonetic constraints of the language, an alternative form is generated instead.

Because this process does not involve affixation, Mathur (2000) considers it a phonological readjustment rule under the framework of Distributed Morphology (Halle and Marantz 1993). However, Rathmann and Mathur (2002) modify this view, recognizing that the earlier proposal fails to account for syntactic effects of agreement. Accordingly, Rathmann and Mathur (2002) develop Mathur's (2000) proposal by putting forth a model of agreement which accounts for the non-affixal nature of agreement in sign languages without taking all aspects of agreement out of the syntax.

We will come back to verb agreement in Unit 5, where we discuss some recent challenges to the view of the process described here as agreement, and to implications for the interaction of linguistic organization, modality, and cognition.

3.1.7 Non-manual marking of agreement

Recently, it has been claimed that subject and object agreement may also be marked non-manually in ASL (Bahan 1996, Neidle, Bahan, MacLaughlin, Lee, and Kegl 1998a, Neidle, MacLaughlin, Lee, Bahan, and Kegl 2000).[21] We will review the description of this phenomenon here and discuss some issues concerning it. Bahan and colleagues also make extensive claims about the phrase structure of ASL based on their observations about non-manual markers of agreement. These claims will be discussed in Unit 4, where the overall phrase structure proposed by this group is presented.

The basic description of non-manual agreement marking concerns transitive constructions. In transitive constructions, the signer's head may tilt in the direction of the locus of the subject, while his or her eyes may gaze in the direction of the locus of the object. According to Bahan, the head tilt is a non-manual manifestation of subject agreement, and the eye gaze is a non-manual manifestation of object agreement. This non-manual marking of agreement is not generally obligatory, but Bahan observes that it occurs frequently and is required in some contexts (to be elaborated shortly). According to Bahan et al., the non-manual marking of agreement may co-occur with agreeing or plain verbs. Head tilt and eye gaze are illustrated in Figure 3.15, with a verb marked for manual subject and object agreement. Although other researchers have noticed

[21] Bahan and his colleagues are members of the American Sign Language Linguistic Research Project (ASLLRP). The material discussed in this section is presented in Bahan (1996), Neidle et al. (1998a), Bahan et al. (2000), and Neidle et al. (2000). As these sources all present essentially the same data and analyses with respect to the issues under discussion here, we will mainly cite only Bahan (1996), unless we are quoting specifically from another reference.

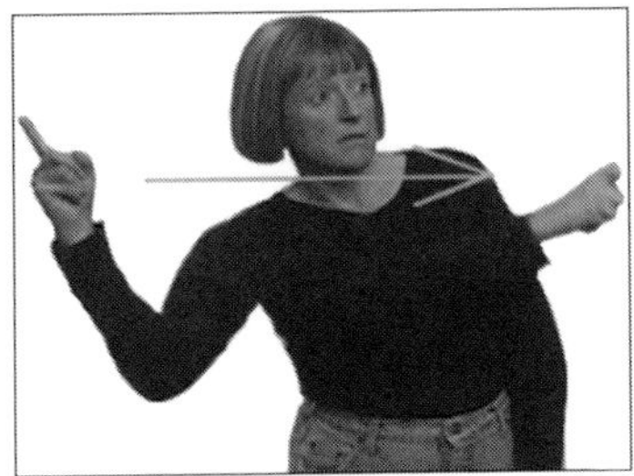

a-ASK-b
(manual and non-manual agreement)

Figure 3.15 Non-manual marking of agreement

the presence of specific eye gaze, head tilts, and body leans during signed discourse and associated them with other functions (e.g., Baker 1977, Baker and Padden 1978, Kegl 1986), this is the first proposal to treat certain instances of eye gaze and head tilt as manifestations of agreement.

There are some complications to the description, however. First, since the eyes cannot gaze toward the locus of the first person, when the object is first person, eye gaze is used to indicate the subject, and the head position indicates the object.

Second, there is an "indefinite" form of object agreement in both manual and non-manual modes. Manually, agreement with an indefinite or nonspecific object involves moving the hand to an unspecified location on a higher plane than definite agreeing forms. Non-manually, with an indefinite object "the eyes do not gaze toward a single point in space, but may wander within an area in space (or may gaze in an unfocused manner)" (Bahan et al. 2000, p. 12).

Third, there is a "neutral" or "unmarked" position for subject agreement, both manual and non-manual. The manual neutral subject agreement form is essentially the same as the first-person form. Bahan (1996, p. 103) says that it is "similar in realization to the 1st person agreement form." It is also essentially the same form Padden (1988 [1983]) and others call a verb with "Agreement Marker Omission." However, Bahan argues that the agreement is not omitted in such verbs, but merely unmarked/neutral. One interesting piece of evidence for this conclusion is that even when the subject agreement is unmarked (for person), number agreement may be apparent. As noted above, subjects do not take multiple agreement, but they can take other forms of plural. The example in (11) shows a plural form involving the two hands reduplicating the verb movement in an alternating fashion. This plural form can be used with either a specific, marked subject locus (a), or the unmarked, neutral position (b).

a. neu-ASK-b (neutral manual and non-manual subject agreement)

b. neu-ASK-b (neutral manual and non-neutral non-manual subject agreement)

Figure 3.16 Non-manual marking of agreement

(11) ASL (Bahan 1996, p. 106)

a. PEOPLE GROUP$_i$ (2h alt)$_i$GIVE$_j$++ JANA$_j$ TOY
'A group of people gave Jana toys.'

b. MANY PEOPLE $_{\text{neutral-position}}$(2h alt)GIVE$_j$++ JANA$_j$ TOY
'Many people gave Jana toys.'

Bahan claims that there is also an unmarked form of non-manual subject agreement, which is also "very close to the form used for 1st person" (1996, p. 121). However, unlike the unmarked manual form, the unmarked non-manual form can be distinguished from the first-person form by "a specific kind of body position that includes a slight forward lean" (ibid.). This lean is clearly visible in the video clips to accompany Neidle et al. (1998a), generously made available at the ASLLRP website (http://www.bu.edu/asllrp). We have replicated it in Figure 3.16, which contrasts the neutral and non-neutral non-manual forms of subject agreement, in both cases with a verb having neutral manual subject agreement. For intransitive constructions, Bahan and colleagues claim that either eye gaze, head tilt, or both are used to express agreement with the single argument.

Bahan and colleagues argue that the non-manual markings described above constitute overt manifestations of the features of agreement. They assume that agreement features constitute heads of syntactic categories which project to full phrasal categories, just as a Noun head projects a Noun Phrase, a Verb projects a Verb Phrase, etc. According to them, the timing and spread of non-manual agreement features support this idea.

Several questions can be raised about the proposal that the movements of the head and eyes constitute non-manual marking of agreement.

Bahan suggests that the neutral form of non-manual subject agreement marking may be more common than the overt head tilt (p. 121). Although the neutral form may have a body lean to distinguish it from lack of non-manual subject agreement, apparently this is not always found. Thus, there may well be many cases which could be analyzed as having non-manual subject agreement but which look no different from cases without non-manual subject agreement. This makes some of the claims about this marker empirically untestable.

Another question about the analysis of these markers as agreement comes from the possible different distribution of the manual and non-manual markers. Recall from Section 3.1.3 that manual agreement is limited to verbs which take two animate arguments, or two arguments which are both possible possessors. Some verbs fail to take agreement because of phonological reasons, but others are simply not in the class of agreeing verbs. According to Bahan, non-manual markers of agreement occur with both agreeing and plain verbs, including intransitives. Apparently, non-manual marking of agreement is not limited to the class of potentially agreeing verbs. If both agreeing and plain verbs take non-manual agreement, but only agreeing verbs agree with source and goal of the possessors in a transfer relation, what is it that the non-manual marking on transitive and intransitive plain verbs is agreeing with?

A third issue concerns Bahan's claims about the timing of head tilt and eye gaze – that head tilt marking subjects precedes eye gaze that marks objects. These differences have not been observed in our examination of videos made available on the ASLLRP website. We conclude that the purported difference in timing may require instrumentation and confirmation.

Examining the timing of the non-manual markers with respect to VP-adverbials might help to clarify their structural position. It is generally assumed that certain adverbs, like *always* and *definitely*, adjoin to VP. Thus, they would be expected to fall within the c-command domain of Agr_S and Agr_O, and should be marked with eye gaze and head tilt. However, data collected by one of us show that head tilt and eye gaze begin only with the verb, after any preverbal VP-adverbials, as in example (12). This weakens the claim that these markers originate in agreement projections dominating VP, if we accept the researchers' claim, crucial for their theory, that timing directly reflects tree structure.

(12) head tilt-a
eyegaze-b
a-JOHN DEFINITELY a-BLAME-b b-MARY
'John definitely blames Mary.'

Finally, Bahan points out that there may be some semantic or pragmatic differences between overt and default head positions. Also, as he points out, eye gaze has several purposes in ASL, concerned with discourse and pragmatic factors. It appears quite possible, then, that head tilt and eye gaze play a semantic and/or pragmatic role rather than a purely formal role like that of agreement. This possibility suggests itself as an important topic for future research.

3.1.8 Verb agreement summary

Verb agreement has played a prominent role in descriptions of sign language morphology. As far as we know, every sign language uses verb agreement, in ways very similar to the system used in ASL and ISL (although some researchers may use different terminology, references to a process like the one described here can be found in, e.g., Bos 1990 on Sign Language of the Netherlands; Brennan 1981 on British Sign Language; Collins-Ahlgren 1989 on New Zealand Sign Language; Engberg-Pedersen 1993 on Danish Sign Language; Fischer 1996 on Japanese Sign Language; Pizzuto, Giuranna, and Gambino 1990 on Italian Sign Language; Smith 1990 on Taiwan Sign Language). The potential sign universality of verb agreement and the particular form that it takes in signed languages are no doubt influenced by the modality, an issue we have not yet discussed.

However, the question of how to account for the use of space in agreement (as well as pronouns) has received considerable attention in recent literature. In fact, it has led some researchers to abandon the notion of agreement in sign language altogether (Liddell 1995, 2000). We will take up this concern in Unit 5.

Phonologically, the form of agreement in sign languages involves changes in the beginning and ending locations of verb roots. This shows that it is crucially necessary to be able to refer to the beginning and ending of a sign – a requirement which has important implications for sign language phonology. This requirement is discussed in Unit 3, where the notion of sequentiality versus simultaneity in ASL is discussed at length.

The syntactic realization and consequences of agreement have received less attention, but some researchers such as the ASLLRP group have begun to address this issue. We will return to it in Unit 4. There we will also address some grammatical differences between sign languages within the verb agreement system. In particular, there is some evidence that some sign languages treat sentences with agreeing verbs structurally differently from sentences with plain verbs (Quadros 1999 on Brazilian Sign Language, Rathmann 2000 on German Sign Language). Also, some sign languages have what is analyzed as an auxiliary verb, which carries agreement marking when the main verb does not (Bos 1994 on SLN, Rathmann 2000 on German Sign Language,

Smith 1990 on Taiwanese SL). The auxiliary element will be discussed in more detail in Chapter 19.

3.2 Verbal aspect

Verbs and predicate adjectives in sign languages may be inflected for aspect by altering the movement shape and/or the rhythmic pattern. Klima and Bellugi (1979) describe a large number of aspectual inflections in ASL, expressing temporal aspect, manner, and focus – eight for verbs and eleven for predicate adjectives. The illustrations in Figure 3.17 demonstrate some of these, using the verb LOOK-AT and the predicate adjective SICK. Aspect markings with similar form and meaning have been described for other sign languages as well (e.g., Bergman 1983 for Swedish Sign Language; Brennan 1983 and Sutton-Spence & Woll 1999 for British Sign Language; Engberg-Pedersen 1993 for Danish Sign Language; Sandler 1996b for ISL), though none of these present as rich a system as that described in Klima and Bellugi.

A comparison with aspectual systems found in spoken languages yields similarities in function with that of ASL, and differences in form. For example, Chukchee has fifteen different aspectual affixes. Two of these – *-lʔet*, prolonged continuous action, and *-sqəcat*, accelerated action – are shown in (13).

(13) Chukchee (data from Skorik 1977, cited in Spencer 1991)

a. *-lʔet* prolonged continuous action

ʔəttʔe	ninepiŋku-*lʔ et*-qin . . .	ottəlgən
dog	jump-*ASP*-3/3	stick

'The dog jumped over the stick over and over again.'

b. *-sqəcat* accelerated action

qənwer	ŋəto-*sqəcat*-gʔə	gəmnin	təletumgin
at last	come-out-*ASP*-3sgSUBJ	my	companion

'At last my companion sprang out.'

While the functions and abundance of aspectual modifications are clearly comparable in ASL and Chukchee, the morphophonological implementation of aspect is just as clearly different in the two languages. Chukchee strings affixes one after another in a sequence, while, according to Klima and Bellugi, ASL "superimposes" different rates, rhythms, degrees of tenseness, and pauses on the basic signs. Is this difference of structure a fundamental modality difference, or is each language choosing from the same universal pool of morphological mechanisms, much as they choose from the same pool of grammatical functions, but just happening, in this case, to come up with different structural mechanisms for the same function? And is the simultaneous nature of the sign language forms unique to the morphology of visual languages?

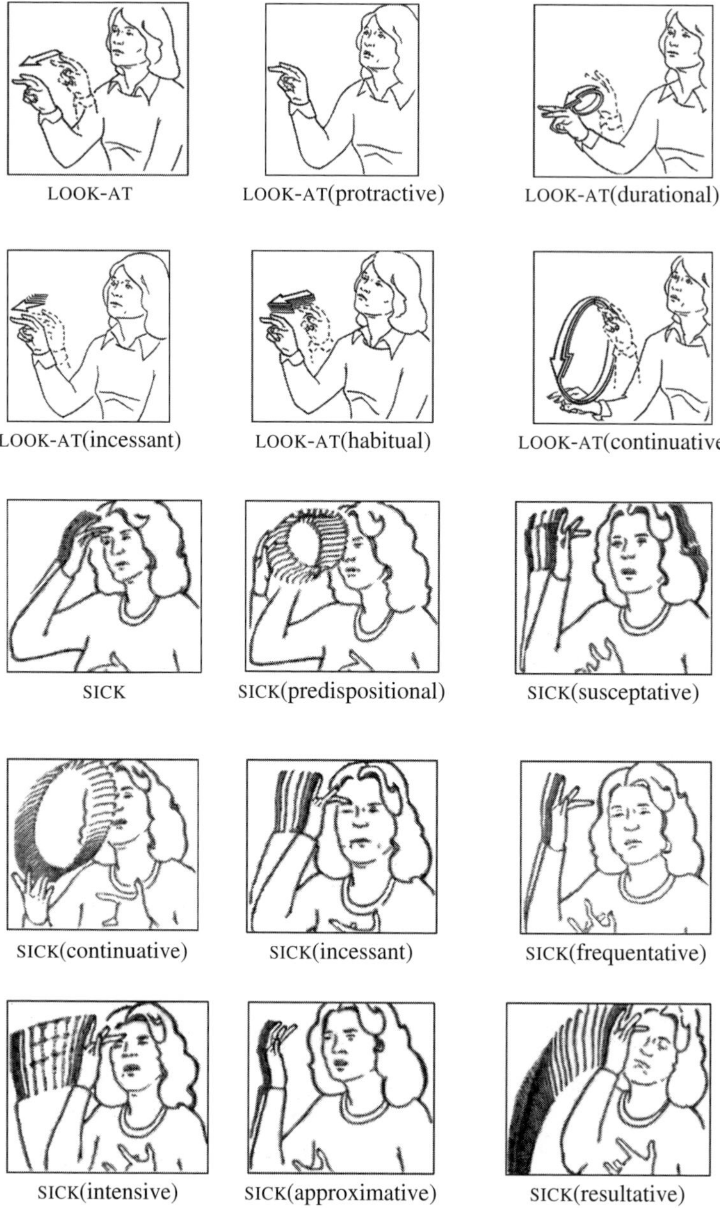

Figure 3.17 Aspect markings in ASL (LOOK-AT, SICK) (© Ursula Bellugi, the Salk Institute)

A step toward an answer to the latter question can be found in a treatment of the Unrealized Inceptive aspect in ASL (Liddell 1984a). This aspect, which conveys the meaning, 'was just about to begin Verbing,' is formed by truncating the base sign and adding inflectional material. Liddell describes three verb classes, each of which enters into an inflectional "syllable frame" with some of

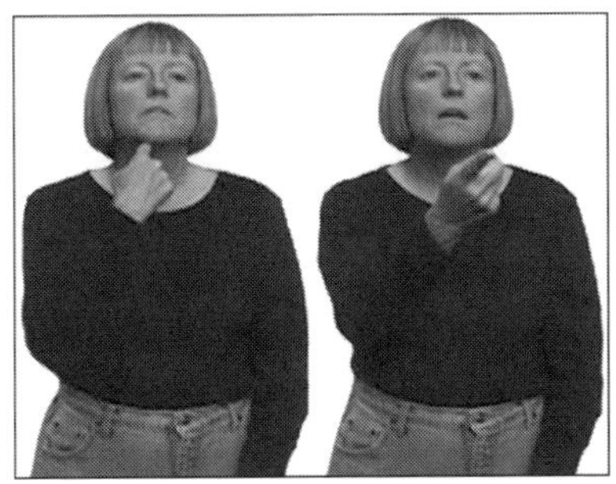

a. TELL (citation form)

b. TELL [Unrealized Inceptive]

Figure 3.18 Two forms of TELL (ASL)

its features prespecified. Here we will consider only verbs of Liddell's class 1, an example of which is TELL, shown in Figure 3.18 in citation form and in the Unrealized Inceptive. In class 1 verbs, the derived sign begins at a place of articulation near the abdomen. The hand follows an arc movement path and ends up at the first place of articulation of the base sign, while the signer inhales and rotates his/her body. The sign TELL is normally produced by placing the index finger at the chin and then moving the hand outward toward the location of the object. In Liddell's analysis, the Unrealized Inceptive frame consists of two segments, a Movement segment, and a Hold or static segment. This is shown schematically in (14). The features and certain other aspects of the representation are simplified here for clarity.

(14) Incompletive Inceptive frame, class 1 verbs (Liddell 1984a, p. 264)

```
RIGHT HAND              -----------------------
    Movement:           |    M    |     H     |
                        |   arc   |           |
                        | -------- | -------- |
                             | \        |
                             |   \      |
                             |     \    |
                        -----------------------
    Hand Config:        |_       _|_         _|
    Pt. of Contact:     |    -    |           |
                        |         |           |
                        |_OpTRt_|_           _|
    Grounding:          |         |           |
                        |_       _|_         _|
    Orientation:        |   BA    |           |
                        |_  EL   _|_         _|
    Non-manual Sig:     |         |   CURB    |
                        |_GZ-Loc_|_GZ-Loc_|
```

According to this analysis, the handshape is specified by the base sign, as is the final place of articulation, to be specified in the empty box in the representation. These features spread onto the initial segment, whose other features are specified by the inflectional frame. In the Unrealized Inceptive form of TELL, the hand moves from a point in front of the abdomen up to contact with the chin, while the signer inhales and rotates the body. Although Liddell believes this kind of morphology to be very unusual, he suggests that his treatment has something in common with the theory developed by McCarthy (1979, 1981) to account for the morphology of Semitic languages. We review that theory and describe a model of sign language morphology that is directly related to it in Section 3.4.

Many of the temporal aspect inflections that have been reported for ASL involve reduplication. Although this device does not appear in the Chukchee aspectual system, the use of reduplication to mark iterative, habitual, or continuative activity is not uncommon in the world's spoken languages. In sign languages, the morphological option of reduplication is exploited for a large number of other inflections and derivations as well. We turn now to a study of noun pluralization in Italian Sign Language that involves a particular type of reduplication.

3.3 Pluralization

A study of pluralization in Italian Sign Language (LIS) was conducted by Pizzuto and Corazza (1996). They found that nominal signs that are produced in neutral space rather than on the body are systematically reduplicated by displacement. That is, the sign is iterated three or more times, each at a different point in space. Signs that are body anchored (including signs in which the non-dominant hand serves as a place of articulation; see Chapter 12) are pluralized non-morphologically, by adding numbers or quantifiers, or by adding several head nods towards different locations in space. The authors also point out that constructions involving nominal classifiers (see Chapter 5) can always take morphological (reduplicative) pluralization. If the phonological form of a sign blocks plural displacement because it requires contact with the body, and if a classifier is available that can represent the noun, then the classifier can undergo plural displacement in place of the noun it represents. Similar methods for pluralization are found in ASL.

Although reduplication involves a sequence of forms, it is considered to be basically non-linear in nature. This is because it involves not only copying some or all of the abstract prosodic structure of the base but also superimposing the features of the base sign upon that abstract template (e.g., McCarthy 1979, Marantz 1982, McCarthy and Prince 1986). In other words, the copied portion linearly precedes or succeeds the base, but the phonological content is associated with the copy in a non-linear fashion. Pluralization, like other sign language reduplicative processes described previously, is non-linear in this sense. How do models of morphology account for non-linear processes?

3.4 Models of templatic morphology

The morphology of sign languages is often described as "simultaneous," for reasons that have by now become obvious. The sequential affixation so common in spoken languages is relatively rare in sign languages (though it does occur, as we show in Chapter 4). Far more common are the kinds of processes described in the previous subsections, in which the base, or root sign, is modified by the superimposition of some element.

While morphological processes in spoken language are typically linear, involving the sequential lining up of bases and affixes, non-linear morphology is also found in spoken languages. Morphology that is non-linear is also sometimes called non-concatenative (McCarthy 1979). These terms are broad enough to include any of a wide range of morphological processes, including ablaut in English *sing*, *sang*, *sung*, for example. The particular type of non-concatenative morphology that involves association of phonological material to an abstract prosodic form or template is called prosodic morphology or **templatic morphology**. It is the templatic type of non-concatenative morphology that is so abundant in sign languages.

In the case of verb agreement (Section 3.1), the beginning and ending locations and facing of the hand are altered, depending on the referential loci established for the source and goal (or subject and object). Note that the source/goal agreement markers are actually sequenced: first the source and then the goal. However, the process is felt to be simultaneous because the addition of the agreement markers does not result in a sign with more sequential segments than in the citation form. In both the citation and the agreement marked forms, the hand simply moves from one location to another. Furthermore, some subject/object markers involve no sequencing at all – just a change in facing.

In the aspectual inflections as well, signs typically do not have sequential affixes like those of Chukchee (example (13) above). Instead, the shape and extent of the movement path and/or the duration of one or both locations is altered. As Liddell noticed, this type of morphological form is somewhat similar to that found, for example, in Semitic languages. Morphology that changes the shape or rhythm of a word rather than adding affixes – called prosodic morphology – is discussed from a phonological perspective in Unit 3, where we also motivate sequential segments in sign language (see especially Chapter 9).[22] We anticipate that discussion now, from the point of view of morphology.

22 Morphology that is not sequential goes by a number of names, depending on which aspects of a given morphological system or theory are the focus of discussion: non-linear, non-concatenative, templatic, and prosodic, among others. In Unit 3, where phonology is in focus, we consider the prosodic properties of the sign language templates, and consequently adopt the term "prosodic morphology" there.

In Standard Arabic, the difference between the three words in (15) is one of duration of consonants and vowels.

(15) Standard Arabic

kataba	'he wrote'
kaataba	'he corresponded'
kattaba	'he caused to write'

McCarthy (1979, 1981) adopted the non-linear representations of autosegmental phonology to express the fact that the morphological alterations here are not linear or concatenative. Rather, they involve association of the root consonants (*k, t, b* in the present example) and of the vowels that indicate voice or mood (here *a*) to a prosodic template consisting only of the sequence and durations of consonants (Cs) and vowels (Vs) specified by the particular derivational category: CVCVCV (*kataba*), CVVCVCV (*kaataba*), and CVCCVCV (*kattaba*). Where one element, such as the vowel *a*, is associated to two vowel (V) slots, it is pronounced as a long vowel. Where one consonant, like *t*, is attached to two consonant (C) slots, it is pronounced as a long or geminate consonant. This type of structure is illustrated in (16).

(16) Templatic morphology in Arabic

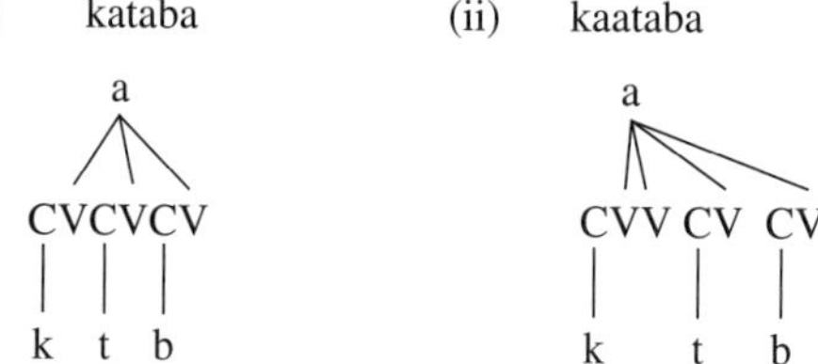

McCarthy's representation makes clear the fact that each prosodic template has a morphological status of its own, regardless of which root is associated to it. In Arabic, most roots are triconsonantal and, as such, different roots attach in the same way to the same templates (those above and many others) with more or less the same semantic-grammatical results.[23]

Similarly, the Intensive inflection of the ASL sign SICK, as represented in (17), may be best analyzed as the association of the base sequence to a prosodic template in which the first and last locations are lengthened (following Sandler 1989, 1990).[24] The base consists of a Location near the

[23] McCarthy's theory successfully captures regularities in the Standard Arabic verb system. There are, however, unpredictable facts about the system, such as restrictions on co-occurrence of certain roots with certain templates and some idiosyncrasies in the semantics. As the lexicon is the repository of the idiosyncratic, this is to be expected in derivational morphological processes of this sort.

[24] The motivation for the sequential model of Locations and Movements used here for illustration is presented in Unit 3.

forehead (in the absence of a simple transcription system, we represent it as x), followed by a straight Movement (y) and another Location in contact with the forehead (z): together, x,y,z. The Intensive template, represented as sequences of L (location) and M (movement) segments, is LLMLL, to which the x,y,z base is associated. The Intensive form is then the same as the base LML sign, but with longer duration (the hand is held in its position) on the first and last locations: xxyzz. The Durational form adds an arc feature to the movement of the base sign. In both spoken and signed languages, bases may be augmented or truncated to fit prosodic templates. More examples and the phonological mechanics of such processes appear in Chapter 9.

(17) Templatic morphology in ASL

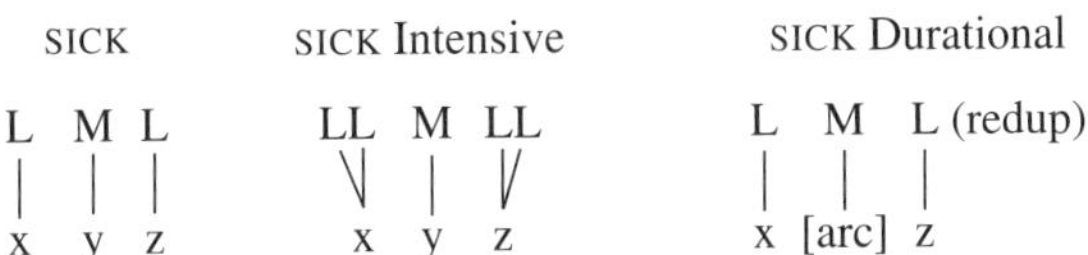

Another aspectual operation in ASL forms the Delayed Completive (Brentari 1998). This operation productively applies to telic verbs, with some phonological restrictions, and adds the meaning, 'delay the completion of x,' where x is the base verb. The first location of the verb is held longer than in the citation form of the base, and is characterized either by wiggling of the fingers or wagging of the tongue. That is, an L segment is added to the beginning of the sign pre-associated with the wiggle feature. All other features of hand configuration and of location spread to that initial L segment. During the movement to the second location, a mouth movement corresponding to the spoken syllable *ap* is articulated. More specific phonological details are provided in Chapter 14.

The nominal and verbal prosodic templates of Semitic languages have both derivational and inflectional properties (Aronoff 1994). We have made the traditional assumption that the ASL temporal aspects described here are inflectional. Temporal aspects are typically part of a language's inflectional system, but there are exceptions to such generalizations: a process that is usually inflectional might be derivational in particular languages and vice versa. Derivational affixes may be quite selective about the base they attach to, and often result in idiosyncratic phonological changes and meanings that cannot be predicted by rule. As inflections are systematically related to other elements in the sentence, on the other hand, it makes sense that they would be less idiosyncratic and more productive. The morphology of the aspectual modulations found in ASL has never been fully investigated. Idiosyncrasies, the interaction of aspect with different categories of verbs, with classifier predicates, and with additional morphological processes all await more detailed study.

In any case, one overriding formal characteristic of sign language morphology is clear: much of the morphology of sign languages is templatic in nature. This is true of its inflectional morphology, and, as we show in the next chapter, it is true of its derivational morphology as well.

4 Derivational morphology

We have described rich systems of morphology in sign languages – specifically, inflectional morphology, the type that is related to the use of words with other words in sentences. But that is not the only kind of morphology that exists in sign languages. The morphology of lexeme formation – derivational morphology – is also to be found in languages of signs. As in the inflectional component, much of the derivational morphology of sign languages is templatic.

4.1 Templatic derivational morphology in sign languages

The clearest earmark of derivational morphology is a change in lexical category (part of speech), and one of the earliest studies of derivational morphology in ASL concerned the relation between certain pairs of nouns and verbs (Supalla and Newport 1978). As we show in Section 4.1.1, this is an example of the typical templatic derivational morphology found in ASL and other sign languages. This subsection also discusses several other templatic derivational processes observed in ASL. Allomorphy is observed in ASL as well. The degree of linguistic abstractness inherent in allomorphy is highlighted by a particular ASL allomorphic alternation that is shown to extend to different homophonic morphemes. The chapter concludes with a discussion of non-manual morphemes. In these morphemes expressed on the face, we find a modality-specific type of simultaneous morphology, but one that is nevertheless strictly constrained.

4.1.1 Templatic derivational morphology in ASL

Supalla and Newport (1978) investigated a class of semantically and formationally related nouns and verbs in ASL. The verbs of this class are activities; the nouns are concrete, and are semantically related to the activity – often as instruments (BROOM, SWEEP; IRON, IRON), but also as locations (CHAIR, SIT) and other roles. Although earlier descriptions (Stokoe, Casterline, and Croneberg 1965) had claimed that related

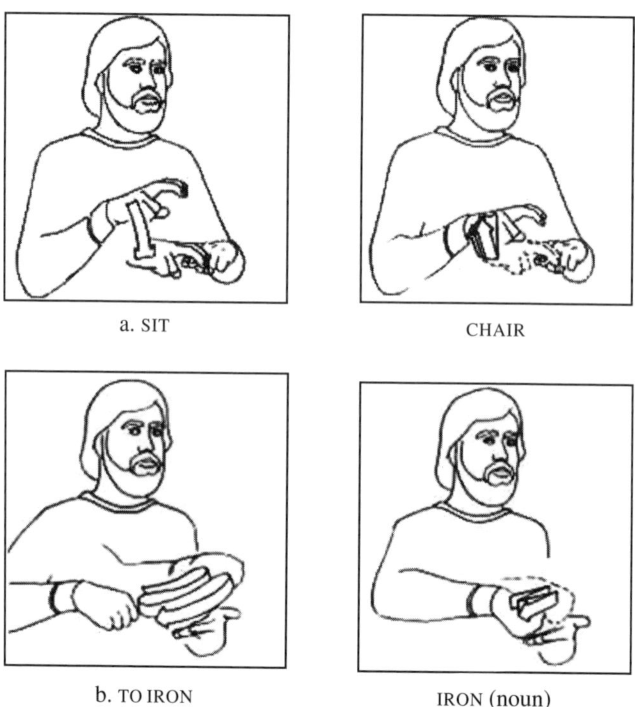

Figure 4.1 Derivationally related noun/verb pairs (reprinted with permission from Supalla and Newport 1978)

nouns and verbs such as CHAIR and SIT were formationally identical and disambiguated only by sentence context, Supalla and Newport took note of a systematic movement pattern which distinguishes the noun from the verb in such pairs, as illustrated in Figure 4.1. Verbs are generally signed using relatively longer movement. Verbs which involve a completed action, such as SIT, have only one movement; verbs that inherently involve duration or iteration, like IRON or SWEEP, are reduplicated. The related nouns are characterized by reduplication always, regardless of whether or not the related verb is reduplicated, and also by short, restrained movement. Supalla and Newport propose that an abstract form not specified for grammatical category underlies both the noun and verb, and they propose separate derivational rules to derive the surface noun or verb form. The appendix to the Supalla and Newport article lists about 100 noun–verb pairs, indicating that this is a productive derivational process.

Klima and Bellugi (1979) and Padden and Perlmutter (1987) describe another derivational process, one which forms activity nouns from verbs, such as ACT, ACTING; SWIM, SWIMMING; WRITE, WRITING; CHAT, CHATTING. Regardless of the form of the verb, the nouns are all

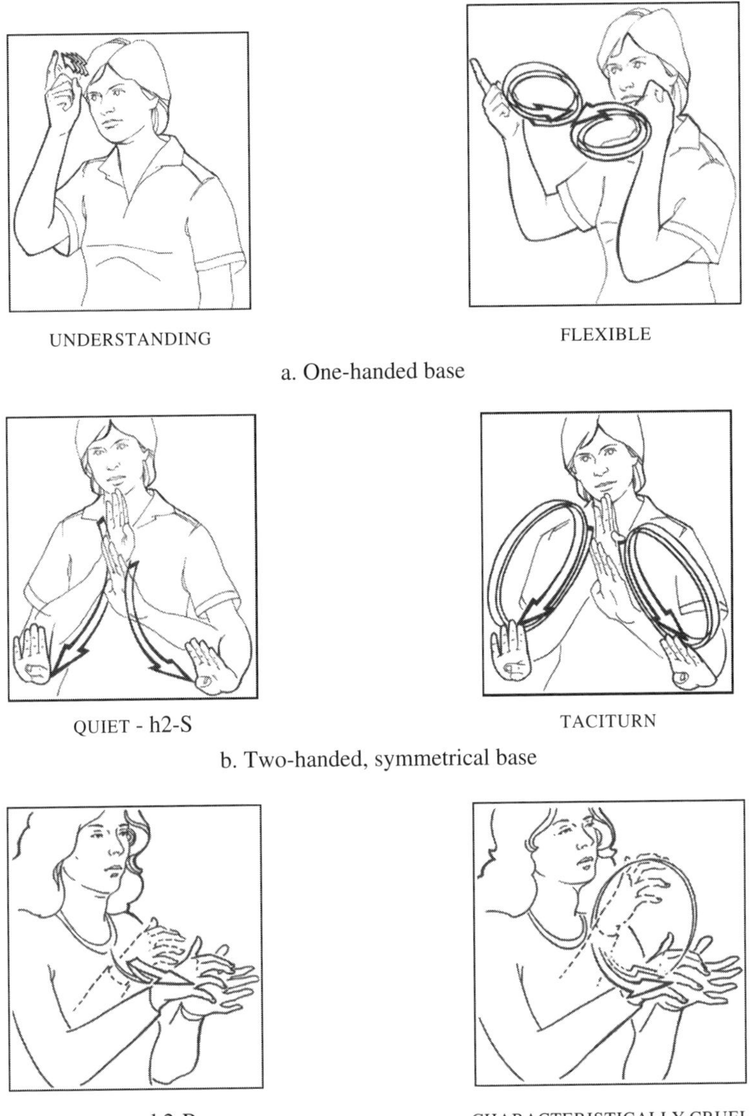

c. Two-handed, non-symmetrical base

Figure 4.2 Characteristic adjective formation (© Ursula Bellugi, the Salk Institute)

characterized by movements described by Padden and Perlmutter as small, stiff, quick movements, repeated numerous times.

ASL adjectives with the meaning 'characteristically x' are derived through a different process (Padden and Perlmutter 1987). In this process, illustrated in Figure 4.2, FLEXIBLE is derived from the adjective

UNDERSTANDING, and TACITURN is derived from QUIET. Padden and Perlmutter describe the morphological change resulting from this derivation as in (1).

(1) Characteristic Adjective Rule (Padden and Perlmutter 1987, p. 346)
Input: adjective
Phonological change in output: reduplicated circular movement
If input is one-handed, output is alternating.

Notice that the output is alternating if the input is one-handed. Since there are more one-handed than two-handed signs, and since alternating movement is more marked than non-alternating movement, we may consider the alternating movement to be the underlying form of movement for this derivation. However, as implied by the qualifying statement in the rule, the derivation has more than one morphological form or allomorph.

4.1.2 Allomorphy

The Characteristic Adjective derivation involves more than one form depending on the characteristics of the base, as shown in Figure 4.2 above. If the base is one-handed, then the derived form gets alternating reduplicated movement. If the base is a two-handed sign in which both hands move symmetrically, then the derived, reduplicated form has plain, non-alternating movement. If the base sign is two-handed but one hand moves while the other serves as a place of articulation, then the derived form is one-handed. This alternation is an example of allomorphy: two different forms for the same grammatical element.

In Section 3.4, we described the Delayed Completive aspect as characterized either by finger wiggle or tongue wag. Specifically, if the lexically specified handshape is , then the first segment is additionally specified for wiggle in the Delayed Completive form; with any other handshape, the tongue wag is specified instead. The two forms of the Delayed Completive provide another example of allomorphy in ASL.

These examples demonstrate that phonologically conditioned allomorphy is not alien to sign language. And, as is often the case with spoken language, it is not a purely phonetic phenomenon. It is physically quite possible to use alternating movement in examples like that in Figure 4.2b above, and it is physically possible to substitute a handshape for a different underlying one and wiggle the fingers in the Delayed Completive. But there is something in the morphological system – in these cases, possibly some requirement on retrievability of the base – that blocks the alternating and the wiggling allomorph in these forms, and produces the other allomorphs instead. This is an interesting result from a cognitive point of view. It means that the word-building mechanisms of human language universally allow alternate forms for a single meaning-bearing element. These forms, though phonologically different from one another, are still interpreted as the "same" in meaning and function.

4.1.3 An ASL morphome

The alternating movement allomorphy represents an even more abstract property of morphology that is shared with spoken language: the existence of "morphomes", often tied to syncretism in spoken languages (Aronoff 1994). In many languages, there are instances of a grammatical marker that has more than one function. Such markers may have originated as distinct morphemes and merged diachronically, resulting in syncretism. In English, for example, an inflectional suffix of the form *-s* has three distinct functions: it marks verbs for third-person singular in the present tense; and it marks nouns both for plural and for possessive. This inflectional *-s* also has three phonologically conditioned allomorphs: [z] following voiced sounds (*jog*[z], *bill*[z], *man'*[z]); [s] following voiceless sounds (*walk*[s], *hat*[s], *shop'*[s]); and [əz], following all sibilants, whether voiced or voiceless (*lunch*[əz]; *church*[əz]; *judge'*[əz]). In each case, the first example is of person/number/tense on the verbs; the second is the plural on nouns; and the third is the possessive. This alternation can be shown to be allomorphy rather than allophony; that is, it is triggered by the morpheme rather than purely by phonological conditions. We can see this in words ending in sonorants, such as *purrs*, *pews*, or *hen's*. They get the [z] allomorph because the sound before the *-s* is voiced, while other combinations of sonorants with final [s], in which the [s] is not a morpheme, may have the voiceless [s] in the same position: *purse*, *puce*, *hence*.

The fact that this inflectional *-s* has the same allomorphy regardless of grammatical function indicates that in some sense, the grammar treats it as one entity. To underscore the abstract basis on which all these distinct *-s* forms are regarded as a single entity by the grammar, Aronoff (1994) gives forms like this their own name: morphome. Thus, *-s* is a morphome of English.

In ASL, alternating reduplication can be shown to be a morphome. It is used for distinct grammatical functions, but regardless of function, it always exhibits the same three allomorphs – alternating, non-alternating, or one-handed reduplicating – depending on the phonological characteristics of the base. Support for this analysis comes from another grammatical function marked by alternating reduplication: one of the distributive inflections, as illustrated in Figure 4.3.

The reduplication associated with the exhaustive inflection clearly has a different function from the reduplication of the characteristic adjective derivation, yet it exhibits the same three allomorphs. The two hands articulate reduplication in alternating fashion when the base is one-handed, like GIVE; they reduplicate in unison if the base is two-handed and symmetrical, such as SIGN-TO-EVERYONE (CHAT); and only

GIVE (Distributive)

Figure 4.3 A distributive inflection in ASL (© Ursula Bellugi, the Salk Institute)

one hand reduplicates the base if the non-dominant hand is a place of articulation in the base sign, as in SEND or REJECT.[1]

The existence of a morphome like alternating reduplication is significant from our perspective. The very fact that the same formal entity has two unrelated functions shows that, as far as the language is concerned, this entity is an arbitrary linguistic form. Note also the irrelevance of iconicity here. In the exhaustive, one could argue that the morphome is iconically motivated; in the Characteristic Adjective process, iconic motivation is far less transparent. But in any case, if the morphology were strictly iconic, one would surely not expect the same formative to have two distinct functions. More interestingly, we would not expect it to have three different forms, each determined by formal properties of the base. This duplication of allomorphy is what enables us to say that in the morphological grammar of ASL, the formative in question is one entity, like the *-s* is in English. It is as if ASL morphology were telling us: "Here is a formal morphological entity; let's use it to mark some grammatical function. Here's another function that needs marking; let's mark it with this morphological entity that we already have." This, of course, is precisely what the morphomes of spoken language tell us, and, according to Aronoff, it is formal properties like this that make morphology a distinct component of the grammar.

4.1.4 Morphemes realized on the face

Despite widespread use of the term "manual language" in describing sign language, this term is a misnomer. The structure and organization of sign language are filtered through the whole body and the face, and are not confined to the hands (see, e.g., Liddell 1978, 1980, Baker and Cokely

[1] We are grateful to Carol Padden for these examples. The inflection pictured in Figure 4.3, which we call a distributive inflection, is labeled "allocative determinative" in Klima and Bellugi (1979). The body movement indicated in the figure characterizes all three allomorphs described here.

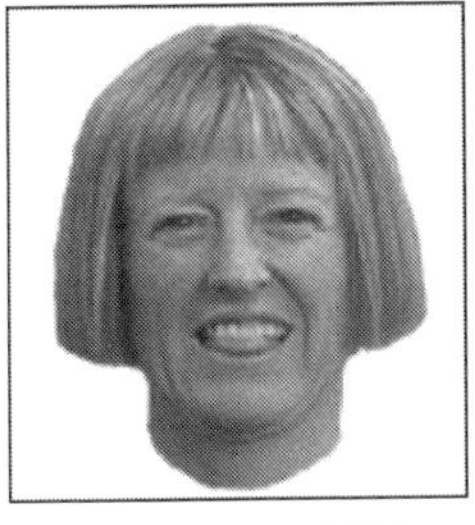

a. NOT-YET (ASL) b. AWESOME (ISL) c. DANGEROUS (ISL)

Figure 4.4 Facial articulations associated with lexical items

1980, Davies 1985, Valli and Lucas 1992). For example, specific facial expressions correspond to certain types of utterances, such as WH-questions (see Chapter 23), and they delineate prosodic constituents, such as Intonational Phrases (see Chapter 15). Both their function and their distribution lead to the suggestion that such expressions are intonational.

A different category of facial articulations, usually articulated with the mouth, are lexically associated with particular words, which are ill-formed without them. Examples are NOT-YET in ASL, and AWESOME and DANGEROUS in ISL, all illustrated in Figure 4.4. The ISL sign AWESOME is minimally distinguished from the sign DANGEROUS by the facial expression.

In addition, an inventory of facial expressions has been described in some sign languages which perform adverbial and adjectival functions (Baker and Cokely 1980, Liddell 1980, Anderson and Reilly 1998, Wilbur 2000). While the upper part of the face is most often noted in intonation, the most salient aspect of adverbial expressions appears to be the configuration of the mouth. Several such forms have been described in ASL. For example, an expression called 'th,' which involves extending the tongue tip between the teeth, means "lack of control, inattention, unintention, and unawareness" (Liddell 1980, p. 50). An expression called 'mm,' made by protruding the lips, conveys "relaxation and enjoyment" (Liddell 1980, p. 45). These two expressions are responsible for the different interpretations of the two sentences in (2).

(2) ASL (Corina, Bellugi, and Reilly 1999)

mm (over COOK [durational])

a. HER HUSBAND COOK [durational] DINNER
'Her husband has been cooking the dinner with pleasure.'

th (over COOK [durational])

b. HER HUSBAND COOK [durational] DINNER
'Her husband has been cooking the dinner inattentively.'

The multichannel nature of the sign language articulatory system allows the adverbial markers, produced by the mouth, and verbs, produced by

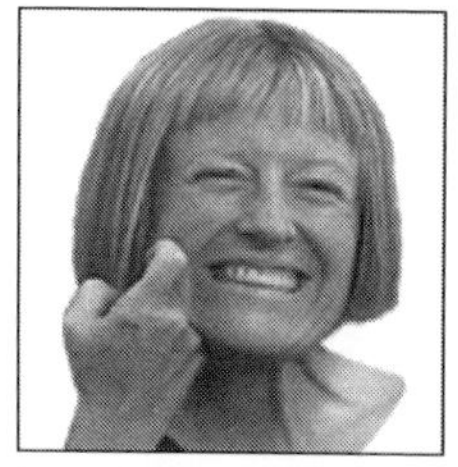
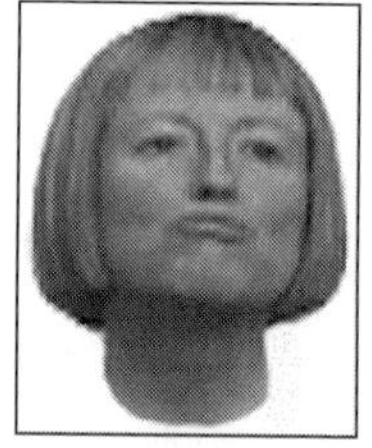

a. 'close' in time or space (ASL)
b. 'with relaxation and enjoyment' (ASL)
c. 'carelessly,' (ASL)

Figure 4.5 Non-manual adverbials (ASL)

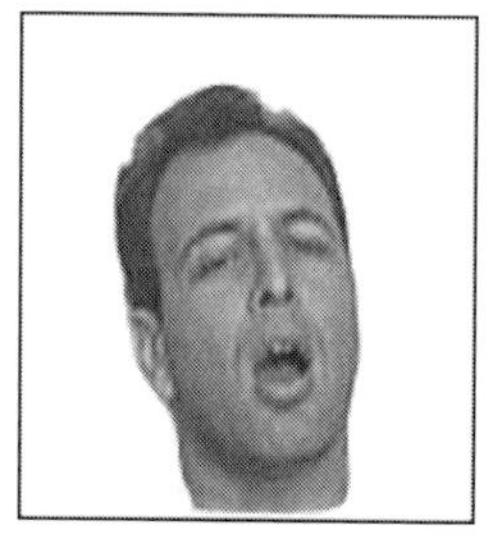
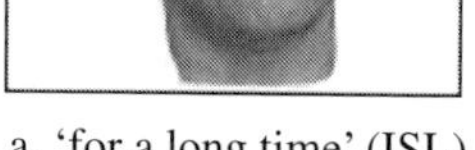

a. 'for a long time' (ISL) b. 'carefully' (ISL)

Figure 4.6 Non-manual adverbials (ISL)

the hands, to co-occur simultaneously, which is precisely what they do. Some adverbial facial expressions of ASL are pictured in Figure 4.5.

Other sign languages have similar markers. For example, ISL also has adverbial markers articulated by the mouth (Sandler 2003; Meir and Sandler 2004). They are not identical to those of ASL, but some of them convey the same meanings. For example, an ISL expression meaning 'carefully' is made by tensing the lips and touching the lower lip with the upper teeth, and 'for a long time' by raising the brows, squinting the eyes, and opening the mouth, as shown in Figure 4.6. An example of such a marker in British Sign Language is given in Figure 4.7.

These facial expressions typically occur simultaneously with verbs and bear adverbial force (Liddell 1980). This is one reason for including these facial expressions here, within the domain of word formation. Another reason for doing so is that they are bound forms, never appearing alone. The third reason is that they manifest a minimal pairing of form and meaning – the classical definition of a morpheme.

Liddell (1980) in his groundbreaking investigation of non-manual signals in ASL, shows that the scope of the facial adverbial meaning 'close in time or space', is precisely that of the full adverbial expression

'exact' (BSL)

Figure 4.7 Non-manual adverbial in BSL (reprinted with permission from Sutton-Spence and Woll 1999)

signed by the hands. For example, in the question in (3), 'Did it happen just last night?', the 'close in time or space' non-manual marker ('cs' – chin close to shoulder) shown in Figure 4.5a above coincides with the signs YESTERDAY NIGHT, while the entire sentence, HAPPEN YESTERDAY NIGHT, is characterized by the facial expression typical of yes/no questions ('q'– raised eyebrows, upper body forward, chin forward).

(3) ASL (Liddell 1980, p. 49)

```
______________________q
           ___________cs
HAPPEN YESTERDAY NIGHT
```

'Did it happen just last night?'

In Units 3 and 4, we argue that facial expressions such as that typically used for yes/no questions correspond to intonation in sign languages. In other words, they have a different pragmatic function and formal distribution than the adverbial forms, which may well be adverbs as Liddell claims. On these assumptions, it is not surprising that the adverbial morpheme 'close in time or space' characterizes only the temporal expression YESTERDAY NIGHT, while the yes/no question expression occurs over the larger, prosodically determined domain.

4.2 Morpheme sequences: non-templatic derivational morphology in sign languages

It is striking that all instances of inflectional and derivational morphology discussed so far have a common characteristic: they are templatic. All involve changes in the quality or length of movement or location of a sign, sometimes with reduplication, and none of them are produced by the type of sequential affixation that is so abundant in spoken languages. In Chapter 5 we describe in some detail another non-concatenative (though not templatic) system: the classifier constructions. It has been suggested that a combination of phonetic and cognitive factors conspire to favor simultaneous layering of linguistic information in sign languages (Bellugi

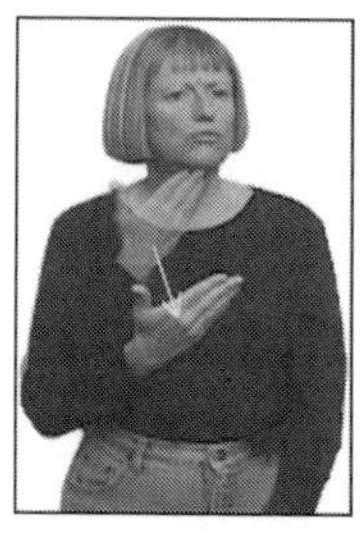

a. GOOD (ASL)

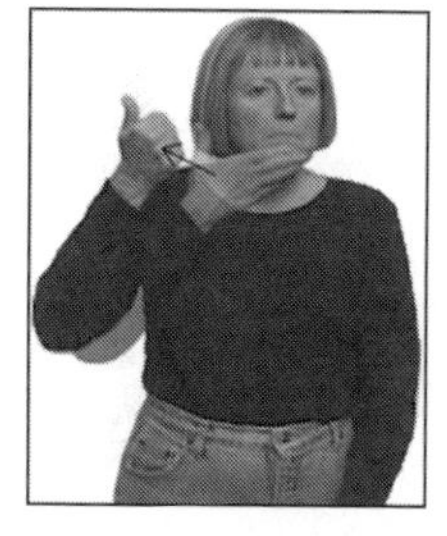

b. GOOD + ER 'better' (ASL)

c. GOOD + EST 'best' (ASL)

Figure 4.8 Sequential affixes: comparative, superlative

and Fischer 1972, Klima and Bellugi 1979, Meier 1993, Emmorey 1995, Meier and Willerman 1995), a suggestion which receives more attention in Unit 5. From the point of view of linguistic theory, the preponderance of abstract morphological templates strengthens current views of morphology as a word-based system of processes, and provides additional evidence against more traditional approaches, according to which words must be built up by stringing morphemes.

Nevertheless, it would be inaccurate to say that all sign language morphology is templatic. In fact, though relatively overlooked in the sign language literature, sequential affixation does exist. We turn now to a description of some clearly sequential morphological processes found in ASL and ISL. It is in this type of morphology that sign languages differ most from one another.

4.2.1 *Sequential morphology in ASL*

A few sequential affixes have been mentioned in the ASL literature, among them the suffixes for comparative and superlative. Since this type of complex word formation is rare in ASL, and since affixes with similar functions exist in English, it has often been assumed that the ASL affixes evolved under the influence of English – from *-er* and *-est* in this example. But the ASL forms do not pattern exactly like their English counterparts. Their distribution is apparently more limited, attaching only to a small subset of the words that take them in English, and to at least one word whose English counterpart is suppletive. Where English has *good, better, best*, ASL has GOOD, GOOD + comparative, GOOD + superlative, shown in Figure 4.8.

Although both English and ASL have an agentive suffix, corresponding to *-er* in English, recent work suggests that the ASL agentive suffix did not arise through translation from English, as had commonly been assumed. Supalla (1998) argues on the basis of evidence from century-old films that the ASL agentive suffix was grammaticized from an early

ASL sign meaning 'person.'[2] Whatever its origin, the synchronic agentive ASL suffix has a different distribution pattern than English agentive *-er*, creating, for example, STUDY-agentive (English: *student*, **studier*), TYPE-agentive (*typist*, **typer*), and OPERATE-agentive (*surgeon*, **operater*). As a large number of unrelated spoken languages have agentive derivational forms, it is quite conceivable that their existence in both English and in ASL is a coincidence, as Supalla's work suggests. The ASL agentive suffix behaves quite independently of the English one, then, but both systems behave normally from a morphological point of view. For example, the principles underlying blocking effects are alive in both languages, but with different derivational results.

In spoken language morphology, Aronoff (1976) noticed that gaps in the application of morphological rules are often not accidental. As they often correspond in meaning and part of speech to more idiosyncratic forms that share the same base, he proposed that the existence of these idiosyncratic forms blocks the application of the word formation rule that would derive the non-occurring forms. For example, the nouns *curiosity*, *monstrosity*, and *pomposity* are derived from the adjectives *curious*, *monstrous*, and *pompous*. However, the rule does not derive **gloriosity*, **famosity* or **furiosity* from *glorious*, *famous*, and *furious*. Aronoff claimed that in such cases the gaps are explained by the existence of the more idiosyncratic noun forms, *glory*, *fame*, and *fury*.

Returning to the agentive affixes in English and ASL, we see different blocking effects in each language. Where forms like **typer*, **studier*, and **operater* (in the sense of performing surgery) are normally blocked by the more common but more idiosyncratic and less productive English forms, *typist*, *student*, *surgeon*, there is no corresponding blocking in ASL, simply because the lexicons and derivational systems are different in the two languages. ASL has forms TYPE + agentive, LEARN + agentive (Figure 4.9), OPERATE + agentive, MACHINE + agentive ('mechanic'), and HAMMER + agentive ('carpenter'). There does not happen to be a more specialized, simpler, or more idiosyncratic way of expressing these concepts in ASL, so there is no blocking effect.

The existence of sequential affixes in a sign language is significant because it indicates that, despite the modality-driven propensity for layered morphology, these languages draw from the same pool of word formation options that spoken languages do. We turn now to a native suffix of ASL that has no counterpart in English. This form, glossed ZERO, and translated 'not (verb) at all,' is apparently grammaticized from an independent word with a similar meaning (Sandler 1996c, Aronoff, Meir, and Sandler 2000,

[2] Supalla's claim gains credence from the observation that it is common in spoken languages for agentive affixes to evolve diachronically from a word for 'person,' as in Dravidian; thanks to Mark Aronoff for bringing this to our attention.

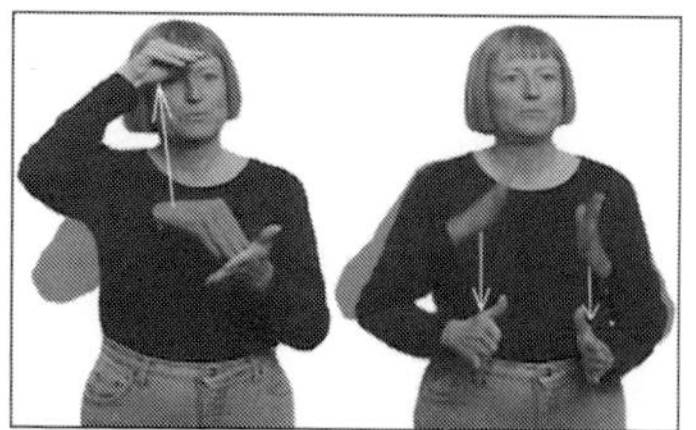

LEARN+ER 'student' (ASL)

Figure 4.9 Agentive suffix

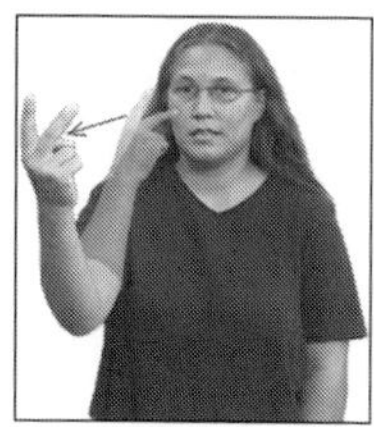

a. SEE (ASL)

b. NOTHING (ASL)

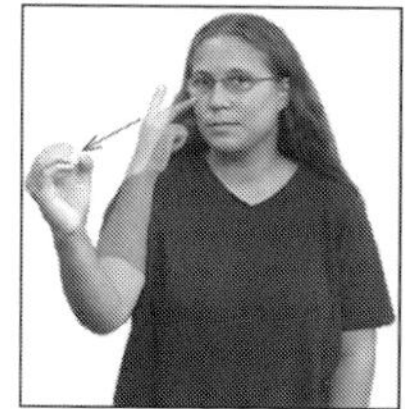

c. SEE+ZERO 'not see at all' (ASL)

Figure 4.10 Negative suffix

Aronoff, Meir, and Sandler 2005). The form is shown in Figure 4.10 c with the base SEE. The meaning of the word is 'not see at all.' The independent words SEE and NOTHING are shown in Figure 4.10 a, b.

In the analysis of language, the line separating one type of complex structure from another may not always be razor sharp, and we cannot assume a priori that –ZERO is an affix, rather than the second member of a compound or a clitic, or simply an independent word. As a context for our argument that it is indeed a suffix, we offer in Table 4.1 criteria that distinguish these different structures.[3] We stress that the table is offered as a heuristic in characterizing the structures and should not be taken as

[3] Under word-level phonological properties, we subsume any changes undergone by the complex form or either part of it as a result of the joining together of the two. That is, we restrict this cell in the table to phonological changes on words, either lexical words or phonological words that are formed postlexically as a result of cliticization. We exclude any postlexical phonological changes that may occur across words. See Chapter 10 with respect to compound reduction, and Chapter 15 for coalescence under cliticization.

Table 4.1 *Characteristics of phrases and complex words*

	phrase (word + word)	host + clitic	lexicalized compound	word + derivational affix
Interruptible by other words	+	+	–	–
Word-level phonological properties	N/A	+	+	+
Idiosyncratic semantics	–	–	+	+
Arbitrary lexical gaps	N/A	–	–	+
Productivity of morphological element	N/A	+	generally not productive	generally productive

definitive in any absolute sense. Yet it can serve as a useful guide for the purposes of this discussion.

In the table, each structure is given a plus or minus value for the relevant properties. "Phrase (word + word)" refers to a sequence of any two words in a phrase, like *black cat*; a compound is a sequence of two or more words that behave as a single word, like *blackboard*; "word + affix" refers here to a word and a derivational affix, such as *happiness*; and an example of a "host + clitic" is the English contraction *'ll*, as in *he'll call tomorrow*, or *all the people who heard the radio broadcast'll call tomorrow*.

The most dissimilar categories in the table are the categories of phrase and word plus affix (the table refers specifically to derivational affixes, as the distinction between them and the other categories may be drawn more crisply). A phrase consisting of two words can be interrupted by other words (*a black silky-coated cat*), and it bears none of the characteristics of complex words, such as idiosyncrasy in meaning or in form. Female blackbirds are brown, but black cats are always black. Not surprisingly, compounds bear some similarities with independent words in a phrase, and some with word plus affix constructions. As with independent words, the word in a particular position within a compound generally cannot be said to be productive. Though *blackbird* and *blackboard* are two compounds that happen to have the same first member, *black* cannot be said to recur productively in this position to form a large number of compounds. If it did so, then *black* would be behaving more like an affix. Compounds that have been lexicalized do share some properties with affixed words. This is not surprising, as lexicalized compounds by definition are listed as words in the lexicon. Thus, neither blackbirds nor blackboards need be black. Derivational affixes often show idiosyncrasy in form and meaning, and normally show some degree of productivity. We are now in a position to evaluate the ASL –ZERO form against these criteria.

First, the verb –ZERO form cannot be interrupted by other words. This criterion distinguishes verb –ZERO from a word + word sequence in a phrase. For some signers, some but not all of the verb and suffix forms are fused phonologically and are obligatorily characterized by the same non-manual articulations and postures. Examples for these signers are SEE–ZERO and FEEL–ZERO. According to criteria proposed in Zwicky and Pullum (1983) for distinguishing affixes from clitics, idiosyncratic phonological properties of this sort – i.e., phonological changes that result from the attachment of an affix with some bases but not others – do not characterize clitics, and –ZERO is thus distinguished from clitics. Two more criteria offered by those authors also favor an affix analysis over a clitic analysis for ZERO. The first is idiosyncratic meaning. Some verb + ZERO forms, such as TOUCH + ZERO, 'didn't use at all,' have taken on special meanings that are not directly retrievable from the components. Second, there appear to be arbitrary gaps in the list of verbs that can take –ZERO. Apparently –ZERO is still undergoing changes in the language, since its use, productivity, and even the lexical category of the base it attaches to vary across signers. Of six signers studied, two (over age 40) were very selective about the verbs taking –ZERO; two younger signers accepted the form very productively, one on verbs and the other on adjectives; and two signers reported that the form was acceptable and familiar but that they never use it themselves. This kind of variation is what might be expected of a relatively new derivational affix, but not of a clitic. Clitics are usually phonologically weak morphemes with inflectional properties, and as such they normally cliticize productively (under the right prosodic circumstances) and not idiosyncratically, as we show in Chapter 15.

According to the table, a word plus affix combination appears to be most like a lexicalized compound. This may seem surprising at first, since affixes are bound, by definition, while each member of a compound may also function as a free word. Yet the fact that in older languages like English affixes do not tend to look like words does not mean they never did. In fact, it is common for affixes to have grammaticized from free words diachronically, becoming obligatorily bound only in the later stages of grammaticization (Hopper and Traugott 1993). We can still see this in forms like English *-man* (*postman*, *chairman*, *horseman*, *clergyman*, etc.). Both the recurrence of the formative *-man* in many words, and its reduced stress, indicate that its synchronic status is somewhere between that of a member of a compound and that of a suffix. So the distinction between compounds and affixed words is not etched in stone, even in English.[4]

[4] Richard Meir (p.c., November, 2002) has pointed out to us that the plural forms of even the most lexicalized words in *-man* is *-men* (*postmen*, *chairmen*, etc.), which indicates that these forms are nonetheless compounds.

Unlike familiar affixes such as English *-ness*, the ASL form, ZERO can also function synchronically as a free word in the language, which makes it seem more like a member of a compound. In fact, in the early list of about 300 ASL compounds compiled at the Salk Institute for Biological Studies, many forms with ZERO were included. But it is precisely the fact that so many complex words were formed with ZERO that led to the suspicion that the morpheme had achieved affixal status (Sandler 1996c). Two related properties distinguish affixes from members of lexicalized compounds according to the table: productivity or systematic recurrence on the one hand, and gaps of occurrence on the other. These properties are related, because it only makes sense to speak of gaps if a form is productive in the first place. The form in question is recognized as occurring in many complex words, but not in all cases where it might be expected. On both counts, –ZERO behaves more like an affix. For example, as we've explained, *black* does not occur in many lexicalized compounds. It doesn't make sense to speak of a word-formation rule with the prefix *black-*. –ZERO, on the other hand, seems to behave as a relatively productive affix for those signers who use it, though the degree of productivity varies with different signers. The process by which –ZERO is becoming an affix appears still to be in the grammaticization stage, and would make an interesting topic for sociolinguistic research.

Another affix that exists for some signers of ASL has been brought to our attention by James MacFarlane and Kevin McClellan (p.c., September, 1996; January, 2002). The form is glossed STRONG, and it combines with base forms to produce adjectives that add the meaning 'excessively' or 'emphatically.' For example, DRINK+STRONG means 'drink excessively.' According to MacFarlane and McClellan, the movement of the STRONG suffix takes a diagonal path instead of the straight path found in the free form from which it evolved. While it is not yet known how widespread the use of this suffix is, it is possible that the suffix has its origins in a commonly used compound that has STRONG as its second member: FACE^STRONG=RESEMBLE (Figure 4.11 a–c), often used in emphatic contexts.[5]

4.2.2 Sequential morphology in Israeli Sign Language

ASL is not the only sign language with sequential affixes. A class of prefixes has been found in another sign language: ISL (Aronoff et al.

[5] While lexicalized compounds in ASL also often involve phonological changes, these are reductions across the two members, different from the changes on the affixes cited here. See Chapter 10.

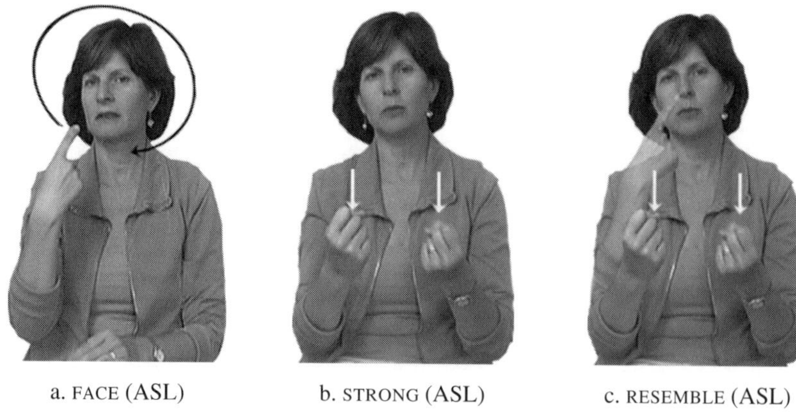

a. FACE (ASL) b. STRONG (ASL) c. RESEMBLE (ASL)

Figure 4.11 Lexicalized compound as a possible source of ASL suffix −STRONG

2000, 2003, 2005). In that language, a group of signs whose meanings are related to the senses attach to verbs as prefixes. Some of the complex signs have meaning that is analyzable from the meaning of the sense prefix together with the meaning of the verb, e.g., SEE + SHARP, 'to discern by seeing.' This form, together with its component parts, is illustrated in Figure 4.12.

The sense prefixes in many other examples, such as SEE in SEE + FOLD-BACK-RABBIT-EARS, 'to chicken out,' have opaque meanings. So far, about seventy such forms have been recorded. Both the semantic opacity and the systematic recurrence of the forms in the same position indicate that the forms are affixes. Regardless of the lexical category of the word they attach to, the prefixed forms are always verbs – making the sense affixes verb-forming derivational prefixes. Like the ASL −ZERO suffix, the sense prefixes of ISL have fixed order with respect to the verb and may not be interrupted by another sign. Taken together, the evidence weighs in favor of an affixation analysis.

Another affix in ISL is a negative form that means 'without,' similar in meaning to English *-less* (Aronoff, Meir, Padden, and Sandler 2004). Also apparently grammaticized from a free form meaning roughly 'none' (glossed '*ein*' in Hebrew), it productively occurs with nouns to form adjectives, as in INTEREST + NONE, shown in Figure 4.13. This suffix has two allomorphs: if the base is one-handed, the suffix is also one-handed, while it is two-handed when attaching to a two-handed base.

The existence in sign language of both non-concatenative and limited concatenative morphology has implications for our understanding of language universals. This issue, as well as some associated cognitive implications, is taken up in Unit 5.

Another type of concatenation of word parts is cliticization. In this process, function words, typically pronouns, come together with content

a. SEE (ISL) b. SHARP (ISL)

c. SEE+SHARP 'discern by seeing' (ISL)

Figure 4.12 Sense prefix

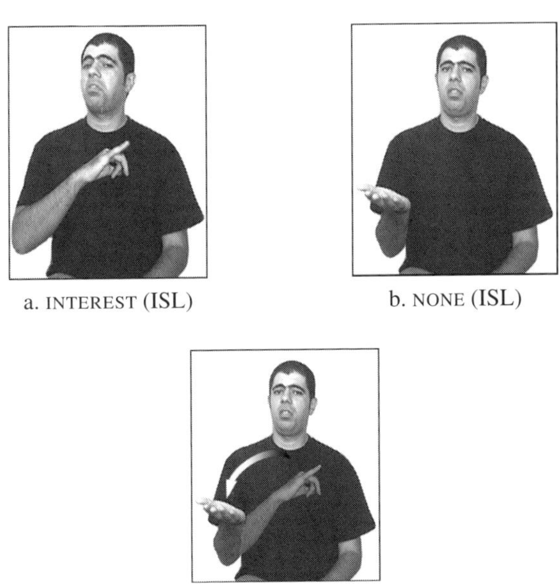

a. INTEREST (ISL) b. NONE (ISL)

c. INTEREST + NONE 'without interest' (ISL)

Figure 4.13 Negative suffix

words to form a single prosodic unit which is demonstrably distinct from affixed forms. In ISL, such cliticized pronouns take two different phonological forms, depending partly on whether or not they are in a prominent position within the phrase (Sandler 1999a, 1999b). Two properties of these clitics should be mentioned in the present context. First, they show none of the idiosyncrasies of affixes described above. Second, the host plus clitic structures are non-structure-preserving, demonstrating that they are formed postlexically. As the sign language examples of cliticization have most relevance for prosodic constituency and other phonological issues, they are dealt with in more detail in Chapter 15. We now turn to the third traditional category of word formation: compounding.

4.3 Compounds

In this section, we deal with two types of compounding: typical compounding, in which two or more words are combined to form a new word with one of them as the head, and coordinate compounding, in which a superordinate category is represented through coordination of basic-level exemplars of that category.

4.3.1 Lexicalized and novel compounds

One of the most common word-formation processes used in ASL and other sign languages is compounding (Klima and Bellugi 1979, Bellugi and Newkirk 1981, Wallin 1983 on Swedish Sign Language). Compounding is synchronically productive in many sign languages including ASL, and noun–noun compounding seems especially so. In ordinary compounds, one sign is the head and the other the modifier. Typically, this sort of compounding may recursively keep adding new members, with each new member modifying the rest of the compound structure. Three-member compounds, such as DEAF^SCHOOL^CLASS (where 'SCHOOL' here is the sign INSTITUTION, used for residential schools) and HOME^MADE^COOKIES, have been recorded in ASL, indicating that the process is recursive, as in spoken languages (see (4)).

(4) Recursive compounding

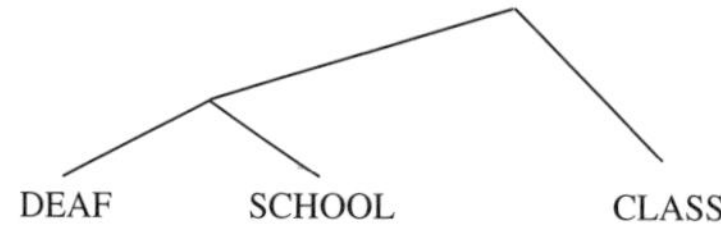

In this example, SCHOOL is the head of DEAF^SCHOOL and CLASS is the head of DEAF^SCHOOL^CLASS. Most of the linguistic work on compounds to date has investigated lexicalized compounds in ASL, and we will deal mainly, though not exclusively, with these here. As is typical with lexicalized compounds, semantic drift sometimes results in meanings that are not transparent. English examples are *movie star*, *high chair*, and *blackboard*, none of which has the literal meaning predicted from its components. Similarly in ASL, the lexicalized compound diachronically formed from RED^SLICE means TOMATO (Frishberg 1975); and lexicalized MIND^DROP means FAINT.

Lexicalized compounds in ASL typically undergo reduction (Liddell and Johnson 1986, Sandler 1989). In ASL, the length of time it takes to sign a compound is about the same as the length of an average single sign, although the compound is formed from two separate signs (Klima and Bellugi 1979). In order to achieve this temporal shortening, both signs of the compound are frequently compressed; the first sign is usually shortened even more than the second sign. Furthermore, the transition between the two elements is speeded and smoothed. The phonological processes that contribute to this "compression, speeding, and smoothing" are discussed in Chapter 10.

4.3.2 Coordinate compounds

In addition to the usual kind of compound, another type of compound exists in ASL: coordinate compounds (Klima and Bellugi 1979). These compounds, which bear some similarity to so-called dvandva compounds in languages of India, are formed by listing basic category-level exemplars of a superordinate category. Examples of coordinate compounds in Kannada are given in (5).

(5) Kannada (Aronoff and Sridhar 1987)

tande tāyi	'father and mother'
kallu maṇṇu	'stones and dirt'
mane maṭʰa	'house and monastery'
gaḍḍa mīse	'beard and moustache'

In ASL, similar compounds exist, in which no member is head or modifier; instead, all members are equal, exemplifying the intended concept. Typically, the ASL compounds of this type include three items, so that the term *dvandva* (*dva* 'two') extends only loosely to them. The concept 'jewelry,' for example, may be signed by stringing together NECKLACE^BRACELET^RING^ETC., with particular prosodic characteristics that distinguish these compounds from simple lists. In particular, items in a list are separated by pauses and sometimes by indicating 'number one, number two, number three,' etc., and are often marked by forward movement of the head or upper body. The signs in coordinate compounds are produced quickly and without such prosodic breaks between them.

Apart from the prosodic differences between coordinate compounds and simple lists, there is additional evidence suggesting that these compounds function as single words: the meanings of the individual words within the compound are not accessible in sentences in which the compounds are used. For example, it is acceptable to say the equivalent of 'I love apples^oranges^bananas^etc. (= fruit), but I don't like oranges' (reported in Klima and Bellugi 1979). If the members of the compound were individually accessible, i.e., if the series represented a list and not a compound, then such a statement would be contradictory. The mirror situation is one in which the compound is introduced and then a different basic-level word from the same superordinate category represented by the compound is used – but not a word from the compound itself. Such an utterance emerged in a preliminary study by one of us: 'As for dance^painting^sports^etc. (= hobbies), I like photography.' The coordinate compound 'dance^painting^sports^etc.' was characterized by the prosodic characteristics described above. Utterances like these indicate that the forms are indeed compounds and not lists.

Unlike dvandva compounds, coordinate compounds in ASL are generally not lexicalized. Klima and Bellugi note that the basic-level items selected to represent a superordinate category vary from discourse to discourse and from signer to signer. Of the three native signers studied by Sandler, the signer who felt most comfortable with these forms commented that her mother used them more than she did. The same signer used a coordinate compound for FAMILY: [MOTHER^FATHER^SISTER^BROTHER]. It is far more common among ASL signers to use the initialized sign FAMILY, based on the sign GROUP, with the handshape of the fingerspelled letter F, . Apparently, the use of coordinate compounds is a device for forming novel words for perceived gaps in the lexicon of superordinate terms. As ordinary lexical words emerge to represent these concepts, they replace the corresponding coordinate compounds. This explanation is compatible with the widespread individual variation found in the constituency and use of these complex word forms.

4.4 Interim summary

The foregoing chapters of this unit have dealt with categories of morphological operations that are commonly found in spoken languages: derivations, inflections, and compounding. Most of these processes are templatic in form, though a number of sequential processes were also described. Some of the processes, such as verb agreement, are known to be fully productive; others, like the sequential affixation of ASL and ISL forms, are less productive; and the productivity of still others, such as various predicate aspects, is still unknown. With the exception of clitics, described briefly above, all processes dealt with so far are clearly lexical. They all involve either some base lexeme that combines with bound grammatical formatives or, in the case of compounds, the combination of two lexemes that are themselves words of the language. On the whole, the kinds of processes described here are not alien to students of morphological systems.

We now move on to another type of morphological complexity found in sign languages, a complex system in which large numbers of bound forms can combine in a unified structure – the so-called classifier system. This system is notoriously difficult to characterize, both because it is different from the rest of the morphology of sign languages, and because it is unlike morphology found in spoken languages in certain ways. But there has been renewed interest in classifier structures of late, both in sign language (e.g., Emmorey 2003) and in spoken language (e.g., Senft 2000a), and their analysis is becoming more tractable.

5 Classifier constructions

There is a rich and complex morphological system in all sign languages we know of that is used for the purpose of denoting spatial relations and motion events and for characterizing shapes and dimensions of objects.[1] The system utilizes forms representing different classes of nominals in combination with other elements. The noun class forms are represented by a set of handshapes, and it is these handshape units that are commonly called classifiers in the sign language literature.

Classifier constructions represent a pervasive but somewhat anomalous subsystem in sign language grammars. Their form, though morphologically complex, is different from that of complex lexical words, and, although classifier constructions may translate as whole propositions, they are not formally like ordinary sentences either. Classifier constructions often capitalize on iconicity, which has led some researchers to question the linguistic status of these forms. The view we present here characterizes classifier constructions as a linguistic system that bears certain significant similarities to verbal classifier constructions in spoken languages, a comparison we develop in detail. But we do not lose sight of the uniqueness of the sign language system. We exemplify its special properties with an analysis of the way classifier handshapes and the coordinate predicate structures they may enter into are extended artistically in sign language poetry.

We begin the chapter with a simple and general description of the sign language classifier system. We then go on to draw parallels with certain types of spoken language classifiers and to point out differences from other types that have sometimes mistakenly been compared to sign language classifiers. We pursue a comparison between the classifier constructions of sign languages and the verbal classifiers that are claimed to have evolved from noun incorporation in spoken languages, especially in work by Marianne Mithun. The chapter then turns to the distribution and interpretation of the elements that comprise sign language classifier

[1] There is published research on classifiers of at least twenty different sign languages. See Emmorey (2003).

constructions, and to a characterization of the resulting linguistic constituent. Classifier constructions, productively formed from an inventory of bound morphemes, are often contrasted with "frozen forms" (Supalla and Newport 1978), monomorphemic words whose components have only phonological but not morphological significance. Yet it has often been observed that many "frozen" words, interpreted as monomorphemic, began life as complex classifier constructions. Here we restrict ourselves to the latter; the path from classifier construction to lexeme is investigated in Chapter 6. These explorations of classifier constructions from several different angles will serve as a basis for morphosyntactic analyses of the system in Chapter 20.

5.1 A basic description

In early linguistic work on sign language, classifier constructions were sometimes relegated to the realm of pantomime; they were dubbed "mimetic depiction" by Klima and Bellugi (1979). The idea that these forms in ASL involve classifiers was introduced in the early literature by Frishberg (1975), Kegl and Wilbur (1976), McDonald (1982), and Supalla (1982, 1986), among others. Ted Supalla was the first to analyze the systematic properties of these constructions as part of a grammatical system (1982, 1986). His work categorizes the classifier handshapes into two basic types: Size and Shape Specifiers (SASSes) and "semantic" classifiers. We adopt here Supalla's SASS term, but use the term "entity classifiers" for the latter type, following Engberg-Pedersen (1994) and Schembri (2003). The SASS category counts among its members handshapes representing visually perceived physical properties of objects.[2] In this system, each finger and the thumb, as well as degrees of bending, may contribute meaning (Supalla 1986). Figure 5.1 shows examples of SASSes from Supalla (1982). Entity classifiers are more abstract, in that their iconicity is more opaque and they refer to general semantic classes rather than to visually perceived physical properties.[3] Examples are shown in Figure 5.2.

A third type of classifier, handling classifiers (McDonald 1982, Schick 1987, Schick 1990), represents the shape of the hand or other object handling or gripping the referent. According to Engberg-Pedersen (1993), handling classifiers are "perceived as the manual articulator imitating a hand or forelimb holding an entity or imitating some other instrument (holding an entity)" (p. 277). Items in this category described for Danish Sign Language by Engberg-Pedersen include handling of a

[2] SASS classifiers correspond to spoken language classifiers that represent "physical categories," in Grinevald's (2000) semantic categorization.

[3] According to Grinevald's (2000) typology, classifiers of this sort exist in spoken languages and fit the semantic profile of "essence categories."

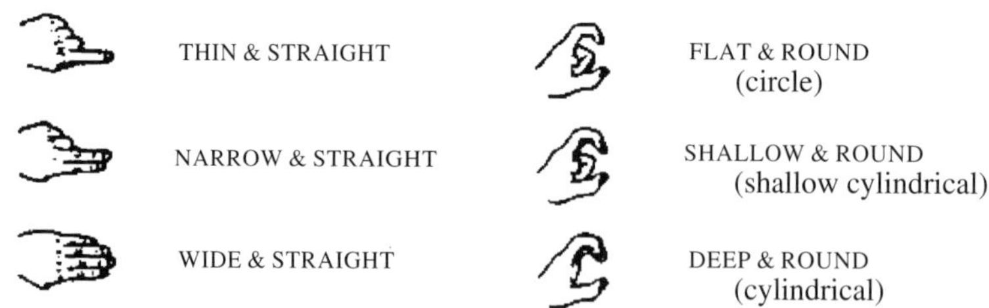

Figure 5.1 Size and shape specifiers (ASL) (reprinted with permission from Supalla 1982)

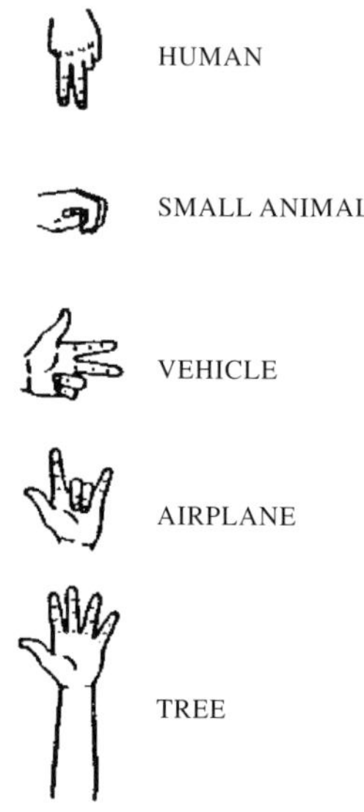

Figure 5.2 Entity classifiers (ASL) (reprinted with permission from Supalla 1982)

handle (e.g., the handle of a cup or suitcase –); a two-dimensional entity like a piece of paper (); a lumplike entity such as a potato or lump of mud (). Examples of two handling classifiers in ASL are shown in Figure 5.3.

We have said that in the classifier system, the handshape – that is, the handshape characterized by the dominant or preferred hand – denotes some entity. One unique property of the system is that the non-dominant hand may simultaneously represent an independent classifier, a Secondary Object with which the Primary Object interacts, in Supalla's analysis. Alternatively, it can represent the Ground in an event involving Figure and Ground. This is a clear indication that structures involving classifiers are in some way separate from the lexical signs of the language. In lexical signs, the non-dominant hand has no morphological status, functioning only phonologically, either articulating symmetrically with

Figure 5.3 Handling classifiers (ASL)

the dominant hand, or providing a place of articulation (see Chapter 12) – in both cases, meaningless. In structures involving classifiers, the dominant and non-dominant hands each have morphological status.

It is not only the two hands that systematically contribute meaning to classifier constructions. The locations articulated by the hand or hands in this system signify precise locations within the space established to represent the event. Thus, locations articulated by the hand(s) are meaningful, and, if both hands are used, the semantic and spatial relation between the two hands becomes significant as well.

The third major parameter of signs, movement, also has a different role in classifier constructions than it has in lexically listed signs of the language. Supalla analyzes classifier constructions into predicates denoting existence, location, or motion. These are conveyed by different types of movements. There are three types of movement "roots" in the system: *stative*, conveying the mere existence of some object; *contact*, which means 'to be located at'; and *active*, used for some kind of motion. Each root type has an anchored form (fixed to a given point in space) and a displaced form. The roots can be modified through repetition at different frequencies, and they can be sequenced while articulated by the same classifier handshape, indicating a sequence of movements enacted by the same referent. Different paths and manners of movement have meanings as well, meanings that are to some extent independent of the handshapes and locations with which they combine.

Now that we have reviewed the components of classifier constructions, we illustrate with a sequence taken from Supalla (1986), given in Figure 5.4.

In the examples of Figure 5.4(a–g), the dominant hand (the right for this signer) represents an entity classifier that reflects relatively abstract semantic characteristics – 'vehicle' in these examples. The same handshape could be used in ASL for cars, trucks, motorcycles, bicycles – virtually any vehicle on land or sea, regardless of physical appearance.

In the examples in Figure 5.4(e) and (g), both hands represent entity classifiers: 'vehicle' and 'tree' in (e), and 'vehicle' and 'human legs' in (g).

The other examples in Figure 5.4 illustrate Size and Shape Specifiers or SASSes. As indicated in Figure 5.1 (compared with Figure 5.2), this set is larger than the set of entity classifiers, and includes categories like the

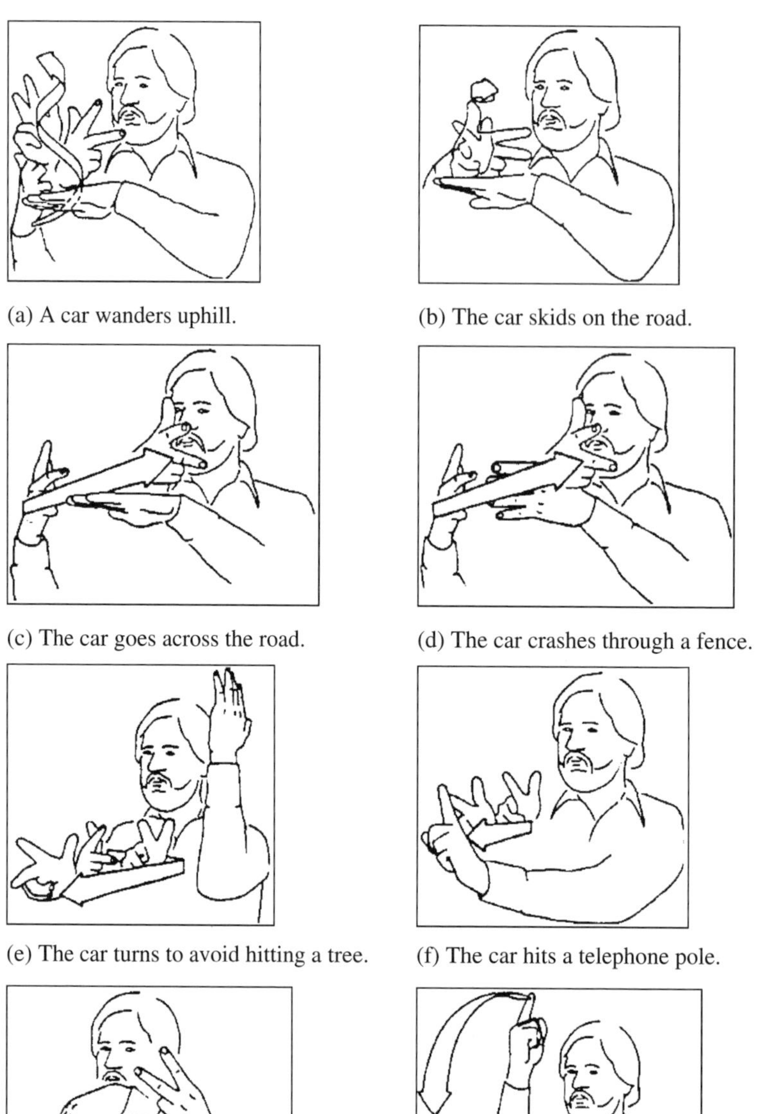

(a) A car wanders uphill.

(b) The car skids on the road.

(c) The car goes across the road.

(d) The car crashes through a fence.

(e) The car turns to avoid hitting a tree.

(f) The car hits a telephone pole.

(g) A person falls out of the car.

(h) The telephone pole falls down.

Figure 5.4 Sequence of verbs of motion (ASL) (reprinted with permission from Supalla 1986)

ones shown in this sequence: small round object, cylindrical object, flat object ((a–c) and (h)), long thin object (h), etc.[4]

The handshapes that represent physical category classifiers have been broken down into smaller units by some researchers. Supalla claims that each finger and the thumb may act as separate morphemes, and that the degree of bending or spreading of the fingers may have morphological status. Wallin (1996) shows that in Swedish Sign Language, different parts of the hand, when configured as a classifier, may stand for corresponding parts of the object it represents.

Just as there are different categories and aspects of nominals that the handshapes may represent in this system, there are also several different categories of motions/locations and of manners of motion. In a preliminary investigation, Talmy (2003) counts thirty properties that can be expressed in ASL classifier constructions, divided according to the categories given in (1). Talmy points out that no spoken language is known to grammatically encode such a large number of motion event properties, an issue to which we return in Unit 5.

(1) entity properties: 5 types (with subtypes)
orientation properties: 3 types
locus properties: 1 type
motion properties: 4 types
path properties: 10 types
manner properties: 2 types
relations of figure or path to ground: 5

Supalla's analysis of the classifier system employs a number of movement roots, modifications, and possibilities for their combination, as well as a list of classifiers, some of which are themselves componential. The point Supalla wishes to make is that the list is finite, its formatives discrete, and the resulting system a grammatical one. The analysis of sign language classifier systems has sparked renewed interest and controversy of late (see Emmorey 2003). The forms of this system are referred to using different terms by various researchers: they are verbs of motion and location according to Supalla (1982, 1986); they have been called classifier predicates by Schick (1990); polymorphemic verbs by Engberg-Pedersen (1993); polysynthetic verbs by Wallin (1994); complex predicates by Schembri (2003); and classifier expressions by Talmy (2003). Each term is actually a claim about the

[4] SASSes that involve movement of the fingers or hands to trace the outline of an object (not exemplified here) are called tracing SASSes (Mandel 1977, Supalla 1986). Supalla includes all classifiers denoting size and shape as SASSes, whether they are tracing or non-tracing in form. The two types have different distribution, however. Tracing SASSes do not combine with movement morphemes. Instead, they serve a more clearly modifying function, often entering into compound relations with lexical signs, like CHAIR + OBLONG for 'bench'. Since the "tracing classifiers" behave quite differently from other classifiers, especially insofar as they do not combine with verbal elements, it is likely, as Zwitserlood (2003) suggests, that they represent a different grammatical phenomenon, and we will not deal with them further here.

internal structure and grammatical role of these forms. We adopt the relatively neutral term, classifier constructions, supporting the claim that classifiers are involved, but taking a neutral position for now on the type of complex structure that results. This system is anomalous in many ways with respect to the rest of the linguistic structure of sign languages, but paradoxically it is also central to fully understanding them.

It is immediately apparent that the constructions shown in Figure 5.4, though consisting of a single (dominant) handshape, movement, and location, like most ordinary signs, are nevertheless different from ordinary signs. As we have noted, the most obvious difference is that each of these formational primitives is meaningful in these constructions, while in ordinary signs they are generally meaningless. Furthermore, well-formedness constraints, such as conditions on the configuration and movement of the non-dominant hand in two-handed signs (Battison 1978 [1973], see Chapter 12), are violated in these constructions. Anomalous as it seems to be, this system of classifier constructions is very prominent in all sign languages, and it provides a lexicalization source for the lexemes of these languages. As such, the system warrants closer attention.

In a recent volume on noun classification, Senft (2000a) writes that classifiers are usually defined as "morphemes that classify . . . nouns according to semantic criteria."[5] If Senft's definition is quite broad, that is only because there are many types of classifiers in spoken language, and we will demonstrate some relevant ones in the following pages. What classifiers must have in order to be so called, is (a) status as a morpheme (bound or free), and (b) the function of grouping, subcategorizing, and classifying nouns. As the handshape forms of sign languages conform to these criteria, the term "classifier" is apt.

A closer look at the constructions into which classifiers enter reveals similarities with those of spoken languages, and some differences as well. Differences have led some researchers to argue that the term "classifier" is problematic for the sign language forms (e.g., Engberg-Pedersen 1993, Sutton-Spence and Woll 1999, Cogill-Koez 2002a, 2002b, Schembri 2003, Slobin, Hoiting, Kuntze, Lindert, Weinberg, Pyers, Thumann, and Biederman 2003). Given the wide variety of structures that are dubbed "classifiers" in spoken languages, however, outright dismissal of the term in connection with sign language may be too hasty, while adopting the term allows us to draw useful comparisons with spoken languages. What is important for our understanding of these constructions is the way in which they pattern in sign languages. As we attempt to show, a

[5] The original quote from Senft was "Classifiers are usually defined as morphemes that classify and quantify nouns according to semantic criteria." (p. 21). He later separates quantifiers into a separate category, saying that classifiers quantify a noun inherently, while quantifiers (i.e., numeral classifiers) do so temporarily. The analogy relevant for our discussion is to classifiers and not to quantifiers.

comparison with classifier constructions in spoken languages – in particular, with verbal classifiers in Grinevald's (2000) taxonomy – provides a useful context in which patterns can begin to emerge and be recognized.

Before proceeding further, let us turn for a moment to two kinds of classification that have mistakenly been compared to the sign language system, explicitly or implicitly: classificatory verbs and numeral classifiers. After removing those types from consideration, we proceed to more fruitful comparisons with verbal classifiers.

Classificatory verb stems are found in a number of Athapascan languages such as Navaho, among others. These verb stems categorize a noun argument in terms of physical properties such as shape, size, and other qualities. Typically, the semantics of the verbs involve handling, motion, existence, or location. As the sign language classifier constructions also involve these notions, it is not surprising that parallels have been drawn (e.g., Newport 1981, McDonald 1982). However, as Engberg-Pedersen (1993) and Schembri (2003) explain, the analogy is misleading. Classificatory verb stems are different from sign language classifier constructions, because there are no noun classifiers in the classificatory verb stem constructions. Instead, the verb stems themselves are suppletive, inherently making the classification. The verbal stem of classificatory verbs is a portmanteau that cumulates the motion and its subject or object in a single unanalyzable unit. By contrast, in the classifier constructions of sign languages, the motion unit, the location unit, and the nominal element are distinct formatives. The nominal element, represented by the handshape, is what classifies.

Another type of classifier that figured prominently in the survey of Allan (1977) is numeral classifiers, the most common type in spoken languages. Senft defines numeral classifiers in the following way: "In counting inanimate as well as animate referents the numerals (obligatorily) concatenate with a certain morpheme, which is the so-called 'classifier'. This morpheme classifies and quantifies the respective nominal referent according to semantic criteria" (Senft 2000b, p. 15). Numeral classifiers are different from verbal classifiers in that they are obligatory, they always occur with numerals or quantifiers, and their classificatory function is the most salient one. In all three of these properties, numeral classifiers also differ from those of sign languages.

5.2 Verbal classifiers and Noun Incorporation

Verbal classifiers, also called verbal classifying affixes, are most comparable to sign language classifiers.[6] Verbal classifiers are morphemes representing

[6] Based on her investigations of classifiers in Sign Language of the Netherlands, Zwitserlood (2003) independently arrived at the same conclusion, namely, that the classifiers of sign languages are comparable to verbal classifiers of spoken languages.

general nominal categories, which attach to verbs as affixes. An example from Cayuga, a Native American language of the Iroquoian family, is shown in (2).[7]

(2) Cayuga (Mithun 1986a, pp. 386–388)
Skitu ake'-**treht**-ae'
skidoo I-CL(vehicle)-have
'I have a skidoo.'

This example (cited in Grinevald 2000) also bears semantic similarity to sign language entity classifiers. The classifier for VEHICLE, *-treht-*, is reminiscent of the ASL VEHICLE classifier in Figure 5.4(a–g) above. Different semantic properties are signified in the classifiers of Digueño, also cited in Grinevald, as shown in (3).

(3) Digueño (Langdon 1970, p. 78)

a*'mi* ...	'to hang (a long object)'
tu*mi* ...	'to hang (a small round object)'
a*.xi.¬* ...	'to drag (a long object)'
c*' xi.¬* ...	'to drag (a bunch of objects)'

In this language, it appears that the prefix is a classifier of some physical property of a nominal: a LONG OBJECT, a SMALL ROUND OBJECT, or a BUNCH OF OBJECTS, in these examples. As a bound form classifying nominals according to physical properties, these prefixes are functionally comparable to SASS classifiers, like those in Figure 5.4(a–c) and (h) above: SMALL-ROUND-OBJECT, CYLINDRICAL-OBJECT, FLAT-OBJECT (a–c), and LONG-THIN-OBJECT (h).

We see in these examples, though different in each language, that in both of them the noun classifier is affixed onto the verb. In Cayuga, the classifier classifies according to a broader semantic category, and in Digueño, according to physical properties. Sign language classifiers exist in both flavors, and also share with classifiers of such languages the characteristic of being bound morphemes, making comparisons with verbal classifiers like those of Cayuga or Digueño seem quite appropriate.

In her influential work, Marianne Mithun (1984, 1986a) proposes that verbal classifiers in spoken language evolved from a morphological structure called Noun Incorporation (NI), and in some cases are indistinguishable from those forms. We discuss that theory briefly now, not to consider an NI analysis of classifiers in sign language directly – that possibility is taken up in Chapter 20. Rather, we present aspects of Mithun's investigation in order to highlight some shared properties between classifiers found in spoken languages and those of sign language: affixation of a generic nominal element; the existence of classifiers of more than one semantic type in the same language; lexicalization

[7] A brand name for a snowmobile, 'skidoo' has become a generic term.

resulting in opacity of the classifier's independent meaning; and the use of classifiers for backgrounding and for other stylistic effects.

5.2.1 *Properties of classifiers that evolved from Noun Incorporation*

Noun Incorporation (NI) is a morphological process found in some spoken languages, in which nominal morphemes are attached to verbs in a particular sort of compounding, and the two together form a single word. The function of the incorporated nominal in NI is to qualify the verb. In example (4b) from Yucatec Mayan, 'I wood-chop,' the incorporated noun, 'wood,' qualifies the verb 'chop'; it describes a type of chopping. In many, though not all, languages with NI, the incorporated noun is similar in form to the full noun which also exists in the language. In the Yucatec Mayan example, they are identical: *ce'*.

(4) Yucatec Mayan (Mithun 1984, p. 857; data from Bricker 1978)

a. *t-in-c'ak-Ø-ah* *ce'*.
COMP-I-chop-it-PERF tree
'I chopped a tree.'

b. *c'ak-ce' -n-ah-en.*
chop-tree – ANTIPASS-PERF-I (ABS)
'I wood-chopped' = 'I chopped wood.'

These structures look different from classifier systems exemplified earlier because the incorporated noun is similar in form and meaning to the free noun. In example (4), *ce'* means 'tree,' whether it is free or incorporated. Also, the incorporated nouns in such structures are not generic; they do not refer to a superordinate class. But even in this straightforward compounding type of noun incorporation, Mithun argues that the process is lexical and not syntactic. The noun is unmodified, and the complex does not necessarily have the full range of meanings predicted by phrasal combination of the noun and verb. Instead, it is interpreted as denoting a unitary activity – in this example, wood-chopping.

But Mithun argues that incorporated nouns like these may evolve diachronically into true classifiers, as they lose the independence and specificity of the nouns from which they originate. On this view, as the function of NI comes to denote some unitary and common activity that Mithun describes as "institutionalized," the independence of the noun is diminished, both syntactically, and semantically. Syntactically, incorporation may affect valency and case assignment,[8] and semantically, the incorporated nouns often become more generic in meaning. Generic

[8] When the object of a normally transitive verb is incorporated into the verb, the verb may behave syntactically like an intransitive. See Spencer (1991) for an analysis of Chukchee, an ergative language, along these lines.

meanings are, of course, a definitive property of classifiers. In example (5) from Mohawk, when referring to a specific type of fish, a bullhead (*rabahbót*), the incorporated noun (*tsy*) has the more generic meaning, 'fish.'

(5) Mohawk (Mithun 1984, p. 870)
.....sha'té:ku nikú:ti rabahbót wahu-tsy-ahní:nu ki rake'níha
eight of them bullhead he-fish-bought this my father
'... my father bought eight bullheads.'

Certain sign language classifier constructions lend themselves to comparison quite readily. In an NI analysis of Israeli Sign Language, entertained in depth in Chapter 20, Meir presents the following example from ISL.

(6) ISL (Meir 1999, p. 304)
BOOK INDEX$_b$ HE $_a$GIVE-CL:flat C_1[9]
book that he wide-flat-object-he-give-me
'He wide-flat-object-handed-me a book'
('He handed me a book.')

In Mithun's treatment of spoken language classifiers, she points out further that classifiers indicating entities may coexist synchronically in the same language with classifiers indicating qualities. Munduruku, for example, includes classifiers that indicate "generic terms such as road, name, village, and kin, alongside of qualifying terms such as 'round objects,' 'long, rigid objects,' 'long, flexible objects,' and 'liquids'" (Mithun 1986a, p. 394).

Here again, a comparison may be made with sign languages, which apparently all have entity classifiers, representing such categories as 'upright human,' 'legs,' 'small animal,' and, in ASL, 'vehicle' and 'upright object.' In the same languages, SASS classifiers stand for physical qualities like 'small, round object,' 'flat object,' 'long, thin, object,' etc.

The NI-classifier analysis offered by Mithun examines the relation between Noun Incorporation and classifier constructions from both diachronic and synchronic perspectives. By examining a range of languages, she shows that NI at any stage may decay, becoming fixed and non-productive. Incorporated constructions existing in the lexicon remain, but their phonological form may be eroded, and morpheme boundaries may cease to be discernible. The meaning too may diverge from the original combined meaning of the components, leaving a list of semantically opaque lexicalized words. Here too, the diachronic stages Mithun argues for may leave their tracks synchronically in a language. Productive NI may exist in a language side by side with completely lexicalized and non-productive forms.

[9] In this example, the gloss GIVE stands for the spatial verb meaning 'to hand,' or 'CARRY-BY-HAND.'

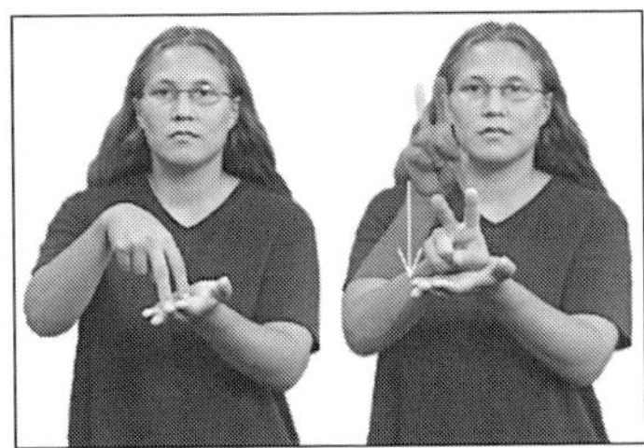

FALL (ASL)

Figure 5.5 Sign that is likely to have originated as a classifier construction

This coexistence of productive, componential forms with non-productive, opaque forms also provides a basis for comparison with sign language. A large number of words in sign language lexicons are believed to have their origins in classifier constructions. An example provided in Supalla (1986) is the sign FALL, illustrated in Figure 5.5.

The sign must have originated through combination of a 'flat object' SASS and the entity classifier for 'legs' of an animate being. Yet the 'frozen' sign FALL is unanalyzed. Hand orientation and movement path are constant, and the sign may be used in sentences in which the theme is animate or inanimate, limbed or blobby, round, etc. At the same time, the classifiers from which the sign evolved are synchronically productive in the language, and may be invoked to describe the falling of a limbed animate creature along various trajectories, in different manners, etc. We will have more to say about classifiers and the lexicon in Chapter 6.

In some spoken languages, noun incorporation tends to be used under particular discourse conditions or for stylistic effect (Mithun 1984). For instance, nouns may be incorporated after they become old information in the discourse. The effect is to background the incorporated noun while still maintaining it in the discourse. In the question of example (7a), the knife is new information and appears as a free noun. In the response in (7b), the knife is old information and it is incorporated. This common function of classifiers is referred to as "backgrounding."

(7) Huahtl Nahuatl (Mithun 1984, p. 861)

a. kanke eltok kocillo? Na' ni-'-neki amanci
where is knife I I-it-want now
'Where is the knife? I want it now.'

b. ya' ki-kocillo-tete'ki panci
he (he)it-knife-cut bread
'He cut the bread with it (the knife).'

Sign language classifiers lend themselves to stylistic backgrounding in a unique way because of the availability of an "extra," relatively independent articulator – the non-dominant hand – and the simultaneity

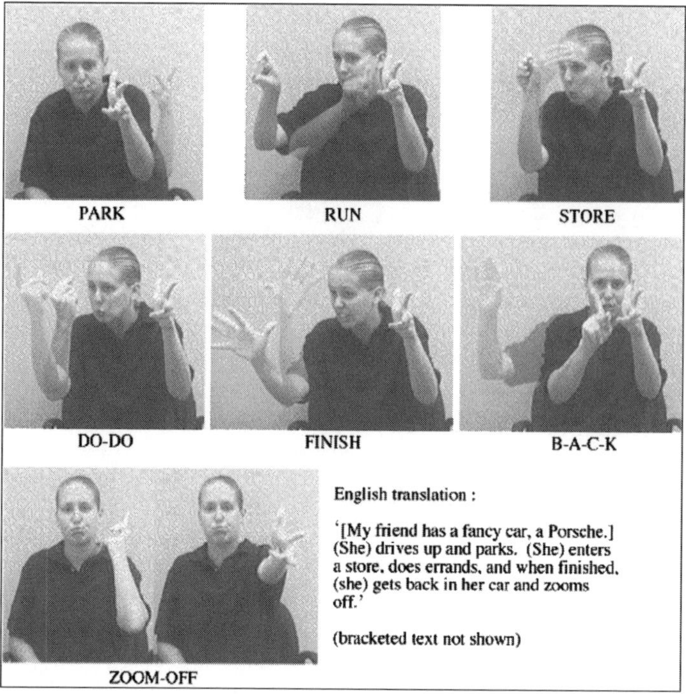

Figure 5.6 VEHICLE backgrounding (reprinted with permission from Emmorey 2002)

afforded by the manual-visual system. In the initial illustration of the system shown in Figure 5.4, the non-dominant hand acts as a "secondary" classifier, in Supalla's terminology, usually the ground in figure–ground relations. In addition to this function, the non-dominant hand may also be exploited to keep background information present in the discourse for as long as it is relevant. Emmorey and Falgier (1999) offer the example in Figure 5.6. The translation is: '[My friend has a fancy car, a Porsche.] (She) drives up and parks. (She) enters a store, does errands, and when finished, (she) gets back in her car and zooms off' (bracketed text not shown). The fancy car remains in the signal, depicted by the non-dominant hand configured for the classifier, VEHICLE.

In spoken languages, the effective use of incorporating constructions indicates special skill or eloquence on the part of a speaker. From Mithun:

> An interesting fact, noted by grammarians for a number of languages, is that innovative NI, as well as the use of a large variety of morphologically complex forms, involves special skill. Speakers of polysynthetic languages often comment on ... (their) consciousness of who speaks their languages especially well. This recognition ... is for stylistic skill, which appears in conversation as well as in

> jokes, anecdotes, legends, and formal oratory. Admired speakers generally share a specific trait: they use a variety of morphologically complex words – particularly incorporating constructions.
>
> (Mithun 1984, p. 879)

Skilled use of classifier constructions is a mark of creative signing in the same way (Klima and Bellugi 1979, Brennan 1990, Blondel and Miller 2000, Sutton-Spence 2000, Sandler and Lillo-Martin 2001, Taub 2001). In performative story-telling and in poetry, signers often make extensive use of classifier constructions, deftly interweaving them with lexical signs, referent projections (stylized use of the whole body to represent nominal referents), and even mime (Aronoff et al. 2003). The availability of classifier handshapes with generic meanings reaches artistic heights in poetry, where some poets exploit the repeated use of the same handshapes as an alliterative device. This poetic device has been noted for ASL poetry (Klima and Bellugi 1979), SLN poetry (Sandler and Lillo-Martin 2001), and BSL poetry (Sutton-Spence 2000). We will illustrate it in Section 5.4.

In sum, we've seen that sign language classifiers share several characteristics of verbal classifiers that have evolved from NI in spoken languages. One of the criticisms sometimes leveled at such comparisons is that in many of the sign language cases, there is no noun around that could be a candidate ancestor for handshape classifiers. This difference between the two kinds of language, however, may be more apparent than real. In spoken languages, the identity of a noun that was incorporated at an earlier stage of a language is often so eroded as to be unidentifiable (Grinevald 2000), so that its diachronic origins are not part of the synchronic competence of speakers. It is similarly possible that at the very nascence of a given sign language, the nominal elements that became classifiers had some nominal function. The SMALL-ROUND-OBJECT classifier signed on the torso may, the first time it was used, have simply meant, 'button.' Even today in ASL, the classifier handshapes for CUP and TREE are the same as those in the corresponding nouns. In any case, as the synchronic lexicons of spoken languages often bear no trace of the diachronic relation between classifier and noun, we do not take the historical origin of classifiers to be a useful synchronic distinction between classifiers in spoken and signed languages.

5.3 Classifier constructions: bound morphemes combined postlexically

Although Supalla dubbed classifier constructions "Verbs of Motion and Location," this appears to be a misnomer. In many ways, they do not behave like ordinary verbs, and their phonological, morphological, semantic, and syntactic structures are different as well. Schick (1987, 1990) refers to them as "classifier predicates," a more satisfying label. We will not take a position on the syntactic properties of these constructions here, although we will discuss some suggestions in Chapter 20. We will simply refer to them as propositions, and describe some of their distributional characteristics.

One of the ways in which entity classifier constructions in ISL and ASL behave differently from ordinary verbs is with respect to aspectual inflection. Recall that verbs like ASL LOOK-AT take on durational meaning when inflected with a reduplicated circular pattern (Chapter 3). But a construction using, for example, the VEHICLE classifier that moves in a reduplicated circular pattern cannot have the meaning, 'car keeps driving' because the path and its repetitions are necessarily interpreted more literally. In fact, the form meets with laughs and derision from ASL consultants.[10]

In their basic morphological structure, classifier constructions differ from lexical words as well, as we've explained, in that each structural element has meaning, constituting a morphological unit rather than a phonological unit as they do in lexical words. Furthermore, each hand may represent a distinct nominal argument in the construction, an additional complexity that does not exist in the "frozen" lexicon.

Third, the phonological form of classifier constructions is different from that of lexical words, as Aronoff et al. (2003) show. Each hand may serve as an independent classifier and may move freely, violating Battison's Symmetry Condition (Chapter 12). Figure 5.7 is a classifier complex in which a man is dragging a dog along (on a leash) behind him. The two hands have different shapes and move independently, the 'dog' wiggling along behind the 'man,' who charges ahead.

The Dominance Condition (Chapter 12), stating that when the non-dominant hand (h2) has a different shape from that of the dominant hand, it must have an unmarked handshape, is also violated in this system, as h2 is an independent classifier, and many classifiers have marked handshapes. These violations have been documented for classifier constructions in ASL (Schick 1990), ISL (Aronoff et al. 2003), Danish SL (Engberg-Pedersen 1993), and Swedish SL (Wallin 1994).[11] The morphological and phonological structure of classifier constructions, then, is unlike that of a word.

The propositional content of classifier constructions and their prosodic structure are different from those of words as well. Here, the prosody offers the key. We anticipate here the analysis of prosody in Chapter 15, to the extent that it can help us gain insight into classifier constructions.

[10] Some constructions with SASS classifiers and many constructions with handling classifiers can take verbal aspect inflections, however. We will return to this issue below.

[11] There are, however, morphological co-occurrence constraints on ASL classifiers. For example, entity classifiers must be treated as whole entities. This means that a handling or SASS classifier representing (handling of) a cap may not be placed on the "head" of the UPRIGHT-HUMAN classifier, nor may one represent the hood emblem of a Mercedes Benz by placing a SASS classifier for ROUND OBJECT on the front of the VEHICLE classifier. These restrictions are morphological and not phonological.

MAN-DRAGS-DOG (ASL)

Figure 5.7 Classifier construction violating Symmetry Condition

First, even extremely complex classifier constructions may span only a single syllable. Brentari (1995) demonstrates a monosyllabic classifier construction glossed, 'two hunched upright beings make their way carefully from point a to point b,' which constitutes one syllable. As a monosyllable is the optimal form of the prosodic word in sign languages (Sandler 1999b, see Chapter 14), we might be led to believe that classifier constructions are indeed words on the basis of this example, albeit morphologically, semantically, and syntactically complex ones.

But such a conclusion is contradicted by the fact that classifier constructions may also span much larger prosodic domains, even traversing several intonational phrases (Aronoff et al. 2003). Consider a construction with the translation, 'the car wove its way uphill, turned left, and ran into a telephone pole.' This string is likely to constitute at least three intonational phrases according to criteria developed in Nespor and Sandler (1999, and Chapter 15): rhythmic cues together with changes in head and/or body position as well as in facial expression. What distinguishes a string like this from other sequences of intonational phrases is that the handshape, and the handshape alone, remains constant throughout the whole utterance without rearticulation. Back translation of classifier strings like the example involving the vehicle and telephone pole, Figure 5.4(a–g), indicates that these strings may indeed span several propositions, each with its own predicate. In that example, the entity classifier for VEHICLE persists throughout seven propositions, functioning as a nominal element involved in events of wandering, skidding, going, crashing, turning, colliding, and falling out.

A partial explanation for this behavior can be found by analyzing classifier constructions as bound morphemes that are combined postlexically. The postlexical level is typically where words combine in syntactic constructions. In the case of sign language classifier constructions, it's not words that combine, we suggest, but bound morphemes. In expressions that include a series of predicates relating to the same classifier argument, a single handshape persists throughout, to form coordinate propositions: sequential strings of predicates articulated with the same classifier. In familiar spoken languages, the subject is often elided in strings of this kind: 'The car wound its way uphill, Ø turned left, and Ø ran into a telephone pole.' And indeed, similar sign language sequences without classifier constructions, in which a subject would be conveyed by an independent sign or signs, would also elide the subject in the second and third clauses, or might have a null subject altogether. But comparable sign language sequences in which the subject is conveyed by a handshape classifier do not elide the subject. Every signed expression must have some handshape, and the simultaneity of the system permits the subject to be articulated only once, while spanning a series of predicates. As postlexical entities, it is not surprising that constraints such as the Symmetry Condition and the Dominance Condition are violated: postlexical forms may be non-structure preserving (Kiparsky 1982).

5.4 Understanding classifier constructions through poetry

In sum, the handshapes available to the classifier system classify sets of referents according to certain, usually physical, properties. And a single classifier may characterize a sequence of predicates without rearticulation of the handshape. In ordinary prose, the classifier handshape in such sequences represents a single referent, the car in the example given in the previous section. Each predicate in the series is predicated of the car. But in poetry, license is taken with both of these properties. A classifier handshape may persist across a sequence of lines of poetic text, but represent a *different* referent in each (Klima and Bellugi 1979, Sutton-Spence and Woll 1999, Sandler and Lillo-Martin 2001). The persistence of a single handshape evoking a series of different images within a poem challenges the viewer to assign an interpretation to these images, achieving semantic versatility in a way that is aesthetically pleasing

In his poem, "Desert Spirit," Dutch poet Wim Emmerik uses the handshape in a manner that might be described as alliterative. The sequence shown in Figure 5.8 depicts a man walking with effort in the desert, viewing the flat, spare horizon, falling to the ground from exhaustion, raising himself with effort, and spotting a vulture overhead. There are many aspects of this passage that are poetic, in the sense that they depart from and heighten the standard form of language for aesthetic and emotional effect. The separation of the observer (indicated with the face and body) from the event (indicated with the hands) in (SEE-) BIRD (-ABOVE) is one such device. The relevant feature for our discussion is the use of a single handshape (in this case, on both hands) throughout

a. FEET-WALK b. FLAT-HORIZON

c. FALL-FLAT d. RAISE-SELF e. SEE-BIRD-ABOVE

Figure 5.8 Classifiers used in poetry (SLN)

the passage. Except for the gesture of raising oneself from the ground, the other expressions in the sequence are all classifier constructions.

5.5 Conclusion

The productive and systematic use of classifier constructions alongside ordinary words provides a rich and variegated means of depicting spatial relations and motion events that is at once grammatical and in harmony with languages produced with the hands, face, and body, and perceived with the eyes. Later chapters will build on the basic description and analysis of classifier constructions presented here. Chapter 6 pursues the common assumption that many lexical words of sign languages evolved from classifier constructions. Some syntactic analyses of classifier constructions are discussed in Chapter 20, and the unique, modality-specific qualities of this subsystem are addressed in Unit 5 on modality effects.

6 Entering the lexicon: lexicalization, backformation, and cross-modal borrowing

The existence of productive inflectional and derivational morphology in sign languages that have been studied indicates that lexicons of sign languages have much in common with those of spoken languages. Form–meaning correspondences must be listed together with part-of-speech and other syntactic properties. Word-formation rules must also be contained there, be they rules of simple affixation or of templatic association. Productive rules afford a language a way of expanding its lexicon, and this option is exploited in sign languages as it is in their spoken counterparts.

Two other ways in which sign language lexicons may expand are through the lexicalization of classifier constructions and through borrowing. Lexicalization and borrowing are commonly found in spoken languages as well, but in sign language, each has properties unique to the modality. Insofar as classifier constructions are often different from words in semantic, syntactic, phonological, and prosodic structure, their transformation to words is necessarily multifaceted, posing different challenges from those found in spoken language lexicalization. And as sign languages may sometimes reach over into the spoken modality to borrow, the borrowing process also has properties that are different from those that characterize borrowing from one spoken language to another. This chapter focuses on those processes, aiming to distill the general linguistic properties from the modality-rich solution in which they are immersed. Most of the chapter is devoted to the lexicalization of classifiers, presenting examples of monomorphemic signs that are obviously descended from polymorphemic classifier constructions. To illustrate this phenomenon, we trace the radical prosodic transformation of a classifier construction to a word in real time. The route from classifier construction to "frozen" word is so transparent synchronically, in fact, that it leads to a sign language-unique kind of delexicalization akin to backformation.

Words are not only characterized by their phonological and morphological form; they are also often characterized by idiosyncrasies. Liddell (2003) has shown that classifier constructions, too, have idiosyncrasies. On that basis, he argues that they are not necessarily made up of fully productive morphemes, and implies that they are more like unanalyzed words. We examine Liddell's argument in detail, as it allows us to pinpoint a number of morphological issues of more general interest. We ultimately reject it, suggesting instead that some classifier constructions may undergo lexicalization, while the morphemes from which they are constructed still retain their morphological productivity. The interesting relationship that emerges between unanalyzed, monomorphemic lexicalized words on the one hand, and polymorphemic classifier constructions made productively from bound morphemes on the other, helps to bridge a well-known gap in sign language analysis. It is the gap between classifier constructions and the amorphous category of verbs that has been likened to them, spatial verbs.

Languages that have regular contact with other languages often borrow from them, and sign languages are no different: when they come into contact with one another, they may borrow as well. Research on ASL has shown that that language has taken many words from French Sign Language (Woodward and Erting 1975). Similarly, Israeli Sign Language also has many words from other sign languages (Meir and Sandler 2004). In fact, the history of ISL implies that it is actually a contact language, a creole. In some situations, a lingua franca may arise under special circumstances through contact among many sign languages (Woll 1990, Supalla and Webb 1995), a fascinating process in itself.

Here we touch briefly on a different kind of borrowing: cross-modal borrowing. Sign languages are unusual as a group in that they always exist alongside languages in a different modality, and their users are often in constant contact with spoken languages through reading and communication with hearing people. This language contact situation results in two kinds of borrowing into sign language: mouthing of spoken words and fingerspelling words from the spoken language. In both cases, the sign languages impose phonological, morphological, and semantic constraints on the borrowed forms.

6.1 Classifier constructions: from postlexical to lexical and back again

Despite the striking differences between classifier constructions and lexical words, many researchers believe that "frozen" monomorphemic signs in sign language lexicons evolved diachronically from classifier constructions, as we mentioned in the previous chapter (McDonald 1982, Shepard-Kegl 1985, Brennan 1990, Schick 1990, Johnston and Schembri 1999, Schembri 2003).[1] Many ASL signs like FALL, illustrated

[1] It is also likely that under certain circumstances the direction is reversed, as was suggested for 'button' > SMALL-ROUND-OBJECT in the previous chapter. For example, in language acquisition or home sign (Goldin-Meadow 2003), holistic signs or gestures may be reanalyzed as consisting of meaningful components, and may then be introduced into a classifier system. Thanks to Richard Meier for stressing this point to us.

WRITE (ISL)

Figure 6.1 A lexical sign derived from a classifier construction

in Figure 5.5, seem clearly to have evolved from entity plus SASS classifier constructions, and many others, like WRITE, in Figure 6.1, from handling + SASS classifier constructions. (The convergence of two classifiers in a single form is possible because each hand may represent an independent classifier.) In each case, the sign is normally interpreted as an ordinary, monomorphemic, monosyllabic word. Conversely, "frozen" signs that normally function as monomorphemic can be reinterpreted within a discourse as morphologically complex. The morphologically simple sign WRITE behaves like an ordinary verb. For example, it can take temporal aspect marking like other verbs (where classifier-predicate forms are more restricted). Yet, as Brentari and Goldsmith (1993) have pointed out, in a discourse, the non-dominant handshape can be interpreted as if it were a classifier for the flat object being written upon. Consider for example a sentence meaning, 'I wrote a letter to the editor yesterday, but then had second thoughts and reconsidered it critically.' In this sentence, the words WRITE and LETTER have the non-dominant hand as a place of articulation. These are sign lexemes or words, in which handshape, location, and movement are phonological parameters and as such meaningless. In signing the sentence above, however, it would be common to leave the non-dominant hand in its configuration and location throughout the entire sentence, and for it to serve as the place of articulation for the later sign CONSIDER, as shown in Figure 6.2. That is, the non-dominant hand of the lexeme WRITE may be reinterpreted as a classifier morpheme for flat object, referring to the piece of paper on which the letter is written. It assumes its backgrounding role, remaining in the signing space as long as it is relevant to the discourse.

One might think of this reanalysis of lexical words into their original classifier components as a sign language-particular type of *backformation*. While spoken language backformation typically creates simple forms by mistakenly interpreting some element as an affix (e.g., removing *-ar* to form *burgle* from *burglar*), however, the sign language version is likely to recapitulate diachrony accurately by arriving at the true multimorphemic origin of the sign. The similarity of the incorrectly analyzed affix in spoken

CONSIDER LETTER (ISL)

Figure 6.2 Place of articulation of lexical sign WRITE reinterpreted as a classifier

language to a real affix is an accident of history, and it is only through knowledge of the actual history of the word that we can recognize back-formation at all. But the classifier morphemes from which the signs evolved are at once extremely productive and often so transparent due to iconicity that there is no room for error.

6.1.1 Prosodic transformation under lexicalization

Classifier constructions continue to be a productive source of new words, then, becoming "frozen" forms in which handshape, movement, and location have only phonological, and not morphological status.[2] Such forms undergo a transformation when they enter the lexicon, conforming to the prosodic constraints on lexical words.

In the course of a comparative study of classifiers in two sign languages, the spontaneous evolution of a word from a classifier construction was observed under laboratory conditions (Aronoff et al. 2003). Asked to describe bones and how they are attached at the joint, an ISL signer first signed the sequence shown in Figure 6.3, in which "||" represents a prosodic break, and the boldface section is the portion that was subsequently spontaneously lexicalized. Between the two sequences printed in boldface type in the caption, there was a long hold and eye contact with the addressee as well as a head nod, clearly marking an intonational phrase break. The whole expression spanned 1,440 ms. Note that the classifier for the roundish object is held in front of the signer's face, to draw special attention to the form and action depicted. As signers typically look at the face of their interlocutors and not at the hands (Siple 1978), ordinary signing generally does not block the face, and placing the hand in front of the face in this way makes the string anomalous compared to lexical signs.

Within moments, the name of this anatomical structure was reduced to a much simpler form, shown in Figure 6.4, which might simply be glossed

[2] Forms referred to as frozen exclude the spatial verbs, which synchronically behave like classifier constructions in terms of their spatial properties. That is, their locations at least are not frozen, but covary with the spatial loci of locative referents. See Section 6.2.1.

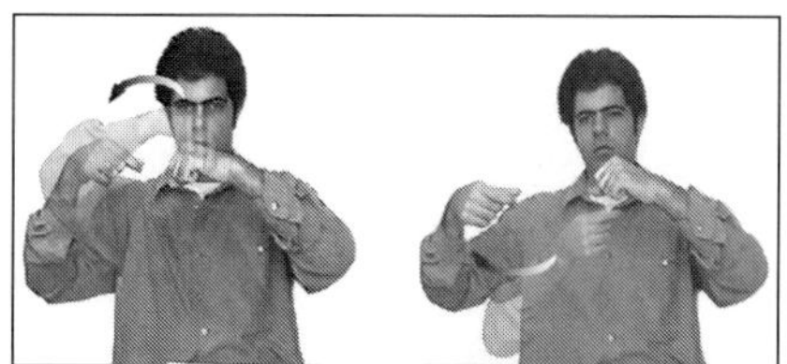

'Arm || Meet, two-roundish-objects-adjacent-rock-together || **Thin-stringy-object-extend-from-top-of-roundish-object-in-arc-shape || Thin-stringy-object-extend-from-under-roundish-object-in-arc-shape-to-meet (other thin stringy object)** || Two roundish-objects-adjacent-rock-together.'

Figure 6.3 Classifier sequence designating a ligament (ISL)

LIGAMENT (ISL)

Figure 6.4 Classifier construction evolved to sign-like form within a discourse

as LIGAMENT. Though not yet in full conformity in every detail, this sign already fits the canonical prosodic structure of a sign language word (Location – Movement – Location; discussed in Chapter 9). It was uttered extremely rapidly, with no intonational or rhythmic break of any kind, and spanned only 280 ms. It is signed in neutral space and does not block the face of the signer, which instead articulates a facial expression – squinted eyes – that is used to represent shared information in ISL (Sandler 1999c, Nespor and Sandler 1999; Chapter 15 here). The signer uses this facial expression while signing his new sign for the concept 'ligament' in order to call the addressee's attention to the previously signed classifier construction from which it had so quickly evolved. This is presumably the way of lexicalization. If the concept behind a sign lexicalized in this manner gains currency, it is added to the common lexicon of the language.

6.2 Productivity and lexicalization: the case of SAUNTER

There is a consensus among researchers that classifiers, movement paths, movement manners, and locations combine quite freely, making the

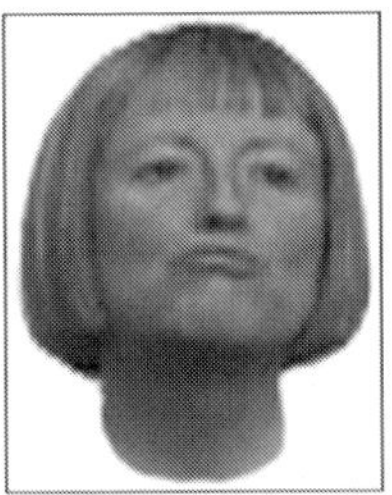

'with relaxation and enjoyment' (ASL)

Figure 6.5 Non-manual adverbial

classifier subsystem extremely productive. Classifier constructions are interpreted componentially, according to the meaning of the individual elements that comprise them. It is also generally acknowledged that frequent combinations of a classifier with a particular movement or location may drift toward lexicalization, as we have seen. Though these two observations are theoretically compatible with one another, Liddell (2003) sees a contradiction. He argues that a perceived drift toward lexicalization in some forms diminishes the degree of productivity usually attributed to the classifier subsystem as a whole. While we take the consensus view that the system is extremely productive, we consider Liddell's point here, because it provides a vehicle for highlighting issues of productivity, of interpretation of classifier constructions, and of the effect that lexicalization has on both the classifier subsystem and the lexicon.

Liddell points out that the handshape classifier representing an upright human may combine with a rhythmic bouncing forward movement, which is interpreted as 'walking along in an unhurried manner.' He also notes the (possibly) obligatory addition of a mouth shape adverbial, pictured in Figure 6.5 (repeated from Chapter 4), which means 'unhurried, relaxed, enjoyable, or not out of the ordinary' (Liddell 1980). Liddell claims further that no other human classifier (e.g., LEGS) can combine with this movement element, nor can a non-human classifier (e.g., SMALL-ANIMAL). He goes on to observe that it is not acceptable to move the hand backwards with this movement to mean, 'walking along backwards in an unhurried manner.' If all elements in the classifier construction system can productively combine, as many researchers claim, then these non-occurring forms are unexpected. Liddell's line of reasoning implies that classifier constructions are less productively formed and more lexicalized than previously believed, implying further that the combination of upright human classifier, bouncy movement, and 'mm' non-manual are stored in the lexicon – as a sign, let's say, SAUNTER. The justification for lexical listing relies on the tacit assumptions that neither this particular co-occurrence nor the nonoccurrence of other

Figure 6.6 Two different classifiers for humans

combinations involving the same morphemes is predictable. We challenge both assumptions.

As humans do not normally locomote by propelling themselves forward by bouncing, the combination of bouncing movement and the upright human classifier must be interpreted metaphorically, as moving forward in a bouncy state of mind. In other words, as this metaphorical interpretation is the only felicitous one, it does not warrant lexical listing of the morpheme combination.

That the LEGS classifier can't combine with the bouncing movement may also be accounted for by a more general restriction on the use of this classifier proposed by Engberg-Pedersen (1993) for Danish Sign Language. She writes, "The choice of handshape unit does not depend only on the choice of noun in the verb's argument or on non-temporary features of the referent, but on the kind of motion event the verb is used to describe." She describes the different conditions under which the human figure classifier and the human legs classifier are used. The or human legs classifier handshape illustrated in Figure 6.6a is used for "(1) motion or locomotion of human beings with special reference to their legs or feet" (e.g., in distinguishing *sit*, *lie*, and *stand*); or (2) "motion by foot in a certain direction, to a goal, or within an area." The handshape classifier illustrated in Figure 6.6b is used for "an individual approaching or passing the holder of the point of view; motion with a goal or route; or two people meeting or parting" (pp. 247–249). While we may not assume blindly that the constraints that hold on Danish Sign Language are the same as those for ASL, constraints of this sort must be sought before resorting to lexical stipulation. If indeed the constraint does hold for ASL, then the non-occurrence of the bouncing movement with LEGS would be explained by the fact that the event being described is not concerned with the physical activity of the feet, and it is not goal-oriented. In that case, another purported reason for lexical listing is removed from consideration.

Let's consider now the claims that the small animal classifier cannot co-occur with the bouncing movement, that the enjoyment facial expression is mandatory, and that the bouncing movement is obligatorily in a forward direction. As it turns out, each can be explained using general principles and without stipulation. Our consultants do accept the co-occurrence of bouncing movement with a 'small animal' classifier. They point out that the 'enjoyment' non-manual would be inappropriate in this case, except perhaps in a cartoon in which the animal is personified. This consideration is pragmatic; it is not a linguistic restriction on the construction.

The facial expression that occurs with the 'upright human' classifier in this construction is also explainable on more general grounds. For humans, the bouncing movement is infelicitous without the 'enjoyment' non-manual, because they do not literally hop along when walking. In other words, we suggest that it is not the construction which requires the facial expression, but the metaphorical interpretation that the construction must have, due to pragmatic reasons.

A 'human bouncing backwards' is also ruled out for two different pragmatic reasons. First, the state of mind that the bouncing movement metaphorically represents with a human classifier is not likely to characterize walking backwards, predicting that the combination of morphemes conveying 'human sauntering backwards with enjoyment' is not acceptable. The second and more basic pragmatic restriction is the fact that humans do not literally bounce backwards, so a 'human bouncing backwards' construction is ruled out for this reason under normal circumstances. But just as a small animal may bounce along with enjoyment under special circumstances (in an animated cartoon), one can imagine that the restriction on 'bouncing along backwards with enjoyment' could also be violated for special effects such as humor. Mr. Bean could be depicted as 'bouncing' himself into a situation that he discovers to be embarrassing, and bouncing himself back out of it with the same, now humorously inappropriate, facial expression.[3] This interpretation suggests that, contra Liddell's arguments, the example is indeed analyzable into its parts, but that not all combinations of elements are equally felicitous under normal circumstances. That is, felicity conditions make the right predictions without lexical stipulation.

Maintaining the bouncing movement in the repertoire of classifier constructions preserves the generalization that the same bouncing movement element may be interpreted literally, for example in combination with the 'small animal' classifier, and with SASSes (notably without the non-manual adverbial indicating an attitude). A bouncing forward movement combined with a SMALL-ROUND-OBJECT SASS may describe a pebble skipping across a pond. Here, the movement is interpreted more literally, and has a different meaning than the same movement has when

[3] Mr. Bean is a character in a television series, played by British actor Rowan Atkinson, famous for his physical humor. Through a combination of enthusiastic determination and utter cluelessness, Mr. Bean manages to entangle himself in impossible situations, and then applies equal enthusiasm and determination to the always daunting task of extracting himself from them.

combined with an entity classifier. Similarly, the 'upright human' and 'mm' facial expression may combine productively with other movement morphemes. Such possibilities are predicted by Supalla's original analysis of the system, which contains a small list of bound movement roots (in the lexicon) that combine productively with different classifier handshapes (Supalla 1982, 1986).

Nevertheless, the example is instructive. If it could be demonstrated that the combination of the bouncing movement with the human classifier and the 'enjoyment' adverbial facial expression co-occurs often and, in the process, has assumed a particular meaning or behavior beyond that predicted by even a metaphorical interpretation of the individual components, then it would indeed be necessary to list the combination in the lexicon with its own definition and simple gloss, e.g., SAUNTER. Presumably, when the construction functions as a lexical item, it conforms to phonological constraints on words, a prediction waiting to be tested. But in any case, as this discussion has made clear, the individual components must be listed as well, as they are still free to be used productively in the system.

Dual listing in the lexicon of morphemes, whether free or bound, in addition to the complex forms in which they occur, is far from anomalous. In fact, it is rampant in spoken languages, and one of the central motivations behind the word-based theory of morphology (Aronoff 1976). For example, the suffix *-able* must be available in the lexicon as an adjective-forming suffix that attaches very productively to transitive verbs. But at the same time many common words in *-able*, like *readable* or *washable*, must be listed in their derived form because not all of their meanings are fully predictable. *Washable* does not have only the predicted meaning, 'capable of being made clean by applying soap and water.' It also has the meaning, 'washes well without being damaged.' The latter meaning is actually more common, but it is not predicted by the *-able* word-formation rule, and therefore not only the productive affix but also the derived form *washable* must be listed in the lexicon.

The foregoing discussion, which has sought to pinpoint more clearly the relationship between polymorphemic classifier constructions and lexical words, allows us to tackle a class of signs that has proved difficult to categorize: spatial verbs. In Section 6.2.1, we take a step toward explaining why it is that these signs may act like classifier constructions but "feel" like lexical verbs.

6.2.1 Spatial verbs as lexicalized classifier constructions

Spatial verbs are the verbs that inflect by changing direction, like agreeing verbs and unlike plain verbs, but whose locations in space are not determined by loci associated with subject and object as are those of agreeing verbs (Chapter 3). Instead, like the locations of classifier constructions, the locations of spatial verbs are determined by the more fine-grained and more literal layout of objects established in the discourse space (Padden 1988 [1983]). We approach the problem by bringing a number of observations and analyses in the sign language literature together with Mithun's treatment of lexicalization in Noun Incorporation.

In Padden's (1988 [1983]) seminal analysis of verbs in ASL, spatial verbs are grouped with classifier constructions on the basis of their locative agreement properties. Engberg-Pedersen (1993) claims for Danish Sign Language that spatial verbs fall somewhere in the middle along a continuum from classifier constructions to lexical verbs. Calling something a verb implies that it is in the lexicon, something we have been claiming that most classifier constructions are not. What, then, defines the line between a construction that is in the lexicon (a spatial verb) and one that is not (a classifier construction)?

Spatial verbs are called verbs for two reasons: they have a simple gloss (e.g., MOVE, PUT, IRON), and they may sometimes inflect for temporal aspect. As Chapter 5 made clear, classifier constructions are glossed by the combination of morphemes (e.g., TWO-LEGGED-BEING-MOVES-ALONG-ARC-PATH-FROM-POINT-A-TO-POINT-B), and they may not inflect for temporal aspect.

The difference, we suggest, is due to the frequent co-occurrence of a particular combination of morphemes. Specifically, if a combination of a classifier handshape with a certain kind of movement is frequently used to label a common concept, the form gets a standard gloss and behaves like other verbs; it is lexicalized.

The example of IRON is instructive. This verb in ASL is listed as one of about a hundred noun–verb pairs found in Supalla and Newport (1978), and, at the same time, its agreement properties also place it in the category of spatial verbs. Its origin as a classifier construction is clear; the handshape is easily recognizable as a handling classifier, and the back and forth movement are similarly transparent. Following Meir's (1999) analysis of instrumental classifiers as noun incorporation (see Chapter 20), we analyze the verb glossed IRON as a combination of a stem meaning something like, 'slide back and forth along a surface,' and an incorporated nominal handling classifier indicating the hand grasping a narrow object. On this view, the spatial verb glossed IRON originates as a classifier construction meaning, 'slide a narrow-handled object back and forth along a surface.' Because of the utility of this expression in everyday life – a factor which Mithun (1986a) says results in lexicalization of noun incorporation in spoken languages – the classifier construction is lexicalized, and gains the more specific meaning, 'to iron.' That is, it gains a conventionalized citation form, which clearly distinguishes it from a classifier construction. Once it is lexicalized in this way, it can freely inflect for temporal aspect like other verbs.

The theoretical implication is clear. A deeper understanding of classifier constructions is gained by explicitly allowing the dual listing of productive morphemes and of lexicalized words – a kind of organization characteristic of spoken language lexicons as well. We now turn to another way of adding to the lexicon: borrowing.

6.3 Foreign vocabulary

In addition to ordinary borrowing among sign languages, sign languages may also borrow cross-modally, through mouthing and fingerspelling.

6.3.1 Mouthing is sign, not speech

In many European sign languages and in Israeli Sign Language, a fair amount of mouthing of words from the ambient spoken languages takes place, more, apparently than is typically the case in ASL (Boyes-Braem and Sutton-Spence 2001).[4] However, it would be a mistake to interpret this mouthing as speech accompanying sign. In fact, mouthing grammatically is not well understood, and it is difficult for second language learners to acquire. First, the word order of the spoken language is not the same as that of the sign language, making it virtually impossible to accompany each sign with its translation in the spoken language. (This would be comparable to speaking Turkish with English words.) Second, as we have seen, the morphological structure of sign languages is different from that of spoken languages, so that each word contains different grammatical morphemes in spoken versus signed language, again making simultaneous transmission of the two impossible. Third, only a relatively small percentage of signs are normally accompanied by mouthing. In some cases, mouthing disambiguates two concepts represented by the same sign. But the function of many other instances of mouthing have yet to be discovered.

Rather, mouthing, though borrowed from the spoken language, appears to perform sign-language-internal functions. Although mouthing patterns are not yet fully understood, one function of mouthing that has been attested is to disambiguate two otherwise similar signs, in this way performing a significant lexical role. Some sign words are

[4] In this section, we refer to mouthing that accompanies real sign languages, and not to contrived systems such as Signed English, Signed Hebrew, etc.

obligatorily accompanied by mouthing, and in some of these, only part of a word is mouthed, apparently conforming to the rhythm of the monosyllabic form of the sign (see Chapter 14). Whatever other role such mouthing performs, it also marks the prosodic form of the sign. Conversely, the mouthing of a word is often "stretched" over more than one sign (Boyes-Braem and Sutton-Spence 2001). In ISL, the mouthing of a content host word may be stretched over its cliticized pronoun as well (Sandler 1999a, 1999b), in this way marking the domain of the prosodic word. Though originating in spoken language, then, mouthing fulfills system-internal semantic and prosodic roles in sign languages. For descriptions of a range of functions performed by the month in various sign languages, readers are referred to the volume edited by Boyes-Braem and Sutton-Spence (2001).

6.3.2 Borrowing through fingerspelling: structure, meaning, and iconicity

A number of sign languages have systems, called fingerspelling, which represent the letters of the alphabet of the ambient spoken language with different handshapes on one or both hands. The extent to which fingerspelling is used and the ways in which it is incorporated vary a great deal from sign language to sign language (see Padden 1998).

In ASL, fingerspelling takes various forms. One of these is a kind of code switching, in which a signer will spontaneously spell the English name, place, or concept if no sign is available. The fate of such forms varies. If the concept which is initially fingerspelled is commonly used within a community of signers, a sign may be coined to replace it. But in American Sign Language, code switching via fingerspelling is sometimes a conduit for borrowing words into the lexicon, words whose forms are based on the shape of the fingerspelled letters. There are three ways in which fingerspelling leads to borrowing. Sometimes two concepts represented by one sign are disambiguated through initialization: replacing the native handshape of the sign with the fingerspelled shape of the first letter of the English word. For example, ROOM and OFFICE are distinguished from each other and from un-initialized BOX by using the R and O handshapes for the first two, respectively, and leaving the location and movement the same for all three, as in the native form. Another way is through abbreviation, which consists of fingerspelling the first English letter of a word or of each member of a compound and articulating it at some arbitrary location. An example of this is the word BACKGROUND, formed by spelling the letters B and G against the open palm of the non-dominant hand – B high on the hand, against the fingers, and then G low, against the heel of the palm. The third type of borrowed forms involving fingerspelling is termed fingerspelled loans (Battison 1978 [1973]). Here, the fingerspelling of the English word is imported into the language, often with changes in form.[5] This last type of borrowing is the most interesting in the present context, because it is this type of borrowing that reveals real interaction between English and ASL within the lexicon.

As it is integrated into the visual language through lexicalization, the fingerspelled loan words often take on sign-language-specific phonological properties of native words in the lexicon. In particular, the forms may alter the handshapes of the fingerspelled letters to conform to shapes of the native lexicon, and some letters may be deleted in order to more closely approximate the monosyllabic form of native signs. The result of these changes may produce a simple hand-internal movement of the kind that is common in native words.

For example, the ASL word NO evolved from fingerspelled N-O. This form underwent precisely the changes described in the previous paragraph, resulting in a monosyllabic form with a change in finger position but not in finger selection. In other words, the loan is phonologically indistinguishable from a native sign. In addition to the phonological changes, this form has also undergone a morphological metamorphosis. Specifically, the word NO is further derived to form a verb with the meaning SAY-NO-TO. The loan verb adds a simultaneous path movement to the hand-internal movement, and, now a verb in the ASL lexicon, it inflects for subject and object agreement.

Another kind of interaction of the ASL and English lexicons via fingerspelling is observed in compounds, which may adopt one or both members from the English. What is interesting in this borrowing is that it reveals differences in the semantics of the words in the two languages (Padden 1998, Brentari and Padden 2001). For example, the compounds DEAD^LINE and TIME^LINE, both borrowed from English through sign-for-word translation, contrasts with S-K-Y-L-I-N-E., where the hyphens indicate fingerspelling of each letter. The first two examples do not involve fingerspelling; but rather translation into signs. The third is fully fingerspelled because, according to Brentari and Padden, the sign LINE refers to a boundary or conduit but not to an outline, as in 'skyline.' Thus, using the sign LINE in this compound would violate the semantic integrity of the sign. Similarly, EYE^B-A-L-L and BLACK^B-A-L-L borrow the first member wholesale through translation to a sign with the same meaning, but fingerspell the second member, because the meaning of the sign BALL is restricted to balls held by the hands and used for playing.

It is noteworthy that the sign language with the most pervasive use of fingerspelling, American Sign Language, also makes less use of mouthing than do European sign languages, and vice versa. It may be, as suggested

[5] Some signs, such as several color signs in ASL, originated as initialized forms; no earlier version with native handshapes is known.

to us by Carol Padden, that the two are functional complements of each other. Of interest in the present context is the fact that in both types of cross-modal borrowing, sign languages impose their own constraints on the borrowed forms, constraints arising from properties that are not modality specific, but linguistic.

7 Morphology: conclusion

If we were to approach sign language morphology from a simplistic and surface-oriented viewpoint, we would be confounded at once. Most of the word formation in sign languages does not consist of the linear affixation of concrete morphemes that bear a one-to-one correspondence with a meaning or grammatical function. Instead, the morphology of sign languages lends support from a different modality for the contemporary generative view of morphology – a morphological component that is word-based, and involves forms and processes that are often abstract and are not necessarily concatenative. Verbal bases may be associated to partially specified skeletal templates to form various verbal aspects; certain verbal forms may be reduplicated and their movements altered to derive nouns; classifier morphemes associate non-concatenatively to movements and locations to create complex forms that depict locative relations and different path shapes and manners of motion.

Classical morphological properties are also found in sign languages. There are sequential affixes that evolved diachronically from free words in the sign languages we have studied. Derivation, inflection, and compounding are all attested in many sign languages. This means that productive word-internal processes for forming new lexemes and for marking syntactic relations among words are robust in sign languages, as they are in most spoken languages – a significant discovery for defining the human language faculty. The sign language system supports allomorphy as well – more than a single form for the same word partial. In fact, ASL was shown to utilize the same set of allomorphy relations for more than one grammatical function – a morphome in Aronoff's terminology. As explained in Chapter 4, this is of theoretical interest because it demonstrates the abstractness and the productivity of the morphological system, and distinguishes it from other components of the grammar.

The system for forming complex words in sign languages, then, is far from random. It is replete with patterns, many of which are found in spoken languages as well. It is a linguistic system.

There are some intriguing generalizations arising in the study of sign language morphology that we have not dealt with here yet. First, certain aspects of morphological structure, such as the amorphous form of classifier complexes, do not seem to be found in spoken languages. Second, there is a core of morphological processes and properties that are found in all sign languages, properties that may be thought of as trademarks of sign language morphology. We will deal with these generalizations in Unit 5.

In Unit 3, the next unit, we go "down" one level, to the word-building elements that are meaningless, and their organization – to the phonology of sign language. We will show that sound is not critical for phonology in natural human language.

Unit 3

Phonology

8 Meaningless linguistic elements and how they pattern

The preceding unit demonstrated that the lexicons of sign languages are rich and diversely structured, containing lexemes and bound morphemes, mechanisms of derivational and inflectional morphology, of incorporation and compounding. In all of these ways, one may naturally compare the words of sign languages with those of spoken languages. But in spoken languages, there is a level of structure beneath the word and the morpheme, a meaningless level, consisting of patterns of sounds. The form and organization of these sounds are constrained in part by the physiology of the oral–aural systems that produce and perceive them. Obviously, one would not expect to find equivalence in the formational units of a different modality. At the same time, there are principles of organization and alternation found at this level that are more abstract than those aspects of the system that can be described on the basis of physiology alone, principles which are in the domain of phonological theory. And it is here, at the level of analysis that abstracts away from the physical system to some extent, that we may look for similarities between the two modalities.

Until quite recently, sign languages were assumed to exist without a meaningless level of structure at all. As we explained in Chapter 1, it had been widely assumed that signs were essentially iconic wholes. It took the work of William Stokoe to demonstrate systematically that there is indeed a level of sign language structure that corresponds to phonology (Stokoe 1960, Stokoe et al. 1965). In particular, he showed that sign languages have duality of patterning: a meaningful level of structure, as well as a level that is made up of a list of meaningless, yet linguistically significant elements. The primary source of evidence adduced for this claim is the traditional one: minimal pairs that are distinguished by a single discrete meaningless element. Stokoe went on to show that the number of meaningless linguistically contrastive elements in the ASL system is finite and reasonably small. This discovery tells us that the human brain is determined to organize the language transmission system in a particular way, even where the physical means of transmission is radically different from that of languages in the more widespread modality. It suggests that defining phonology in terms of sound patterns is too narrow, and that the following definition is better: *phonology is the level of linguistic structure that organizes the medium through which language is transmitted.*

The study of sign language phonology has a unique contribution to make towards understanding language universals and the contribution of modality to language structure. This enterprise is valid to the extent that it is approached with the right balance of two elements: knowledge about spoken language and open-mindedness about the possibility of significant modality differences. Researchers have grappled with the challenge of finding the right balance, and, in the process, some have leaned farther to one side or the other. The result has been a substantial body of literature on sign language phonology, much of it detailed and complex, often difficult for linguists approaching this literature to probe. An additional problem is presented by the fact that sign language is, after all, transmitted in an entirely different physical modality, so that descriptions of sign language elements attributed to a phonological level, and analogies with constructs in spoken language, are sometimes quite difficult to grasp. If that's not enough, the plethora of different theories of phonological structure in sign languages, some of them partly overlapping, some of them incompatible with one another, may cause the person attempting to access the work in this field to wring his or her hands, or even to throw them up in despair.

The present unit sets three goals. One is to make the study of sign language phonology more tractable for linguists of both the spoken and sign varieties. Another is to make significant findings in sign language phonology accessible to phonologists in particular, whether or not they have any familiarity with sign language research. The third and perhaps most important goal is to show how the study of phonology in a visual-gestural language can raise unexpected questions about phonological universals and about the relation between phonetics and phonology, and, sometimes, suggest answers to them.

The study of sign language phonology forces a reexamination of concepts that are often taken for granted. When one thinks of phonological theory, one may think of such proposals as autosegmental phonology (Goldsmith 1976), hierarchical feature organization (Clements 1985), dependency relations (Anderson and Ewen 1987), syllable theory (Blevins 1995), or prosodic morphology and phonology (McCarthy and Prince 1995). But as soon as we turn our attention to language in another modality, we are reminded that even the most basic elements of phonological analysis, such as the feature, the feature class, the segment, or the syllable, are actually no more than theoretical constructs that have served us well in formulating generalizations about spoken language. There is no reason to assume that they are relevant for sign languages. If a particular

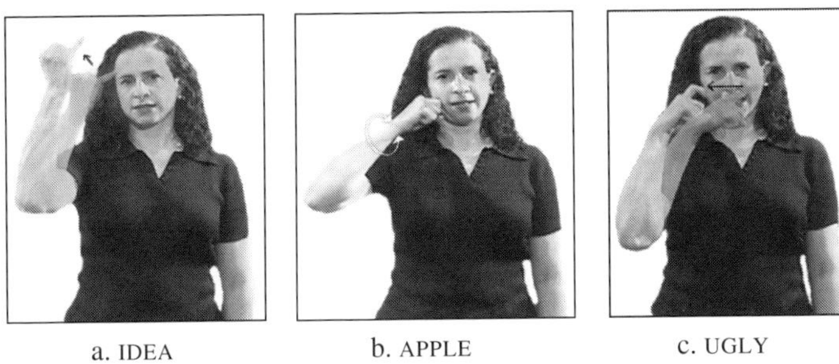

Figure 8.1 Three ASL signs with different specifications for hand configuration, location, and movement

construct *is* found in the phonology of languages in both modalities, however, then that construct reflects a universal organizing principle of language at the phonological level, one that is not directly dependent on physical constraints. If a construct is found in only one modality, then it is generated by the physical design of that modality, and the discovery casts the relationship between the design and the structuring in high relief. Throughout the unit, we will briefly introduce general theoretical issues and models as they become necessary in dealing with sign language phenomena and analyses. The unit does not aim to present a comprehensive overview of all research on sign language phonology. That would be impossible in the space we have here, and utterly indigestible to boot. Nor does it presume to deal with all important issues of phonology in general. Rather, we hope to show how specific and central problems in the phonological description and analysis of sign languages have been approached, and ways in which investigators have appealed to general phonological theory in order to understand the phonology of this particular subset of human languages. The question of the universals arises naturally along the way, and is addressed explicitly in Chapter 16.

Let us begin now with a pretheoretical characterization of the sublexical structure of sign language words, providing a context for the phonological analyses that will follow in subsequent chapters. Consider the following three ASL signs: IDEA, APPLE, UGLY, shown in Figure 8.1.

The examples in Figure 8.1 are distinct from one another, and characterizing these distinctions raises key issues in sign language phonology. First we must entertain the null hypothesis and ask, should each sign be considered a holistic unit with no internal structure? Although such a view was tacitly assumed at the dawn of sign language research, had it been correct, this book would be considerably shorter. Instead, we now know that the signs in Figure 8.1 must be distinguished by analyzing their internal structure. Each has a different hand configuration, and each is signed on or near a different part of the face. Furthermore, each has a different type of movement. IDEA involves a *path movement*, from contact with the forehead outward; APPLE involves only an *internal movement*, twisting of the hand; and UGLY is characterized by internal movement (curving the finger) and path movement (from one side of the face to another) together. Is each such difference contrastive in the language? How are they to be characterized?

Working in a structuralist framework, William Stokoe demonstrated that changing a single meaningless element within a sign could produce a change in meaning; i.e., he showed that there are minimal pairs in sign language. In his 1960 monograph, *Sign Language Structure*, Stokoe provided an inventory of elements that are contrastive in ASL. He divided these elements among three categories: handshape, location, and movement.[1] Figure 8.2 shows minimal pairs that differ in handshape, location, and movement, respectively.[2] CANDY and APPLE share location (the side of the chin) and movement (rotation of the hand), but differ in handshape. UGLY and SUMMER have the same extended index finger handshape, and the same movement – closing of the finger while moving the hand from the contralateral to the ipsilateral side of the face. The two differ in location: the nose for UGLY and the forehead for SUMMER. TRAIN and CHAIR differ in movement. In TRAIN, the fingers of the dominant hand slide forward and backward on those of the non-dominant hand. In CHAIR, they move down (twice) to contact the fingers of the non-dominant hand.

While the signs shown here and in Figure 8.1 above may have iconic origins, there is a good deal of evidence that the primitives from which they are formed function like meaningless phonological elements in the language. Early psycholinguistic studies on ASL showed that errors in word-list recall tests are in the direction of formational similarities to the target words, and not semantic similarities that might be triggered by iconicity (Klima and Bellugi 1979). Those results indicate that a signer is more likely to mistakenly produce CHAIR when the target was TRAIN, than s/he is to produce TABLE, for example. CHAIR and TRAIN have nothing in common semantically, but they are a minimal pair phonologically: they are identical in hand configuration and location, differing only in type of movement. These results are similar to those of hearing subjects, who may erroneously respond with *vote* [vot] instead of *boat* [bot] (and not with *lake*).

[1] Stokoe invented different terminology than that used here. He called handshape dez (designator), location tab (tabulator) and movement sig (signifier). Similarly, rather than use the sound-based word "phoneme," Stokoe gave the name "chereme" to what he considered to be the sign language equivalent, from the Greek word *cher*, which he translated as 'handy.' These opaque terms have fallen out of use.

[2] The sign choices in Figure 8.2 are from Klima and Bellugi (1979). In the sequential view of sign language structure that we will adopt here, minimal movement contrasts are characterized somewhat differently. See Chapter 13.

Figure 8.2 ASL minimal pairs

Diachronic studies confirm the primacy of abstract phonological form over transparency of meaning. In particular, iconicity tends to be minimized in favor of arbitrariness over time, and the resulting ASL structures are phonologically simpler and more regular (Frishberg 1975). Similar diachronic findings are reported for a much younger sign language, Israeli Sign Language (Meir and Sandler 2004). More strictly phonological evidence will emerge in the chapters to follow.

Stokoe considered each of the values within the three categories he posited to be analogous to a phoneme in spoken language. The organization of these elements within a sign, however, is different in the two modalities, according to Stokoe. In a spoken word, phonemes are arranged sequentially, whereas in a sign, Stokoe's phonemes occur simultaneously.

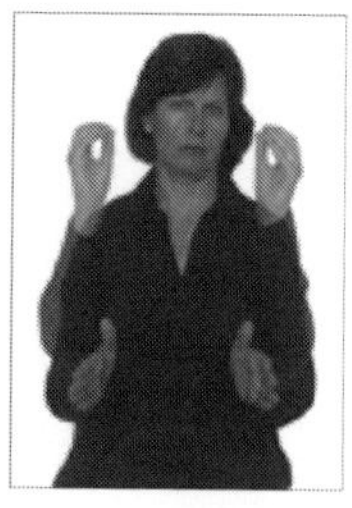

TEACHER (ASL)

Figure 8.3 Two-handed sign with a sequence of two movements: outward and downward

Subsequent work has delved more deeply into the structure of the sign and questioned some of Stokoe's claims. It has asked whether each hand configuration, location, and movement "phoneme" is better described in terms of features, like those of spoken languages. If so, are the features randomly bundled together, or are they organized in classes? Are the major phonological elements of hand configuration, location, and movement simultaneously organized at the phonological level within a word, or does it make sense to speak of sequences of segment-like elements? If the latter, then are these units comparable to the consonants and vowels found in spoken languages?

More questions arise when we consider a suffixed sign like (ASL) TEACHER, shown in Figure 8.3. One property of interest in TEACHER is the use of two hands in the articulation of the sign. The presence of two anatomically identical articulators is unique to sign language, and raises the question of whether this characteristic leads to significant differences in the phonological structure of the two modalities. Another way in which this sign is different from the signs in Figure 8.2 is in the sequence of two movements that characterizes it, each with a different hand configuration. Clearly there is sequential structure here: the base, TEACH, is followed by the agentive suffix. But is it only at the morphosyntactic level that we have sequences, i.e., is it only morphemes and words that are sequenced? Or is there any motivation for a prosodic unit for such sequences, a unit like the syllable? Stating the question in other words, we can say that TEACHER is bimorphemic, but can we also say it is disyllabic? Consideration of prosodic structure at the level of the syllable raises the question of whether there is prosody in sign languages at higher levels of structure, such as the prosodic word, the phonological phrase and the intonational phrase.

In this unit, we will address every one of the questions just raised. The chapters will tap the work of a number of researchers, and converge on a particular picture of the phonology of sign language. We will support the claim that even morphologically simple signs have sequential segments, though the number and type of segments in a sign is severely restricted. One particularly complex phonological category that is typically realized simultaneously across the entire sign is hand configuration. Taken together, the restrictedness of sequential elements and the complexity of the simultaneous ones yield a structure that is descriptively quite different from that of spoken words, but remarkably similar from a number of key theoretical perspectives. Hierarchically organized models of the internal structure of sign language phonological categories will be presented. Finally, we will describe studies of the prosodic constituents of sign language, for which a hierarchy has also been proposed, extending from the syllable through the intonational phrase. The higher constituents of the prosodic hierarchy signal syntactic constituency, leading us up to the next and last unit on grammatical structure in sign language, unit 4, on syntax.

Much of the theoretical work on sign language phonology has been done on American Sign Language, and a good deal on the phonology of Israeli Sign Language and Sign Language of the Netherlands as well. The illustrations in this unit are mostly taken from American Sign Language and Israeli Sign Language. In some cases, we use the pictures to illustrate language-specific properties or rules. But unless so indicated, the choice of language was determined by technical convenience and is therefore arbitrary, and the illustrations are put forward as examples of general phonological properties of sign languages. Sign language phonologies appear to have much in common with one another at the level of complexity investigated so far (as spoken language phonologies do), and many of the claims and analyses made here may be relevant for other sign languages as well. Such purported similarities must be rigorously investigated, however, and finer grained studies must be initiated to establish differences between sign languages. We hope the present unit will provide some contexts and strategies for doing so.

9 Sequentiality and simultaneity in sign language phonology

In spoken language, segments follow one another in a sequence within a morpheme, and morphemes usually follow each other sequentially within a word. In fact, it seems so obvious that spoken words are linearly structured that discoveries of non-linear aspects to this structure in the 1970s and 1980s were considered revolutionary.

In sign language, the situation seems to be just the opposite. In the previous chapter, minimal pairs were shown in Figure 8.2 to demonstrate a phonological level of structure. The pairs were distinguished by some meaningless feature of hand configuration, location, or movement. Although minimal pairs distinguish spoken words as well, Stokoe (1960, Stokoe et al. 1965) viewed the sign language pairs as different from minimal pairs in spoken words, which are distinguished by features of a particular segment in the same linear position in the two words (e.g., the voicing feature of [p] and [b] in the minimal pair *pin* and *bin*). In Stokoe's conception of the structure of an ASL sign, the features that distinguish minimal pairs co-occur simultaneously with all other features in the sign.[1]

Indeed, when one looks at a sign, there is a feel of simultaneity about it. One reason for this may be that the iconic origin of many signs, while often irrelevant synchronically (see, for example, Chapter 6), is still retrievable, triggering the gestalt impression of the whole object or activity. Consider the sign GIVE in ASL, illustrated in Figure 9.1.

The sign looks like the act of giving something to someone, in some sense a unitary event. In the notation Stokoe developed, the sign is represented with a symbol for place of articulation (the torso, using the notation [ ]), a symbol for the handshape (, using the notation O), and a symbol for movement (away from the body, using the notation ⊥). While Stokoe et al.'s (1965) *Dictionary of ASL* adopted the convention of listing these symbols in a sequence – [ ] O ⊥ – Stokoe stipulated clearly that they were to be interpreted as occurring simultaneously.

[1] Stokoe contrasts typical signs with compounds, where sequentiality is acknowledged.

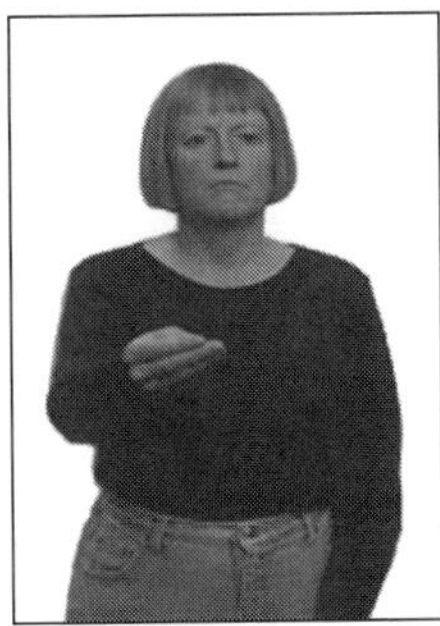

GIVE 'to give' (ASL)

Figure 9.1 Citation form of GIVE (ASL)

But other researchers have subsequently argued that there is significant sequential structure in signs. In the GIVE example, the hand moves from one location to another. As GIVE is an agreement verb, those locations must be explicitly referred to by the morphology, indicating that each of them is linguistically significant. Nowadays, based on evidence to be presented in Section 9.2, there is a consensus that such sequential structure exists, although not all investigators are in accord about its nature and representation.

Sequential structure notwithstanding, it is also clear that sign languages have more simultaneously occurring structure in their words than spoken languages have in theirs. For example, in GIVE, there are at most three segments: the starting point, the movement, and the endpoint. Furthermore, a phonologically complex category, the category of hand configuration, simultaneously characterizes the whole sign. These two properties are canonical and common to all known sign languages; the vast majority of signs share very limited sequential structure and the same simultaneous instantiation of hand configuration. The optimal model of sign language phonological structure will represent both sequential and simultaneous aspects of signs in such a way as to capture significant generalizations about its makeup and behavior.

To sum up: in spoken language, it is simultaneous or non-linear properties that are the Johnny-come-lately of linguistic analysis. In sign language, it is the opposite: simultaneous properties are self-evident, while sequential properties are the big surprise. But is this an accidental artifact of the history of the field, or does it reflect a real difference in phonological structure in the two modalities? We believe the latter to be true: signs are more simultaneously structured than spoken words. Yet sequentiality and simultaneity are a matter of degree, and the existence of both types of structure in both modalities reflects a universal property of language.

We begin this chapter by introducing non-linear theories of spoken language phonology and morphology as a frame of reference. Section 9.2

then presents some of the evidence for sequentiality of structure in signs. On the basis of this evidence, a model of phonological structure was developed that departs from that of Stokoe and represents sequential structure explicitly as sequences of dynamic and static segments. That model, the Move–Hold model of Liddell and Johnson, is presented in Section 9.3. As the model focuses especially on the sequential aspects of sign language structure, and also pays much needed attention to previously neglected phonetic detail, other things are inevitably overlooked. In particular, simultaneous aspects of structure and certain significant phonological generalizations are not accounted for. A different model builds on the insights of the Move–Hold model, while attempting to arrive at a phonologically motivated representation of both the sequential and the simultaneous in sign language phonology. The outlines of that model, Sandler's Hand Tier model, are introduced in Section 9.4, and its details presented in subsequent chapters.

9.1 Liberation of the segment: excursus on non-linear theories of phonology and morphology

A major turning point in phonological theory was the adoption of the phonological feature as the atomic element in the system, rather than the phoneme as a whole. This discovery led to a vast body of illuminating and elegant solutions to problems in spoken language phonology. For many decades, these features were viewed as anchored to segments in a sequence of cohesive bundles (see especially Chomsky and Halle 1968). The study of African tone languages, in which tones may behave independently of other features and cannot be viewed as part of a cohesive feature bundle, led to the breaking up of these bundles, and to the representation of some features on different "tiers" with the temporal freedom to move around among segmental positions (see especially Goldsmith 1976, 1990).

These non-linear theories of phonology led to new ideas about morphological structure as well, this time growing out of research on Semitic languages (McCarthy 1979, 1981), explained briefly in Chapter 3. By adopting a non-linear representation, in which the root is separated from the vowel pattern, and both are separated from the morphologically determined sequence of consonantal and vowel positions, more satisfying analyses of the phonological and morphological properties of such languages were attainable.

The early models of non-linear phonology and morphology led to crucial innovations in sign language phonology, because they posited an integration of simultaneous structure with sequential structure within words.

Thanks to Stokoe, sign language researchers were well aware that signs were characterized by simultaneous phonological structure. Some researchers assumed that the simultaneous layering of both phonological

CHRISTIAN (ASL) COMMITTEE (ASL)

Figure 9.2 Minimal pairs differing in final location

and morphological information was determined by the physical modality (e.g., Bellugi and Fischer 1972; see Chapter 16 and Unit 5). It was the discovery of sequentiality in sign language that made it possible to begin to explore the interaction of the two types of structuring in sign language phonology as well. Let's turn to the evidence for sequential structure.

9.2 Sequential structure in the sign

There are some monomorphemic signs which are distinguished by one feature at a particular temporal point in the sign's structure. For example, one version of ASL CHRISTIAN is distinguished from COMMITTEE by different final locations only, as illustrated in Figure 9.2 (example from Emmorey 2002).

Sign languages differ from spoken languages, however, in that such simple and clear examples of sequential structure in non-complex sign language words are rare. The best evidence for linguistically significant sequentiality in sign language comes from the analysis of morphologically complex forms. Let us return to the sign GIVE. When this sign is inflected for agreement with first-person subject and non-first-person object, it changes in a way that reveals independent structural elements. Specifically, the end of the sign occurs at a different location than that of the citation form. This can be seen by comparing Figure 9.1 with Figure 9.3.

As we explained in Chapter 3, most agreeing verbs involve movement from some particular location to another particular location in order to mark agreement with their referents. Thus, verbs may be modified with respect to the initial location as well as the final location, as can be seen by comparing Figure 9.3 with Figure 9.4. Regardless of how the rules for agreement are stated formally, they must make reference to the beginning and ending locations of the sign independently. The first and last locations are discretely referred to by the grammar, indicating, according to

1-GIVE-a 'I give her' (ASL)

Figure 9.3 GIVE with first-person subject, third-person object agreement

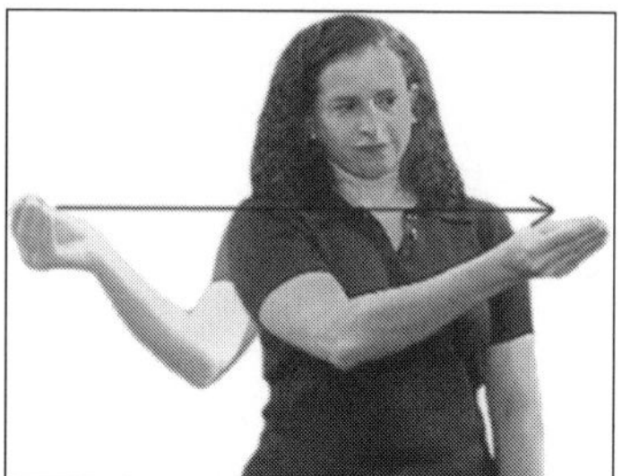

a-GIVE-b 'she gives him' (ASL)

Figure 9.4 GIVE with third-person subject, third-person object agreement

standard assumptions in linguistic investigation, that each location is a grammatical element in the language. This means that a Stokoean model, according to which there is a single location, simultaneously realized with hand configuration and movement, is inadequate. Rather, two sequenced locations must be part of the representation.

Another ASL process making crucial reference to discrete locations is metathesis, which switches the first and last locations of a sign (Liddell and Johnson 1989 [1985]). In signs in which the signing hand makes contact at two different settings within one major body area (such as the head or chest), the order of the two may be reversed, as shown in Figure 9.5. In 9.5a, DEAF follows FATHER. FATHER is signed at the forehead and the first location for DEAF is at the cheek, followed by the second location, at the chin. In 9.5b, DEAF follows MOTHER, a sign made at the chin. Influenced by this lower location, the sign DEAF begins with the chin location in this context, and ends at the cheek. Liddell and Johnson claim that the conditioning environment for metathesis is the location of the preceding sign.[2] In order to

[2] In a sociolinguistic study, Lucas (1995) claims that metathesis is not predictable on phonological grounds alone. She found that the only significant correlation between metathesis

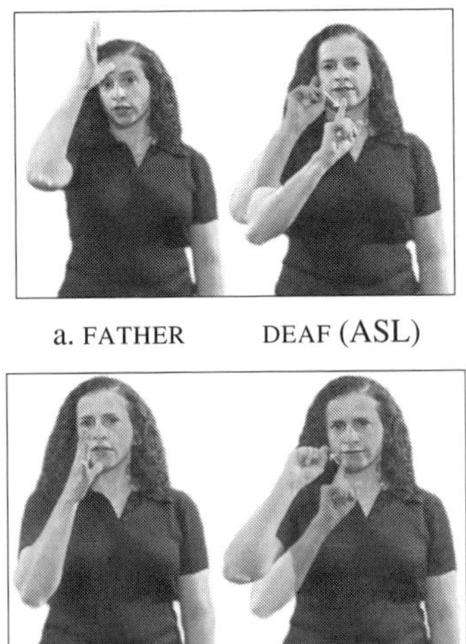

Figure 9.5 Metathesis of locations for the sign DEAF in different phonological environments

characterize such a process, it is necessary to refer independently to the beginning and ending of adjacent signs.

In an influential paper, in which evidence is presented for a class of derivationally related nouns and verbs (see Chapter 4), Supalla and Newport (1978) show that signs may be distinguished underlyingly by what they call the manner of movement. One such "manner of movement" is restricted to the end of the sign only, where the hands may either remain stationary in space (hold) or not (continuous). For example, the movement at the end of the ASL sign THAT'S-THE-ONE is continuous, while at the end of the otherwise identical sign, STAY, the hands are held in place.

Supalla and Newport show that the hold at the end of a sign can be added derivationally, distinguishing for example the sign for FLY (by plane), which employs continuous movement, from FLY-THERE, with a hold. While the authors make no arguments for sequential phonological structure, we may deduce that the rule for this locative morpheme glossed 'there' or 'specified

and other factors for the sign DEAF is its lexical category: if DEAF functions as an adjective, it may undergo metathesis. It is possible, however, that a finer-grained linguistic analysis – one that takes prosodic structure into account – will explain this seemingly odd result. Adjective-noun phrases are likely often to comprise a single prosodic constituent. As such constituents commonly serve as the domain for phonological rules that involve adjacent words (see Chapter 15), it is reasonable to hypothesize that metathesis tends to occur within but not across such prosodic domains. If this hypothesis is borne out, Liddell and Johnson's analysis of metathesis as a phonological process can be maintained. Brentari (1998) argues that plane of articulation is also important for the application of metathesis. In any case, some signs certainly metathesize, and the description of this process requires reference to the first and last location of a sign, i.e., to sequential structure.

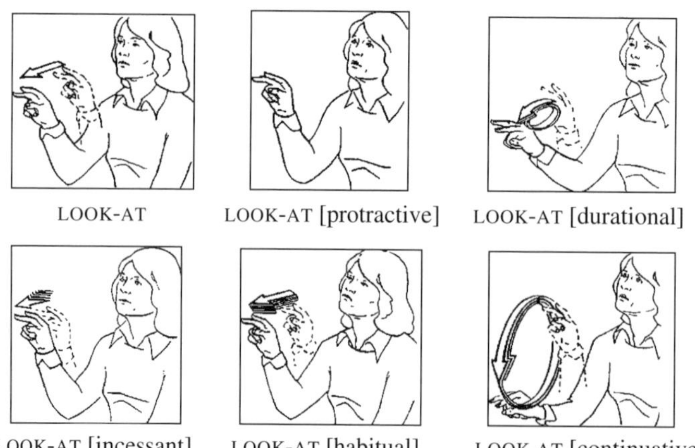

Figure 9.6 Some inflections for temporal aspect on LOOK-AT (© Ursula Bellugi, the Salk Institute)

location' must make explicit reference to the end of the sign, showing that the end is phonologically discrete.

Around the same time and, like Supalla and Newport, also working at the Salk Institute, Newkirk (1978, 1979) shows that temporal aspects such as Iterative, Durational, Continuative, Habitual, and Facilitative in ASL contrast according to features of the onset, the movement core, or the offset. Illustrations of these aspects appear in Figure 9.6, repeated from Chapter 3.

By distinguishing onset, movement, and offset, Newkirk proposes the first explicitly segmental analysis of sign language structure, one in which canonical signs have three segments. The new observation here is that not only the beginning and ending location, but also the movement between them can be seen as sequentially significant.

The Delayed Completive aspect (Brentari 1998) provides additional evidence for sequential segments in ASL. This operation productively applies to telic verbs, with some phonological restrictions, and adds the meaning, 'delay the completion of x,' where x is the base verb. The process consists of a sequence of two elements, the first of which associates to the beginning of the sign, which is also geminated (given added duration), and the second spreads over the rest of the sign. The first element is wiggling of the fingers, if the handshape of the base sign is (all fingers extended and spread). Otherwise, it is a rapidly repeated tongue wag if the base has any other handshape, an allophonic alternation described in Chapter 4. The second element consists of a mouth movement which, if pronounced as a spoken syllable, would be something like [op]. That is, at the beginning of the sign, the hands are held in their first location while the fingers wiggle or the tongue wags; then the movement and second location are executed, while the visual equivalent of the syllable [op] is articulated by the mouth.

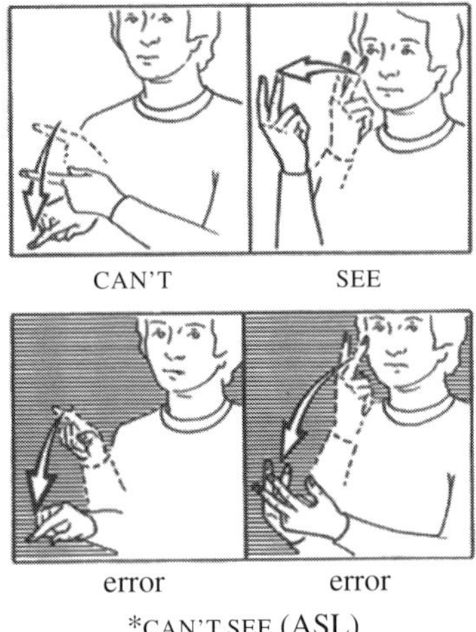

Figure 9.7 Slip of the hand *CAN'T SEE (ASL). (© Ursula Bellugi, the Salk Institute)

As Brentari points out, what is significant phonologically about this process is the temporal distribution of the Delayed Completive morpheme. The first part must co-occur with the beginning of the sign, coinciding temporally with the first location and hand configuration, and the second part, [op], is evenly distributed over the lexical movement of the sign, ending with the final location. The fact that either allomorph – finger wiggle or tongue wag – must discretely coincide with all the other features that occur at the beginning of the sign, before the hand moves, supports the claim that there is linguistically significant sequential and segmental structure to signs.

Finally, performance data also support the claim that segments exist in ASL. The example we are about to describe is from the only extensive study done to date on slips of the hand in ASL (Newkirk, Klima, Pedersen, and Bellugi 1980). In the example, illustrated in Figure 9.7, the signs CAN'T and SEE are produced so that the last segment of CAN'T, i.e., the location reached by the hand after the movement portion of the sign, is erroneously switched with the last segment of SEE.

The investigators in the error study did not notice that this is an example of a segment switch (like *hash and grass* → *hass and grash*, Fromkin 1973) because they had a simultaneous model in mind. It was one of a small number of errors pictured in Klima and Bellugi's book and its sequential nature was noticed and described in Sandler (1989). If the same error data were reanalyzed allowing for the possibility of sequential structure in signs, our interpretation promotes the expectation that other such sequential segment switching errors would be found.

How can this group of observations be incorporated into a model of the structure of the sign? The next section, 9.3, describes the first attempt to incorporate sequential structure into a phonological model. Section 9.4 deals with another model, one that represents both sequential and simultaneous structure, and that incorporates some of the constraints on that structure as well.

9.3 The Move–Hold model: sequential segments in sign language

The first detailed model of sign language structure that attempts to account for observations such as those just described is the Move–Hold model proposed by Liddell and developed together with Johnson (Liddell 1984b, 1990b, Liddell and Johnson 1989 [1985]). In effect, the Move–Hold model rejects two fundamental properties that had been introduced by Stokoe: the tripartite categorization of major phonological categories as handshape, location, and movement; and simultaneity of organization among all categories and their features. The Move–Hold model proposes a basic distinction between two types of sequentially ordered segments, a distinction that is determined by a single phonetic criterion: whether or not the hands move. If the articulating hand or hands move, then the segment is a Movement (M) segment; if they are held still, then the segment is a Hold (H) segment. Signs consist of sequences of Hs and Ms, just as spoken words are made up of Cs and Vs. In fact, Liddell and Johnson make the radical proposal that movements are analogous to vowels, and holds are analogous to consonants.

While focusing primarily on the sequential segmental aspect of sign structure, the Move–Hold model borrows certain ideas from the theory of autosegmental phonology (Goldsmith 1976), described briefly in Section 9.1 above. In particular, the idea that phonological elements may have a one-to-many or many-to-one temporal relationship to one another is adopted. While the beginning and ending segments may be characterized by different features of location, handshape, and other elements, the movement between them is often – but not always – just a straight path with no other independent features. In these cases, the movement is redundantly characterized by the same features as the surrounding "hold" segments, and serves as the anchor for a contour that phonetically results between one hold and the other. Another idea that Liddell and Johnson adopt from general phonological theory is the concept of an abstract timing skeleton to which features are associated (McCarthy 1979, 1981, Clements and Keyser 1983) The sign IDEA is illustrated in Figure 9.8. Its representation in the Move–Hold model (Liddell and Johnson 1989 [1985]) is given in (1).

IDEA (ASL)

Figure 9.8 Sign with path movement

(1) Representation of the ASL sign IDEA in the Move–Hold model (Liddell and Johnson 1989 [1985])[3]

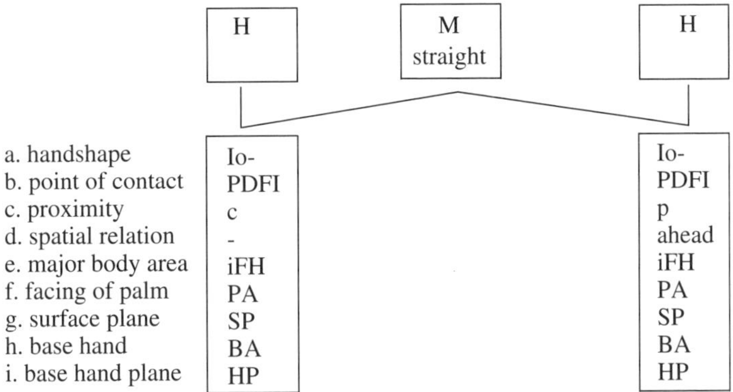

Liddell and Johnson offer new evidence for sequential structure in their work, such as the metathesis rule described above. Within their framework, the rule switches the first and last hold segments. Liddell (1984a) also shows that a certain morphological process involves deletion of one segment of the base form and insertion of the remaining features into a "frame" consisting of three segments. This process, which forms the Unrealized Inceptive form of some verbs (e.g., STUDY → 'was just about to study when . . . '), may be interpreted as a kind of templatic morphology, similar to the morphology of Semitic languages for example (McCarthy 1979, 1981). The templatic theory of sign language morphology (Sandler 1989) was introduced in Chapter 4 and is explained in more detail in Section 9.4 below.

[3] Line (a) represents the handshape: Io- means that all but the pinky are closed and the thumb is opposed and closed; (b) is fingerpad contact (of the pinky with the forehead); (c) is proximity, where c means contact and p means proximal; (d) is spatial relation, from contact with the location to a place ahead of it; (e) is the major body area location, the side of the forehead ipsilateral with the signing hand; (f) refers to the fact that the palm faces the location, on (g) the surface plane; and the base of the hand (h) is on the horizontal plane (i).

The Move–Hold model of Liddell and Johnson offers a wealth of phonetic detail, from which all subsequent research on sign language phonology has benefited. It provides thirteen features for handshapes alone, which specify a total of 150 handshapes claimed by the authors to exist in ASL. Some eighteen major places of articulation are listed as well. The result of relying on purely descriptive motivations as the Move–Hold model does is that the model overgenerates, predicting the existence of many types of signs that are in reality unattested, while leaving unexplained significant predictable properties of signs. One of the goals of subsequent work by other sign language phonologists has been to eliminate the redundancy inherent in the Move–Hold model, to arrive at a smaller set of features and distinctions. The other, related, major challenge has been to understand the inter-organization of the categories and features, and constraints on their co-occurrence.

Overgeneration is due mainly to redundant representation of features. In the sign IDEA, for example, pictured in Figure 9.8 and represented in (1), there is no change of handshape from the first H to the second H, yet a second representation of the same handshape features appears in the representation. As most signs have no change in handshape, a representation such as this one is clearly redundant. In many signs, however, there is a change in certain particular features of handshape (see Chapter 10, Section 10.2). While Liddell (1990b) considers the possibility of eliminating the second representation of handshape features, he argues that this is not possible in signs that have handshape change, because that change is not predictable – a claim which has been disputed, as we shall see. But it is not only handshape features that are redundant in the Move–Hold model. In fact, the majority of the features that characterize one hold segment are identical to those characterizing the other hold segment, and yet they are listed independently in the original Move–Hold model. This type of representation is undesirable from a theoretical point of view, as it implies that the recurrence of the same features is coincidental, rather than the result of constraints on the structure of signs, and it inaccurately predicts that any other, non-redundant combination is equally possible. In the wake of criticism along these lines, Liddell (1990b) alleviated some of these problems in a revised version of the Move–Hold model, specifying repeated features only once, and doubly associating Hs or Ms instead. However, certain key specifications argued by other researchers to be predictable, specifically, certain features of both handshapes in signs with handshape change and features of the place of articulation, are still represented twice in the Move–Hold model, associated independently to different segments. These redundancies are eliminated in the Hand Tier theory described in Section 9.4.

Dealing as it does with purely surface phenomena, the Move–Hold theory is forced to propose blanket rules of epenthesis and deletion. For example, Liddell and Johnson propose that a rule of movement epenthesis inserts a transitional movement between signs. To sign FATHER DEAF (Figure 9.5a above), for example, the hand must move from the final location of FATHER (i.e., on the chin) to the initial location of DEAF (cheek). Liddell and Johnson propose a rule to insert this movement. But such a rule is seen as redundant in phonological theory, since it is required by the physiology of the system, and no manual language could do without it.

The authors also propose a rule of hold deletion, which allows the hands to move smoothly between signs in a string, rather than holding them still at the beginning and/or end, as is done in citation forms. In the same sequence, FATHER DEAF, the final hold of FATHER and the initial hold of DEAF are both deleted. The features associated with the holds are not influenced; they remain in the signal, spreading to the neighboring Ms in the Move–Hold model. Only the stillness of the hands is deleted.

The main problem with this analysis is the assumption that the citation form is the same as the underlying form. This assumption triggered the proposal of a phonological rule that deletes a structural element that is absent more than it is present: holds only appear (a) at the beginning and/or ending of a rhythmic unit; or (b) as a result of morphological processes.

This leads to the alternative suggestion that the holds of the Move–Hold model are not underlying at all. Instead of proposing a hold-deletion rule, we assume instead that holds appear either as a rhythmic effect of prosodic chunking, or as a result of a morphologically conditioned process of gemination. By this reasoning, citation forms induce holds because they are by definition surrounded by intonational phrase boundaries (Sandler 1986, 1989, Perlmutter 1992, Wilbur 1993).[4] Morphological insertion of "holds," i.e., gemination as a morphological process, hinted at in Supalla and Newport's discussion of continuous versus hold endpoints, is returned to in Section 9.5 below on templatic morphology.

We leave the Move–Hold model for now, returning in later chapters to other insights uncovered by the model. A different model of the sequential properties of signs will be described next, one that provides a greater role for simultaneous structure than the Move–Hold model does, and attempts to provide a more constrained representation of phonological elements.

[4] Prosodic constituency and phonology are the topic of Chapter 15 in this unit.

9.4 The Hand Tier model: hand configuration as an autosegment

Non-linear theories, those sketched in Section 9.1 and others that evolved later, forged a new view of the phonological structure of spoken languages. The universally available pool of phonological form is now seen as including structure that is sequentially segmented, yet still allows a degree of autonomy from that segmentation. The meaningful units of language, morphemes and words, are poured into this structure. Each such unit may have an abstract form underlyingly, and may only take on the linear properties observed on the surface when they join up with all the other elements of the word.

Advances in autosegmental phonology and morphology provide a conceptual and formal framework for exploring the relationship among sequentiality, segmentation, and simultaneity in sign languages, a framework first tapped for sign language in the Move–Hold model of Liddell and Johnson, described in the previous section. This approach led to the Hand Tier model of sign language structure (Sandler 1986, 1987b, 1989), which proposes the representation of a canonical monomorphemic sign given in (2).[5] In this representation L stands for location and M for movement. HC represents the hand configuration, which has its own complex structure, to be expanded on in Chapter 10.

(2) Canonical form of a monomorphemic sign in the Hand Tier model (Sandler 1986, 1987b, 1989)

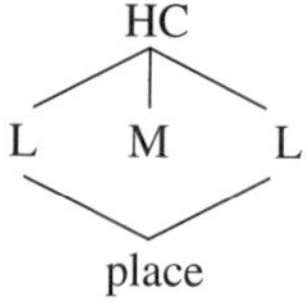

The Hand Tier model adopts some aspects of Stokoe's original categorizations as well as elements of the Move–Hold treatment, while rejecting others. In the Hand Tier model schematized in (2), sequential segmental structure established in the Move–Hold model is maintained, as are some of the phonetic features. Movement as a sequentially represented category is also adopted.[6] But most other aspects of the representation are different. Locations replace the holds of the Move–Hold model as a major segmental category. Lengthened holding of the hand or hands

[5] The Hand Tier model first appeared in Sandler (1986). The model was motivated in detail and also modified significantly in Sandler (1989).

[6] The place category is associated only to the Ls and not to the M. This convention is adopted to reflect the fact that place features belong to the location category. Phonetically, place spreads to characterize the movement as well.

at some location is seen as related to prosody or to morphological structure, as described above, and not as an underlying property or category of signs. The second difference between the Hand Tier model and the Move–Hold model is the revival of Stokoe's view of hand configuration, location, and movement as the major category types. But the major categories are not simultaneously organized with respect to each other as in Stokoe's model. Instead, locations and movements are organized in a sequence, like the moves and holds of Liddell and Johnson's theory, while hand configuration typically characterizes the whole sequence simultaneously. In this way, the model captures both sequential and simultaneous aspects of sign language structure. The three major categories are not seen as containing "phonemes," as Stokoe proposed. Rather, like the major phonological categories of spoken languages, they are comprised of subclasses of features. These subclasses and the hierarchical organization they manifest are dealt with in Chapters 10–13. For now, we focus on the major categories, their interorganization within a sign, and some of the motivation for these in the Hand Tier model.

Locations stand for the starting and ending point that the hand traverses in articulating the sign. As such, there are typically two locations in a sequence. In the citation form of the sign, IDEA, for example, pictured in Figure 9.8 above, the first location is in contact with the head of the signer, and the second location is a slight distance in front of the first. The major body area, or place of articulation, is the head, and that place characterizes the whole sign, as indicated by the one-to-many association of the place category in (2) above. Unlike Stokoe's model, which characterizes the movement of the hand in a sign like IDEA with a simultaneous movement feature, 'away' (⊥), the Hand Tier model adopts the view that the beginning and ending locations must be separately and sequentially represented, in order to be accessible to the rules and other generalizations outlined in Section 9.2. The hand moves from one location to another in relation to that place of articulation. This theory of sign structure obviates the need to posit the hold-deletion rules postulated by Liddell and Johnson, and also assumes that the M epenthesis they offer as a rule applying between signs is a phonetic effect that need not be accounted for by a phonological rule.

While the hand or hands usually move from one location to another in the articulation of signs, it is generally the case that a morpheme is characterized by one and only one handshape, like IDEA, shown above in Figure 9.8. The representation of IDEA in the Move–Hold model was shown in (1) above. Compare it with a partial representation of this sign in the Hand Tier model, in (3). In advance of deeper exploration of each category later, diagram (3) is still partially schematized, and a handshape icon is substituted for representation of that complex category.

(3) Hand Tier representation of IDEA

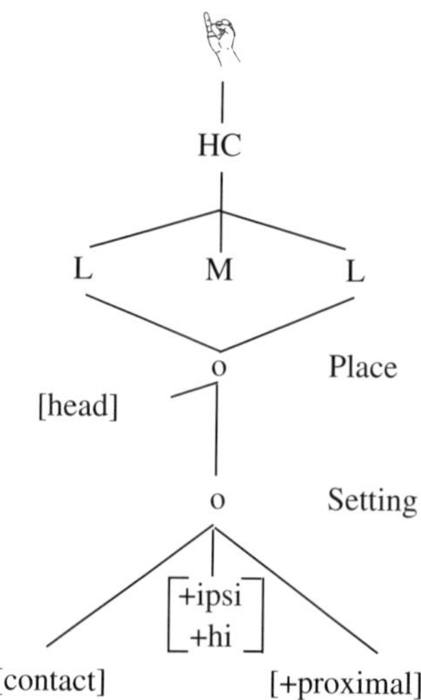

In the Move–Hold representation, all features are doubly represented, but the only feature that changes is the location feature: the hand moves from contact with the forehead to a location ahead of and close to the forehead. The Hand Tier model attempts to eliminate the redundancy in the representation while capturing generalizations about the form of signs. Only the changing features are represented sequentially; the rest are multiply associated. The major categories of hand configuration (HC) and place are always multiply associated in this model, reflecting the fact that they are predictably instantiated simultaneously across all segments. The first location of the sign IDEA, specified by the feature [contact], means that the hand is in contact with the head; and the second, specified as [proximal], means that the hand is a short distance in front of the head.

The representation of hand configuration as a single, multiply associated category in the Hand Tier model is motivated first and foremost by the fact that most signs are characterized by a single hand configuration in which no features vary throughout the sign. Many signs are characterized by some change in the handshape, however, a characteristic that prompted Liddell and Johnson to represent each handshape in a separate segmental cell. In the sign SEND (Figure 9.9), for example, the selected fingers are closed at the beginning of the sign, and open at the end; while the opposite is true for LIKE (Figure 9.10).

The problem is that the term "handshape change" for such signs overstates the case. A closer look reveals that it is not the whole handshape that changes, but only the position of the fingers. The choice of fingers is constant, as established in Mandel (1981). Mandel's Selected Finger Constraint is given in (4).

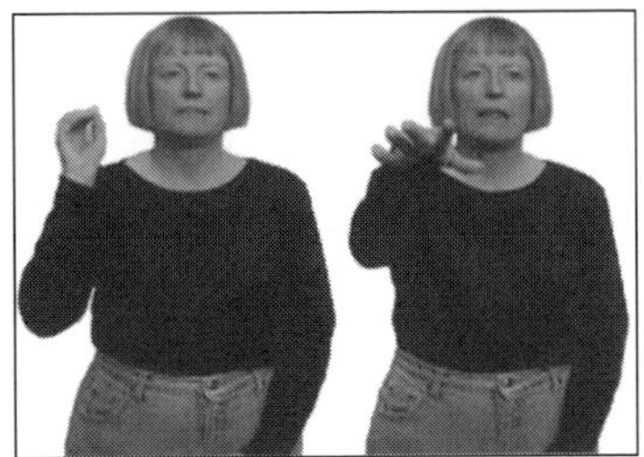

SEND (ASL)

Figure 9.9 Sign with change in finger position: closed to open

LIKE (ASL)

Figure 9.10 Sign with changed finger position: open to closed

(4) Selected Finger Constraint (Mandel 1981)[7]
Only one group of fingers may be selected in a sign.

In SEND, all five fingers go from closed to open, and in LIKE, the selected middle finger and thumb go from open to closed. *Contra* the claims of Liddell and Johnson, the relationship between the first and second positions is largely predictable in such signs (Friedman 1977, Wilbur 1987, Sandler 1989), as we show in detail in Chapter 10, Section 10.2. We will see there that the problem of capturing the Selected Finger generalization while allowing for "handshape change" is solved by dividing the HC category into two feature classes, Selected Fingers and Finger Position. For now, suffice it to say that the Selected Finger Constraint and the simultaneous instantiation of hand configuration across a sign are represented by one-to-many association of categories in the Hand Tier model.

Another indication that HC has a somewhat independent status is the fact that hand configuration alone often functions as a morpheme. For example, classifiers generally consist of handshapes only, joining with

[7] In Chapter 10, we will revise this constraint as a constraint on the morpheme and not the sign.

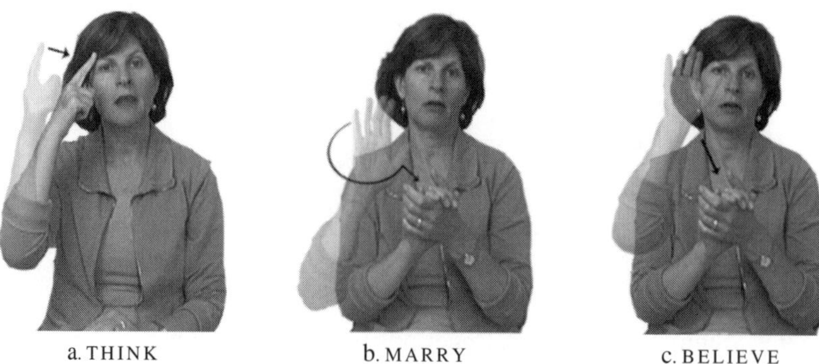

Figure 9.11 Lexicalized compound (ASL)

meaningful locations and movements to form classifier constructions. As we showed in Chapter 5, Section 5.2, some classifier constructions have the phonological appearance of lexical signs, while others may span several phrases. In both cases, the utterance is interpreted as predicated of the same nominal referent as long as the same primary classifier, that is, the same handshape, persists.

The generalizations about hand configuration are captured by representing the HC category autosegmentally, on a separate tier from the features of locations and movements, associated in one-to-many fashion to the L and M positions, as in (2). The representation eliminates the redundancy of listing the same hand configuration for each segment in a sign, throughout the lexicon. The phonological and morphological autonomy of hand configuration are the central motivations for the Hand Tier model (Sandler 1986, 1987a, 1987b, 1989).

In addition to capturing generalizations in the lexicon, this representation also offers a coherent account of processes in which hand configuration with all of its features behaves as an autonomous unit, i.e., as a long-distance autosegment. An example is the behavior of HC in many lexicalized compounds, which have undergone hand configuration assimilation as part of a common pattern of reduction (Frishberg 1975). First of all, some sequential segments of both members of the compound delete (Liddell 1984b, Liddell and Johnson 1986, Sandler 1987b, 1989). In addition, the hand configuration of the first member also deletes, and that of the second member characterizes the whole surface compound (Sandler 1986, 1987b, 1989). The compound THINK^MARRY = BELIEVE is an example, illustrated in Figure 9.11.

What is significant in this reduction process is that the hand configuration is not lined up temporally with the locations and movements. Rather, one segment of the first member of the compound survives, but its original hand configuration deletes, and the hand configuration of the second member spreads to characterize it. This is an example of autosegmental stability, a defining property of autosegments. In (5) is a schematic representation of the compound reduction process.[8]

(5) Compound reduction

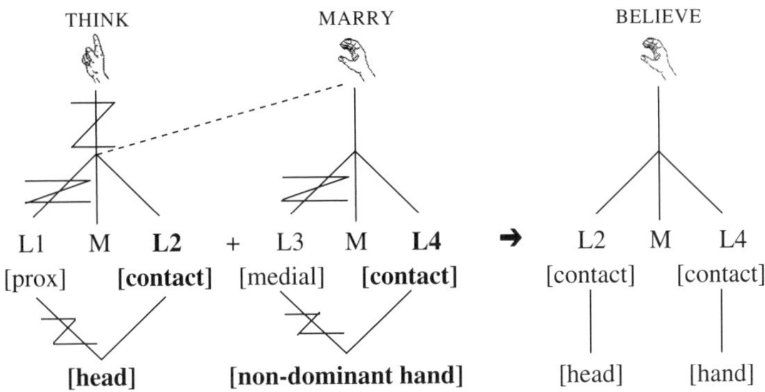

The representation reflects the autonomy of the hand configuration from the sequential segments. It does this by representing the LML segments sequentially, allowing for the selective deletion of some of them (deletion of L1 and L3 here), and representing the HC autosegmentally, expressing the autonomous spreading behavior of this category.

Not all compounds reduce. Some maintain all segments and both hand configurations. Others, like (ASL) PRAISE, reduce in their segmental structure only, maintaining two hand configurations. In the latter, the two underlying handshapes of the member signs characterize the surface representation in this model, just as the two underlying places of the members of BELIEVE characterize that compound, seen in (5). In having two HC or two place specifications, such signs are readily distinguishable from monomorphemic signs and from reduced lexicalized compounds, each of which is represented with only one HC. The difference between simple signs and morphologically complex ones is thus clearly represented in the model.

There is some evidence that this assimilation process is synchronic as well as diachronic: some compounds, such as THINK^TOUCH = OBSESS, can optionally be signed with or without handshape assimilation.[9] The same

[8] In the Hand Tier model, the orientation of the hand is part of the hand configuration category (Chapter 10, Section 10.3). We were unable to graphically indicate orientation in (5), which is offered as an abstract schema.

[9] The observation that there is synchronic variation in the form of THINK^TOUCH = OBSESS, with and without hand configuration assimilation, is based on data videotaped in the late 1970s at the Salk Institute, which Ursula Bellugi kindly made available to Sandler.

kind of assimilation exists in ISL compounds, indicating that assimilation of this sort is not idiosyncratic but reflects basic phonological properties of signs.

The other category that remains constant throughout most signs is the major body area, called place of articulation in the Hand Tier model. Specifically, the two locations that are typically articulated by the hand are contained within a single major body area, such as the head or the trunk (Battison 1978 [1973]). We can state Battison's observation as a constraint, as in (6).

(6) Place constraint (Battison 1978 [1973])[10]
There can be only one major body area specified in a sign.

Both of these constraints are represented by the many-to-one autosegmental model shown in (2), and the full representations of each of these categories are argued for in detail in Chapters 10 and 11. Unlike hand configuration, no evidence of spreading of the place category has come to light to date.

The picture that emerges is one in which signs have sequential structure of a limited and largely predictable kind (typically, but not exclusively, LML on this analysis). But it is also one in which much of the phonological material of signs co-occurs simultaneously (in particular, the complex hand configuration category and the place of articulation). The Hand Tier model is designed to capture these generalizations through grouping features into categories, and one-to-many autosegmental associations of these categories.

As mentioned, several researchers, beginning with Liddell (1984b), have proposed that the alternation of static and dynamic segments is comparable to the alternation between consonants and vowels in spoken languages. In the terminology of the Hand Tier model, we can express this claim by thinking of the static Ls as consonant-like and of the dynamic Ms as vowel-like. This comparison is not meant to be taken literally here. It will be evaluated (and essentially rejected) in Chapter 14 on the syllable in sign language.

Regardless of whether or not the analogy with consonants and vowels is adopted, there does appear to be an alternation between static and dynamic parts of signs, giving signs a canonical prosodic shape. The basic prosodic shape of signs is then systematically manipulated by the morphology of sign languages, which provides prosodic templates for a variety of morphological processes. We now take a closer look at that templatic morphology.

[10] This constraint as well will be shown in Chapter 14 to hold over the morpheme rather than the sign.

9.5 The phonology of non-linear morphology in sign language: prosodic templates

As in the morphology of Semitic and other types of spoken languages, in ASL too some morphological entities are best described as abstract skeletons that mark the position, the length, and sometimes the quality of segments. The phonetic material from the root and from the inflectional or derivational morphology are the flesh and blood that are incorporated by the skeleton to give the complex word a recognizable form (Liddell 1984b, Sandler 1987b, 1989, 1990). In Chapter 4, Section 4.2, we foreshadowed the present discussion by demonstrating how material from the ASL base adjective SICK associates with the Resultative and Durational templates of the kind proposed in the Hand Tier model, which follows McCarthy's early work on Semitic languages. We repeat those representations here in (7) for convenience, with the addition of an HC icon.

(7)

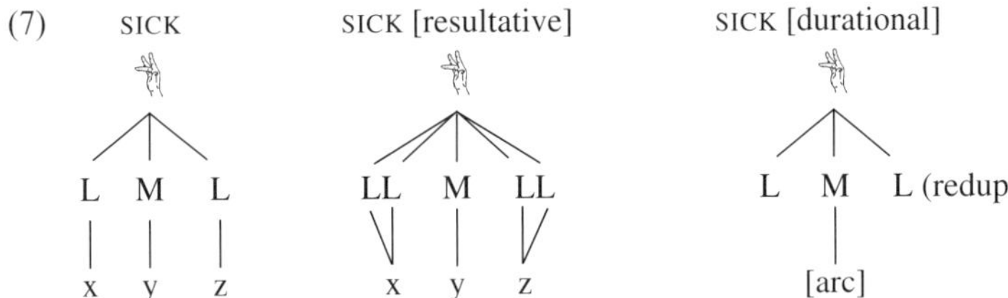

To form the Resultative, the underlying specifications of the base for handshape, place of articulation, and settings are associated to the LLMLL template, much as the *k-t-b* root in the Arabic examples in Chapter 4 are associated to templates consisting of Cs and Vs. The Resultative template merely alters the timing of the base sign, by doubly associating the features of the first and last locations to additional timing slots and thereby lengthening them, creating geminates.[11] Similarly, the Durational inflection can be seen as associating a root consisting of specifications for a handshape and two locations to an LML template in which the movement is prespecified for an arc feature (Sandler 1989, 1990).[12] The underlying form of LOOK-AT and the inflected form LOOK-AT[durational] with a circular movement pattern were shown in Figure 9.6.

[11] The form with lengthened beginning and ending segments is sometimes described as "Intensive" in the literature. In the Klima and Bellugi (1979) drawing and feature description, this form maps to what those authors call "Resultative." More research to clearly motivate and distinguish the array of temporal aspects that has been reported would be welcome.

[12] In spoken languages, too, templates may be prespecified. See McCarthy (1979) and Marantz (1982).

a. STUDY[citation form] (ASL)

b. STUDY[durational] (ASL)

Figure 9.12 Citation and inflected forms of an underlyingly L-only sign

The introduction of more abstract and less temporally rigid structures into the universal inventory of grammatical possibilities provides the framework for a more satisfying explanation of such sign language processes.

The representations in (7) demonstrate the association to templates of signs whose underlying form is the canonical one, represented here as LML. However, some signs consist of only one L, for example, the ASL sign STUDY, shown in Figure 9.12a. This sign is produced by holding the dominant hand above the non-dominant hand, the fingers pointed toward the palm of the non-dominant hand, and wiggling. As there is no movement from one location to another, the sign STUDY only has one location, and may be represented schematically as in (8a).

(8)

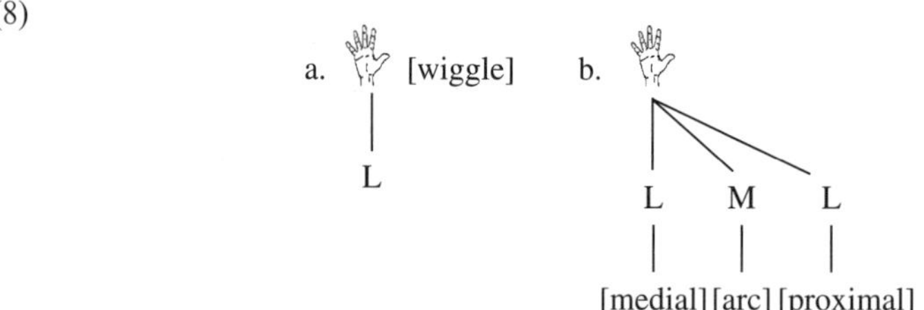

When STUDY is inflected for durational it assumes a path movement from one location to another, as shown in Figure 9.12b and represented in (8b), just as the underlyingly LML sign LOOK-AT does (Figure 9.6). For each aspect, the whole complex is then reduplicated. In addition, for the durational aspect an arc feature is associated to the movement section. The transitional movement between reduplications is given features creating arcs with the opposite value for concavity to that of the M in the template. The result is the circular movement observed on the surface (Sandler 1989, 1990).

The fact that L-only bases like STUDY conform to LML templates through augmentation of their underlying form is evidence for the existence of such abstract templates (Sandler 1999b). Similar augmentation is found in Arabic, where underlyingly biconsonantal roots (e.g., *s.m.*) double their last consonant to conform to a triconsonantal template (e.g., *samam*; McCarthy 1979, 1981). In a range of other languages, extra elements occur under reduplication in order to fill out a template with more material than is present in the underlying base word (McCarthy and Prince 1986, 1993). This augmentation of the base to fit a more elaborate template is an earmark of templatic morphology.

Moreover, a model that includes sequential segments perspicuously reflects the distinction between the uninflected form of L-only signs like STUDY and DIRTY and their forms when they are inflected for temporal aspect (Newkirk 1998 [1981]). Such inflectional templates, then, are evidence for sequential structure in signs. Similarly, an LML template in which the M segment is prespecified for an arc shape lends further support to the sequential segment model, and, as we will argue in Chapter 13, to the M category it posits as well.

In a later development of the theory of prosodic morphology, McCarthy and Prince (1986, 1995) suggest that only actual prosodic constituents such as the mora or the syllable are relevant for prosodic morphology, and that the segmental level should be eliminated from consideration. Whether a purely prosodic analysis of this kind can be independently motivated in sign language remains to be seen. In either case, this type of morphology, with abstract formational templates with particular prosodic shapes, is found frequently in sign languages.

The Hand Tier analysis described here implies that all the processes previously described as "superimposition" or "simultaneous layering" of morphemes are more appropriately analyzed as non-concatenative templatic morphology of this sort. The similarity between Semitic languages and sign languages should not be overemphasized, however. Unlike the Arabic examples shown above, in which consonants and vowels have the status of separate morphemes, it is not the case in sign languages that each tier is morphologically motivated. In particular, in lexical signs, the hand configuration, location and movement "melodies" typically all belong to the root.[13] The autosegmental status of HC and place are phonologically rather than morphologically motivated. In Semitic languages, the morphological tiers conflate eventually, so that the consonants and vowels are actually sequentially ordered on the surface (McCarthy 1986). In sign language too there is reason to believe that some (but not all) autosegmental features must link to sequential positions, but the categories in

[13] The situation is actually more complicated than this. The content of locations may be determined morphologically, as in the case of verb agreement. In the classifier subsystem of the grammar, which involves polysynthetic combinations of bound morphemes rather than lexical signs, hand configuration always functions as a morpheme.

question are phonological and not morphological.[14] We return to the issue of linearization of non-linear features in the next chapter.

9.6 Conclusion

Spoken languages, long represented as strictly linear in their internal organization, are now understood to possess significant non-linear properties as well. This new understanding led to models of phonological and morphological structure that allow for a certain amount of temporal autonomy of structural units. Conceptions of the phonological structure of sign languages have the reverse history. Their phonological and morphological elements, first thought to have only simultaneous organization, are now understood to have a certain amount of linearity as well. Several diverse pieces of evidence from a number of different studies have been presented here to support the claim that signs have sequential structure: minimal pairs differing in the place features of one sequential segment; marking of verb agreement on the first and last segment; metathesis; underlying and derivational distinctions in the timing of the final location; verb aspect inflections that selectively alter locations, movements, or both; a sign error.

The theories that arose to account for temporal autonomy of linguistic units in spoken language have helped to explain the relation between linear and non-linear structure in languages of both modalities. Such models reveal that spoken languages as well as signed languages have both linear and non-linear structure, providing support for the universality of the basic insights underlying non-linear theories. But the overall architecture of languages in the two modalities is not the same. Sign languages have a good deal less sequential structure and a good deal more simultaneous structure than do spoken languages. This difference, which resurfaces throughout this unit, is surely related to modality, and as such it will be addressed in Chapter 16 and more broadly in Unit 5.

Because the Hand Tier theory has tried to come to terms with a wide range of phonological issues and sought to integrate them in a single model, that model will stay with us throughout much of the unit. Yet there are many unresolved issues, as well as a proliferation of other models that have been proposed to deal with them. The unit will reflect these as well where useful. Some of the most interesting controversies surround movement, questioning, for example, whether it has equal

[14] In the classifier subsystem discussed at length in Chapter 5, it is shown that hand configurations are independent morphemes, classifiers. This independence was one of the original motivations for placing the category on a separate tier. However, within the phonology of lexical words, the category behaves as a meaningless element with autosegmental properties, the primary motivation for the representation.

status as a timing unit with static segments, whether or not it constitutes a major class, and, if so, whether this class is like the class of vowels in spoken language. Another hotly debated topic is the role of the non-dominant hand, a dual articulator with no parallel in spoken language. These issues will be tackled in later chapters. First we take on the complex category of hand configuration, in the next chapter, replacing the icons used thus far with hierarchically organized features.

10 Hand configuration

Of the three major categories – hand configuration, location, and movement – the hand configuration category is the most complex. The hand has many degrees of freedom, and sign languages exploit this articulatory range, though subject to certain constraints. The four fingers and the thumb can be selected in various combinations in the articulations of handshapes. The fingers can bend at any joint, or at more than one joint at once. The thumb can be adducted or abducted, can contact fingertips, or can close over the fingers. In addition, the whole hand may be oriented in various directions.[1] In this chapter, we present generalizations that have been discovered about the way in which these possibilities are both exploited and constrained in sign languages, and some models that have been proposed to reflect these generalizations. A chart of some common handshapes is offered in Figure 10.1 for reference.[2,3]

We begin by presenting parameters along which lexical contrasts are made, each of which will later be shown to constitute a subcategory of hand configuration features. After these preliminaries, the chapter proceeds to construct a model of hand configuration that is motivated by the clustering of features in classes, both in underlying representations and in phonological processes. The overall structure of the model relies on the theory of feature geometry (e.g., Clements 1985, Sagey 1986, Halle 1992). The representation of the terminal features is facilitated by appealing to the theory of dependency phonology (Durand 1986, Anderson and Ewen 1987, van der Hulst 1989). As usual, we find that the strategy of holding sign language phenomena up against spoken

[1] See Ann (1992, 1993, 1996), for anatomical and physiological descriptions, and for algorithms devised to calculate ease of articulation of various handshapes.

[2] The handshape drawings in the chart and throughout the book are reprinted with permission from HamNoSys (Hamburg Notation System, Prillwitz 1989).

[3] This chart is offered for convenience and is not intended to represent the phonemic handshape inventory of any sign language. Shapes that only occur in handshape changes in the sign languages with which we are familiar are omitted. Some of those included may only function as allophones.

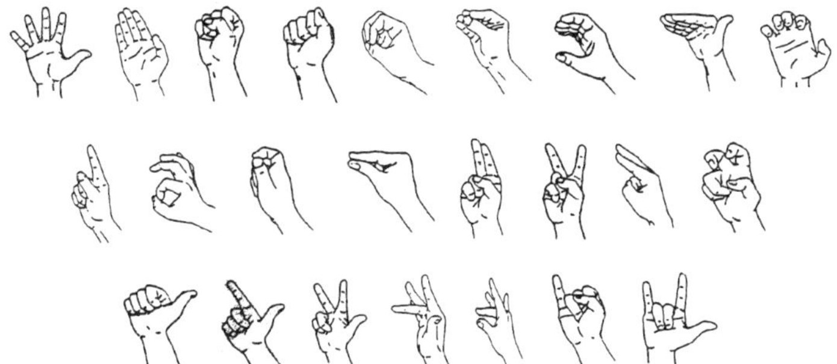

Figure 10.1 Some common handshapes

a. DANGEROUS (ISL)

b. INTERESTING (ISL)

Figure 10.2 Minimal pair distinguished by different specifications for selected fingers

language models helps to illuminate both similarities and differences between the two modalities.

10.1 Parameters of contrast

Hand configurations may contrast along several parameters. The examples in this section are from Israeli Sign Language, but the same contrasts are found in ASL and other sign languages. The most salient way in which signs may contrast is in the selection of fingers, as in (ISL) DANGEROUS, INTERESTING, shown in Figure 10.2. DANGEROUS is specified for all fingers selected, while INTERESTING is specified for pinky and thumb. Signs may also contrast for the shape or position of the fingers, as in (ISL) ALREADY, DOCUMENT, shown in Figure 10.3. In both members of this pair, all fingers are selected. In ALREADY, they are open, and in DOCUMENT, they are closed.

In addition to shape, the orientation of the hand may also be responsible for lexical contrasts (Battison 1978 [1973], Klima and

a. ALREADY (ISL)

b. DOCUMENT (ISL)

Figure 10.3 Finger position minimal pair

a. COMPARE (ISL)

b. VACILLATE (ISL)

Figure 10.4 Minimal pair distinguished by different specifications for orientation

TAKE-ADVANTAGE-OF (ISL)

Figure 10.5 Internal movement: change of finger position

Bellugi 1979). Signs minimally contrasting for orientation are pictured in Figure 10.4.[4]

Finally, the hand configuration may change in particular ways: either the finger position may change or the orientation of the hand may change within a sign, creating what is usually referred to as internal movement. Each of these two types of internal movement is illustrated in Figure 10.5 and Figure 10.6. Different types of internal movement may also create

[4] Facing is included as a category by Liddell and Johnson (1989 [1985]), who showed that it varies independently of orientation. Meir (1998a, 1998b) shows that facing plays a grammatical role in verb agreement. Facing has not been accounted for in phonological models to date.

DEAD (ISL)

Figure 10.6 Internal movement: change of orientation

WIN (ISL)

Figure 10.7 Handshape and orientation change together

a. WINE (ISL)

b. FLAT-TIRE (ISL)

Figure 10.8 Minimal pair for internal movement (WINE) and path movement (FLAT-TIRE)

contrasts. The sign WIN shown in Figure 10.7 involves handshape change, as well as orientation change. It is distinct from TAKE-ADVANTAGE-OF (Figure 10.5), which involves handshape change only.

Presence or absence of internal movement may be contrastive. In Figure 10.8, we see WINE, with internal movement (opening of the index finger) and short path movement to contact the neck, and FLAT-TIRE, with path movement to contact but no internal movement.

Stokoe's (1960) phonemic ASL handshape inventory of twenty-one shapes is compiled on the basis of minimal pairs. An ambitious attempt to list all of the handshapes found in all sign languages, the HamNoSys notation (Prillwitz 1989) is useful from a phonetic point of view, but makes no claims about

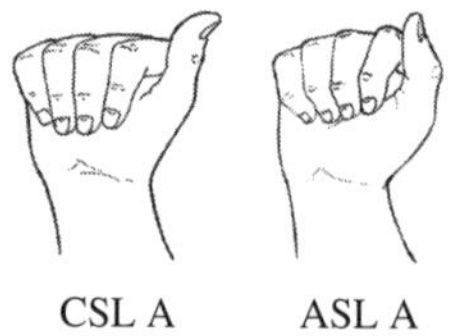

Figure 10.9 Cross-sign-language handshape differences: ASL and CSL (© Ursula Bellugi, the Salk Institute)

contrastiveness. Stokoe's phonologically based inventory may not be exhaustive for ASL, and there are certainly some shapes that exist in other sign languages, but not in ASL. Only systematic cross-linguistic research on the phonology of handshapes will ultimately enable us to speak with confidence about the pool of possible shapes available to the sign language learner.

In the oral modality, different languages have different phoneme inventories, and foreign accents often reflect different phonological structure of the same phonetic space. Aspiration of voiceless stops, for instance, can be phonemic (as in Hindi), allophonic (as in English), or non-existent (as in French). Adult speakers of each of these languages transfer their own phoneme inventories and allophonic rules to any foreign language they learn, resulting in the foreign accents we perceive. In sign languages as well, there are differences in handshape phoneme inventories and in the pronunciation of similar shapes, both across sign languages and across dialects of the same sign language. For example, Thai SL has an extended ring finger handshape that doesn't exist in ASL or ISL (Mandel 1981). Russian SL has an extended ring finger and pinky shape. In addition, casual observation indicates that shapes in different sign languages that seem the same are actually different in subtle ways. For example, Klima and Bellugi (1979) show that there is a difference between the handshape *A* in ASL and a similar shape in Chinese SL. In CSL *A*, the fingers are more tense than in the ASL version. These differences are illustrated in Figure 10.9.

Presumably, an American signer learning CSL would have a foreign accent which is partly definable by the features that distinguish similar but not identical shapes in the two languages. But most investigations to date have been based on one sign language only, and, until recently, models of handshape structure were developed on that basis alone.

Attempts to arrive at a universal inventory of underlying handshape features are confounded by two other factors which are unique to sign languages: iconically motivated shapes that may occur in only one sign, and the limited borrowing of shapes from fingerspelling alphabets (see Chapter 6, Section 6.3).[5] Some researchers (e.g., Brentari 1998) attempt

[5] Liddell and Johnson (1989 [1985]) add many shapes, to arrive at a grand total of 150 handshapes. The reason for this huge disparity appears to be Liddell and Johnson's inclusion of small variations in handshape that Stokoe and other researchers have ignored on the assumption that they are phonetic only and not contrastive. The problem may relate in part

to incorporate such shapes into their feature inventories in order to be able to represent all shapes with features. Another approach is to represent anomalous handshapes holistically, refraining from positing special features for them alone, and predicting that the resulting feature inventory will capture all and only the phonological generalizations of the language (e.g., Sandler 1989, 1995b, 1996a).

The notion of feature inventories for hand configuration is in itself a departure from the Stokoe proposal. For Stokoe, who was trained in the structuralist linguistic tradition, each hand configuration is the equivalent of a phoneme, indivisible. Generative phonologists have shown that phonemes of spoken languages must indeed be broken down into smaller units in order to give a satisfactory explanation for distinctions within and among inventories, as well as to account for the set of phonological processes that occur in the world's languages (Chomsky and Halle 1968, Jakobson, Fant, and Halle 1951). We take the position that feature theory is more explanatory than a holistic phonemic approach in sign language as in spoken language.

Investigations of hand configuration abound, most of them seeking to define handshapes using a set of features, and numerous inventories have been proposed. Unfortunately, we cannot begin to do them all justice here.

Our goal is to isolate and account for central generalizations about the category of hand configuration. We do so by appealing to phonological theories developed on the basis of spoken language which account for similar phenomena. Facts about the behavior of the fingers, their position, and the orientation of the hand within signs and in phonological rules find an explanation in the theory of Feature Geometry, according to which features are hierarchically organized in classes corresponding to physical articulators. Another robust generalization is that some handshapes are more marked than others according to the definition and range of criteria set out in Jakobson (1968 [1941]). The theory of Dependency Phonology is concerned with reflecting the relative markedness of phonological elements, as well as with parsimony in the feature inventory, and we appeal to that theory as well. The question of whether or not the two approaches can be integrated coherently within general phonological theory will not be resolved here. In the new science of sign language phonology, each approach makes a significant contribution.

A basic generalization about the hand configuration category is its temporal autonomy from locations and movements exemplified by assimilation in compounds, discussed in Chapter 9 and illustrated in Figure 9.11. We repeat the schematic representation of that process here for convenience. As shown in (1), the entire category of hand configuration undergoes total assimilation, and some of the locations and movements independently delete.

to iconic motivation inherent in some handshapes, which causes subtle variants of basic shapes. This issue has yet to be resolved, but serious consideration of the effect of iconicity on the phonology of Sign Language of the Netherlands appears in van der Kooij (2002).

(1) Autonomy of hand configuration

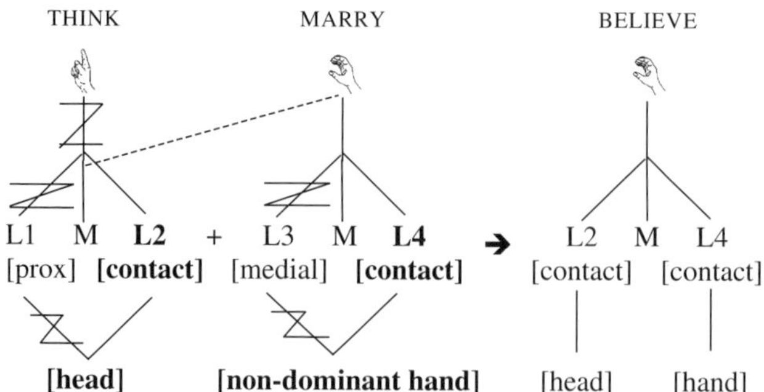

The present chapter aims to break down the category of hand configuration into its features and motivate a particular hierarchical organization of the classes into which those features are organized.

The central claims of the model to be supported are these: (1) hand configuration is made up of both the shape and the orientation of the hand; (2) the shape consists of finger selection and their position; and (3) orientation is a subclass of handshape, i.e., of selected fingers (Sandler 1987b, 1989). Other aspects of the model shown in (2), to be elaborated here, are drawn from Sandler (1995c, 1996a), van der Hulst (1995), Crasborn and van der Kooij (1997), and van der Kooij (2002).

(2) A hierarchical model of hand configuration features (based on Sandler 1989, 1995c, 1996a)

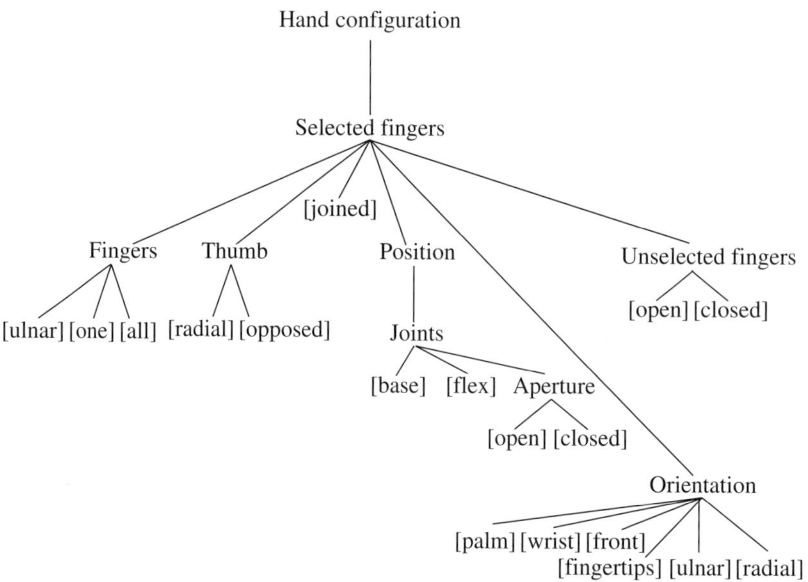

We now proceed to take the model apart and put it together again, beginning with handshape (selected fingers) and finishing with orientation. The relation between these two categories in an assimilation process motivates their representation and completes the hierarchy.

10.2 Hierarchical representation of feature classes: handshape

Let us begin with a division of the category of handshapes into two subcategories first proposed by Mandel (1981). Mandel observes that any morpheme has only one set of selected fingers, but that these fingers may change their position within the morpheme. In other words, while a morpheme may be characterized by internal movement in which the handshape changes, this is restricted to a change of position, and not of selection of fingers. A sequence such as – may not occur within a morpheme.[6] But the sequence – occurs commonly, as in the ASL sign SEND, pictured in Figure 9.9 above. This important observation motivates a model of handshape in which there are two categories: selected fingers and finger position.[7]

Liddell and Johnson (1989 [1985]) present some signs that are purported to counterexemplify Mandel's generalization. Words such as JOB (characterized by the handshape sequence –) include two groups of selected fingers. Sandler (1986, 1989) rejects the claim that these are counterexamples, on the following grounds: these are fingerspelled borrowings from English orthography (Battison 1978 [1973]); orthography is an arbitrary symbol system for representing language in a different modality; in spoken language, borrowed sounds often go beyond native phoneme inventories (e.g., [x] sometimes used in English for *Bach*); and the selected fingers constraint remains strong in the native lexicon. According to the latter view, a good phonological model should make perspicuous precisely which forms are well behaved and which are exceptional; i.e., it should favor phonological generalizations over a purely descriptive taxonomy.[8] But how can we represent the generalization that selected fingers must remain constant across a sign while their position

[6] Numbers and fingerspelling are excluded from these generalizations. In numbers, each finger is an icon or a symbol for a digit, so that the finger combinations are arithmetic rather than linguistic. Fingerspelling is a borrowed system dictated by orthography, which is itself parasitic on spoken language, and does not reflect the natural properties of sign language.

[7] Another argument for the separation between selected fingers and finger position is the fact that they can be affected independently in slips of the hand (Newkirk et al.1980, Sandler 1989).

[8] Another type of sign that Liddell and Johnson claim is a counter example to the selected finger generalization is signs like (ASL) THROW, which they claim consists of –. Sandler (1989) argues instead that the first handshape is actually a closed version of the second both phonetically and phonologically – i.e., only two fingers go from closed to open and the others are unselected – making the sequence: – and in keeping with the selected finger generalization.

may change, if the two belong to the same phonological element, namely, the hand configuration?

Non-linear theories of phonological structure in spoken language, introduced in Section 10.2.1, liberated features from their strict segmental straitjackets. Later developments went further, and allowed for a multidimensional conception of sound structure in which each feature is autonomous, whether or not it has the broad scope of features such as tone. In this view, all assimilation rules are represented as multiply connected lines that associate the assimilating feature to various positions in a string. And all deletion rules simply delink the feature from the string; i.e., they cut the association lines. As we will show shortly, these theoretical innovations influenced sign language research, making it possible to capture certain generalizations in a principled way.

10.2.1 Feature geometry in spoken language phonology

Though features are potentially autonomous, they often cluster together in classes. According to the theory of Feature Geometry, the classes are motivated by the physical architecture of the vocal tract as well as by the behavior of features in rules, especially assimilation rules (e.g., Clements 1985, Sagey 1986, Halle 1992). In particular, features that tend to cluster together in rules – such as place features – are represented as a class that may assimilate as a group. In Chapter 1, the example was given of nasal consonants that assimilate the place of articulation of a neighboring segment, whatever it is, without losing their nasal quality: *can* becomes [kæm] before *be* and [kæŋ] before *go*. Hierarchical Feature Geometry models capture the generalizations that all oral place features involve articulators in the oral cavity, and that they may assimilate together, by grouping them together as a class. In the case of [ŋ] resulting from the assimilation of the place features of [g] in *go* to the [n] segment of *can*, the rule will automatically assimilate both the [high] and [back] features responsible for velar consonants, while leaving the [nasal] specification unaffected, as shown in example 1 in Chapter 1.

10.2.2 The geometry of selected fingers and finger position

We now turn to the representation of handshape in sign language, in the context of the theory of feature geometry, following the Hand Tier model introduced in Chapter 9 (Sandler 1987b, 1989).[9] To take the anatomy as a starting point, one might consider Mandel's separation of the selection

[9] Other hierarchical models are proposed in Ahn (1990), Corina (1990a), and Corina and Sagey (1989). Space does not permit a comparison here, but see Corina and Sandler (1993) for an overview.

Figure 10.10 Four finger positions: open, closed, bent, curved

of the whole finger or fingers from the position of those fingers, i.e., the extension or flexion of the joints. ASL may select a single finger, a combination, or all fingers together. The position of the fingers may be considered a separate category because whatever fingers are selected, they must all be in the same position; i.e., they must all extend or bend at the same joints. All are open, all bent, all curved, or all closed, each illustrated in Figure 10.10 for shapes in which all five fingers are selected.

In terms of phonological behavior as well, there is a separation of the two feature classes, selected fingers and finger position. In a morpheme with handshape change, it is only the position that changes, as we have seen. Position may also be altered by morphological rule, for example by wiggling or flicking the fingers; but these rules may not affect the selection of fingers (Battison 1978, Mandel 1981, Sandler 1989). Taken together, these facts motivate a feature hierarchy in which the selected fingers node dominates the position node, as in (3).

(3) Hierarchy of selected finger and finger position features (Sandler 1987a, 1987b, 1989).

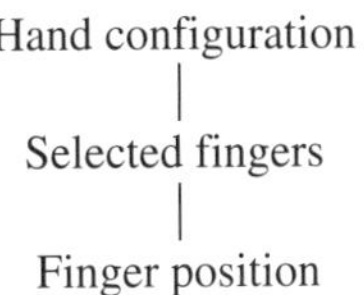

By design, whichever position feature is specified must characterize all the selected fingers that are specified. Also, if the selected fingers node spreads (i.e., assimilates) or deletes, then the position features must go along. Yet position features are predicted to potentially behave independently.[10]

There is some evidence from ASL that this prediction is correct. In the Unrealized Inceptive (Liddell 1984a), the second handshape deletes; i.e., both the selected finger and the position features delete. Under other circumstances, only the position feature is affected. In particular, some signs with handshape change have variants without the change (Corina

[10] Corina and Sagey (1989) independently propose a hierarchical model of handshape. In their model, each finger dominates position features independently, a representation motivated by cases of individual finger assimilations between words. Since such assimilations are postlexical, we assume here that the representation motivated by them is not underlying in the lexicon.

1990a). This means that one finger position deletes, but the selected finger specification persists throughout the sign. For example, the sign UGLY is specified for the index finger only, and the position is first open, then curved, as the hand moves across the face. In the variant, the hand, index finger selected, traverses the same path across the face, but only the curved position surfaces. As the model also predicts, processes affecting the selected finger specification but not the position are not attested.

10.2.3 The representation of internal movement

There are two broad types of movement in sign languages: path movement, from one location to another; and internal or local movement, i.e., change of handshape or change of orientation. In the case of handshape change, illustrated in Figure 10.5 above, only position features may change; selected finger features remain constant. This was presented in the previous section as a motivation for the representation of handshape with the feature classes of selected fingers and finger position.

The Hand Tier model that we have been describing represents internal movement by branching at the finger position node, or at the orientation node, as shown in (4).[11] This branching creates a contour transition between the two states represented on each branch, comparable to contour tones in tone languages (Sandler 1987b, 1989).

(4) Representation of handshape contour

There is a constraint on the sequences of handshapes, given in (5), originally proposed in Sandler (1989) and refined in Brentari (1990).

(5) Handshape Sequence Constraint (HSC)
If there are two finger positions in a sign, then one must be open or closed.

The HSC means that there cannot be a sequence in which at least one position is not either open or closed. In other words, sequences such as open–closed, or bent–open are okay, but the sequences *bent–curved and *curved–bent are ruled out. The feature [closed] is interpreted as involving contact between the thumb and the fingers; i.e., thumb involvement is redundant.

[11] See Corina (1993) for a proposal that handshape changes be represented with the contour features [opening] and [closing], rather than with branching position nodes.

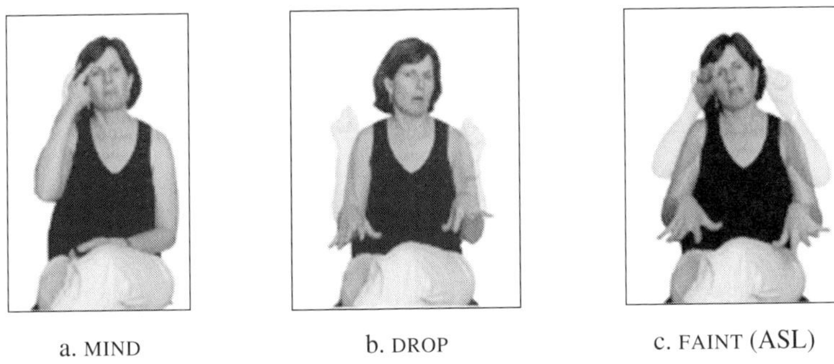

a. MIND b. DROP c. FAINT (ASL)

Figure 10.11 Independent members of a compound (MIND^DROP) and the compound (FAINT) with selected fingers and Finger position assimilation

Evidence for the representation of internal movement as part of hand configuration comes from assimilation under compounding in ASL. Total assimilation of hand configuration includes features of finger position, unitary or contour, independently of the L and M segments. For example, in the compound MIND^DROP = FAINT, the HC from DROP spreads to the beginning of the compound in the same total assimilation process schematized in (1) above. As FAINT has handshape-change-internal movement (–), both finger positions spread with all other hand configuration features. Figure 10.11 illustrates this compound, and (6) shows a partial representation of the spreading process.

(6) Total hand configuration assimilation in FAINT

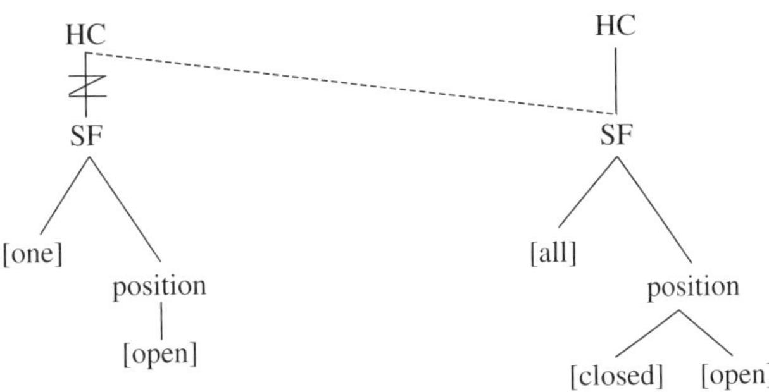

The geometry of handshape (i.e., the selected fingers category) has now been laid out. Before dealing with the terminal features in Section 10.4, we now complete the overall architecture of hand configuration by placing the category of orientation in the model.

10.3 Orientation and the hand configuration hierarchy

In a sign, the hand articulator is characterized not only by its shape, but also by its orientation. Battison (1978) notices that orientation is sometimes contrastive, as shown in Figure 10.4, and proposes it as a fourth major phonological category. The discovery that orientation is contrastive can be separated from the claim that it constitutes a major category, however, since any distinctive feature is, by definition, contrastive. Orientation might function instead as a part of the hand configuration category, an idea that is suggested by an error study (Newkirk et al. 1980), in which handshape substitutions included orientation as well (Sandler 1989). Since the patterning together of handshape and orientation is not required on phonetic grounds, such substitutions indicate that orientation and handshape are indeed phonologically related.

In fact, there is independent phonological motivation for the idea that orientation is a phonological subcategory of hand configuration, and not, as Battison suggested, an independent category on a par with hand configuration, location, and movement. The evidence consists of the behavior of orientation under assimilation. In ASL compounds, orientation alone may assimilate without the fingers and their position, but if the fingers and their position assimilate, then orientation is not independent – it must assimilate as well (Sandler 1987a, 1987b, 1989). This observation prompts the representation of orientation as subordinate to the selected finger node.[12]

A good example is the compound OVERSLEEP (from SLEEP^SUNRISE), introduced in Chapter 1. In one variant, only orientation assimilates, as illustrated in Figure 10.12.

a. SLEEP (ASL)

b. SUNRISE (ASL)

c. OVERSLEEP (ASL) orientation assimilation

Figure 10.12 Independent members of compound and partial assimilation form

[12] In the original model, orientation was subordinate to a handshape node, making it a sister of the position node. That representation is motivated by different considerations that complicate the discussion and is less desirable for reasons of perspicuity, so we opt for the representation shown here.

The partial assimilation process of orientation only is represented in (7), where only the HC category (and not the location and movement categories) is shown for simplicity. The feature representation is transparent and somewhat oversimplified in advance of the discussion of features in the model.

(7) Assimilation of orientation only in OVERSLEEP

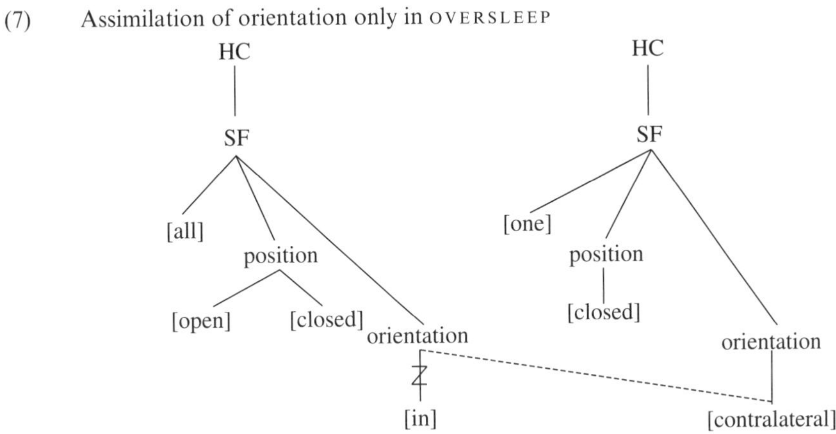

Partial assimilation, assimilation of orientation only, characterizes one version of this compound. In another attested version, selected fingers may assimilate, but if they do, then their position and the orientation of the hand assimilate as well, resulting in total assimilation, as illustrated in Figure 10.13.

Here, the selected finger node spreads, taking along all the other features of hand configuration, as shown in (8). These data motivate the representation of hand configuration in the Hand Tier model shown here, which allows total hand configuration assimilation (selected fingers, finger position, and hand orientation) to be represented simply as spreading of the highest node in the hierarchy dominating all the other features.

OVERSLEEP (ASL)

Figure 10.13 Total assimilation of handshape and orientation

(8) Total hand configuration assimilation in OVERSLEEP

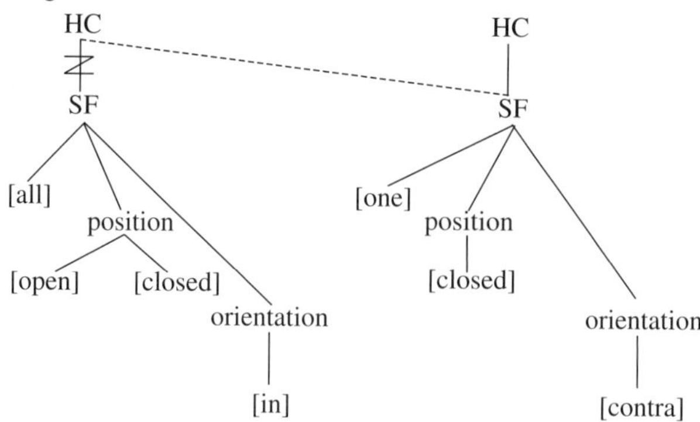

What is striking about this pattern is that it is not required by the phonetics. It is phonetically quite easy to assimilate the selected fingers and their position without orientation. In fact, such assimilation occurs postlexically (see Chapter 16, Section 16.1). But in assimilation processes at the lexical level shown here, selected fingers do not assimilate without orientation in ASL.

Most of the documented cases of assimilation of this kind involve lexicalized compounds, raising the question of whether the structure argued for is synchronically relevant (Perlmutter 1996). There are three reasons for thinking it is. First, even if such assimilation processes were not synchronically productive, they could still point to structural properties that are synchronically relevant. In English, there is a small group of lexicalized alternations involving plurals of certain words ending in *f*: *wife*, *wives*; *knife*, *knives*; *half*, *halves*; *calf*, *calves*. This process is not synchronically productive, as we can see from *fife*, *fifes* (**fives*); *staff*, *staffs* (**staves*), but it is structure preserving, deriving words whose sounds and sound combinations exist in English, and it relies on a feature that still functions as distinctive in English: voicing. In other words, the stem allomorphy is frozen in the lexicon and not productive, but the feature contrast that it relies on is still relevant, and both the base and derived forms are synchronically well formed. In the same way, lexicalized compounds can lend insight into phonological structure even if the phonological processes involved in forming them were no longer productive. Considering how few truly phonological processes there are in ASL, it is a useful strategy to exploit any evidence we can find in order to understand the phonological structure of the language.

But in fact, there is a good reason to believe that this process is not dead. Recordings of the compound THINK^TOUCH = OBSESS support this model as synchronically relevant.[13] The compound THINK^TOUCH = OBSESS has

[13] This analysis of compounds (Sandler 1987a, 1987b, 1989) relies on Salk Institute data collected in the 1970s.

a. MIND

b. STOP (suspend)

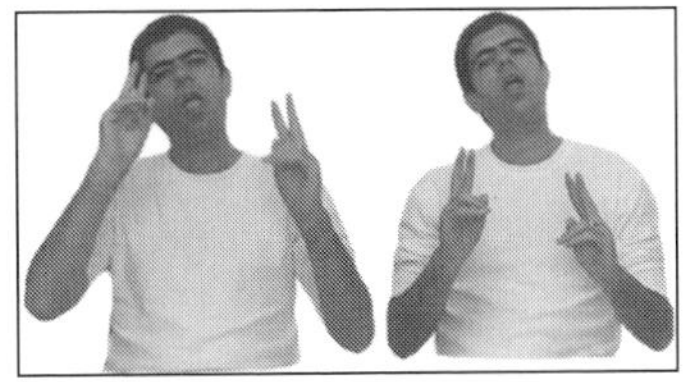

c. MIND^STOP=DAYDREAM

Figure 10.14 Total HC assimilation in an ISL compound

three synchronic variants, one with orientation only assimilation, one with total handshape assimilation, and one with no assimilation. Crucially, there is no variant attested for this or any other compound in which only handshape assimilates without orientation (Sandler 1987a, 1987b, 1989).

Furthermore, lexicalized compounds in Israeli SL behave the same way: if handshape assimilates, orientation does as well. The lexicalized compound DAYDREAM from MIND^STOP, given in Figure 10.14, illustrates this.

This supports the claim that the type of feature organization shown in (2) may characterize all sign languages – just as spoken language feature geometry is claimed to be universal for all spoken languages.[14] In the original Hand Tier model, orientation refers to the palm of the hand, and the features are defined accordingly. A different proposal for orientation features derived from a relation between handpart and place of articulation will be presented in Section 10.4.2.

The feature geometry model is in the spirit of the spoken language models in grouping features together by articulator (Sagey 1986). The fingers, finger joints, and palm of the hand are each articulator nodes, and all together belong to the hand articulator. Such a representation is arguably more explanatory than one in which the feature groupings bear no relation to the anatomy of the system.

10.4 Terminal features

Having established the architecture of handshape feature categories, we now move on to the features themselves. For two reasons, the theory of Dependency Phonology has provided a useful framework for dealing

[14] We have not noticed any examples of partial (orientation-only) assimilation at the lexical level in ISL, and therefore cannot yet confirm that handshape dominates orientation in that language. However, the ISL total assimilation data do confirm that orientation and handshape group together, i.e., that they are both dominated by the higher hand configuration category.

with handshape features. First, the theory admits only unary and not binary features, and second, it aims to reflect relative markedness directly in the representation (Durand 1986, Anderson and Ewen 1987, van der Hulst 1989). Each of these principles facilitates the expression of generalizations about handshape.

There are two principles of dependency phonology that are appealed to in the model of hand configuration we espouse. One is the idea that the simplest and most useful theory of phonological features is one in which features are unary, not binary as in the classical generative model. The second principle holds that relative markedness should be reflected by relative complexity in the representation: the simpler the representation the less marked the form, and vice versa.

10.4.1 Unariness and markedness in handshapes

Researchers have proposed feature-based hierarchical models of handshape that can represent all the shapes of all sign languages (e.g., Corina and Sagey 1989, Sandler 1989). But certain robust generalizations are missed by these models.

First, no evidence has been provided for minus values of the binary features used in handshape specifications. A sign may be characterized for index finger, but if a sign is specified for pinky, for example, then the notion of non-index fingerness is superfluous. Other criteria for constructing a feature theory are parsimony and perspicuity. Here, too, we fail to find advantages for binary features in the representation of sign language phonological form. Sandler's (1989) model of the location category proposes binary values for pairs of features which, when combined, can yield a third specification for free, just as [-hi,-lo] yields "mid" in spoken vowel systems. But the absence of processes that refer to the lack of some feature encourages us to seek other equally parsimonious ways of specifying phonological properties, and the representation in (2) models such a system.

The second generalization about handshapes that is supported by several disparate types of evidence, but that is not reflected in the models presented so far, is this: certain handshapes consistently behave as less marked than others. The term "markedness" is used in a variety of ways in linguistics. For discussions within the theory of dependency phonology, the reader is referred to Durand (1986) and Anderson and Ewen (1987). In connection with hand configuration, we refer to Jakobson's theory of markedness, which posits the following cluster of properties for elements that are relatively *less* marked: they are frequent cross-linguistically, easier to produce, acquired early by children, and resistant to loss in aphasia (Jakobson 1968 [1941]). A summary of the evidence for an unmarked set of handshapes given in (9) is from Sandler (1995c, 1996a). These generalizations are mainly from the literature on American Sign Language, but ISL is reported to have the same set of unmarked shapes based on such properties as frequency and the shape of the non-dominant hand in two-handed signs (see (2) and (3) in Chapter 12), and a subset of these shapes is reported to be an unmarked set in Sign Language of the Netherlands (Harder and Schermer 1986).[15]

(9) Evidence for this set of unmarked handshapes:

1 The unmarked shapes are "maximally distinct, basic geometrical shapes" (Battison 1978).
2 They are the easiest to articulate motorically (McIntire 1977, Woodward 1978, Klima and Bellugi 1979, Mandel 1981, Whittemore 1986, Ann 1993, Greftegreff 1993).
3 They are the most frequently occurring shapes in ASL and in other sign languages (Battison 1978).
4 They are the first to be acquired by children (McIntire 1977, Boyes-Braem 1981, Siedlecki and Bonvillian 1997).
5 When the non-dominant hand is involved in a sign but is not in the same shape as the dominant hand, its shape is restricted to one of the unmarked shapes (Battison 1978). (See footnote 16.)
6 These shapes are less restricted in terms of how they may contact the body or the other hand than are the other shapes (Battison 1978).
7 Aphasics make fewest errors on these shapes (Whittemore 1986).

[15] We include both and in the unmarked list here, but the two are probably not contrastive in unmarked contexts (e.g., non-dominant handshape in h2-P signs [see Chapter 12], acquisition substitutions, etc.). If this is the case, only one of them should be included in the list. Battison includes . As the latter shape sometimes alternates allophonically with , we've chosen to leave it out pending further evidence that the distinction is relevant for markedness. Battison also includes the shape among the shapes that may occur independently on the non-dominant hand, and classifies it as an unmarked shape. However, as Mandel (1981) points out, this shape occurs in signs in which the dominant hand makes contact in the opening made by the non-dominant hand (e.g., VOTE, TEA). That is, the underlying shape in such signs is the closed shape, , and the curved shape is allophonic. is also included by Battison. In the analysis presented here, this handshape, when specified, is more marked than , because it requires the feature [joined]. Here too, we list only the unmarked spread-finger shape, hypothesizing that in the unmarked contexts the two are not contrastive.

8 These are the shapes most likely to be substituted for other shapes by children (McIntire 1977) and by aphasics (Whittemore 1986).

A principled way of constraining the representation of handshapes, then, is to seek a model that reflects relative markedness in terms of relative complexity, and ignores irrelevant phonetic detail. The theory of Dependency Phonology (Anderson and Ewen 1987) provides the underpinning for the dependency hand configuration model (Sandler 1995c, 1996a), in which the main opposition for selected fingers is determined by whether the hand is relatively pointy (one finger) or relatively broad (all fingers) in appearance. Finger positions are relatively open or relatively closed. Features expressing these characteristics are proposed and representations of handshapes combine the features and their head-dependency relations in various ways, resulting in a model in which relative complexity of representation corresponds to the relative markedness of the handshape. This model does away with individual representations of each finger and each position found in other models, proposing instead only two features for fingers and two features for positions.

These two features are either alone in a representation or enter into different dependency relations with each other. The number of features and their structural relationship with each other reflect the relative markedness of the handshape. Shapes with only one feature in each category and therefore no dependency relations comprise precisely the class of unmarked shapes. Sandler's dependency model of features was strongly influenced by a general theory of sign language structure that is developed in van der Hulst (1993, 1996). We will have more to say about van der Hulst's dependency model in connection with the non-dominant hand (Chapter 12) and movements (Chapter 13). The revised model of hand configuration, repeated in (10), is based on Sandler's (1995c, 1996a) proposal, but also incorporates improvements from work by van der Hulst (1989) and van der Kooij (2002). For example, van der Hulst (1995) refines the representation by splitting finger position into joint selection and aperture, a change we have adopted. We also adopt here the straightforward selected finger feature labels [all] and [one] proposed by van der Kooij (Brentari, van der Hulst, van der Kooij, and Sandler 1996, van der Kooij 2002).[16]

[16] The thumb feature [radial] is intended for signs in which the thumb is selected non-redundantly, like (ASL) CIGARETTE-LIGHTER or (ISL) PEN. The thumb feature [opposed] helps to distinguish (ASL) FORBID from LATER, for example. Addition of either of these features and the Thumb node with it adds markedness to a sign. For detailed argumentation for the model, see Sandler (1996a).

(10)

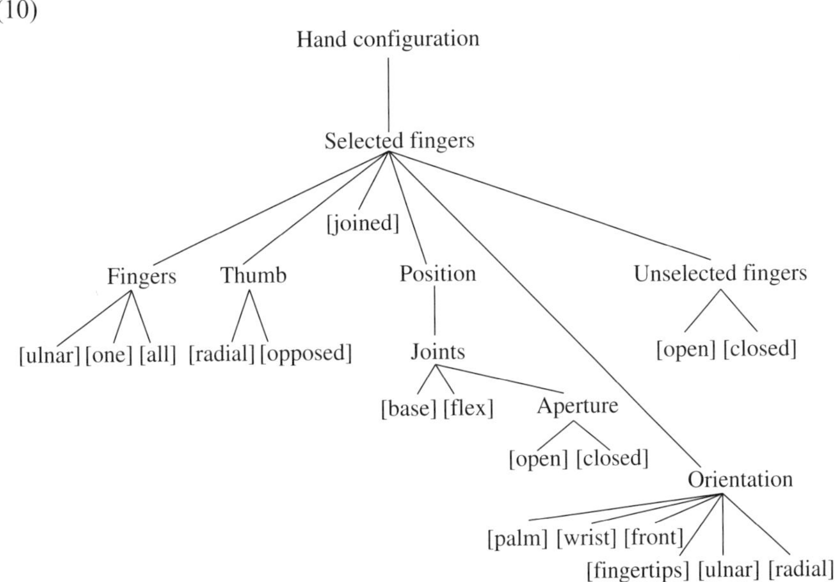

Only specified nodes are activated; nodes that dominate default specifications are not included in representations. The default features are called upon in underlying representation only when required to interact in a dependency relation in order to represent very marked shapes. This requirement simplifies representations and also reflects relative markedness: the more nodes represented, the more complex the handshape.

An example of a node that is rarely activated is the Unselected Fingers node. According to Corina (1993), in most ASL signs, the position of the unselected fingers is redundant. While selected fingers may occur in any of four positions, the fingers not selected – the unselected fingers – are more constrained: they must be either open or closed, and, in most cases, the position is predictable. The redundancy rule Corina proposes is shown in (11).

(11) Unselected Fingers Redundancy Rule (Corina 1993)
If specified fingers are closed, unspecified fingers are open; otherwise unspecified fingers are closed.

The "otherwise" part of the rule is interpreted as follows: if the selected fingers are anything except closed – if they are open, curved, or bent – then the unselected fingers are closed. In the spirit of suggestions in Mandel (1981), van der Kooij (1998) suggests that this bifurcation of foregrounded and backgrounded fingers may be considered a type of phonetic enhancement. By assuming an extreme position that is as different as possible from that of the selected fingers, the unselected fingers make the selected fingers more perceptually salient.[17]

The model includes a node for the position of unselected fingers, although their position is usually redundant. There are two cases in which the positions of unselected fingers is not redundant: and . In , the middle finger is selected and bent, and the unselected fingers should be closed according to the redundancy rule in (11) but they are open instead. In , the index is selected and closed (through fingertip contact with the thumbtip), and the unselected fingers are expected to be open . While such a shape exists and is even more common than , the latter also exists. Unselected finger position must be specified for these configurations, indicating correctly that they are marked shapes.

Returning to Battison's unmarked shapes , the first thing we now notice is that only two selected finger specifications are involved, each of them maximally simple: [all] and [one].

The examples in (12) illustrate the way this model works, by giving representations for the unmarked shape , the somewhat more marked shape , and the still more marked shape . The unmarked shape has only one feature under the selected finger node and one under the finger position node. The marked shapes have combinations of features in dominance relations to one another. The handshape, which selects the index and middle fingers, is represented with [all] as head and [one] as dependent. The bent position is represented with [closed] as head and [open] as dependent.

(12) Representations of less and more marked shapes (from Sandler 1995c, 1996a)

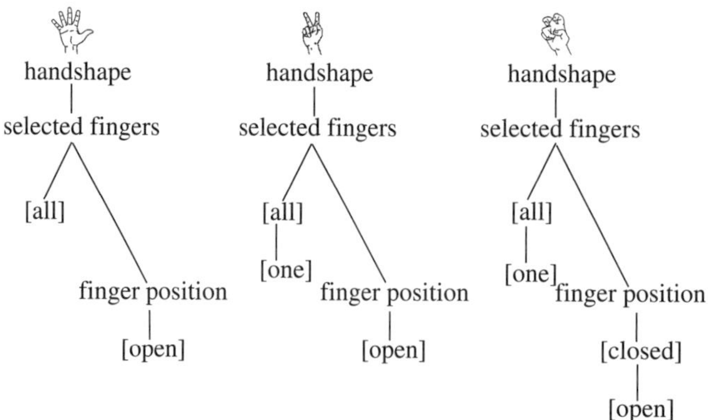

We follow van der Hulst (1995) in representing dependency relations among features in tree structures (instead of using the punctuation

[17] Similarly, if the fingers are in the unmarked spread position, the feature [joined] does not appear in the representation. The thumb node is also usually redundant and therefore not represented (see Sandler 1995c, 1996a, for details).

convention of Durand 1986). In our model, this means that structures in which features are subordinate to other features (and not to feature classes as in Feature Geometry) are interpreted as feature complexes according to the conventions of Dependency Phonology.

The unmarked shape has the simplest possible representation: one selected finger feature and one position feature. The more marked shape has two selected finger components: [all] and [one] in a dependency relation. The most marked shape has the same complex selected finger representation plus a combination of finger position components, [closed] and [open]. The model represents other more marked shapes with the additional categories of thumb and unselected fingers, used when these articulators are in a configuration that is other than the default.

The resulting model preserves the original feature-geometric tree structure as far as the relationship of the categories to each other is concerned; only the level of the terminal features themselves is different, now proposing unary features organized in dependency relationships. Feature Geometry represents the relationship between physical articulators and the way in which features that are produced by those articulators function in forms and rules of languages. Dependency Phonology representations reflect feature groupings according to their patterning in languages, as in Feature Geometry, but the relationship of the features to their articulators is not a motivating factor. Rather, Dependency Phonology representations aim to reveal relative markedness, as well as head-dependent relations that are argued to characterize all phonological structure, and to restrict the feature inventory by allowing combinations of a very small set of unary primitives. Because of advantages offered by both theories, we adopt this mixed model of handshape for now, and recommend future investigations of the consequences of a hybrid model such as this. For models of sign language phonology that are constructed entirely according to the principles of Dependency Phonology, see van der Hulst (1993, 1996) and van der Kooij (2002).

We are now in a position to return to finer details, for example, distinguishing the following three shapes, all represented as all five fingers selected ([all]), and a [closed] position: . A solution to this problem is proposed by van der Hulst (1995), who further refines a suggestion in Uyechi (1996 [1994]) that separates flexion at the base joints (the joints closest to the hand body) and the non-base joints (the other two joints). In van der Hulst's model in the Dependency Phonology framework, the finger position node is split to include joint selection (which articulates bending and curving) and aperture (which articulates opening and closure). Representations of finger position for these three shapes in van der Hulst's model are shown in (13). The selected finger specification for all three examples is [all].

(13) Three closed handshapes (from van der Hulst 1995)

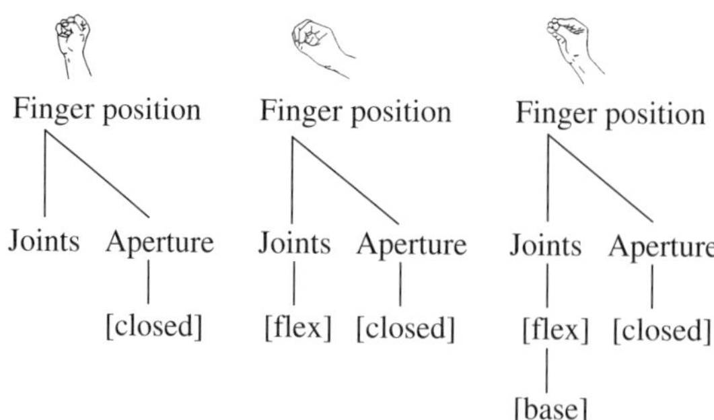

The categories Joints and Aperture are in a dependency relation with each other: Joints is the head, represented with a straight line, and Aperture the dependent, represented with an angled line in van der Hulst's model. A model that provides separate features for Joints and Aperture has the advantages of unambiguously spelling out the first and last shape in signs with handshape change, and of limiting all handshape changes to changes of aperture. Here as above, the more marked shapes have more complex representations.

10.4.2 Orientation features

The observation that the orientation of the palm can be minimally contrastive (Battison 1978) prompted phonologists to take the category seriously, and there is a place for it in all models. The articulatory status of orientation as well as assimilation facts in lexicalized compounds motivate a model in which orientation is a member of the hand configuration category, as explained in Section 10.3. In addition to features of orientation, so-called "facing" features have also been argued for (van der Hulst 1993, Liddell and Johnson 1989 [1985]) to refer to the part of the hand that faces the location toward which the hand moves. Verb agreement must refer to facing because some part of the hand faces the syntactic object, as we saw in Meir's (1998a) analysis, described in Chapter 3, Section 3.2. Two questions require answers with respect to this parameter: what are the features of orientation, and is orientation distinct from facing?

These questions relate to the broader question of where redundancy lies. From a phonetic point of view, specification of handshape, place of articulation, orientation, facing, and the part of the articulating hand that makes contact with the place of articulation (in signs in which the hand contacts the body) will make all necessary contrasts. However, if only some of these features must be specified and the others are redundant, then the redundant features do not belong to the underlying representation. But which features are redundant? Asked differently, which features, if specified, consistently predict the values of other features?

Figure 10.15 AT-THAT-MOMENT (ISL)

Let's take the ISL sign AT-THAT-MOMENT, pictured in Figure 10.15, as an example. In this sign, the handshape is ; the palm orientation is down, facing is the selected fingertips, handpart of contact is also selected fingertips, and place of articulation is the non-dominant hand.

If the shape of the hand, the orientation and the place are specified, then facing and handpart of contact are redundant. That is, if the palm is oriented downward, the location is the non-dominant hand, that location is specified for the feature [contact], and the handshape selects the fingers that it does, then both the direction in which the hand is facing and the handpart making contact are predictable. Alternatively, if the handpart making contact and the location are specified, then the orientation of the palm and the facing are predictable. What, then, should be specified in underlying representation?

A recent proposal takes a step toward solving the problem. According to Crasborn and van der Kooij, working on SLN, orientation is a relative notion, realized relative to the other elements mentioned in the previous paragraph (Crasborn and van der Kooij 1997, Crasborn 2001, van der Kooij 2002). They explain that restricting orientation to the palm is the wrong approach, as it forces independent specification of the facing handpart and the point of contact. However, if orientation is reinterpreted as that part of the hand that relates to the place of articulation, then the old classes of orientation, facing, and point of contact can be reduced to one, which they call relative orientation. The features Crasborn and van der Kooij propose are the following: [palm], [back], [wrist], [front], [fingertip(s)], [ulnar], and [radial], adopted in the representation in (2)/(10) above. They propose that only relative orientations be specified in the hand configuration subtree, and that these are interpreted in relation to handshape and location features which must be represented for independent reasons. The rest falls out from redundancy and phonetic interpretation rules, which they leave to future research.[18]

[18] Brentari (1998) also proposes that orientation is a relative notion, interpreted from a combination of handpart and plane of articulation. See the representation in Chapter 13, example (10).

In support of their proposal that relative orientation should be represented in terms of a part of the hand in relation to the place of articulation is the following observation: the relative orientation value (i.e., the relation between handpart and location) is sometimes more robust – more resistant to alternation – than either the finger position or the orientation of the palm. An example in which relative orientation is more robust than finger position is in the SLN sign PEOPLE, a sign in which the fingertips contact the body. In the citation form of the sign, the handshape is . But the sign is often pronounced with a curved handshape . Regardless of finger position, the relative orientation [fingertips], interpreted together with the place of articulation on the body, remains constant. Exemplifying the latter observation, that relative orientation is more robust than orientation of the palm, is the SLN sign IDEA, in which the fingertip must always articulate at the forehead, but the palm orientation may vary.

The analysis has yet to be fully worked out in order to make the right predictions about how orientation and facing interact with verb agreement. This is an important test of any model, as the direction in which the hands are facing is part of the verb agreement morphology (see Chapter 3, Section 3.2). Crasborn and van der Kooij suggest that it is the second location in the agreeing form that somehow determines the relative orientation. That is, the part of the hand that faces the second location is specified as the relative orientation feature. For example, in the ASL sign LOOK-AT, the handshape is , the palm is oriented downward, and the fingertips lead the hand toward the locus of the object referent; i.e., they point toward the locus. The relative orientation specification is presumably [fingertips], interpreted in relation to the second locus of the sign. However, in this particular sign and others like it the wrist is also morphologically accountable; it must be oriented toward the locus of the subject, i.e., the first location of the sign, distinguishing YOU-LOOK-AT-ME from SHE-LOOKS-AT-ME, for example. Future research is also needed to specify how to interpret the surface form from the underlying representation.

10.4.3 Phonetic redundancy and other predictable properties

A model cast entirely in the dependency framework is offered in van der Kooij (2002).[19] The frequency of shapes in the lexicon, which needs to be tallied in order to determine relative markedness, is calculated in a computerized database – the SignPhon database of Sign Language of the Netherlands (SLN). Van der Kooij's is the first phonological handshape study we know of that uses such a database, which includes 3,000 signs.[20]

[19] An early version of the model initiated by van der Kooij, developed in an unpublished working paper (Brentari et al. 1996), is adopted with some revisions in Brentari (1998).
[20] The SignPhon website is http://www.leidenuniv.nl/hil/sign-lang/signphon2.html

In an effort to represent only those features which are contrastive in SLN, thereby eliminating features that are predictable, van der Kooij proposes a set of redundancy rules (called Phonetic Implementation Rules or PIRs). The model simplifies underlying representations by positing rules to derive surface forms. For example, PIRs are proposed to specify thumb features such as [adducted, abducted, crossed (= restraining)] according to the selection and position of the other fingers, and the presence and type of internal movement (van der Kooij 2002). Noting that flexion of the base joints depends on the articulatory context, she proposes the phonetic implementation rule in (14). The rule is clearly phonetic, as it is gradient.

(14) A Phonetic Redundancy Rule (van der Kooij 2002, p. 127)
Base joints are flexed if a combination of the specification of a part of the hand and a specified location (i.e., the relative orientation) requires it for articulatory reasons.

A radical step is taken in van der Kooij's theory. She attributes to iconicity a significant role in the specification of handshapes. Staying with the example of base joints, their position may also be determined by the shape of the object depicted by the sign. If the object is a ball, for example, the base joints are not flexed, as flexing would make the resulting shape angular instead of round. To account for such conditions, van der Kooij proposes Semantic Implementation Rules. This idea, which is influenced by Boyes-Braem (1981), is beyond – even incompatible with – phonology as we know it, and we will return to it in Unit 5.

10.5 Where is hand configuration in the overall phonological model?

In the model under consideration, hand configuration is conceived of as a complex category with long-distance autosegmental properties. As such, the whole category associates in one-to-many fashion to the segments on the LM tier, exemplified schematically in example (15).

(15) Linking of hand configuration to the LM tier

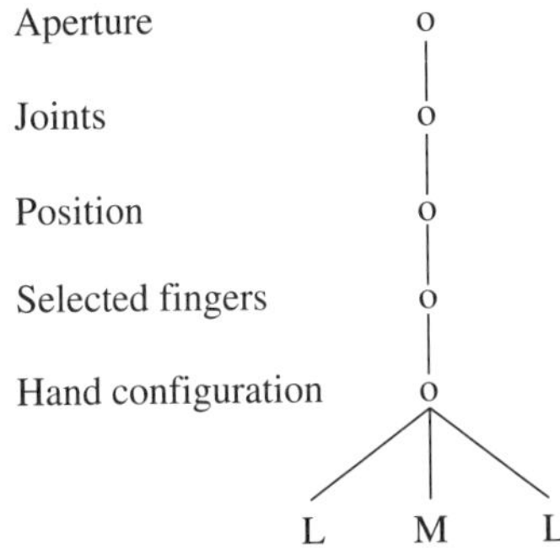

This representation is self-explanatory for most signs. If a sign has hand-internal movement, as shown in example (10) with a branching Aperture node, linking becomes a bit more complex.

(16) Underlying representation of a sign with hand-internal movement

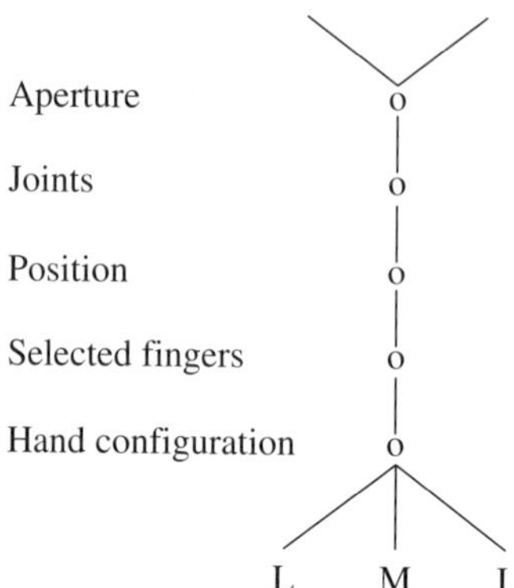

This representation is somewhat abstract, differing from the surface representation in the actual temporal realization of each member of the aperture (or orientation) contour. On the surface, the first and second branches of the contour are articulated with the first and second locations, respectively. In the sign SEND (Figure 9.9) for example, the closed finger position is co-temporal with the first location, and the open finger position is co-temporal with the second location. But this is problematic: is the HC category, including finger position and orientation, temporally autonomous of the LM tier? Or are the contour features in signs with two positions or orientations linked to the timing tier? The answer is: both.

Position is part of the selected finger category, so it spreads with it, whether there is one aperture or two. The representation is explanatory, because the position of the fingers is directly related anatomically to the fingers themselves, it characterizes all selected fingers in the same way, and position spreads with the fingers, in compound reduction, for example, as we have seen. Yet on the surface, each finger position in a sign with handshape change does end up aligned with a different timing slot. On this evidence, one might expect the temporal linking of features to occur only at the surface, perhaps in phonetic implementation.

This leads to indeterminacy, however, since some processes require the two features making up a contour to be associated to the first and last timing slots before phonetic implementation. For example, when the ASL Resultative inflection (Klima and Bellugi 1979), which geminates the first location segment, applies to a sign with internal movement, the first finger position geminates too.[21] This can only happen if the first and last positions are lined up with the first and last locations, as shown in (17). The point at which this linking occurs must be "after" compounding, so that assimilation can affect all HC features without reference to the timing tier, but "before" aspectual inflections occur.[22] The schematic representation in (17) shows only the relevant position features (strictly speaking, aperture features) that create an internal movement contour, labeled pos x and pos y.[23]

(17) Linking of finger positions and spreading for Resultative

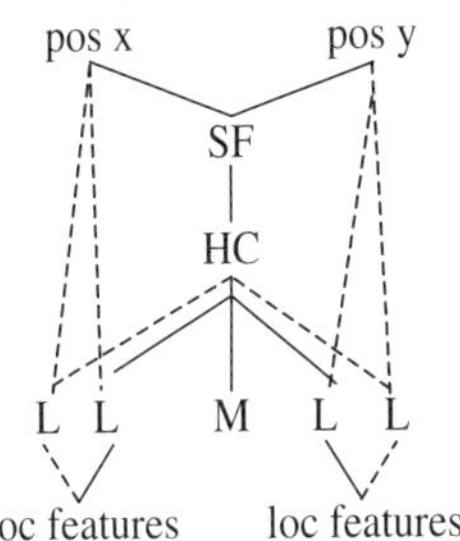

10.6 Summary and conclusion

The hand has many degrees of freedom, but it does not exploit them all when it acts as an articulator in a linguistic system. Instead, its configuration is subject to constraints. The main constraint on hand configuration operating at the level of the morpheme is that only one group of fingers may be selected. An additional phonological constraint is that all selected fingers must be specified for the same position in native handshapes of the sign languages we have studied. If there are two finger positions in a sign, one must be either fully open or fully closed, another constraint on the structure of hand configuration. Finally, the unselected fingers may also be either open or closed, and their position is usually predictable from that of the selected fingers.

21 Finger position features must be interpretable as aligned to the first and last location in order to undergo "negative incorporation" as well. This process is exemplified in Chapter 14, on syllables.

22 This explanation is couched in a theory entailing rule ordering and the ordering of lexical levels. A constraint-based approach might instead posit different constraints and rankings to achieve the survival of different parts of the structure of HC under compounding and aspectual inflection.

23 The solution chosen in (17), in which features align themselves without breaking down the feature geometry, is simpler than that suggested in earlier work (Sandler 1993d). However, such double linking of phonological material is admittedly ad hoc, and the theoretical and empirical implications should be investigated.

The investigation of hand configuration illuminates some of the similarities between spoken and signed languages, and reveals differences as well. We focus here on similarities, leaving differences for the final chapter in this unit, Chapter 16.

In both modalities, phonological categories are comprised of distinctive features, and these features are classed in groups. Hierarchical organization of feature classes is also shown to be universal. The theory of feature geometry launched by Clements (1985) seeks to encode the insight that anatomical architecture and phonological architecture are synchronized. At first glance, this seems unsurprising; after all, phonology is carried by physical articulators in a much more direct way than is, say, syntax. However the link between physical structure and phonological structure becomes more interesting when the latter is distinguished from phonetics. To quote Hayes (1999), "There is a considerable gap between the raw patterns of phonetics and phonological constraints." Both modalities have systematic rules of assimilation that are phonological rather than phonetic in the sense that they involve whole categories of features and are discrete rather than gradient.

In the hand configuration assimilation that occurs in compounds, the category of orientation is shown to be subordinate to handshape (selected fingers). Involving as it does the direction in which the hand is turned, orientation is anatomically part of the hand, motivating a representation in which it is dominated by a higher structure in HC, proposed in the Hand Tier model to be the selected fingers category. However, from a purely phonetic point of view, the selected finger specification is independent of the orientation. There is no phonetic barrier to the assimilation of fingers independently of orientation, a type of assimilation that actually occurs postlexically between pronominal clitics and their hosts (see Chapter 15, Section 15.1).[24] Yet in the lexical phonological process of compounding, assimilation of the finger selection category carries along the orientation category, encoding an anatomical relation phonologically.

Finally, the study of sign language handshapes gives renewed credence to Jakobson's notion of markedness, which links relative complexity or difficulty with other properties such as frequency, distribution, the course of acquisition, and the course of language loss. The relative markedness of handshapes is captured in a model of terminal features that relies on the theory of Dependency Phonology.

[24] Even gradient assimilation of a single finger in signs that select more than one finger can occur on the surface (Corina 1993), a fact that supports a distinction between phonology and phonetics. We will return to this idea in Chapter 14.

A model of the overall architecture of the hand configuration category emerges from the investigation in this chapter, offered in (18). The model shows only feature classes and not terminal features.

(18) The architecture of hand configuration

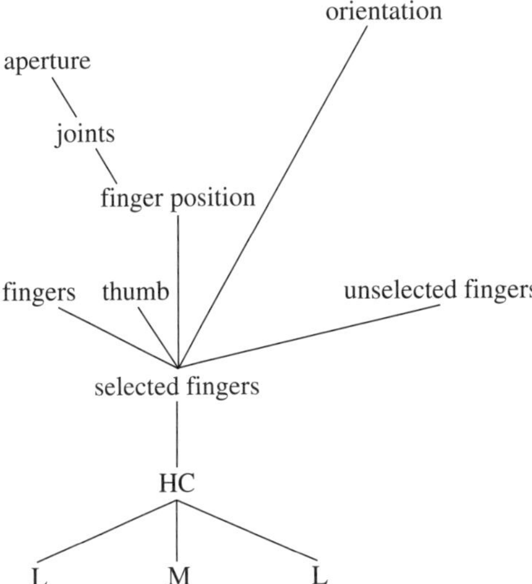

The category of hand configuration is represented as multiply associated to locations and movements because there is only one per morpheme, and because it exhibits a degree of temporal autonomy as explained in Chapter 9, and demonstrated again in (1) in this chapter. The other two major categories, location and movement, are elaborated in Chapters 11 and 13.

11 Location: feature content and segmental status

The designation of location as a major phonological category in sign language is unquestioned. Clear evidence is presented in Chapter 8, where the ASL minimal pair UGLY, SUMMER, distinguished only by some feature of location, is illustrated in Figure 8.2b. Like hand configuration, the location category is made up of subcategories with different characteristics. In particular, the major body area (such as the head) remains constant within a morpheme, while different subareas (such as the forehead or the chin) may have two different specifications in that domain (Sandler 1989). This categorization, too, is widely accepted. There is, however, one area of controversy with respect to locations that may be stated in terms of the following two views: (1) locations are a sequential segment type (as consonants are in spoken language); or (2) locations are a category on a par with hand configuration in a single feature hierarchy (like the place features of a segment in a Feature Geometry model). In this chapter, we will demonstrate the category-internal organization about which there is a consensus. We adopt the Hand Tier framework to represent it, making certain changes from the original model. The more controversial issue and what is at stake in it are laid out in the conclusion to the chapter. As this issue is related to the notion of syllables in sign language, it will be taken up again in Chapter 14.

11.1 Two classes of location features

A robust generalization with respect to locations is that there is only one major body location per morpheme (Battison 1978, Stokoe 1960). Yet the hand moves to articulate a sign, with the result that in some sense it articulates two locations, the beginning and the ending locations. For example, in the ASL sign IDEA, repeated in Figure 11.1 for convenience, the major body area is the head, while the beginning and ending locations are: (1) in contact with the forehead and (2) at a small distance in front of the forehead, respectively.

There are two different ways to account for these facts. One is to propose that there is only one location in a morpheme, and that the

Figure 11.1 IDEA (ASL)

Figure 11.2 DEAF (ASL)

hand moves in some direction with respect to it, i.e., that there is a direction or path feature, such as 'toward' or 'away' (Stokoe 1960, Brentari 1990, 1998). The other is the position we adopt here, representing IDEA with two distinct locations (Liddell and Johnson 1989 [1985], Sandler 1989). One reason for our choice is that it provides a unified representation for signs like IDEA and signs like DEAF, repeated in Figure 11.2. DEAF, like IDEA, also has the head as its major body area. But here the first location is at the cheek, while the second is at the chin. Both signs are represented with the same LML structure.[1]

In order to capture the generalization that there is only one major body area, this model divides the location category into two features classes: place, which is the major body area, and setting (Sandler 1989). The place category includes the unary features [head], [trunk], [non-dominant hand], and [arm]. As there is only one per morpheme and usually only one per sign, place is multiply associated, as shown in (1). Place is a category of location, and as such it is associated to the L segments in representations. Its features spread to the intervening M phonetically. The bare bones of the hand configuration category are shown here as a reminder of the rest of the structure. There is a single class of setting features that may characterize any place – in the same way that the same finger position features (e.g., [open] or [closed]) can characterize any specification of selected fingers.

[1] The Hand Tier representation offered here contrasts with both Liddell and Johnson's Move–Hold model and Brentari's Prosodic model (Brentari 1998), which both assume IDEA and DEAF represent two different types of signs with distinct types of representations.

(1) Representation of the place category

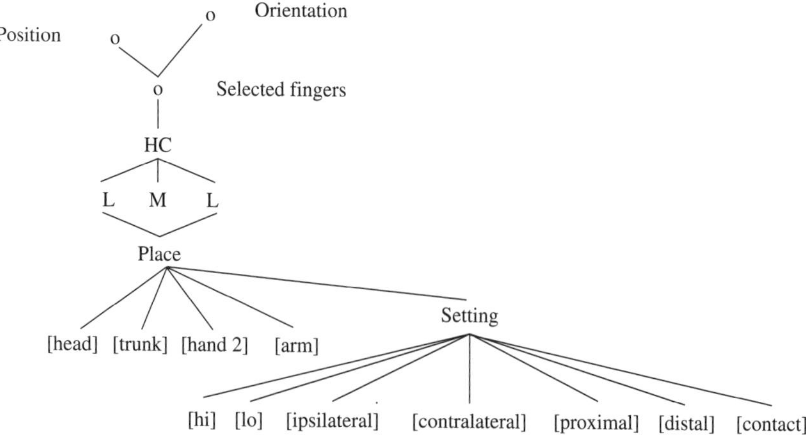

The features [hi, lo, ipsilateral, contralateral, proximal, distal, contact] are binary in the original model (Sandler1989), in which "mid" or "central" or "medial" settings are represented as [-hi, -lo], [-ipsi, -contra], and [-prox, -dist], respectively, following spoken language binary feature theory. Here we make the assumption that all features are unary, and that the values "mid," etc., are to be represented through combinations of unary features in dependency relations instead, as explained in the previous chapter. HEAD and LIST are illustrated in Figure 11.3, and partially represented in (2). Instead of positing settings like "ipsilateral temple" and "chin" for the sign meaning HEAD in ASL, and "fingers" and "heel" of the non-dominant hand for the sign meaning LIST, the same height features are used to characterize both signs: [hi] and [lo]. [h2] stands for the non-dominant hand, the place feature of LIST. This analysis and representation significantly cut down and constrain the location feature inventory and feature combinations.

(2) Distinct place features for HEAD and LIST

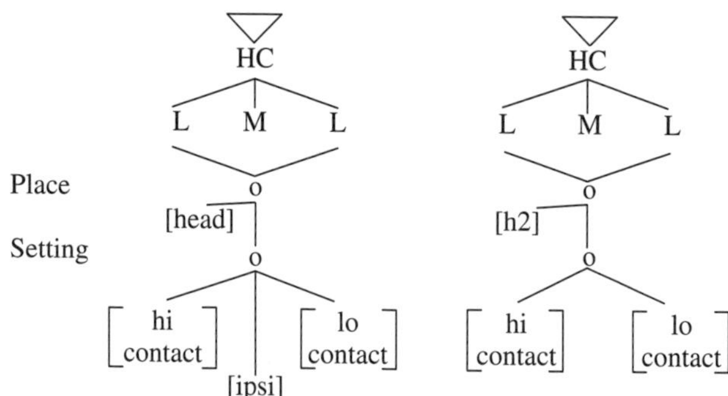

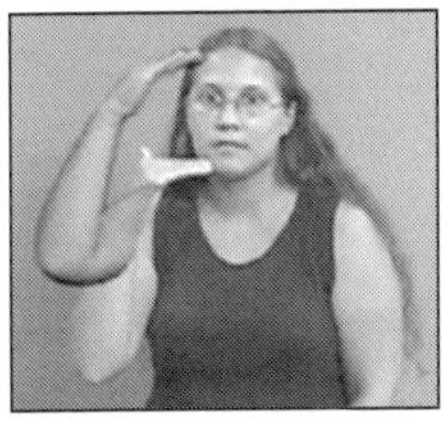

a. HEAD (ASL)

b. LIST (ASL)

Figure 11.3 Signs with distinct place features and the same setting features: [hi] and [lo]

A sign like IDEA, illustrated in Figure11.1, is of similar form. The main difference is that only one of the settings involves contact with the place; the other is a short distance in front of it, as partially represented in (3).

(3) Place representation of IDEA

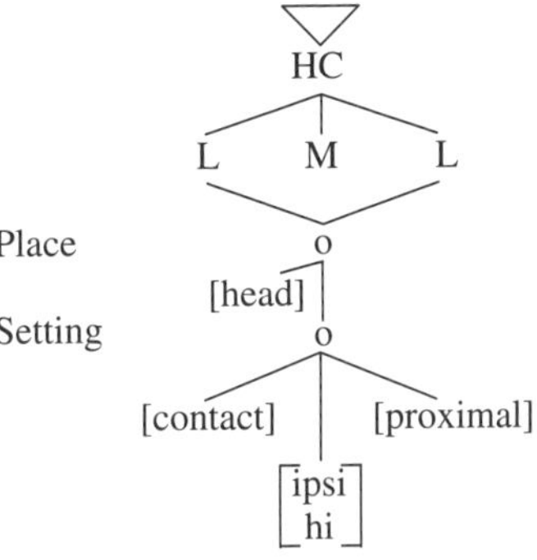

The model also shows which features are invariant across a morpheme, and which are not: the parameter that has different specifications in each location (i.e., the height, laterality, or distance features) branches from the setting node. In HEAD and LIST, the height features branch; in IDEA, the distance features branch. Setting features that are invariant like [ipsi, hi] in IDEA do not branch. But note that in HEAD and LIST, [contact] is not represented as branching, despite the fact that each location is characterized by contact. This is in order to distinguish signs with two contacts like these from signs with continuous contact across movement as well, like CLEAN, represented in Chapter 13, Figure 13.7.

The representation here, in which place is constant and setting features may branch, is essentially a mirror image of the HC representation, in which the selected finger node is constant, while its dependents, finger position or orientation, may branch. And as with those categories, the branching features must link to the L timing units because they may truncate independently of the major place feature under certain morphological operations, such as compound reduction (discussed in Chapter 9, Section 9.4) or negative incorporation (discussed in Chapter 14, Section 14.5).

In bimorphemic signs, such as compounds, with two major body areas, each location has its own place specification.[2] Because of the place constraint introduced in Chapter 1, stating that a morpheme may have only one place of articulation, any sign represented with two places of articulation is revealed to be bimorphemic. An example is BELIEVE, formed from THINK and MARRY, and illustrated in Chapter 9, Figure 9.11. In simplified form, emphasizing the individual place specifications, BELIEVE is represented in (4). Although this reduced compound has only one HC specification (as a result of assimilation) and only one movement, and therefore has the general appearance of a canonical monomorphemic sign, the presence of two place specifications gives away its bimorphemic origin.

(4) Representation of Place in the lexicalized compound, BELIEVE

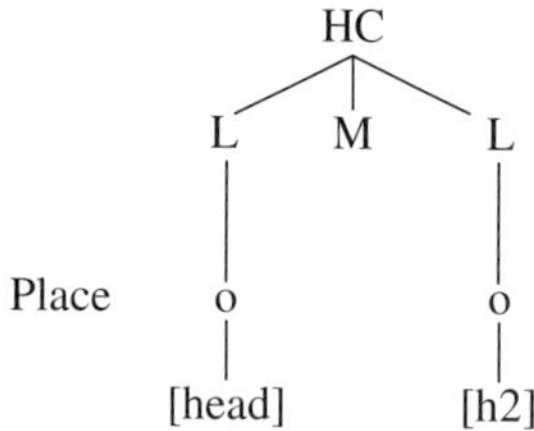

This model makes two testable predictions: (1) that finer setting distinctions (such as a setting somewhere between the ipsilateral temple and the center of the forehead) will not be minimally contrastive within a sign language and (2) that features such as [high], [ipsilateral], etc. will figure in phonological processes, to the exclusion of specifications such as "cheek" or "chin" that are posited by other models.

The first prediction, while promising because we know of no counter-evidence, remains to be thoroughly tested on a variety of sign languages. There is some suggestive evidence for the second prediction, that processes will refer to features of laterality or height rather than to specific phonetic settings like cheek or chin. The evidence comes from metathesis in ASL (Liddell and Johnson 1989 [1985]), a process which also supports the division of locations into two categories, place and setting. As discussed in Chapter 9, Section 9.2, metathesis works in the following way. Signs that are characterized by contact on two different settings within the same place of articulation fit the structural description for this process. An example is the

[2] The model shown here is different in some respects from the original Hand Tier model. In particular, settings are subordinate to place here, while they were sisters in the earlier model. This change is in the spirit of van der Hulst (1993), which proposes that setting is a dependent of place, and it is compatible with the feature geometry approach of the Hand Tier model, in the sense that settings are a refinement of place.

sign for DEAF, from the sentence, FATHER DEAF ('father is deaf'), shown in Chapter 9, Figure 9.5. In this sequence, DEAF is signed in its citation form. If a sign such as this one is preceded by a sign closer to the second setting (here, the ipsilateral side of the chin), such as MOTHER, then the two settings are reversed.

Metathesis also applies to signs made elsewhere on the body, such as the chest. An example is the sign COMMITTEE, shown in Chapter 9, Figure 9.2. In citation form, it is normally signed by making contact first on the contralateral side of the chest, and then on the ipsilateral side. If this sign occurs after a sign articulated on the ipsilateral side of the chest, such as VOLUNTEER, then it may metathesize. Metathesis is triggered by signs that make contact at high and low settings on a place as well, such as DEAF or HOME. However, the two settings must be on the same place of articulation. The process does not occur if the two settings are on different places of articulation, such as the (lexicalized) compound MAN, which contacts the head and the trunk.

To clarify the advantage of this model, consider first the fact that signs can metathesize whether they are made on the head or the trunk, provided the settings are [high], [low], or [contralateral], [ipsilateral]. In order to state the process in the most general way, to account for metathesis of DEAF and COMMITTEE with the same rule, the metathesis rule should refer to these settings, and not to specific (phonetic) locations like cheek or chest. More support for the use of a single set of setting features is seen in Negative Incorporation; described in Chapter 14, Section 14.5, and footnote 12 in that chapter.

Furthermore, the metathesis rule is constrained to apply only where the contacts are made within the same body area. This is evidence that major body areas are seen by the phonology as distinct from settings, a distinction later adopted by other models as well (Brentari 1998, van der Hulst 1993, 1996). Finally, the rule as it applies in ASL requires the sign to have two locations with [contact], providing evidence for the existence of this feature. The metathesis rule, then, provides evidence for several aspects of the model: the separation of place from setting; the dominance of place over setting in the hierarchy; the use of the same setting features dominated by different places of articulation to characterize different locations; and positing [contact] as a phonological feature.

11.2 A 3-D hierarchy of signing spaces

A novel and intriguing approach to location is introduced in Uyechi (1996 [1994]). That work proposes that the visual phonology of sign languages is inherently different from the auditory phonology of spoken languages, and should be investigated entirely on its own, without the contamination of theories based on spoken language. Uyechi proposes that there are three different signing spaces, inhabiting a nested structure. Local Signing Space (LSS) is the space occupied by the hand in a lexical sign. For example, the ASL sign LOOK-AT requires specification of a particular position and orientation of the hand in local signing space. Morphological specification of the spatial path, as in verb agreement, is represented in Global Signing Space (GSS). To sign 'I look at you,' for example, the Global Signing Space must indicate the spatial relation of the hand with respect to the signer and the addressee. At the discourse level, where areas of space can be used to designate different discourse topics, and where the whole body may shift its spatial perspective to indicate different points of view, another space obtains: Discourse Signing Space (DSS). If the signer assumes the point of view of a third person looking at another third person, for example, the body shift must be represented in Discourse Signing Space. Schematically, these spaces are seen as nested in a three-dimensional hierarchy, as shown in (5).

(5) Hierarchy of signing spaces (Uyechi 1996 [1994])

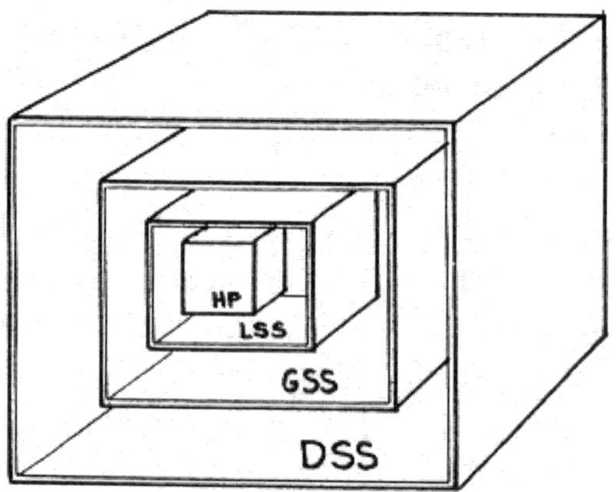

The notion of three independent yet interdependent spaces is compelling on the intuitive level. It reflects the fact that the articulating hand retains the features of LSS when it is implanted in GSS, and both the hand and the articulating arm retain their spatial features as they are implanted in DSS.

This conception of the space utilized in signing highlights a unique problem in the phonological treatment of locations in sign languages. Notice that only the Local Signing Space is required to be represented as part of a sign in the lexicon. Global Signing Space and Discourse Signing Space are only relevant for the syntactic and discourse levels. But these locations in space are unlike the syntactic aspects of words in spoken language, such as agreement markers, or discourse-related elements, such as anaphoric pronouns – all of which are represented phonologically in the same way as any other form in the oral modality. The locations of the verb agreement or classifier systems in sign language defy phonological characterization, as they can be designated at any point in the signing space. It seems that the best we can hope for is a representation that designates a linear position for locations where this is predictable (as in verb agreement; see Chapter 3), and leaves the precise locations to the interpretive devices like coindexation. Uyechi's model is instructive in distinguishing differences in the use of space at different levels of the grammar, and in revealing their interaction in the physical system. The linguistic use of space is discussed further in Unit 5.

11.3 Summary and unresolved issues

This chapter adopts a phonological view of locations that originated with the Hand Tier model: that the location articulated in a sign is a major phonological category, comprised of two subcategories, place of articulation and setting. As setting is a refinement of place, the two are represented hierarchically (following van der Hulst 1993; see footnote 2). The constraint that a morpheme may only have one place specification is represented by association of the place category to both (or all) locations. These place and setting features belong to a superordinate category in this model, locations, which are sequentially represented on a timing tier with movements.

The notion that there are two categories of features comprising locations – place features and setting features – has been incorporated into other models (Brentari 1998, van der Hulst 1993). One way in which these models differ from the Hand Tier model presented in this chapter is that they do not represent movement as a sequential position separating the two locations, a difference we will examine in Chapters 13 and 14. One aspect of locations is not likely to be resolved by any phonological model, and that is the specification of locations whose articulation is not related to a part of the body, but to referential loci in space. Such loci, assigned to Global Signing Space and Discourse Signing Space in Uyechi's model, were shown to be important in the verb agreement and classifier systems (Chapters 3 and 5). They involve a potentially infinite number of points in space established for different referents in a discourse. This use of location is modality specific – and universal within the sign language modality – and will be addressed in Unit 5.

With discussions of hand configuration and location behind us, we are now equipped to turn our attention to an element which is claimed by some researchers to belong to each of those two categories: the non-dominant hand.

12 The non-dominant hand in the sign language lexicon

A striking difference in the transmission system of languages in the two modalities is the existence of two anatomically identical articulators in sign languages: the two hands. Spoken languages have no such potential. On the assumption that the human organism will make full use of its articulatory system, within the relevant modality, in the service of communication, one would expect that both hands would be used in sign language. And indeed they are. But do they function linguistically as two independent articulators in the words of sign language, resulting in a significant phonological difference between the two modalities? Researchers are in agreement that the answer to this question is "no." The physiological existence of a second articulator generally does not mean that there are two completely independent articulators in the formation of words in the sign language lexicon. Rather, the non-dominant hand (h2) is always in some sense subordinate to other structural elements at the phonological level. This is the most important discovery about the non-dominant hand, as it offers novel insight into the relationship between phonetics, phonology, and the lexicon. What we see is a potential articulator with many degrees of freedom that behaves in a highly restricted way in the words of sign language lexicons.

But the non-dominant hand behaves quite differently within words than it does at other levels of structure, such as discourse and prosody. At the end of the chapter, we suggest that the seemingly anomalous articulator of sign languages conforms to aspects of grammatical organization that are not anomalous at all.

An independent question that is harder to answer is the one to which much of this chapter is devoted: does the non-dominant hand have two distinct phonological roles in sign language words, or only one? Is it sometimes an articulator and sometimes a place of articulation, as Stokoe asserted, or is it always essentially an articulator that is subordinate to the primary articulator, the dominant hand? Although the answers that have been proposed are more complicated than the question, and controversial as well, the debate over h2 is well worth considering, for three reasons. First,

a. FEEL

b. THRILL

Figure 12.1 One-handed versus symmetrical two-handed signs (ASL)

the main opposing positions are clearly spelled out and supported, and can be compared to each other directly. Second, the two models examined here reveal the way in which distinct phonological theories can influence sign language analysis. Finally, considering the two views raises interesting questions about the relation between phonetics and phonology. One theory, the one that we ultimately adopt, claims that while h2 is phonetically unitary, it has two distinct phonological roles. The other claims that h2 is a single element, both phonetically and phonologically.

12.1 The two-role theory

According to Stokoe's (1960) original analysis of the phonological components of ASL, there are descriptively two main types of two-handed signs. In one type, both hands articulate, and in the other, only one hand articulates. That is, the distinction is made on the basis of whether or not the non-dominant hand *moves* in the underived form of the sign. Compare THRILL, a two-handed sign, with FEEL, which is one-handed. The two signs are illustrated in Figure 12.1. According to the two-role theory, in signs in which both hands move, such as THRILL, h2 is a duplicate articulator, performing the same phonological role as h1. We will call signs like THRILL h2-S (symmetry) signs.[1]

In signs in which only h1 moves, h2 performs the phonological role of place of articulation. We refer to signs of this type as h2-P (place) signs.[2] In Figure 12.2 compare TOUCH, which has h2 as place of articulation, with SICK, in which the head is the place of articulation.

[1] Despite their similarity, FEEL and THRILL are *not* a minimal pair distinguished by use of one versus two hands. In FEEL, the dominant hand moves from a midpoint on the torso to a higher point, maintaining contact with the body. In THRILL, the hands start at about the same location as FEEL, but then they lose contact with the body and describe an arc shape outward while changing their orientation. In fact, signs minimally distinguished by number of hands are exceedingly rare across sign languages.

[2] Different types of two-handed signs have been called many things in the literature. We hope that the transparency of the labels we choose in this book offsets the potential confusion that the plethora of different terms might otherwise cause.

a. SICK

b. TOUCH

Figure 12.2 [head] and [h2] as places of articulation (ASL)

In order to understand these various roles of h2, let us consider two overall conditions on two-handed signs observed by Battison (1978 [1973]). Battison formulated the constraints on the non-dominant hand paraphrased in (1)–(2).

(1) The Symmetry Condition
states that (a) if both hands of a sign move independently during its articulation, then (b) both hands must be specified for the same handshape, the same movement (whether performed simultaneously or in alternation), and the specifications for orientation must be either symmetrical or identical.

(2) The Dominance Condition
states that (a) if the hands of a two-handed sign do not share the same specification for handshape (i.e., they are different), then (b) one hand must be passive while the active hand articulates the movement and (c) the specification of the passive handshape is restricted to be one of a small set: A,S,B,G,C,O.[3]
(Battison 1978 [1973], pp. 34–35)

This formulation leaves out the set of signs like ISL ALREADY (Figure 8.3) in which the non-dominant hand has the same handshape as the dominant hand, but it is passive – signs which Battison calls Type 2 signs. The two-role model categorizes such signs simply as h2-P signs, since they behave phonologically just like any other signs in which h2 does not move. Under this analysis, the Symmetry Condition is assumed to refer to h2-S signs and the Dominance Condition to refer to h2-P signs. If this is the case, however, the Dominance Condition requires revision, as follows in (3).

(3) Revised Dominance Condition
In signs in which h2 is passive (i.e., does not move), h2 must either be unspecified underlyingly, or it must be characterized by an unmarked handshape.

[3] The shapes that Battison designates as unmarked, based partly on the Dominance Condition, are A,S,B,G,C,O: . We've narrowed the list of unmarked shapes down to . See Sandler (1995b, 1996a) and Chapter 10, footnote 15 for an explanation.

Under the condition in (3), it is assumed that an underlyingly unspecified h2 takes on the shape of h1 by a redundancy rule (Sandler 1989, 1993a).

The argument about how to represent h2 is not about whether two general types exist at the descriptive level; no one disputes that. What has become a source of controversy is whether the non-dominant hand is playing two distinct roles phonologically, and therefore should be represented in different ways in models of sign language phonological structure, or whether it is fundamentally a single element from a phonological point of view, deserving of only a single representation.

The basic dichotomy of Stokoe is adopted in the Hand Tier model (Sandler 1989, 1993a). In the two-role view, the diagnostic for categorihood is whether or not h2 is active. In h2-S signs (like THRILL, Figure 12.1b), h2 is represented as an additional node in the HC hierarchy, essentially copying all the features of h1, and associating to all the same locations and movements. The representation in (4) requires h2 to have the same handshape as h1, and to articulate in the same way.[4]

(4) Hand Tier representation of h2-S signs (Sandler 1989, 1993a)

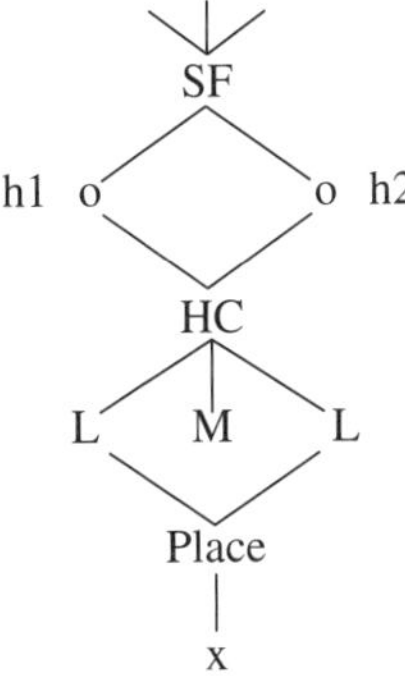

In h2-P signs (like TOUCH, Figure 12.2b), in which h2 functions as a place of articulation, h2 is simply represented as such, as the feature of place, just like the head or the trunk, as shown in (5). If its shape is different from that of h1, it must be specified. Otherwise it is left unspecified and a redundancy rule will copy the shape of the dominant hand.

[4] Blevins (1993) supports Sandler's (1989, 1993a) two-role view, but proposes a change in the model for h2-S signs, according to which h2 is a dependent of h1 rather than a sister to it. Like Brentari (1990, 1993), Blevins argues that h2 is weaker than h1, and that it is phonologically dependent on it, as h2 does not occur by itself in lexical signs, and it is synchronized with h1 if both hands move. She proposes the dependency representation for h2-S signs only, agreeing with Sandler that in h2-P signs, h2 is represented as a place of articulation.

(5) Hand Tier representation of h2-P signs (Sandler 1989, 1993a)

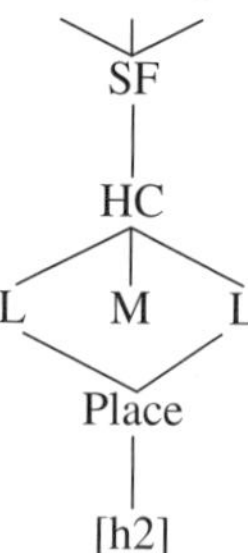

Some of the arguments for this model follow. Unless otherwise indicated, the arguments are from Sandler (1993a).

1. The Symmetry and Dominance Conditions on h2 ((2) and (3)) treat the non-dominant hand differently, depending on whether it moves (h2-S) or not (h2-P).
2. As Perlmutter (1991) points out, signs in which h2 functions as a place of articulation (h2-P signs) normally may not be specified for any other place of articulation. Signs in which h2 functions as a symmetrical articulator (h2-S signs) must have a place specification.[5]
3. Under morphological operations, h2 behaves like h1 in h2-S signs and like places of articulation in h2-P signs, as predicted by the model. For example, under inflection for Characteristic Adjective (Klima and Bellugi 1979, Padden and Perlmutter 1987), the non-dominant hand behaves differently, depending on whether the sign is one-handed, h2-S or h2-P.[6] The rule forms adjectives meaning 'characteristically X' from plain adjectives by reduplicating the movement of the sign in the following way. If the sign is underlyingly one handed, then it becomes h2-S, with the two hands moving in alternating fashion. If it is underlyingly h2-S, then the movement of the two hands does not become alternating. If it is underlyingly h2-P, then h1 reduplicates its movement, but h2 remains stationary, like any other place of articulation. Figure 12.3a shows QUIET, an h2-S sign. In the derived characteristic adjective, TACITURN (Figure 12.3b), both hands move the same way, as predicted from the representation in (4), as both hand (h) nodes are associated with the same L and M slots and their features. The sign ROUGH, shown in Figure 12.3c, is an h2-P sign. When it inflects for characteristic adjective to form CHARACTERISTICALLY CRUEL, shown

[5] Perlmutter (1991) presents a view of h2 that is similar to that of Sandler (1989, 1993a). The main difference is that Perlmutter proposes a different set of features for h2 in h2-P signs with the goal of including each feature set for h2-P as a different place of articulation. Since the handshapes available to h2-P are precisely the unmarked subset of those that may characterize h1, the Hand Tier model is able to capture this generalization without increasing the inventory of phonological features. It does so by using the same features for both hands.

[6] The Characteristic Adjective derivation is described in Chapter 4, Section 4.1.1.

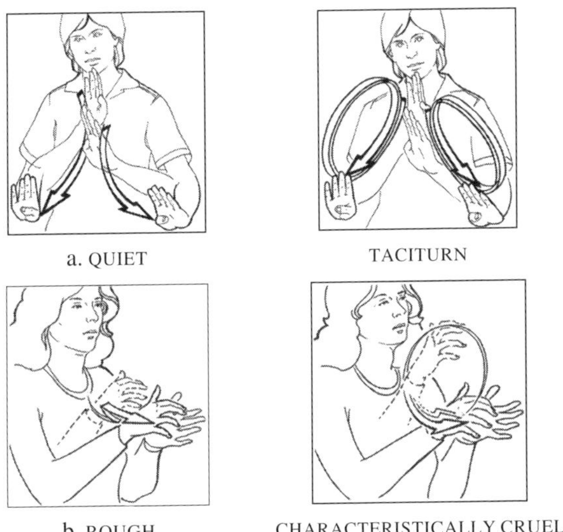

Figure 12.3 Characteristic Adjective formation (ASL) (Figure 12.3a reprinted with permission from Padden and Perlmutter 1987; Figure 12.3b © Ursula Bellugi, the Salk Institute)

in Figure 12.3d, only h1 moves, which is also predicted by the model, reflected in (5), where h2 is a place of articulation and not an articulator.[7]

4. In lexicalized compounds in which hand configuration assimilates (discussed in Chapter 10, Section 10.2), h2 assimilates together with h1 only in h2-S signs, but not in h2-P signs. For example, in FAINT, in which the second sign is an h2-S sign, the two hands assimilate. Assimilation of FAINT (pictured in Figure 10.11) is represented schematically in (6).

(6) Representation of hand configuration assimilation from an h2-S sign (FAINT)

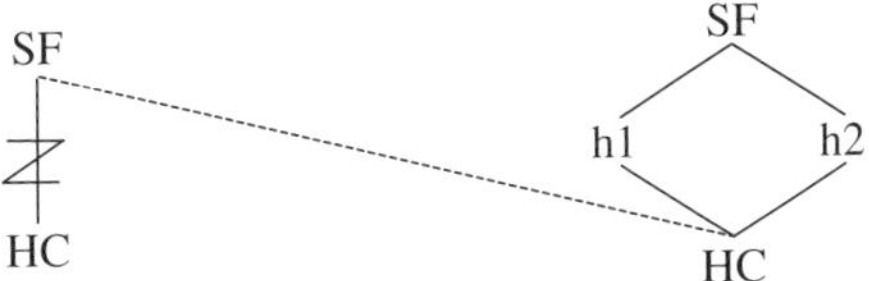

But in SLEEP^SUNRISE = OVERSLEEP, pictured in Figure 10.12, in which the second sign is an h2-P sign, only h1 assimilates. In this as in all h2-P signs, h2 is a static place of articulation. As the two-role theory predicts, h2 does not assimilate with h1 under compound reduction because it is represented under the place node (see (7)).

[7] Note that the non-dominant hand behaves the same in the Distributive inflection allomorphy described in Section 4.1.3, further supporting the Hand Tier two-role model.

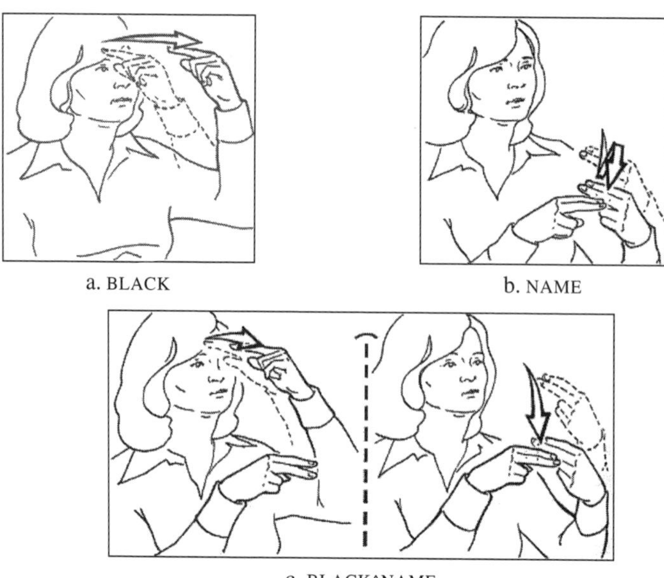

Figure 12.4 BLACK^NAME = BAD-REPUTATION (ASL) © Ursula Bellugi, the Salk Institute)

(7) Representation of hand configuration assimilation from an h2-P sign (OVERSLEEP)

5. Another rule, h2 anticipation (Liddell and Johnson 1986, Sandler 1989, 1993a), causes h2 in h2-P signs like BLACK^NAME to be present in the signing space at the beginning of the compound, as can be seen in the picture in Figure 12.4c. This spreading is different from the assimilation rules shown in (6) and (7), since in anticipation, h2 does not assimilate any features from the first sign; it only changes its temporal scope, appearing in the signing space while the first member of the compound is signed by h1.[8]
6. There are a few attested compounds in which the second member is an h2-S sign, while the first is one-handed; in these compounds the first sign becomes h2-S instead of one-handed – i.e., the symmetrical two-handedness of the second sign spreads to the first member. An example is SLEEP^CLOTHES = NIGHTGOWN in ASL. This spreading of two-handedness does not occur in compounds whose second member is a h2-P sign.

[8] In Chapter 15, we will see evidence from ISL that the domain of the anticipation rule is larger than the compound.

7. Weak Drop,[9] a process by which h2 is deleted from a sign (illustrated in Chapter 16, Figure 16.1), is far more common in h2-S signs than in h2-P signs, in adults (Battison 1974) and in children acquiring ASL (Siedlecki and Bonvillian 1993). The latter researchers attribute the stability of h2 in h2-P signs to the salience of place of articulation generally in the signing of young children, supporting the claim by the two-role model that h2 in h2-P signs is a place of articulation and not an articulator.

12.2 The one-role theory: a dependency model

The opposing position views h2 as a unified category with a single representation. Its proponents (Brentari 1990, Brentari and Goldsmith 1993, van der Hulst 1993, 1996) suggest that h2 is always in some sense a weaker version of h1, and that the representation should reflect this. This theory of h2 is also motivated phonologically, but relies on a different set of arguments. The strongest of these follow, from Brentari (1998) unless otherwise indicated:

1. In any type of two-handed sign, h2 may always either have the same shape as h1, or one of a subset of the shapes that may characterize h1. This is taken to be evidence for a general dominance relationship between the two hands (Brentari and Goldsmith 1993, Brentari 1998).[10]
2. There is a relatively large number of h2-P signs in which h2 has the same shape as h1. Indeed, it is only when h2 = h1 that h2 may have a marked handshape in h2-P signs. The argument is that this redundancy must have something to do with the fact that the hands are phonologically related to each other, even when only one is articulating.
3. There are five ASL signs which are known to have changed diachronically in a way that supports a relationship between the two hands in h2-P signs. These signs have remained h2-P signs, but h2 has assumed the handshape of h1. While the two-representation model of Section 12.1 can represent this change, that model does not predict that there should be interaction between the two hands in this way.
4. There are three signs in ASL which have changed diachronically from h2-S to h2-P signs; i.e., h2 historically behaved as a symmetrical articulator, with the same handshape as h1 and mirrored movement, but over time, h2 lost its movement and became a place of articulation. An example given in (Brentari 1998) is the sign DEFEAT.

[9] The process of h2 deletion was first described in Battison (1974) and was later given the name Weak Drop in Padden and Perlmutter (1987), where its interaction with morphological rules was investigated.

[10] This observation led to the proposal that h2 is a syllable coda (Brentari 1990, 1993).

5. One type of sign (e.g., SHOW) is somewhere in between the two types described above as h2-S (like THRILL, pictured in Figure 12.1b and represented in (4) above), and h2-P (like TOUCH, pictured in Figure 12.2b and represented in (5)). Though otherwise like h2-P signs, in the sense that h2 has a different configuration from that of h1 and one that is unmarked, SHOW-type signs involve uninterrupted contact between the two hands, so that h2 moves with h1, and does not remain stationary as in more typical h2-P signs. This suggests that movement of h2 does not clearly distinguish two distinct types of two-handed signs.
6. Brentari (1998) shows that a clear distinction between h2-S and h2-P signs cannot be made on the basis of Weak Drop. It is the particular lexical feature specifications of a sign that determine whether or not the rule of Weak Drop applies, and not whether the sign is h2-S or h2-P. The following types of signs may *not* undergo weak drop.[11]

   a. Signs with alternating movement (by definition, these are also h2-S).
   b. Signs with continuous contact between the two hands (h2-S or h2-P).
   c. Signs with *both* contact between the two hands at any point in the sign, *and* an orientation in which the two hands face each other (h2-S or h2-P).

7. It has been suggested that two of the processes affecting h2 in compounds, HC assimilation (represented in (6) and pictured in Figure 10.11), and h2 anticipation (pictured in Figure 10.13) may be reducible to a single process, in which h2 spreads regressively, regardless of whether the input is h2-S or h2-P (van der Hulst 1996).

Let us look at a model of h2 under this view, and then go on to further evaluate the two theories of h2. The representation proposed in van der Hulst (1996) reflects his one-role analysis, in accord with the empirical observations of Brentari (1990) and Brentari and Goldsmith (1993), and also determined by the overall theory of sign language structure that he adopts. Van der Hulst proposes that the type of structural relationship holding between the two hands that best explains their interaction is one of dependency: h2 is a dependent of h1 in all two-handed signs.[12] His theory of the structure of signs is guided by general principles of Dependency Phonology (Anderson and Ewen 1987) and by his view of the nature of head-dependent relations in all human languages (Dresher and van der Hulst 1998). Specifically, van der Hulst proposes that linguistic structures (morphosyntactic or phonological) are best represented in tree structures, in

[11] See Unit 5 for a suggestion that there are also semantic conditions on weak drop.
[12] Van der Hulst's dependency view has something in common with that of Blevins (see footnote 4), but he extends the dependency relation to all two-handed signs, h2-S and h2-P, whereas Blevins adopts Sandler's view that h2-P signs are in a different category.

which the character of non-terminal constituent nodes is determined by one of its daughters, which is called the head of the constituent. This is familiar from syntax, in which Noun Phrase nodes necessarily dominate nouns, for example. His theory further claims that each element of structure within a tree has two branches (i.e., is binary branching, van der Hulst 1989).

The theory is further developed in Dresher and van der Hulst (1998), in which it is claimed that there is a typology of asymmetries between heads and dependents. The relevant type of asymmetry for treatment of the non-dominant hand in his view is that in which the head and dependent are elements of basically the same type (like, e.g., two syllables forming a foot), but one is dominant. This dominance is reflected in the relative complexity of the two elements: the head is more complex than the dependent. In the case of syllables in a foot, the head is the stressed syllable (often more complex in its segment or timing structure); and in the case of the two hands, the dominant hand is more complex. The lack of complexity of h2 is expressed in the fact that h2 is limited to either copying the properties of h1, or to allowing a small unmarked subset of handshapes (Brentari 1990, 1993). Dresher and van der Hulst support the analogy with heads and dependents within a foot with the observation that the handshapes that may occur on h2 in h2-P signs are a subset of those that may occur on h1, just as the vowels that may occur in weak (dependent) syllables are a subset of those that may occur in strong (head) syllables.

This theory, developed on the basis of spoken language, provides the foundation for a model of the phonological structure of signs in general (van der Hulst 1993) and for that of two-handed signs in particular (van der Hulst 1996). Provided in (8) are representations of h2-S ("balanced" two-handed) and h2-P ("unbalanced" two-handed) signs, respectively, in the dependency model, slightly simplified. In the first representation, explanatory terms are added in parentheses for clarity.

(8) a. Dependency model representation of h2-S ("balanced") signs (van der Hulst 1996)

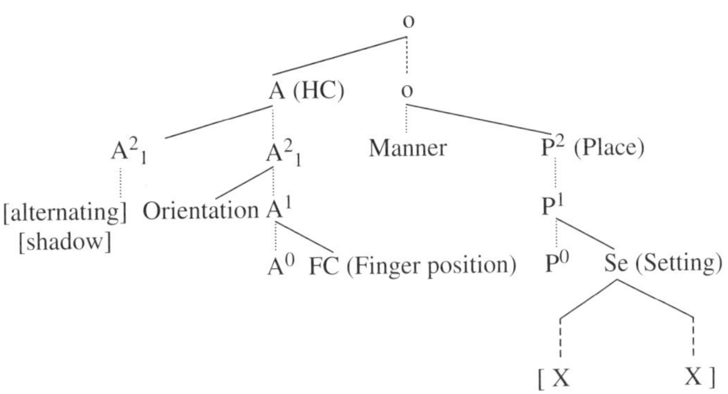

b. Dependency model representation of h2-P ("unbalanced") signs (van der Hulst 1996)

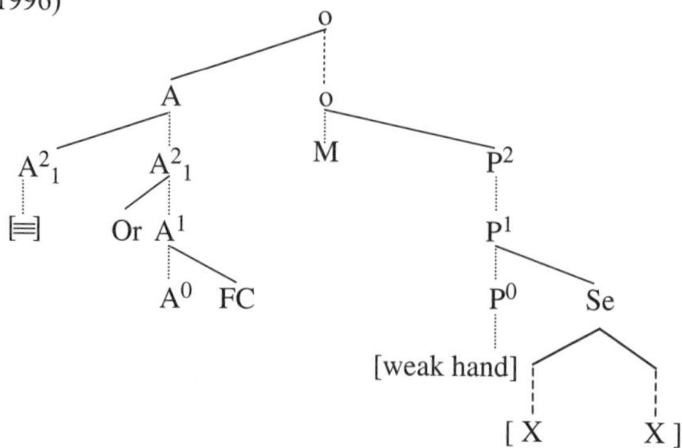

We cannot provide a detailed discussion of this model and its motivations here, as it would take our eye off the h2 ball, the topic of this chapter. Instead we describe only the general architecture of the model and then focus on the representation of h2.

This model represents a typical sign as branching off from a single root node at the top of the tree. The two main branches of structure are place (P) and hand or articulator (A). As the hand is more likely to spread or change in a sign, a property typical of dependents, it is hypothesized that hand is dependent, and place is the head. Manner (M) corresponds to movement in other models, and is deemed equivalent to spoken language manner features such as [continuant]. The model does allow for sequential timing units, however, represented as X slots with which phonological elements are aligned. Here, the settings are aligned with sequential X slots to create a path movement.

Let's now focus on the representation of the non-dominant hand. In both h2-S signs and h2-P signs, h2 is represented as a dependent of h1. In h2-S signs, the two hands (A) are coindexed, indicating that they are essentially the same in shape and articulation. In h2-P signs, h2 may optionally be further specified for its own handshape features, and the place branch of structure also specifies that h2 is the place of articulation. That is, in h2-P signs, the non-dominant hand is represented in two different places in the hierarchy, once as an articulator (A), and once as a place (P).

12.3 Advantages and disadvantages of each theory of h2

While each theory has points in its favor, each has undesirable consequences as well. We synthesize here what we see as advantages and disadvantages for each theory and its claims (see also van der Hulst and Sandler 1994), and go on to argue in favor of only one of them in Section 12.4.

The main advantage of the two-role (HT) theory is that it reflects the generalization attested to by the grammar that there are basically two types of two-handed signs, and that h2 behaves differently in each type. In h2-S signs (h2 has the same shape and same movement as h1), it behaves like h1 in the morphophonology, e.g., in processes like Characteristic Adjective and different types of spreading in lexicalized compounds. In h2-P signs (where h2 often has a different configuration from h1 and is normally static), h2 behaves like any place of articulation, remaining static and not affected by morphophonological processes affecting h1.

The disadvantage of the two-role model is that it does not predict that there will be any phonological interaction whatsoever between the two hands in h2-P signs. We have seen that there is such interaction, though marginal, diachronically. A few h2-P signs in ASL have become h2-S signs, and the handshape of several h2-P signs which were once different from the shapes of h1 have taken on the same shape as h1 over time. It is reasonable to hypothesize that many of these signs were originally asymmetrical in handshape and changed over time, a situation which appears anomalous in the two-role representation.

The advantages and disadvantages of the one-role theory are the mirror image of those of the two-role theory. The main advantage of the one-role theory (Dependency model of van der Hulst and Prosodic model of Brentari) is that it does reflect the fact that h2 may be influenced by h1 regardless of the type of two-handed sign it occurs in, i.e., even when h2 functions as a place of articulation.

In only one case has it been argued (by van der Hulst) that the actual phonological behavior of h2 in the distinct sign types might be collapsed – in the assimilation of h2 in compounds where the second member is an h2-S sign, and the spreading h2 in compounds where the second member is an h2-P sign. But this suggestion fails on closer examination. First, the details of the spreading are quite different in the two processes: one results in assimilation of handshape and orientation (shown in Figure 10.13); the other does not affect hand configuration at all, instead affecting only the timing of the appearance of h2. Not even the Dependency model can represent these two phenomena in a single coherent rule. In addition, the particular rule of hand configuration assimilation that assimilates orientation together with handshape applies only to compounds. The spreading behavior of h2 in h2-P signs is a different rule, applying at a higher prosodic level, as we show in Chapter 15, Section 15.2.

Another disadvantage of the one-role model is that it is actually a closet two-role model which forces a redundant representation of h2 in h2-P signs. In the representations in (8)b, h2 appears both under the articulator node and under the place node. This is disadvantageous insofar as it makes the unmotivated prediction that h2 will normally behave both like h1 and like a place in the same sign.

12.4 Phonology vs. phonetics, and the central consensus

Each of the two main schools of thought captures complementary generalizations, and neither offers an account of all of the data. We suggest that the reason for this complementarity in the two theories is a battle between the phonetics and the phonology of sign languages. Phonetically, there are two anatomically identical articulators, whose activity is motorically coordinated (Blevins 1993). This leads to certain symmetries, such as the existence of h2-S signs in the first place, assimilation of shape between the two hands, and diachronic overlap of function, emphasized in the Prosodic and Dependency one-role models. But phonologically, the system allows only one major articulator, possibly due to some abstract organizing principle that is at work regardless of physical modality (see Gijn et al. in press). The Hand Tier two-role model reflects the relevant generalization: when h2 is an articulator, it must be largely redundant; elsewhere, it's not an articulator at all. We view the generalizations motivating the two-role model – i.e., the behavior of h2 in lexical rules – as more phonological in nature, while those motivating the one-role model – e.g., diachronic interaction between the two hands – as reflecting the phonetics of the system. For these reasons, we opt for the two-role theory and the Hand Tier representations in (4) and (5) as a phonological model of h2.

What is missing is a detailed and well-motivated *phonetic* model of the sign in sign language that is phonologically informed, along the lines of the model of spoken language developed by Browman and Goldstein (1989). Such a model, and the research required to develop it, will help to better understand the interaction of the two hands.

This interesting disagreement should not obscure the consensus view that h2 is not an independent phonological element within the ordinary words of the ASL lexicon. That is, despite the fact that signed languages have at their disposal two anatomically identical articulators, the phonology of the *words* of the language only exploits one major articulator: the dominant hand. Considering the fact that spoken language has only one major articulator, the tongue, this generalization about sign language may reveal a fundamental modality-free organizing principle (Perlmutter 1991).[13,14]

[13] Spoken languages have additional articulators (e.g., the lips and the pharynx; see McCarthy 1988), but the tongue is certainly predominant.

[14] The model of Liddell and Johnson is an exception, however, as it implies that h2 is an independent articulator, and therefore misses the generalization that the behavior of h2 is far more constrained than that of h1.

12.5 The roles of the non-dominant hand beyond the lexicon

At the beginning of the chapter, we mentioned the assumption that the human organism is likely to make full use of the articulatory system at its disposal – predicting that both hands would be exploited by the system. And, despite the modest role of h2 in the lexicon, this expectation does not go unfulfilled. In fact, the non-dominant hand performs important tasks elsewhere in the grammar of sign languages: at the levels of discourse and of prosody. An example of the former is the role of h2 in classifier constructions, where it has morphemic status and phonological independence from the dominant hand (see Chapters 5 and 15, respectively). Within this system, the non-dominant hand may represent some referent with respect to which the dominant hand can interact throughout a whole chunk of discourse (see Chapter 6, Section 6.1). Even outside the classifier subsystem, the non-dominant hand can act like a secondary dominant hand for certain discourse effects, maintaining the hand configuration of a lexical sign that simultaneously backgrounds some aspect of a discourse. In such cases, the signal is carrying more than one word (or classifier morpheme) simultaneously.[15] The second grammatical role played by the non-dominant hand outside the lexicon is in the prosodic system. There, it delineates prosodic constituents at two levels of the prosodic hierarchy. This function of h2 is examined in detail in Chapter 15.

By contrasting the active role of h2 in other areas of the grammar with the redundancy that it exhibits in words of the lexicon, we arrive at an interesting hypothesis (Sandler 2002). The predictability and redundancy of h2 in sign language words may provide a perceptual cue to wordhood within the language, offering a significant advantage for language acquisition and for language processing.

[15] Other interesting ways in which h2 behaves independently at the level of discourse are discussed in Padden (1988 [1983]), Frishberg (1985), Zimmer and Patschke (1990), Brentari and Goldsmith, (1993), and in Emmorey and Falgier (1999).

13 Movement

All signs have movement in them – either a path made by the hand or hands as they go from one location to another, a change in handshape, a change in orientation, or some combination of these (Wilbur 1987, Stack 1988, Brentari 1990). In the classifier subsystem (introduced in Chapter 5), there is a sizeable inventory of movements, and a rich array of combinatory possibilities, both simultaneous and sequential. In words of the lexicon, the main focus of this chapter, the inventory of path movements is far more limited, and the possibilities for their combination strictly constrained. Yet they are part of the system, not only phonetically, but phonologically and morphologically as well, and many models of sign language phonology treat movement as an important phonological property of signs (e.g., Stokoe 1960, Liddell and Johnson 1989 [1985], Sandler 1989, 1993d, Brentari 1990, 1998, Perlmutter 1992, Wilbur 1993, 1999a). These investigators are in agreement about the importance of movement, but not about the way in which it is integrated into the phonology of sign language, and the following questions remain unresolved: how is movement instantiated in a sign, and how should it be represented in a model of sign language? Do movements constitute a sequential segment type, or do they characterize the sign as a whole? Are they like vowels, carrying the sonority of the sign language syllable?

The issue is especially interesting because movements, especially path movements, are often redundant; i.e., they are often no more than straight paths between two locations. This redundancy has even led some researchers to make different claims, either that movement is non-existent at the underlying level altogether (Nagahara 1988, Stack 1988, Hayes 1993, Uyechi 1996, Osugi 1997) or that it should not be considered a phonological primitive (Miller 1991, van der Hulst 1993, Channon 2002a, 2002b). Following Ahn (1990) and Wilbur (1993), van der Hulst (1993) proposes that all features that define the type of movement present in a sign belong to the category Manner, represented as characterizing the whole sign rather than as a sequential segment. Channon (2002a, 2002b) also refrains from representing movement as a segment type. In fact, her model takes the extreme position that the canonical monomorphemic sign has no internal sequential structure, that it is unisegmental.

The position to be supported here is that movements do exist as a phonological category, that their sequential position should be reflected in the representation, and that they define the sign language syllable. The first two of these issues are dealt with in this chapter; the syllable and the comparison of movements with vowels are taken up in Chapter 14. We begin by describing some common movements, and then provide some arguments for movement as a phonological category. After that, evidence for the sequential status of movements will be presented, completing the arguments for the model we adopt. A different model is then described, one that also assigns an important role to movement, but that motivates a non-sequential representation of the category – Brentari's Prosodic model. That model, which integrates all types of movement into one of the two major branches of structure in the sign, is contrasted with the LML model we adopt here. A summary and conclusion provide a transition to the next chapter, which focuses on syllables.

13.1 The movement category: preliminary description

The main kinds of movement found in lexical signs are path movement and internal movement. The latter can be broken down into handshape change and orientation change. These types and their combinations are illustrated in Figure 13.1. The examples are from ISL, but are typical of ASL and other sign languages as well.

The shape of path movements can be straight, arc, or, in ASL, '7,' the last used almost exclusively for initialized city names. Circling movement is considered a movement type by some researchers; others analyze circles as consisting of a sequence of arcs with different values for concavity (Sandler 1989, 1990, Corina 1990b). Different types of handshape and orientation changes result in an inventory of internal movements, such as hooking, flattening, releasing, squeezing, rubbing, twisting, nodding, circling, and swinging (Stack 1988, van der Hulst 1993).

Another kind of internal movement, called secondary, oscillating, or trilled,[1] involves uncounted rapid repetition of handshape or orientation change, or else finger wiggle.[2] Like the other kinds of internal movement, secondary movement may also occur either together with a path movement, or by itself, as shown in Figure 13.2.

[1] The term "trilled movement" was coined by Padden and Perlmutter (1987), who include in this category not only trilled internal movements as we do here, but uncounted, rapidly repeated path movements as well.

[2] Signs with secondary movement (rapidly repeated handshape change or orientation change) and no path movement (BIRD in Figure 13.2) are decidedly more common in ASL than in ISL, where they are hard to find at all. Finger wiggle is also more common in ASL than in ISL.

AT-THAT-MOMENT (ISL)
a. Path movement

TAKE-ADVANTAGE-OF (ISL)
b. Handshape change

DEAD (ISL)
c. Orientation change

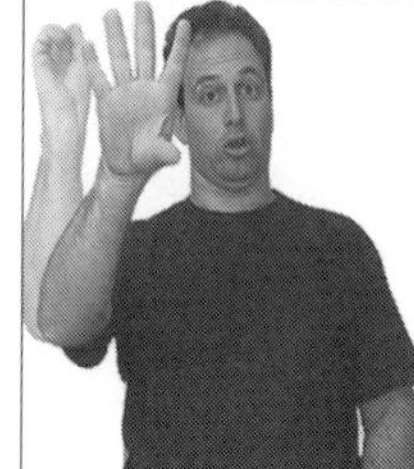
SEND (ISL)
d. Path movement plus handshape change

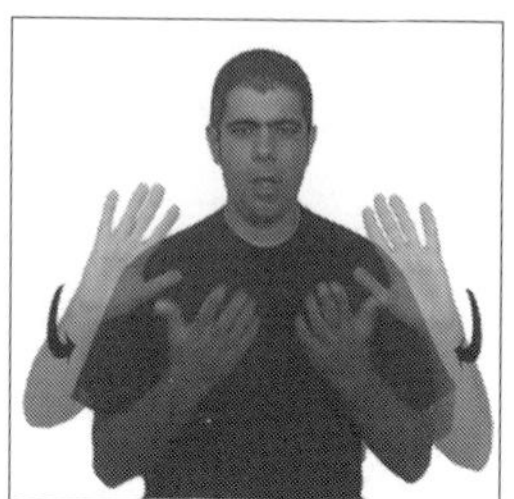
FAST (ISL)
e. Path movement with orientation change

Figure 13.1 Movement types

BUG (ASL)
a. Secondary movement: rapidly repeated finger curving

WORM
b. Secondary movement with path movement

Figure 13.2 Secondary movement with and without path movement

Perhaps the most fundamental argument for the significance of movements is this: signs are not well formed without them (Wilbur 1987, Stack 1988, Brentari 1990). This is important because of the surprising fact that it is phonetically possible to pronounce many, perhaps most, signs without their flowing straight or arc movements, and even to do so in a sequence, connecting them only with transitional movements in between. Normally, only one or two features of the setting, [hi]/[lo], [proximal]/[distal], or [ipsilateral]/ [contralateral], distinguish the first location from the last, so that the meaning of the sign would probably be retrievable if one setting is deleted and with it the sign's movement. Such movementless signs can be strung together into sentences, connected only by phonetic transitional movements, and can even be quite intelligible, though annoying to signers (p.c., Ted Supalla). No natural sign language we know of makes general use of such signs. The movements in the signs of natural sign languages are an intrinsic part of the sign. Phonetically, these movements are different from transitional movements, and phonologically, they carry both lexical and morphological contrasts.

13.2 Evidence for a movement category

One way of determining the nature of the movement within a sign phonetically is by comparing it with transitional movements between signs. A measure that has been applied is the tracking of handshape change in signs that have both path movement and handshape change, and comparing that change to transitional handshape changes occurring during the movement between signs. This measure determined that the timing of the handshape change in ASL is systematically more evenly distributed across the co-occurring path movement within signs than between them (Brentari and Poizner 1994, Brentari, Poizner, and Kegl 1995). These findings provide phonetic evidence for distinguishing lexical from transitional movement. According to Brentari (1998), this result also unifies handshape change and path movement in a single movement category, a point to which we will return.

There is phonological evidence for lexical movements as well. The next several arguments are from Sandler (1996b). First, movement features can be contrastive. The ASL minimal pair YOU and INSULT, for example, illustrated in Figure 13.3, is distinguished by movement features. Partial representations of these signs are given in (1). As we explain below, the feature [straight] is the unspecified default movement feature.[3]

[3] In addition to the shape of the movement path, there are other small differences in the articulation of YOU and INSULT, such as the direction in which the fingertip is facing and the orientation of the hand. These features are all clearly connected phonetically

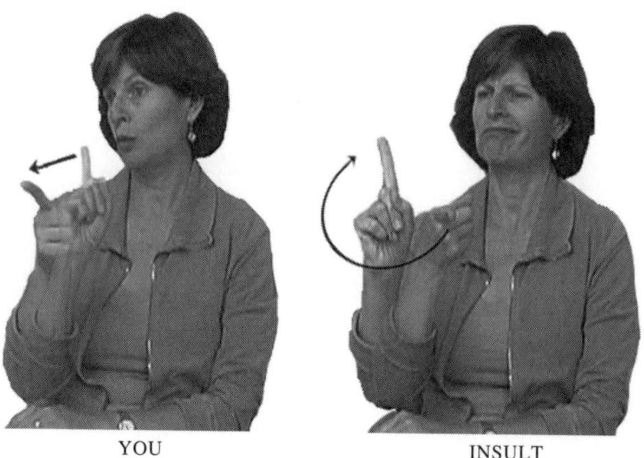

YOU INSULT

Figure 13.3 Two ASL signs distinguished by path movement features

(1)

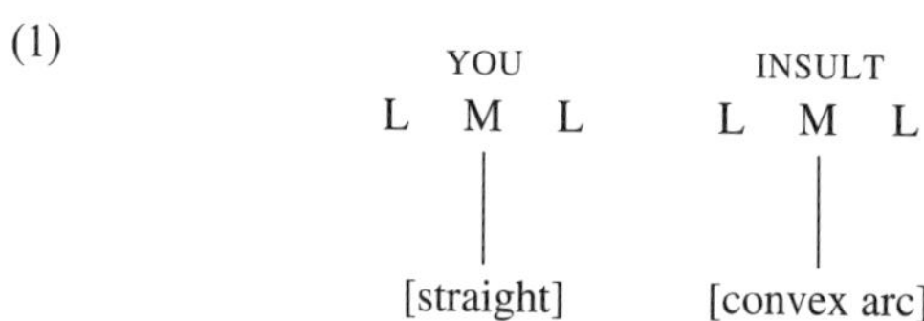

A minimal pair in ISL distinguished by arc shape is NEXT-YEAR (concave) and THIS-YEAR (convex), pictured in Figure 13.4. Single movement in a sign is sometimes contrastive with lexically specified double movement, as in (ISL) LUCK (single movement) and LOAN (double movement), shown in Figure 13.5.

Another argument for a movement category in ISL specifically comes from the behavior of movement features under inflection for multiple agreement. ISL verbs specified for any feature belonging to the class of movement features, [arc, tense, restrained], are subject to a constraint that blocks the multiple agreement inflection (Sandler 1996b). [arc] is a shape feature; [tense] means muscle tension in producing the movement; [restrained] refers to shortened and doubled movement, and is specified in all signs that are lexically (not morphologically) reduplicated (like (ISL) LOAN above).

ISL verbs that take singular agreement marking also take multiple agreement marking, characterized by a horizontal arc, as illustrated for the sign SUPERVISE in Figure 13.6a and 13.6b. This process takes place *unless* the verb base is specified for a movement feature, like the sign GUARD in Figure 13.6c, specified for [restrained] movement. That is, GUARD is an agreeing verb (see Chapter 3, Section 3.2), but does not take the multiple marking because it is underlyingly specified for a movement feature. Since both the blocking features and the blocked feature ([horizontal arc]) are features that characterize movements, it can be argued

(see Chapter 10, Section 10.4.2 for relevant discussion), but a fully satisfactory analysis of their interrelation and (under-) specification awaits further research.

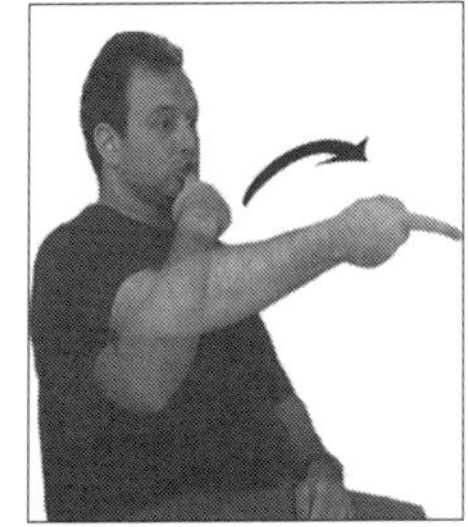
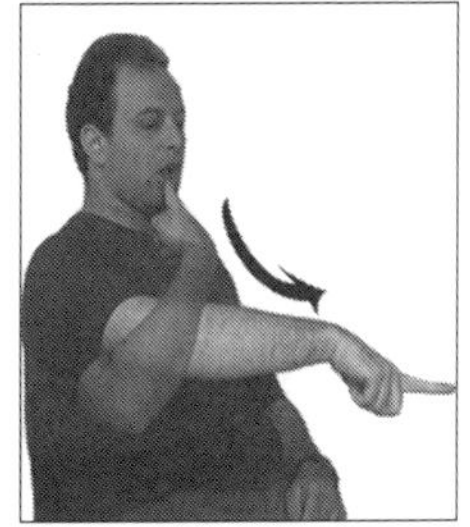

a. NEXT-YEAR (concave) (ISL) b. THIS-YEAR (convex) (ISL)

Figure 13.4 Minimal pair distinguished by arc shape

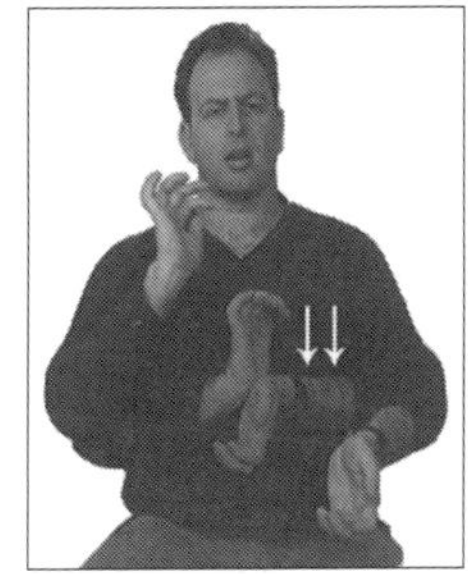

a. LUCK (one movement) (ISL) b. LOAN (two movements) (ISL)

Figure 13.5 Minimal pair distinguished by number of movements

a. SUPERVISE (uninflected)

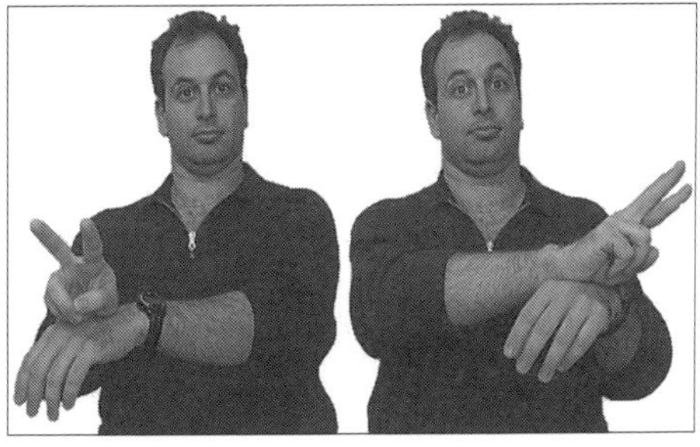

b. SUPERVISE-ALL (multiple form)

c. GUARD (uninflected)

Figure 13.6 Evidence for a movement category: lexical double movement in GUARD blocks the multiple form

that the relevant constraint here refers to a phonetically unified movement category (Sandler 1996b).

While the multiple form on signs specified for movement, like GUARD, is blocked, it is possible to pronounce it, either by rearticulating the specified movement across the horizontal arc, or by coalescing the two types of movement together, which result in more complex path movements. Apparently, it is this complexity of movement that is being avoided. These arguments are based on ISL, but there is some indication that ASL behaves the same way. ASL multiple agreement takes a similar form to that of ISL, and, while not all movement features have been checked in verbs of that language, Padden (1988 [1983]) reports that one of them, the feature [arc], blocks multiple agreement inflection in ASL, as it does in ISL.

Further research on all proposed movement features is called for. But the weight of the evidence presented suggests that these generalizations must be stated on a phonological movement category of some type, arguing against proposals that deny the existence of such a category.

Phonologists who accept this view have proposed different types of representations to accommodate it. There are essentially two camps: those who think that movement should be associated with a sequential position in representations, and those who do not.

13.3 Representation of movement as a sequential segment

Models that propose a sequential position for movements are the MH model (Liddell and Johnson 1989 [1985]), the Hand Tier model (Sandler 1989), and the Moraic model (Perlmutter 1992, 1993). These researchers adopt the sequential theory of sign language structure described in Chapter 9, Section 9.2. In all three models, there are two major segment types, those that move (Ms in all three models) and those that don't (holds, locations, or positions, respectively). There are differences among the models in the way in which an element qualifies as a segment, especially a non-movement segment, and we abstract away from those differences here.

One argument for representing movement as a sequential segment type is the distribution of the feature [contact]. This feature may occur on either location segment (creating either an initial contact or a final contact sign), on the movement segment of a sign (creating a so-called brushing movement), or on all segments (for so-called continuous contact), as illustrated in Figure 13.7 and represented in (2).[4] This distinction

[4] See Channon (2002a) for a discussion of the distribution of [contact] within a monosegmental model of the sign.

a. NUDE
Contact during movement

b. SHINY
Contact on first location

c. TOUCH
Contact on second location

d. CLEAN
Contact on all segments

Figure 13.7 ASL signs with discrete contact on one location segment, a movement segment, or all segments

is argued to support both the existence of a sequential movement segment as well as a sequential representation of movements and locations (Sandler 1989).

(2) Representations of signs with contact on:
a. the movement segment (NUDE)
b. the initial location (SHINY)
c. the final location (TOUCH)
d. all three segments (CLEAN)

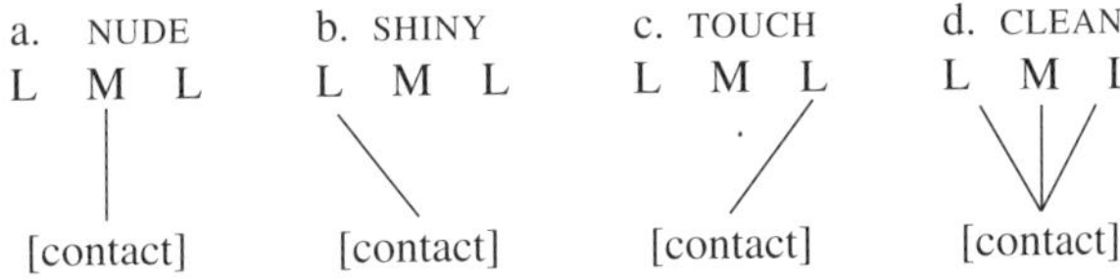

Another argument for the validity of a movement category is the fact that movements must be referred to by morphological operations. For example, in Israeli Sign Language, the movement segment is geminated (temporally lengthened) in the intensive form of verbs and adjectives, as represented in (3a) (Sandler 1993b), resulting in a movement that is longer in duration. In the same language, the final location is lengthened in the continuative form, shown in (3b), resulting in a geminated location, i.e., a hold.

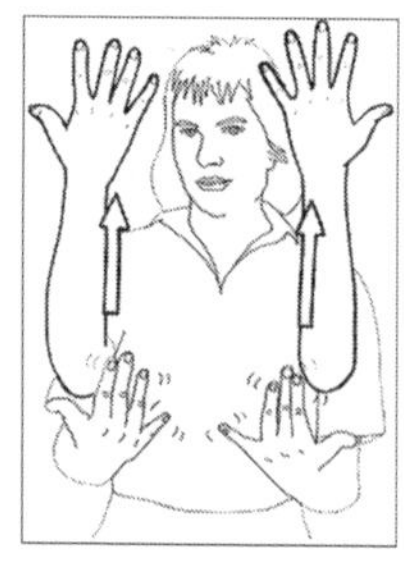

GO-UP-IN-FLAMES (ASL)

Figure 13.8 A sign with path movement and secondary movement (reprinted with permission from Perlmutter 1993)

(3) Gemination in two ISL forms

a. Movement in Intensive

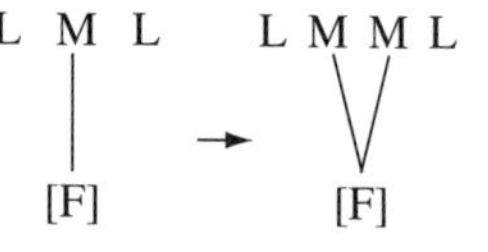

b. Location in Continuative

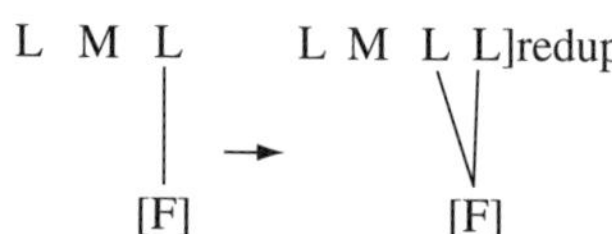

In ASL as well, characteristics of movements are contrastively altered in the temporal aspect system (Klima and Bellugi 1979, Newkirk 1981) and in certain adjectival derivations. For example, the feature [arc] is added (among other changes) to the movement segment to derive Characteristic Adjectives as well as the Durational and Continuative aspects (Sandler 1990, 1993d).

The distribution of secondary movement under phrase-final lengthening, described by Perlmutter (1992, 1993), provides another argument in favor of an M segment. He observes that secondary movement, such as rapid repetition of handshape change or wiggling of the fingers, co-occurs with the path movement in any syllable that has a path movement, as in GO-UP-IN-FLAMES, Figure 13.8. But signs without path movement may also be characterized by secondary movement. The wiggle or other secondary movement is associated with the static location in such signs as GERMANY, shown in Figure 13.9.

Under phrase-final lengthening, accounted for by mora insertion in Perlmutter's analysis, the secondary movement persists on the lengthened segment in signs with no path movement (P(osition)-only, using Perlmutter's notation), but not in PMP (LML) signs.[5]

[5] Perlmutter represents GO-UP-IN-FLAMES as MP. According to the analysis of location in Chapter 11, this sign has the form LML (equivalent to PMP in Perlmutter's model). This difference does not affect the point made here, because in both representations, the sign ends with a non-movement segment.

GERMANY (ASL)

Figure 13.9 A sign with secondary movement only (reprinted with permission from Perlmutter 1993)

According to the analysis, this behavior can be explained by associating secondary movement with the M segment in signs like GO-UP-IN-FLAMES, and with the P segment in signs like GERMANY. The process is shown in (4).

(4) Phrase-final lengthening (adapted from Perlmutter 1992)

These phenomena are made clear by a sequential representation that includes movements.

Finally, some temporal aspects in ASL augment signs that have no internal movement underlyingly to fill an LML template in which the movement is prespecified with an arc movement, as illustrated in Chapter 3, Section 3.3. Such signs, like STUDY or DIRTY (formally similar to GERMANY) when not inflected for aspect, have finger-wiggle-internal movement but no path movement, and they are represented with only one L segment, as shown in (5)a. Under continuative, they take the form in (5)b.

(5)

The evidence presented indicates that there is such a thing as a movement category and that typical signs have path movements situated sequentially between two locations, as shown in (6). In the spirit of Sandler (1995c, 1996a) and the model set out in Chapter 10,

Section 10.4, we leave out two default features from the representation: [straight] and [concave]. We assume that [straight] is the default path shape, so that a sign with a straight path movement will have no feature represented. If [arc] is the shape, we assume that [concave] is the default arc shape. The marked feature [convex] is represented as a dependent of [arc].

(6) Path movement in the Hand Tier model

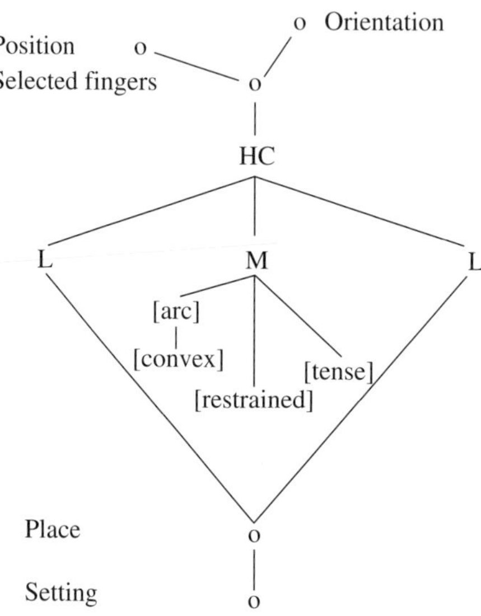

13.4 Another proposal: movement as prosody

The Prosodic model of sign language phonology views movement as the principle determinant of class membership within a sign, but unlike the Hand Tier model, the Prosodic model denies it any sequential position in the representation (Brentari 1998). In the theory behind the Prosodic model, movements are considered very important, providing necessary salience to the sign. Brentari offers additional phonological arguments for a category that unifies path and internal movement. One is the uniform behavior of internal and path movement in the morphological process of Delayed Completive. In Chapter 9, Section 9.2, it was shown that the Delayed Completive morpheme is a sequence of two elements: first, finger wiggle (or tongue wag), and second, a mouth movement corresponding to the spoken syllable *op*. The wiggle or wag is aligned with the first segment or timing unit of the base sign, while the mouth movement distributes itself over the lexical movement of the sign – crucially, regardless of whether that movement is path or hand internal.

This is compelling evidence for sequential structure as well as for a movement category that includes both path and hand-internal movement, especially in light of the fact that either type of movement is sufficient for the well-formedness of a sign. The theory behind the Hand Tier model also recognizes path and internal movement as a single category, but does not represent it in a unified way in the model. The Prosodic model adopts the position that movement should be represented as a unified category.

In order to unify the representation of movement, Brentari's Prosodic model divides the phonological features of ASL into two major categories: (1) inherent features, all features that characterize the whole sign and have no internal sequencing or other dynamic quality; and (2) prosodic features, those that result in movement on the surface. In some cases, following Wilbur and van der Hulst, movement falls out from sequencing of features. Specifically, there are the finger position handshape features, orientation features, and setting features of location. The two features that do not involve sequencing in the Prosodic model but are still considered prosodic features are the path features of direction (toward or away from the place of articulation) and of tracing (following some other path with respect to the place of articulation, such as the arc path traced by the hand in neutral space in front of the body, in the ASL sign RAINBOW).[6]

The representation proposed in the Prosodic model is shown in (7). For clarity, we have chosen a partial representation, including only main feature classes but not including either smaller classes (such as joints and fingers under the h1 articulator node) or terminal features (such as [all] under the finger node). The main innovation of the Prosodic model is the division made in the model between static ("inherent") and dynamic ("prosodic") properties of signs.

[6] Brentari (1998) proposes the following movement features for ASL: [direction], [tracing], [pivot], [repeat], and [alternating]. Behind Brentari's feature inventory lies a different analysis of the underlying properties of signs from that of Sandler's Hand Tier model. For example, the inventory proposed by Brentari includes a [direction] feature, motivated by an asymmetry in movement under reduction in compounding. Some simple path movements do not delete in compounds, while other phonetically identical ones do. On this basis, Brentari argues that the signs that reduce (often but not always signs with final contact) have no underlying movement and that the surface movement in such signs is epenthetic. Those signs that block reduction in compounds are assigned the movement feature, [direction]. See Brentari (1998) for motivation of movement features in the Prosodic model. In the Hand Tier theory, all movements along a path are represented the same way: as setting changes.

(7) The Prosodic model with branching setting features for one type of path movement (adapted from Brentari 1998)

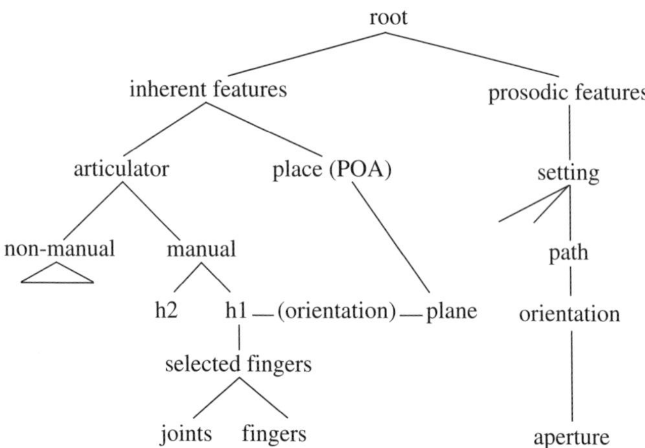

In this model, categories and their features are separated from the movement that they articulate. Place is segregated from setting in different branches of structure; inherent orientation from orientation change,[7] and finger position (joints, fingers) from handshape change (aperture change). Articulators and their configurations are thus segregated from the movements they make. A further characteristic of this model is that path movement is seen as independent of setting change, a point we will return to below.

One of the ways in which signs are made more prominent serves as a central motivation for the model. Under certain discourse conditions, path movement and hand internal movement can be added to one another and/or substituted for one another.[8] In general, to make the movement of a sign more prominent, e.g., for public signing or emphasis, a larger movement is made by producing the movement from a joint closer to the body. For example, a sign whose citation form involves movement at the elbow will substitute movement at the shoulder for more prominence. Movement at either joint results in path movement, so the observed path movement in itself does not constitute an argument in favor of collapsing the two. But a sign that involves movement at the wrist, which can articulate an orientation change, a kind of internal movement, can also be enhanced by substituting movement at the elbow, changing such a sign into one with path movement instead.

[7] In the Prosodic model, orientation is conceived of and represented in two ways. Inherently, it is seen as a relation between hand part and the plane of articulation. It is also represented in the prosodic branch with features such as [supination], [pronation], etc., if there is an orientation change in the sign being represented.

[8] Some of these alternations were first observed and analyzed by Corina (1990a, 1996).

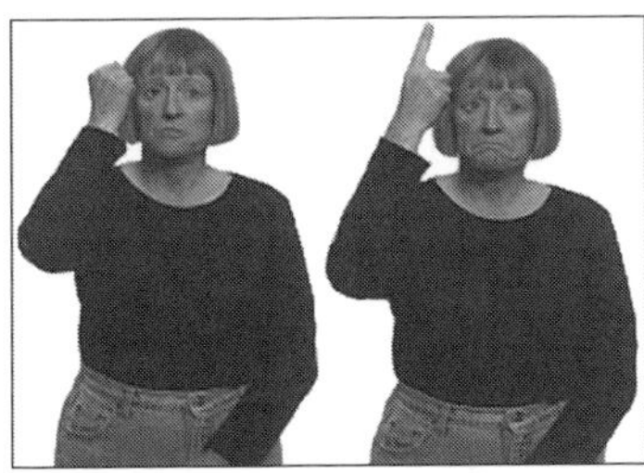

a. UNDERSTAND (ASL)

b. UNDERSTAND ('enhanced') (ASL)

Figure 13.10 Process adding path movement to internal movement for emphasis

Alternatively, a sign that in citation form involves movement at the elbow, can be made less prominent under certain discourse conditions, reducing to movement at a joint more distal from the body instead, such as the wrist, resulting in a visibly smaller sign. In the latter case, path movement becomes internal movement, or, in other words, a change in orientation or handshape features may replace a change in setting features, while all other features are kept constant. Since these alternations appear to be systematic, it follows that these changes involve the same sort of features – movement/prosodic features – and Brentari argues that the representation ought to be able to reflect the fact that the features belong to one and the same category, while facilitating statement of the rules involved in the alternations.

For example, the (ASL) sign UNDERSTAND is shown in Figure 13.10 in its citation form (a) and in its more prominent form (b). In citation form, there is an opening handshape change and no path movement. In the emphatic form, a path movement is added. To achieve this, an association line is added, linking a direction feature to the path node.[9] Extrapolating from Brentari's model and discussion, we assume the process would look like (8). The Prosodic model recognizes sequential structure, adopting van der Hulst's two X timing slots for anchoring the branching features.

[9] Direction features are also used to represent verb agreement in the Prosodic model (Brentari 1998).

(8) Addition of path movement by associating a [direction] feature in the Prosodic model

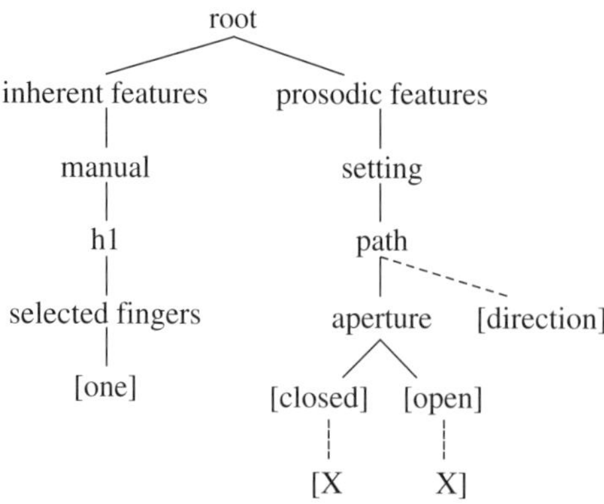

A set of translation statements is expected to be worked out, which will govern relative prominence operations, saying, for example, that an opening handshape change is made more prominent (enhanced, in Brentari's terms) by a path movement away from the place of articulation. In this example, the model succeeds in unifying path and internal movement features, both within the representation of lexical forms, and in its ability to express the relationship between more and less prominent signs. The example of relative prominence shows that the relationship between path and internal movement features and their interaction are natural within this model, all represented in the prosodic category, an advantage for the model.[10]

The segregation of prosodic and inherent features from one another is not without cost; that is, the internal organization of categories like hand configuration and place is disrupted in the Prosodic model, which divides up the pie primarily on the basis of movement. In order to evaluate the model, both its motivation and the implications of its organization of feature categories must be gauged.

13.4.1 Discussion

The Prosodic model represents both path and internal movement in the same branch of structure. This is a plus for the model, as there are good arguments for considering movement to be a unified category. The two types of movement are not formally integrated in the Hand Tier model, which represents internal movement as branching structure in the hand configuration category, and path movement as an M position on the

[10] Whether or not this relative prominence is a matter of sonority, as Brentari claims, is a separate question. We will argue in Chapter 14, Section 14.6 that it is best understood not as sonority but as the sign language equivalent of loudness.

segmental tier, as shown in (9).[11] A sign with both path and internal movement is a combination of these; it has LML structure as well as a branching finger position or orientation node.

(9) Two Hand Tier representations

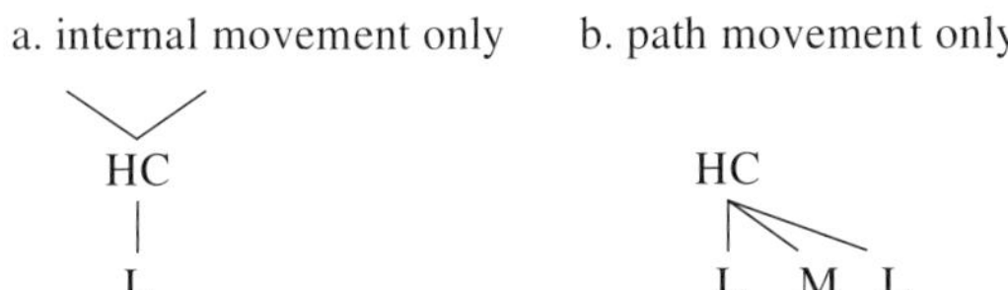

In the Prosodic model, each type is represented under the prosodic features branch of structure, as shown in (10).

(10) Two Prosodic model representations

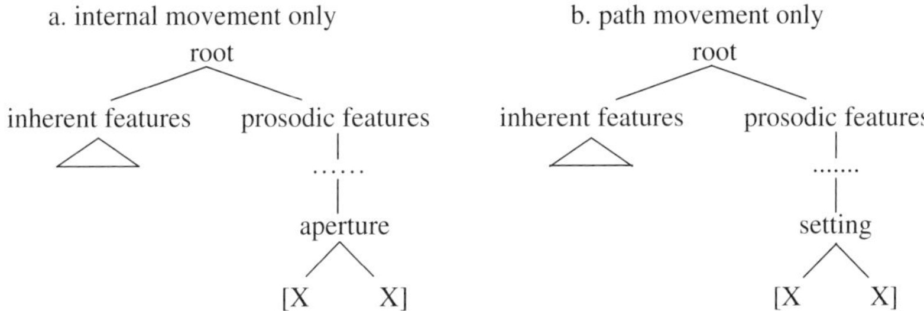

We now consider Brentari's empirical arguments for unifying path and internal movement structurally. The distribution of the two parts of the Delayed Completive morpheme is presented as one argument. While Brentari does not offer a representation of this process, she explains that the wiggle or wag would associate to the first X slot. But the unelaborated non-manual node in the Prosodic model, appearing as it does in the inherent branch of structure, makes the wrong predictions about the Delayed Completive. As an inherent feature, the *op* non-manual unit in Delayed Completive is predicted to characterize the whole sign instead of just the attested second syllable. Therefore, at least until the non-manual component is worked out, the representation of the Delayed Completive cannot be considered an advantage of the Prosodic model and does not help us choose between the two models.

[11] The representation of signs with internal movement but no path movement in (5a) and (9) is true to the original Hand Tier model. In a paper on a sonority cycle in ASL, Sandler (1993d) makes a change in the model, proposing that not only signs with path movement have an M segment, but that signs with some types of internal movement and no path movement do as well, contra the earlier Hand Tier model. We hesitate to accept that revision here, because it obscures the distinction between signs with and without path movement. Also, as there seems to be a conspiracy in favor of path movement (see Chapter 14), we wish to leave that distinction encoded in the representation for clarity, as in (9).

Another phenomenon that figures prominently in motivating the Prosodic model is the range of alternations created by generating the movement at different joints, in other words, differences in the size of the movement. We will argue in Chapter 14 that these alternations are phonetic, and that they are directly comparable to loudness in spoken language. On that interpretation, they do not reflect a phonological property, and therefore do not constitute an advantage for the Prosodic model.

The most convincing argument in favor of unifying path and internal movement is that each of them makes a sign well-formed, constituting something like a syllable nucleus. In this regard, the Prosodic model offers the aesthetic advantage of putting both types of movement in the same branch of structure. And if movement defines the syllable, a claim we support in the next chapter, then there should be some way to identify this movement, whether it is internal or path, and the introduction of a prosodic branch of structure is a way to do this. This choice has consequences, however. It results in a bifurcation of the categories of hand configuration and place. What is the effect of this organization?

The inherent features of handshape (in the articulator category of the inherent branch of structure in the Prosodic model shown in (7)) include those that distinguish open and closed finger positions by specifying the relevant joints and whether or not they are flexed. In signs with handshape change, the prosodic features specify the same properties with the features [open] and [closed]. There is a certain amount of redundancy here, and with it a missed generalization: that it is the finger positions that change in handshape change.

Another generalization that does not find expression in the Prosodic model is the unity of handshape change with handshape in phonological processes. For example, recall that under total hand configuration assimilation, selected finger, finger position, and orientation features all spread together. Where there is internal movement, represented by branching position or orientation features in both models, then that movement assimilates as well, as in the sign MIND^DROP = FAINT (see Figure 10.11). The Hand Tier model represents assimilation of this kind simply by spreading at the hand configuration node, as shown in example (6) of Chapter 10, Section 10.2.3. This process can't be represented in a unified way by the Prosodic model because the relevant features are in two different branches of structure: the inherent finger and joint specifications are under the inherent feature branch, while the [closed][open] handshape change features are under the prosodic feature branch.

According to common representational conventions, the organization of the Prosodic model raises the expectation that the prosodic features should spread or be affected as a group. This expectation does not appear to be borne out, although they do interact with one another in the "enhancement" effects, to which we have promised to return in the next chapter. In this sense, the Prosodic model implicitly rejects the central motivation for feature geometry, and with it, the phenomena that it explains. According to the theory of feature geometry, grouping features in a single branch of structure predicts that they are affected together in rules and/or constraints. The explanatory power of the theory lies in the linkage between the anatomical organization of the articulators and the phonological behavior of the features they control (Clements 1985, Sagey 1986). That is, the features assume an organization that mirrors that of the physical structures that articulate them, and their spreading and deletion as a group confirms both the class status and the hierarchical organization among classes so represented (see Chapter 10, Section 10.2). The geometry of hand configuration in the Hand Tier model achieves this theoretical goal, as argued at length in Sandler (1989). The fact that generalizations such as these are lost in the Prosodic model is a drawback.

Finally, by representing movement as a branch of structure, the Prosodic model rejects the notion that M is a type of sequential segment, as claimed by Sandler, following Liddell and Johnson. The primary generalizations captured by the sequential movement representation of models like the Hand Tier model are prosodic. First, positing an M segment makes perspicuous the timing differences introduced by various morphological operations. As shown in (3) above, ISL morphology distinguishes between gemination of movement and gemination of location. Second, as we explain in more detail in the next chapter, ASL (at least) clearly favors an LML structure in its signs (Sandler 1989, 1993d, 1999b). Other structures – that is, signs with internal movement only and no path movement, represented as just L, as well as longer signs with more than one syllable – often expand or reduce in the direction of the canonical LML template, as we will show in Chapter 14. This distinction is encoded by the Hand Tier model with an M timing slot for each path movement, but is obscured in the Prosodic model.

Another argument for LML structure is the distribution of [contact]. The feature may characterize the first location, the last location, or the movement, or it may alternatively characterize all three, in signs with so-called "continuous contact," as shown in example (2) of Section 13.3 above.[12] Representing contact on the first location in SHINY and the last in TOUCH is a perspicuous representation of the temporal distribution of this feature. Similarly the most coherent representation of signs like NUDE, in which the contact takes place during the movement from one

[12] Van der Kooij (2002) suggests that the feature [contact] may be eliminated from the phonology in Sign Language of the Netherlands. This does not seem to be an option for ASL, which refers to [contact] (a) in distinguishing the sign types presented in this chapter (Sandler 1989), (b) in determining allophonic variation of handshapes (Wilbur 1987), and (c) in predicting which elements will delete under compound reduction (Liddell and Johnson 1989 [1985]).

location to another, is simply to specify the feature [contact] on the movement segment, as the Hand Tier model does.

Because of the coherence of the feature geometry, the ability to distinguish path movements from other movements, the perspicuous representation of the distribution of [contact], and the possibility of representing movement length and other movement features needed for prosodic templates, the Hand Tier representation is adopted here.[13]

13.5 Movement in words is constrained

Before leaving the topic of movement, we wish to draw attention to an instructive contrast between the restricted role assumed by movement in words of the sign language lexicon and its form and use in more expressive aspects of sign languages, like classifier constructions and poetry. We suggest that this difference is another indication of the special status of words.

The classifier subsystem (Chapter 5) exploits a rich variety of movement shapes, such as upwards arc, pivot, and zigzag, as well as movement manners, which manipulate speed, size, and rhythm – each argued to have morphemic status in ASL. These possibilities are finite and constrained according to Supalla (1982, 1986), but both the primitives and their combinations are far more numerous than the movements of lexical signs.

In poetry, the movement parameter is also used in a versatile way for artistic effect. For example, consider a haiku performed in sign language in the film, *The Human Language*.[14]

Since my house burned down,
I now have a clear view
Of the rising moon.

In presenting the poem, the signer signs the burning down of her house by violent whirling motions which gradually diminish and fade like the fire itself. Expressing hope and wonder in the face of this devastation, she then signs MOON-RISE very slowly, denoting the rising of the moon over the now flattened landscape. Without these possibilities for producing a wide range of movement shapes and rhythmic variations, sign languages lose some of their expressive power.

However, once movement assumes a role that is phonological, rather than either morphological or poetic/affective, its inventory is drastically reduced (see also Wilbur, Klima, and Bellugi 1983). This bifurcation is reminiscent of the behavior of the non-dominant hand (Chapter 12). There we explained that when h2 behaves as a morpheme or an

[13] See Miller (1996) for a treatment of rhythmicity of movement in LSQ.

[14] Apparently, the sign language haiku was adapted from an English one by Bob Holman (http://www.poetrysociety.org.holman.html). The sign language version appears in *The Human Language, Part I*. A film series by Gene Searchinger.

independent sign in classifier constructions and for special discourse purposes, it has many degrees of freedom. But when it assumes a phonological role within words, it is far more restricted. We now see that movement too is much more constrained and exhibits more redundancies in lexical signs than in other kinds of expression. While sign languages take advantage of iconic and other motivated forms of expression afforded by the modality, in what we will call "non-lexical" subsystems (Chapter 16), they are still subject to the imperative of language to clearly identify its central unit, the word.

In the next chapter, we deal with the phonological distinctions between the word, the morpheme, and the syllable, and the role of movement in these constructs.

14 Is there a syllable in sign language?

The opposition between relatively static elements and relatively dynamic elements in signs was first reported in the work of Newkirk (1998 [1981]), and the idea that ASL signs have a formal unit like the syllable can be traced back to Chinchor (1978). The first comprehensive model to encode such a distinction is that of Liddell (1984b). That model, developed in Liddell and Johnson (1989 [1985]), makes the radical claim that there is a sequentially organized static–dynamic alternation that can be compared to consonants (holds) and vowels (movements), leading to the concept of a sequentially organized syllable in ASL, adopted also by Sandler (1989) and Perlmutter (1992). Others conceive of a sign syllable that is simultaneously organized, one that is projected from, and organized in relation to, a dynamic element (Brentari 1990, Corina 1990b). The notion of sonority has also been employed in describing syllables of sign language (e.g., Brentari 1990, 1998, Corina 1990b, Perlmutter 1992, Sandler 1993d).

But is use of the terms "syllable" and "sonority," "consonants" and "vowels" with regard to sign language merely metaphorical, or should we understand the analogy with those concepts in spoken language to be direct, and therefore approachable through the general assumptions of linguistic theory? We will show first that there is such a thing as a syllable that is distinct from the morpheme and the word. We'll then argue that "syllable" as a formal concept does have an analogue in American Sign Language, but that both its phonetic and its phonological properties are quite different from those of spoken language. Considering the notion of sonority as visual salience, we find some distributional evidence to suggest that it plays a role in the form of signs. However, we show that a direct comparison with sonority in spoken language is premature and probably untenable, given the radically different properties of the transmission systems in the two modalities. Despite these differences, or, more interestingly, because of them, we conclude with the suggestion that further linguistic and experimental investigations of the syllable and visual salience in sign language will move us closer to a comprehensive theory of phonology.

This chapter focuses almost exclusively on ASL. Comparison with other sign languages awaits future research.

14.1 The sign language syllable: preliminary description

Syllable-based generalizations in spoken language rely on such factors as the organization of sounds around a sonority peak and the assignment of relative stress. In sign language, movement has been likened to a syllable peak. But there is a strong tendency for each sign to contain only one movement. This raises two questions: whether the two concepts, the word and the syllable, are even distinguishable, and whether it makes sense to talk about relative stress in a sign language word. Moreover, the property of sonority is grounded firmly in the anatomy and physiology of the vocal tract and acoustics, and it typically organizes sequences of consonants on either side of the most sonorous element in the syllable unit. Now, no matter how sequential one's theory of sign language phonology, there can never be any clusters of static elements (i.e., holds or locations), because the physiology of the system requires the hand to move in between. And, as we show in Section 14.6, the physical properties of the production and perception system are so different from those of spoken language as to make any meaningful comparison of sonority in the two modalities extremely difficult.

Against these odds, a number of investigators have devoted serious thought to the notion of a syllable in sign language that is defined in terms of movement. A central observation that has figured in this work is the requirement described in the previous chapter, that a sign must have at least one movement in order to be well-formed, even if this movement is a default straight path movement. This observation alone would not argue for a defining role for movements in syllables, though, since both hand configurations and locations are also obligatory in well-formed sign words. Two additional ideas, together with the obligatoriness of movements, lead to the suggestion that movements may be the nuclei of sign language syllables. One is the possibility that movement is more visually salient than stasis, just as the nucleus is the most auditorily salient element in a spoken syllable. The other idea was presented in Chapter 13: most signs are pronounceable, and many are intelligible, *without* movement – a generalization which does not hold of the other two major phonological categories – and yet the movements are still required for well-formedness. This reasoning has led to the proposal that one movement (or more than one movement occurring simultaneously) constitutes a syllable nucleus (Chinchor 1978, Coulter 1982, Wilbur 1982, Liddell and Johnson 1989 [1985], Sandler 1989, Brentari 1990, 1998, Perlmutter 1992).

Let us assume the definition of a syllable given in (1).

(1) Definition of a sign language syllable (Brentari 1998, p. 205)

a. The number of sequential phonological movements in a string equals the number of syllables in that string. When several shorter dynamic elements co-occur with a single dynamic element of longer duration, the single movement defines the syllable.

b. If a structure is a well-formed syllable as an independent word, it must be counted as a syllable word-internally.

The mention of shorter and longer dynamic elements in (1a) refers to secondary movement: finger wiggle or rapidly repeated handshape or orientation change. If any of these occur on a path movement, they don't count as individual syllables; rather, the number of path movements determines the number of syllables. An implication of (1a) is that if a single path movement co-occurs with a single internal movement, then that unit also counts as one syllable. Only if movements occur in a sequence can we count more than one syllable. Reference to "phonological movements" is intended to exclude transitional movements between signs and between reduplications of a sign.

The literature on syllables and sonority in sign language is confusing, in part because the conclusions of different researchers often have different empirical bases. We will try to present a coherent picture of some of the results and arrive at some useful generalizations. We gather support for the following claims:

(2)

i. there is a prosodic unit that organizes the timing of phonetic gestures

ii. there are constraints on the content of this unit

iii. it is referred to by rules

iv. there is distributional evidence for the following saliency hierarchy: path movement > internal movement > location

We will also argue that the analogy that has been proposed between movements and vowels is too strong, and that certain phenomena that have been attributed to relative sonority in sign language are better understood as relative loudness instead.

Before pursuing the question of whether syllables exist in sign language and what their properties might be, it is useful to consider the basic characteristics of syllables in spoken language as a frame of reference.

14.2 Theoretical background: the syllable in spoken language

Evidence for syllables in spoken language comes from phonetics and psycho-linguistics, in addition to standard linguistic patterns. Syllables are organized according to the relative sonority of segments; speech errors respect the onset-nucleus-rhyme structure of the syllable, as well as the number of syllables in a word; and many phonological generalizations require reference to the syllable and its constituents.

EXTRACT-INFORMATION (ISL)

Figure 14.1 Movements coordinated in the second syllable

14.3 The sign language syllable as a timing unit

The canonical syllable in sign languages, defined as in (1), consists of a simple path movement from one location to another; we have seen many examples of this form. If internal movement – change of handshape or change of orientation – occurs in addition to the path movement, then the first shape or orientation co-occurs temporally with the first location, and the second with the last. Another movement element that is temporally organized by the syllable is non-manual movement, e.g., by the eye or mouth. We are not referring here to adverbial mouth movements, which span whole predicates or larger discourse stretches, nor to co-occurring mouthings of spoken language that are superimposed on signs and may also span longer prosodic constituents (see Chapter 15). Rather, it is those mouth movements that are lexically specified for individual signs that are organized temporally by the syllable. The native sign language lexical mouth movements we are now focusing on have been reported in many sign languages (see Boyes-Braem and Sutton-Spence 2001), and also exist in ISL. They typically consist of a gesture made by the mouth, which, if whispered or voiced, would be perceived auditorily as a CV or VC syllable (Woll 2002). Lexically specified mouth movements are temporally distributed over the syllable in the same way that the specifications of internal movement are.

The ISL sign meaning 'to get information out of someone' illustrates both aspects of timing within a syllable: internal movement and non-manual movement. This sign consists of the EYE sense prefix (see Chapter 4, Section 4.2) and a second sign with no independent meaning, together glossed as EXTRACT-INFORMATION. The complex word, shown in Figure 14.1, is disyllabic, consisting of an (epenthetic) movement from the eye to a point in space in front of the signer, and another path movement to a point closer to the signer. In the second syllable, two kinds of movement are synchronized with the path movement toward the signer. First, there is a hand-internal movement in which the index finger goes from an open (extended) position to a curved position. Second, there is a mouth movement in which the corners of the mouth are pulled back, exposing the teeth, and then relaxed. The internal handshape movement and the mouth movement are clearly coordinated with the path movement of the second syllable only, and not with the whole word.[1]

Such synchronization within a syllable might not be significant if it were not for the contrast it presents with the transitional movements that occur between signs. Brentari measured handshape changes that occur within a sign syllable with those that occur on transitional movements. She found that within a syllable, the transition between the two handshapes is evenly distributed over the path movement, as mentioned in Chapter 13. This contrasts with handshape and orientation changes that occur during the transitional movement between signs, which are only about 40 percent as long as the transitional path movement, and are not linked temporally with the beginning and ending of that path movement (Brentari and Poizner 1994, Brentari et al. 1995, Brentari 1998).

14.4 Distinguishing the sign language syllable, the morpheme, and the word: constraints on structure

In Unit 2, we equated the concept "sign" with "word," and from a morphosyntactic point of view the analogy is apt. In terms of syllable content and structure, though, there are differences between the signed word and the spoken word. In many spoken languages, the prosodic form of words can vary greatly, consisting of one or many syllables, which are simple or complex, open or closed, as the following examples from English show: *go*, *cri.mi.no.lo.gists*. But in all sign languages that we know of, most words correspond to the same phonological template, repeated in (3) (Sandler 1989, 1993d, 1999b).

(3) The canonical form of the sign

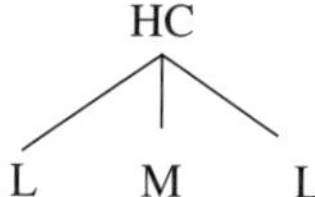

According to the definition of a syllable in (1), this means that most words consist of a single syllable because there is only one movement. Saying that LML is canonical means that, although there are many signs with internal movement only, the typical sign has a path movement, represented by M.

[1] Woll (2002) suggests that the structure and timing of these lexical mouth movements point to a common rhythmic base for spoken and signed syllables.

There are constraints on this LML form, but since a syllable usually corresponds to a word and a word may also be monomorphemic, it is not immediately apparent whether these constraints hold on morphemes, words or syllables. So, it is important at the outset, in our pursuit of the sign language syllable, to distinguish these three kinds of structures – the morpheme, the word, and the syllable.

We will approach the issue from the point of view of constraints on structure and the domains over which those constraints hold. Most of the constraints we refer to here are either inviolable or would be very highly ranked in an Optimality framework (McCarthy and Prince 1993, Prince and Smolensky 1993). By looking mostly at constraints that cannot be violated within their domains, we may clearly distinguish different levels of structure. As the phonology of sign language is still in its infancy, we can take nothing for granted, and must use the clearest possible means to determine the viability of structures such as the morpheme, the syllable, and the word, whose independent existence is usually a foregone conclusion in spoken languages. Throughout the discussion that follows, it will be useful to keep in mind the definition of the syllable, which stipulates that any path movement constitutes a single syllable regardless of whether or not internal movement occurs with it simultaneously, and that internal movement alone may also constitute a syllable.

We summarize the generalizations we will be making with respect to words, morphemes, and syllables in Table 14.1.[2]

14.4.1 Constraints on the syllable

Let's begin with the syllable. A constraint that holds exclusively on syllables – and not on morphemes or words – limits finger positions and orientations to a maximum of two within this domain (Wilbur 1993, Uyechi 1996 [1994], Brentari 1998). Such a sequence results in internal movement, which is timed with the beginning and end of the syllable, as described above. A different kind of internal movement is called secondary movement or trill, and it involves either rapid repetition of these two finger positions or orientations throughout the sign, or finger wiggle.[3] There are very few signs in ASL or ISL that have both handshape and orientation change with or without path movement. If these languages are representative, then under the hypothesis

[2] The first work to systematically distinguish the syllable, the morpheme, and the word is Brentari (1990). That approach is revised and extended in Brentari (1998). Some but not all of the generalizations cited here are compatible with Brentari's. Unfortunately, a detailed comparison would exceed the scope of this work.

[3] The term "trill" is used differently by different authors, some of whom include uncounted rapid repetitions of path movements in the category (footnote 1 in Chapter 13). We assume here that only internal movement may be trilled.

Table 14.1 *Distinguishing the word (ω), the morpheme (μ), and the syllable (σ) in ASL*

Word	Morpheme	Syllable
Hand Configuration Assimilation domain	Selected Finger Constraint (5)	Hand Configuration Binary Branching Constraint (SHCC) (4a)
	Place Constraint (6)	Timing Constraint (definitional) (STC) (4b)

Non-isomorphism between syllable, morpheme, and word:
(a) words may be monosyllabic but multimorphemic (e.g., a-GIVE-b with subj-obj agreement);
(b) words may be disyllabic but monomorphemic (JOT-DOWN)

All of the following forms are attested:

ω | μ | σ	ω | μ / \\ σ σ	ω / \\ μ μ \\ / σ	ω / \\ μ μ | | σ σ
monomorphemic monosyllabic words	monomorphemic disyllabic words	**bimorphemic monosyllabic words**	bimorphemic, disyllabic words

that handshape and orientation both belong to the hand configuration category (Sandler 1987a, 1987b, 1989), we may restate the constraint on finger positions and orientations as follows:

(4) Syllable Structure Constraints

a. Syllable-level Hand Configuration Constraint (SHCC)
The hand configuration category may dominate at most one binary branching constituent (finger position or orientation) within a syllable.

b. Syllable-timing constraint (STC; preliminary formulation)
   i. The two branches of (a) are temporally aligned with syllable edges.
   ii. Lexically specified non-manual movements are temporally aligned with syllable edges.

So, a word like (ISL) SEND, repeated in Figure 14.2, has open and closed finger positions, and these are aligned with the beginning and end of the path movement, i.e., the locations. Similarly, a sign specified for a non-manual movement like (ISL) EXTRACT-INFORMATION shown in Figure 14.1 has internal or mouth movements that are aligned with the beginning and end of the path movement of the second syllable.

SEND (ISL)

Figure 14.2 Sign with a sequence of finger positions: closed and open

A monomorphemic word in ASL may have more than two finger positions, as does DESTROY, with the finger positions open to closed and closed to open. By definition, this word is disyllabic. This shows that constraint (4a) holds within the syllable and not the morpheme. There is only one binary branching finger position structure in each syllable of (ASL) DESTROY, as constraint (4a) prescribes. The timing of the handshape change satisfies constraint (4b): each position is temporally aligned with the first and last timing slot. This example also demonstrates that the syllable and the morpheme are not isomorphic: the ASL word DESTROY consists of a single morpheme, but it has two sequential handshape changes, each aligned with a path movement, and therefore two syllables.

The constraints on syllables are essentially the definition of the syllable, and an attempt to motivate the constituent solely through definitional constraints would be circular. Independent evidence is provided for the phonological significance of a syllable unit in Section 14.5.

14.4.2 Morpheme structure constraints

We now move on to the morpheme. The Selected Finger Constraint described in Chapter 10, Section 10.2 (Mandel 1981) – stating that only one selected finger specification is allowed – is a constraint on the morpheme, not on the syllable or the word. Mandel's constraint above is revised in (5) to refer to the morpheme instead of the word (Sandler 1989).[4]

(5) Revised Selected Finger Constraint (Sandler 1989)
There can be only one specification for selected fingers in a morpheme.

The disyllabic word DESTROY observes the Selected Finger Constraint – selecting all five fingers throughout – even though it is disyllabic, because it is monomorphemic. That the Selected Finger Constraint operates on

[4] As explained in Chapter 10, the Selected Finger Constraint may be violated by fingerspelled borrowings from English orthography.

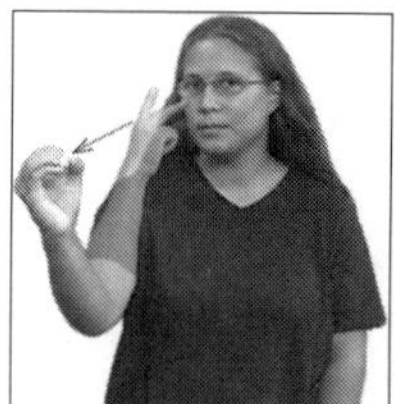

SEE + ZERO 'not see at all' (ASL)

Figure 14.3 Two selected finger specifications in two morphemes of one word

THINK^MARRY=BELIEVE (ASL)

Figure 14.4 Monosyllabic compound sign with two selected finger specifications

the morpheme and not on the word is shown by the fact that neither words with linear affixes nor compounds are constrained by it. For example, the ASL suffixed sign SEE-ZERO, illustrated in Unit 2 and repeated in Figure 14.3, is a single word that has two morphemes and two selected finger specifications, and . That the SFC is not a constraint on the syllable can also be seen from those compounds which reduce to one syllable (one path movement) but maintain their two handshapes. As seen in the partial assimilation variant of the compound THINK^MARRY=BELIEVE, shown in Figure 14.4, which keeps its two distinct handshapes and , a single syllable may have two selected finger specifications if it is bimorphemic. We conclude, then, that (5) is correct as a condition on the morpheme.

Similarly, the place constraint mentioned in Chapter 11 (Battison 1978 [1973]) – stating that only one place of articulation (major body area) is allowed in a sign – is a constraint on the morpheme, as claimed in Sandler (1989), shown in the revised constraint, (6).

(6) Revised Place Constraint
There can be only one place of articulation per morpheme.
(Sandler 1989)

Both of these constraints hold in the disyllabic monomorphemic word, DESTROY, but neither holds in compounds (lexicalized or not), even if

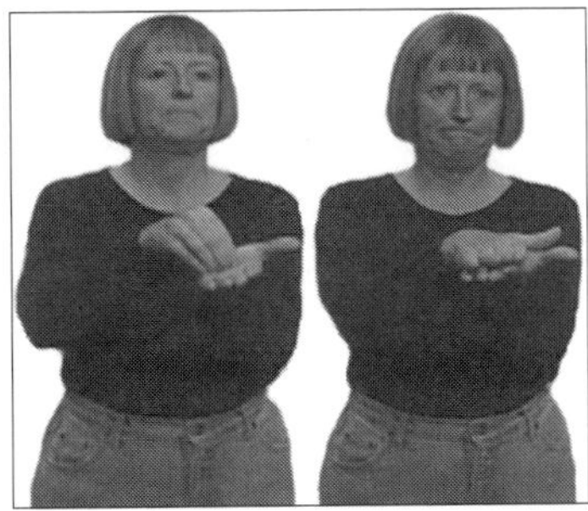

JOT-DOWN (ASL)

Figure 14.5 Disyllabic monomorphemic sign with different finger positions in each syllable

they are monosyllabic. The ASL compound BELIEVE shown in Figure 14.4 above reduces to a single syllable, but maintains its two distinct places of articulation, the head and the non-dominant hand.

The specification of the non-dominant hand is also determined at the level of the morpheme, rather than the syllable or the word. Interestingly, the behavior of the non-dominant hand in monomorphemic, disyllabic words is compatible with the two-role theory described in Chapter 12, Section 12.1. In the disyllabic monomorphemic sign DESTROY, a symmetrical h2-S sign, h2 acts as h1 does, articulating the same single selected finger specification and the same open–closed, closed–open finger positions as h1. That is, there are two hand-internal movements on each hand, one per syllable. In the disyllabic monomorphemic sign JOT-DOWN, shown in Figure 14.5, in which h2 is a place of articulation (in an h2-P sign), h1 articulates two different finger positions, one in each syllable, but h2 can only have one specification, constrained by the place constraint in (6) stipulating a maximum of one place of articulation per morpheme.[5] DESTROY and JOT-DOWN also show that a word may be monomorphemic and disyllabic. The selected finger and place constraints are constraints on morpheme structure, and h2 abides by those constraints according to its role in a given morpheme.[6]

[5] JOT-DOWN is interpreted here as disyllabic because there are two movements to contact with the hand, each characterized by a different handshape. The two handshapes share the same selected fingers specification as required by the SFC on morphemes. The same sign would be monosyllabic if the handshape change occurred during a single movement.

[6] Brentari (1998) argues that the prosodic word governs specification of h2, and not the morpheme as we claim. Specifically, on the basis of lexicalized compounds that have only one specification for h2, Brentari proposes that there is a limit of one h2 specification per prosodic word. Her consultants judged the specially invented compounds presented to them, with two different h2 specifications, to be unacceptable. However, grammatical novel compounds such as PRACTICE+VOTE with h2 + h2 falsify that claim. (Thanks to Carol Padden for the example.) We speculate that the rejection by Brentari's

MAN^MARRY=HUSBAND (ASL)

Figure 14.6 Hand configuration assimilation in a reduced monosyllabic compound

SLEEP^SUNRISE=OVERSLEEP (ASL)

Figure 14.7 Hand configuration assimilation in an unreduced disyllabic compound

14.4.3 The word

We move on to the morphosyntactic word. One way in which the grammar identifies the constituent "word" is in stating the rule of HC assimilation in compounds, illustrated and analyzed in Chapter 10. The domain of this rule is neither the morpheme nor the syllable, but the word. Compounds are by definition single words comprised of two or more base words. Partial and total assimilation of hand configuration in compounds takes place within the compound word (across the two members of the compound). As indicated in Chapters 9 and 10, compounds may reduce to a single syllable, but this is certainly not obligatory, and hand configuration assimilation may take place regardless of whether or not the compound loses a syllable. For example, total hand configuration assimilation occurs on the reduced monosyllabic compound (MAN^MARRY=) HUSBAND in Figure 14.6[7] and on the unreduced disyllabic compound (SLEEP^SUNRISE=) OVERSLEEP in Figure 14.7.[8] This shows that the domain for the rule is the word.

More evidence that the morpheme, the syllable, and the word are clearly distinguishable comes from other kinds of morphologically

consultants was not due to a phonological constraint, but rather due to the fact that the compounds that were used as examples (e.g., WORD+HELP, 'thesaurus') were too semantically opaque to be accepted as novel compound forms.

7 Note that HUSBAND is homophonous with BELIEVE.

8 In the discussion of hand configuration assimilation, we do not distinguish between the morphosyntactic word and the prosodic word. Prosodic words are discussed in Chapter 15.

complex words. A verb marked for subject and object agreement such as ASL ASK, shown in Chapter 3, Figure 3.4, is typically monosyllabic but trimorphemic, as shown in the representation in (7) in the following section. Temporal aspect marking, also discussed in the following section, may add a morphemic movement feature to a verb marked for agreement, adding another morpheme without disturbing the monosyllabic nature of the base.

We concur with Brentari (1990), then, that syllables, morphemes, and words are distinguishable. Still, we feel that we would be missing a generalization were we to ignore the fact that words often overlap with syllables. Apart from full reduplications, sign language words, be they morphologically simple or complex, are usually monosyllabic (Coulter 1982, Wilbur 1987). That is, most words take the first or the third form, shown in boldface, in Table 14.1 above. It has been suggested that this tendency is a conspiracy, in the sense that it is a prosodic form that signs seem to settle on, regardless of their morphosyntactic structure (e.g., Sandler 1993d, 1999b). We discuss this conspiracy in the next section, making the supposition that if a conspiracy exists, there must be something to conspire about. We then go on to provide phonological evidence for the syllable explicitly.

14.5 The monosyllable conspiracy and other syllable level generalizations

Most phonologists consider the best evidence for the existence of theoretical constructs, such as the syllable, the feature, or the feature class, to be the behavior of that element in the grammatical processes of a language or languages. In particular, if the statement of rules or constraints in a language must make reference to the proposed element, especially if there is more than one independent process that must refer to it, then the existence of that element is supported. The syllable was not given much credence in Chomsky and Halle's *Sound Pattern of English* (1968), in which generalizations were stated on sequences of segments, morphemes, and words. It was only when researchers such as Kahn (1976) demonstrated clearly that many independent generalizations are best accounted for by assuming the syllable as an independent element of structure that this construct was legitimized in generative phonology. In sign languages, we have seen that syllables can be defined phonetically as in (1), and that they have certain phonotactic constraints on their structure, shown in (4). Is that where the story ends? Or does the morphophonology have further use for the syllable?

Here we provide three independent pieces of evidence from ASL to support the claim that the syllable is a bona fide phonological construct in that language, over and above the structural constraints in (4) above. These are (1) the tendency of morphologically complex signs to be monosyllabic; (2) word-level stress; and (3) final syllable reduplication.

14.5.1 *The monosyllable conspiracy*

The tendency of morphologically complex words to be monosyllabic (Sandler 1989, 1993d, 1999b) is one way in which the grammar is telling us that the syllable unit is real. The first indication of this conspiracy is reflected in the so-called simultaneity of many of the morphological processes in sign languages, i.e., the combination of morphemes without adding sequential structure. Common and productive processes such as verb agreement and verbal aspect morphology are clear examples. Verb agreement, whose morphological properties are described in Chapter 3, can be described phonologically as associating an agreement morpheme with the first and last locations of a sign, as shown schematically in (7). Durational aspect involves associating an arc specification with the M segment, as shown in (8), and then reduplicating the whole form. In fact, a word may be inflected for both verb agreement and temporal aspect, as sketched in (9).

(7) Verb agreement (Sandler 1989)

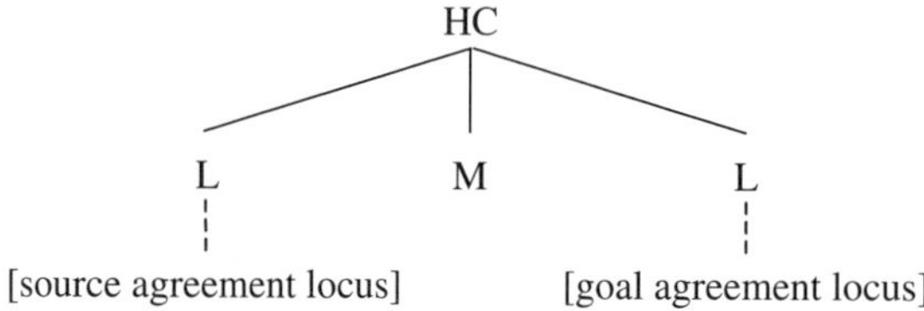

(8) Durational aspect (Sandler 1990)

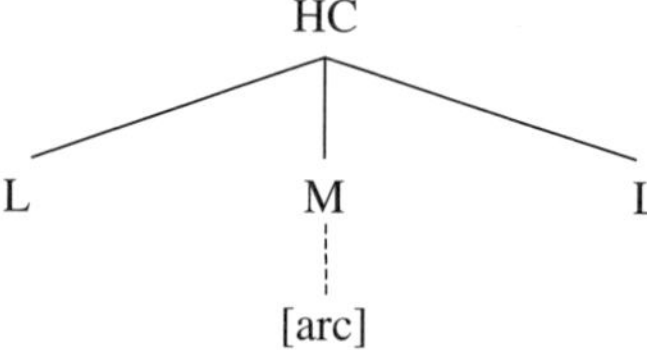

(9) Verb agreement and durational aspect

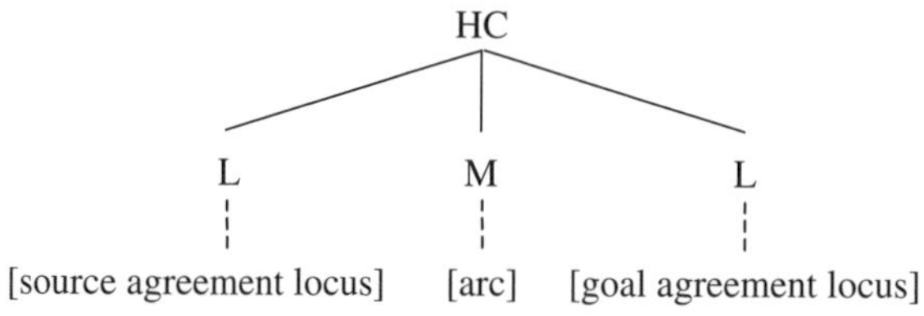

In these and many similar morphological processes, morphemes such as [arc] are added without adding sequential movements, resulting in morphologically complex bases that are monosyllabic.[9] Other templatic

[9] We exempt the total reduplications that are typical of temporal aspect morphology from the syllable count, and return to them in Section 14.5.2.

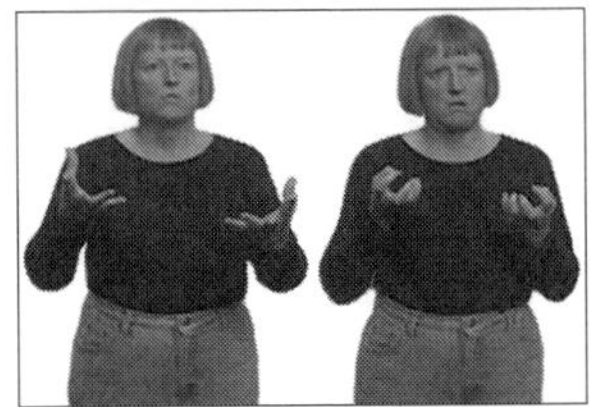

a. WANT (ASL)

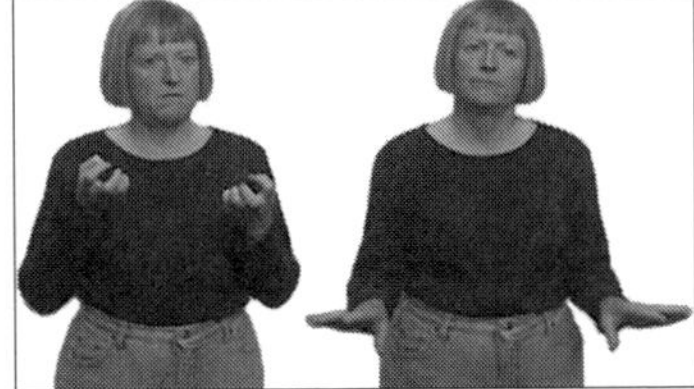

b. DON'T-WANT (ASL)

Figure 14.8 Negative incorporation – reduction to a monosyllable

morphological forms that add timing slots to form geminates without adding syllables are shown in Chapter 13, example (3).

When classifier constructions lexicalize and become words (see Chapter 6), they too become monosyllabic. Since classifier constructions may constitute more than one syllable and even more than one intonational phrase, it is striking that the lexical items that evolve from them are overwhelmingly monosyllabic.

Even processes that are by their nature sequential may result in truncation to produce the favored monosyllabic words. One example is the process known as negative incorporation (Woodward 1974) shown in Figure 14.8. These forms involve suffixing a location that is lower than the last location of the base sign and that is specified for a prone orientation and an open finger position. Adding the additional location sequentially would result in a disyllabic sign, as the hand moves to the lower position and adds the additional open finger position: LML + L → LML(M)L. But disyllabicity is prevented by truncation: the first location and handshape are deleted. The process is shown for the sign DON'T-WANT in (10) (following Sandler 1989). The representations are schematic, suppressing some of the hierarchical structure and using transparent feature specifications for clarity. Those features of the base that will characterize the derived sign are printed in bold. The suffix is lexically underspecified, bearing only the features represented, features of finger position, palm orientation, and setting, but not specified for selected fingers or for place. The latter specifications are spread from the base sign.[10]

[10] The negative incorporation process supports the Hand Tier model of locations presented in Chapter 11, since the setting features such as [low] behave independently of the place features. In WANT/DON'T-WANT, the place is [trunk], while in KNOW/DON'T-KNOW,

(10) a. WANT base + underspecified NEG suffix

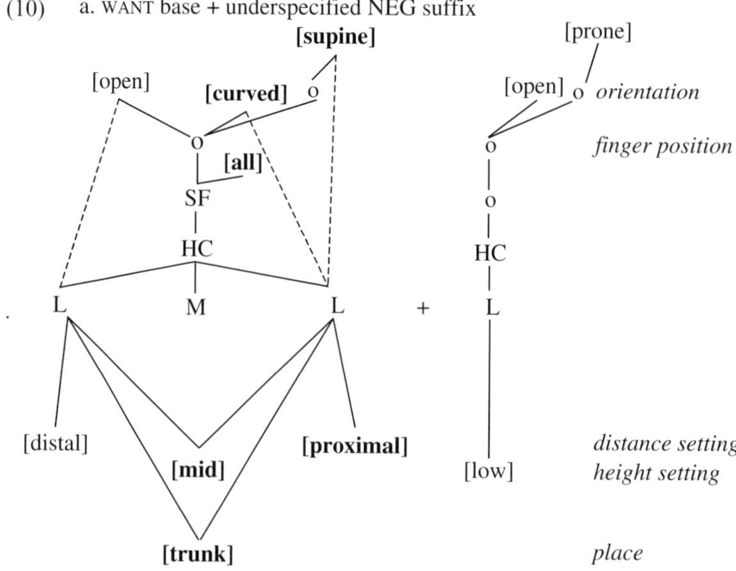

b. DON'T-WANT surface form

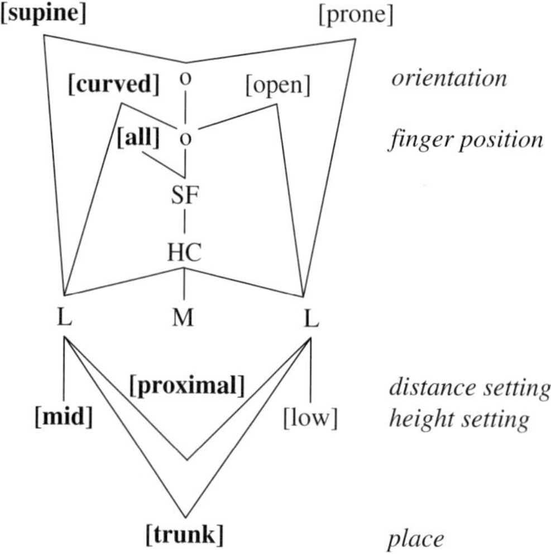

The result, in which the movement is the default straight movement necessarily intervening between two locations, is the canonical LML monosyllabic form. Similarly, we have seen that in both of the sign languages with which we are familiar, ASL and ISL, compounds may reduce when they are lexicalized, and that a common type of reduction

the place is [head]. Negative incorporation always results in a final setting that is lower than the first, but articulated with respect to the place that is lexically specified for the specific base sign.

is the elimination of one of the movements, resulting once again in monosyllabic forms: LML + LML -> LML. Examples are ASL MAN^MARRY=HUSBAND, pictured above in Figure 14.6, and ISL MIND^STUCK=DAYDREAM, pictured in Chapter 10, Figure 10.14. All of these processes point to a conspiracy of monosyllabicity.

It is likely that the monosyllables we see are due to an output constraint in the form of an LML syllable template (Sandler 1989). This suggestion is compatible with the proposal of Miller (1991) that the negative incorporation form results from right-to-left syllabification. Further support for Miller's suggestion can be seen in the fact that total hand configuration assimilation in compounds also preserves the right HC at the expense of the left. The details of how and under what circumstances signs reduce to monosyllables remain to be investigated, and a constraint-based approach like OT in which constraints are ranked and may be violated suggests itself for future research in this area. In any case, the fact that we see such monosyllables so pervasively supports the syllable as a valid prosodic organizing unit in sign language phonology. We'll deal with the distinction between the syllable, the morphosyntactic word, and the prosodic word in Chapter 15, on prosody.

14.5.2 Stress

We now turn to stress, a system that crucially involves the relative prominence of syllables. Although most lexical signs are indeed monosyllabic, not all of them are. In fact, all novel compounds and many lexical compounds are disyllabic, and we may look to the stress patterns in such forms for further linguistic support for syllables. Researchers have claimed that compounds in ASL have regular stress patterns. First, disyllabic compounds have been described (by Klima and Bellugi 1979) as having what may be interpreted as a weak–strong stress pattern, where stress is characterized as increased muscle tension and increased speed.[11] The discussion in Klima and Bellugi (1979) describes the relation between the first and second sign in compounds, and not syllables explicitly. However, many of their examples are uncontroversially disyllabic, consisting of a sequence of two path movements (e.g., BLACK^NAME 'bad reputation' shown in Chapter 12, Figure 12.6; THRILL^INFORM 'news, entertainment'), so it is reasonable to interpret their description as applying to disyllabic feet. In particular, the first sign is always weakened (losing repetition, shortening in duration and displacement, and

[11] The judgments about word-level stress are impressionistic, as are most phonological treatments of spoken language stress. Wilbur and her colleagues have measured stress instrumentally; see Wilbur and Schick (1987) and Wilbur (1999a) for an overview. These studies have concentrated on phrase-level stress (prominence) and stress used for emphasis or focus.

weakening in stress), and the second sign either remains normally stressed or receives additional stress. ASL words that are lexically reduplicated such as NAME or CHAIR – a type described with the feature [restrained] in the ISL data in Chapter 6 – are described in Coulter (1990) as stressed on the first syllable, i.e., on the first iteration of the base.[12] These stress assignment rules, then, must refer to the last or first syllable of a word. Finally, bidirectional words, whose movement is from one location to another and back again ($L_1ML_2ML_1$), like PLAY-PIANO, have been described as having equal stress on both syllables (Supalla and Newport 1978, Wilbur 1999a), distinguishing them from unidirectional reduplicated words like FINGERSPELL ($L_1ML_2(M)L_1ML_2$), whose stress is on the lexical movement and not on the epenthetic return movement. While a full analysis of these different stress patterns on different types of ASL words has not yet been undertaken, it is clear that in order to contrast these three different patterns, it is necessary to refer to the syllable.[13] This is evidence that the phonology of ASL recognizes the syllable unit.

14.5.3 Final syllable reduplication

Another process that makes reference to the syllable is morphological reduplication. Unlike underlying reduplication found in monosyllabic words like NAME, which has exactly one reduplication (two iterations), morphologically introduced reduplication may involve three or more iterations. Many of the temporal aspects described for ASL (Klima and Bellugi 1979), in particular those expressing duration or iteration, involve total reduplication of the base. When ASL compounds are reduplicated, the reduplicated element is the final syllable (Sandler 1987b, 1989). If the compound is reduced and monosyllabic, like MIND^DROP = FAINT (shown earlier in Chapter 10, Figure 10.11), then the whole form is reduplicated, as schematized in (11).

(11) FAINT [reduplicated]

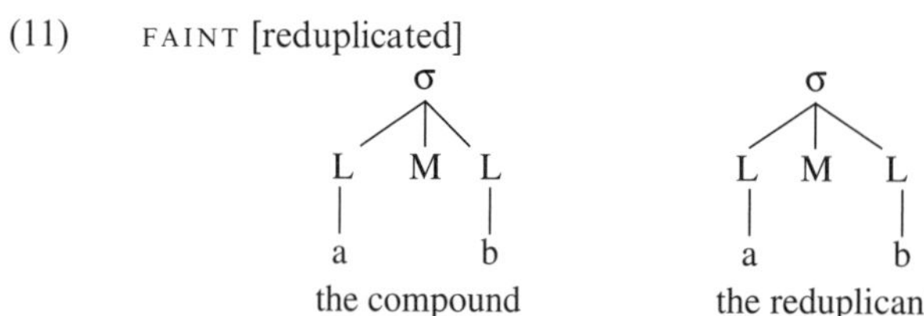

[12] Lexically reduplicated words are represented with the feature [restrained], and not by a sequence of syllables in Sandler (1996b), as mentioned in Chapter 6. In any case, on the surface these signs are disyllabic by our definition, and it is at that level that the stress pattern is revealed.

[13] See Miller (1996) for an analysis of stress and prosody in LSQ.

However, if the compound is disyllabic, like SLEEP^SUNRISE = OVERSLEEP, shown in Figure 14.7, then only the final syllable is reduplicated, as schematized in (12).

(12) SLEEP^SUNRISE = OVERSLEEP [reduplicated]

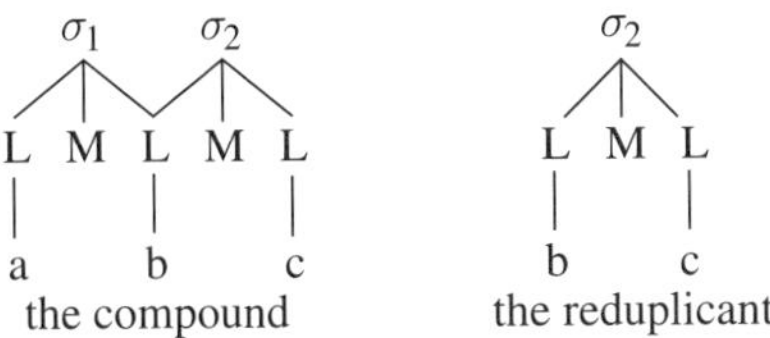

It doesn't matter whether the last syllable has path movement only or internal movement only; each type of movement is regarded as a syllable nucleus by this reduplicatory process. The second member of the compound WRONG^HAPPEN = ACCIDENT has internal movement only, specifically, orientation change. It is that syllable that gets reduplicated, and not the whole compound, as shown in (13). In the representation of ACCIDENT, the M in parentheses is epenthetic, and the branching structure above the L in the second syllable schematically indicates a handshape change. As the reduplication rule refers to the last syllable regardless of its structure, this supports the existence of the construct "syllable" (Sandler 1989).

(13) ACCIDENT [reduplicated]

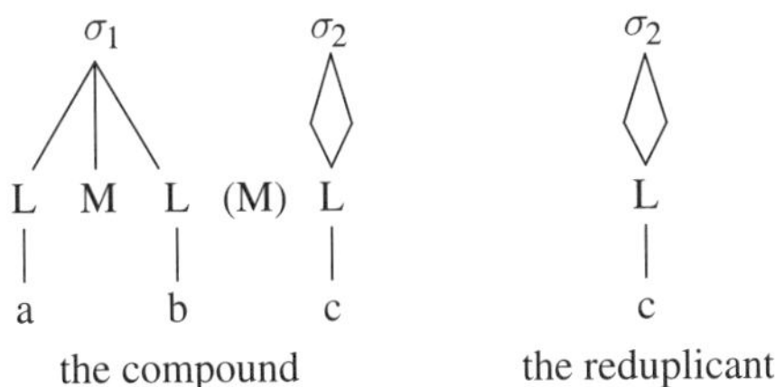

We now have both phonetic/phonotactic and phonological generalizations about the prosodic unit consisting of a single movement (which may be complex, i.e., consist of two or even three simultaneous movements), commonly called a syllable in the sign language literature, and summarized in Table 14.2.

The table illustrates both phonetic and phonological evidence for a unit that is prosodically defined and distinct from the morpheme and from the word, an interesting discovery in itself. It is reasonable to call such a unit a syllable for two reasons: (1) it is defined prosodically, in terms of movement which is hypothesized to be visually salient and (2) it shows some effects that are typical of a prosodic unit at the same level in spoken language, specifically, behavior regarding stress and reduplication. At the same time, we have already seen some significant differences. Two of the ubiquitous characteristics of the spoken language

Table 14.2 *Evidence for a syllable unit in sign language*

Sign language syllable generalizations
Hand Configuration Binary Branching Constraint (4a)
Timing Constraint (definitional) (4b)
Final syllable stress in ASL compounds
Initial syllable stress in lexically doubled words
Final syllable reduplication for temporal aspect in ASL compounds
Non-isomorphism
a. A single syllable may be monomorphemic, bimorphemic, or multimorphemic.
b. Words may consist of two or more syllables (though they are usually monosyllabic).

syllable are the asymmetry between onset and coda, and the complex category, rhyme, consisting of nucleus and coda. For example, onsets are more obligatory than codas cross-linguistically; the set of consonants that may characterize the coda is a subset of those that may occur in the onset (Goldsmith 1990); and the rhyme constituent alone may determine syllable weight and stress assignment. The only asymmetry we are aware of in sign language syllables has to do with signs with handshape change in which one finger position is open. In LSQ, and most likely in other sign languages as well, if the first handshape is closed, then it is typically characterized by thumb restraint, while if it is the last handshape that is closed, there is not necessarily thumb restraint (Miller 1991). Otherwise, no asymmetries have been attributed to onset and rhyme in the sign language syllable, a clear difference from spoken language.

Another difference from spoken language is in the nature of the two sequentially organized categories that have been proposed to characterize the sign language syllable. The sequential model as first introduced by Liddell and Johnson explicitly draws an analogy between static elements (holds in their model, locations in the Hand Tier model) and consonants, and between dynamic elements (movements) and vowels. Other researchers have followed suit. On more careful consideration, it appears that this analogy is either too sweeping or else only trivially viable, for the following reasons. (1) While spoken languages often have consonant clusters, there are no location clusters. (2) In a typical CVC syllable of spoken languages, there is not necessarily any similarity between the first and last consonant. In fact, in many languages, there is a strong tendency for consonants to have different places of articulation within a morpheme (McCarthy 1988). In sign language, the two locations in a typical syllable always share many features, especially place of articulation (see Chapter 16). (3) While some spoken languages have small vowel inventories, we know of no spoken language in which most vowels are default vowels like the straight path movements of sign language. (4) Spoken languages vary in terms of the number and types of consonants and vowels that constitute the onsets, nuclei, and rhymes of syllables (see footnote 1). Apparently, sign languages universally have the same syllable structure. More differences emerge from an examination of sonority, which we undertake in Section 14.6.

The phonetics of the spoken syllable offers some insight into the differences between spoken and signed syllables. MacNeilage (1998) and Davis and MacNeilage (1995) argue that the basic shape of syllables in spoken language is determined by the oscillation of the mandible (jaw). Although there are other articulators, such as the tongue and the lips, the authors claim that the "frame" for the consonant and vowel alternations in syllables is provided by the repeated raising and lowering of the mandible. They also bring evidence from infant babbling to suggest that the distribution of particular consonants and vowels is influenced by the same mandibular oscillation. Clearly, the sign unit we have been describing is different. As Meier (2002b) observes, there is no single predominant oscillator in sign languages. The hand is sometimes compared to the tongue as a primary articulator, but that analogy cannot be extended to actual phonological behavior in relation to other elements within the system. This is because the places of articulation that the hand must reach are often not anatomically contained within the same coherent unit as the hand in the way that the tongue is connected to the jaw and contained within the mouth. In particular, though the hand often articulates at some point on the body, it also commonly articulates at points in space, and these seem to be determined by spatial and perceptual factors more than by any constraints imposed by the physiology of the articulatory system. From a physical point of view, then, we must conclude that there are no significant similarities between the spoken syllable and the syllable of sign language. This also means that phonological generalizations that result from physical properties of syllables and their primitives will not be the same in the two modalities. So it seems that there are clear modality differences at this level of structure (see Wilbur 1999a). Implications of these differences are considered in the conclusion to this chapter.

14.6 Sonority in sign language

Another property that has been appealed to in defining the sign language syllable is sonority. As we've explained, in spoken languages, it is the relative sonority of sounds that establishes the peak (nucleus) of the syllable and organizes other sounds around it. If sonority is the property that lends salience and well-formedness to a syllable, and relative sonority organizes the phonetic material within the syllable, then this leads to the hypothesis that in sign language, movement of any kind is sonorous

(Brentari 1990). In spoken language, syllables are organized in terms of the *relative* sonority of their component parts. What evidence is there for relative sonority and its role in sign language?

We review a number of investigations into sonority in sign language, beginning with approaches that are most compatible with the sequential structure that we have been favoring throughout. The question asked is whether the sequential alternation between static and dynamic elements in sign language that Liddell and Johnson originally posited is related to sonority. We then consider, and argue against, other approaches which view sonority as a simultaneous property of the whole sign.

While all the studies reported have yielded interesting generalizations, the claims of different researchers are often incompatible or conflicting. There are three reasons for this. One is that each study relies on a different model of sign language phonology. Another is that they rely on different empirical data. The third reason, a more fundamental one, is that none of the treatments has been informed by an understanding of salience in a visually perceived language, simply because of a lack of experimental research in this domain. Our survey of the various theories and their empirical bases leads us to suggest that some of the phenomena attributed to relative sonority in sign language are more likely to have other explanations, such as articulatory reduction or relative loudness.

We hypothesize that the requirement for movement on the one hand, and the restricted nature of the sign language syllable and canonical word on the other, are indeed related to visual "sonority" or salience. But we also conclude that progress in phonological research on sign language sonority can only be made if conducted in tandem with empirical experimental investigations into salience in these languages.

14.6.1 Sonority in a sequentially organized syllable

Perlmutter (1992) follows Liddell and Johnson (1989 [1985]) and Sandler (1989) in arguing for sequences of static elements, which he calls "positions" (comparable to locations), and dynamic elements, called "movements" (similar to the movements of the other sequential models). As mentioned in Chapter 13, Perlmutter observes that secondary movement, such as rapid repetition of handshape change or wiggling of the fingers, co-occurs with the path movement in any syllable that has one. He claims that secondary movement co-occurs with a location only if there is no path movement in the sign. Schematic representations are shown in (14).

(14) Secondary movement distribution

In this representation, we use Ls instead of the Ps or positions of Perlmutter's model, for continuity. Assuming that secondary movement always co-occurs with a syllable nucleus, the conclusion offered is that a position (≈ location) can only be a syllable nucleus if it is not adjacent to a movement. The generalizations in (15) and (16) are derived from this distribution of secondary movement:

(15) Secondary movement features can occur only on the nucleus of a syllable. (Perlmutter 1992, p. 417)

(16) A P can be the nucleus of a syllable only if it is not adjacent to an M. (Perlmutter 1992, p. 417)

The sonority hierarchy proposed is simply that movements are more sonorous than positions: M > P (≈ M > L). The analysis implies that a P will be a nucleus if it can't be syllabified with a nearby M, and that secondary movement will then (and only then) have no choice but to be realized on the P. In a sense, Perlmutter uses the distribution of secondary movement as a diagnostic for the relative sonority of Ps and Ms.

The Delayed Completive aspect described in Chapter 9, Section 9.2, presents a problem for this analysis. It shows that there are signs in which a secondary movement does occur on a location that is adjacent to a path movement, contrary to (16). It demonstrates that secondary movement may define a syllable nucleus even if it is adjacent to an M, as in the sign RUN-OUT-OF] Delayed Completive, represented schematically in (17), in which the syllable nuclei [wiggle] and the M segment are shown in bold. That sign inflected for Delayed Completive aspect is not ill-formed, as Perlmutter's analysis predicts; it is simply disyllabic according to the definition offered in (1) above.

(17) Delayed Completive

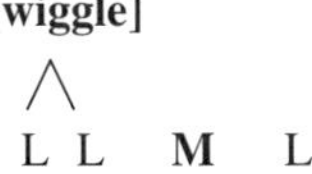

This means that secondary movement isn't a diagnostic for sonority; instead it manifests sonority, constituting a syllable nucleus. If it co-occurs with a movement, then the two types of movement together constitute a single syllable nucleus. If it co-occurs with a location, then the secondary movement alone is the nucleus.

Sandler (1993d) further pursues the idea that movement is related to sonority, and that movement segments are more sonorous than the static type, a claim with roots in Liddell and Johnson's and Sandler's early work, and adopted also in Blevins (1993).[14] Following Corina (1990b)

[14] Blevins' (1993) sonority scale for ASL is path movement > nonstatic articulator (= internal movement) > static articulator > location hold. Sandler's scale is similar, except for "static articulator," i.e., a secondary classifier morpheme held in place. Classifier

and Brentari (1990), Sandler assumes that sonority in sign language corresponds to visual salience. Observing the overwhelming preponderance of LML structure over signs with L-only plus internal movement, she surmises that path movement is preferred over internal movement as a syllable nucleus because it is more sonorous (salient) than internal movement.

Not only are morphologically simple signs typically L M L – i.e., signs that move from static L to sonorous M and back to static L – but, as demonstrated in Section 14.5, morphologically complex signs are as well. Morphological operations that involve simultaneous structure (like verb agreement) as well as those that alter sequential structure (like compounds reduced under lexicalization, and negative incorporation) tend to surface as LML syllables, i.e., as syllables with one path movement, as we have seen. Temporal aspect templates, illustrated in Chapter 13, Section 13.3, and Section 14.5 above, tend to have LML form, so that bases with no path movement (such as DIRTY, STUDY, etc.) are augmented to fit the template with path movement. Sandler (1993d) suggests that this LML conspiracy is guided by a constraint preferring a rise–fall sonority cycle (in the sense of Clements 1990) in the sign language syllable. Such phenomena are used to argue for the following sonority hierarchy, motivated primarily by the relative degree of movement.

(18) (Partial) sonority hierarchy adapted from Sandler (1993d)
path movement > internal movement > locations > contacting locations

14.6.2 Other theories of sonority

Two other proposals about relative sonority are reviewed briefly here. We will argue that each proposal uncovers significant generalizations, but that these generalizations are not likely to be related to sonority.

The first researcher to introduce the concept of relative sonority in sign language is Corina (1990b). He adopts a simultaneous model rather than a sequential one, and argues that there are no sequentially organized sonority differences in sign syllables. But Corina does propose a simultaneously instantiated sonority scale in ASL, shown in (19), on the basis of interesting alternations that he observes.

(19) Sonority hierarchy according to Corina (1996)
Movement sequence > full handshape change or orientation change > location change (i.e., path movement) > partial handshape change

First, he studies signs like (ASL) ASK, that are lexically specified for both path and internal movement, but in which one of these two movements is

constructions are not taken into consideration in Sandler's sonority scale or other work on the phonology of lexical words because these constructions are not words, and exhibit generally anomalous phonological behavior (see Chapter 5).

optionally deleted. In such signs, he finds that internal movement survives while path movement may delete. On that basis, he argues that internal movement is more sonorous than path movement, the opposite conclusion from that of Sandler (1993d).

An alternative explanation for Corina's observations suggests itself: the tendency of the hand-internal movement to survive in the signs Corina cites is due to lexical retrievability. On this view, the internal movement cannot delete because it carries so much information about the sign that the sign would not be recognizable without it. This suggestion is compatible with the fact that path movements add little information that is not predictable to the sign, as explained in Chapter 13, so that deleting them barely reduces retrievability of many signs. Relative retrievability is a phenomenon that can be studied empirically under experimental conditions, and resolution of the opposing views awaits such research.

Another observation made by Corina (1990b, 1996) is that some types of handshape change always co-occur with secondary movement; i.e., they are always rapidly repeated. The type of handshape-change signs that behave this way are precisely those in which neither of the shapes in the sign is open or closed; instead, the two positions are curved and bent, like ASL BUG, shown in Figure 14.9. Corina's claim is that such partial handshape changes are not sonorous enough and that they must therefore be rapidly repeated several times in order to reach a minimum sonority threshold.

Here too, an alternative analysis is at least equally plausible. Notice that the handshape changes in question are precisely those that seem to violate the Handshape Sequence Constraint (Chapter 10, example (7)). That is, neither of the shapes is open or closed. The alternative analysis now becomes clear: it is the rapid repetition that creates the partial handshape change, and not the other way around. Under such an analysis, signs like BUG are underlyingly specified for open and bent handshapes, thus satisfying the HSC, and they are specified for rapidly repeated movement as well.[15] The rapid repetition has the phonetic effect of preventing the hand from opening all the way.

Support for this alternative comes from signs with internal movement that are demonstrably not underlyingly specified for rapidly repeated movement but that gain such movement through morphological derivation. For example, DOUBT, produced with the handshape sequence open and then bent , may be derived to form the adjective DOUBTFUL by adding rapidly repeated handshape change (Liddell 1990b). In the

[15] For different representations of secondary movement, see Sandler (1989, 1993d), Corina (1990b, 1996), Liddell (1990b), Perlmutter (1992), Brentari (1993, 1998), van der Hulst (1993).

BUG (ASL)

Figure 14.9 Sign with secondary movement and partial handshape change

process, according to the illustrations provided by Liddell, the fingers do not reach the fully open shape, but rather phonetically articulate two degrees of bent shape instead. We are suggesting that the same may be true of signs like BUG. That is, such signs actually do conform to the HSC by being underlyingly specified for one shape that is fully open, and, in words like BUG, are underlyingly specified as well for rapidly repeated movement. The effect of this movement is to phonetically reduce the handshapes.

We now turn to a different theory of relative sonority, one that we mentioned in the previous chapter in our discussion of the Prosodic model. The theory of sonority adopted in that model is motivated by variations in signs that are made under circumstances in which signers want their signing to be perceived at greater distances, such as on a stage (Brentari 1998).[16] Under those circumstances, signers may substitute an underlying movement with a movement made at a joint that is closer to the body (substituting the shoulder for the elbow, for example), creating a larger movement. Brentari's proposal suggests that this joint substitution is a form of phonetic enhancement.[17] The citation forms of UNDERSTAND and its enhanced form were shown in Figure 13.10. As explained, Brentari argues that such substitutions unify all movements into one phonological class, regardless of how they are produced, a claim independently motivated and one we find compelling.

She also makes a different claim based on the same observation, a claim that we challenge: that the degree of proximity to the body of the joint responsible for a given movement determines the sonority of that movement. The hierarchy in (20) is proposed on that basis.

[16] Rapidly repeated movement, variously called trills, trilled internal movement (TIM), or secondary movement, are not included in these alternations.

[17] Brentari cites Stevens and Keyser's (1989) theory of phonetic enhancement. Their theory, however, relates to relative markedness of features belonging to different categories, where the relation between enhancement and sonority is indirect and partial. We interpret Brentari's use of the term enhancement in a more straightforward way, as simply increasing the relative visual salience of a movement.

(20) Brentari's (1998) sonority scale[18]
shoulder joint > elbow joint > wrist joint > base-of-finger joints > middle finger joints

We will argue that the alternations she describes are analogous to loudness rather than sonority. Distinguishing the two in sign language reveals an important difference between the two modalities.

14.6.3 Sonority versus loudness

The phenomenon under consideration has been observed before, notably by Uyechi (1996 [1994]). She uses as an example the chant in the famous 1988 demonstrations at Gallaudet University[19] in favor of hiring a Deaf president: DEAF PRESIDENT NOW. She compares the very large signs used in that chant with the way in which the signs would be produced in an imaginary police state where it was forbidden to openly express such an opinion. The differences are similar to those that Brentari attributes to sonority. Uyechi's loudness explanation seems to us to be the more straightforward interpretation of the observations of different sized signs, that "bigger" signs are shouted and "smaller" ones are murmured!

This interpretation is supported by Crasborn's (2001) study of SLN (Sign Language of the Netherlands) phonetics. He conducted an experiment in which signers of SLN were asked to sign to each other across a large room in one condition, and sitting very close to each other in another. The subjects made adjustments similar to those Brentari describes, and the types and degrees of adjustments made under different conditions varied across signs and signers, as is expected for phenomena that are not phonological in nature.

The challenge in sign language becomes one of distinguishing between a linguistic property (sonority) and a non-linguistic property (loudness). Loudness in spoken language depends on the intensity of the sound source, specifically, the rate at which the lungs collapse and push the air through the vocal cords. The faster the rate at which the air is pushed through, the greater the amplitude of vocal cord vibration, and the louder the perceived sound. Loudness is a matter of degree; differences in loudness are gradient – both in terms of physical properties and in terms of the way loudness differences are used and interpreted in the system.

Sonority in spoken language is quite different. After the lungs push the air through the larynx, the configuration of the vocal tract filters the resulting sound in such a way as to enhance certain frequencies and their

[18] In Brentari's scale, the base-of-finger joints have the technical name, metacarpal, and middle-of-finger joints are called interphalangeal. We use the more transparent terminology here.

[19] Gallaudet University is a university for Deaf students in Washington, DC.

harmonics at the expense of others. The amount of sonority a sound has is determined mostly by how open the mouth is, i.e., by the filter rather than by the source. The configurations of the oral cavity filter the sound, so that a more open mouth permits more energy to radiate from it, hence more sonority. Vowels are more sonorous than consonants, and the vowel [a] is more sonorous than the vowel [i].[20] And this is true regardless of the amplitude of vocal cord vibration, i.e., regardless of whether you shout or murmur, whether you are declaiming from a stage or intimately confiding in a friend.

While relative sonority is phonetically scalar just as relative loudness is, sonority is a linguistic property, encoded in language in a way that is discrete. Different amounts of sonority are encoded in the discrete phoneme inventory of a language; there is no gradient continuum of [a] sounds; rather [a] is distinct from other vowels in any phoneme inventory, corresponding to a particular configuration of the vocal tract. Similarly, all of the sounds in a language are typically treated by the phonology of that language as either plus or minus sonorant; the relation is binary and not scalar. Relative sonority is relevant for syllabification in spoken language. But here too, sonority is distinguished from loudness. Sonority is relative across sounds, not within sounds. Specific phonemes do not alter their relative sonority value in the way that any sound can be altered for loudness.

In sign language, the closer to the body the articulating joint is, the larger the perceived signal – the "louder" it is visually. And, according to Crasborn's findings, differences observed for sign language loudness are gradient, like loudness in spoken language. Loudness spans three kinds of internal movement (middle finger joints, base-of-finger joints, and wrist joint) and two kinds of path movement (elbow and shoulder).

Irrespective of both sonority and loudness, the difference between internal and path movement is a discrete one within the phonology. Signs are underlyingly specified for a particular path or internal movement, and not for any variant along a continuum from path to internal. For example, FLAT-TIRE and WINE in ISL, shown in Figure 14.10 are very similar, but WINE has only internal movement while FLAT-TIRE has only path movement.

The grammar does not recognize incremental distinctions between joints of relative proximity. According to Sandler's sonority hierarchy shown in (18), this two-way distinction between path and internal movement is the only one within the movement category that might be relevant for a sign language counterpart to sonority.

[20] Thanks to John Kingston for helping us understand the phonetics of sonority and loudness.

a. FLAT-TIRE (ISL)
path movement

b. WINE (ISL)
internal movement

Figure 14.10 Minimal pair for path and internal movement

We have tried to draw a distinction between sonority and loudness in sign language. Why should this be such a challenge in sign language, while the two are clearly distinct in spoken language? Here we get to a fundamental problem in finding an analogue to sonority in sign language.

14.6.4 *Sonority summary: assessing the relation between visual salience and linguistic sonority*

As mentioned, the source of energy in spoken language is the lungs, and the filter responsible for creating different sounds is the vocal tract. The acoustic signal that results is created by sound waves as they emerge from the vocal apparatus, displacing the air, which sets up vibrations in the auditory system, and the signal is then interpreted as sounds of language. Syllables organize themselves around the element with the most sonority. More energy at the source (the lungs) results in loudness regardless of the configuration of the filter (the vocal tract); the source and the filter are independent physically, and have independent effects, i.e., loudness on the one hand and sonority on the other.

In sign language, the situation is quite different, because the configurations of the articulatory system are perceived directly. We are not in a position to speculate about the relation between manual articulation, the resulting visual signal, and its perception. But it seems clear that this relationship is qualitatively different from the source-filter-signal-perception relationship that exists in spoken language. This difference should not be taken lightly, and exploring it will lead to a deeper understanding of phonetics and phonology in each modality.

As there is no obvious distinction between source and filter in sign language, the *physical* difference between linguistic salience (sonority) and loudness is harder to pinpoint in this modality than it is in the spoken modality. Nevertheless, this does not mean that distinguishing the two is hopeless. Rather, we look to linguistic patterning as the key. The gross distinction between internal movement and path movement is encoded linguistically as two different categories of movement, and it seems that the greater salience of syllables with path movement makes it the preferred type in the system. Gradient differences created by degrees of proximalization at any of five joints is interpreted non-linguistically, as loudness.

Clearly, the concept of a syllable in sign language, its internal organization, and the relative salience of its components are areas requiring more experimental work.[21]

14.7 Syllables and sonority: conclusion

Our approach to sign language research is one that takes full advantage of linguistic description and linguistic theories that have been developed on the basis of spoken language. We take this approach because we think it is reasonable to expect human language to conform to certain organizing principles regardless of physical modality. At the same time, the extent to which sign language and spoken language are alike is still an empirical question whose answer must not be taken for granted if we are ever to achieve a comprehensive theory of language (Sandler 1993c, 1995b). The construct "syllable" and the property of sonority are instructive here.

The syllable is a unit determined partly by the physical properties of the production and perception systems, and as such there are significant differences between syllables in the two physical modalities. But the syllable is also a prosodic unit referred to directly by the phonology, e.g., in rules of aspiration in spoken language or thumb restraint in sign language, and rules of stress and reduplication in both. These grammatical parallels justify a relatively direct analogy in the two modalities, and even use of the same label, *syllable*.

At the same time, the properties and internal organization of signed and spoken syllables have very little in common with those of the spoken syllable, and should be studied in their own right. For instance, the property of sonority is so intrinsically tied to the modality of production and perception as to render any direct comparison across language modalities difficult. Yet the patterning of the system does offer us some hints about where to look for relative salience in sign language.

The evidence in this chapter and the previous one suggests the syllable types shown in (21) below. The LML structure on the left is a sign with path movement like (ISL) FLAT-TIRE shown in Figure 14.10a, and the L-only structure represented schematically on the right with two finger (or orientation) positions in (21) is like (ISL) WINE shown in Figure 14.10b).[22]

[21] Some experimental work has already been undertaken, but space considerations do not permit discussion of it here. See, for example, Grosjean (1981), Clark and Grosjean (1982), Emmorey and Corina (1990), an interpretation of some studies by Kingston (1999), and Corina and Hildebrandt (2002).

[22] Other researchers propose a greater variety of syllable types (e.g., Liddell and Johnson 1989 [1985], Perlmutter 1992, Brentari 1998). Our investigations and analyses yield a sparer inventory. Unfortunately, space does not permit a comparison here.

(21) Sign language syllable types

The difference in salience in these two syllable types might be compared to the difference in sonority between the two syllables in the English word, *rhythm* [rɪðm̩]. The first syllable nucleus, with a full vowel, is more sonorous than the second, containing a nasal consonant as nucleus. Unlike spoken language, though, there is no conclusive evidence in sign language that different degrees of sonority determine the organization of elements within the syllable.

We've mentioned two observations suggesting that signs with path movement (LML) may be more "sonorant" or salient than those with internal movement only (L). First, they are far more common in the lexicon, and second, under derivation and inflection, signs tend to be augmented or reduced to the LML form rather than reduced to L. Most other arguments for sonority were shown to fall through or to be explainable with equal plausibility by other factors.

The differences in organization between spoken and signed languages at this level of analysis raise important theoretical issues about the relation between the biology of language and linguistic form. If the manual/corporal-visual modality is responsible for the form of syllables in sign language, then the oral–aural modality is responsible for the form of syllables in spoken language. This implies that constraints on spoken syllables are not an arbitrary set, supplied to language by UG. Instead of taking them as given, we stand to reach a deeper understanding of those linguistic constraints by motivating them, through investigation of the physical channels in which they are produced and perceived. (See, e.g., Hayes 1999 for a relevant discussion of phonetically grounded constraints in spoken language.)

Similarly, the details of the interaction between production, perception, salience, and sign language form must be determined by experimental work in tandem with more linguistic research. As those details begin to emerge and to be compared with the spoken language system, our understanding of phonology will be considerably advanced.

We now turn our attention to higher levels of prosody, the description of which is more tractable: the prosodic word, the phonological phrase, and the intonational phrase.

15 Prosody

In spoken language, the flow of speech is not a steady unbroken stream, nor is it uttered monotonally. Instead, it is broken up into rhythmic chunks; some of its elements are more prominent than others; and it is characterized by meaningful excursions of pitch, called intonational tunes. This prosodic pattern is such an integral and systematic part of language that it enables newborn babies to notice when a speaker changes from one language to another, even when the segmental information is filtered out of the signal, leaving only prosodic properties (Mehler, Jusczyk, Lamberz, Halsted, Bertoncini, Amiel-Tison 1988). We intend to show that central properties of the prosodic system are common to languages in both modalities, spoken and signed.

Prosody is often thought of as an area of phonology, and that is understandable, under the broad definition of the term *phonology* proposed in Chapter 8: *phonology is the level of linguistic structure that organizes the medium through which language is transmitted.* This broader definition implies that the realm of phonology includes material above the word as well, encompassing, for example, the phrase, the utterance, or even the discourse. However, many linguists maintain that prosody comprises a separate component of the grammar, independent of other levels of linguistic analysis, because it has units and rules for their distribution and combination that are specific to the prosodic component. This prosodic component systematically interacts with all other components – with phonology, syntax, semantics, discourse, and pragmatics.

Research has motivated a hierarchy of prosodic constituents (Selkirk 1984, Nespor and Vogel 1986). The hierarchy shown in (1), adapted from Nespor and Vogel,[1] ranks prosodic constituents, from smallest to largest. These constituents exist alongside morphological and syntactic constituents, but are often not isomorphic with them. For example, *Jane's* in the sentence *Jane's singing* is two morphosyntactic words, *Jane* and *is*, but a single prosodic constituent – one syllable. The non-isomorphism of

[1] We have omitted the clitic group, which has proved controversial in spoken language research, and subsume it with the prosodic word.

prosodic constituents with morphosyntactic constituents is one of the strongest arguments that prosody is an independent component of the grammar, and cannot be relegated exclusively to an interaction between syntax and phonology without mediation.

(1) Prosodic hierarchy
mora < syllable < foot < prosodic word < phonological phrase < intonational phrase < phonological utterance

In earlier chapters, we have dealt with the prosodic unit, syllable, and with prosodic templates employed by the morphology. The discussion of prosody in the present chapter will move up to higher levels of the hierarchy: to the prosodic word, the phonological phrase, and the intonational phrase.

Our goal here is to describe the elements that go into the prosodic system in sign languages, and in this way to demonstrate that sign language grammar has a prosodic component. We'll also take a close look at the claim that sign language has intonation, expressed on the face. The discussion lays the groundwork for investigations of non-manual elements in connection with syntax, to be explored further in Unit 4. As intonation is part of prosody, and prosody is related to syntax, it is not surprising that some scholars have attributed to facial expression an explicitly syntactic role. We will suggest instead that the function and distribution of the relevant facial articulations correspond more closely to an intonational system.

15.1 The Prosodic Word

Just as morphemes and syllables are not isomorphic, morphosyntactic words and prosodic words are not always the same thing. It's very common, for example, for unstressed function words to group together with a nearby word prosodically, to form one prosodic word. Examples in English are contractions formed with auxiliaries like *Bill is* → *Bill's*. In many languages, like French, pronouns cliticize onto verbal hosts: *je aime* → *j'aime*. In these examples, the function word loses its syllable nucleus altogether, so that it would be ill-formed if pronounced as a full syllable; instead, it attaches prosodically to the host. In ISL, and apparently in ASL as well, there is also a distinction between morphosyntactic and prosodic words. In particular, pronouns can cliticize to lexical words, losing some of their phonological integrity, and forming one prosodic word together with the host. We will describe two such phenomena.

It has been noticed that in ASL, the handshape of pronouns can assimilate to that of a neighboring sign (Corina and Sandler 1993). This phenomenon has also been reported for Quebec Sign Language (LSQ – Parisot 2000), as well as for Danish Sign Language (Engberg-Pedersen

a. I (ISL)

b. I-READ (ISL)

Figure 15.1 Cliticized pronoun and host with handshape assimilation

1993). It occurs in ISL as well for personal, possessive, and deictic pronouns, and has been attributed to cliticization (Sandler 1999b, 1999c). In Figure 15.1, the pronoun 'I' takes on the handshape of the verb READ.

It is clear that cliticization of a function word to a host is involved, rather than a more general phonological assimilation rule, since it is always the case that the pronoun is the word that loses its underlying handshape, and never the neighboring full lexical word. Pronouns are typically unstressed in all languages, and are commonly cliticized. Given relative freedom of word order in ISL, assimilation can be either progressive or regressive; it is the lexical status of the words that determines the direction, and not the word-level phonology.

Another type of pronoun cliticization, coalescence, has also been observed in ISL (Nespor and Sandler 1999, Sandler 1999b, 1999c). In this type, in which the host is a two-handed h2-S sign, the host and pronoun reduce to a single syllable. Specifically, the non-dominant hand completes the full lexical sign, but the dominant hand only signs half of the host sign, and then signs the pronoun clitic while h2 completes the host. The sequence of two movements of the dominant hand is simultaneous with the single movement of the non-dominant hand, which creates a monosyllabic envelope for the newly formed prosodic word (see Chapter 14, example (1) for a definition of the sign language syllable). The coalescence process is illustrated in Figure 15.2. Figures 15.2a and b illustrate the signs SHOP and THERE uttered independently. In Figure 15.2c we see that the dominant hand switches from SHOP to THERE in "midstream," while the dominant hand simultaneously completes the sign SHOP.

The prosodic words formed by assimilation and coalescence are different from lexical words in some ways and similar to them in others. Let us examine the two cliticization processes more closely.

The handshape assimilation pictured in Figure 15.1 produces a single handshape specification for the host and clitic. The resulting form conforms to the Selected Finger Constraint (Chapter 14, Section 14.4),

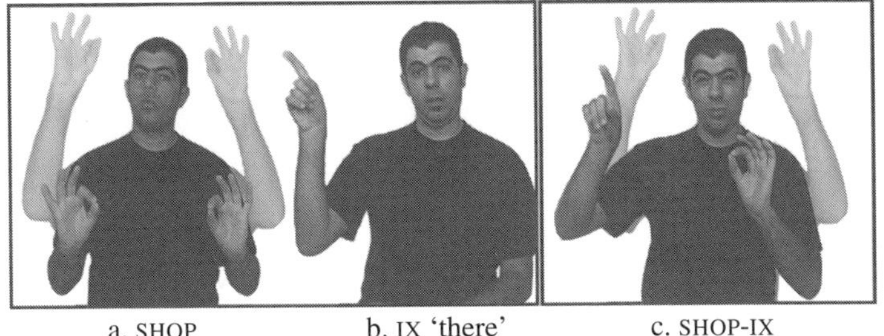

a. SHOP b. IX 'there' c. SHOP-IX

Figure 15.2 Independent signs and cliticized host plus pronoun

rendering a surface form that bears a certain resemblance to a monomorphemic sign. However, this assimilatory process violates a constraint encoded in the hand configuration hierarchy presented in Chapter 10, Section 10.3, and results in an anomalous form. According to that hierarchy, if handshape assimilates, as in compounds, then orientation assimilates as well. This means that complex lexical words like compounds can have the same orientation on the two member signs with two different handshapes, through orientation assimilation. But it also means that assimilation can't result in the same handshape on the two member signs with two different orientations.[2] Yet in host plus clitic forms like I-READ, just such a form is created: handshape assimilates (→ one handshape), while orientation does not (→ two orientations).

The prosodic words formed by the other type of cliticization, coalescence, shown in Figure 15.2 (SHOP-IX), also serve to make the prosodic word so formed more like lexical words. Like most lexical words, the prosodic envelope provided by the non-dominant hand is monosyllabic (see Chapter 14, Section 14.5). But, like assimilation, this process is also non-structure preserving, in this case violating the Symmetry Condition on the behavior of the non-dominant hand (see Chapter 12, example (1)). In morphemes in which both hands move, the Symmetry Condition requires the two hands to have the same shape, path, and movement. It seems that this constraint holds not only for the morpheme, but for the syllable and the morphosyntactic word as well – we know of no counterexamples at any of these levels of structure. But as Figure 15.2 shows, in the prosodic word, the dominant hand changes its shape from to , while the non-dominant hand remains throughout, and the dominant hand changes its movement trajectory in mid-word, while the non-dominant hand completes the full movement of the host, SHOP.

[2] Monomorphemic, disyllabic lexical words, like ASL COOK, may have two different orientations of the hand with the same handshape, but these orientations are always mirror images of each other, e.g., supine and prone, and always signed with respect to the same place of articulation, here, h2. In cliticization, which is postlexical, these constraints are violated.

The explanation for these apparent violations is this: clitic formation is a postlexical process, occurring not in the lexicon – not through a process of word formation – but rather "later," at the point where words are strung together in sentences. Such a form is permitted because the assimilation process that creates it is postlexical and therefore may be non-structure preserving, as are many postlexical processes generally (Kiparsky 1982, 2002). In English, for example, a geminate [t:] may occur in *night time* although English does not have lexical length distinctions, and lexically prohibited consonant clusters occur freely in connected speech as well. In the same way, the prosodic words formed by handshape assimilation as in Figure 15.1 (I-READ) are non-structure preserving, but permitted postlexically.

The discussion leads us to three conclusions about these cliticized prosodic words in ISL: they are not isomorphic with morphosyntactic words; they are non-structure preserving; at the same time, they take on certain characteristics that make them more like lexical words.[3]

15.2 The Phonological Phrase

The constituent in the prosodic hierarchy that is above the Prosodic Word is the Phonological Phrase. According to Nespor and Vogel (1986), this unit is projected from syntactic phrases according to an algorithm that starts with a phrasal head belonging to a major lexical category: Nouns, Verbs, or Adjectives. Once constructed, phonological phrases can be restructured or merged, especially if they are short. Phonetically, this prosodic constituent is identifiable by minor rhythmic breaks. For example, the square brackets divide the following sentence into phonological phrases that would be likely to occur at a normal to slow rate of speech: *[The very tall] [construction worker] [carefully walked] [under the ladder]*. In English, the rhythmically prominent or strong position in the phonological phrase is the last stressed syllable in the phrase.[4]

To further support their claim that the prosodic hierarchy includes phonological phrases, Nespor and Vogel provide evidence that is independent of phonetic rhythmicity. The evidence consists of phonological rules in several languages that have the phonological phrase as their domain. For example, the Italian rule of *Raddopiamento Sintattico* (RS) applies only within phonological phrases. RS is an external sandhi rule

[3] A constraint competition analysis of these facts is suggested in Sandler (1999b), in which the Symmetry Condition, the Selected Finger Constraint, and Monosyllabicity are in competition, and the constraints have different rankings lexically and postlexically.

[4] According to Nespor and Vogel's theory, the direction in which phonological phrases are formed from the head, and the position of prominence within them, are predicted by the direction of syntactic recursivity – i.e., the word-order properties – of the language.

(i.e., a rule of assimilation across a word boundary). The rule geminates a consonant at the beginning of a word after a lexically stressed syllable: *p* and *l* after the stressed *é* of [*é* ***p****iú* ***l****oquace*] shown underlined and in boldface in (2a). But if a phonological phrase boundary separates the consonant from the stressed syllable, as in (2b), then RS does not apply and the consonant *p* of [*piú attentamente*] does not get lengthened, because the preceding stressed [*ó*] is in a different phonological phrase.[5]

(2) a. [Il tuo pappagallo]$_P$ [é **p**iú **l**oquace]$_P$ [del mio]$_P$
'[your parrot] [is more talkative] [than mine]'
b. [Guardó]$_P$ [piú attentamente]$_P$ [e vide]$_P$ [che era un pitone]$_P$
'[He looked] [more carefully] [and saw] [it was a python]'

A study of prosodic constituents in ISL (Nespor and Sandler 1999) has shown that there are phonological phrases in that language. This investigation coded and analyzed thirty elicited sentences, each signed by three signers, providing a corpus of ninety sentences. The rhythmic phonetic cues that mark the end of phonological phrases are: hold (freezing the signing hand or hands in their shape and position at the end of the sign), pause (relaxing the hands briefly between signs), or reiteration of the last sign. Nespor and Sandler's findings suggest that the end of the phrase is the prominent position in the phrase.

The study also discovered that the surface number of iterations of a sign is often determined by position in a phrase. The lexical representation of signs usually specifies a single iteration. But some signs have two, a distinction that may be contrastive (see Figure 13.3). In Chapter 13 on movement, the feature [restrained] was used for signs with two iterations, i.e., signs that are reduplicated once lexically.[6] If a sign that is underlyingly marked for the feature [restrained], i.e., reiterated once, occurs in a weak position in a phonological phrase (i.e., not phrase finally), it is often signed only once, losing the reiteration that occurs in citation form. However, if a sign that is underlyingly non-reduplicated occurs in the prosodically strong position at the end of the phrase, it often is reduplicated, even as many as three times (four iterations).[7] In an investigation of the phonology of the sign language of Quebec (LSQ), Miller (1996) finds that reduplication is influenced by prosodic context in that sign

5 Phonological phrases with a small number of words in them can be restructured into a neighboring phrase (Nespor and Vogel 1986).

6 Lexical reduplication and phrase-final reiteration are each distinct functionally and distributionally from morphological reduplication that occurs for example in temporal aspect inflection.

7 Laura Downing points out that a citation form is in a phonological phrase, implying that all signs should potentially be reiterated in citation form. However, this is not the case: the lexical distinction between single and double movement is observed in citation form but may be neutralized by higher level prosodic cues. A possible explanation rests on Nespor and Sandler's (1999) suggestion that reiteration marks prominence. As prominence is a relative property, it requires the presence of more than one word in order to surface.

language as well, suggesting that this may be a general property of sign language prosody.[8]

Phonological phrases in spoken language are marked not only by phonetic cues but by phonological processes, like RS in Italian. In ISL as well, a rule of external sandhi provides further evidence for the domain in that language – it is a rule of Non-dominant Hand Spread (NHS). Specifically, if there is a two-handed sign within a phonological phrase, the non-dominant hand can anticipate or perseverate the triggering sign by articulating the configuration and location of that sign. This spreading extends to the beginning and/or end of the phonological phrase, while the dominant hand articulates other signs. Crucially, the researchers found that NHS stopped at the boundary of the phonological phrase. Example (3) is divided into two intonational phrases (each labeled with an I subscript), the first containing three phonological phrases, and the second containing two phonological phrases. Each phonological phrase (labeled with φ) was marked by a characteristic phonetic cue – hold, pause, or reiteration of the last sign.

(3) [I-TELL HIM]$_{\varphi}$ [BAKE CAKE]$_{\varphi}$ [TASTY]$_{\varphi}$]$_{I}$ [[ONE FOR ME]$_{\varphi}$ [ONE FOR SISTER]$_{\varphi}$]$_{I}$
'I told him to bake a tasty cake, one for me and one for my sister.'

Unlike Italian RS, NHS does not involve sequential segments. Rather, the spread of the non-dominant hand from the triggering two-handed sign is simultaneous with the signing of other words by the dominant hand.

Figure 15.3 illustrates NHS in an excerpt from (3). The illustration shows the signs BAKE and CAKE with NHS. Also shown are the sign HIM in the phonological phrase that precedes BAKE CAKE, and the sign TASTY in the phonological phrase that follows it. In this example, the non-dominant hand from the sign BAKE spreads to the end of the phonological phrase by remaining in the same configuration as in the source sign, BAKE, throughout the next sign, CAKE, which is a one-handed sign. The end of the phonological phrase is marked by a hold – holding the hand in position at the end of the last sign. Precisely at the onset of the next phonological phrase, [TASTY]$_{\varphi}$, the sandhi stops, and the hand assumes a neutral shape. In the actual signing of this sequence, the change in the handshape and location between HIM and BAKE, and the rapid retraction of the fingers to a neutral position between CAKE and TASTY, are both perceptually salient (Sandler, in press).

NHS is an optional process, and does not always occur. Unlike hold, pause, and reiteration of the last sign, NHS is not a phonetic cue to a phonological phrase boundary. Instead, it is a rule of external sandhi

[8] If reiteration is influenced by prosodic position in ASL as it is in ISL and LSQ, this could explain why the underlying distinction between nouns and verbs in noun/verb pairs (Supalla and Newport 1978; Chapter 4, Section 4.1) was not discovered earlier.

Figure 15.3 Non-dominant Hand Spread in the phonological phrase

which, by stopping at the phonological phrase boundary, is argued to provide further evidence for the existence of that constituent. What is important in the context of prosodic constituency is what the boundaries of NHS are when it does occur. In order to be convinced that the domain for the rule is the phonological phrase, we must rule out two other factors that might explain why the spread of the non-dominant hand stops where it does: the occurrence of another two-handed sign before or after the phonological phrase boundary, or the co-occurrence of a phonological phrase boundary with an intonational phrase boundary. When sentences with such co-occurrences were removed from consideration in two studies involving a total of seven signers and about eighty sentences, there were still no examples of h2 spreading beyond the phonological phrase boundary (Nespor and Sandler 1999, Sandler and Dachkovsky 2004). Therefore, the domain of the sandhi rule must be the phonological phrase boundary, and the rule provides evidence for the existence of this constituent.

15.3 The Intonational Phrase and intonation in sign language

At the next higher prosodic level, that of the Intonational Phrase, even more obvious prosodic breaks occur. Parentheticals, non-restrictive relative clauses, topicalizations and other extrapositions, vocatives, expletives, and tag questions form intonational phrases in many languages (Nespor and Vogel 1986). The salience of this break is due to clear rhythmic cues – IPs are typically separated by pauses and often by breaths – and also due to the distribution of intonational contours, to which we will return shortly. Sign languages have intonational phrases and intonational tunes as well, the latter expressed through facial expression. In ISL as in spoken languages, clear prosodic breaks were found for such syntactic constituents as those listed above. For example, when the elicited sentences in (4) were signed, they were broken up into intonational phrases in the expected way.

(4) Intonational phrases in ISL

a. Parenthetical

[DOGS THOSE]$_I$ [(YOU) KNOW]$_I$ [LIKE EAT COOKIES]$_I$

'Dogs, as you know, like cookies.'

b. Non-restrictive relative clause
[BOOKS HE WRITE PAST]$_I$ [I LIKE]$_I$ [DEPLETE]$_I$
'The books he wrote, which I like, are sold out.'
c. Right-dislocated element
[THEY TIRED]$_I$ [PLAYERS SOCCER]$_I$
'They're tired, the soccer players.'
d. Topic
[CAKE]$_I$ [I EAT-UP COMPLETELY]$_I$
'The cake, I ate up completely.'

Pronouncing the English translations of sentences (4a-d) above will give you a feel for the intonational phrase in spoken language, whose boundaries typically fall where the commas are. The breaks separating the intonational phrases in these ISL sentences of the Nespor and Sandler corpus had the following characteristics: they were marked by a change in head or body position and an across-the-board change in all aspects of facial expression. They were also optionally characterized by eyeblink. Eyeblinks often characterize phrase boundaries in American Sign Language as well (e.g., Baker and Padden 1978, Wilbur 1994b, Wilbur 1999a). The phrases described in the ASL studies appear to correspond to the Intonational Phrase (and not to the lower level Phonological Phrase).[9] This suggests that when eyeblinks occur, they are a reliable indicator of intonational phrase boundaries in sign languages generally, as breaths are in spoken language.

Comparison of the same sentences in different sign languages suggests that the change in head and body position together with facial expression at intonational phrase boundaries is common cross-linguistically (Sandler and Dachkovsky 2004). But one study indicates there may be some cross-linguistic variation in prosodic marking. Boyes Braem (1999) describes rhythmic side-to-side body sways for structuring certain kinds and levels of discourse in Swiss-German Sign Language, a cue not reported in other languages. Her work also shows that body sways of late learners differ from those of early learners on a range of measures, implying that the system is indeed linguistic.

In ASL and ISL, the ends of intonational phrases are prominent. In ISL, the last word in intonational phrases typically has more reiterations and larger signing than the last word in phonological phrases. In a study of prominence in American Sign Language, Wilbur and Zelaznik (1997) used an instrumental tracking device to determine prominence. They found that the final position in the intonational phrase was characterized by highest peak velocity, which they interpreted as prominence.

[9] For a comparison of methods and findings of Wilbur and those of Nespor and Sandler, see Sandler (1999a).

Intonational phrases in spoken languages are an important domain for intonational tunes (Pierrehumbert 1980). Intonational tunes impose a wide range of meanings on spoken utterances. In some languages, such as Hebrew, intonation may distinguish a declarative sentence from a yes/no question, as exemplified in (5) below. There is no syntactic difference between the two in these languages; only intonation distinguishes them.

(5) Hebrew intonational minimal pair

a. Yoni	halax	laxanut.
Yoni	go-3rd-sg-m.-pst	to-def-store
'Yoni went to the store.'		
b. Yoni	halax	laxanut?
Yoni	go-3rd-sg-m.-pst	to-def-store
'Did Yoni go to the store?'		

Within intonational phrases, the pitch accents fall on relatively prominent elements, and the boundary tones come at the edge, together forming the phrase's melody. The pitch accents and boundary tones themselves have meanings, and have been referred to as morphemes (e.g., Hayes and Lahiri 1991). This means that they have the dual function of delineating prosodic constituents and adding meaning to utterances. While dramatic pitch excursions tend to occur at intonational phrase boundaries, smaller changes at phonological phrase boundaries may also occur, effecting subtle nuances of meaning. Furthermore, intonational tunes in some languages have been analyzed as componential, building up complex meanings through sequences of meaningful tones and tone combinations.

An example from Bengali (Hayes and Lahiri 1991) given in (6) illustrates some of these properties. The $L^* H_P L_I$ tune is the focus tune, consisting of an L^* pitch accent – that is, an accented low pitch – followed by an H (high) phonological phrase boundary tone and an L intonational phrase boundary tone. The focus tune has the effect of emphasizing the part of the sentence on which it falls. The succeeding H tone is a continuation rise, indicating that more information follows. As we can see here, phrasal tunes are componential.

(6) [jodio ram [harlo,]$_P$]$_I$ (o k^{h}ub b^{h}alo k^{h}elec^{h}ilo)

$L* \ H_P \ L_I \ H_I$

'Although Ram lost, (he very well played).'

We now return to sign language. The corpus examined in the prosody study of Nespor and Sandler, in addition to coding the behavior of the hands, coded each non-manual element of the face independently: eyebrows, eyes (upper and lower lids), cheeks, mouth, head position, similar to the system devised by Baker and Padden (1978). A (different-colored) line was drawn opposite the facial articulator label, and extended across the glosses of the signs with which they co-occurred. An example is given in (7).

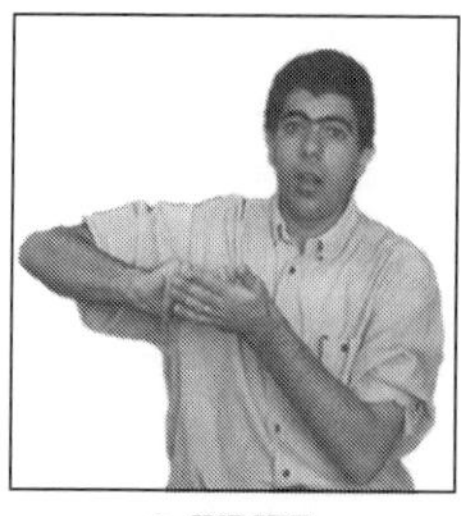

a. WRITE

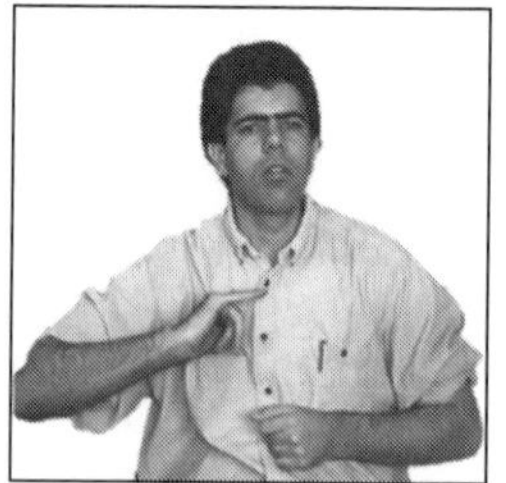

b. INTERESTING

Figure 15.4 Complete change in non-manual markers in two adjacent intonational phrases in ISL

(7) Prosody coding (Nespor and Sandler 1999)

	[[BOOK-THERE]$_P$	[HE WRITE]$_P$]$_I$	[[INTERESTING]$_P$]$_I$
brows	up ________	________	down ________
eyes	squint ______		droop ________
mouth		'O' _____	down ________
tongue			
head	tilt ________	________	
mouthing	*'book'* ______		*'interesting'* ___
torso	lean ________	________	
hold	=		
reiteration	−1	×3	×4
pause			
speed			slow
size		big	big

The findings were consistent. The lines in that corpus were systematically discontinued at the intonational phrase boundary. In the example in (7), there are two phonological phrases in the first intonational phrase: BOOK THAT and HE WRITE, and one phonological phrase in the second intonational phrase, INTERESTING. The first IP is interpreted as the topic and the second as the comment (see also Rosenstein 2001). Although there is some small difference in non-manual articulation between the first two phonological phrases (in particular, there is a squint on the first phonological phrase only, and a non-neutral mouth shape only on the second), *all* facial configurations and the head and body positions change at the intonational phrase boundary in this example, and throughout the Nespor and Sandler corpus. This change is clearly indicated by the fact that all the lines on the coding sheet break between intonational phrases. Pictures of the two adjacent signs on either side of the intonational phrase boundary in this example, WRITE and INTERESTING, are given in Figure 15.4.

The fact that facial expressions coincide with intonational phrases is one of the motivations for the claim that they correspond to intonation, a claim we will support further in the next section.

15.4 Superarticulation: facial expression as intonation

It has long been known that facial expression and other non-manual markers play a significant linguistic role in sign languages.[10] Liddell (1978, 1980) presented the first detailed analysis of these markers in ASL. In that groundbreaking study, he demonstrated that yes/no questions, sentence topics, negated constituents, relative clauses, and other structures have characteristic facial expressions and head postures. He also examined the interaction between the scope of non-manuals and the scope of the constituent, finding that they were coextensive. His investigation provided evidence for word-order properties of ASL, to be presented in Chapter 18. Liddell also distinguished non-manual signals of emotional states such as surprise or anger from grammatical signals, pointing out that the emotional ones are more gradient, a claim confirmed in Baker-Shenk (1983). Analyses of the upper face/head and body positions in ASL showed that specific non-manual articulations mark questions, relative clauses, topics, conditionals, WH-questions, and rhetorical questions (Baker and Padden 1978; Baker-Shenk 1983; Liddell 1978, 1980). Baker-Shenk (1983), Liddell (1986), Wilbur (1994b), Wilbur and Patschke (1999), and Bahan (1996) subsequently have identified functions for additional components. Together with all researchers since Liddell, we concur that non-manual signals are grammatically significant. But unlike Liddell and some recent researchers such as Neidle et al. (2000), we do not claim that facial expression is a direct reflection of syntax. Instead, we support the position taken by Reilly, McIntire, and Bellugi (1990b), and Wilbur (1991), that facial expression corresponds to intonation. We present evidence for this claim here, and take up the issue again in connection with WH-questions in Chapter 23.

In this discussion, we refer only to facial expression that corresponds to intonation, and not to other uses of facial expression such as lexical marking or adverbials, which were mentioned in Chapter 4.[11] To avoid the pitch-based label, "intonation," we call the intonational system of sign language *superarticulation*, and we use the term *superarticulatory arrays* for the combination of articulations corresponding to tunes (following Sandler 1999c).

[10] See, for example, Stokoe (1960), Baker and Padden (1978), Liddell (1980), Reilly, McIntire, and Bellugi (1990a), Nespor and Sandler (1999).

[11] We also exclude iconic mouth gestures (Sandler 2003) from our purview here, as they are argued to be the sign language equivalent to co-speech gesture, and therefore outside the formal linguistic system.

Studies of ISL have demonstrated that certain facial expressions consistently bear certain meanings in that language (Nespor and Sandler 1999, Sandler 1999c, Sandler and Dachkovsky 2004, Dachkovsky 2004) as they do in ASL. As in spoken language intonation, superarticulatory meaning is broad, and gains more specific interpretation through its interaction with the meaning of the text with which it is associated. Furthermore, like the tones comprising intonational tunes in spoken languages, these superarticulations may combine componentially with one another to give complex meanings. Finally, grammatical facial expressions in sign language can be distinguished from emotional facial expressions, just as linguistic and paralinguistic intonation in spoken language are distinguishable from each other. In the sections that follow, we will illustrate each of these characteristics.

15.4.1 Superarticulation is linguistic

Superarticulatory arrays similar to those that mark yes/no questions and WH-questions in ASL (Baker and Cokely 1980, Liddell 1980), in British Sign Language (Sutton-Spence and Woll 1999), Sign Language of the Netherlands (Coerts 1992), Danish Sign Language (Engberg-Pedersen, 1993), and many others, are found in ISL as well (Nespor and Sandler 1999, Sandler 1999c, Sandler and Dachkovsky 2004). Typical yes/no questions in ISL are marked by brow raise, wide eyes, and a forward head position – Action Units 1, 2, 5, and 57 in the Facial Action Coding System of Ekman and Friesen (1978). Typical WH-questions are marked by lowered brows (AU 4) and head forward (AU 57). A common systematic facial expression in ISL is a kind of squint used to mark shared information (lower lid contraction, AU 7). What appears to be the same superarticulation with the same interpretation is reported for Danish Sign Language (Engberg-Pedersen 1990). These superarticulatory arrays are illustrated in Figure 15.5

Finer grained superarticulatory arrays have also been found in ISL. For example, factual and counterfactual conditionals are distinguished by different superarticulatory arrays in that language, discussed in the next section.

The meanings attributed to these arrays are independent of the sentences they are articulated on, like the "morphemes" of spoken language intonation. This independence is exemplified by the fact that the superarticulations may combine with sentences whose syntax or lexical meaning do not match directly. For example, while prototypical WH-questions are accompanied by the articulatory array shown in Figure 15.5b, sentences that are WH-questions syntactically may be accompanied by different facial expressions if their pragmatic intent is not that of a WH-question. Conversely, the typical WH facial expression

a. Yes/no Q b. WH-Q c. shared information

Figure 15.5 Three grammatical superarticulatory arrays in ISL

may accompany strings that are not syntactically WH-questions, if the pragmatic intent is to ask a WH-question. We will provide examples of this dissociation in Chapter 23, where we present more specific arguments in support of our position that grammatical facial expressions in sign language are best understood as intonational "tunes." The next section demonstrates that meanings of superarticulatory arrays are built up componentially.

15.4.2 Superarticulation is componential

Coulter (1979) was among the first to identify component pieces of non-manual articulations, and to ascribe potential functions to them in ASL. Superarticulatory arrays can combine to form more complex arrays with more complex meanings in ISL as well (Nespor and Sandler 1999, Sandler 1999c). For example, in that language, a WH-question about information designated as shared is marked by a furrowed brow (WH) plus squinted eyes (shared), shown in Figure 15.6.

Current work on ISL is showing that even arrays often interpreted holistically may be complex, i.e., that each individual action unit makes a contribution to meaning.[12] For example, brow raise in that language can co-occur with yes/no questions, factual conditionals, adverbial clauses, relative clauses and topics.[13] Dachkovsky (2004) proposes that brow raise conveys the general meaning of prediction. In these structures, it predicts that the first part of the utterance is going to be followed by some relevant information or consequence. In simple yes/no questions, the brow raise can be interpreted as predicting that a response will follow. Both yes/no and WH-questions are characterized by a forward head position (AU 57). Wilbur and Patschke (1998) suggest that the forward head position that occurs in these structures in ASL as well indicates inclusion of the addressee, a suggestion that is also compatible with the ISL data.

[12] A micro-component analysis of this sort might account for Reilly et al.'s (1990a) interesting finding that children master the non-manual components of the ASL conditional array bit by bit between the ages of 5 and 8, rather than all at once.

[13] Wilbur and Patschke (1999) and Wilbur (2000) isolate brow raise in ASL, a component in a large number of superarticulatory arrays, and provide an analysis predicting its occurrence on syntactic grounds. See Chapter 22 for discussion.

Figure 15.6 WH-Q plus shared information: componential facial expression

Similarly, lower-lid squint (AU 7) in ISL occurs, often with various other superarticulations, on topics, relative clauses, parentheticals, and counterfactual conditionals, contributing to each array the same general meaning: designating the information so marked as shared between the interlocutors for the purpose of the utterance.

Dachkovsky (2004) analyzed counterfactual conditionals in ISL, sentences such as *If Ilan had more self-confidence, he would have passed his driver's test*. The first clause in such sentences is characterized by raised brows and lower-lid squint. Each superarticulation makes an independent contribution to the meaning, at once sharing with the addressee the knowledge that the event did not occur, and predicting the information in the next clause, i.e. what would have happened otherwise. This analysis demonstrates that the meanings associated with each action unit in the system are broad, gaining specificity and adding subtlety by combining with each other and with the meaning of the sentences they characterize. Intonation works like that.

15.4.3 *The physical instantiation of intonation versus superarticulation*

Superarticulation in sign language and intonation in spoken language, then, have three principal characteristics in common: (1) their functions, which are illocutionary, semantic, and pragmatic, (2) componentiality, and (3) the prosodic constituents that provide their domain: the phonological phrase and especially the intonational phrase. But the physical instantiation of tunes and arrays in each system is strikingly different, both in terms of the number of independent articulators that convey the tunes/arrays, and in terms of temporal distribution with respect to each other and to the co-occurring text.

In spoken language, the only intonational source is the vocal cords, which can vibrate at faster or slower frequencies resulting in higher or lower pitch. Intonational tunes are produced by changes in the frequency at which the vocal cords vibrate (the fundamental frequency or F_0) and are perceived as pitch excursions. Because only one articulator is involved, each tone is produced independently, and tunes consist of sequences of these tones. Although a range of tones is implemented in this system phonetically, from a phonological point of view it is sufficient to distinguish only the two extremes, H (high) and L (low), and to account for the rest by rules of implementation (Pierrehumbert 1980). The sequences of individual H and L tones that comprise tunes typically are arranged at particular points of the text: on the stressed syllable of the head of focused constituents (see Selkirk 1984) and at phonological and intonational phrase boundaries (Beckman and Pierrehumbert 1986). While the tones occur simultaneously with particular syllables (hence the traditional term, "suprasegmental"), the syllables themselves are arranged in a sequence, and even tones falling on a single syllable also follow one another in a sequence.

In sign language, the physical system is quite different. There are several independent articulators – the brows, the upper and lower eyelids, the cheeks, the lips – and each articulator can perform more than one articulation. For example, the brows may rise or lower and the eyelids may contract or widen. The result is a system with a larger potential inventory of articulatory possibilities than spoken language intonation has. Whether or not this results in a richer intonational system is an empirical question. But one aspect of the physical instantiation is clearly different in the two modalities: the temporal instantiation of tones/superarticulations with respect to each other and in relation to the text. Instead of a linear sequence, the arrangement in sign language is simultaneous. Superarticulatory arrays typically co-occur with the entire prosodic constituent they characterize, and not only with the stressed syllable of a focused or boundary word as in spoken language, so that there is nothing in sign language that directly corresponds to pitch excursions, nor has the equivalent of a pitch accent been isolated. Furthermore, the superarticulations themselves within each array – i.e., whole "tunes" – co-occur simultaneously.

15.4.4 Grammaticization and language specificity of superarticulation

All humans use facial expression when they communicate, and many of these expressions are universal (Ekman and Friesen 1975). How otherwise could we explain our ability to communicate attitudes and emotions to people with whom we have no common language? Or to empathize with people in news reports or characters in movies who speak different languages and come from cultures very different from our own? As communication through facial expression is universal, it should not be at all surprising that deaf people, for whom the visual medium is primary for communication, use facial expression as well. However, it should be clear by now that the use of facial expression in sign language is different. What is an idiosyncratic means of communication, one that may occur independently of language or as a supplement to it, has been grammaticized into a conventional system in sign language.

In an attempt to track the process of this grammaticization in ASL, Janzen argues that the yes/no question facial expression (raised brows and head tilted forward) evolved from a universal questioning expression, and that topic marking in that language evolved in turn from the yes/no non-manual configuration (Janzen 1998, 1999, Janzen and Shaffer 2002).

Evidence for the nonlinguistic source may be seen in a situation in which a person holding a drink makes eye contact with someone and then holds up the drink while raising his/her eyebrows. The interlocutor understands this to mean, 'Do you want a drink?' According to Janzen, this facial expression forms the basis of a conventional non-manual marker in ASL.

In Janzen's analysis, topics are seen as information from the interlocutors' shared world of experience, either new or old in the discourse. The meaning of the topic marker is associated with one of the meanings of yes/no questions: *Do you know x?*... This overlap in meaning is claimed to underlie the further grammaticization of topics from yes/no questions. The phonetic difference between yes/no questions and topic marking in ASL is the direction of head tilt: forward for yes/no questions and backward for topics. Janzen cites Wilbur and Patschke's (1998) explanation mentioned above: the forward head tilt on yes/no questions indicates inclusion of the addressee, while the backward head tilt found on the otherwise similar topic marking is interpreted as exclusion of the addressee.

An approach like Janzen's can explain why certain basic superarticulatory arrays, like yes/no questions, seem to be widespread across sign languages, and reveals another similarity between this system and spoken language intonation. In spoken language, for example, yes/no questions are nearly universally marked by a high tone (rising pitch) (Bolinger 1986, 1989). One explanation that has been offered for this universality is that certain pitch patterns evolved from purely biological factors and are now innate (Ohala 1984). Subsequently, such patterns are grammaticized (Gussenhoven 1999). A similar explanation for the grammaticization of universal facial expressions is suggested in Campbell, Woll, Benson, and Wallace (1999). In both modalities, the emotional or non-linguistic system exists alongside the grammatical intonation system. But if that is the case, how can we tell them apart?

15.4.5 Linguistic and nonlinguistic superarticulation

While differences between emotional or paralinguistic intonation and linguistic intonation in spoken language are not obvious, the two can

Figure 15.7 Grammatical "shared information squint" for three signers on the same phrase: 'Yossi's brother' in the utterance 'I just got a fax. Yossi's brother was killed in an accident.'

be distinguished. First, paralinguistic intonation reflects emotion and is therefore idiosyncratic, while linguistic intonational tunes have meaningful pragmatic functions and are conventionalized (Ladd 1996). Second, paralinguistic intonation is gradient. One can express more or less excitement, sadness, etc. by the degree of pitch excursion. Linguistic intonation, in contrast, is discrete and categorical (Gussenhoven 1999). The interpretation of a yes/no question melody does not depend on the mood of the asker, and small differences in the contour of a linguistic tune do not correspond to incremental changes in meaning or illocutionary force.

Signers use facial expression in both non-linguistic and linguistic ways, another parallel with intonation of spoken language. Linguistic use of superarticulation is conventionalized, while paralinguistic non-manual articulations are idiosyncratic. Furthermore linguistic superarticulation is distributed across prosodic constituents discretely. Its onset is abrupt (Baker-Shenk 1983); and it does not begin before the constituent or continue after it (Baker-Shenk 1983, Sandler and Dachkovsky 2004). In all of these ways, linguistic superarticulation is different from nonlinguistic use of facial expression.

An utterance signed by three signers in a study of superarticulation in ISL illustrates the difference clearly (Sandler and Dachkovsky 2004). The elicited utterance is, *I just got a fax. Yossi's brother was killed in an accident*. In this utterance, the string *Yossi's brother* was characterized by the "shared information squint" (AU 7) superarticulation, shown in Figure 15.7. The onset and offset of this grammatical superarticulation were synchronized within three video frames of the onset and offset of the prosodic constituent established by manual signs in the string. (There are 25 frames per second of PAL videotape.)

But each signer produced a different array of facial articulations and head positions on the rest of the sentence, idiosyncratically reflecting different kinds, nuances, and intensities of emotion. Furthermore, these arrays, exemplified in Figure 15.8, were not synchronized with the signed text, instead beginning or ending up to 17 frames from the constituent boundary, and optionally crossing intonational phrase boundaries.

Figure 15.8 Idiosyncratic emotional facial expressions characterizing other parts of the same utterance

The distinction between linguistic and non-linguistic facial expression is supported by acquisition and aphasia studies as well. Anderson and Reilly (1998), Reilly and Bellugi (1996), and Reilly, McIntire, and Bellugi (1990a) provide evidence that affective (non-linguistic) and grammatical (linguistic) facial expression are acquired differently by children, and Corina, Bellugi, and Reilly (1999) report case studies on signers with brain lesions which indicate that the linguistic and non-linguistic uses of facial expression are represented in different hemispheres of the brain.

15.5 Nonisomorphism

Although phonological and intonational phrases often correspond to syntactic constituents like the phrase or the clause, they are not strictly isomorphic with them. Rate of speech or signing, length of the syntactic constituent, and other factors have a clear influence on prosodic constituency. The two forces of syntax and rhythmicity in language don't always pull in the same direction, so that syntactic and prosodic constituents are not fully isomorphic, as shown in the excerpt from the children's story in (8).[14]

(8) Syntactic constituency vs. prosodic constituency
Syntactic: [This is [the cat that killed [the rat that ate [the malt]]]]
Prosodic: [This is the cat] [that killed the rat] [that ate the malt]

If the syllable were isomorphic with the morpheme, or the phonological phrase with the syntactic phrase, then there would be no need to posit a separate level of prosodic constituents in the grammar. Is such non-isomorphism found in sign language?

In Chapter 14, we presented evidence from sign language for non-isomorphism between the syllable, a prosodic unit, and the morpheme and the word, morphosyntactic units. In Section 15.1 above, we showed that the prosodic word and the morphosyntactic word are not one and the

[14] The example is taken from *The House that Jack Built*, a children's story compiled recursively into one long sentence.

same. Evidence is presented in the Nespor and Sandler study for non-isomorphism at the phonological and intonational phrase levels of structure in Israeli Sign Language. Specifically, syntactic units which project their own prosodic constituents may be restructured and incorporated into nearby constituents if these syntactic units are short, or if the rate of signing is fast.

Especially compelling evidence of the dissociation between syntax and prosody can be found in the superarticulation system. This runs counter to a good deal of current research on ASL syntax, which relies on the assumption that facial expressions are explicit syntactic markers determined entirely by the syntax. We've provided a number of arguments here that the system is intonational instead, and will provide evidence of the dissociation between syntax on the one hand, and the rhythm and intonation of prosody on the other, in Chapter 23.

15.6 Summary, conclusion, and future research

Like all human behavior, communication among humans is subject to rhythmicity. It appears that language recruits this rhythmicity to interpret constituents that are not inherently rhythmic in nature, such as words, clauses, sentences, utterances, and higher discourse segments. This results in a prosodic system in which a hierarchy of prosodic constituents corresponds to morphosyntactic constituents to some extent, but not fully. Intonation superimposes itself upon this combination of syntactic structuring and rhythmic accentuation, systematically adding particular kinds of semantic information to the message. The existence of a prosodic system is a linguistic universal.

This chapter has served to substantiate the claim that prosody exists in sign language, and that it has certain key features in common with the spoken language system. But we have just begun to understand the structure of the sign language prosodic system in general, and of the intonational system in particular. How should intonational meanings best be characterized? How are they distributed and associated with the text? How are they interpreted? Is there an underlying system of intonational tunes that is altered by phonological and phonetic rules to produce the surface arrays, as has been demonstrated for spoken language (Pierrehumbert 1980; Gussenhoven 1984)? What are the prosodic differences across sign languages? Neither instrumental tracking and transcribing of this system in sign language, nor experimental work on its perception and interpretation, have yet been done. Our work is cut out for us.

16 Phonology: theoretical implications

In this unit, we have taken apart the phonological elements that contribute to making a sign and examined each of them in detail. Now it is time to put them back together again and to look at the system from a somewhat broader perspective. First, we attempt to draw together areas of consensus among researchers with regard to the phonology of sign language. Still unresolved issues emerge at every turn, which point the way to future research.

From this broader perspective, the overall architecture of the phonological component comes into view, and with it the relation of that component to the rest of the grammar. We will review some of the differences between the phonological patterning of words in the lexicon and phonological patterning at the level of phrases and sentences. This bifurcation is found in spoken languages as well, and may be considered universal.

At the same time, sign languages have a third level of structure to draw on, one that we will call *non-lexical*, which is particular to the modality. At this level, the dividing lines between phoneme and morpheme on the one hand, and form and meaning on the other, are blurred, as are certain constraints on structure. But the contrast between lexical and non-lexical does not erode the imprint of linguistic structure on sign language; on the contrary, it places it in high relief.

The last topic is that of the differences between the two modalities. We review the differences between signed and spoken phonologies, and consider the implications for our understanding of language in general.

16.1 Consensus and unresolved issues

Within each aspect of sign language phonology, areas of consensus and of disagreement can be found. Let's begin with the major phonological categories. There is across-the-board consensus on the centrality of Stokoe's categories of hand configuration and location (regardless of what these categories are called and how they are represented in each model). There is broad agreement on the centrality of movement as well, though there are some voices of dissent, mainly over how it should be represented. Most models of sign language phonological structure now accept sequentiality, whether it is a sequence of static and dynamic segments (Liddell 1984b, Liddell and Johnson 1989 [1985], Sandler 1986, 1989, Perlmutter 1992), or a sequence of abstract timing units with which only the non-dynamic endpoints ultimately associate (van der Hulst 1993, Brentari 1998). The notion of a sign syllable, defined as a movement unit, is very widely accepted.[1]

Another area of consensus is the division of handshape features into the categories of selected fingers and positions (Sandler 1987a, 1987b, 1989, 1996a, Corina and Sagey 1989, Corina 1990a, Perlmutter 1992, van der Hulst 1993, Brentari 1998). The hierarchical representation proposed in Sandler (1987a, 1987b, 1989) is also widely accepted.

The claim that orientation is a subcategory of hand configuration (Sandler 1987a, 1987b, 1989) remains unrefuted so far and is also incorporated into the DP model (van der Hulst 1993, 1996) – although other models are either not fully compatible with it (e.g., Brentari 1998) or do not reflect it (Liddell and Johnson 1989 [1985], Perlmutter 1992). Taken together, the models of the handshape category support the view that phonological features are grouped in classes that are hierarchically organized (Sandler 1987a, 1987b, 1989, Corina and Sagey 1989).

An area of healthy dispute is the phonology of the non-dominant hand, but even here there is significant consensus. All researchers agree that the non-dominant hand is a subordinate category and not a "separate but equal" articulator in the lexical representation of signs (see Chapter 12 for details and references). This is a significant claim, since it implies that languages with two anatomically identical potential articulators (sign languages) are like languages with only one (spoken languages). Each modality has only one primary articulator at the phonological level: the hand and the tongue. The area of dispute is essentially whether the non-dominant hand plays two different subordinate roles in the phonology, or only one.

The models of the phonological structure of sign language vary, sometimes dramatically. This is to be expected in a new field attempting to define language in a different modality. Even so, consensus has been reached on several key issues, as we have shown. A clear exception is sonority.

Though a number of investigators have explored the notion of sonority or visual salience in sign language, and have claimed that it plays a role in the syllable, it is not possible to draw firm conclusions. Nearly every investigation has a different empirical basis, leading to disparate claims that are difficult to compare with one another. The reason suggested

[1] An exception is van der Hulst (1993), who suggests that what is considered a syllable by other researchers is instead a rhyme, and that the transition between signs provides the onset.

(Chapter 14, Section 14.6) is that the importance of modality cannot be marginalized here, and oral sonority cannot be fruitfully compared with visual salience at this stage. Experimental research is needed to assess the property in sign language, how it is perceived, and what effect it has on the structure of the sign.

16.2 The architecture of the phonological component: lexical, postlexical, and non-lexical

We would like to aim the camera at a comfortable distance now in order to compare the phonology of the lexicon with phonological processes that occur "later," when words are inserted into sentences. The addition of morphemes changes the phonology of signs in the trivial sense that they are pronounced differently than their morphologically simple counterparts. Such changes in the phonological form of words that are the result of morphological processes are often described as part of the lexical phonology. Other phonological changes that occur whenever the phonological conditions are met (including across words), without reference to morphological structure or operations, are not part of word formation, and are assigned to the postlexical level, where words are put together in sentences (Kiparsky 1982, 2002).[2]

A model of grammar that is divided into lexical and postlexical levels has certain characteristic features, and interesting implications as well. First, lexical-level processes must be structure-preserving, in the sense that they may not result in the creation of forms that do not belong to the underlying inventory of phonological elements or that violate well-formedness constraints. Second, lexical processes may only apply within words. Postlexical processes, on the other hand, may be non-structure-preserving, and they may apply between words. An important implication is that all lexical processes are ordered before all postlexical processes. The ordering metaphor, as Goldsmith (1990) calls it, reflects the fact that word formation is in some sense independent of sentence formation. When sentences are formed from words, then the contact between the words may result in alternations that can be different in kind from those that may only occur within words. In particular, they may fail to respect lexical phonological and morphological constraints.

From a functional point of view, the distinction between lexical and postlexical phonological alternations makes sense. Communication is not significantly impeded by postlexical processes which create ambiguities or other confusions, because sentence context is so good at resolving these potential problems.

[2] In phonological theory of spoken language, there is no longer a unanimous consensus concerning the lexical/postlexical distinction. See Kiparsky (2002) for a defense of the distinction in the context of Optimality Theory. As we show here, respecting this distinction allows us to state several interesting generalizations about sign language.

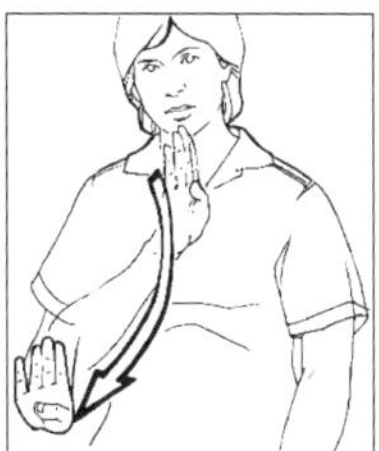

Figure 16.1 QUIET (ASL) with Weak Drop (reprinted with permission from Padden and Perlmutter 1987)

16.2.1 Lexical and postlexical phenomena in sign language

Some clear arguments are made for a similar architecture in ASL in an article by Padden and Perlmutter (1987), where they show that a lexical morphophonological process must occur before a postlexical phonological process. The lexical process in question derives characteristic adjectives from plain adjectives. The formational change involved is as follows: if the input is a one-handed sign, then the Characteristic Adjective is formed by adding the non-dominant hand, making the derived form two-handed, and producing reduplicated, alternating movements, as shown in UNDERSTAND and its corresponding Characteristic Adjective, FLEXIBLE, shown in Chapter 4, Figure 4.2. If the input is two-handed, the surface form is different: the whole sign is reduplicated, but with synchronized rather than alternating movement, as shown in Chapter 12, Figure 12.3b.[3]

Now that the phonology of the lexical rule is clear, we turn to the postlexical phonological process involved: Weak Drop. It deletes the non-dominant hand from two-handed signs. For example, the underived sign QUIET, shown in its citation form in Figure 12.3a, is shown in Figure 16.1 after the application of Weak Drop.

Since the conditions for application of Weak Drop are entirely phonological, having nothing to do with morphological processes, it is assumed to be postlexical. As such, it is predicted to apply after morphological operations, if the architecture of sign language grammar is similar to that of spoken language. Indeed, Padden and Perlmutter showed that Weak Drop must apply after Characteristic Adjective formation, and may not apply before. Were Weak Drop to apply before Characteristic Adjective formation that derives TACITURN from QUIET (see Figure 12.3b), then

[3] The description of Padden and Perlmutter requires some modification. If the input sign is two-handed and symmetrical (h2-S), then the derived form is reduplicated and synchronized, as the authors state. However, if the input is two-handed but h2 is a place of articulation (h2-P), then h2 remains stationary like any other place of articulation, while h1 alone reduplicates the sign's movement (Sandler 1993a). In addition to being necessary for deriving the correct surface form, the additional distinction required by the rule provides support for the Hand Tier model that suggests two different representations for h2 (see Chapter 12, Section 12.1).

the input to Characteristic Adjective would be one-handed, and the rule would then produce alternating movement. Instead, the architecture of the grammar prevents such forms from occurring.

More evidence for a postlexical level in sign language comes from cliticization in Israeli Sign Language, discussed in Chapter 15, Section 15.1. Both cliticization processes must be postlexical because they occur in the syntax, where function words combine with content words to form phrases and sentences. In addition, they are non-structure-preserving, forming prosodic words that violate lexical well-formedness constraints (Sandler 1999b). In the syllable coalescence process, both hands begin to sign the lexical host sign, and the non-dominant hand completes it while the dominant hand changes its path half-way through, and signs the pronoun (see Figure 15.2). This form violates the Symmetry Condition (stated in Chapter 12, example (1)), which says that if both hands move, they must have the same hand configuration and the same or symmetrical movement. Syllable coalescence is therefore non-structure-preserving: no lexical process produces such forms.

The other ISL cliticization process, handshape assimilation (Figure 15.1), is also non-structure-preserving, but in a different way. It disrupts the lexical representation in which orientation is subordinate to handshape, and must therefore assimilate together with it (see Chapter 10, Section 10.3). So far, we have seen no counterexamples to this proposed hierarchical structure of handshape and orientation in any lexical processes of ASL or ISL, and even the error data of Newkirk et al. (1980) confirm its robustness. However, in the non-structure-preserving postlexical process of cliticization, the integrity of the relationship between selected fingers and palm orientation is violated in both sign languages. An even more obviously non-structure-preserving assimilation reported in ASL (Corina and Sandler 1993) involves coalescence of handshape, such that the resulting form has two different selected finger specifications simultaneously. In particular, the sign HAVE in the sequence HAVE IX (where HAVE specifies all fingers bent and contacting the chest, while IX (index) is a pronoun specified for extended index finger only), undergoes single-finger assimilation. The middle, ring, and pinky fingers are all curved and making fingertip contact with the chest, while the index finger only is extended, assimilated from IX. Once again, this must be postlexical, as the assimilation occurs across words. Such facts support the claim that sign language grammars, like those of spoken languages, are structured into lexical and postlexical components. Finally, the external sandhi rule of Non-dominant Hand Spread (Chapter 15, Section 15.2) results in non-structure-preserving configurations in which there may be two places of articulation simultaneously present in the signal. In the example shown in Figure 15.3, BAKE CAKE, the place of articulation for BAKE, the non-dominant hand, co-occurs with the place of articulation for CAKE, the chin.

16.2.2 A non-lexical level in sign language

In addition to the lexical and the postlexical, sign languages are unique in possessing linguistic structures that we might call "non-lexical."[4] In particular, the classifier system, described at length in Chapter 5, consists of underspecified morphemes of hand configuration, location, and movement, the same elements which are meaningless phoneme-like units within lexical words. While most of the elements that comprise classifier constructions must be in the lexicon, their combination does not result in "words," and that is why we are including them under the heading of non-lexical. Instead, these morphemes combine to form complex predicates.

The non-lexical forms that result apparently enter into grammatical subsystems with different properties from those of ordinary words and sentences. For example, we showed in Chapter 5 that classifier constructions often consist of strings of complex predicates with a single classifier argument which span any number of intonational phrases. Such constructions may translate as a sequence of propositions. The non-dominant hand can simultaneously represent an additional argument in such constructions, adding to their complexity and to their departure from lexical form. The gestural roots of these languages and the fact that they are perceived visually afford them kinds of expression that are simply not available to the aural–oral modality.

From the point of view of phonology, what is interesting about these forms is that they do not obey the phonological constraints of the lexicon. For example, each hand may articulate a different classifier morpheme in a single construction, in violation of the Dominance and Symmetry conditions on the non-dominant hand (Chapter 12, examples (1) and (2)). Similarly, movement patterns are permitted in this system that do not occur in lexical signs (Chapter 13). The classifier subsystem provides a basis for more creative uses of language in story telling and poetry, also subsumed under the category of "non-lexical." Using the basic principles of the subsystem, nonce forms may be created that are immediately understandable (see Sutton-Spence and Woll 1999, Sandler and Lillo-Martin 2001; and Chapters 5 and 6). The building blocks of both lexical and non-lexical systems may be selectively interpreted and combined in the service of metaphor (Wilcox 2000, Taub 2001). Forms in the non-lexical system may exhibit gradience (e.g., the use of movement in the poem described in Chapter 5), typically not exploited in linguistic systems, the forms of which are instead discrete.

In fact, even the lexicon itself is not hermetically sealed against non-lexical influences. Since many words in the lexicon originated as classifier

[4] Non-lexical should not be interpreted as non-linguistic. See Chapters 5 and 20 for morphological and syntactic analyses of the classifier subsystem, a linguistic system which we analyze as non-lexical.

constructions, the lexicon may "leak" when such words are reanalyzed into their component classifier parts (Figure 6.2). In Chapter 5, this was described as a sign language special kind of backformation, a phenomenon that is reflected in the phonology too. For example, it has the effect of violating a constraint that holds at the level of the phonological phrase. If there is a two-handed sign that undergoes this kind of backformation, where each handshape is reanalyzed as a classifier rather than a meaningless phonological element, then the non-dominant hand may spread across phonological phrase boundaries, which is otherwise prohibited (Chapter 15, Section 15.2).

The pervasive presence in sign languages of both lexical and non-lexical systems, and the clear formal dichotomy between these systems, do not, in our view, point to a non-linguistic explanation for sign language structure. On the contrary – the clarity with which the two are formally distinguished, i.e., the strict constraints on phonological form of the morpheme and the word (Chapter 14), make the identification of a *word* in sign language straightforward.

Consider the significance of this result. The existence of the word is a necessary condition for any language, and its identification is essential for acquisition and for processing. In these languages that also have a non-lexical component, the formal constraints on words, and by extension the clear distinction between words and nonwords, provide a significant advantage for acquisition and processing of the words and sentences of sign languages.

What we are calling the non-lexical system, manifested productively in the classifier subsystem and exploited for special effect in story telling and poetry, offers an auxiliary type and range of expression that are unique to the modality.

16.3 Universals and modality effects in both modalities

What can we learn about language from the phonology of signed languages? In some very significant ways, signed languages are surprisingly like spoken languages at the phonological level of structure, supporting the view that there are phonological universals regardless of language modality. At the same time, there are significant differences. These differences should not be dismissed as "modality effects," but instead they should motivate us to look more closely at the role of the physical system in the shaping of phonological structure in *both* modalities (see also Sandler 1995a, in press, Lillo-Martin 2002). Let's be more specific about universals that emerge from comparison of the phonology in the two modalities, noting the differences that are revealed as we go.

The first universal is the existence of a sublexical level of structure that is meaningless, discrete, finite, and systematically organized. Given the different modality, it is not at all obvious a priori that sign languages would have this level of structure. Nor is it necessarily to be expected that the elements of this component may be altered in rule-governed ways under certain morphological and/or phonological-contextual conditions. In other words, it is a significant discovery that sign languages, like spoken languages, have phonologies, and the properties just listed are indeed universals of human language. Considering the likelihood that sign languages certainly evolve from an iconic base, it is all the more remarkable that this abstract level of structure inevitably arises. This tells us that human minds create this kind of system wherever they get together to make language.

In each language modality, certain features are common across languages, and are frequently referred to by constraints and rules, while others are less active in phonological systems. This observation leads to the (Jakobsonian) notion of markedness, a notion which is clearly exemplified by the distribution and behavior of handshapes and of the interaction between the two hands. A comparison of the relative markedness of phonological elements in the two modalities may provide deeper insight into the nature of phonological markedness in general, its relation to articulation, and its influence on phonological systems.

The internal organization of features reveals another interesting similarity between the two modalities. In particular, there is compelling evidence in both modalities that features cluster into categories that correspond to their articulators, and that these categories are organized hierarchically (see especially Chapter 10). At each level of the hierarchy, the features subordinate to it behave as a group. If the evidence accrued so far is representative, then these aspects of the organization of features and feature categories appear to be universal.

The features themselves are of course different. While distinctive features apparently exist in any natural language, and may be considered a universal property, the quest for a universal set of them must now be conducted according to modality. This discovery should not elicit the complacent response that some things are simply "modality effects." If the set of features required to describe sign languages is a function of modality, then the set of features required to describe spoken languages is also a function of modality. If each modality carves out a different set of features, then the set arrived at must therefore somehow be *explained*, motivated on the basis of production, perception, and processing constraints, rather than assumed to be simply innately specified. Articulation-based constraints on the system may also be approached in this way.

In all natural languages, the phonetic features define natural classes of sounds. Since the features are different in the two modalities, it follows that the natural classes must necessarily also be different. Just as spoken languages have processes or constraints affecting all stop consonants or all vowels, for example, sign languages have processes or constraints affecting all handshapes or all movements.

Languages in both modalities have sequential structure, but there are big differences in the nature of that structure. Spoken languages show variation along the following parameters: the makeup of syllables (e.g., whether clusters are allowed in the onset or the rhyme, and if so, what kinds); the minimal and maximal length of words; stress patterns among syllables. Sign languages appear to have very few options. A signed word generally consists of one syllable; there are no clusters; whatever word-level stress pattern may exist must be very simple, since there are so few words with more than one syllable (apart from fully reduplicated forms and compounds).

The simplicity of the sequential structure in sign languages in no way precludes complexity of word structure, however. As explained in Unit 2, sign languages have complex morphology. Morphological complexity in sign languages strongly tends to be templatic, incorporating morphological material non-linearly, and resulting in sequential form that is monosyllabic and simple. We will return to this unusual combination of morphological complexity, non-linear structure, and sign language universals in Unit 5.

Non-linear phonological structure exists in all languages, but here too we have striking modality differences. Ignoring for now the fact that all features bear a relationship with segments that in some sense is not strictly linear (cf. feature geometries), let us consider only those elements that are dramatically non-segmentalized, those with long-distance scope and spreading effects, such as tones in tone languages, or nasality or vowel features in harmony systems. Comparing these with the sign language elements that have similar scope, we see some big differences. Unlike spoken language autosegments, which typically consist of one or two features, the hand configuration autosegment of sign languages is the most complex element in the whole system, consisting of several hierarchically organized classes of features (Sandler 1987a, 1987b, 1989, 1995c). The other element that has scope over the whole sign is the place of articulation (major body area), which, though not as complex, is visually very salient in a word. In fact, very few features are actually sequenced in any signed word. In spoken words, the opposite is true: most features are sequenced. Also, only a subset of spoken languages even have long-distance autosegments, while the phonological structure of sign languages seems universally to be characterized by long-distance features of hand configuration and place of articulation.

Compare representations of the English word *fit* (1a, b), with the ASL sign, IDEA (2a, b). The word *fit* is represented using a feature geometry in the spirit of Halle (1992), and then with SPE-type feature matrices. The ASL sign IDEA is represented using a feature geometry in the spirit of Sandler (1989), and also with feature matrices.[5]

[5] In the Halle (1992) model, the features [stiff, slack] are intended to account for voicing (Halle and Stevens 1971). Here we use the more common feature, [±voiced].

(1) English *fit*

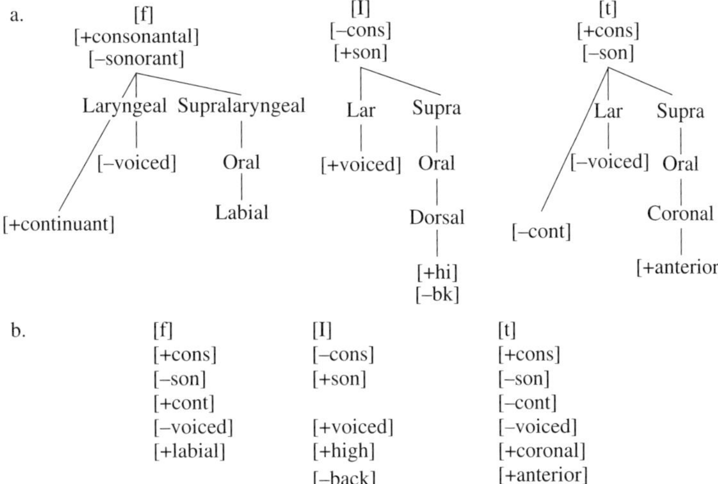

(2) IDEA (ASL)

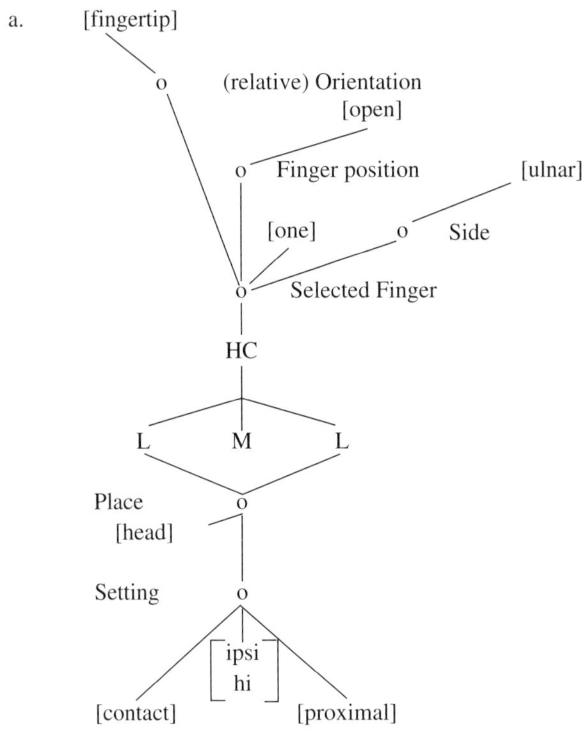

b.

x	x	x
Location	Movement	Location
one	one	one
ulnar	ulnar	ulnar
open	open	open
fingertip	fingertip	fingertip
head	head	head
ipsi	ipsi	ipsi
high	high	high
contact		proximal

The English word *fit* has three segments, like the ASL sign IDEA. Few features and values are the same in the three segments of *fit*, and fewer of them are predictable from the features in the other segments. The only feature value that is fairly predictable given a word with three segments is that the second segment is likely to be a vowel. In ASL IDEA, almost all the features are the same in the three segments. Apart from what might be considered major class features, location and movement, only the features [contact] in the first segment and [proximal] in the last segment differ. While it is not predictable which features will be different, it is predictable that in a monomorphemic sign with three segments, only two (setting features) or at most four (two setting and two finger position or orientation features) will be different. Whether each segment is a location or a movement is also predictable.

These examples illustrate why the overall impression in spoken language is one of sequentiality, while in sign language the overall impression is one of simultaneity. In the English word *fit*, there are no features that have scope over more than one segment phonologically. In the ASL sign IDEA, almost all of them do.

If we think of the hand configuration category as a long-distance autosegment as Sandler proposes, and compare it with tones, prototypical long-distance autosegments in spoken language, we again see a difference. Consider the Shona word, *ákàònápó*, 'he saw there.' This word has three tones, the last of which has scope over three vowels. Unlike the hand configuration category, which is very complex, the tones of Shona are simple, consisting of one feature only. Even vowel harmony generally involves one or two features at most.

(3) Shona *ákàòná#pó* 'he saw there' (data from Odden 1980, cited in Kenstowicz 1994)

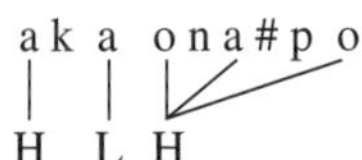

So, while the formal properties of linearity and of non-linearity are common to both spoken and signed languages, the relative centrality of each in the phonological organization of each modality is different.

A numerical comparison of features and their organization in Halle's spoken language model and in Sandler's sign language model (as revised here) is useful. The number of feature classes is similar: nine in spoken language and ten in sign language. But there is a big difference in the number of features. Spoken language has eighteen features while sign language has thirty (of which fifteen are hand configuration features).

We might speculate that the reason for this difference is related to the relative amount of sequentiality in the two modalities. Each modality must have the potential to produce a great number of lexical contrasts. In spoken language, this can be achieved through different configurations of sequentially arranged phonemes. In sign languages, sequentiality is limited and simultaneity favored by the modality. In order to create a similar number of lexical contrasts with far fewer sequential positions available, a larger number of features may be required.

This idea is compatible with the results of a study of ten languages conducted by Nettle (1995) in which he compared the number of contrastive segments in the inventories of ten languages to the mean number of segments in the words of each language. He found that as the number of segments in a language increases, the mean word length decreases. The languages at the two extremes were Nahuatl and !Xu. Nahuatl has an inventory of 23 segments and a mean word length of 8.69, while !Xu has 119 segments and a mean word length of 4.02.

A comparison of segment inventories in signed and spoken languages is not very meaningful, because of the differences we have seen here in the nature of the sign segment compared to that of spoken language, and the number of contrastive segments in any given sign language has not been calculated. But a comparison of feature inventories is instructive. Both language modalities are presumably structured in such a way as to accommodate a large vocabulary of distinct words. In sign languages, the small number of sequential distinctions in a sign – i.e., both the small number of segments in a typical sign and the small number of feature distinctions across them – may be compensated for by a larger number of features.

That the organization of phonological elements in words tends to be more simultaneous in sign language than in spoken language has a direct effect on phonological rules. Relatively few rules that are purely phonological, like aspiration in English or final devoicing in Russian, have been discovered in sign languages. By purely phonological, we mean rules that are not triggered by the morphology. We suggest that the apparent dearth of purely phonological rules is due to the relative lack of sequential structure in sign words. It is precisely under morphological and syntactic processes in sign language that concatenate morphemes and words – i.e., linear affixation, compounding, and cliticization – that significant sequential structure arises within words. As soon as such concatenation does occur in sign languages, a plethora of concomitant phonological effects arises: hand configuration assimilation, orientation assimilation, truncation, coalescence, selected finger assimilation. These effects only arise under morphological operations and cliticizations because it is primarily under those circumstances that phonological elements are conjoined linearly.

Finally, the existence of prosodic structure is a language universal, regardless of modality. Investigations conducted to date demonstrate that sign languages have prosodic constituents that are similar to those of spoken language, and that they also have the equivalent of intonational systems. The main differences discovered so far are in the phonetic makeup and scope of the primitives of intonation. The high and low tones of intonational tunes are sequential in spoken language, while the configurations of the face and body features that comprise superarticulation in sign language are simultaneous. The way in which these markers are superimposed on the text is different too. In spoken language, the pitch excursions of intonational tunes co-occur with syllables, typically at constituent boundaries, while in sign languages superarticulatory arrays co-occur with the entire prosodic constituent with which they are associated.

Research on sign language phonology leads to two conclusions, which are also important directions for future research in this relatively new field: (1) there are universal properties of phonological organization common to natural language in radically different physical modalities, but (2) there are substantial areas in which the physical production and perception systems mold the phonology of *both* modalities. Clearly, this conclusion has implications for our conception of phonological universals, and for how we "do" phonology as well. If modality effects in sign language are isolated by comparing them with spoken language, then the mirror image of these properties are precisely the modality effects of spoken language. This should lead us to ask not only what phonology is like, but why it should be as it is.

Unit 4

Syntax

17 Syntax: introduction

17.1 Unit overview

Our aim throughout this book is to probe more deeply into the human capacity for language by seeking properties which are truly universal – those that hold for sign language as well as spoken language. In this unit, devoted to studies of sign language syntax, the goal is the same. Do sign languages respect the claimed universal properties of sentence structure? Where there are similarities, are the proposals that have been developed to account for universals adequate for encompassing sign languages as well? Where there are differences, can they be explained – not just described? In order to ask these questions, it is crucial that we begin here as in previous units with some kind of understanding of universals of spoken languages.

Over the past decades, many linguists have sought to understand the abstract properties which underlie all languages. These properties have been captured by a variety of mechanisms developed within a number of theoretical frameworks. We find that detailed, formal theories often provide an excellent starting point for our investigation, because they lead researchers to ask specific questions which might not otherwise come up. Thus, we concentrate largely on work conducted within such frameworks. In this unit in particular, most of the work we present has exploited the theoretical devices made available by generative grammar, as introduced by Chomsky (1957, etc.) and subsequently pursued by many others as well. In Section 17.2, we present a brief overview of essential components of this framework which are used throughout the unit. As we progress through the unit, additional theoretical material will be presented as a backdrop to the proposals for analyzing sign language syntax.

In order to account for the patterns found at all levels of grammar, generative theoreticians posit certain structural devices, and constraints on structure, which are posited to hold cross-linguistically. The framework provides specific tools for analysis. As these tools are tested against an increasing range of data, they may be amended or dropped, and new tools added. Occasionally, a major shift in the metatheory takes place in an attempt to refine the theoretical machinery, applying criteria used more generally to fine-tune scientific theories.

Research on sign language syntax takes place within this milieu, so a variety of existing tools have been used to probe the structure and constraints of sign language sentences. While we are interested to see how well a particular analysis succeeds at explaining certain phenomena, we are also interested in the phenomena themselves. We attempt to highlight issues that bear on our major questions, and to critically examine the analyses proposed. In each area, we find that the similarities between sign language and spoken language are impressive, despite the potential for vast differences.

We begin in Chapters 18 and 19 by examining basic clausal structure, and ask, do sign languages display evidence of structural organization? Do different sign languages behave similarly to each other in this regard? Chapter 18 focuses on ASL, and in Chapter 19 we discuss some of the theoretically based research on other sign languages. We will see that sign languages do not adhere to a strict surface word order as English does, and that some variability in order may be related to the use of spatial locations to represent referents in the verb agreement system (cf. Chapter 3). This leads us to the question of modality effects – differences between signed and spoken languages attributable to the differences between the manual–visual and vocal–auditory modalities. Does the fact that sign languages seem to be produced spatially rather than simply temporally lead to modality effects? We will see that the evidence for order and for hierarchical structure of the kind found in spoken languages is abundant in sign languages. We will show as well that sign languages operate similarly to spoken languages that are unlike English, in that they make use of morphologically complex elements to license word order variation.

After examining the structure of basic sentences, we turn in Chapter 20 to review the analyses of a few sentence types that go beyond the basics. We hold off on the two most-studied extensions of basic sentence structure, topic structures and WH-questions, because these constructions require their own chapters (22 and 23, respectively). Some of the more recent research has begun to look beyond basic sentences and to probe other issues, and future work is sure to be developed in these domains. Thus, we review the structure of noun phrases (or Determiner Phrases),[1] the syntax of classifier constructions, several contexts in which non-basic order is derived, and negative sentences, all in Chapter 20.

[1] In current usage within generative grammar, noun phrases are often referred to as DPs, highlighting the notion that the noun is actually a complement of the determiner. We will use this term when such proposals are discussed, but otherwise we will stick with the more familiar NP.

In Chapter 21, we turn to examine the distribution of null and overt pronouns. Pronouns have received quite a bit of attention, in large part because of the glaring need to explain their use of spatial locations. In fact, in some ways pronouns seem to be the clearest candidate for a modality effect to be found in the syntax of sign languages: they unambiguously pick out referents, not classes of referents, within a discourse. We discuss the impact of this fact for syntactic structure here, leaving some broader implications and a more detailed discussion until Unit 5, as this is an area where sign languages do go beyond linguistic universals based on spoken languages.

As already mentioned, the next two chapters – 22 and 23 – explore the structure of sentences with particular pragmatic functions: topic, focus, and questions. Sign languages have characteristics of so-called discourse-oriented spoken languages (like Chinese, or Serbo-Croatian), including pragmatically determined variability in word order, and proliferation of null elements. While these aspects are discussed to some extent in other chapters, in Chapter 22 we consider in much more detail the operations languages use to highlight and background certain kinds of information. Even spoken languages with these characteristics show that a broader conception of grammar is required, in comparison with what might be considered for languages like English. Only with fuller development of such a conception of discourse-oriented languages will it be possible to see whether the ultimate analyses of these aspects of sign languages will require mechanisms that are distinct from those needed for spoken languages.

The structure of WH-questions has received considerable attention in the literature, in part because the availability of various options for questions has made the core data controversial. Yet the issue is crucial, as we see in Chapter 23, because some of the analyses proposed have made use of structures quite different from those needed for spoken languages. Do sign languages require the postulation of structures not found in spoken language questions? Or is there an analysis available which accounts for the variety of data observed within a theoretically universal set of assumptions?

The sentence types discussed in Chapters 22 and 23 are marked by the use of particular non-manual markers – one of the most obvious areas in which sign language syntax might appear to be distinct from that of spoken language. As we have seen in the earlier units, sign languages are more than "manual" – there is an active non-manual component involving particular facial expressions, and certain head and body positions. Specific non-manual markers are observed to co-occur with particular syntactic structures. Since non-manual markers apparently "spread" over a particular syntactically defined domain, they seem to have no spoken language syntactic analogue. However, we have seen reasons in Chapter 15 for considering some non-manual markers to be analogous to spoken language intonation. We take up this possibility again in Chapter 23, where we pursue an alternative analysis of WH-questions based on this proposal, and find that a sign-unique structure is not required.

Finally, Chapter 24 summarizes the material of the syntax unit, and discusses issues of most concern to theoretical linguistics. There we also highlight some of the needed future research, as research on the syntactic structure of sign languages has only scratched the surface.

Recall that our main focus is on the question, Just how successfully do purported linguistic universals account for sign languages? It was pointed out in Unit 3 that differences in the articulatory and perception systems of signed and spoken languages naturally lead to the expectation that many differences might be found in the area of phonology. We showed there, however, that there are remarkable similarities across signed and spoken languages, even in phonology, and that comparative study of languages in the two modalities leads to the discovery of true linguistic universals. At the level of syntax, there are also potential sources of modality effects – the use of space and non-manual markers being the most obvious. Yet, here again, we find impressive similarities in structure and organization which support the postulation of linguistic universals. Are there no differences between signed and spoken languages then? There are some, at all levels, but we postpone detailed discussion of them until Unit 5.

Now, we turn to an overview of generative grammar, and pick up the discussion of sign language syntactic structure in Chapter 18.

17.2 The generative approach

Most of the work discussed in this unit follows some version of a generative approach to syntax (among many others, Chomsky 1957, 1965, 1981, 1995).[2] Many details of the model have changed over the years, so each researcher whose work is presented may employ a different set of theoretical tools, even when working within the generative approach. Here we provide an overview of this theoretical approach.

In general, these studies employ the idea that hierarchical syntactic structure is represented at two levels: deep structure or D-structure, which provides information about a verb's thematic relationships (such as its need for an agent or patient), using information that comes from the lexical component; and surface structure or S-structure, which is close to the arrangement

[2] For introductory or overview material, see among others van Riemsdijk and Williams (1986), Lasnik and Uriagereka (1988), Haegeman (1991), Webelhuth (1995), Baltin and Collins (2001).

of words as actually pronounced. Furthermore, constituents must be licensed in various ways, such as their thematic relation to the verb (or θ role) and Case marking of noun phrases. These markings need not be overtly realized in each language, but the structural relationship is assumed to be universal. Noun phrases which have no way of being licensed will cause a string to be considered ungrammatical – for example, an "extra" noun phrase in a sentence like **Julia cooked dinner the fish*, or a noun phrase in an inappropriate position, such as **It seemed Fred to be intelligent*.

Universal principles, such as the requirements for noun phrases to be theta- and Case-marked, play an important role in generative theory, and in much of our discussion we will refer to such principles. However, the theory of Chomsky (1981, Chomsky and Lasnik 1993, et seq.) also hypothesizes that there is limited variation between languages in certain areas. These areas of limited variation can be explained by positing *parameters*, choice-sets among which languages select. For example, heads precede their complements generally in languages like English (Verb–Object; Preposition–Object), but the complements precede the heads in languages like Japanese (Object–Verb; Object–Postposition). As another example, in some languages (like English) WH-elements appear in the sentence-initial position, while in others WH-elements remain in sentence-internal positions (again, Japanese is an example).

In the theory of Principles and Parameters, then, languages are expected to adhere to certain principles universally, but not every generalization about a language will necessarily be related to a universal principle – some will be related to parameters (and still others might reflect language-particular idiosyncrasies). In our discussion of sign languages, we will be interested in observing where they seem to follow universal principles, and where they fall into the range of variation permitted by parameters. We would also be very interested in discovering where the theory of Principles and Parameters falls short in accounting for observations from sign languages.

It has been found that many phenomena are sensitive to the hierarchical relationship between elements that may be linearly distant from one another. Thus, just as structure is a primitive notion of syntactic theory, it is necessary to be able to define certain structural relationships. Many of the constraints and generalizations to be discussed in this unit relate to the notion called c-command. C-command is a structural relationship defined on hierarchical trees. Beginning with the notion "in construction with," due to Klima (1964), c-command grew out of Langacker's (1969) "command." Reinhart's (1976) definition has been widely adopted, though various modifications have also been proposed. A basic definition of c-command is given in (1), and we illustrate the notion using the abstract tree in (2).

(1) C-command (from Haegeman 1991, p. 198)
A node A c-commands a node B iff

i. A does not dominate B;
ii. B does not dominate A;
iii. the first branching node dominating A also dominates B.

(2)

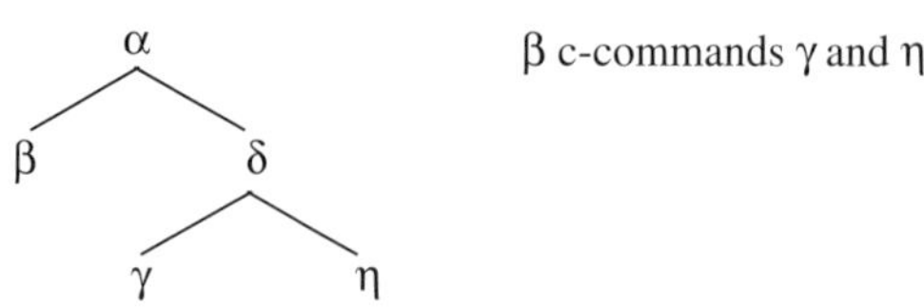

It is sufficient to think of a c-commanding element as occupying a higher (but not dominating) position in the tree. This will be true whether the higher element precedes or follows the lower one. C-command is used in all of the following chapters, since it is an important structural relationship.

Some constituents will undergo movement in the mapping from D-structure to S-structure; at S-structure elements will (generally) be in their surface position, reflecting the order in which they are produced. Much syntactic theorizing concerns the mechanisms involved in movement operations, since they provide evidence of universal constraints. In more recent versions of generative theory (echoing some of the earliest theories), movement is seen as an operation which copies an element, and later deletes the original (Chomsky 1995). The difference between movement and copy + delete is that on the latter view, real copies are available at various points in the derivation.

Movement can also take place during the mapping from S-structure to Logical Form (LF), the level which is input to the interpretation component. This kind of movement is considered covert, since it does not affect the order of elements pronounced.

Many of the discussions in the chapters to follow rely on the conceptions of syntactic movement just summarized. The motivation for positing movement operations in sign language syntax, as in that of spoken languages, is evidence that a constituent bears some relationship to an element it is linearly distant from.

Many of the constraints on movement are known as "island constraints," a term intended to evoke the idea that constituents cannot escape from their syntactic island by moving to a position outside the island. This term is due to Ross (1967), who describes several constraints on "reordering transformations" and the contexts of their use.

Syntactic movement and constraints on movement will be discussed extensively in this unit. Whenever constituents appear in positions other than their postulated deep structure positions, movement is involved, and such manipulations of word order occur with great frequency in sign languages. Discussion of movement naturally leads to the question of constraints on movement, since such constraints are universally found. Thus, whether sign languages employ the same types of movement operations as spoken languages, and whether these movements are subject to the same kinds of constraints, is clearly an issue of some interest.

Under a variety of circumstances, some constituents of a sentence may be left unexpressed. When a syntactically real element is unpronounced, it is known as an empty category, and it is subject to universal principles on licensing, with some cross-linguistic variation. Syntactic movement creates one kind of empty category, a "trace" (represented as *t*), which is a phonologically empty but syntactically real marker of where an element has been. In some languages, the empty category *pro* is permitted as a null pronominal subject (or object). These empty categories will be discussed to differing degrees in the following chapters, where it will be seen that the properties of empty categories in sign languages are like those of spoken languages in general.

In sum, the approach to syntax adopted here is one that posits a distinction between the basic syntactic structure provided by the phrase structure rules of a language and the observed sentence form that results when that structure is rearranged. The movements which achieve this reordering are not completely free, and one of the goals of syntactic theory is to provide a universal set of constraints that will prevent the generation of ungrammatical sentences in any language.

This concludes our brief summary of relevant aspects of the generative approach to syntax. Additional background information is provided as needed in the coming chapters. In some cases, sign language data are employed to address issues which are of most interest to those who aim to argue for one syntactic theory over others. But most of the time, the questions transcend partisan theoretical points, and endeavor to reach the proper analysis of particular phenomena, in sign language and in language more generally. As we have stated, we find that adopting a particular theoretical approach is often very illuminating, as it enables the researcher to ask and address questions that a less formal approach might miss completely. Thus, we will point out the narrow concerns but also bring the reader back to the broader questions which would call for consideration in any theoretical approach. This, we hope, is how future progress will be made.

18 Clausal structure

Syntax begins with phrase structure. However, in over twenty-five years of research on the syntactic structure of ASL, there are still controversies about its phrase structure. Initially, these stemmed from debate over the basic word order. Word order is flexible in ASL and other sign languages, and therefore the basic structure of the clause is not immediately obvious. Around 1980, a consensus seemed to have been reached that the basic order of elements in ASL is Subject–Verb–Object (SVO). This is the order which is used in pragmatically neutral contexts, such as the answer to a general question like, *What happened*?

However, as recently as the mid-1990s (Bouchard and Dubuisson 1995, Bouchard 1996), the proposal that sign languages (in this case, ASL and Quebec Sign Language – Langue des Signes Québecoise, LSQ) have no set basic word order has been resurrected. We will review some of the history of this debate, as it provides data which in many cases still today require adequate analysis. It also encompasses two fundamental controversies in the pursuit of universals: whether sign languages are structured differently from spoken languages, and whether all languages (spoken or signed) require hierarchical structure.

Even with the adoption of S–V–O as the "basic" word order for a language such as ASL, the underlying clausal hierarchy is not automatically determined. In recent years, several variants of phrase structure for ASL have been proposed. In a language with frequent disruptions of word order, an explanation of the mechanisms for such changes rests on assumptions about the hierarchical structure of the sentence. We will discuss these proposals in some depth, as they form the core of current theoretical controversies in sign language syntax. Furthermore, they bear more generally on syntactic analyses of languages with variable word order, and the question of whether there is one universal hierarchical structure or language-particular variation in structure.

Because so much of the theoretical analyses of word order and clause structure in sign languages focuses on or starts with ASL, we focus the present chapter almost exclusively on this language. In the next chapter, we review some proposals for sign language clause structure based primarily on data from other sign languages. Much further theoretically based cross-linguistic research on the structure of sign languages is desperately needed and eagerly awaited.

18.1 Basic word order

Many of the earlier studies examining the issue of word order in ASL concentrated mainly on the relative ordering of the subject, verb, and object. Researchers debated the underlying structure of ASL by considering the types of conditions in which different orders are used.

The proposal that basic word order in ASL is Subject–Verb–Object was supported by Fischer (1975). She indicates the possibility for orders other than SVO by adding that this order is found "in a sentence with reversible subject and object," and that "any other order will have intonation breaks" (p. 5). Fischer notices that intonation breaks are accomplished by pausing and non-manual markers. She cites the examples in (1), showing SVO, OSV, and VOS orders. Fischer claims that in (1b), the object is topicalized, and in sentence (1c), "the subject or perhaps the verb phrase is topicalized" (p. 5).[1]

(1) ASL (Fischer 1975, p. 5)
a. MAN NOTICE CHILD. (SVO)
'The man noticed the child.'
b. CHILD, MAN NOTICE. (OSV)
'As for the child, the man noticed it.'
c. NOTICE CHILD, MAN. (VOS)
'He noticed the child, the man did.'

Fischer asserts that "it becomes possible to have SOV word order – indeed even OVS becomes possible – when there is only one plausible way to interpret the grammatical relations in the sentence" (p. 9). For example, she cites (2) and (3), illustrating alternative orders for semantically "non-reversible" propositions.[2]

(2) ASL (Fischer 1975, p. 10)
a. MAN MUST B-I-L-L-S PAY (SMOV)
b. MAN MUST PAY B-I-L-L-S (SMVO)

(3) ASL (Fischer 1975, p. 14)
a. BOY LIKE ICE-CREAM (SVO)
b. BOY ICE-CREAM LIKE (SOV)

[1] Note that if the subject were topicalized in (1c), this would necessarily be movement to the sentence-final position. Most sign language researchers now analyze only sentence-initial elements as topics (and indeed, it is the sentence-initial position in which topics appear cross-linguistically).

[2] Fischer only gives the cases in (3a, b, c), indicating that such an example would also permit "the two perturbations allowable in reversible cases," which we have interpreted to mean (3d, e). No intonation breaks are marked in these examples.

c. ICE-CREAM LIKE BOY (OVS)
d. LIKE ICE-CREAM BOY (VOS)
e. ICE-CREAM BOY LIKE (OSV)

Furthermore, she says that other "near-idiomatic" cases only permit OV order, as in (4).

(4) ASL (Fischer 1975, p. 10)
a. WATER TURN-FAUCET (OV)
'turn on water'
b. MOVIE FLASH-FLASH (OV)
'take movies'
c. NECK CUT-OFF (OV)
'slaughter, as a chicken'

Finally, Fischer discusses the process which has come to be known as verb agreement (see Chapter 3), and indicates that it is related to the possibility of orders other than SVO. Recall that some verbs agree with their subject and object, by facing toward the object and away from the subject, moving from the location associated with their source to the location associated with their goal (cf. Figure 3.4 in Chapter 3). Thus, if an agreeing verb is used, it will be clear which NP is subject and which is object, so, apparently, a strict order is not required. According to Fischer, with agreeing verbs OSV is preferred over SOV, for articulatory reasons. If the object is signed in location (a), then the subject in another location (b), the hand will then be in the proper position for the verb to move from the second location to the first location (a-NOUN, b-NOUN, b-VERB-a). However, if the subject is signed in location (a) first, then the object in another location (b), an extra movement (back to a) is required to then move the verb from the first location to the second location (a-NOUN, b-NOUN, a-VERB-b). Fischer's claim is that the extra movement required in an S–O–sVo sequence will make it dispreferred.

An alternative to the idea that ASL employs an underlying SVO order is the claim that order is actually free. Friedman (1976) argues against Fischer's analysis, claiming that "word order is relatively free, with the exception of the tendency for the verb to be last" (p. 142). She finds that SVO order is infrequent in discourse excerpts she analyzed; instead, she proposes that SOV is the underlying order in ASL. Like Fischer, she claims that semantic "reversibility" will determine the interpretation of nouns; furthermore, she claims that context and rewording avoid potential ambiguity. Although she does not assume that ASL has a grammatical process of verb agreement, she describes the movement of the hand in pronouncing the verb (which is now considered agreement) as an iconic device to aid interpretation.

How is the proposal that underlying order is SVO to be reconciled with the variety of surface orders observed? Liddell (1980) discusses both Fischer's and

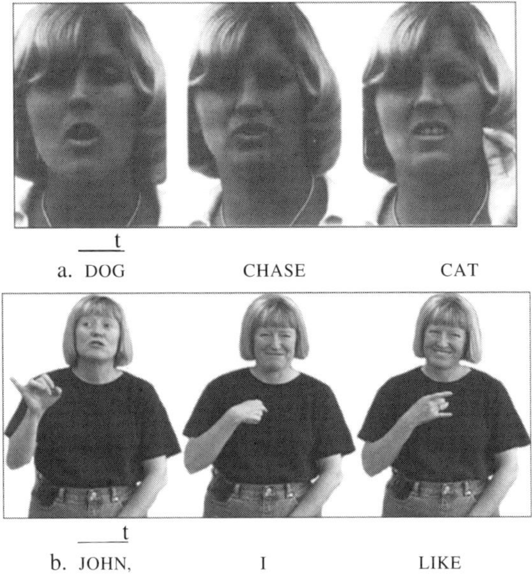

Figure 18.1 Non-manual marking of topic (18.1a reprinted with permission from Liddell 1980)

Friedman's accounts and argues that Friedman's proposals are not convincing. He also provides additional empirical support for the SVO analysis.

For example, although there is some variability in word order for declaratives, Liddell claims that the only grammatical word order corresponding to the yes/no question *Did the woman forget the purse?* is SVO, as in (5).

(5) ASL (Liddell 1980, p. 77)

q
WOMAN FORGET PURSE
'Did the woman forget the purse?'

Liddell proposes a specific rule of topicalization, by which NPs may be fronted. He claims that specific timing, facial expression, and head position mark topicalization. Topics are held longer than NPs in other parts of the sentence, and even in comparison with non-topic sentence-initial NPs. During the topic, the head is tilted back a bit, with the brows raised slightly. The contrast between the non-manual marking accompanying the topic and the rest of the sentence is shown in Figure 18.1.

Liddell proposes a particular structure associated with topicalization, using evidence from the interaction of topic marking and the headshake marking negatives ('n'). He shows that a topic can be outside the scope of a negative marker, as in (6), where only the verb phrase is associated with the negative headshake.

(6) ASL (Liddell 1980, p. 81)

t n
DOG CHASE CAT
'As for the dog, it didn't chase the cat.'

Liddell proposes the structure in (7) for (6). First, note that Liddell "tentatively analyze[s] the negative headshake as a higher verb which takes the clause as its subject" (Liddell 1980, p. 82).[3] According to the structure in (7), the NP DOG is Chomsky-adjoined to the clause containing the negative "verb" and its "subject."[4] Liddell says, "any element that is commanded by 'n' is subject to its negating force. Thus, where the subject has been topicalized, it is no longer commanded by 'n' and does not fall under the scope of the negation" (p. 83).[5] In (7), S_2 is commanded by 'n,' and falls under the scope of negation (both in its interpretation and in the spreading of the non-manual marker). However, the NP DOG is not commanded by "n," and is therefore outside of its scope.

(7) (Liddell 1980, p. 83)

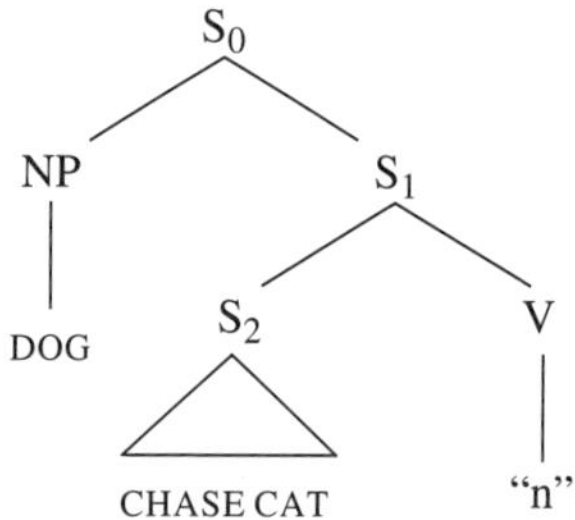

Liddell shows, in accord with Fischer's claims, that an Object or a VO sequence can also be topicalized, with the expected interaction with negation, as shown in (8a), where the topicalized object is not marked for negation, and (8b), where the topicalized Verb Phrase is not marked for negation.

(8) ASL (Liddell 1980, pp. 84, 86)

a. t n
CAT DOG CHASE
'As for the cat, the dog didn't chase it.'

b. t n
CHASE CAT DOG
'As for chasing the cat, the dog didn't do it.'

[3] This treatment of the negative marker has not been assumed in other works. See Chapter 20, Section 20.4.

[4] When an element A is Chomsky-adjoined to a node X, they form a new category of type X. Thus, in example (7), the new category dominating the NP DOG and the clause containing the negative (i.e., S_1), will also be a clause (S_0).

[5] The notion "command," due to Langacker (1969), is a predecessor to the modern notion c-command, defined in Chapter 17. Liddell defines command as follows: "To determine if one element commands another, simply trace up the tree structure until an S node is reached. If it is possible to trace *down* from that S node to the other element, the first element commands the second" (Liddell 1980, p. 83).

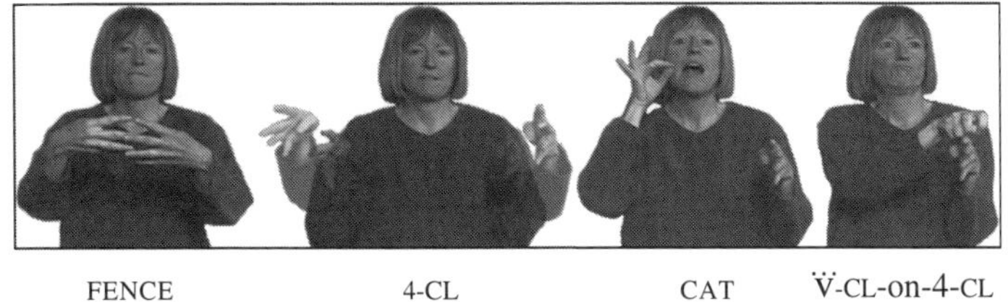

FENCE 4-CL CAT V̈-CL-on-4-CL

Figure 18.2 Classifier construction

Liddell shows that a complication in his analysis of basic word order arises because certain sequences of SOV are grammatical (without any special non-manual marking). He provides the examples in (9)–(10).

(9) ASL (Liddell 1980, pp. 88–89)
a. MAN BOOK READ
'The man read the book.'
b. WOMAN PIE PUT-IN-OVEN
c. ME BICYCLE BUY

(10) ASL (Liddell 1980, p. 90)
a. *MAN MOVIE SEE
b. *MAN NUMBER FORGET
c. *BOY CANDY NOT LIKE

Liddell claims that the acceptable examples in (9) are distinguished from the ungrammatical ones in (10) by some kind of "mimetic" relationship. For example, with respect to (9)b, he claims "for this sequence to be acceptable, the hand which is used as the base hand for PIE is used as the active hand for the sign PUT-IN-OVEN ... It seems that the iconicity of the sequence is important for this SOV sequence" (p. 89). We will see an alternative to this appeal to iconicity in Chapter 20, Section 20.3.

Another class of apparent exceptions involves *classifier* constructions (see Chapter 5). For example, (11) seems to show an order other than SVO. In this example, pictured in Figure 18.2, the non-dominant hand holds the 4-CL (a size-and-shape classifier representing the fence) in place (this hold is indicated by the dashes following the 4-CL), while the dominant hand articulates the sign CAT, followed by the V̈-CL (a semantic classifier for small animals) being placed on the 4-CL, to represent the relative spatial locations of the cat and the fence.

(11) ASL (Liddell 1980, p. 93)
FENCE 4-CL----------------------
CAT V̈-CL on 4-CL
'A cat is lying on the fence.'

The classifier subsystem involves spatial or locative relations with verbal components. Liddell argues that FENCE in (11) is not a grammatical object, as in the English translation, but a *ground* in a figure–ground relationship with CAT. In such cases, Liddell argues that the basic order is Locative Object – Locative Subject – Locative Predicate (as opposed to the basic Subject–Verb–Object order for ordinary transitive verbs).

Liddell also notices that alternative word orders not marked as topics can be found with verbs which are marked for *aspect* (see Chapter 3, Section 3.3). For example, he cites (12), in which the object appears before the aspect-marked verb.

(12) ASL (Liddell 1980, p. 103)

______________________q
TOMATO GIRL EAT[I:durative aspect]
'Did the girl eat tomatoes for a long time?'

Liddell speculates that "The reason for this may be due to the heaviness of the verb" (p. 103). He mentions Heavy NP Shift in English, but does not explain how the sentence in (12) might be derived. We will come back to this example in Chapter 20, where we present analyses of this kind of structure based on the construction known as "object shift."

There is support, then, for the proposed underlying SVO word order, but still many recalcitrant apparent counterexamples. In her dissertation, Padden (1988 [1983]) proposes an analysis which unifies Liddell's disparate word-order statements for regular verbs and classifier constructions. Working within the framework of Relational Grammar (Perlmutter 1983, Perlmutter and Rosen 1984), she proposes that basic order in ASL is Subject–Predicate. Furthermore, she argues that examples such as (11) are multiclausal. Her analysis of (11) consists of two subject–predicate sequences, roughly as in (13).

(13) ASL (after Padden 1988 [1983])

FENCE 4-CL
'The fence is here

- - - - - - - - - - - - - - - -
CAT V̈-CL on 4-CL
(and) the cat is sitting on the fence.'

Padden has a set of arguments for the clausehood of Noun + Classifier sequences such as FENCE 4-CL. She concludes from the clause-like properties of Noun + Classifier sequences that classifier constructions are predicates in examples like (11)/(13) (pp. 178 ff) (cf. discussion of classifiers in Chapter 5).

Padden's first argument for the clausal status of classifier constructions concerns sentential complements. Padden observes that a matrix predicate like THINK takes a clausal complement, but not an NP, as shown by the contrast in (14a, b). The fact that (15) is grammatical indicates that the classifier sequence WOMAN $_i$CL:V is a clause.

(14) ASL (Padden 1988 [1983], p. 205)

a. $_1$INDEX THINK $_2$INDEX FINISH LEAVE
'I thought you already left.'

b. *$_1$INDEX THINK CAR

(15) ASL (Padden 1988 [1983], p. 205)

$_1$INDEX THINK WOMAN $_i$CL:V
'I think the woman stood over here'

Padden's second argument comes from short answers. Verbs can be short answers to questions, but NPs cannot, as shown in (16). The fact that the short answer in (17A) is grammatical indicates that the classifier is a predicate.

(16) ASL (Padden 1988 [1983], p. 206)

--------- -q- ---------------
Q. $_2$INDEX HAVE MONEY, CAN PAY
'Do you have enough money to pay for it?'

---hn----
A. (i) YES, HAVE
'Yes, I do.'

-----hn-----
(ii) * YES, $_1$INDEX

-----hn----
(iii) *YES, MONEY

(17) ASL (Padden 1988 [1983], p. 207)

-------q-----------
Q. QUESTION COW $_i$CL:VV
'Was the cow standing there?'

A. YES, $_i$CL:VV
'Yes, it was.'

Padden also provides an argument based on facial adverbs (cf. Chapter 4, Figure 4.6). She points out that facial adverbs appear with verbs, as in (18). As they can also appear with classifier constructions, as in (19), this is evidence for their predicate status.

(18) ASL (Padden 1988 [1983], p. 124)

--mm-
$_1$INDEX DRIVE.
'I was driving along easily.'

(19) ASL (Padden 1988 [1983], p. 209)

-mm-
CAR $_i$CL:3
'The car is parked there without any apparent problem.'

Finally, Padden presents an argument from modals. Only subjects can precede modals, as illustrated in (20). Since the "locative object" can appear before the modal in (21), it should be analyzed as the subject of the classifier predicate.

(20) ASL (Padden 1988 [1983], pp. 158, 160)

a. $_i$INDEX SHOULD LEAVE BUTTER
'He was supposed to leave the butter here.'

b. *BUTTER SHOULD LEFT
'The butter should leave it here.'

(21) ASL (Padden 1988 [1983], p. 210)
L-hand: $_i$CL:B- - - - - - - - - - - - - - - -
R-hand: TABLE MUST MONKEY CAN $_j$CL:V$_k$
'The table has to be positioned here so the monkey can jump onto it.'

Padden's analysis of classifier constructions can also account for Liddell's observation that certain "mimetic" SOV sequences are allowed, and for some facts not yet discussed concerning pointing signs, or indices. According to Padden's analysis, examples like Liddell's in (9) above, the first of which is repeated in (22), are also multiclausal. Padden's multiclausal analysis of (22) is given in (23).[6]

(22) ASL (Liddell 1980, p. 88)
MAN BOOK READ
'The man read the book.'

(23) ASL (Padden 1988 [1983], p. 228)
L-hand: $_i$CL:B]$_0$
R-hand: $_0$[MAN $_1$[BOOK $_i$CL:BB-OPEN]$_1$ READ]$_0$.
'The man with the book open, began to read.'

The fact that the sequence in (23) can include two modals, as in (24), strongly supports the analysis Padden gives. This is because only one modal can appear per clause in ASL, as she shows independently. The occurrence of MUST with the classifier for a flat object, together with the modal CAN with READ, indicates that the classifier construction forms a clause that is independent from the clause with READ.

(24) ASL (Padden 1988 [1983], p. 229)
L-hand: $_i$CL:B
R-hand: MAN [BOOK MUST $_i$CL:BB-OPEN BIG-LETTER] CAN READ.
'The man, his book has to be in large type then he can read it.'

Padden shows that an additional factor which influences apparent surface word order concerns pointing (also known as indexing). Points serve a number of functions in ASL, such as those of determiners and pronouns

[6] The notation CL:BB-OPEN indicates a two-handed sign. The non-dominant (left) hand stays in position while the right hand continues signing until the final sign READ is signed using the left hand as its location.

(Chapters 20 and 21). Points are also used with nominals to indicate the location to be associated with them. It is this latter use of pointing that Padden is concerned with. An example with two such points is given in (25).

(25) ASL (Padden 1988 [1983], p. 229)
BOY $_{i}$INDEX, GIRL $_{j}$INDEX, $_{i}$KICK$_{j}$
'The boy kicked the girl.'

Padden cites Kegl's (1976) proposal, which claims that sign order is more flexible in clauses containing inflecting verbs like KICK in (25), and treats such sentences as having SOV word order. However, employing some of the same tests for clausehood used to determine that classifier constructions involve independent clauses, Padden shows that at least in many cases, these pointing signs are also properly analyzed as predicates, and the sequence given in (25) thus consists of three separate clauses (perhaps conjoined, or perhaps three separate sentences), adhering to the basic Subject–Predicate word order, as in (26).

(26) ASL (Padden 1988 [1983], p. 236)
[BOY $_{i}$INDEX]$_{1}$ [GIRL $_{j}$INDEX]$_{2}$ [$_{i}$KICK$_{j}$]$_{3}$
'The boy is here; the girl is there; he kicked her.'

After the spurt of proposals regarding how best to analyze the basic word order of ASL culminating in Padden's dissertation, the field has generally accepted the idea that the basic order of ASL is SVO. However, the various ways in which this order can be altered, including topicalization, the use of verb agreement, aspect, and "mimetic devices," have continued to be studied, and will be discussed in various places in this unit, particularly in Chapters 20 and 22.

Basic word order has received a fair amount of attention for sign languages other than ASL as well. For example, Quadros (1999) argues that the basic word order of Brazilian Sign Language (Lingua de Sinais Brasileira, or LSB) is SVO, as does Smith (1990) for Taiwan Sign Language (TSL). SOV is the proposed basic word order for Austrian Sign Language (ÖGS; Wilbur 2002), German Sign Language (Deutsche Gebärdensprache, DGS; Glück and Pfau 1998, Rathmann 2000), and Japanese Sign Language (Nihon Shuwa, NS; Fischer 1996, Torigoe 1994).

However, many researchers emphasize the variability of word orders present in the sign languages they are studying, and argue that a description such as "topic-comment" should be used to define word order in these languages. Such proposals have been made for British Sign Language (BSL; Deuchar 1983); Danish Sign Language (DSL; Engberg-Pedersen 1994); Israeli Sign Language (ISL; Rosenstein 2001); Sign Language of the Netherlands (SLN; Coerts 1994); and Quebec Sign Language (Langue des Signes Québecoise, LSQ; Nadeau and Desouvrey 1994); see also papers in Brennan and Turner (1994). Some of these researchers have challenged the idea that sign languages, with the variability of word orders permitted, should be assigned a "basic word order" or structure at all. We will return to this important issue in Section 18.3.2.

18.2 Embedding

One of the most definitive properties of human language is recursiveness, the ability of phrases to be repeated with no theoretical limit. Subordinate structures display a special kind of recursiveness, as they are generated by including a sentence inside another sentence. Embedding also testifies to the importance of hierarchical structure, as the elements of an embedded clause act as a group. If sign languages adhere to universal properties of language, then they would be expected to have this essential property.

It comes as a surprise then that Thompson (1977) claims that ASL has no subordination. He claims that apparently complex structures (or translations of complex embedded structures) consist of strings of coordinated clauses. However, his arguments are largely the result of his failure to detect an overt marker of subordination. Liddell (1980) shows convincingly that ASL has both subordination and coordination, with subordinate clauses as sentential complements, relative clauses, or adverbials. He claims that many of the subordination markers are non-manual, including movements of the signer's body as well as facial expressions.

Liddell agrees with Thompson that certain verbs (predicates) do not take sentential complements in ASL, such as HAPPY, ANGRY, SURPRISED, RELIEVED, SORRY, and PROMISE. However, Liddell points out that verbs such as KNOW, WANT, EXPECT, and others, do take embedded sentential complements. And he shows that relative clauses, another structure involving embedding, are marked in ASL with a specific non-manual marker.

Padden (1988 [1983]) gives a number of structural arguments which distinguish between embedded and coordinate clauses, providing good tests for other aspects of structure as well. For example, she shows that a pronoun copy of the subject of a clause can be tagged onto the end of the sentence by a process she calls Subject Pronoun Copy.[7] As (27) shows, a pronoun may be a copy of the first subject in a string only if the string contains an embedded clause – not a coordinate clause. In (27a), which contains an embedded clause, the sentence-final subject pronoun copy ($_i$INDEX) can refer back to the matrix subject, MOTHER. Example (27b),

[7] Bos (1995) provides an interesting discussion of pronoun copy, focusing on Sign Language of the Netherlands. She argues that the final subject pronouns are not emphatic, contrary to Padden's analysis of the seemingly very similar phenomenon in ASL. Her observation is that final pronouns are most often used with plain verbs, and she suggests that their presence is due to an overall tendency for subjects to be identified, either through a pronoun or through agreement.

on the other hand, contains a conjoined clause (the first clause contains just the verb $_{1}$HIT$_{i}$, whose subject and object are null but licensed by the agreement; see Chapter 21 for a full discussion of null arguments). The subject pronoun copy ($_{1}$INDEX), referring back to the (null) subject of the first conjunct, is not allowed.

(27) ASL (Padden 1988 [1983], pp. 87–88)

a. MOTHER SINCE $_{i}$PERSUADE$_{j}$ SISTER $_{j}$COME$_{i}$ $_{i}$INDEX.
'My mother has been urging my sister to come and stay here, she [mother] has.'

b. *$_{1}$HIT$_{i}$, $_{i}$INDEX TATTLE MOTHER $_{1}$INDEX.
'I hit him and he told his mother, I did.'

Another argument that distinguishes embedded and conjoined clauses comes from negation. Padden shows that the non-manual marker for negation extends over the clause it modifies.[8] Therefore, if a clause is embedded under a negative clause, it will necessarily have the negative marker, as in (28a). However, a conjoined clause must be negated independently; otherwise it will not have the negative marker, as in (28b).[9]

(28) ASL (Padden 1988[1983], pp. 89–90)

```
   -------n----------------
a. 1INDEX WANT iINDEX GO-AWAY
```
'I didn't want him to leave.'

```
   -----n-----------  ---hn------------
b. 1INDEX TELEPHONE, iINDEX MAIL LETTER
```
'I didn't telephone but she sent a letter.'

Padden also shows that topicalization can apply to an element in an embedded clause, as in (29a). In this example, the topic, EXERCISE CLASS, is understood as the object of the deeply embedded verb, TAKE-UP. If the clauses were conjoined, such movement would violate the Coordinate Structure Constraint (CSC, Ross 1967).[10] In fact, Padden shows that extraction out of coordinate clauses does violate the CSC, as in (29b). Here, the topic FLOWER cannot be understood as the object of the second verb, GIVE. The difference between (29a) and (29b) indicates that different structures must be involved – embedding in (29a) and coordination in (29b). Topicalization will be discussed further in Chapter 22, in the context of discourse-related syntactic operations.

[8] See Chapter 20, Section 20.4 for discussion of just how far the non-manual marker spreads.
[9] 'n' stands for the negative headshake; while 'hn' stands for an affirmative head nod.
[10] The Coordinate Structure Constraint (Ross 1967) prohibits extraction of an element from a conjoined clause. It is one of the island constraints referred to in Chapter 17. This constraint rules out deriving examples like (ii) from (i).

i. Mary went to Paris and John went to Rome.
ii. *Where did Mary go to Paris and John go to __ ?

(29) ASL (Padden 1988 [1983], pp. 92–93)

- - - - -t- - - - - - - -
a. EXERCISE CLASS, $_{1}$INDEX HOPE SISTER SUCCEED PERSUADE MOTHER TAKE-UP.
'The exercise class, I hope my sister manages to persuade my mother to take (it).'

- - -t- - -
b. *FLOWER, $_{2}$GIVE$_{1}$ MONEY, $_{j}$GIVE$_{1}$.
'Flowers, he gave me money but she gave me.'

Finally, Padden shows that there are, indeed, overt lexical (manual) markers for coordinate clauses, including BUT, as in (30a), as well as AND, FINISH ('then'), WELL ('so'), PLUS ('and'), and others. (Padden suggests that they may be discourse markers rather than true coordinate markers.) Importantly, these signs appear before coordinate clauses, but not embedded clauses. If (30a) involved an embedded clause, then it should be possible for a pronoun copy of the first ("main clause") subject to appear. As (30b) shows, this is not acceptable – so the second clause must be coordinate, not embedded.[11]

(30) ASL (Padden 1988 [1983], pp. 95–96)

a. $_{1}$PERSUADE$_{i}$, BUT CHANGE MIND.
'I persuaded her to do it but then I/she/he changed my mind.'

b. *$_{2}$PERSUADE$_{i}$ BUT $_{i}$INDEX CHANGE MIND $_{2}$INDEX.
'You talked her into it but she changed her mind, you did.'

These tests are solid indications of embedded structures in ASL, and have been used in various other ways to be discussed throughout this chapter.

Although linguists studying the structure of ASL in the early years of ASL syntactic research had to struggle with questions of basic word order and subordination, it is now widely accepted that ASL does have embedding, and that SVO is the basic word order. However, this is not to say that all issues about the phrase structure of basic sentences are settled. Recent work on ASL has again turned to phrase structure, but now the questions concern a wider range of syntactic elements. In particular, several researchers have recently asked how the basic structure of ASL fits within current syntactic theory, and what the implications may be for other aspects of sentential structure. In preparation for discussing these sign language questions, we turn to a brief summary of developments in generative approaches to phrase structure, and return immediately to the sign language issues.

18.3 Phrase structure

In recent decades, more and more unified theories of phrase structure have been developed. Accordingly, even though it is clear that languages differ

[11] In these examples some of the verb's arguments are null. We will discuss the licensing of null arguments in ASL in Chapter 21.

widely with respect to the ordering of elements, linguistic theory has attempted to narrow down the possible types of phrase structures posited to characterize these cross-linguistic differences. For example, the proposal that various syntactic categories behave similarly both within and across languages led to the development of a parameterized X′-theory ('X-bar theory'). Certain data may appear to be recalcitrant: in some languages, not all categories seem to employ the same ordering; in other languages, order itself seems unimportant. What the developing theories attempt to do is to account for these empirical differences, but maintain increasingly restrictive theories of phrase structure. Of course, restrictiveness in one component may lead to greater power in another. For example, if it is hypothesized that headedness is uniformly in one direction, it may be necessary to employ movement rules to reorder constituents. The optimal analysis will account for a range of empirical data within a maximally restrictive theory.

In the past few decades, sign language researchers have explored the question of whether sign language data are amenable to analysis under such systems. What is the basic clausal structure for any particular sign language? Is there uniformity in the phrase structure? Are there sentence types which provide empirical support for one hypothesis or another? These are the questions we will be addressing in the following sections. First, we provide a brief overview of the generative approach to phrase structure in Section 18.3.1. Then, in Section 18.3.2, we consider a recent proposal that the variability of word order in sign languages should be taken as an indication that structure is not needed. This proposal would make sign languages significantly different from spoken languages in important respects. We then turn to a series of proposals regarding the phrase structure of ASL in Sections 18.3.3–18.3.6. These proposals attempt to account for basic phrase structure and a varying set of additional facts. Establishing the basic phrase structure is a crucial first step for deeper investigation of sign language structure.

18.3.1 Generative approaches to phrase structure

In the 1970s, generative grammarians found that different syntactic categories behave similarly with respect to hierarchical organization (see, for example, Chomsky 1970, Jackendoff 1977). According to X′-theory, generalizations can be made over the syntactic categories (noun, verb, adjective, preposition) to describe their organization. X′-theory captures generalizations about phrases in each of these categories: XP's generalize over Noun Phrases (NPs), Verb Phrases (VPs), Adjective Phrases (APs), and Prepositional Phrases (PPs). In this way, X′-theory captures generalizations that earlier phrase structure theories missed.

Each phrasal category XP must have a *head* of category X (sometimes known as X^0). A head may combine with a *complement*, creating an intermediate category known as an X′ (V′, P′, etc.). This intermediate X′ category can combine with a *specifier* to make the phrasal category XP. A tree diagram showing this hierarchy is given in (31).

(31)

XP

specifier X′

X complement

According to parameterized theories of phrase structure, the X′ phrase structure rules are universal, but the order of constituents may vary across languages. So, while the order shown in (31) describes English, a language like Japanese would have the complements preceding the heads.

For English and Japanese, the ordering of constituents is constant for all X. This captures cross-linguistic generalizations across syntactic categories, such as the tendency for VO languages to use prepositions (P-NP), while OV languages use postpositions (NP-P). However, there have been some proposals that languages such as German and Dutch may require different ordering statements for different categories. This issue will be addressed with respect to sign language data in the following subsections.

Pollock (1989) gives extensive arguments that the category I (inflection or Infl), which had been considered the head of a sentence (Chomsky 1986), should actually be broken up into its component categories T (tense) and Agr (agreement), which themselves project phrasal categories (TP – tense phrase, and AgrP – agreement phrase). He also proposes that negative elements head their own projection called NegP. This theory, some version of which has been widely adopted, is sometimes known as an "expanded" or "articulated" theory of Infl. Under this theory, the structure of a basic clause will be as in (32).

(32) Basic clause structure (Pollock 1989, p. 397, adapted)

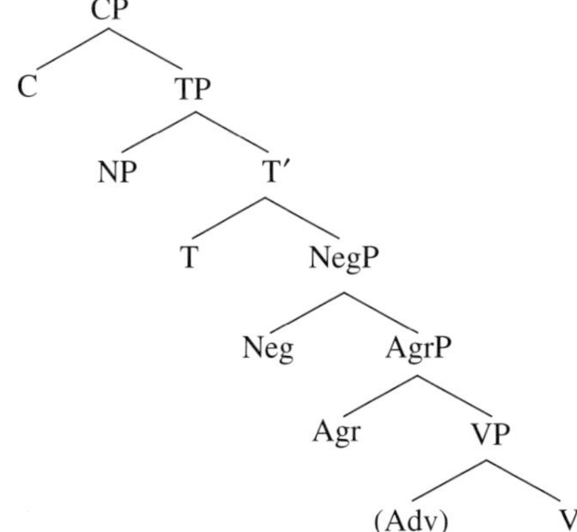

Pollock allows for certain aspects of the structure he proposes to vary across languages. Following the spirit of Koopman and Sportiche (1991) and Kuroda (1988), who argue that the subject is generated as the specifier of VP,[12] Pollock suggests that the subject might be generated in a lower position and raised to its surface position (which in French is [Spec, TP]), but languages may differ with respect to this proposal. Additionally, he suggests that languages may differ with respect to which functional categories are used and the order in which they are generated. On the other hand, in the interest of a more restrictive theory, others have assumed uniformity across languages with respect to the categories used and their order.

These issues have been relevant to the syntactic analysis of sign languages. Some researchers have assumed that the type and hierarchical order of functional projections is variable across languages, and have tried to find evidence for which order is used in the sign language being analyzed. Others have adopted proposals for universal structure, and have sought to fit sign language data to such structures. We will discuss these different analyses in the coming sections.

Since Pollock's work, it has been proposed that other functional categories in addition to Agr and T are also heads of full phrases. For example, Pollock's AgrP has been divided into subject agreement (AgrS, also known as S-Agr and various other notations) and object agreement (AgrO, O-Agr). Asp (aspect), D (determiner), Q (quantifier), F (focus), and other categories have also been proposed as phrasal heads. Some functional projections are posited based on morphological features expressed by lexical items; others are based on abstract features used for licensing, movement, or other operations.

Another development which will be relevant to the discussion of sign languages concerns feature checking. Feature checking is essentially a mechanism to ensure agreement (broadly speaking), such as that between a verb and its subject, or more abstractly, between a WH-phrase and a [+Q] feature.[13] The abstract syntactic features of an element can be checked with those of another element when they are in the appropriate syntactic configuration. According to Chomsky (1993, 1995), this configuration is restricted to the specifier/head relationship. That is, the phrase in a specifier position [Spec, XP] and the head of XP [X] are in the correct configuration for feature checking. This means, of course, that an element may need to move in order to check its features. If the surface order indicates that no movement has taken place, it may be assumed that movement is covert, that is, it takes place on the way to LF.

Much recent work in generative theory has been aimed at developing the notions of hierarchical structure, determining the full list of projected

12 This allows the verb's argument structure to be represented within the VP at some level.

13 Abstract Case must also be checked. Feature checking is how a lexicalist approach to morphology ensures that the correctly matching forms are chosen for the syntactic derivation.

categories, whether or not the list varies across languages, the hierarchical order of these categories, and whether or not the order varies across languages. Other work has concentrated on the theory of feature checking and how feature checking and syntactic movement interact. (See papers in Baltin and Collins 2001 for an excellent overview of recent developments in generative theory and the forces behind them.) Work on sign languages has contributed to this debate by making use of different proposed structures for analyses of different sentence types, with differing assumptions about universality. It should be noted that the theory is such that certain assumptions are made on theoretical grounds, in order to use empirical evidence to support or develop other hypotheses. Many aspects of the theory are controversial or changing, so one researcher may adopt assumptions which another researcher rejects. Through this process, the less successful aspects of the framework are eventually winnowed away. Sign language research is no different. Each researcher or group starts with their own set of assumptions, consistent with one version of a theory if not another. Eventually, consistent empirical generalizations lead to the selection of the most felicitous set of hypotheses, though in the midst of this process the end result is usually clouded.

We come to a summary of several of these proposals momentarily. But first, we take a side step to a recent discussion of whether sign languages make use of hierarchical structures such as the one in (32) at all.

18.3.2 Do sign language sentences have structure?

Reviewing the literature on basic word order in ASL, Bouchard and Dubuisson (1995) note that many authors have recognized greater flexibility of word order in ASL than that found in a language like English, as discussed in Section 18.1. As we have seen, eventually, the field has settled on the assumption that the underlying order of ASL is SVO. But one repeated claim (particularly in the early work) is that order is more flexible in semantically "non-reversible" sentences, such as (2)–(3) above, repeated as (33)–(34); and in sentences with verbs marked for agreement with subject and object, such as (25), repeated as (35).

(33) ASL (Fischer 1975, p. 10)

a. MAN MUST B-I-L-L-S PAY (SMOV)
b. MAN MUST PAY B-I-L-L-S (SMVO)

(34) ASL (Fischer 1975, p. 14)

a. BOY LIKE ICE-CREAM (SVO)
b. BOY ICE-CREAM LIKE (SOV)
c. ICE-CREAM LIKE BOY (OVS)
d. LIKE ICE-CREAM BOY (VOS)
e. ICE-CREAM BOY LIKE (OSV)

(35) ASL (Padden 1988 [1983], p. 229)
BOY ${}_{i}$INDEX, GIRL ${}_{j}$INDEX, ${}_{i}$KICK$_{j}$
'The boy kicked the girl.'

Bouchard and Dubuisson conclude that order is just "one means among others of expressing the combination of elements" (p. 108). When other means – such as verb agreement – are used, according to Bouchard and Dubuisson, word order is free. In particular, they argue against a possible alternative account which uses an underlying order plus order-changing operations to derive different orders; rather, they claim, in such circumstances there is no particular underlying order: "order is free, since it is not functionally necessary" (p. 109).

A problem for this conclusion is that order is not completely free, even with agreement or spatial information, as we have seen. VSO is not a permitted order in ASL, for example. And the extent to which non-SVO orders are permitted is actually a matter of some dispute. While sequences of SOV such as (25), and their OSV counterparts, are sometimes found with verbs showing agreement, they are not completely free. Furthermore, recall that Padden (1988 [1983]) argued that such cases should receive a three-clause analysis: Noun-1 is here; Noun-2 is here; null-subject Verb null-object.

There are also interesting cases in which SOV or OSV may be found with verbs marked with spatial, aspectual, or classifier information. But these cases may be analyzed in relation to another order found with such constructions, SVOV (cf. Fischer and Janis 1990, Matsuoka 1997, Chen Pichler 2001, Braze 2004). These constructions will be discussed in Chapter 20.

There is also plenty of evidence that with or without special morphology on the verb, in many cases non-SVO orders are associated with particular discourse markers – indicating topic or focus for example (see Chapter 22 and, among many others, Liddell 1980, Fischer 1990, Aarons 1994, Wilbur 1994a, 1996, 1997). In any case, whether the constituents in non-canonical position are analyzed as moved or base-generated, this type of behavior is far from unique to signed languages. Rather, they seem to behave like those spoken languages which use discourse structure or morphological information to permit variation from the more neutral order. In ASL, these alternative orders are associated with both a particular discourse context, and prosodic cues – and they show other classical effects of derived structures (such as constituency restrictions and constraints on long-distance relations) (Padden 1988 [1983], Lillo-Martin 1991, Petronio 1993).

Bouchard and Dubuisson's position, however, was not intended solely to distinguish signed languages from spoken languages with respect to order. Instead, they advocate a much stronger position (expanded on and clarified in Bouchard 1996), which is that languages may vary in the extent to which they rely on abstract hierarchical structure to provide information about the relationships between elements in a sentence (or discourse). They advocate the approach that all languages may choose from two universally available means for establishing a relationship between elements. The first means is to put the elements in a physical relation, so that they share an edge or space. For spoken languages, this can only be done by temporal ordering. For sign languages, however, this can be done either by temporal sequencing *or* by using the same physical space for the elements. Signed languages are distinct from spoken languages in that they may (and invariably do) make use of this latter mechanism. The second mechanism is modification of the elements, as in Case marking. Bouchard claims that structure is unnecessary when means other than temporal sequencing are used (such as Case marking or physical locations) – and so the most minimal conception of the human language mechanism would omit structure in these cases.

Bouchard and Dubuisson argue that structure-based analyses of ASL have not proven the necessity for structure over some other mechanisms such as those they propose. In particular, they argue against the proposals by Aarons Bahan, Kegl, and Neidle (1992), which include a complex phrase marker containing multiple functional categories with mixed headedness. The proposals by Aarons et al. (1992, 1994, 1995), defended in Kegl, Neidle, MacLaughlin, Hoza, and Bahan (1996), were not intended to argue for the notion that sign language sentences have structure; rather, presupposing this common idea, they apply a particular structural proposal to ASL data. While their particular hypotheses may be debated (see Section 18.3.5), completely dispensing with the notion of structure is unwarranted, and fails to account for the full range of data.

For example, even Bouchard and Dubuisson concede that structure and order are required for sign language sentences which do not use spatial relations, such as utterances with plain verbs. They "conclude that ASL is a mixed language, with an 'elsewhere' approach to order" (p. 109). That is, if the use of spatial locations allows all relevant information to be expressed without order, then order is free, but elsewhere ASL reverts to order. This conclusion puts Bouchard and Dubuisson in a rather awkward position. If sign languages don't need order because they have space, why do they need order sometimes after all? Furthermore, as Carol Padden (p.c.) points out to us, there are pairs of verbs with very similar meanings which differ in exactly this respect: one is spatial and the other is plain or agreeing (e.g. CL:V-'walk' vs. WALK; PASS-BY-HAND vs. GIVE). Why would the non-spatial verbs even exist if spatial relations are to be exploited whenever possible?

A further concern for the approach advocated by Bouchard and Dubuisson concerns the "elsewhere" condition. What is it that determines the "elsewhere" order? And why should sign languages, like spoken languages, vary with respect to what looks like the "elsewhere" order (ASL is SVO, but German Sign Language – Deutsche Gebärdensprache

(DGS) – is SOV)? Bouchard and Dubuisson's argument is that if order is not needed, a minimal conception of the human language capacity would not include it. But it is not the case that order is not needed; since it must be part of the human language capacity, there is not necessarily an additional cost to the assumption that it is always used. Questioning whether the analyses which assume structure make use of too many additional, unwarranted, assumptions in order to derive the correct structure, as Bouchard and Dubuisson do, is legitimate, to be sure. But arguing against particular analyses which include structure is different from arguing against the whole idea of structure.

This debate is reminiscent of the state of affairs in the formal linguistic investigation of various so-called "free word order languages." One example comes from the study of Japanese in the early 1980s. Some authors claimed that Japanese is "non-configurational" (Hale 1980, 1983, among others), because of its apparently "free" word order and other properties. Non-configurational languages were thought to have no ordering requirements or hierarchical structure. A broad set of facts about the language could be captured using this notion. However, Hoji (1985) and Saito (1985), among others, showed that hierarchical structure is required in Japanese, and employed the movement operation known as scrambling to account for the variations of word order found. Scrambling in Japanese moves noun phrases to the sentence-initial position – but starts with a phrase structure employing both a verb phrase hierarchically separate from the subject and verb-final ordering within the verb phrase. Thus, a relatively free word order is derived from an ordered hierarchical structure. Saito quotes from Kuroda:

> Word order is quite free in Japanese. This is obvious. But to transform this trivial observation of a phenomenon into a grammatical principle is another matter. There are good indications that the linear order of certain constituents is grammatically relevant, if one pays attention to the interaction between so-called word order and certain other grammatical phenomena.
>
> (Kuroda 1983, pp. 153–154, cited by Saito 1985, p. 54)

The debate about configurationality in Japanese has been repeated for numerous other languages, and the conclusion has always been in favor of hierarchical structure. The same can be said for ASL (and presumably other sign languages). Bouchard's idea emphasizes that if it were possible for the human language capacity to work without structure, this would be apparent in sign languages, since spatial information could presumably carry out the same function. If even sign languages require hierarchical structure, such structure must be a basic, primitive component of all languages. The discussion in this section therefore supports the claim that structure dependence is a criterial component of language, whether spoken or signed.

If we accept the arguments presented above that sign language sentences do display hierarchical structure, what is the nature of this structure? How does the structure proposed account for the various word orders and sentence types observed? We turn now to several proposals concerning the hierarchical structure of sign language sentences.

18.3.3 Mini-topicalization

In view of the underlying SVO order argued for above, it might seem that ASL is a right-branching language, with a structure like that of (36).

(36)

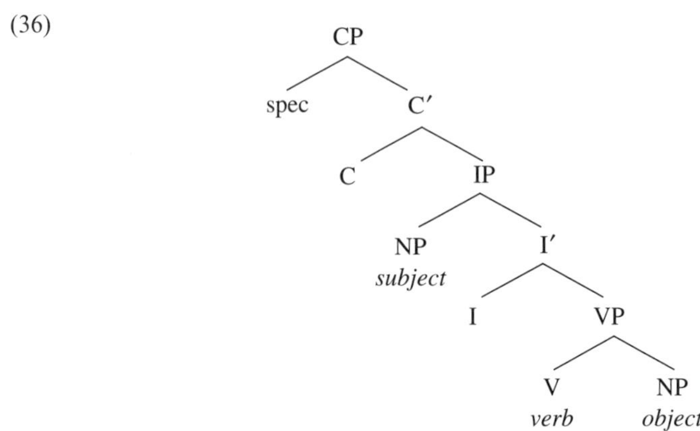

In this structure, heads uniformly come before their complements, and specifiers precede their heads. Although this conclusion seems to be mainly true, there are reasons to question its broad generality. On the one hand, in ASL there is more variability in the ordering of some constituents than one might expect. For example, adjectives come either before or after the nouns they modify, modals can appear in a variety of positions, and other structures show variability.

In order to account for these phenomena, Fischer (1990) argues that ASL is uniformly head-initial, but allows topicalization to any available specifier position. She calls this topicalization within a phrase "mini-topicalization," and she uses this idea to account for some of the variations observed. For example, she claims that an object can mini-topicalize to the [Spec, VP] position to derive SOV order; that the complement to an auxiliary or modal can topicalize to leave the auxiliary or modal in sentence-final position; and that some nouns, complementizers, and conjunctions might be found following their complements because the complements have topicalized.

Alternatives to Fischer's proposal regarding the basic clausal structure of ASL have been suggested by Romano (1991), Aarons et al. (1992), and Petronio (1993). As discussed in some detail immediately following (Sections 18.3.4, 18.3.5, and 18.3.6), all three of these works propose as an alternative to mini-topicalization that ASL is not uniform in the directionality of headedness of the different categories (although the works disagree on just which categories have which directionality).

The controversy regarding the underlying phrase structure of ASL is interesting not just for ASL syntacticians. Since ASL displays a variety of surface word orders, it provides empirical data on the variability found within X-bar syntax. The account of Aarons et al. also proposes new phrasal categories and adjunction structures, not used (so far) in the analyses of spoken languages. If ASL displays a variability or a phrasal category not found in spoken languages, this would have important ramifications for syntactic theory. The analysis of ASL might even suggest new parameters which turn out to be needed in spoken languages as well.

Alternatively, an analysis of ASL within the range of variation found for spoken languages might be made. A development along these lines was proposed by Quadros (1999) for Lingua de Sinais Brasileira (LSB), and will be presented in Chapter 19. Although there are some important interesting differences between LSB and ASL (cf. Quadros, Lillo-Martin, and Chen Pichler 2000, 2004), many of the proposals made by Quadros could be applied to ASL. This approach would lead to an analysis of ASL more in line with those proposed for spoken languages.

18.3.4 Split headedness

Given the evidence for SVO basic word order, it is relatively clear that Verbs and Prepositions are head-initial. The types of structures which appear to contradict a uniformly head-initial analysis involve CP and IP. Recognizing this, Romano (1991) proposed a headedness split between lexical and functional categories in ASL. She proposed that lexical categories (i.e., V, N, P, A) are uniformly head-initial, while functional categories (C(complementizer), I(inflection), CL(classifier)) are uniformly head-final. This proposal results in a phrase structure tree like that in (37) (CL phrase is omitted from this tree, as it will not be considered further).

(37)

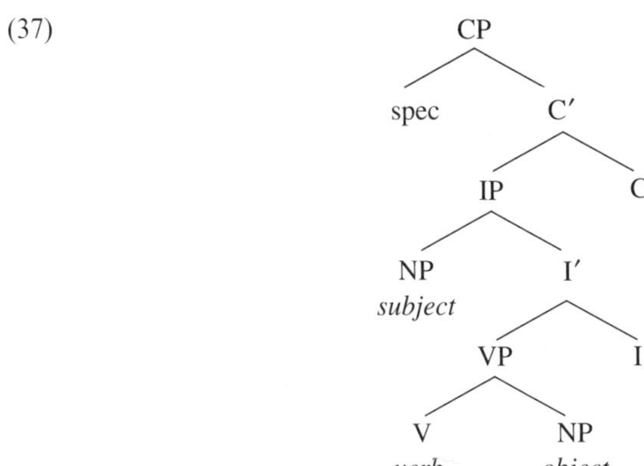

Romano's argument for the headedness of IP comes from sentences with lexical tense markers, such as FINISH and WILL. She provides the

examples in (38a–c). These examples show that FINISH can appear in either the sentence-final position or between the subject and verb.

(38) ASL (Romano 1991, p. 245)

a. ME SEE MOVIE FINISH

b. ME FINISH SEE MOVIE

c. *ME SEE MOVIE FINISH (with "t" marked over ME SEE MOVIE)

'I saw the movie.'

As Romano points out, under Fischer's head-initial theory, (38a) cannot be derived. The constituent SEE MOVIE cannot be fronted to a position between the subject and the Aux, on the assumption that the subject is in [Spec, IP] and the tense element is in I (cf. structure (36)). Furthermore, since it is ungrammatical for these two signs to be marked with the topicalization non-manual marker, as (38c) shows, it is unlikely that they could be fronted through topicalization. As an alternative, Romano argues that (38a) should represent the deep structure position of FINISH in I, and that (38b) is derived via affix hopping (by which the element in I hops to the preverbal position). Since Romano also argues for the head-final structure of Classifier Phrase, she furthermore proposes that for reasons of parsimony all functional categories (including, specifically, C) might be head-final in ASL.

On further investigation, it seems that there may indeed be a split between categories which are head-initial, and those which are head-final, but it is not clear that the split falls along the lines of functional vs. lexical categories. Recent works have investigated this in some detail, namely Aarons et al. (1992 and following works), and Petronio (1993). These approaches have also invoked the expanded IP structure discussed above, employing the categories TP, NegP, AgrSP, and AgrOP. Both of these approaches reject the lexical-functional split in headedness; in fact, both adopt structures which uniformly have the order specifier–head–complement from TP down. These models also agree with respect to the ordering of projections as T–Neg–Agr-S–Agr-O. However, they provide different arguments for this ordering, and they furthermore differ in the structure above TP. Here, we will discuss their proposed clause structure up to TP, reserving discussion of higher positions for Chapters 22 and 23.

18.3.5 Non-manual markers as key to phrase structure

In a series of articles summarized in their book,[14] Neidle, Kegl, and their colleagues (Neidle et al. 2000) present arguments for a phrase structure of ASL which, like Romano's, shows mixed headedness, but unlike hers is

[14] Aarons, Bahan, Kegl, Lee, MacLaughlin, and Neidle are members of the American Sign Language Linguistic Research Project (ASLLRP). The material discussed in this section is presented in similar forms in various works, particularly Aarons et al. (1992, 1994, 1995),

left-headed from TP down. Other details of their proposal are also rather different from Romano's, and their arguments go beyond basic word order.

The basic clause structure of ASL (from TP down) argued for by Neidle et al. (2000) is given in (39).[15]

(39) Partial syntactic tree (Neidle et al. 2000, p. 3)

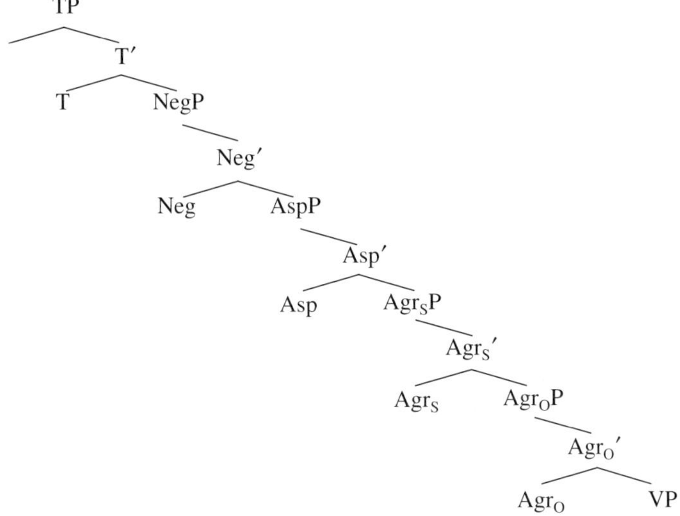

Their arguments for this structure, going back to Aarons et al. (1992), are based on certain assumptions they make regarding the status of non-manual markers in ASL. These assumptions are summarized in the following comments, taken from Neidle et al. (2000, pp. 43–45).

- Non-manual syntactic markings are frequently associated with syntactic features residing in the heads of functional projections.
- The non-manual marking may spread over the c-command domain of the node with which it is associated (reflecting relations at Spell-Out).[16]
- Spread of the non-manual marking is optional if manual material is available locally. However, in the absence of such manual material, the

Aarons (1994), Bahan (1966), Bahan et al. (2000), and Neidle et al. (1998a, 2000). Some details of their analyses have changed over time. For coherence, we will mainly present the version from Neidle et al. (2000).

15 Structures higher than TP will be discussed in Chapters 22 and 23.

16 The definition of c-command was given in Chapter 17. To repeat, A c-commands B iff A and B do not dominate each other, and the first branching node dominating A also dominates B.

Neidle et al. adopt the notion of Spell-Out from the Minimalist Program (Chomsky 1993, 1995), in which the distinction between D-Structure and S-Structure has been modified. Spell-Out is the point at which some portion of a derivation is sent to PF (Phonological Form), so it is similar to the pre-Minimalist notion of S-Structure. The point of the parenthetical remark is that it is the surface order of elements which determines the spread of non-manual markings. We will return to this in Chapter 23.

marking spreads obligatorily so that it may be coarticulated with manual material.
- The intensity of the non-manual marking is greatest at the node of origin and decreases gradually as distance from the source increases.[17]
- As in the manual channel, perseveration (maintenance of a particular articulation that will recur later) is found with non-manual expressions.[18]

Note that the statements above are generalizations based on the particular analyses proposed by Neidle et al. There are other ways to analyze non-manual markings which do not make the same claims. For example, the intonation analysis discussed in Chapter 15 makes different claims about the spread of non-manual markers. This issue will be discussed extensively in Chapter 23.

As an example of how non-manual markers are used by Neidle et al. to determine syntactic structure, consider the case of negation, illustrated in (40). The manual negative sign appears between the subject and the Verb Phrase. Neidle et al. assume that the manual negative is represented in the Neg head, and that the non-manual marker of negation is associated with the [+neg] syntactic feature also residing in the head of the functional projection Neg°. Since manual material is available locally (i.e., in the Neg° position), the non-manual syntactic marking begins simultaneously with the manual negative, and may optionally spread over the c-command domain of the node with which it is associated, NegP.

(40) ASL (Neidle et al. 2000, p. 44)

$\underline{\text{neg}}$

a. JOHN NOT BUY HOUSE
'John is *not* buying a house.'

$\underline{\text{neg}}$

b. JOHN [NOT [BUY HOUSE]$_{VP}$]$_{Neg}$
'John is not buying a house.'

It is also possible to produce a negative sentence with no manual negative marker, just the non-manual marker. In this case, as Neidle et al. claim, the non-manual negative marker *must* spread over the full c-command domain, i.e., the rest of the sentence (41).

[17] This claim may lie behind some controversies between their analysis of WH-questions and that of Petronio and Lillo-Martin (1997, Petronio 1993). We will return to this issue in Chapter 23.

[18] By this it is meant that aspects of the articulation of non-manual markers or lexical signs which occur at two separate positions in a string may be extended throughout the intervening material. This may be similar to the process of sandhi discussed in Chapter 15.

(41) ASL (Neidle et al. 2000, p. 45)

a. $\overline{\text{neg}}$ *JOHN [+neg]$_{\text{Neg}}$ BUY HOUSE

b. JOHN $\overline{\text{[+neg]}_{\text{Neg}}\text{ BUY HOUSE}}^{\text{neg}}$

'John is not buying a house.'

The data presented in (40)-(41) are in accord with the tree proposed by Neidle et al. given in (39), on the assumption that the subject appears in [Spec, TP]. However, other researchers claim that the negative non-manual marker may extend over the subject as well. This dispute is one source of different theoretical positions, and is discussed in Chapter 20.

We now turn to Neidle et al.'s arguments for other aspects of the structure in (39).

Tense

Although ASL clauses do not require an overt tense marker, tense can be marked through time adverbials or lexical tense markers (Aarons et al. 1995). Lexical tense markers appear between the subject and negation (42), and cannot appear in structures analogous to infinitivals (43). Aarons et al. also provide examples to show that modals are distributed like lexical tense markers; i.e., they appear between the subject and a negative, but not in infinitives. The ordering of tense (and modals) vis-à-vis negation leads the ASLLRP group to posit that T is higher in the tree than Neg, as shown in (39).

(42) ASL (Neidle et al. 2000, p. 80)

JOHN FUTURE$_{\text{tns}}$ $\overline{\text{NOT BUY HOUSE}}^{\text{neg}}$

'John will not buy a house.'

(43) a. JOHN PREFER GO MOVIE

'John prefers to go to a movie.'

b. *JOHN PREFER FUTURE$_{\text{tns}}$ GO MOVIE

Agreement

As we have seen in Chapter 3, a class of verbs in ASL may be marked for subject and object agreement. Since this agreement marking attaches to the verb, it alone tells us little about the ordering of AgrS and AgrO with respect to other categories. However, as discussed in Chapter 3, Bahan (1996) argues that there is a non-manual marker of subject and object agreement in ASL whose ordering does testify to the hierarchical phrase structure given in (39).

In particular, Bahan (1996) and Neidle et al. (1998a) argue that the non-manual marker for subject agreement, head tilt, begins *after* the subject and any negative sign, and *before* the non-manual marker for object agreement, eye gaze, which likewise precedes the Verb Phrase. This ordering is illustrated in (44).

(44) ASL (Neidle et al. 2000, 84)

neg
head tilt$_i$
gaze$_j$
JOHN$_i$ NOT [+agr$_i$]Agr$_S$ [+agr$_j$]Agr$_O$ VISIT$_j$ MARY$_j$
'John is *not* visiting Mary.'

This is exactly the ordering predicted by the tree given in (39), together with their assumptions about non-manual markers. Note that this proposal includes the assumption that verbs do not move overtly in ASL, but stay in their position within VP.[19]

In Chapter 3, we pointed out problems for the proposal that eye gaze and head tilt constitute non-manual markers of agreement. Of particular relevance here is the accuracy of the claim that the relative timing of head tilt and eye gaze reflect the hierarchical ordering proposed in (39). Although the transcription given in (44) makes the pattern seem obvious, in fact this is not observed to be the case. In this example, both non-manual markers begin only one or two video frames before the verb. In other examples without manual material intervening between the subject and the verb, both head tilt and eye gaze may actually begin during the subject. In several of the examples posted at the ASLLRP website, the eyes are closed at the relevant moment, or the eye gaze clearly begins one or two frames prior to the head tilt. Thus, the claim that head tilt and eye gaze reveal hierarchical structure is not empirically supported.

Aspect

Lexical aspect markers, such as FINISH, appear after lexical negatives (45), and before non-manual markers of agreement (46). This is the ordering expected if lexical aspect markers appear in the head of AspP, and this projection is placed lower than Negation, but above both Agr projections, as it is in (39). There will be additional discussion of the placement of AspP in Chapter 20, where we discuss structures involving aspect and alternative word orders.

[19] In this way, ASL is unlike French, since Pollock (1989) argued that verbs must raise overtly in French. It is now sometimes assumed that verbs which do not raise overtly, such as English main verbs, raise covertly (i.e., in LF).

(45) ASL (Neidle et al. 2000, p. 84)

neg
JOHN NOT FINISH READ BOOK
'John hasn't read the book.'

(46) ASL (Neidle et al. 2000, p. 84)

head tilt$_i$
eye gaze$_j$
JOHN$_i$ FINISH [+agr$_i$]Agr$_S$ [+agr$_j$]Agr$_O$ VISIT$_j$ MARY$_j$
'John has visited Mary.'

Summary

On the assumption that lexical and/or non-manual tense, negation, aspect, and agreement elements appear on the surface in the heads of their respective projections, and that non-manual markers function in the way claimed by Neidle et al., the data in (40)–(46) motivate a phrase structure hierarchy like that given in (39). We stress these assumptions here, because they are not trivial. The first assumption is that phrase structure is directly reflected in surface order. This is the appropriate default assumption, since any proposed movement operations should be justified. However, the "generalizations" about non-manual markers proposed by Neidle et al. do not provide independent evidence for the hierarchical structure they use, and the non-manual markers do not constitute overt evidence of functional categories, as claimed. As we have seen, there are numerous reasons for treating (at least some) non-manual markings as analogous to intonation. On such an interpretation, they are not necessarily expected to reflect syntactic structure directly. We take up this issue again in Chapter 23. There will be some discussion of other evidence, for or against the proposed hierarchy, in the following sections and chapters.

18.3.6 Modals provide evidence for phrase structure

Is there any additional evidence regarding the relative structural positions of TP and AgrSP in ASL? Petronio (1993) sets out to use modals to test the ordering of T with respect to SAgr, on the common assumption that (as in many languages) modals are located in T. She provides additional arguments for the independently arrived-at ordering of phrasal categories in (39), repeated (using Petronio's notation) linearly in (47).

(47) [TP [(NegP) [SAgrP [OAgrP [VP]]]]]

First, Petronio considers Padden's (1988 [1983]) argument that modals in ASL must be main verbs, rather than auxiliaries. If modals are main verbs, they do not provide evidence about the position of T, which is assumed to be the host for auxiliaries. Padden's argument is based on the observation that while nominals (in particular, subjects and direct objects, including clausal objects) may participate in topicalization (48a), predicates do not (48b).

(48) ASL (Padden 1988 [1983], pp. 151–152)

    ____________t
a. WOMAN STAY, $_{1}$INDEX HOPE
    'As for the woman staying, I hope she does.'

    ____t
b. *STAY, $_{1}$INDEX HOPE WOMAN

On the other hand, the material following a modal may topicalize, as in (49).

(49) ASL (Padden 1988 [1983], p. 152)

- - - - - -t- - - - -
STOP SMOKING, SISTER MUST
'My sister has got to stop smoking.'

Padden accounts for this by hypothesizing that modals are predicates, rather than auxiliaries, and that they take clausal complements. Under this hypothesis, (49) is derived from a structure where STOP SMOKING is a clause following the (modal) predicate MUST. As a clausal object, STOP SMOKING can participate in topicalization.

Petronio argues that Padden's observation does not require modals to be main verbs. Instead, the facts can be explained by considering the licensing requirements on traces. As the traces of movement generally are required to be in a particular licensing configuration, Petronio asks what would license the trace of the constituent which moves in (49). Following Lobeck's (1986) proposal based on spoken languages, Petronio suggests that an overt element in T can license a trace in its complement. Thus, the modal can be in T, and the position of modals is therefore informative regarding the ordering of T with respect to other elements.

For this information, Petronio examines the co-occurrence of modals with agreeing verbs, as in (50). This example shows that modals and agreeing verbs can co-occur (unlike English, **He should shows me*).

(50) ASL (Petronio 1993, p. 86)

$_{2}$INDEX SHOULD $_{2}$SHOW$_{1}$
'You should show me.'

Petronio assumes that an agreeing verb moves to Agr during the overt syntax in ASL. This is so the verb, moving through the Agr projections, will have the appropriate agreement features (cf. Pollock's analysis of French). Since modals can co-occur with agreeing verbs, the modal in T must be higher than the verb in SAgr, yielding the structure in (51).

(51) (Petronio 1993, p. 86)

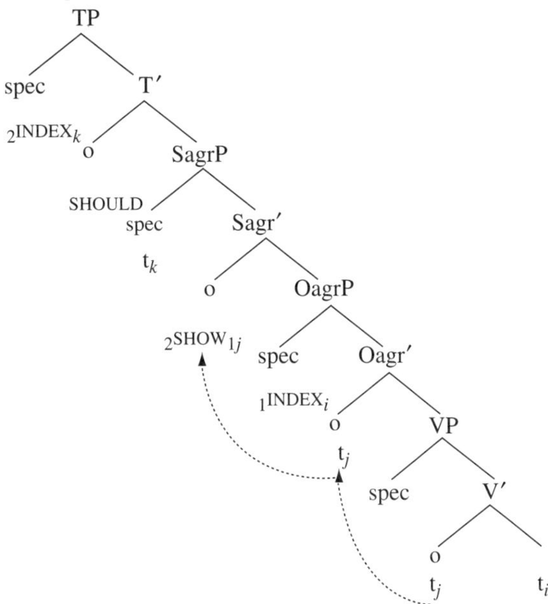

Recall that Neidle et al. (2000) do not assume that agreeing verbs raise overtly. In their analysis, agreeing and plain verbs remain in V during the overt syntax, raising covertly to check features.[20]

Another piece of evidence regarding the positions of T, SAgr, and OAgr comes from the structure of infinitival embedded clauses. Although in ASL there is no overt tense marking on the verb to distinguish tensed and infinitival complement clauses, complements of matrix verbs such as TRY and WANT behave like non-finite complements in many spoken languages, and most researchers consider them members of this class in ASL. Petronio points out that such complements disallow overt subjects and modals (52), but do show agreement (53).[21]

(52) ASL (Petronio 1993, p. 92)

a. *$_a$JOHN TRY $_a$INDEX WIN

b. *JOHN WANT SHOULD WIN

(53) ASL (Petronio 1993, p. 89)

$\overline{\qquad\qquad\qquad\text{hn}}$

$_a$JOHN WANT $_a$SHOW$_1$

John wants to show me.

[20] This issue will come up again in several of the following chapters. We will see that there is independent evidence for the conclusion of Neidle et al. (2000) that verbs do not raise overtly to SAgr, but do raise to Asp(ect) when they are morphologically marked for aspect.

[21] It is possible that (52b) is unacceptable for semantic reasons, but not syntactically ungrammatical. A more complete investigation of this issue would be needed to rule out this possibility.

Because such complements can show agreement marking, Petronio concludes that infinitival complements employ structures headed by SAgr (recall that she assumes that verbs move overtly to the Agr projections when marked with morphological agreement). However, if infinitival complements were full TPs, Petronio assumes they should have all the properties of TPs, including allowing elements which would appear in the head of T and overt subjects. Since neither are permitted, Petronio concludes that infinitival clauses do not project all the way to TP, and therefore that TP (when present) is higher than the Agr phrases, as in the structures in (39) and (47).

Petronio also noted that modals may appear sentence-finally (SVOM), or twice in one clause: either SMVOM, or MSVOM. She relates both of these phenomena to a more general process of doubling elements in the sentence-final position, which will be addressed in Chapter 22. There we will see a number of discourse/pragmatic variations on word order found in sign languages. We will see that ASL has a strong discourse tendency to place old information in initial position, and emphasized, focused information in final position. Just how these word order changes are achieved will be considered in that context.

18.4 Summary and conclusion

Over the years, various proposals have been put forward that ASL and other sign languages have no basic word order, or no hierarchical structure. However, we have presented evidence that this notion is as mistaken for sign languages as it is for spoken languages. Order and structure are a basic part of language, and they apply to sign languages as well as to spoken languages. ASL is an SVO language with the hierarchical structure of an SVO language.

However, languages do vary in the amount to which they make use of order-changing operations to reflect discourse notions such as topic and focus. ASL – and, most likely, other sign languages – can be considered "discourse oriented," as it makes extensive use of such order-changing operations. These will be discussed in more detail in the coming chapters, particularly Chapters 20 and 22.

But first, we consider another analysis of phrase structure in sign language, and the question of cross-sign-language variation in clause structure. We take a rather detailed look at one proposal in particular. This proposal is based on data from Brazilian Sign Language, Lingua de Sinais Brasileira (LSB). We examine this proposal in detail because it follows a recent theoretical development towards a very restricted theory of cross-linguistic variation in phrase structure, that of Kayne (1994). Kayne's proposal is that all languages are underlyingly SVO – i.e., that specifiers uniformly precede, and complements uniformly follow, their heads. This proposal has been very controversial, but highly influential, as it restricts the power of the "base" component of grammar. Can the structure of a discourse-oriented language be accounted for under Kayne's system?

We will see that the properties of LSB can be accommodated by a Kaynian approach to clause structure. We will also make comparisons between LSB and ASL which help to illuminate the phrase structures used by both languages. Additional research comparing the clause structures of unrelated sign languages would be most welcome.

19 Clausal structure across sign languages

We have seen that despite the fact that there is considerable flexibility of word order, ASL can be described as a language with the underlying or basic word order SVO. Typically, an SVO language (like English) has the ordering head–complement for all phrasal categories. While it is clear that ASL employs this ordering for some categories, there have been various proposals for some kind of mixed headedness to account for the full range of surface orders observed. These proposals were discussed in Chapter 18, but they will come up again as we discuss additional aspects of order-changing operations in Chapters 20 and 22.

While a number of researchers have proposed that languages may vary in their headedness, and even in the hierarchy of functional projections employed, others support an analysis which restricts the possible variation in these domains. Perhaps the most strictly restricted theory is that of Kayne (1994). Kayne proposes that all languages have the same underlying phrase structure, and that this structure requires the order specifier before head, head before complement. If a language has the surface order complement–head, then this order must be derived, on Kayne's theory.

Given the proposals for mixed headedness in ASL, is it possible to apply a theory like Kayne's to account for ASL data?

In this chapter, we will address this question. But, since Kayne's proposal is about where cross-linguistic variation is found, it will be most informative for us to consider the question in the light of cross-sign-language data. Thus, the broader context of this chapter concerns variability in basic clause structure across sign languages. The issue of variability vs. strict uniformity of phrase structure will come up again in Chapters 20 and 22, where we discuss additional order-changing operations that apply in ASL and other sign languages.

In this chapter we discuss in most detail data from Brazilian Sign Language (Lingua de Sinais Brasileira, LSB). Recently, Quadros (1999) has presented an analysis of the basic clause structure of LSB which makes use of the restricted theory of structure proposed by Kayne. This permits us to directly evaluate the efficacy of Kayne's proposal for sign language data. In the concluding section of this chapter, we briefly directly compare LSB and ASL. Additional cross-sign-language comparisons will help in the evaluation of theories such as Kayne's, and in understanding the extent of possible syntactic differences within the sign modality.

We begin our discussion with a description of signs sometimes analyzed as auxiliaries. ASL has no sign comparable to the signs described for several other sign languages in Section 19.1. These auxiliary signs are used with non-agreeing verbs – conveying the information normally carried by agreement. LSB, like Taiwan Sign Language, Sign Language of the Netherlands, and Japanese Sign Language, uses an auxiliary sign with non-agreeing verbs (although there are differences in the use of these signs across the various languages which have them). The description and analysis of auxiliaries is important for understanding the structures associated with plain and agreeing verbs, the issue on which we focus in Section 19.2.

19.1 Auxiliary signs

We have seen some claims that the availability of verb agreement to indicate the subject and object permits the ordering of these constituents to be more free in ASL (and indeed, similar claims have been made for some other sign languages). However, the situation is more complicated in some sign languages other than ASL, which have an element ASL lacks. This element is considered by many researchers to be a type of auxiliary.

Three such elements in Taiwan Sign Language (TSL) are described by Smith (1990). The form he called AUX-1 is shown in Figure 19.1. By Smith's description, this sign consists of an index (hand with index finger extended) which moves, like agreeing verbs, from the location of the subject to the location of the object.[1]

Smith argues that AUX-1 is an auxiliary on the basis of its behavior. It shows agreement, but appears immediately preceding a main V, in sentences like (1). It also permits gender marking, like many agreeing main verbs in TSL. AUX-1 can be used with any verb, but tends to be used more frequently with verbs from the non-agreeing class. When used with potentially agreeing verbs, "the main verbs tend to appear in an uninflected form," which "suggest[s] that when an auxiliary is present, it is ungrammatical to also mark subject or object agreement on the main verb" (p. 219). Smith says, "The sole function of AUX-1 appears to be to

[1] Recall that we have seen in Chapter 3 that on Meir's (2002) analysis agreeing verbs move from the location associated with their source to the location associated with their goal. Smith indicates that while TSL does have verbs of the sort known as "backwards" verbs, AUX-1 shows the "regular" pattern of agreement.

Figure 19.1 AUX-1 (TSL) (reprinted with permission from Smith 1990)

carry subject and object agreement information" (p. 219). Although Smith describes two other signs which he calls auxiliaries, it is AUX-1 which seems most comparable to auxiliaries in other sign languages, and we will not describe the others here.

(1) TSL (Smith 1990, p. 217)
THAT FEMALE 3p-AUX1–1p NOT-LIKE
'That woman doesn't like me.'

Bos (1994) describes a similar element in Sign Language of the Netherlands (SLN), which she glosses ACT-ON. She describes its form as similar to the SLN sign GO-TO, but with the mouthing /ɔp/, corresponding to a Dutch word for 'on.' Bos characterizes the function of ACT-ON as, "to agree in person with one or two arguments of the verb in the clause" (p. 40). It usually appears immediately preceding or following the verb, though other material may intervene. Usually, the verb appears without agreement (even a potentially agreeing verb), but there are plenty of examples where both the verb and ACT-ON show agreement. An example of the typical use of ACT-ON is given in (2). ACT-ON immediately follows the non-agreeing verb LOVE.

(2) SLN (Bos 1994, p. 39)
_____________________topic /eg3a/[2]
INDEX$_1$ PARTNER INDEX$_{3a}$, LOVE $_{3a}$ACT-ON$_1$
mij vrien op
'My boyfriend loves me . . .'

Bos notes that while the AUX-1 Smith describes for TSL seems in many ways similar to her description of ACT-ON for SLN, there are some differences between the two. In particular, while AUX-1 immediately precedes the main verb (or is in clause-initial position), there is a strong tendency for ACT-ON to appear adjacent to the verb, either before or after it. Also, AUX-1 tends to occur with plain verbs, and Smith says that when AUX-1 appears with verbs of the agreeing class they appear uninflected. ACT-ON, on the other hand, appears with both types of verbs, and when

[2] In Bos' notation, /eg3a/ indicates eye gaze to the third person locus 'a.'

co-occurring with an agreeing verb, agreement may appear on the verb as well as on ACT-ON.

Japanese Sign Language (JSL) also seems to have an auxiliary sign (Fischer 1996). Like TSL but unlike SLN, the JSL sign (glossed AUX1 by Fischer) cannot co-occur with agreeing verbs. Unlike TSL, the JSL AUX1 cannot co-occur with gender agreement. Its placement with respect to the verb is freer than that found for AUX1 in TSL. An example of the use of AUX1 in JSL is given in (3). Here AUX1 appears preceding the verb.

(3) JSL (Fischer 1996, p. 107)
CHILDa TEACHERb aAUX1b LIKE
'The child likes the teacher.'

Other researchers have noted similar elements in other sign languages, including LSB (Quadros 1999), German Sign Language (DGS; Rathmann 2000), and Israeli Sign Language (ISL; Meir 2003); however, they do not all agree on the "auxiliary" analysis in the languages they study. We will come back to these elements in Section 19.3, where we compare the structure of ASL, a sign language lacking an AUX, with LSB, which has one. First, we turn to our detailed examination of LSB phrase structure.

19.2 LSB phrase structure

19.2.1 A universal theory of phrase structure

Basic word order has been studied in a number of sign languages. As cited in Chapter 18, researchers have proposed sign languages with basic orders SVO and SOV, as well as several proposals that particular sign languages have no basic order, but only discourse-dependent orders.

Is the potential variability in word order across languages unbounded? If so, then conclusions about the structure of one sign language would have little bearing on the next, or even on syntactic theory. An extreme alternative viewpoint starts with the assumption that languages do not vary with respect to underlying phrase structure. Surface differences must then be accounted for by differing application of universally available movement rules.

This approach has been adopted by Quadros (1999; Quadros and Karnopp 2004) in her study of aspects of the phrase structure of LSB. Quadros is guided by a theory of syntax which postulates that *all* languages share particular hierarchical characteristics (Kayne 1994), and her proposal for LSB is compatible with this model, unlike those of Neidle et al. or Petronio for ASL. Furthermore, she suggests that many aspects of her analysis do apply to ASL. We will discuss her analysis as it applies to LSB first, and later bring in comparisons with

ASL. But first, we introduce some of the central notions of Kayne's proposal relevant to the present discussion.

Kayne (1994) makes a radical new proposal to restrict the possible variation in grammar. He puts forth the idea that phrase structures do not allow for the variation in order between heads, complements, and specifiers which had been assumed. Rather, he argues that specifiers uniformly precede heads, and heads uniformly precede complements. What then, if a complement follows its head overtly? Kayne argues that in such cases, the complement has moved to a higher position – namely, the specifier of the head (this is very similar to Fischer's (1990) proposal for "mini-topicalization"; see Chapter 18, Section 3).

Kayne's proposal requires viewing hierarchical structure at a more abstract level than simple surface order. It is not, however, just a notational variant of a theory with flexible order for complements and heads, as constraints on movement will rule out some possibilities allowed under the traditional view. Furthermore, it predicts an asymmetry between heads and complements which precede them, unlike the theory that allows complements to be directly generated preceding their heads. To illustrate, the traditional theory would generate a complement–head order (such as Object–Verb in SOV languages) as in (4a). However, Kayne's theory would require the complement to be generated to the right of the head in all languages, and then to move to the specifier position when necessary, as in (4b). Thus, in his theory preceding complements will asymmetrically c-command their heads. That is, the complements will behave as though they are structurally higher than their heads when they precede them, but not when they follow them.

(4)

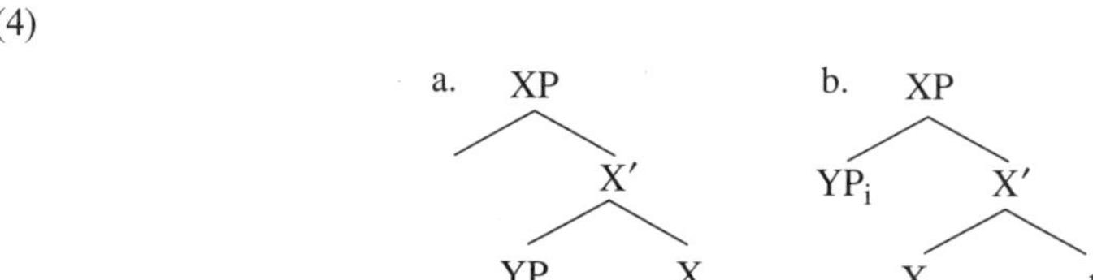

Kayne's proposal is one which postulates greater cross-linguistic uniformity. Since it is a more restrictive theory, Quadros makes use of some of Kayne's ideas in her analysis of LSB. In particular, she assumes that all specifiers precede their heads, and all heads precede their complements. As a result, analyses using mixed headedness (like most of those discussed in Chapter 18 for ASL) are not employed. She also assumes that the hierarchical order of functional categories in LSB should be the same as that hypothesized by some to be universals for spoken languages, and uses the common ordering [AgrSP [TP [AgrOP]]], unlike the proposals made by Petronio and by Neidle et al. for ASL.

19.2.2 Verb types in LSB

Quadros shows, using many of the same arguments employed by Fischer, Liddell, and Padden for ASL, that the basic word order for LSB is SVO. When considering how to represent this in the phrase structure, however, she also notices that structures used with plain verbs differ from those used with agreeing verbs in LSB. Her analysis attempts to account for these differences in a systematic way.

We begin with a summary of differences Quadros notes between plain and non-plain verbs in LSB.[3]

(5) Summary of differences between plain and non-plain verbs:

i. negation with plain verbs is different from negation with non-plain verbs; i.e., with non-plain verbs a sentential negative element can intervene between the subject and the verb, but not with plain verbs
ii. only plain verbs can co-occur with the sign glossed AUX, which is an agreeing auxiliary verb
iii. sentences with non-plain verbs have more freedom in word order than sentences with plain verbs; in particular, SOV order is permitted with non-plain verbs in many instances
iv. null arguments with non-plain verbs differ from those with plain verbs (this characteristic will be discussed further in Chapter 21)

Characteristic (i) most clearly shows the difference between plain and non-plain verbs in LSB. As shown in (6) and illustrated in Figure 19.2, negation with non-plain verbs in LSB is similar to that seen earlier for ASL: the negative element (NO) appears between the subject and the verb.

(6) LSB (Quadros 1999, p. 116)[4,5]

neg (over NO <a>GIVE<b>)
IX<the> JOHNa NO <a>GIVE<b> BOOK (SNVO)
'John does not give the book to (her).'

However, with plain verbs negation cannot appear between the subject and the verb (7a); nor can it appear after the verb (7b). Instead, the negative element appears in the sentence-final position (7c), or negation

[3] Because Quadros finds similar behavior for agreeing and spatial verbs, she groups them together under the name "non-plain."

[4] Like ASL, LSB uses a pointing sign to establish the relationship between a referent and a location in the signing space. Quadros glosses this pointing sign as IX<the>, to indicate the definiteness such a relationship implies. See discussion of ASL IX in Chapter 20.

[5] Quadros uses angle brackets rather than subscripts to indicate the beginning and ending locations of moving verbs, as in <a>GIVE<b>. Lower-case letters following nouns represent the loci with which the nouns are associated (they may not be signed in this location as long as the association is accomplished in some other way; cf. Chapter 3). We cite using her notation, standardizing in a few examples.

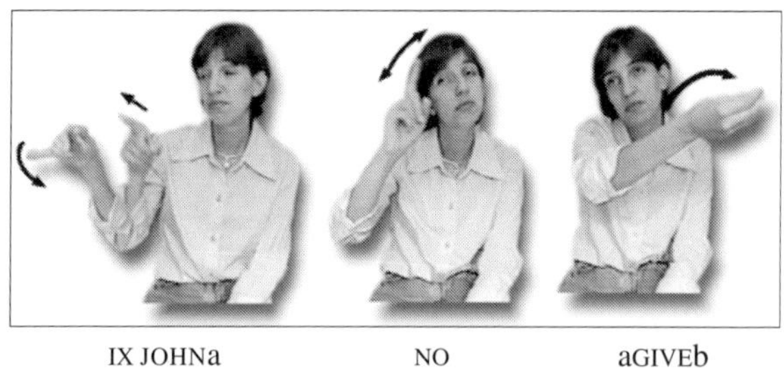

Figure 19.2 Sentence with negation preceding agreeing verb (LSB) (illustrations provided by Ronice Müller de Quadros, p.c.)

is only marked non-manually (options which are also available for non-plain verbs). The relevant aspects of (7a, c) are illustrated in Figure 19.3.

(7) LSB (Quadros 1999, pp. 116, 117, 124)

a. *JOHN $\overline{\text{NO DESIRE CAR}}^{\text{neg}}$ (SNVO)

b. *IX<the> JOHN $\overline{\text{DESIRE NO CAR}}^{\text{neg}}$ (SVNO)

c. JOHN $\overline{\text{DESIRE CAR NO}}^{\text{neg}}$ (SVON)
'John does not like the car.'

Compare these patterns with the following facts concerning the order of negation and main verbs versus auxiliaries in English. Main verbs in English cannot precede negation (8a). Rather, main verbs must follow the negative element, and *do*-support is required to provide a host for the verbal morphology (8b, c).

(8) English main verbs (Pollock 1989)
a. *John likes not Mary.
b. *John not likes Mary.
c. John does not like Mary.

Auxiliary verbs in English, on the other hand, do precede negation (9a, b), and do not use *do*-support (9c).

(9) English auxiliaries (Quadros 1999)
a. John has not read about the game results.
b. *John not has read about the game results.
c. *John did have not read about the game results.

The differences between main verbs and auxiliaries in English motivated Lasnik (1995) to hypothesize that main verbs are inserted into the phrase structure bare, and must combine with their affixes through a merger process like the old-fashioned Affix Hopping, which requires the verb and the affix to be string-adjacent. A negative element between the affix and verb block merger; so, following negatives, the verb surfaces bare and *do*-support is required to host the stranded affix.

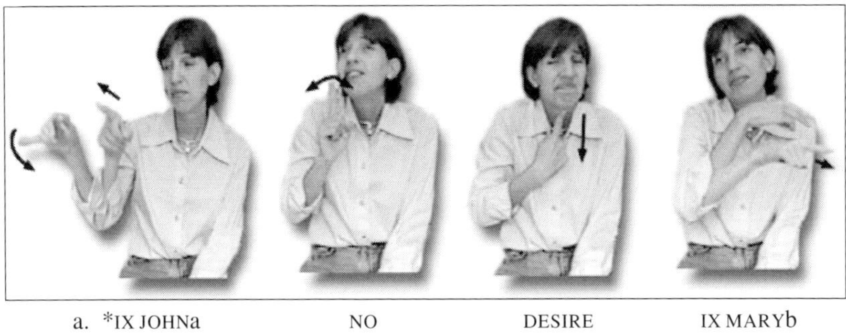

a. *IX JOHNa NO DESIRE IX MARYb

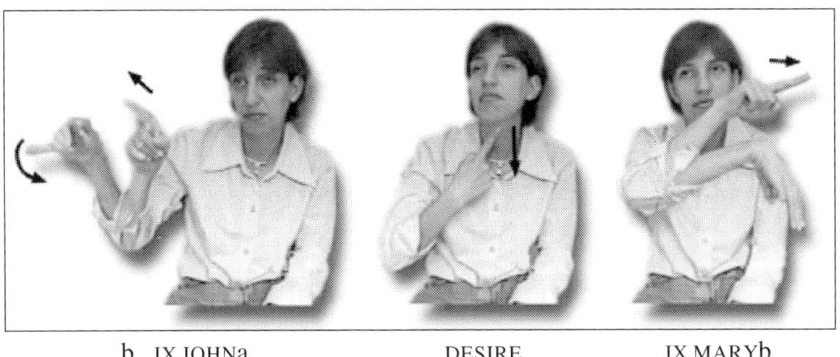

b. IX JOHNa DESIRE IX MARYb

NO

Figure 19.3 Sentences with negation and plain verb (LSB) (illustrations provided by Ronice Müller de Quadros, p.c.)

Auxiliaries, on the other hand, are inserted fully inflected. In this, they are like main verbs of French, which also appear fully inflected before negation (*pas*), as in (10).

(10) French main verbs (Pollock 1989, p. 367)
Jean n'aime pas Marie.
'John does not love Mary.'

Quadros (1999) accounts for the distribution of verbs and negation in LSB by assuming that a virtual affix is inserted in sentences with plain verbs, which are bare. As with English main verbs, the LSB plain verb

Figure 19.4 Sentence with AUX (LSB) (illustrations provided by Ronice Müller de Quadros, p.c.)

must merge with the affix, but negation blocks the adjacency required for merger. A different negation structure must be chosen.

Non-plain verbs, on the other hand, are presumably inserted fully inflected, like auxiliaries in English and French main verbs. Since there is no (virtual) affix for them to combine with, a negative element can appear in the preverbal position.

Plain and non-plain verbs appear in different negation structures in LSB. Neither of the negation structures we have seen employs an auxiliary verb, as in English. LSB does, however, have an auxiliary sign like the ones in Taiwan Sign Language and Sign Language of the Netherlands, discussed in Section 19.1. The properties of this sign, which Quadros glosses AUX, are slightly different from those of TSL and SLN. As in those languages, the AUX sign appears with a main verb, marking inflection but carrying no independent meaning. In LSB, the AUX always appears preceding the main verb. Also, in LSB the AUX cannot co-occur with a non-plain verb (11), but only with plain verbs, where it is optional (12). Video grabs of the sentence in (12a) are provided in Figure 19.4.

(11) LSB (Quadros 1999, p. 134)

                                                            eg
*JOHNa MARYb <a>AUX<b> <a>MEET<b>
'John meets Mary.'

(12) LSB (Quadros 1999, pp. 54, 63)

                        eg   eg   hn
a. IX<the> JOHNa IX<the> MARYb <a>AUX<b> LIKE

                                              hn
b. IX<the> JOHN LIKE IX<the> MARY
'John likes Mary.'

Quadros says, "The AUX in LSB is a pure expression of agreement" (p. 91). It is, perhaps, like *do*-support: a host for an affix which cannot combine with the verb (for morphological reasons). As such, it might be predicted to appear with a preverbal negative element. Recall that negation is not permitted before plain verbs, because (by analysis) of the stranded virtual affix. If AUX can host this affix, the negation should be able to appear before the plain verb. This prediction is, in fact, borne out, as shown in (13).

(13) LSB (Quadros p.c.)

neg
IX<the> JOHNa IX<the> MARYb <a>AUX<b> NO DESIRE
'John does not like Mary.'

Quadros goes beyond arguing for distinct properties of plain and non-plain verbs. She argues that in addition to their differing lexical characteristics, plain and agreeing verbs project different phrasal structures. This argument is based on the observations of Lasnik (1995) regarding main versus auxiliary verbs in English, combined with the proposals of Bobaljik (1995). Bobaljik argues that languages fall into two types: free-agr languages and non-free agr languages. The non-free-agr languages display the properties of English sentences with main verbs, while free-agr languages display the properties of French main verbs. Quadros argues that these properties are not properties of languages as a whole, but of the structures that different verb types project. Thus, English and LSB are languages which have both non-free-agr structures (with main or plain verbs, respectively) and free-agr structures (with auxiliary or non-plain verbs).

Non-free-agr structures (as in English) have only one functional projection for verbal morphology (such as tense and agreement): Infl. Therefore, only one morpheme, an agreement morpheme or a tense morpheme, can occur. Free-agr structures (as in French) have projections of both Agr and Tns, hence, separate agreement and tense morphemes can co-occur. Bobaljik also uses the more complex structure of free-agr languages to account for other properties they may have. We will see that one of them, object shift, is relevant to the study of LSB.

Accordingly, plain and non-plain verbs in LSB project different phrasal structures, given in (14) and (15), respectively.[6]

(14) Structure for plain verbs (Quadros 1999, p. 161)

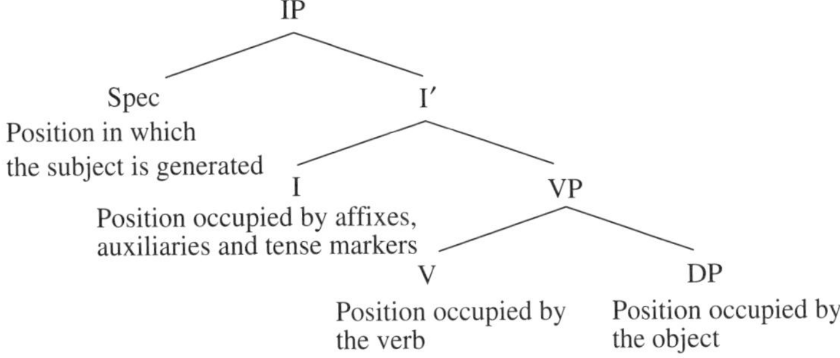

[6] Quadros assumes, following Bobaljik (1995), that subjects are generated outside the VP.

(15) Structure for non-plain verbs (Quadros 1999, p. 162)

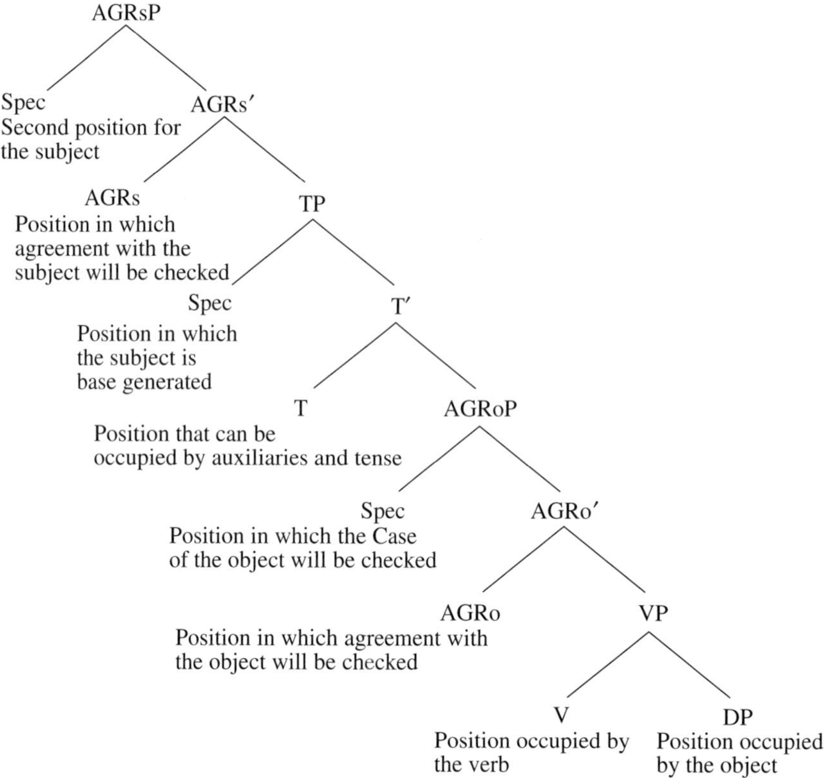

One consequence of the two trees provided here is that there should be complementary distribution between agreement and tense morphemes with plain verbs, but not with non-plain verbs. The only way to check the compatibility of tense and agreement with plain verbs is to use AUX, the auxiliary verb which hosts inflection with plain verbs. As predicted, the combination of AUX and a tense sign results in ungrammaticality, as shown in (16).

(16) LSB (Quadros p.c.)

$\overline{\text{\hspace{6em}}}$eg $\overline{\text{\hspace{6em}}}$eg $\overline{\text{\hspace{14em}}}$hn
*IX<the> JOHNa IX<the> MARYb FUTURE-TNS <a>AUX<b> LIKE
'John will like Mary.'

The prediction for non-plain verbs is also accurate. As shown in (17), lexical tense markers and manual agreement can co-occur in LSB structures with non-plain verbs.

(17) LSB (Quadros 1999, p. 154)

eg/bs (over <a>GIVE<b> BOOK)

IX<the> JOHNa FUTURE-TNS <a>GIVE<b> BOOK

'John will give (her) the book.'

A further consequence comes from the more complex structure used with non-plain verbs. This structure involves the presence of an AgrO projection, which is not present in the structure for plain verbs. The availability of AgrO leads to the possibility that the object can move in front of the verb, to [Spec, AgrOP]. Following the arguments given by Quadros, then, this should be possible in LSB with non-plain verbs, but not with plain verbs. This prediction is associated with characteristic (5iii), greater freedom of word order with non-plain verbs than with plain verbs.

As shown in (18), the prediction is true for non-plain verbs in LSB: they can be preceded by their objects.

(18) LSB (Quadros 1999, p. 147)

eg/bs (over MARYb <a>HELP<b>)

JOHNa MARYb <a>HELP<b>

'John helps Mary.'

The situation is a bit more complicated with plain verbs, however. It is not the case that the O–V order is completely ruled out with plain verbs. Instead, Quadros argues that when this order appears it is generated by a separate mechanism (focus doubling, to be discussed in Chapter 22). Evidence that O–V order with plain verbs is generated by a different mechanism from O–V order with non-plain verbs comes from the distribution of non-manuals accompanying these examples, which are different for the two verb types.[7]

To summarize, Quadros finds a number of syntactic differences between plain and non-plain verbs in LSB. Some of these can be accounted for by analyzing plain verbs as comparable to Bobaljik's (1995) "non-free-agr" verbs (that is, plain verbs appear in structures with a non-expanded IP), and non-plain verbs as "free-agr" (that is, appearing in structures with Agr and T projections). This means that rather than breaking languages into two types, it is verbs which fall into two types, projecting distinct structures depending on their categorization. As a result, verb class has effects which go much beyond morphology, extending into a variety of syntactic consequences. Although this difference was noted by Lasnik (1995) for the main/auxiliary verb distinction in English, the LSB analysis provides much greater support for the conclusion that a single language may employ two different basic phrase structures.

[7] Another mechanism producing O–V order with plain verbs is the kind of object shift which occurs with aspectual marking in ASL also. This construction is discussed in Chapter 20.

19.3 LSB compared with ASL

The data amassed in favor of two distinct phrase markers corresponding to the two verb types in LSB is impressive. Quadros (1999) argues that ASL like LSB also has two distinct structures according to the same two verb types, based on data in the literature. How strong is the evidence for two structures in ASL? This is the question addressed by Quadros, Lillo-Martin, and Chen (2000, 2004).

As Quadros (1999) noted, ASL is different from LSB in not having differing patterns of negation in sentences with plain and agreeing verbs. As shown in (19), negation precedes the verb in both types of sentence. The (a) example illustrates this with plain verbs, and the (b) example with agreeing verbs.[8]

(19) ASL (Quadros et al. 2000)

    ______neg
a. JOHN NOT EAT MEAT
   'John does not eat meat.'

    ______________________neg
b. JOHNa NOT <a>HELP<b> MARYb
   'John didn't help Mary.'

What about property (5iii), the possibility for greater flexibility in word order with agreeing verbs? Quadros argued that plain and non-plain verbs in LSB differ in precisely this way: non-plain verbs freely allow object shift, but plain verbs have more restrictions on the use of O–V order. As we have seen, there are several contexts in which O–V order is permitted in ASL. Is there a difference between plain and agreeing verbs with respect to allowing O–V order?

Recall that Fischer (1975) observes that O–V order is permitted with non-reversible verbs (i.e., those for which there is only one plausible way for the arguments to fill the semantic roles); for certain "near-idiomatic" cases; and in cases with verb agreement. She says that verb agreement allows for freer word order than verbs with no agreement, but that OSV is preferred over SOV. Liddell (1980) finds that O–V order is possible with certain "mimetic" information, with classifiers, and with verbs whose directionality indicates their arguments.[9] Both of these authors, then, seem to support the idea that object shift is possible in ASL with agreeing verbs, but not with plain verbs. This supports the idea that a kind of object shift is possible with agreeing verbs but not plain verbs, making ASL similar to LSB in this respect.

[8] ASL permits sentence-final negation as well as preverbal, but the interpretation of negation in the final position is marked. See Chapter 20 where these distinctions are described.

[9] However, Padden (1988 [1983]) argues that apparent cases of O–V order with agreeing verbs should be analyzed as multiclausal. Her analysis was given in Chapter 18, Section 18.1.

Overall, then, ASL and LSB are most similar in sentences with agreeing verbs, where preverbal negation and a sort of object shift are both permitted. The two languages seem to use the same structures for such sentences – plausibly, structures with a full complement of functional categories. The languages are different with respect to sentences with plain verbs. In LSB, preverbal negation is not permitted, whereas in ASL it is. Whether this means that the two languages use different hierarchical structures for such sentences, as Quadros et al. (2000) conclude, or the same structures with other factors accounting for the differences, as Quadros et al. (2004) conclude, is a matter for continued research.

To sum up, we have seen a variety of proposals to account for the basic SVO word order of two sign languages. What these proposals have in common is that they make use of hierarchical structure, although they make use of different assumptions and conclusions regarding which categories are present, their left–right ordering, and their hierarchical ordering.

The lack of consensus on an issue as basic as clausal structure can be attributed to two factors. One is that the study of the syntax of sign languages is still relatively young. Researchers are still discovering new patterns and generalizations to be explained, leading to different proposals. However, perhaps a stronger reason for the variability is that researchers have been attempting to use the changing tools of contemporary syntactic theory to account for the data of sign languages. As the theories have become more restrictive, the new tools which are proposed on the basis of spoken languages are employed in the sign language research. Importantly, more restrictive theories have not led to the exclusion of sign languages. Instead, these theories have led to restrictive analyses of sign language data.

Of course, we have only scratched the surface of sign language syntax, in that we have examined only a limited number of languages and a limited subset of the structures allowed in each. We cannot evaluate many sign languages because of the regrettable dearth of detailed theoretical research to date. However, some variations on basic sentences in the better-studied sign languages have been investigated, and we turn to these in the next chapters.

20 Variations and extensions on basic sentence structures

We have seen how basic sentences are structured in ASL (Chapter 18) and LSB (Chapter 19). We turn now to the structures associated with additional sentence types. What these sentence types have in common is that they all may involve functional categories – those categories other than the lexical categories, N, V, A, P. Functional categories (such as Determiner, Agreement, Aspect, Negation, and Tense) may host lexical items (words or affixes) in their heads, but in some cases they are postulated to host only features. In either case, the presence of a functional category will often have an effect on some other part of the structure – for example, by requiring movement of some other element to its specifier. The element in the head of a functional category and the element in its specifier "agree" through "spec–head agreement." This process is used in accounting for a number of phenomena. For example, we have already seen that the subject of a sentence may appear in [Spec, TP]. If the verb moves (through Agr) to T, then the subject and verb will check each other's features, so that subject–verb agreement is obtained.

It has been proposed that it is in functional categories where the differences between languages are coded (Borer 1983, Chomsky 1993, but see Snyder 2001 for support of the view that not all cross-linguistic parametric differences are associated with functional categories). In current terms, the features of some functional categories are strong, forcing overt movement to some Spec for feature checking. When the features of a functional category are weak, then this movement is in the covert component – that is, not visibly reflected in surface word order (but arguably there – perhaps because of an effect on interpretation). Again, we have seen an example already in the movement of verbs: while verbs must raise overtly in French, accounting for the ordering verb–neg, they raise covertly in English, which has the ordering neg–verb.

The functional categories we examine in this chapter include Determiner, Agreement (and agreement-like categories), Aspect, and Negation. As usual, the bulk of analyses concern ASL, but some interesting potential cross-sign-language differences have been observed in some of these areas, and they will be noted. Additional research to determine the range of cross-sign-language differences would be welcome.

20.1 DP structure

If the X'-theory of phrase structure (cf. Chapter 18) is applied to the structure of noun phrases it soon becomes clear that additional structure beyond head, specifier, and complement is needed to account for the distribution of elements. For example, in English, noun phrases may contain a determiner, quantifier, and several adjectives before the noun, as illustrated in (1).

(1) The three large brown dogs jumped over a pile of cans.

Furthermore, it has often been observed that the structure of noun phrases has parallels to the structure of clauses (Chomsky 1970), particularly for complement-taking nouns, as illustrated in (2).

(2) a. The barbarians destroyed Rome completely.
b. The barbarians' destruction of Rome was complete.

According to early X'-theory, the structure of a noun phrase should be as in (3).

(3)

NP
Spec N′
N Compl

How should the structure of noun phrases accommodate examples like (1) and (2)? In order to capture these and other facts, Abney (1987) proposed that noun phrases have a more complex structure than that given in (3). In particular, he argued that a noun phrase is headed by a functional category D(eterminer), which projects a full phrasal structure, like other functional projections. The complement of the Determiner may be an NP, as illustrated in (4), or it may be an intermediate functional projection accommodating a Quantifier or Modifier Phrase, according to various proposals.

(4)

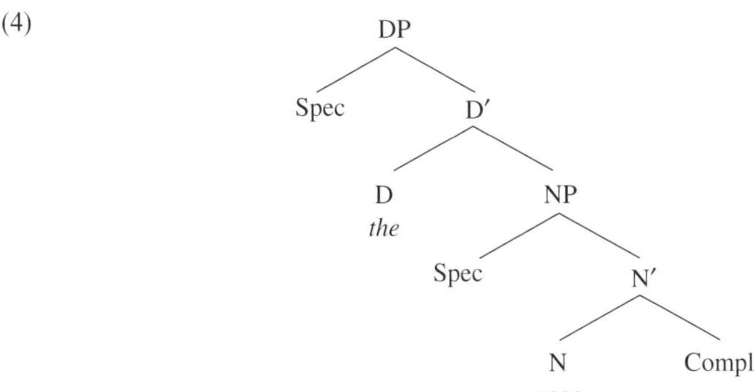

Abney's proposal captures parallels between Determiners and other functional categories, especially the similarities between D and I(nflection). It is a part of the movement to generalize the structures of different phrases so that a uniform principle applies to the analysis of various types of categories.

The proposal that noun phrases are really Determiner Phrases (DPs) has been generally accepted. However, some questions and controversies have arisen concerning other aspects of the structure of DPs. For example, is there a different structural position for definite and indefinite determiners? How are pronouns structured? What accounts for the ordering of adjectives? How are possessives represented?

The sign language literature has only begun to address these questions. The internal structure of DPs in sign languages has not been extensively studied. This may be in part because it seems that ASL has no argument-taking nouns (like *destruction* in (2)) (cf. Fischer 1990, MacLaughlin 1997). Furthermore, early literature assumes that ASL has no determiners and flexible placement of adjectives. It would seem that DP structure in sign language would be of little interest. However, recent works have reopened the issue, examining determiners and modifiers to establish the structure of the DP in ASL. Such studies contribute to an overall understanding of the universal possibilities for structuring noun phrases.

The most comprehensive study of DP structure in ASL is that by MacLaughlin (1997).[1] Her study examines determiners, adjectives, and possessive phrases to support a DP-based theory of noun phrase structure in ASL. She also considers agreement, both manual and non-manual, arguing that DPs in ASL display agreement properties strikingly parallel to those found in clauses. The structure MacLaughlin proposes for the possessive phrase in (5) is given in (6). Note that the index on JOHN and the one on FRIEND are enclosed in parentheses. These indicate that the nouns may optionally be signed in a particular location in space, or in neutral space.

(5) ASL (adapted from MacLaughlin 1997, p. 233)
JOHN$_{(i)}$ POSS$_i$ OLD FRIEND$_{(j)}$
'John's old friend'

(6) ASL (adapted from MacLaughlin 1997, p. 240)

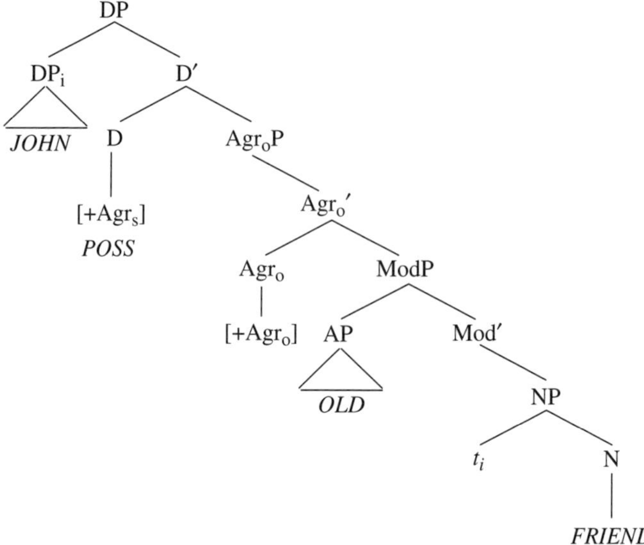

[1] Some of MacLaughlin's arguments and conclusions are summarized in Neidle et al. (2000).

Of note about the structure in (6) are the agreement features, $[+\text{Agr}_S]$ in the head D position and $[+\text{Agr}_O]$ heading its own projection as the complement of D. These features represent two places where agreement can be expressed within the DP in ASL: on the possessor phrase and POSS sign, and on the possessee. This structure is intended to capture strong parallels between the DP and clausal structure (cf. Abney 1987, Szabolcsi 1994).

Agreement in the DP is expressed through spatial locations, like verbal agreement (cf. Chapter 3). MacLaughlin proposes that nouns and adjectives, like verbs, can be divided into two categories: those which are capable of expressing agreement ("agreeing"), and those which are not ("plain"). Although MacLaughlin does not say how to distinguish the classes, it seems to us that a phonological criterion distinguishes the two categories: if a noun or adjective sign has obligatory body contact, it must be plain. In any case, MacLaughlin states that only specific noun phrases may be associated with a location.

MacLaughlin points out, however, that what has generally been referred to as signing a noun "at a particular spatial location" should be understood as orienting the sign toward the location, since the distance of the sign from the body may not be affected. This distinction is illustrated schematically in (7).[2] The image on the left shows the neutral, default position for nouns. In the middle image, the notation "i" is used to indicate the locus associated with a referent. The gray dot shows where a noun might be signed when showing agreement with that referent. In the right-hand image, the gray dot shows where an agreeing verb would be produced – overlapping the locus.

(7) Spatial modification of a sign (MacLaughlin 1997, p. 140)

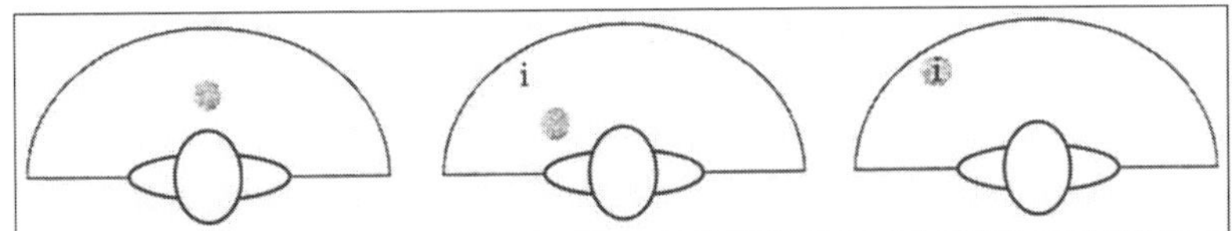

The sign glossed POSS is roughly equivalent to possessive pronouns such as *my/her*, *mine/hers*, and the possessive affix *'s* in English. POSS, like personal pronouns in ASL, is articulated with respect to loci associated with referents (cf. Chapter 3). In ASL, POSS is articulated with the handshape, while ISL employs the handshape. Examples of POSS in ASL are given in Figure 20.1.

The POSS sign must be signed in a location associated with the possessor. MacLaughlin analyzes this as obligatory agreement. The possessor itself, provided the sign is agreeing, may also express agreement, by being

[2] A similar comment about agreeing verbs is made by Padden (1990), when she speaks of reference to vectors. See Chapter 3, Section 3.1.

a. 1-POSS (my)

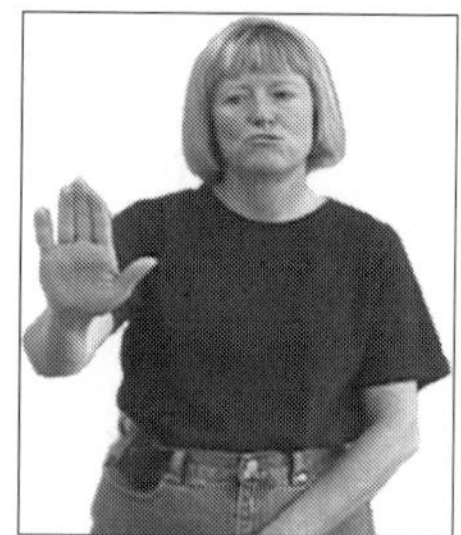

b. a-POSS (her)

Figure 20.1 Possessive pronouns (ASL)

a-JOHN a-POSS b-FRIEND

Figure 20.2 Manual expression of agreement within a possessive DP (ASL)

signed toward the location it is associated with. However, this agreement is not obligatory, as the sign may be produced in neutral space.[3]

Finally, the possessee may also express agreement, by being signed with orientation toward its location. The possessee's location will be consistent before and/or following the DP in question. For example, a subsequent pronoun referring to the possessee will be signed in the same location.

The manual expression of agreement within a possessive DP is illustrated in the sequence in Figure 20.2.

In addition to the observations about manual expressions of agreement within the DP summarized above, MacLaughlin also claims that DPs in ASL display non-manual markers of agreement which are parallel to the putative non-manual markers of agreement within the clause described by Bahan (1996). In particular, she claims that head tilt expresses agreement with the possessor, and eye gaze with the possessee (see also Neidle et al. 2000). The distribution of head tilt and eye gaze within the DP is claimed to be entirely parallel to that found in transitive clauses. See Chapter 3 for further discussion.

The structure given in (6) gives a hint as to the analysis proposed by MacLaughlin for determiners and modifiers. However, each of these DP elements has been the source of some controversy. We discuss them now in turn.

[3] Although not discussed, the optionality of this agreement deserves explanation. In addition, the POSS sign itself may be omitted in some situations. This too requires explanation.

20.1.1 Determiners

Most descriptive grammars have claimed that ASL lacks determiners. However, the view that some pointing signs are related to determiners has been public since the 1970s. Wilbur (1979) summarizes Kegl's (2003 [1976]) view that "indexing" may serve to distinguish definite versus indefinite noun phrases (although the main issue concerns establishing the locations in space with which noun phrases are associated). We have already described (Chapter 3 and elsewhere) pronominal pointing signs. However, pointing signs can co-occur with nouns, and several researchers have argued that they may be determiners.

Zimmer and Patschke (1990) examined one type of pointing sign in particular. They looked at "signs that move slightly or not at all, never arc or jab, and most often point slightly upward." Zimmer and Patschke claim that this upward pointing sign, which they gloss DET, is a determiner which may occur before, after, or simultaneously with a noun. They do not find a definite/indefinite contrast expressed through the use of the DET sign, and claim that the pointing sign is not used with generic nouns, but only with specific entities. They therefore conclude, "that pointing determiners in ASL are used only with concrete nouns that refer to specific entities.... [with] no process marking the definite/indefinite distinction" (p. 207).

MacLaughlin (1997) also considers certain pointing signs in ASL to be determiners, but she argues against several of Zimmer and Patschke's conclusions. First, she includes a much wider range of pointing signs; her data "include various articulations of index signs, all involving the basic index handshape and pointing function, but incorporating potentially different movements" (p. 116). Using this wider range of data, she finds that prenominal and postnominal pointing signs are distinctive. Furthermore, she claims that cases which appear to display simultaneous articulation of pointing sign and noun actually involve a sequence.

MacLaughlin observes systematic differences between prenominal and postnominal pointing signs. In particular, she finds that the prenominal index expresses definiteness, and may be marked for plural using a sweeping movement. These characteristics are illustrated in (8a–c). MacLaughlin concludes that the prenominal index is a definite determiner. On the other hand, the postnominal index may be used in definite and indefinite contexts, but may not be marked for plural, as shown in (9a, b) respectively. She analyzes this sign as an adverbial.

(8) ASL (MacLaughlin 1997, p. 121)

a. JOHN LOVE [IX_i WOMAN $]_{DP}$
'John loves the/that woman.'

b. *JOHN LOOK-FOR [IX_i MAN $]_{DP}$ FIX GARAGE
'John is looking for a man to fix the garage.'

c. $[IX_{pl-arc_i}$ MAN IX_i 'over there' $]_{DP}$ KNOW PRESIDENT
'Those men over there know the president.'

(9) ASL (MacLaughlin 1997, p. 122)
a. [SOMETHING/ONE WOMAN IX_i $]_{DP}$ KNOW PRESIDENT
'Some woman (there) knows the president.'
b. $*[IX_{pl-arc_i}$ MAN $IX_{pl-arc_i}]_{DP}$ KNOW PRESIDENT
'Those men over there know the president.'

The sign glossed SOMETHING/ONE, in which an upward pointing index finger is produced with a tremoring motion, is analyzed by MacLaughlin as an indefinite determiner. Its distribution is said by her to be strictly prenominal, like the prenominal definite determiner. According to MacLaughlin, only specific NPs may be associated with a location in space. Since the indefinite determiner SOMETHING/ONE does not involve a location, it is used with non-specific indefinites. On the other hand, MacLaughlin identifies the sign ONE, similar to the sign SOMETHING/ONE, but without the tremoring movement, as a determiner used with indefinite specific (or identifiable) NPs.[4]

The differences between the prenominal and postnominal pointing signs have led to their distinct analyses. Notice that it is possible for a single DP to contain both a prenominal and a postnominal index, as in (8c). MacLaughlin proposes the structure in (10) for these elements.

(10) (MacLaughlin 1997, p. 170)

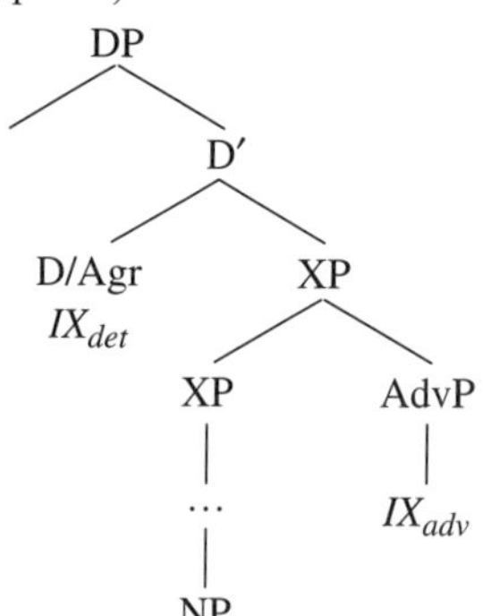

Note that the structure in (10), like the more complex structure for possessive DPs in (6), indicates that the D position hosts agreement. Specific Ns may be associated with locations in space. Specific Determiners agree with these Ns by being produced with respect to the same spatial locations. Furthermore, MacLaughlin claims that definite DPs are like intransitive verbs in allowing either head tilt or eye gaze to express agreement non-manually.

Several aspects of agreement in DPs illustrated in (10) deserve further attention. The mechanism for agreement between the determiner and noun

[4] The sign ONE is also a quantifier. In this case it is more stressed than the determiner ONE.

is not Spec–Head agreement, like most other instances. Instead, MacLaughlin proposes that the head N moves to D covertly to have its agreement features checked. In this way, agreement within the DP (i.e., agreement between two heads) is different from agreement within the clause (which is ultimately agreement between a head and a phrase). In addition, as in other cases of agreement using spatial locations, either an overtly marked or a neutral form of agreement can be used: that is, the noun may be signed with orientation towards a specific location or without any obvious change in articulation.

Another interesting and unexplained observation about pointing signs as determiners in ASL is that they are apparently optional. Noun phrases articulated without any determiner are perfectly acceptable, and seem to have the same range of interpretations as those with determiners.

Finally, with the many similarities between the definite determiner pointing sign and the pronominal pointing sign, it may not be surprising that MacLaughlin analyzes them as the same lexical element, base-generated in the determiner position. This concurs with proposals by Abney (1987) and Stowell (1991) regarding the status of pronouns, and goes against the alternative by Cardinaletti (1994).

20.1.2 Adjectives and quantifiers

It has been observed that ASL permits both pre- and postnominal adjectives. What accounts for the distribution of adjectives within NPs?

If the adjective is base-generated before the noun, then perhaps a process such as Fischer's (1990) "mini-topicalization" (cf. Chapter 18, Section 18.3) could raise the noun to a higher position. Alternatively, Boster (1996) suggests that adjectives are freely generated either before or after the nouns they modify, adjoined to N′.

Both of these possibilities imply that adjectives are freely ordered before or after the noun they modify. However, MacLaughlin (1997) finds that there are distributional differences between pre- and postnominal adjectives, leading to her proposal that they are generated in distinct structures.[5]

To summarize, MacLaughlin finds that prenominal adjectives in ASL have the characteristics of attributive adjective phrases. Postnominal adjectives, on the other hand, have the characteristics of predicative phrases. These differences mean that prenominal adjectives follow the typical ordering for head-initial languages: Evaluating–Size–Color–N, as shown in (11) (cf. Cinque 1994). Postnominal adjectives are freely ordered (12). Furthermore, prenominal adjectives may have idiosyncratic meanings, but postnominal adjectives may only have their predicative meaning.

[5] It should be noted that MacLaughlin worked with a single consultant. She points out that other authors have reported possible dialectal and contextual differences in judgments. It is quite possible that the pattern observed by MacLaughlin does not hold for other consultants.

(11) (MacLaughlin 1997, p. 194)

	Evaluating	Size	Color	N
English	beautiful	big	red	ball
German	schoener	grosser	roter	Ball
ASL	BEAUTIFUL	BIG	RED	BALL

(12) ASL (MacLaughlin 1997, p. 193)

a. [OLD ITALIAN MAN IX_{adv_i} $]_{DP}$ $POSS_{1p}$ FATHER

b. ??[ITALIAN OLD MAN IX_{adv_i} $]_{DP}$ $POSS_{1p}$ FATHER

c. [MAN OLD ITALIAN IX_{adv_i} $]_{DP}$ $POSS_{1p}$ FATHER

d. [MAN ITALIAN OLD IX_{adv_i} $]_{DP}$ $POSS_{1p}$ FATHER
'The old Italian man there is my father.'

(13) ASL (MacLaughlin 1997, p. 196)

a. [$POSS_{1p}$ OLD FRIEND $]_{DP}$
'my old friend'

b. [$POSS_{1p}$ FRIEND OLD $]_{DP}$
'my friend who is old'

These observations lead MacLaughlin to propose the structures in (14) and (15) for prenominal, attributive adjectives and postnominal, predicative adjectives, respectively.

(14) (MacLaughlin 1997, p. 198)

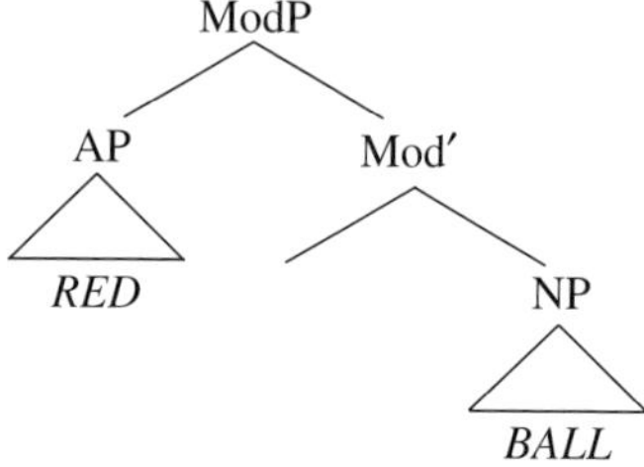

(15) (MacLaughlin 1997, p. 203)

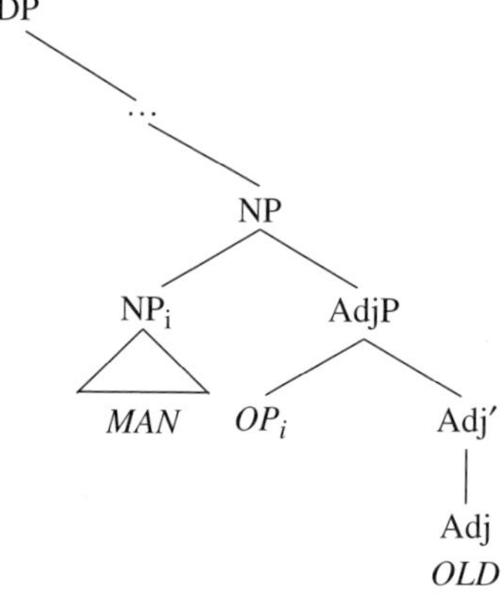

Evidence for a different aspect of the structure of DPs is presented by Boster (1996). She observes that in ASL, a quantifier may be stranded by the topicalization of the NP it modifies, as illustrated in (16).

(16) ASL (Boster 1996, p. 159)

a. $\overline{\text{BOOK}}^{t}$ I WANT THREE
'I want three books.'

b. *$\overline{\text{THREE}}^{t}$ I WANT BOOK
'I want three books.'

According to Boster's data, adjectives may topicalize with the noun they modify, stranding a quantifier, as in (17a); but they may not be left behind when the noun moves, as in (17b).

(17) ASL (Boster 1996, p. 170)

a. $\overline{\text{RED BOOK}_i}^{t}$ I WANT THREE t_i
'I want three red books.'

b. *$\overline{\text{BOOK}_i}^{t}$ I WANT THREE RED t_i
'I want three red books.'

This pattern leads Boster to postulate the structure in (18) for quantified noun phrases.[6] In this structure, the quantifier (Q) heads a functional projection taking NP as its complement.[7] This is an alternative to proposals putting Q as a specifier or adjunct to NP.

(18) (Boster 1996, p. 173)

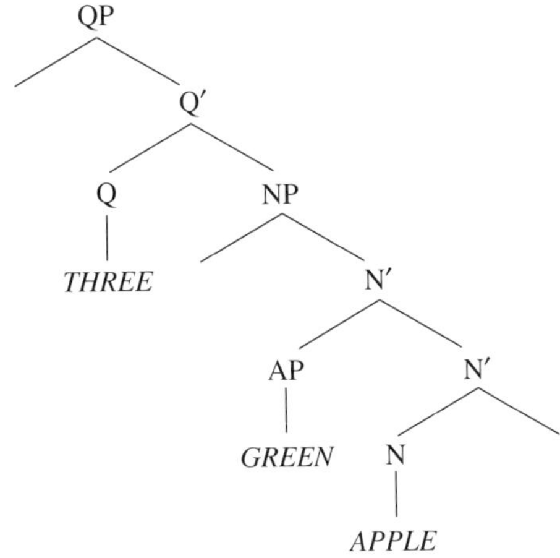

[6] Note that Boster allows for the possibility of a higher, DP structure, but presents no evidence for it.

[7] Boster cites Abney (1987), Lobeck (1990), and Murasugi (1991) for the same proposal.

Boster shows that the NP, including the adjective, may topicalize, leaving behind the quantifier. On the other hand, an N′ cannot topicalize, leading to the impossibility of (17b).

MacLaughlin does not discuss the structural position of quantifiers. Presumably, a QP complement to DP would be compatible with her analysis of ASL. However, since she proposes that adjectives are specifiers of ModP, it is not obvious what would block extraction of the NP stranding the adjective, as in (17b). Further research is needed to reconcile the observations made about quantifier and adjective placement by Boster and MacLaughlin.

According to many syntactic theories, noun phrases have structures with clear parallels to sentences. Thus, we have not yet drifted far from our starting point of basic sentence structure. The next section, however, considers the syntactic structure of a construction far from basic, and not widely considered even in the spoken language literature. In Chapter 5, we presented several aspects of classifier constructions. We saw that they are ubiquitous in sign languages, but difficult to analyze, and many different proposals have been put forth. We showed that sign language classifiers are most similar to spoken language verbal classifiers, which are morphemes representing general nominal categories, attached to verbs as affixes. The question we address now is whether these morphemes combine with verbs only lexically, or whether a syntactic representation of this combination is necessary.

20.2 The syntax of classifier constructions

In Chapter 5, we presented characteristics of sign language classifier constructions. We showed that they are most comparable to verbal classifying affixes found in languages such as Cayuga and Digueño, although classifiers are used in different contexts in sign languages as compared with these spoken languages. We concluded that classifier constructions are predicate-like, sometimes entering into strings of coordinated predicates unified by a single classifier.

What is missing is an account of the syntactic structure of classifier complexes. How are they represented syntactically? Few works discuss this point, but some recent ones begin to address it. We review here two lines for approaching the analysis of classifier constructions: as Noun Incorporation or as a kind of agreement.

20.2.1 A Noun Incorporation analysis

As we saw in Chapter 5, Mithun (1984, 1986a) treats classifiers in spoken languages as evolving from Noun Incorporation structures. Rosen (1989) divides Noun Incorporation into two types: Compound NI and Classifier

NI. Compound NI is a lexical process which combines a noun with a verb such that the incorporated argument is saturated within the V + N complex, affecting the verb's argument structure. That is, since the incorporated noun satisfies the verb's requirement for an argument of a certain type, it no longer requires that argument to occur independently. In the other type, Classifier NI, a noun combines with a verb lexically, but the incorporated argument is not saturated within the V + N complex. Thus, the verb's argument structure remains unaffected by the incorporation.

One consequence of Rosen's analysis of Compound and Classifier NI is that the two types will display different patterns with respect to processes dubbed doubling and stranding. In Classifier NI, since the incorporated noun does not saturate the verb's argument structure requirements, the noun may be realized as an independent NP, resulting in a doubling structure. Alternatively, the associated argument's head N may be null, but its modifiers can be realized – in a "stranding" structure. These two properties of classifier NI are illustrated in (19)–(20), respectively. In (19), the incorporated noun *luq*ʷ 'dish' is doubled. In (20), the modifier *sha'té:ku* 'eight' is stranded.

(19) Kʷakʷ'ala (Anderson 1992, p. 30)
Classifier NI [doubling]
luqʷ-ila-imuxʷa-xa luqʷ-i?
dish-make-expert-OBJ dish-NOMINAL
'the dishmaker (of dishes)'

(20) Mohawk (Rosen 1989, p. 303, citing Mithun 1984, p. 870)
Classifier NI [stranding]
sha'té:ku nikú:ti rabahbót wahu-tsy-ahní:nu ki rake'níha
eight of.them bullhead 3M.3N-fish-bought this my.father
'My father bought eight bullheads.' (= My father fish-bought eight bullheads)

Since the incorporated noun does saturate the verb's requirement for that argument in Compound NI, neither doubling nor stranding will be permitted. Instead, the verb will be inserted with an altered argument structure – one that does not require an argument of the saturated type.

Meir (1999) shows that two different kinds of classifier complexes in ISL behave like Classifier NI and Compound NI, respectively. She divides classifiers into two types: instrumental and theme.[8] Meir's "theme" classifier category includes semantic (entity) classifiers, and some SASS (descriptive) and handling classifiers, determined by whether the classifier has the semantic role of "theme," the object that moves. Theme classifiers are analyzed by Meir as displaying Classifier NI. SASS and handling classifiers that are instruments manifest Compound NI. Note that the distinction between classifier types is based on the thematic role of the entity which the classifier

[8] Body part (limb) classifiers are not included in either group.

Table 20.1 *A partial list of theme classifiers and instrumental classifiers in ISL*

Theme classifiers	Instrumental classifiers
CL:C 'a cylindrical object'	SPOON (SPOON-FEED)
CL:flat C 'a wide flat object'	FORK (FORK-EAT)
CL:CC 'a wide cylindrical object'	KNIFE (KNIFE-CUT)
CL:BB 'cubic object'	TELESCOPE (TELESCOPE-LOOK)
CL:bCbC 'round flat object'	NEEDLE (NEEDLE-SEW)
CL:B 'vehicle'	SAW (SAW-CUT)
CL:bO 'grasp a long thin object'	STRAW (STRAW-DRINK)
CL:F 'grasp a thin object'	HAMMER (HAMMER-BREAK)
CL:FF 'handle (with care) a thin flat object'	SCISSORS (SCISSORS-CUT)
	KEY (KEY-OPEN/CLOSE)
	GUN (GUN-SHOOT)

represents, not the form of the classifier. Examples of theme and instrument classifiers are given in Table 20.1.[9]

As predicted, these two types of classifier differ with respect to whether doubling and stranding are allowed. While theme classifiers permit both, instrumental classifiers permit neither. This contrast is shown in (21)–(22). In (21a), with a theme classifier (comparable to Classifier NI), the overt noun BOOK is signed even while the classifier predicate indicates that the theme is a wide flat object. In (21b), the classifier predicate indicates that the theme is a cylindrical object. Although the overt noun (e.g., CUP) is not expressed, the stranded adjective shows that the argument position is still licensed. In the instrumental classifier examples in (22), on the other hand, the instruments (SPOON, TELESCOPE) are incorporated in the classifier predicate, saturating the verb's need for an expressed instrument argument.

(21) ISL (Meir 1999)
Theme classifiers – Classifier NI
a. BOOK INDEX_b He_a $_a\text{GIVE}$-cl:flatC_1 [doubling]
book this he wide-flat-object-he-give-me
'He gave me this book.'
b. NEW INDEX_a $_a\text{GIVE}$-cl:C_1 [stranding]
new this give-cylindrical-object-me
'Give me the new cup (over there).'
(=Cylindrical object-give-me the new)

(22) ISL (Meir 1999)
Instrumental classifiers – Compound NI

[9] Some of Meir's instrumental classifiers may function as nouns of ISL and their classifier construction counterparts as spatial verbs. In Chapter 6, Section 6.2.1, we suggest that spatial verbs are actually classifier constructions that have become lexicalized through repeated conventional usage.

a. *I SPOON BABY INDEX$_3$ $_1$SPOON-FEED$_3$ [*doubling]
I spoon baby this me-spoon-feed-him
'I fed the baby with a spoon.'
(= I spoon-fed the baby with a spoon)

b. *STAR$_{(distributive)}$ NEW I TELESCOPE-LOOK [*stranding]
stars new I watch-with-telescope
I watch the stars with the new telescope.
(= I telescope-watch the stars with the new (one))

Meir's evidence shows that ISL instrumental and theme classifier predicates are clearly different in their argument structures. She also points out that the instrumental classifiers involve independent noun roots, which carry a non-specific, generic meaning when incorporated. These characteristics strongly support the explicitly lexical Compound Noun Incorporation analysis for instrumental classifiers.

There is one possible complication for the Compound Noun Incorporation analysis not discussed by Meir. This complication comes from ASL data. Whether ISL and ASL are different in their classifier structures is not yet clear. The classifier systems across sign languages are certainly very similar (cf. Chapter 5). But it is quite possible that there are subtle differences, especially with respect to syntactic phenomena. With this in mind, we consider the following argument.

Benedicto and Brentari (2004) divide ASL instrumental classifiers into two types, based on the form of the classifier: descriptive (dICL) and handling (hICL). In descriptive instrumental classifiers, the handshape classifier represents the shape of the instrument. This includes classifiers like to represent a toothbrush, or to represent a spoon. In handling instrumental classifiers, the handshape classifier represents a hand holding an instrument – so might be used to represent a hand holding a toothbrush or a spoon. Both types are considered instrumental classifiers in Meir's work. However, Benedicto and Brentari show that they should be distinguished in ASL.

Benedicto and Brentari, in agreement with Kegl (1990), show that descriptive and handling instrumental classifiers differ with respect to whether or not they take an agentive subject. Constructions with hICLs, but not dICLs, have an agentive subject, either explicit or null. This is confirmed by their syntactic tests, including the fact that only sentences with handling instrumental classifiers can combine with the agent-oriented adverb WILLING, as shown in (23). This pair of examples involves two differing instrumental classifiers representing a saw. The handling classifier, shown in Figure 20.3a, represents a hand grasping a saw handle. The descriptive classifier, shown in Figure 20.3b, represents the shape of the saw itself.

(23) ASL (Benedicto and Brentari 2004)

a. S+SAW_WOOD ($\surd$WILLING) [hICL]
obj/instr_grab$_{hICL}$+cut_wood voluntarily
'S/he is cutting wood voluntarily.'

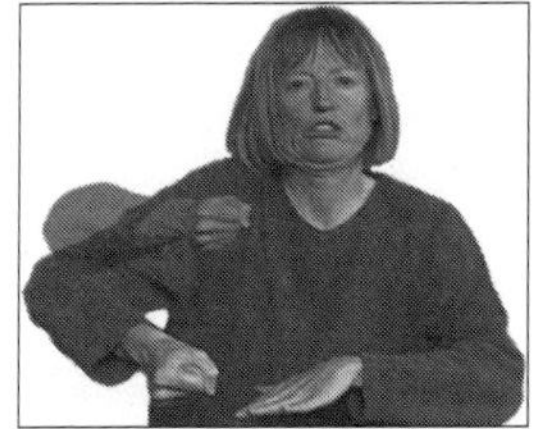

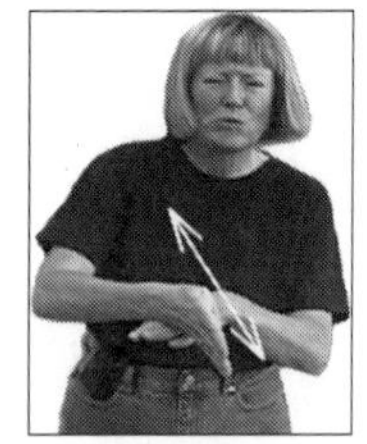

a. handling CL:S 'grasp a saw'   b. descriptive CL:B 'vertical long flat object'

Figure 20.3 Two different instrumental classifiers for SAW (ASL)

b. B+SAW_WOOD (*WILLING) [dICL]
2D_thin_obj$_{dICL}$+cut_wood voluntarily
'S/he is cutting wood voluntarily.'

In (23a), the handling instrumental classifier is used. Although the agent is not overtly expressed, it must be present as a null element of the structure, since the agent-oriented adverb WILLING is licit. On the other hand, in (23b), the descriptive instrumental classifier is used. Even though the two examples are very similar in meaning, no agent is part of the structure in (23b). This is clear since the agent-oriented adverb is not permitted. (Perhaps a better translation of (23b) would therefore be 'there is cutting of wood (*voluntarily).')

This test, and others offered by Benedicto and Brentari (2004), indicate that the two types of instrumentals have different argument structures. So, although the evidence presented by Meir for a (Compound) Noun Incorporation analysis of instrumental classifiers is strong, the two types of instrumental classifiers do need to be distinguished. In argument structure terms, some instrumental classifiers have an agent-external argument (i.e., a subject), and others do not. This distinction might be made within the lexical theory advocated by Meir. A full range of tests needs to be run to determine what generalizations hold across the categories of classifiers as determined by form versus thematic role. Benedicto and Brentari, together with other researchers, argue instead that (certain) classifier constructions are derived syntactically, rather than lexically, as a form of agreement. We turn now to this line of analysis.

20.2.2 Classifiers as agreement

Glück and Pfau (1998, 1999) argue that classifier constructions in German Sign Language (DGS) manifest a kind of agreement, and they argue explicitly against a Noun Incorporation analysis (although they do not consider Meir's particular analysis). As they do not provide any examples with instrumental classifiers, we will take their analysis to be a claim about theme classifiers alone. Citing Rosen's (1989) analysis, they point out that under a (Classifier) Noun Incorporation analysis, structures with classifiers would be expected to allow stranding – the same test Meir used. However, they claim that in DGS, stranding (with theme classifiers) is not allowed, giving the example in (24). That is, GIVE (more accurately, HAND) with a handling classifier indicating 'to handle a thin object' is ungrammatical in this sentence in DGS without the overt noun argument, FLOWER. DGS (24) contrasts with the ISL sentence (21b), in which such stranding is grammatical.

(24) DGS (Glück and Pfau 1998, p. 62)
*MAN-IND$_1$ WOMAN-IND$_2$ THREE $_1$GIVE$_2$-CL$_{flower}$
'The man gives three flowers to the woman.'

Glück and Pfau also claim that in DGS, doubling is obligatory. That is, both the full noun and the classifier must occur in all DGS sentences that involve theme classifiers – another unexpected phenomenon under an NI analysis. However, the classifier can be associated with a null argument (*pro*), as will be shown shortly.

Glück and Pfau argue that "classification" is inflectional in DGS; specifically, that it is an agreement phenomenon. The properties which verbs agree with, according to their analysis, are inherent properties of NPs similar to gender.[10] They claim that the classifier is a morpheme occurring on a verb, marking agreement with a nominal referent.

Glück and Pfau support their agreement analysis by reporting that null arguments can occur with classifier constructions in the same way that null arguments occur with agreeing verbs (see also Chapter 21). In particular, they point out that an argument with which a classifier agrees can be null, and associated with a distant sentential topic. In the same context, an argument that does not correspond to a classifier is not permitted to be null. This contrast is illustrated in (25).

(25) DGS (Glück and Pfau 1998, p. 70)

a. $\overline{\text{MAN-IND}_1}^{\,t}$, CHILD THINK, HE$_1$ TABLE$_2$ GLASS$_a$ $_2$TAKE-CL$_a$
'The man$_i$, the child thinks, he$_i$ takes the glass off the table.'

b. $\overline{\text{GLASS}_a\text{-IND}_1}^{\,t}$, CHILD THINK, MAN (IT$_1$) TABLE$_2$ $_2$TAKE-CL$_a$
'The glass$_i$, the child thinks, the man takes it$_i$ off the table.'

c. *$\overline{\text{MAN-IND}_1}^{\,t}$, CHILD THINK, pro$_1$ TABLE$_2$ GLASS$_a$ $_2$TAKE-CL$_a$

The sentence without any null elements is given in (25a). In (25b), the argument with which the classifier agrees (GLASS) is in the sentence-initial position, and the pronoun IT (an index) referring to the glass can be either

[10] In fact, in current morphological theory, the term *gender* refers to any noun class that triggers agreement.

overt or null. In (25c), however, a different argument (MAN) is in initial position. With no agreement to license the null pronoun associated with MAN, the example is ungrammatical.

Since classifier systems are apparently very similar across sign languages, it is surprising that theme classifiers seem to behave differently in ISL and DGS. These differences should be examined more closely, to see if some additional factor lies behind them. It is important to discover just where sign languages differ with respect to classifier systems, since they appear so similar on the surface.

Additional evidence for an agreement-like analysis of ASL classifiers is presented by Benedicto and Brentari (2004). Although their analysis is like Glück and Pfau's in treating classifiers as a kind of agreement, it takes a very different line of approach. Benedicto and Brentari focus on the argument properties of classifiers in ASL. We have already seen their reasons for claiming that descriptive and handling instrumental classifiers behave differently. Recall that they argued that only sentences with hICL (handling instrumental classifiers), not those with dICL (descriptive instrumental classifiers) have an agentive subject (an external argument), based on examples like (23). They also show that both of these types also have internal arguments – in these examples, the object 'wood.' Thus, they are like transitive verbs.

Benedicto and Brentari provide similar tests to determine the argument structure characteristics of other classifier constructions. Utterances with body part classifiers (BPCL – classifiers depicting a body part, such as for a head), descriptive classifiers (DCL – which we have called SASSes in Chapter 5), and semantic classifiers (SCL – which we have called entity classifiers in Chapter 5), all appear to be intransitive – i.e., they show up with only one argument. However, Benedicto and Brentari show that these fall into distinct classes. Like hICL, verbs with BPCL have external arguments. This makes them similar to unergative verbs (i.e., verbs like *laugh* whose single external argument behaves like a subject at all levels). However, verbs with DCL and SCL take a single internal argument, like dICL (i.e., they are unaccusative, behaving similarly to verbs like *arrive*, whose single argument has the characteristics of an internal argument – an object – but whose surface syntactic placement is that of a subject). This pattern is summarized in Table 20.2.

Brentari and Benedicto account for this alternation by postulating that the classifier types fall into two different functional categories, both of which enter into agreement relations. Those classifiers which take internal arguments are heads of one functional category (labeled $f_2{}^0$), which is generated close to the VP (making it similar to AgrO). Those classifiers which take external arguments are heads of a different functional category, $f_1{}^0$, which is generated higher in the phrase marker (comparable to AgrS). The structure they propose is given in (26).

Table 20.2 *Benedicto and Brentari's classification of classifiers*

	Internal argument	External argument (agentive subject)	Predicate type
BPCL	*	√	Unergative
DICL	√	*	Unaccusative
SCL	√	*	Unaccusative
DCL	√	*	Unaccusative
HICL	√	√	Transitive

(26) Syntactic sturcture for agreement analysis of classifiers (Benedicto and Brentari 2004)

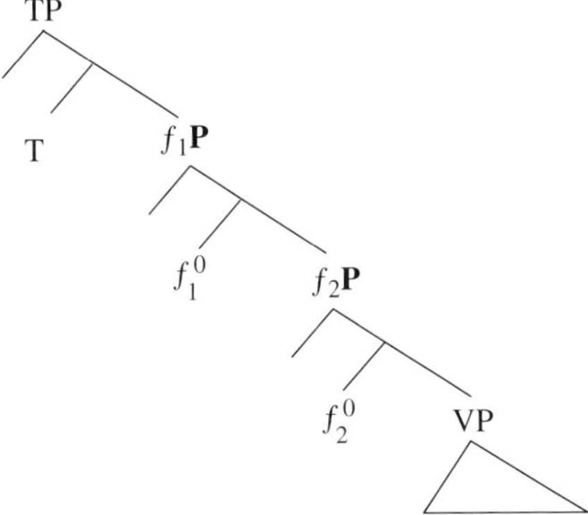

The intransitive classifier types (unergative or unaccusative) will have only one of these functional projections, while the transitive classifiers (hICL) will have both. The arguments associated with the classifiers move to the specifiers of the functional projections, just as with traditional agreement. The verb will combine with the classifier via head-to-head movement.

In support of their syntactic analysis, Benedicto and Brentari observe, like Glück and Pfau, that null arguments are licensed with classifiers, a fact consistent with the agreement analysis. Although their proposal does not explicitly argue against a lexical/ incorporation analysis, such an analysis would require an alternative explanation for the null argument phenomenon.

Meir's argument against a syntactic analysis of classifiers is simply that the two types of classifiers (instrument and theme) must be distinguished. Under a common syntactic analysis of both types, they might not be distinguished. However, with a lexical analysis of instrumental classifiers, this leaves open the possibility for a syntactic analysis of theme classifiers. Such a combination might be able to account for a wider range of facts than either analysis alone. Another issue left unresolved is whether a lexical analysis like Meir's is compatible with our proposal (in Chapter 6) that classifier constructions are formed postlexically. We leave these issues open for future research.

So far, we have seen analyses of noun phrases involving the functional category Determiner, and proposed analyses of classifier constructions involving agreement or agreement-like functional projections. We now turn to some constructions involving the proposed functional category Aspect. Sentences containing verbs with aspect allow some grammatical options not found without aspect, and these have drawn the attention of several syntacticians. Some analyses of these constructions explicitly involve the movement of a noun phrase to the specifier position of a functional projection – a prototypical use of functional projections. Whether the further use – to record cross-language differences – applies in the present case remains to be determined.

20.3 Verb sandwiches and object shift

Although Liddell (1980) argued that Subject–Verb–Object is the basic word order of ASL, he noted several types of sentences which follow an alternative order. We have discussed cases where the verb is marked for agreement, and locative classifier constructions, in Chapter 18. These cases were analyzed by Padden (1988 [1983]) as conforming to the basic Subject–Predicate order of ASL. Another set of cases concerns verbs marked with other kinds of morphology, including aspect, handling or instrument classifiers, and spatial agreement. We turn now to a discussion of these cases, which require postulation of a movement operation to produce the non-canonical order.

ASL has constructions in which a verb appears twice: once in its sentence-internal position and again in the sentence-final position, marked with morphology such as aspect or a classifier. Fischer and Janis (1990) noted such constructions and, since the object is "sandwiched" between the two verbs, dubbed them "verb sandwiches." Two examples are given in (27). In (a), the object HER TERM PAPER is sandwiched between two occurrences of the verb TYPE (the second one crucially being marked for aspect), while in (b) the object R-I-C-E is sandwiched between the lexicalized verb EAT, and the classifier construction with an instrumental classifier, glossed EAT-WITH-CHOPSTICKS (also marked for aspect, presumably, given the + signs).[11]

[11] As Carol Padden points out to us, the facts in this section help to rule out a simpler alternative analysis of examples like that in (27) – namely, that they are simply coordinate. For example, under a coordinate analysis, (i) should be acceptable, counter to fact.

(i) ASL (Matsuoka 1997, p. 139)
*TERM PAPER SALLY TYPE *t* TYPE[asp]

(27) ASL (Fischer and Janis 1990, pp. 280, 284)

a. STUDENT NAME S-A-L-L-Y TYPE HER TERM PAPER TYPE$^{[asp:cont]}$, WRONG! . . .
'A student named Sally is typing her term paper, but . . .'

b. ELIZABETH EAT R-I-C-E EAT-WITH-CHOPSTICKS+++ . . .
'While Elizabeth was eating her rice with chopsticks . . .'

Fischer and Janis suggest that the sandwich constructions are generated because of a "general constraint on the amount of information that can be carried by a single verb . . . When this limit is exceeded, another verb must be presented to carry some of the load" (p. 285). They also show that similar constructions involving verb doubling are found in Vata and Chinese. However, they do not offer a more detailed analysis of the ASL construction.

Verb sandwich constructions with aspect bear some resemblance to two other sentence types with aspectually marked verbs. Ordinarily, objects do not show up preverbally (unless they are marked as topics), as illustrated in (28). However, when the verb is morphologically marked for aspect, two types of preverbal objects are permitted: verb-final constructions (see (29)), in which the object comes between the subject and the aspectually marked verb, and object-raising constructions (see (30)), in which the object appears in the sentence-initial position, preceding the subject and the aspectually marked verb.[12] While Liddell (1980) noticed such structures, he simply listed them as exceptions to the SVO rule.

(28) ASL (Matsuoka 1997, p. 131)
*GIRL TOMATO EAT
'The girl eats a tomato.'

(29) ASL (Matsuoka 1997, p. 131, citing Romano 1991)
S-H-E R-A-D-I-O LISTEN[asp: cont]
'She was continuously listening to the radio.'

(30) ASL (Matsuoka 1997, p. 131)
TOMATO GIRL EAT[I: durative aspect][13]
'The girl eats tomatoes for a long time.'

In order to understand these constructions in ASL, let us first look at a possibly similar situation in some spoken languages. In Scandinavian languages, it is observed that objects may raise to a structural position higher than the VP just in case the verb also raises out of the verb phrase. In (31a), from Icelandic, the NP *bókina* stays within the verb phrase along with the verb *lesið*. It is clear that both are within the verb phrase, because

[12] In fact, some signers reject examples with an object following an aspectually marked verb (i.e., SV[+asp]O), but there is variability in this case.

[13] Liddell (1980, p. 103) cites an example like this one, but with the yes/no question non-manual, given in example (12) of Chapter 18. Liddell points out that although the question marker does not extend over the object, it is not marked as a topic by facial expression or a hold.

the adverb *aldrei* 'never' marks its left edge. The NP cannot raise out of the verb phrase in (31b), because the auxiliary *hefur* blocks the verb from raising. In (32), however, the main verb *máluðu* raises. Although the indefinite *hús* stays within the VP in (32a), in (32b) the definite NP *húsið* raises out of the VP (with its edge marked by *ekki*).

(31) Icelandic (Bobaljik 1995, p. 78, citing Thráinsson 1994, p. 20)

a. Hann hefur [$_{VP}$ aldrei lesið bókina]
he has never read book.the
b. *Hann hefur bókina [$_{VP}$ aldrei lesið]
he has book.the never read
'He has never read the book.'

(32) Icelandic (Bobaljik 1995, p. 76)[14]

a. Í fyrra máluðu stúdentarnir [$_{VP}$ ekki hús]
last year painted students.the not house
'The students did not paint a house last year.'
b. Í fyrra máluðu stúdentarnir húsið [$_{VP}$ ekki]
last year painted students.the house.the not
'The students did not paint the house last year.'

The raising of the object out of the verb phrase is known as Object Shift (see Thráinsson 2001 for a comprehensive overview of this phenomenon and various analyses proposed). Facts like those presented here led Holmberg (1986) to the generalization that now bears his name. A version of this generalization is given in (33).[15]

(33) Holmberg's Generalization (Bobaljik 1995, p. 118)
Object shift is possible only if the (main) verb raises out of the VP.

Chomsky (1993) accounts for Holmberg's Generalization by proposing that the movement of the verb to a higher head position makes the specifier of that position an eligible landing site for the movement of the verb's complement. Ordinarily, the object would only be able to move as far as the closest specifier. Since the [Spec, VP] position is filled by the subject, this would prevent the object from moving out of the VP. In Chomsky's terms, movement of the verb makes the higher specifier position "equidistant" to the object, allowing it to raise. His formulation is more general, but for our purposes this description and the illustration in (34) will suffice.

[14] A typographical error in Bobaljik's original example has been corrected.
[15] Bobaljik (1995) argues that while Holmberg's Generalization holds for the SVO Germanic languages, it does not hold for the SOV ones, nor for some other languages investigated. The analyses to be discussed here make the assumption that it is a general principle, and apply it to the ASL data.

(34) Equidistance illustration (from Bobaljik 1995, p. 121)

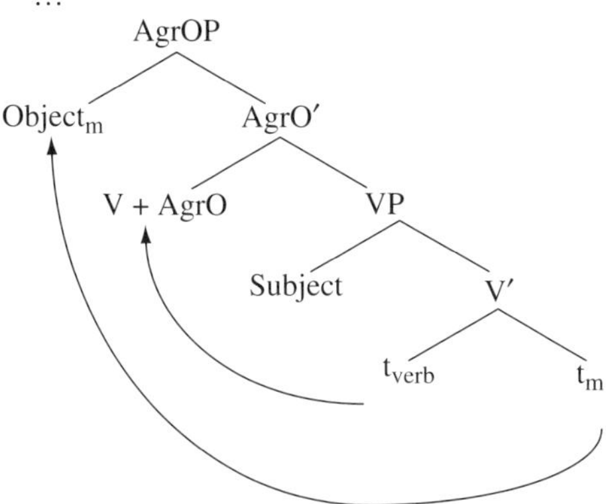

Let us return to the ASL case. Matsuoka (1997) notes similarities between the constructions in (27)–(28) and the "object shift" structures of Scandinavian as in (32b), and she offers the following proposal. First, she assumes, following Romano (1991) (see Chapter 18, Section 18.3), that in ASL functional categories are head-final and lexical categories are head-initial. However, she also assumes that the hierarchical order of functional categories in ASL is the same as that now generally assumed for other (spoken) languages, namely the one given in (35) (Chomsky 1991, and elsewhere). As we have seen, the extent to which languages may vary in terms of hierarchical order is a matter of some debate, but a theory without variation in this component is a more restrictive one, and therefore to be preferred if empirically adequate.

(35) [AgrSP [TP [AspP [AgrOP [VP

Matsuoka proposes that the aspect marker found with aspectually marked verbs in ASL is generated as an affix in the head of AspP (which is, on her account, on the right). Since the affix must have a host (it cannot be stranded for morphological reasons), the verb moves overtly to the Asp head to serve as its host.[16] Thus, the verb moves up out of the VP in structures with aspect marking.

According to the Copy Theory of Movement (Chomsky 1995), syntactic movement involves two steps: copying of the target and deletion of the original at PF. Adopting this theory, Matsuoka proposes that PF deletion

[16] In English, *do*-support rather than verb movement is used to save stranded affixes (we thank Željko Bošković for reminding us of this). Matsuoka appeals to Lasnik's (1995) principle of "Enlightened Self-Interest" – as opposed to Chomsky's (1995) "Greed" – to motivate the verb movement for the satisfaction of the requirements of the affix rather than the verb's own requirements.

of some duplicates is optional in ASL. In particular, when the VP-internal copy of the verb is not realized (i.e., when it is deleted), then the verb-final structures are derived. When the VP-internal copy of the verb is realized, then the verb sandwich is derived. These derivations are illustrated in (36).[17]

(36) ASL (Matsuoka 1997, p. 136)
a. Original array of words: SALLY TYPE PAPER[asp]
b. Overt V-raising: SALLY TYPE PAPER TYPE[asp]
c. PF Merging: SALLY TYPE PAPER TYPE[asp]
d. Optional PF Deletion #1: SALLY *e* PAPER TYPE[asp]

When the verb raises out of VP to host an aspect affix, the object may shift to [Spec, AgrOP], following Holmberg's Generalization discussed above. To derive the object shift examples (with the object first, such as (30)), Matsuoka assumes that overt raising of the subject from the VP-internal position is "stylistic" (i.e., optional) in ASL. If the verb and object move to AspP but the subject fails to raise, the object-shift examples are derived. This derivation is illustrated in (37).

(37) (Matsuoka 1997, p. 138)

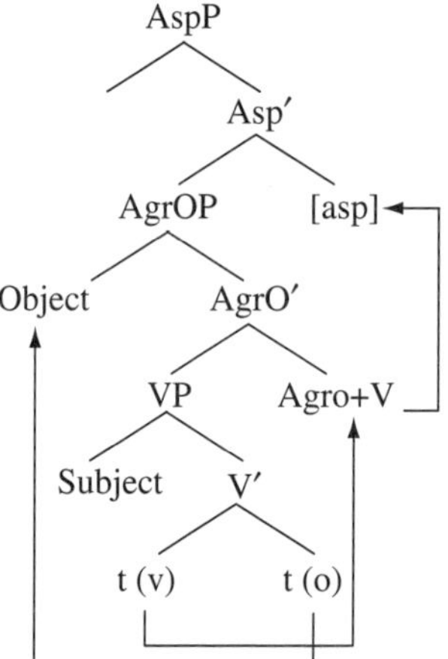

Braze (2004) further considers the data on object shift presented by Matsuoka, and investigates the possible position of the shifted object. Like Matsuoka, he assumes that the hierarchical structure of functional categories in ASL is the same as that generally proposed for spoken languages (crucially, [AgrSP [TP [AgrOP [VP]]]]). Braze also adopts a form of split headedness for ASL, but he proposes a version under which only certain functional categories in ASL are head-final. The categories identified as head-final in Braze's analysis are the non-argument (that is,

[17] The difference between (36b) and (36c) is the PF merging of the sentence-final verb TYPE with the [asp] affix, leading to the aspectually modified form of the verb.

non-A or A′ "A bar") categories, which includes the aspect projection but not Agr or T projections.

Braze sets out to use adverb placement as a diagnostic for the surface position of the shifted object in object-shift sentences such as (30). First, he observes that temporal (sentential) adverbs can be in initial, postsubject, or final position (in agreement with Aarons et al. 1995 and Boster 1996). This can be accounted for by assuming that such adverbs can adjoin to AgrSP or TP.[18] Frequency adverbs (such as ALWAYS) appear preverbally or in final position, consistent with the expectation that they adjoin to VP. Since subjects may follow (38a) or precede (38b) temporal adverbs, but must precede frequency adverbs (39), this leads to the conclusion that the surface position of the subject is Spec AgrSP.

(38) ASL (Braze 2004, citing Boster 1996)
a. TODAY THREE STUDENT ARRIVE CLASS LATE
b. THREE STUDENT TODAY ARRIVE CLASS LATE
'Today three students arrived to class late.'

(39) ASL (Braze 2004)
a. *ALWAYS JOHN LOSE PAPER
b. √JOHN ALWAYS LOSE PAPER
'John always loses his papers.'

Recall that object shift is derived under Matsuoka's analysis when the subject stays in [Spec, VP] and the object moves to [Spec, AgrOP]. At least in sentences without aspect, it seems that the subject must raise from [Spec, VP], since it must appear before frequency adverbs. This fact casts doubt on the analysis of object shift involving subjects remaining in [Spec, VP]. Evidence that the subject raises even in object-shift examples is given in (40). According to Matsuoka's analysis, (40a) should be perfectly grammatical, with the object in [Spec, AgrOP], the adverb adjoined to VP, and the subject in VP-internal position. On the other hand, if the subject is in [Spec, AgrSP], (40b) shows that the shifted object must be still higher in the structure.

(40) ASL (Braze 2004)
a. *PAPER ALWAYS SHE $\text{TYPE}_{[\text{cont}]}$
b. √PAPER SHE ALWAYS $\text{TYPE}_{[\text{cont}]}$
'She is typing papers all the time.'

Braze's alternative analysis has AspP much higher in the structure, as part of an articulated CP, such as that proposed by Rizzi (1997). According to Rizzi's analysis, CP is a cover term for a variety of functional categories which should project their own phrases, along the lines

[18] But see Cinque (1999) for a detailed proposal about the structures associated with adverbs.

of the expanded Infl proposed by Pollock and others, which we have discussed in Chapter 18. Braze proposes that whatever else might be included, the expanded CP should include a projection for Asp. He proposes that this category will be right-headed in ASL. Then, when the verb moves to the head of Asp, the object can shift to [Spec, AspP], following Holmberg's Generalization. Recall that according to Equidistance, the specifier of the position to which the verb moves is a legitimate landing site for the movement of the verb's complement. With the verb – and thus the object – so structurally high, the correct order is achieved if other sentential elements (subject, adverbs, modals, negation, etc.) are in their usual places.

Braze's analysis of object-shift examples like (30) uses some of the insights of Matsuoka's analysis but improves on it by considering additional data. It maintains the essence of employing Holmberg's Generalization to account for ASL, allowing objects to raise when the verb raises to a higher position.

Verb sandwich and verb-final examples are also found with verbs having morphology other than aspect, such as handling/instrumental classifiers or spatial locations. This was noted by both Fischer and Janis (1990) and Matsuoka (1997), though it was not the focus of either paper. Matsuoka (2000) and Chen Pichler (2001) address such constructions directly. Matsuoka analyzes what she calls "lexical sandwiches" differently from aspectual sandwiches, assuming that each verb selects its classifier lexically, so the sandwich construction is not created by verb movement (copying). Chen Pichler proposes to collapse the types, using a functional projection tentatively called "MannerPhrase" to host any of the morphological modifications used in these constructions. Her analysis for both types is very similar to Matsuoka's proposal for aspect sandwiches. Further comparison of the types and more detailed analyses are needed.

Our final extension on basic structures presents a more detailed look at sentences with negation. We have already seen (in Chapters 18 and 19) that sentences with negation can be used to help identify the basic syntactic structure of a language. Now we investigate the structure of certain sentences with negation in order to address two questions. The first question concerns the extent of cross-linguistic variation found in the placement and positioning of functional categories. The second concerns the analysis of the nonmanual marker most often accompanying negation, the headshake.

20.4 Negatives

One type of sentence in which both strong similarities and interesting differences are found across sign languages is basic negative constructions. All sign languages for which relevant data have been reported employ a negative headshake to indicate sentential negation. In most cases, the negative headshake may suffice to indicate negation, as in (41a), while a manual negative sign may optionally also be used, as in (41b, c).

(41) ASL (Neidle et al. 2000, pp. 44–45)[19]

a. $\ \overline{\text{BUY HOUSE}}^{\,neg}$ JOHN BUY HOUSE
'John is not buying a house.'

b. $\ \overline{\text{NOT BUY HOUSE}}^{\,neg}$ JOHN NOT BUY HOUSE
'John is not buying a house.'

c. $\ \overline{\text{NOT}}^{\,neg}$ JOHN NOT BUY HOUSE
'John is *not* buying a house.'

The use of the negative headshake seems to be a sign language universal. However, the extent of spreading of the negative headshake varies across languages. In addition, the position of the negative element varies, following the basic word-order differences (i.e., preverbal negation in VO languages, and postverbal negation in OV languages). The study of sentences with negation thus contributes to an understanding of phrase structure and of the nature of non-manual markers. We look at each of these issues in turn.

20.4.1 Phrase structure of negation

As we have seen in Chapter 18, some syntacticians have argued that sentential negative elements head their own functional category, usually known as NegP (Laka Mugarza 1990, Pollock 1989, Zanuttini 1997). In English and French, the NegP is situated between TP and VP. Because main verbs in French and auxiliary verbs in English appear before negation, it is proposed that they move to T overtly. Since English main verbs appear after the negative element, their movement must be covert.

Some researchers have proposed that languages may differ in the placement of the NegP with respect to other functional categories, and that the sentential negative element may appear as the head of NegP in some cases, but in [Spec, NegP] in other cases (Ouhalla 1990, Pollock 1989). Just how much variability is found across languages – and how much need be permitted theoretically – is a matter of some debate, however. A major issue concerns the power of the theoretical machinery. Most researchers at least implicitly take the view that the theory should be as restricted as possible – hence, a universal pattern for the placement of NegP (below TP, as in the examples above) is used. However, if this more restricted theory is adopted, can the full range of data found across languages be explained?

[19] We have omitted structural diacritics from the notation used by Neidle et al. in examples (41a, b).

It seems that the cross-linguistic study of negation in sign languages can contribute to this debate, since sign languages do seem to vary in the placement of negation. Only a few works have directly addressed the issue, and more work is needed, but the results so far are intriguing.

We start with ASL. In addition to the preverbal position of negation illustrated in (41), ASL allows the negative element to appear in the sentence-final position, as in (42). ASL also permits two negative elements to appear in the same sentence, in a type of negative concord (that is, the two negatives do not cancel each other out – the sentence remains negative). The two negative elements may be the same sign, repeated, as in (43a), or different negative signs, as in (43b).

(42) ASL (Wood 1999, p. 21)[20]
JOHN BREAK FAN NOT.
'John did not break the fan.'

(43) ASL (Wood 1999, pp. 72, 76)
a. JOHN WILL NEVER EAT FISH NEVER
'John will never eat fish.'
b. JOHN NOT BREAK FAN NOTHING
'John did not break any part of the fan.'

The occurrence of more than one negative sign in the same sentence will be discussed in more detail in Chapter 22, where we discuss a number of cases of doubling. There we will also present an argument that sentences with sentence-final elements are generated in a similar way to those with doubles. For the present purposes, our goal is to determine the position of NegP, and the placement of the various negative signs.

As discussed in Chapter 18, Neidle et al. (2000) propose that in ASL, NegP occurs below TP, above AspP and VP. This portion of their proposed syntactic structure is reproduced in (44), which omits the positions of Agreement projections.

(44) Partial syntactic tree (modified from Neidle et al. 2000, p. 3)

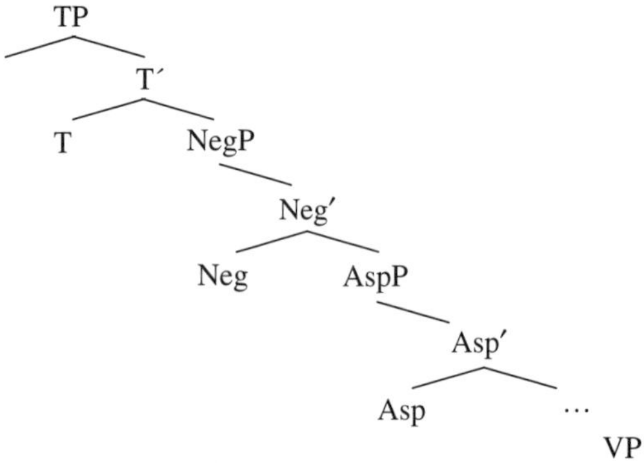

[20] In these and other examples from Wood (1999), no negative headshake or other non-manual markers are indicated. This should not be taken to mean that no non-manual markers are present; they were not included in her transcriptions.

Their reasons for using this structure come from the placement of NOT with respect to other signs in examples like (41), and from the spread of the non-manual marking. Since modals or lexical tense markers (presumably occupying T) occur before NOT (as in (45a)), and lexical aspect markers and verbs appear after NOT (as in (45b)), this motivates the positioning of NegP as seen in (44) (on the assumption that the surface ordering reflects the syntactic structure, i.e., that no movement across elements has occurred). Neidle et al. assume that the sign NOT occupies the head of the NegP, and that the [+neg] feature which is realized as a negative headshake also occurs in this position.

(45) ASL (Neidle et al. 2000, pp. 80, 84)

a. JOHN SHOULD/FUTURE$_{\text{tns}}$ $\overline{\text{NOT BUY HOUSE}}^{\text{neg}}$
'John should/will not buy a house.'

b. JOHN $\overline{\text{NOT FINISH READ BOOK}}^{\text{neg}}$
'John hasn't read the book.'

Similarly, Wood (1999) proposes that in ASL NegP is located between TP and VP, and that NOT occupies the head of NegP. Her analysis of sentence-final stressed NOT involves movement of the VP to [Spec, NegP]. This movement is motivated by the prosodic requirement shown by ASL to have focused elements in sentence-final position (Wilbur 1997). This phenomenon will be discussed in detail in Chapter 22.

Wood also observes that there are important differences across negative signs. Although the interpretations do not differ for negative sentences with NOT in the preverbal versus sentence-final position (except for an emphasis of the negation in the sentence-final position), the placement of the negative sign does make a difference for the interpretation of NEVER. Thus, she argues that sentences with NEVER involve movement of the negative sign, whether it appears in the preverbal or sentence-final position.

According to Wood, preverbal NEVER has an interpretation much like that of *never* in English: it indicates negation of an event that takes place over time. So, (46a) has the interpretation that it is not the case that Bob has ever eaten fish. On the other hand, the sentence-final NEVER, as in (46b), indicates a characteristic of the subject – in this case, Bob simply will not eat fish. Wood puts these interpretations in terms of possibility – in the preverbal case, it is possible that the event would take place, but it hasn't happened. In the sentence-final case, NEVER negates the possibility of this subject participating in this event.[21]

[21] A possible loose translation of the sentence-final version might be, 'Bob eat fish? Never!' More detailed information about the prosody of the ASL utterance in (46b) is needed to determine whether the structure should reflect such an interpretation.

(46) ASL (Wood 1999, pp. 31, 32)

a. BOB NEVER EAT FISH
'Bob has never eaten fish.'

b. BOB EAT FISH NEVER
'Bob won't eat fish.'

Because of this difference in interpretation, Wood proposes that NEVER moves from Neg to T, where it appears when preverbal. In the sentence-final case, NEVER moves on to C, which Wood assumes (following Wilbur 1996, 1999b, Petronio and Lillo-Martin 1997, Neidle et al. 1998b) is sentence-final in ASL. The structures she proposes for these two cases are given in (47).

(47) ASL (Wood 1999, pp. 31, 32)

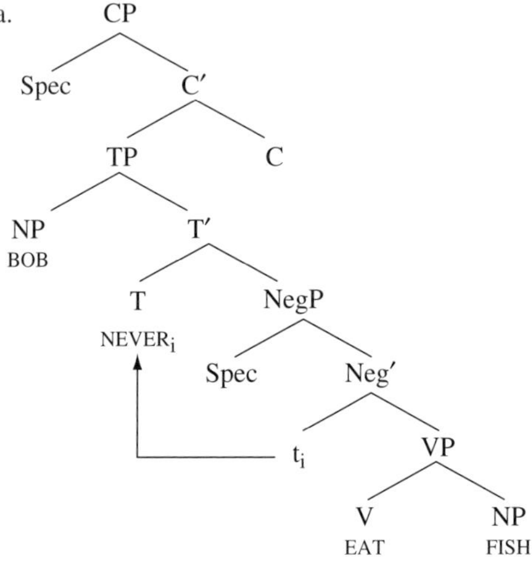

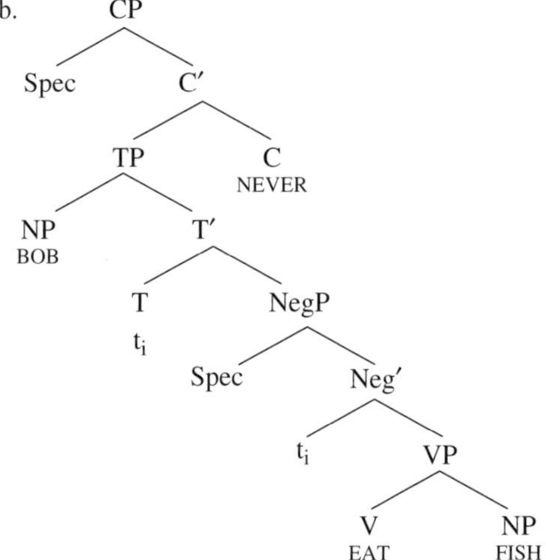

Wood also discusses the interpretation and placement of two additional negative signs: NOTHING, and NO^{o}.[22] These signs are analyzed as negative determiners, contributing the interpretation 'no part of.' Although they are analyzed as determiners, and can appear prenominally (48a), they usually appear in the same surface position as NOT and NEVER: i.e., preverbally (48b), or sentence-finally (48c).

(48) ASL (Wood 1999, pp. 38, 40)
a. ? JOHN BREAK NOTHING/NO^{o} FAN
b. JOHN NOTHING/NO^{o} FAN BREAK
c. JOHN BREAK FAN NOTHING/NO^{o}
'John did not break any (part of) the fan.'

Wood provides the following analyses for these elements. She proposes that NOTHING and NO^{o} are generated as D heads. When nothing else happens, the prenominal versions are derived (as in (48a)). However, Wood proposes that two other options are available. On one, the NP complement can be raised to [Spec, DP] (as perhaps also found with the complements to other determiners; see Wilbur and Zelaznik 1997). In the present examples, this derives the sentence-final negatives, as in (48c). Finally, the negative element can overtly raise to Neg, resulting in the preverbal negative as in (48b).

Wood observes an important asymmetry between NOTHING and NO^{o}. While both elements can modify syntactic objects, only NO^{o} can modify a subject. Furthermore, even when NO^{o} modifies a subject, the subject cannot be in its canonical position, but must appear sentence-finally. These contrasts are shown in (49).

(49) ASL (Wood 1999, pp. 50, 53)
a. SHOW-UP ON-TIME INTERPRETER NO^{o}
'No interpreters showed up on time.'
b. * NO^{o} INTERPRETER SHOW-UP ON-TIME
c. * INTERPRETER NO^{o} SHOW-UP ON-TIME
d. * SHOW-UP ON-TIME INTERPRETER NOTHING

The finding that NOTHING only modifies objects can be refined. In sentences with unergative verbs, as in (50a), NOTHING cannot modify the subject. However, in sentences with unaccusative verbs, as in (50b), NOTHING can be used. This is consistent with the common analysis of unaccusatives as involving base-generation of their sole argument as an object, which overtly raises to the subject position.[23]

[22] NO^{o} is the notation Wood uses for a sign often glossed NONE. It crucially involves lip rounding, and also differs from other similar signs by its downward twisting movement.

[23] See Kegl (1990) for discussion of unaccusative and unergative verb categories, as well as other aspects of verb categorization in ASL.

(50) ASL (Wood 1999, pp. 54, 55)
   a. *RUN FAST DOG NOTHING
      'Not any of the dogs ran fast.'
   b. FAN NOTHING BREAK
      Lit.: fan not-anything break
      'There was not anything broken with the fan.'

As far as the hierarchical position of NegP is concerned, ASL seems to pattern with English and French: TP is higher than NegP. Although many syntacticians assume this is the universal pattern, Cinque (1999) and Zanuttini (1997) argue that two options are available: TP selecting NegP, or NegP selecting TP. Pfau (2002) and Quer (2003; Pfau and Quer 2003) propose that the second option is the one chosen by German Sign Language (Deutsche Gebärdensprache, DGS) and Catalan Sign Language (Llengua de Signes Catalana, LSC). Their argument is interwoven with their analysis of the negative headshake in these languages, so we will present it in this broader context.

20.4.2 Negative headshake

As mentioned, it seems that all sign languages employ a negative headshake in basic negative sentences, and in most cases, the negative headshake is sufficient to indicate negation without a manual negative sign. We have seen that in ASL, the negative headshake may spread over some syntactic domain. Unlike other non-manual markers, however, there are situations in which the negative headshake may be used without any accompanying manual elements (Liddell 1980, Veinberg and Wilbur 1990, Dively 2001). For example, Veinberg and Wilbur (1990) cite the following example (51). These cases seem to be limited, however; for example, headshakes without manual signs do not interrupt a sentence.

(51) ASL (Veinberg and Wilbur 1990, p. 221)
   _______n __n
   [   ] [NOT HURT]
   'S/he was not hurt.

Since Liddell (1980), attempts to account for the spread of the non-manual marker have invoked the structural hierarchy. As seen in Chapter 18, Liddell proposed that the negative element commands the rest of the sentence, and the spread of the non-manual is determined by this command relationship. According to Liddell, the non-manual marker spreads over the whole sentence, including the subject (as in (52a)) – except for any element which has been topicalized, and therefore is not commanded by the negative, as in (52b).

(52) ASL (Liddell 1980, p. 81)

a. DOG CHASE CAT (n over DOG CHASE CAT)

'It is not the case that the dog chased the cat.'

b. DOG CHASE CAT (t over DOG; n over CHASE CAT)

'As for the dog, it didn't chase the cat.'

Neidle et al. (2000) claim that the negative non-manual marker spreads only over the c-command domain of NegP, excluding the subject. They say that a version of (41) with non-manual marking on the subject is only permitted when interpreted as, 'No, John didn't buy the house.' Given that Liddell's and Padden's (1988 [1983]) examples indicate use of the non-manual marker over the subject, and Veinberg and Wilbur's (1990) examples include both types, this issue requires further investigation.

The question of the spread of the non-manual marking in ASL is made all the more intriguing by the observation that sign languages differ even more dramatically in the amount of spreading of non-manual marking employed. Pfau (2002) and Quer (2003; see also Pfau and Quer 2003) provide the following distributions of the negative headshake in DGS and LSC.

In DGS (which is an SOV language, as illustrated in (53a)), the negative element NICHT optionally appears following the verb, as in (53b). Unlike ASL, the negative headshake may co-occur with the verb without spreading to the object, and may not co-occur with the negative manual sign without spreading, as in (53c). Spreading over the verb and object, as in ASL, is optionally allowed, as indicated with a broken line in (54).

(53) DGS (Pfau 2002, pp. 273, 277)

a. MUTTER BLUME KAUF
mother flower buy
'Mother buys a flower.'

b. MUTTER BLUME KAUF (NICHT) (hs over KAUF; hs over (NICHT))
mother flower buy.neg (not)
'Mother does not buy a flower.'

c. *MUTTER BLUME KAUF (NICHT) (hs over (NICHT))
mother flower buy.neg (not)
'Mother does not buy a flower.'

(54) DGS (Pfau and Quer 2003)

MUTTER BLUME KAUF (broken line over BLUME; hs over KAUF)

DGS is an SOV language. Accordingly, it would be expected that the heads of functional projections such as TP and NegP would be to the right of the verb. Pfau further proposes that the [Spec, NegP] position is on the right, and (as mentioned earlier) that NegP dominates TP. This structure is illustrated in (55).

(55) DGS negation structure (Pfau 2002, p. 273)

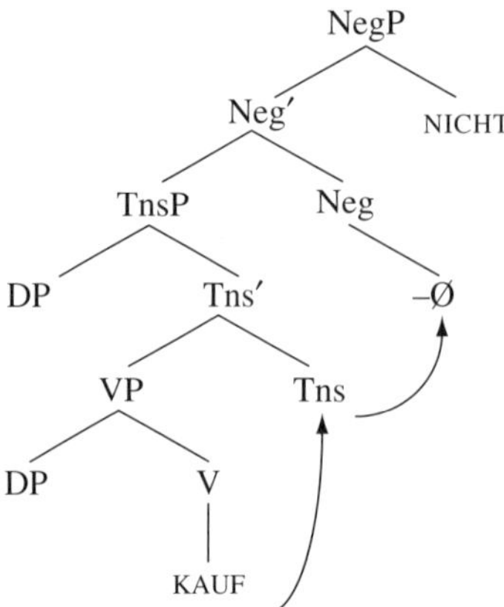

By employing this structure, Pfau is able to account for the facts of negation in DGS. First, note that he proposes that the negative headshake is analogous to tone, in languages such as Gã which mark negation using tone (Pfau cites data from Ablorh-Odjidja 1968). He proposes that the negative element [+neg] is affixal (cf. discussion of affixal vs. featural agreement in Chapter 18), and is located in the head of Neg, as is common, but that the negative manual sign NICHT occupies the [Spec, NegP] position rather than the head. Using the framework of Distributed Morphology (Halle and Marantz 1993, 1994), he proposes that a readjustment rule adds the negative headshake where the negative affix is found. Thus, the verb moves, through T, to Neg, to host the negative affix. The negative sign follows the verb in [Spec, NegP]. When the readjustment rules apply, the negative headshake is realized with the verb.

The situation in LSC is somewhat different. In this SOV language, the negative sign also optionally appears following the verb, as in (56a). As in DGS, the negative headshake may co-occur with the verb without spreading to the object, as in (56b). Unlike DGS, in LSC the negative headshake may co-occur with the negative manual sign NO without spreading. Spreading over the verb and object, as in ASL and DGS, is optionally allowed (57).

(56) LSC (Pfau and Quer 2003)

a. SANTI CARN MENJAR $\overline{\text{NO}}^{\text{hs}}$
Santi meat eat not
'Santi doesn't eat meat.'

b. SANTI CARN $\overline{\text{MENJAR}}^{\text{hs}}$
Santi meat eat.neg
'Santi doesn't eat meat.'

(57) LSC (Pfau and Quer 2003)

```
        ____   _______hs
SANTI   CARN   MENJAR
```

In addition to the negative sign NO, Pfau and Quer discuss the negative signs NO-RES ('neg') and MAI ('never'), which they claim occupy the [Spec, NegP] position. Evidence in favor of this includes the fact that they may co-occur with NO, following it (58)–(59).

(58) LSC (Pfau and Quer 2003)

```
             _____hs       _____hs
a. INDEX1    FUMAR         NO-RES
   I         smoke.NEG     NEG
   'I haven't smoked (at all).'
```

(59) LSC (Quer 2003)

```
                   __n
a. IX-1   FUMAR    MAI
   I      smoke    never
   'I never smoke.'

                   __n   __n
b. IX-1   FUMAR    NO    MAI
   I      smoke    no    never
   'I have never smoked.'

                     __n   __n
c. * IX-1   FUMAR    MAI   NO
```

Taking these facts into account Pfau and Quer propose the structure in (60) for LSC negation.

(60) LSC negation structure (Pfau and Quer 2003)

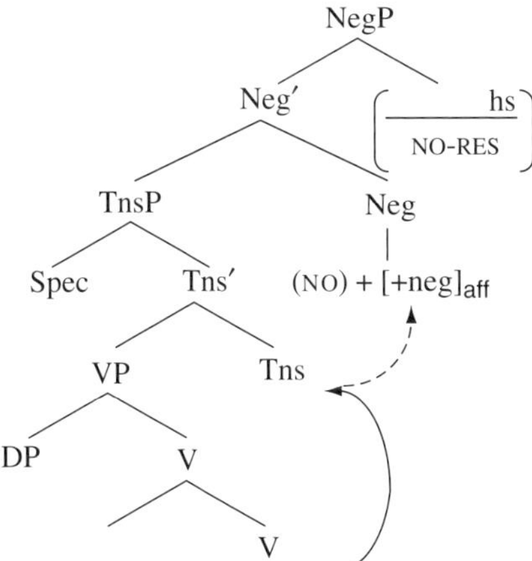

The analysis proposed for negation in LSC is similar in many ways to that proposed for DGS. The placement of NegP dominating TP, and the ordering of the Spec and head of Neg on the right, are both like the proposed structure for DGS. The [+ neg] element is similarly argued to be an affix appearing in the head of Neg. However, in LSC the negative sign NO may also appear in the head.

Thus, when NO appears in Neg, it suffices to bear the negative headshake. Unlike DGS, then, the negative headshake can appear on the negative sign NO only. However, if no manual negative sign is used – or if the negative signs NO-RES or MAI are used, without NO – then there is nothing generated in the Neg head position. Accordingly, the verb must raise, through T, to host the affix, so the negative headshake appears on the verb. The dotted line in (60) indicates the fact that the verb only moves in certain cases – i.e., when Neg does not have an overt negative manual sign.

If the analyses proposed by Pfau and Quer are correct, they provide support for the view that the position of NegP with respect to TP can vary across languages (Zanuttini 1997). Furthermore, the analyses presented account for the cross-sign language differences in the order of negative elements and in the spreading of the negative headshake. The analyses make use of overt verb raising to T. As we saw in Chapters 18–19, spoken languages differ with respect to whether or not verbs raise overtly. Evidence was presented that such overt verb movement is not generally found in ASL or LSB. The observation that overt verb movement is found in DGS and LSC indicates that sign languages, like spoken languages, may vary on this point. In spoken languages, overt verb raising tends to go along with richer verbal morphology. Since the sign languages under consideration have very similar verbal morphology, the findings here indicate that there is not a strict correspondence between richness of verbal morphology and overt verb raising. Further research in all of these areas would be welcome.

21 Pronouns

NPs, the subject of the first section of the previous chapter, are interpreted by virtue of their inherent properties, within a particular domain of discourse. On the other hand, pronouns and anaphors[1] are not interpreted by virtue of their inherent properties, but by how they relate to other linguistic entities within the domain of discourse. Consider the examples in (1) for instance.

(1) a. Ozzy saw Marie.
b. She waved at him.

Suppose we are talking about members of Ozzy's and Marie's families. While there are other men named Ozzy in the world, within this domain of discourse the NP *Ozzy* will pick out a unique referent. However, the pronouns *she* and *him* do not pick out unique referents, even within the domain of discourse. They only narrow down the set of possible referents, by virtue of the features they encode. These features, sometimes known as ϕ-features, generally include person, number, and gender. By principles of pragmatics, particular referents from the candidate set are most likely to be construed.

The form and distribution of pronouns in sign languages has received a fair amount of attention. Most of the work has addressed the question of what features pronouns encode. In what way do sign language pronouns narrow down the set of potential referents they pick out? Do they represent person features, like spoken language pronouns do? This issue is the topic of Sections 21.1.1 and 21.1.2 in this chapter.

In some languages, pronouns may serve functions beyond reference to antecedents. In Ewe and Gokana, for example, pronouns can be used "logophorically," in point-of-view contexts, where the point of view of someone other than the speaker is being conveyed. They indicate whose

[1] Anaphors are expressions which refer back – that is, they take their reference from some other expression. In this sense, personal pronouns (such as *s/he*) and reflexive pronouns (such as *herself/himself*) may be used anaphorically. Within the Binding Theory (Chomsky 1981), the term "anaphor" refers exclusively to reflexive and reciprocal anaphors, as distinguished from pronouns.

point of view is, or is not, considered. In Section 21.1.3, we discuss the possibility that the first-person pronoun in ASL can be used in this way.

Much of the literature on pronouns and anaphors in spoken languages is concerned with general principles governing the syntactic and pragmatic domains in which each type of element can be found (e.g., Chomsky 1981, Koster and Reuland 1991, Reinhart 1976, Reinhart and Reuland 1993). One version of these principles is known as Binding Theory, which requires that (reflexive and reciprocal) anaphors be bound within a certain syntactic domain, while (non-anaphoric) pronouns must not be bound within this domain.

In the 1980s, generative linguists reported data from a variety of languages to develop and refine constraints on the interpretation of pronouns and reflexives. It has become clear that there is (limited) cross-linguistic variability in this domain, and that pragmatic information is relevant to the distribution of pronouns and anaphors in many languages (for a nice overview, see Reuland and Everaert 2001). Much less work has addressed issues concerning the syntactic distribution of pronouns and reflexives in sign languages, and the constraints on their distribution across different sentence types. It remains to be seen exactly how sign languages fit into the range of possibilities discovered for spoken languages. It is clear only that the distribution of the ASL sign glossed SELF is not identical to that of the English word *himself/herself*. Some examples of this will be seen in the context of analyzing the so-called "role shift" in terms of logophoricity in Section 21.1.3.

Across sign languages, it seems that null pronouns (or, more generally, null arguments) are universally found. Of course, null arguments are found in spoken languages too. Researchers have discussed two types of spoken languages which allow null arguments. In one type (exemplified by Spanish), a rich system of verb agreement is found. Information on the verb permits aspects of the reference of the null arguments to be identified. An example from Spanish is given in (2).

(2) Spanish
Hablo Español.
'(I-)speak Spanish.'

In the second type of spoken language (as in Chinese), verbs do not encode information about their arguments. Missing arguments are understood within the domain of discourse as topics. An example is given in (3).

(3) Chinese (Huang 1984, p. 533)
Speaker A: Zhangsan kanjian Lisi le ma?
Zhangsan see Lisi ASP Q
'Did Zhangsan see Lisi?'

Speaker B: e kanjian ta le.
[He] see he ASP
'(He) saw him.'

While some researchers consider these two types of null arguments to be identical syntactically, others have proposed distinct licensing mechanisms with particular syntactic structures involved. In ASL, it has been argued that two distinct mechanisms are involved in licensing null arguments, corresponding to verbs of the agreeing and plain categories. However, this proposal has been recently challenged. The issue is particularly interesting, as no single spoken language has been found to have both types of null argument. Evidence for and against the two-mechanism approach will be the topic of Section 21.2.

We begin now with a brief description of sign language pronouns and anaphors.

21.1 Overt pronouns

21.1.1 Personal pronoun system – description

The ASL pronominal system was briefly described in Chapter 3; here we provide a summary of that description. Referents in a discourse are associated with locations in space. For physically present referents, their current locations are generally used; for non-present referents, other locations (often arbitrary) are established as associated with these referents (the referents are "imagined" at these locations; Liddell 1990a). Pronoun signs then point to these locations. ASL singular personal pronominals are illustrated in Figure 21.1.[2]

Pronouns make use of the referential loci associated with referents. Thus, not only can the signer differentiate reference to self from reference to others, he or she may also differentiate reference to multiple non-addressees, as illustrated in (4)–(5).[3] Pictures of these examples are provided in Figure 21.2.

[2] While handshapes are known to differ, as far as we know every sign language uses the same type of pronominal system. Discussions of pronouns in various sign languages include Berenz and Ferreira Brito (1990) on Brazilian Cities Sign Language (BCSL); Engberg-Pedersen (1993) on Danish Sign Language (DSL); Bos (1990) on Sign Language of the Netherlands (SLN); and Ahlgren (1990) on Swedish Sign Language (SSL). See Unit 5 for discussion of the theoretical implications of this sign language universal.

[3] In this chapter, as throughout, we do not adapt the notation in cited examples, but follow the notation used by the sources. In our own examples, a pointing sign is glossed as a-IX (referent). The 'a' indicates the use of a locus; the (referent) points out which referent is being picked out at this occasion of use, to aid in understanding the examples. In Lillo-Martin's earlier work, pointing signs used as pronouns are glossed $_{a}$PRONOUN. Other sign language researchers use IND, INDEX, and PT to gloss various pointing signs, which may include pronouns, locatives, and determiners.

a. 1-IX

b. a-IX (you)

c. a-IX (s/he)

Figure 21.1 ASL personal pronominals (singular)

(4) ASL
1-IX SEE a-IX(you).
'I know you.'

(5) a-MARY a-LOC; b-JOHN b-LOC.
'There$_j$'s Mary and there$_i$'s John.'
a-IX(Mary) LOVE b-IX(John).
'She$_j$ loves him$_i$.'
b-IX(John) EXTREME-DISTASTE-a.
'He$_i$ doesn't like her$_j$.'

In sign languages, reflexive pronouns make use of the same deictic system as personal pronouns, but they have a different phonological form, involving a distinct handshape or orientation. In ASL, the handshape is used for reflexives; in ISL it is the handshape, produced with the index finger pointing upward and the back of the hand facing toward the referent locus. These forms are illustrated in Figure 21.3. It is also possible to produce the ASL SELF sign with the dominant hand while the non-dominant hand articulates the 'upright being' classifier (usually the SELF hand taps the classifier).

The ASL sign glossed SELF clearly has more uses than a simple reflexive (just as the pointing sign has more uses than personal pronouns), some of which have been mentioned in the literature. We will restrict our attention to regular reflexive contexts.

The ASL reflexive pronoun can be used when the object of a plain verb is coreferential with the subject, as in (6a). Meir (1998b) described the reflexive form of agreeing verbs in ISL as signed facing the location of the subject/object, beginning in a neutral location, with minimal movement in the direction of the goal, as shown in Figure 21.4. This is the same form that the verb takes in ASL; in such cases the reflexive may also be used, as in (6b). Verbs which may be considered inherently reflexive, such as BATHE in (6c) and SHAVE are often signed on the body, with no reflexive sign, using a body lean toward the locus established for the subject of the verb. These forms are illustrated in Figure 21.5.

Figure 21.2 Sentences using pronouns (ASL)

a. MYSELF (ASL)

b. HIMSELF (ISL)

Figure 21.3 Different handshapes for reflexive pronouns in two sign languages

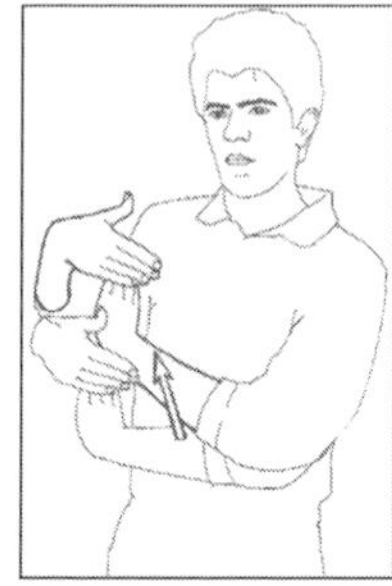

Figure 21.4 $_{1}$HELP$_{1}$ (ISL) (reprinted with permission from Meir 1998b, p. 18)

(6) ASL

a. a-JOHN LIKE a-SELF.
'John likes himself.'

b. a-JOHN a-HELP-a a-SELF.
'John helps himself.'

c. a-JOHN a-BATHE.
'John bathed himself.'

21.1.2 Personal pronoun system – issues

As the pronominal system is so described, several important issues become apparent. The most striking is the observation that there would seem to be an unlimited number of pronoun signs in ASL, each of which unambiguously picks out a referent, rather than a class of referents.[4] The unambiguous reference of ASL pronouns is illustrated in (7)–(8).

[4] Emmorey (2002) points out that Janis (1992) observes that referential locations may be ambiguous between a location and a referent at a location. There may be differences in the articulation of signs indicating these two concepts, however. Pronoun signs are generally directed in a horizontal plane, but locative points may be directed toward a lower location, using a small arc movement. Alternatively, distant locations (including loci representing cities and countries) may use pointing directed slightly higher, as Carol Padden reminds us. See Unit 5 for further discussion.

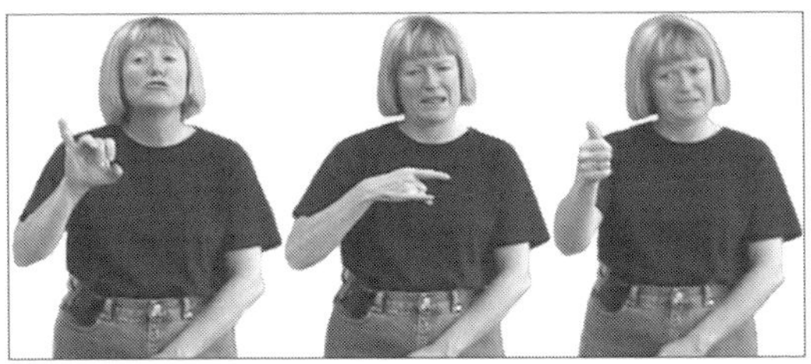

a. a-JOHN LIKE a-SELF

b. a-JOHN a-HELP-a a-SELF

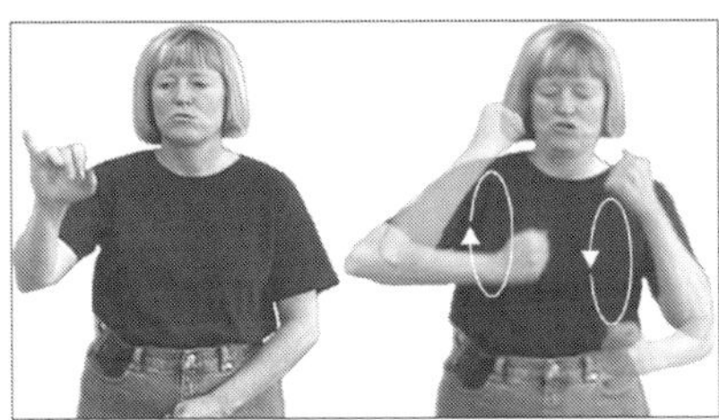

c. a-JOHN a-BATHE

Figure 21.5 Reflexive forms (ASL)

(7) ASL

a. a-GOVERNOR FEEL a-IX(Gov) INTELLIGENT.
'The governor$_i$ thinks he$_i$ is intelligent.'

b. a-GOVERNOR FEEL b-IX(he) INTELLIGENT.
'The governor$_i$ thinks he$_j$ is intelligent.'

(8) ASL

a. a-GOVERNOR TELL-b b-SENATOR c:e-IX(they) SHOULD c:e-LEAVE.
'The governor$_i$ told the senator$_j$ that they$_k$ should leave.'

b. a-GOVERNOR TELL-b b-SENATOR b:d-IX(they) SHOULD b:d-LEAVE.
'The governor$_i$ told the senator$_j$ that they$_{j,k}$ should leave.'

c. a-GOVERNOR TELL-b b-SENATOR a:b-IX(they) SHOULD a:b-LEAVE.
'The governor$_i$ told the senator$_j$ that they$_{i,j}$ should leave.'

Pronouns in spoken languages do not identify particular referents, even within a domain of discourse – they establish which referents within the domain are among the possibilities, by virtue of the features they encode. This means that in (9) for example, *they* is ambiguous between the governor and the senator, people other than the governor and the senator, or any combination of these. In sign languages, however, there is no such ambiguity, as the pronouns pick out a unique locus for each referent. What kind of grammatical model is required for such a system?

(9) The governor told the senator that they should leave.

First, let us consider the question, what features do sign language pronouns indicate? Features commonly marked in pronouns across spoken languages are person, number and gender (see McBurney 2002 for an insightful summary of spoken language pronominal systems and comparison with ASL and five other sign languages). We consider them in reverse order.

As there is no distinction between masculine and feminine pronouns in ASL and many other sign languages, it is clear that gender features are not marked in these languages. However, Japanese Sign Language is reported to have gender marking in its pronominal system. Fischer (1996) gives (10) as an example of gender marking in JSL pronouns. In this example, the sign glossed INDEX$_{a\text{-}I}$ is produced with two hands. While the non-dominant hand articulates the "I" handshape which indicates females in a particular location ("a"), the dominant hand points to this handshape/location.[5]

(10) JSL (Fischer 1996, p. 110)
MOTHER$_a$ COOK CAN INDEX$_{a\text{-}I}$.
'Mother can cook, she can.'
(INDEX$_{a\text{-}I}$ simultaneously indicates gender and location)

What about number? Pronoun signs do show marking for number. There are distinct forms for singular, dual, and both distributive and non-distributive multiple forms in ASL and other sign languages. Some examples of these are given in Figure 21.6. McBurney (2002) provides a more detailed description of sign language differences with respect to number marking.

Finally, what about person? It has frequently been said that sign language pronouns distinguish first, second, and third person, like pronoun systems in spoken languages (e.g., Friedman 1975; see also Berenz and Ferreira-Brito 1990 on BCSL). The first-person form involves pointing to oneself; and the second-person form involves pointing to the addressee, with concomitant eye gaze to the addressee (Baker and Padden 1978, Friedman 1975). What form does the third-person pronoun take? It involves pointing to the locations associated with present or non-present referents.

Meier (1990) and Lillo-Martin and Klima (1990) point out problems with the earlier assessments of ASL pronouns, which treated them as expressing person features. They observe that the location of the addressee (as opposed to other referents) is not something the grammatical system

[5] McBurney (2002) reports that such examples might be better analyzed as a separate morphological process rather than gender marking in the pronominal system.

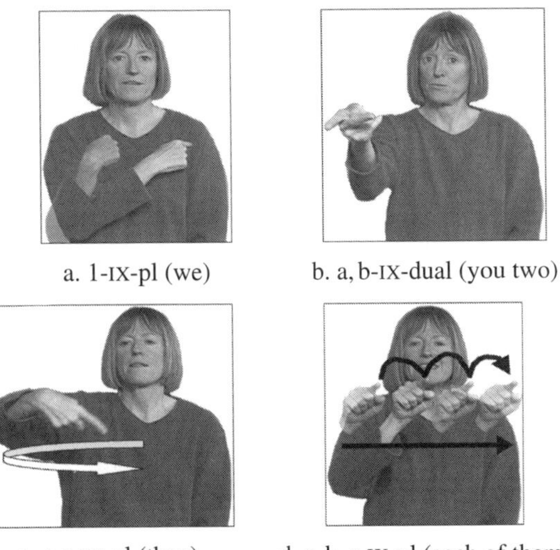

a. 1-IX-pl (we) b. a, b-IX-dual (you two)

c. a-c-IX-pl (they) d. a, b, c-IX-pl (each of them)

Figure 21.6 ASL personal pronominals (plural)

by itself can determine – it requires access to the specific discourse situation to determine which referent is currently addressed. Worse, the description of the third-person form cannot be specified for location – any location in the signing space can be used for a referent, and this requires a non-finite number of locations. Thus, the distinction between second and third person does not appear to be linguistically significant in ASL.

Meier does, however, provide arguments to support the grammatical distinction in ASL between first and non-first person. First, he notes that the form for first person doesn't vary across signers or discourse situations, unlike the non-first form. Thus, this form could be listed in the lexicon without any problem. Then, he notes differences in the plural forms of first and non-first pronouns. The non-first plural form is compositional: it combines the handshape and location of the singular form with an arc movement (as in Figure 21.6c). However, the first-person form is not compositional: rather than an arc at the first-person location, it consists of two contacts on the signer's chest (as shown in Figure 21.6a). Meier also notices the special use of first-person forms in what is commonly called "role play," to be discussed further in Section 21.1.3. In order to pick out the first-person sign as special in these circumstances, a distinct lexical entry for first person is needed. Thus, Meier argues that ASL makes a person distinction between first and non-first, but not between second and third. Numerous other sign language researchers have adopted this point of view as well (e.g., Engberg-Pedersen 1993).

If there is a grammatical distinction between first and non-first person, but not between second and third, what is it that accounts for the variety of non-first forms observed? In some cases, researchers have explicitly (or implicitly) considered the different forms to be representing distinct person features. Neidle et al. (2000, p. 31) claim explicitly that "spatial locations constitute an overt instantiation of ϕ-features (specifically, person features)," specifying further, "although … there is a primary distinction between first and nonfirst persons, nonfirst person can be further subclassified into many distinct person values" (pp. 166–167). This state of affairs makes ASL typologically quite unusual.

Lillo-Martin and Klima (1990) focus on the linguistic status of the various non-first-person forms. They consider it an unacceptable state of affairs for linguistic theory to have to posit an unlimited number of pronoun signs in signed languages (though not in any spoken language). Instead, they analyze ASL pronouns into two parts: one PRONOUN sign listed in the lexicon and a referential index. The referential index is the sort linguistic theory hypothesizes is assigned to every noun phrase, used to indicate interpretation and to check adherence to Binding Theory constraints on pronominals and anaphors. Suppose NPs in ASL, like those of spoken languages, have assigned referential indices. Then, for ASL, unlike for spoken languages, the referential indices can be overtly realized, in the form of distinct locations in signing space.[6] Thus whether coreference or non-coindexing is intended (as in (11)-(12)) will be clear.[7]

(11) ASL

a. a:c-SENATOR a:c-ALL FEEL a,b,c-IX INTELLIGENT.
'Every senator$_i$ thinks that he$_i$ is intelligent.'

b. a:c-SENATOR a:c-ALL FEEL d-IX INTELLIGENT.
'Every senator$_i$ thinks that he$_j$ is intelligent.'

c. a:c-SENATOR a:c-ALL FEEL a:c-IX INTELLIGENT.
'All the senators$_i$ think that they$_i$ are intelligent.'
(both group and individual readings)

(12) ASL

a. $\overline{\text{WHICH SENATOR a:c-IX FEEL b-IX INTELLIGENT WHICH?}}^{\text{whq}}$
'Which senator(s)$_i$ thinks that he$_i$ is intelligent?'

b. $\overline{\text{WHICH SENATOR a:c-IX FEEL d-IX INTELLIGENT WHICH?}}^{\text{whq}}$
'Which senator(s)$_i$ thinks that he$_j$ is intelligent?'

c. $\overline{\text{WHICH SENATOR a:c-IX FEEL a:c-IX INTELLIGENT WHICH?}}^{\text{whq}}$
'Which senators$_i$ think that they$_i$ are intelligent?'

[6] When phonologically permitted, NPs can also be signed in particular locations – as an overt realization of their referential index. Cf. Chapter 20, Section 20.1.

[7] Lillo-Martin and Klima suggest that for optimal generality only one pronoun need be listed in the lexicon, rejecting the distinction between first and non-first forms made by Meier. However, in more recent work Lillo-Martin (1995, 2002) has adopted Meier's proposed first vs. non-first distinction, while maintaining the account she and Klima proposed for the apparent multiplicity of non-first forms. This approach maintains that ASL makes a grammatical distinction between first and non-first person, but *not* between many different non-first referents.

How, then, do SL pronouns fit into the scheme of pronouns cross-linguistically? There is an important effect of modality, in that the referential index associated with pronouns is realized overtly in sign languages, but not in spoken languages. Note, however, that this effect in itself has no bearing on syntactic structure: even if it is true that sign and spoken languages differ in this way, the syntactic representations of pronouns and the sentences that contain them is not different (see also Lillo-Martin 1997, 2002).[8] In both modalities, pronouns bear a referential index and are subject to the same constraints.

However, there are remaining questions regarding this analysis, such as how it relates to the analysis of verb agreement, and how the overtly realized indices are analyzed linguistically. These issues are discussed further in Chapter 25, because they relate to the way that spatial information is used in sign languages, a case of the non-universal cropping up.

21.1.3 Point of view and logophoricity

Many papers have described a phenomenon known as "role shift," "role switching," or "referential shift" in sign languages. As usually described, this is a process whereby a signer "takes on a role" of a character in a discourse (Loew 1984, Kegl 1986, Lentz 1986, Padden 1986, 1990, Liddell 1990a, Lillo-Martin and Klima 1990, Meier 1990, Poulin and Miller 1995). By shifting the body position, and possibly changing aspects of the facial expression, the signer presents another's words, thoughts, or "point of view."

On the first encounter, "role shift" may seem to be something very unlike anything in spoken languages. For example, Mandel (1977, pp. 79–80) says,

> It is common for a signer to take the role of a person being discussed ... When two or more people are being talked about, the signer can shift from one role to another and back; and he usually uses spatial relationships to indicate this ROLE-SWITCHING. In talking about a conversation between two people, for instance, a signer may alternate roles to speak each person's lines in turn, taking one role by shifting his stance (or just his head) slightly to the right and facing slightly leftward (thus representing that person as being on the right in the conversation), and taking the other role by the reverse position ... Similar role-switching can occur in nonquotative narrative ... A signer may describe

[8] As Željko Bošković points out to us, adding indices during the syntactic derivation is a violation of the "Inclusiveness Condition," part of the most recent theoretical framework known as the Minimalist Program (Chomsky 1995, Chapter 4). According to the Minimalist Program, a derivation is seen as starting from a "numeration," which is a set of all the lexical elements to be employed. The Inclusiveness Condition requires that no new elements be added during the syntactic computation, but indices have traditionally been added during the derivation. In order for the analysis proposed here to be compatible with the Inclusiveness Condition, it would probably be necessary to consider the indices as part of the numeration. As Chomsky points out, such a step should only be taken "when forced by empirical properties of language" (p. 381).

> not only what was done by the person whose role he is playing, but also what happened to that person.

While this description of role switching is mainly about quotation, Thompson (1977, p. 190) claims that there is no distinction between direct and indirect speech in ASL. Is role switching how signers indicate both direct and indirect speech? What about the non-quotative uses of role switching? Is this an area where the visual modality permits sign language to do something unique? Role shift clearly involves discourse structures. However, a better understanding of the syntax of structures with role shift will help us to see whether this is a special effect of the modality or not.

In many ways role shift or referential shift does behave like direct discourse in spoken languages (cf. Banfield 1973). It is frequently used in contexts of direct discourse, when quoting another's words. An example of an extended quoted discourse is given in (13).[9] Video grabs of another example are given in Figure 21.7.

(13) ASL (Lillo-Martin 1995, p. 157)[10]

a. HUSBAND SAY

< $_{a}$shift>

($_{a}$SHIFT) FINE, YES, TAKE-PILLS MEDICINE.

'My husband said, "OK, fine, (you) must take your medicine." '

< $_{b}$shift>

ynq

b. ($_{b}$SHIFT) $_{1}$PRONOUN WILL BETTER?

'(His mother replied), "Will I get better?" '

< $_{a}$shift>

c. ($_{a}$SHIFT) WILL, WILL.

'You will.'

< $_{b}$shift>

whq

d. ($_{b}$SHIFT) HOW LONG?

'How long will it take?'

< $_{a}$shift>

e. ($_{a}$SHIFT) $_{1}$PRONOUN DUNNO.

'I don't know.'

What is frequently called role shift is used much more extensively than simply for direct discourse, however, as noted in the quote from Mandel. It can be described as quoting the thoughts of another or simply representing a scene from the point of view of another (this terminology is used by Engberg-Pedersen 1993, 1995, Lillo-Martin 1995, Poulin and Miller 1995, and others). Additional examples are given in (14)–(15).

[9] In these examples, the shift of the body/facial expression is notated both in the gloss line and above the non-manual line as "shift."

[10] This example has been changed slightly from the published text to fix a formatting error.

Figure 21.7 Referential shift (ASL)

(14) ASL (Meier 1990, p. 184)

YESTERDAY INDEX$_S$ SEE$_j$ GIRL.

WALK $_j$PERSON-WALK-TO$_k$

gaze down

mm .... gaze i

$_1$[WALK. .... LOOK-UP$_i$.

gaze i .... gaze i .... gaze i

MAN $_i$PERSON-MOVE-TO$_s$. .... INDEX$_s$ SCARED. .... HIT$_s$]$_1$

'Yesterday I saw this girl. She walked by in front of me. She was strolling along, then she looked up and saw this man come up to her. "I'm scared" [she said]. He hit her.'

(15) ASL (Padden 1986)

< $_a$shift >

$_a$HUSBAND (SHIFT) WORK.

'The husband was like – "here I am, working." '

Lillo-Martin (1995) notices that what referential shift conveys is very similar to what is conveyed with the colloquial English use of *like*, as in, *He's like, I can't believe you did that! Like* need not convey direct discourse, but portrays the point of view of its subject. This usage is reflected in Padden's translation of (15).

Engberg-Pedersen (1993), working on Danish Sign Language, divides role shifting into three separate phenomena, as given in (16).

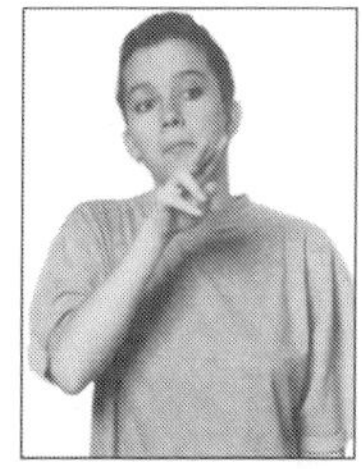

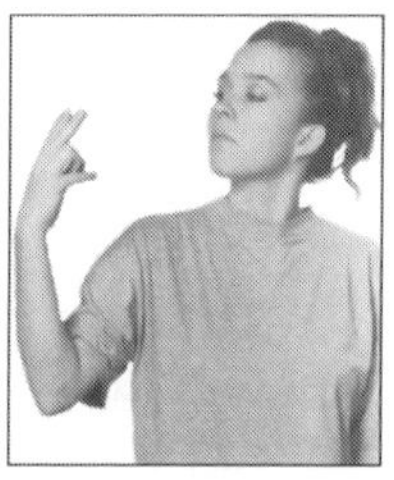

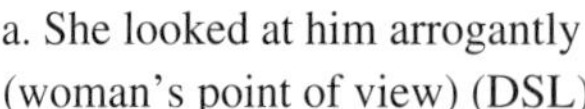

a. She looked at him arrogantly (woman's point of view) (DSL)

b. She looked at him arrogantly (man's point of view) (DSL)

Figure 21.8 Distinction between shifted attribution of expressive elements and shifted locus (illustrations provided by Elisebeth Engberg-Pedersen, p. c.)

(16) (Engberg-Pedersen 1993, p. 103)

i. *shifted reference*, i.e., the use of pronouns from a quoted sender's point of view, especially the use of the first-person pronoun 1.p to refer to somebody other than the quoting sender;

ii. *shifted attribution of expressive elements*, i.e., the use of the signer's face and/or body posture to express the emotions or attitude of somebody other than the sender in the context of utterance;

iii. *shifted locus*, i.e. the use of the sender locus for somebody other than the signer or the use of another locus than the locus *c* for the signer.

In shifted reference, which Engberg-Pedersen says is confined to direct discourse, the first-person pronoun (1.p in her notation) is used to refer to someone other than the signer; that is, the person quoted. In shifted attribution of expressive elements, the signer's signs, face, and body express the emotions or attitude of another. This may be within a direct discourse, but does not necessarily have to be; it may be within "represented thought." Engberg-Pedersen compares shifted attribution of expressive elements to the use of voice quality to distinguish speakers in reported dialogues in spoken languages. Shifted locus is similar to shifted reference, in that the signer's locus is used for reference to another. However, it is not limited to direct discourse, and unlike shifted reference, the signer may also be referred to through a distinct locus. Shifted locus is not always marked overtly by a change in body position.

Engberg-Pedersen shows interesting ways in which these different characteristics of "role play" are separable. For example, the signer's locus can be used to refer to one character under shifted locus, while the facial expression conveys the attitude of a different character under shifted attribution of expressive elements. An example is given in Figure 21.8.

Both panels of Figure 21.8 show the verb LOOK-AT and, in both, the signer's face is used to express the woman's (subject's) point of view.

However, the verb agreement is different in the two panels. In Figure 21.8a, the verb shows regular agreement with the object/goal (the man). However, in Figure 21.8b, the verb uses the first-person locus for the object/goal agreement. This means that while the signer's locus is used to represent the man for purposes of verb agreement (under shifted locus), it is representing the woman for the shifted attribution of expressive elements.

How can these distinct uses of the signer's locus be accounted for? We agree with Engberg-Pedersen's analogy to voice quality in the use of facial expressions to convey expressive elements. That is, while changes in facial expressions to convey the attitudes of others is used along with language, it is not a part of the grammatical system, but paralinguistic (Ladd 1996).

On the other hand, the use of the first-person locus – a grammatically significant contrast – for referents other than the signer should be accounted for within the grammar. According to Engberg-Pedersen, this use of the first-person locus for verb agreement can be found in direct speech and in other contexts. However, the use of the first-person pronoun for referents other than the signer as in (13b) above is restricted to direct speech contexts. This distinction also requires further consideration. In general, the mechanisms for pronouns and verb agreement involve the same features. It is difficult to see how to reconcile the use of the first-person locus for verb agreement, but not for pronouns, since pronouns and verb agreement pick out the same features. However, perhaps the "shifted locus" does not truly use the first-person locus, but the same sort of mechanism described by Bahan (1996) as subject agreement, involving head tilt and body lean. If this is the case, then the agreement under shifted locus does not mark first person.

Another consideration regarding Engberg-Pedersen's distinction between shifted reference (16i) and shifted locus (16iii) is the restriction to direct discourse she says holds only for shifted reference in DSL. In ASL, as we have seen, shifted reference is not so restricted: the first-person pronoun can be used to refer to someone other than the signer in contexts that go beyond direct discourse, quoting the words of another, to "quoting" the thoughts or point of view of another. Further investigation of this potential difference between the languages is desirable.

While "referential shift" has received a fair amount of attention in the literature, there have not been many attempts to analyze it syntactically. One analysis (Lillo-Martin 1995) compares shifted reference with the use of a logophoric pronoun in some spoken languages. In languages such as Abe, Ewe, and Gokana, a so-called "logophoric pronoun" is used in the embedded clause of certain verbs, especially verbs which convey another's point of view, to indicate coreference with a matrix subject or object (Clements 1975, Hyman and Comrie 1981, Sells 1987, Koopman and Sportiche 1989). An example from Ewe is given in (17b).

(17) Ewe (Clements 1975)

a. Kofi se Kɔku wò-nɔ e dzu-m
Kofi hear Koku pro-be pro insult-Asp
'Kofi$_i$ heard Koku$_j$ insulting him$_i$.'

b. Ama se be yè-xɔ nunana
Ama hear that Log-receivegift
'Ama$_i$ heard that she$_i$ had received a gift.'

In (17a), a regular embedded clause is used with no logophoric pronoun. In (17b), however, the complementizer *be* introduces an embedded clause which takes a logophoric pronoun, *yè*. The logophoric pronoun is triggered by this complementizer, which is historically related to a main verb for 'say.' The logophoric pronoun must be coreferential with the matrix subject.

Lillo-Martin (1995) proposes that the ASL first-person pronominal form can serve as a logophoric pronoun in addition to its normal use. Thus, in logophoric contexts (within the scope of a referential shift), the logophoric pronoun refers to the matrix subject, not its usual first-person referent.

Lillo-Martin further proposes that ASL referential shift involves a point-of-view predicate, which she glosses as POV. POV takes a subject which it agrees with, and a clausal complement. This means that the "quoted" material is understood as embedded whether or not there is an overt matrix verb. Any first-person pronouns in the complement to the POV predicate are logophoric; they are interpreted as coreferential with the subject of POV. According to Lillo-Martin's proposal, the structure of a sentence with POV, such as (18), is as in (19).

(18) < $_a$shift>
$_a$MOM $_a$POV $_1$PRONOUN. BUSY.
'Mom (from mom's point of view), I'm busy.'
='Mom's like, I'm busy!'

(19) (Lillo-Martin 1995, p. 162)

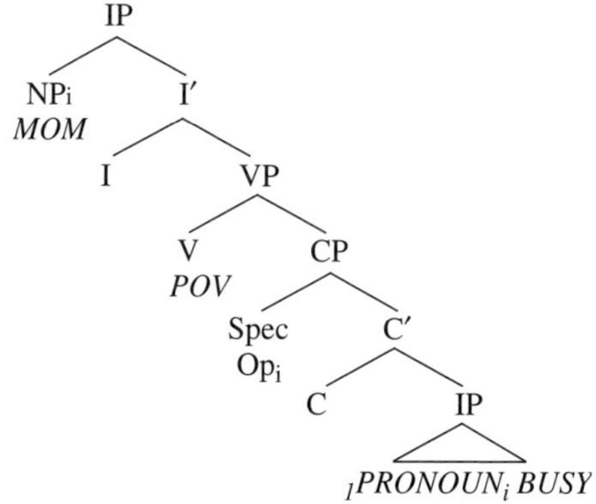

According to the structure in (19), POV takes a complement clause. This CP may be introduced by an abstract syntactic operator, labeled Op.[11] The operator is bound by the subject of POV – the subject c-commands it and they are coindexed. The operator also binds all logophoric pronouns which it c-commands – hence, all "$_{1}$PRONOUN$_{s}$" in the complement clause are interpreted as coreferential with the subject of POV.

Lillo-Martin provides various kinds of supporting evidence for this proposal.[12] The first involves reflexives. In order to present this argument, it is necessary to briefly go over aspects of the distribution of reflexives in ASL.

In ASL, as in English, a reflexive may be bound within a certain syntactic domain. Lillo-Martin finds that in ASL, the domain for binding a reflexive is somewhat different than that for English. In particular, ASL, but not English, permits a reflexive in embedded subject position to be coreferential with a noun phrase in the immediately higher clause. This is illustrated in (20).

(20) ASL (Lillo-Martin 1995, p. 166)
$_{a}$LOWELL FEEL $_{a}$SELF/$_{a}$PRONOUN INTELLIGENT.
Lowell$_{i}$ thinks himself$_{i}$/he$_{i}$ is intelligent.

However, this broadening of the syntactic domain for binding an anaphor seems to be quite limited. A reflexive in embedded object position cannot be bound by an element outside the embedded clause, as in (21a). And a subject reflexive cannot be bound by an element two clauses up, as in (21b). An account of these facts must await a more wide-scale study of the distribution of pronouns and anaphors in ASL, but the observations just made will play a role in supporting the logophoric pronoun analysis.

(21) a. $_{a}$LOWELL WANT $_{b}$WORKER RESPECT *$_{a}$SELF/$_{a}$PRONOUN
'Lowell$_{i}$ wants the worker to respect *himself$_{i}$/him$_{i}$.'
b. $_{a}$LOWELL THINK $_{b}$WORKER FEEL *$_{a}$SELF/$_{b}$SELF RIGHT
'Lowell$_{i}$ thinks the worker$_{j}$ feels *he$_{i}$/he$_{j}$ is right.'

An important generalization from the observations just made is that a reflexive may be bound by an element in the next highest clause only. Lillo-Martin finds that a reflexive may follow a "role shift" in certain circumstances. Under the POV predicate analysis, a reflexive can occur in what would be the embedded subject position following a POV predicate. As with other reflexives in embedded subject position, the reflexive must be coreferential with an element in the matrix clause – in this case, the subject. As expected if POV is a predicate, a reflexive in a further

[11] Operators A′-bind variables, and contribute in some way to the interpretation.
[12] Additional evidence concerning WH-questions and topics will not be addressed here.

embedded clause may be coreferential with the next highest subject or object; but it cannot be coreferential with the matrix subject if further embedded. In other words, the reflexive can only go one clause up to seek its antecedent – and the clause is defined by the POV predicate. This is illustrated in (22). The contrast between (22a) and (22c) is important to the postulation of a POV predicate. If there is no POV predicate (remember, there is no manual sign in these examples), the relationship between the first noun GOVERNOR and the rest of the sentence is not one of embedding. Possibly, the noun simply introduces the speaker, as in a script. In this case, the impossibility of the reflexive referring back to the speaker in (22c) is understandable: the reflexive is not bound. However, if this logic is applied to (22a), the reflexive should be ruled out. If (22a) is allowed because the reflexive can somehow access the noun or does not require binding, why does (22c) not allow the reflexive to be coreferential with GOVERNOR?

(22) ASL (Lillo-Martin 1995, p. 167)

< $_a$POV >
a. $_a$GOVERNOR $_a$POV $_1$SELF PAY TAX HIGH.
'The governor's like, "I pay high taxes." '

<
b. $_a$GOVERNOR $_a$POV
$_a$POV >
$_b$SENATE $_b$PERSUADE$_c$ $_c$WORKER $_{b/c}$SELF PAY TAX HIGH.
'The governor's like, "The senate persuaded the worker that it/he pays high taxes." '

<
c. $_a$GOVERNOR $_a$POV
$_a$POV >
$_b$WORKER FEEL $_{b/*a}$SELF PAY TAX HIGH.
'The governor's like, "The worker thinks he/*I pays high taxes." '

The second piece of supporting evidence Lillo-Martin provides comes from VP ellipsis. She follows a conventional assumption that the interpretation of the second conjunct in VP ellipsis involves copying the interpretation of the first conjunct (Reinhart 1983), as illustrated in (23).

(23) ASL (Lillo-Martin 1995, p. 167)
a. $_a$ROSS $_a$GONE; $_b$JERRY SAME.
'Ross is gone; Jerry is too.'
b. Interpretation:
Ross is gone; Jerry is gone.

When VP ellipsis involves pronouns, the second conjunct is interpreted according to the interpretation of the pronoun in the first conjunct. This pronoun can be bound, if it is in the proper structural relationship to another element (as we have seen). In this regard, consider (24).

(24) ASL (Lillo-Martin 1995, p. 168)

a. ${}_{a}$JOHN THINK ${}_{a}$PRONOUN HAVE MUMPS, ${}_{b}$MARY SAME.
'John$_i$ thinks he$_i$ has the mumps, and Mary$_j$ does too.'

b. Interpretations:

i. John$_i$ thinks he$_i$ has the mumps, and Mary$_j$ thinks Mary$_j$ has the mumps.
ii. John$_i$ thinks he$_i$ has the mumps, and Mary$_j$ thinks John$_i$ has the mumps.

If the ${}_{a}$pronoun in (24a) is interpreted as bound (by the matrix subject ${}_{a}$JOHN) in the first conjunct, then it will be interpreted as bound in the second conjunct. That is, in the second conjunct the pronoun must be bound by an appropriate binder – the subject of the second conjunct. Under this interpretation, Mary thinks Mary has the mumps (this is the so-called "sloppy" interpretation).

However, if the pronoun is not bound, it will be interpreted as coreferential with John (that is, it has the same reference but is not coindexed). In this case, the pronoun will be interpreted as coreferential with John in the second clause. Under this interpretation, Mary thinks John has the mumps (the so-called "non-sloppy" or "strict" interpretation).

On the analysis of the logophoric ${}_{1}$PRONOUN as operator-bound, if it appears in the first conjunct of a VP ellipsis structure then this clause can only have the bound pronoun reading. This is because the non-bound reading is only possible when the pronoun is free to take reference – but a pronoun bound by an operator is not so free. Therefore, the VP ellipsis conjunct should only permit the sloppy interpretation. This prediction is accurate, as illustrated in (25).

(25) ASL (Lillo-Martin 1995, p. 168)

< ${}_{a}$POV >
a. ${}_{a}$JOHN ${}_{a}$POV ${}_{1}$PRONOUN THINK ${}_{1}$PRONOUN HAVE MUMPS, ${}_{b}$MARY SAME.
'John's like, "I think I have the mumps"; and Mary is too.'

b. Interpretation:
John$_i$ thinks he$_i$ has the mumps, and Mary$_j$ thinks Mary$_j$ has the mumps.
Not:
John$_i$ thinks he$_i$ has the mumps, and Mary$_j$ thinks he$_i$ has the mumps.

This analysis has focused on the use of the first-person pronoun. However, the use of the signer's locus for non-signer reference is also employed in the verb agreement system, since verb agreement makes use of referential loci, as we have seen. This may take place even when there is no overt first-person pronoun accompanying the verb, since ASL permits null arguments (as we will see in Section 21.2). This use of "logophoric verb agreement" does not require any mechanisms beyond those already discussed. Agreeing verbs agree with their arguments, so if the verb's subject or object is first-person logophoric, the verb will also be marked for first person.

A different analysis proposes that the clause following a verb of saying is simply another sentence, with a discourse-based relationship to the first clause, as in (26) (Lee, Neidle, MacLaughlin, Bahan, and Kegl 1997). The authors of this proposal argue against Lillo-Martin's logophoric analysis of referential shift, specifically within the context of direct discourse, i.e., with an explicit verb of saying.

(26) ASL (Lee et al. 1997, p. 24)

$\overline{\text{JOHN}_i \text{ SAY IX}_{1pi} \text{ WANT GO}}^{rs_i}$
'John said: "I want to go."'

Lee et al. point out that under the POV analysis, it would be expected to be possible to have an overt subject, a verb of saying, then an embedded subject of POV distinct from the matrix subject, as in (27).

(27) ASL (Lee et al. 1997, p. 42)

$\text{*JOHN}_i \text{ TELL}_j \text{ MARY}_j \text{ [BILL}_k \overline{\text{IX}_{1pk} \text{ WANT GO}}^{rs_i}\text{]}$

Lee et al. do not provide a target interpretation for the example in (27). However, it would be acceptable with the following interpretation: 'John told Mary that Bill was like, "I wanna go!."' Since Lee et al. only consider cases with overt verbs of saying, they do not consider this possibility.

As for the arguments provided by Lillo-Martin from reflexives, Lee et al. suggest that the embedded subject reflexive in sentences like (22) is simply an emphatic, as in, *The governor said, "I myself pay high taxes."* However, their proposal does not account for the restrictions on this reflexive observed in (22c). If it is an emphatic form, there is no explanation for why it cannot occur in those contexts. Under the logophoric analysis, the distribution falls out from the structure proposed and the observation that certain long-distance binding of reflexives is generally permitted in ASL. Lee et al. do not respond to Lillo-Martin's arguments using VP ellipsis, as in (25).[13]

We conclude that the logophoric analysis of pronouns under referential shift accounts for their syntactic distribution. Further aspects of their usage in discourse require more extensive study and analysis. Furthermore, ASL should be explored more systematically in light of the distinction Engberg-Pedersen (1995) found in Danish Sign Language between shifted reference and shifted locus.

We have seen that what appeared at first to be highly unusual, play-acting in the middle of syntax, is, on closer observation, not unlike the properties of spoken language. The use of facial expressions to indicate attitudes is very similar to the parallel use of voice quality, and should be considered paralinguistic. On the other hand, the use of the first-person

[13] They do argue against Lillo-Martin's evidence from WH-questions and topics. These arguments are not presented here, as they involve other areas of dispute to be discussed in Section 21.2 below and Chapter 23.

pronoun to pick out referents other than the signer is a linguistic characteristic which occurs in particular structural configurations with predictable systematic interpretations. Both of these, then, indicate that the mechanisms needed to account for spoken languages are those used by sign languages as well.

We have so far concentrated on overt pronouns – the kind that can be seen and heard. However, in many languages, it is argued that noun phrases can be null – syntactically present, but not pronounced. Such "null arguments" come in two types of languages – those with rich agreement morphology, and those with none. Since sign languages have verbs of both types, how do they fare with respect to null arguments? The proposal that both kinds of null arguments are found in one and the same language is the topic of the next section.

21.2 Two kinds of null arguments in ASL?

21.2.1 Null arguments and agreement

Certain spoken languages permit pronouns to be phonologically null, in examples like (28).

(28) Spanish
a. Hablo Español.
'(I-)speak Spanish.'
b. Hablas Español.
'(You-)speak Spanish.'
c. Habla Español.
'(She/he/it-)speaks Spanish.'

In these examples, the agreement on the verb (*-o*, *-as*, *-a*) marks the identity of the subject as first, second, or third person singular, respectively. Thus, although there is no overt subject pronominal, it can be inferred that a pronoun with which the verb agrees is present – a null pronoun. This null pronoun, called *pro*, has the properties of an overt pronoun except that it has no phonological form (Chomsky 1982). It is because such examples behave as if an overt pronoun were present that linguists have come to assume the presence of a null pronoun. For example, it is well-known that different verbs require particular types of subjects (referential, expletive, etc.). In languages which permit null pronouns, this requirement is met even if the subject is null. More strikingly, null pronouns can "save" a structure from violating constraints on movement, just the way overt pronouns can (McCloskey and Hale 1984).

Languages with a rich system of overt morphological agreement tend to allow null pronouns. Most examples have subject agreement only, and null arguments are generally limited to subject position in such languages (e.g., Spanish, Italian,[14] Catalan, Modern Hebrew). Others, with object agreement, also permit null objects (e.g. Choctaw, Palauan, Pashto, Warlpiri). It is said that the rich verbal morphology "licenses" the null arguments in these cases. This trade-off is not absolute, however. Some languages with relatively rich verbal morphology do not freely allow null arguments (e.g., Brazilian Portuguese, German, Insular Scandinavian). In some cases, such languages may be in transition between a null-argument language and a non-null-argument language; in others, some mechanism other than agreement may be relevant to the licensing of null arguments.

In addition to being licensed, referential null pronouns must be identified – that is, the pronominal features should be determined (Rizzi 1986). In the cases under discussion here, licensing and identification both come from agreement. It is the rich agreement which licenses the null pronouns and determines their pronominal features (e.g., first person singular). A distinction between licensing and identification can be seen in languages which allow only non-referential, expletive subjects to be null (e.g., Icelandic). In these cases, null subjects are licensed, but the agreement morphology is not rich enough to identify the person/number of the subject. Thus, only subjects which don't need identification – non-referential subjects – are allowed to be null.

21.2.2 Null arguments without agreement

Null arguments are not restricted to languages with rich verbal morphology. Some languages which do not inflect for agreement at all nevertheless permit productive null arguments.[15] Prominent examples include Japanese and Chinese.

Researchers disagree as to whether the null arguments in languages like Japanese and Chinese are *pro*, the null pronominal, or another empty category. Huang (1984) argues that null arguments in Chinese are not licensed by agreement, but by other aspects of the grammar of Chinese. In particular, he discusses the characterization of Chinese as a *discourse-oriented* language, and says that null arguments are licensed because of these characteristics. As we will see, this means that most null arguments in Chinese are not *pro*, on his account.

Huang proposes that Chinese has "a rule of coindexation in the discourse grammar . . . , which coindexes an empty topic node with an appropriate preceding topic" (Huang 1984, p. 550). This means that a string of sentences may be constructed with the same discourse topic, and

[14] See Rizzi (1986) for a discussion of some contexts in which objects may be null in Italian.

[15] Jaeggli and Safir (1989) observe that languages which allow null arguments are generally morphologically uniform – verbal paradigms are either uniformly inflected or uniformly uninflected.

that each sentence may have a syntactic topic even if it is a null element. This condition is schematized in (29). What the schema shows is that a particular sentence may have a null topic, which is coindexed with another topic earlier in the discourse. Although the sentential topic is null, it is syntactically present and participates in the syntax.[16]

(29) [Overt topic]$_i$, Sentence ... [Null topic]$_i$, Sentence ...

Because the null topic is syntactically present, it can bind an empty category (null element) within the sentence, on Huang's analysis. This situation is schematized in (30), and examples from Chinese are given in (31).[17] As the Chinese examples show, either the subject or the object – or both – may be null. Huang argues that in discourse-oriented languages, arguments are allowed to be null because they can be associated with null topics.

(30) [Null topic]$_i$, ... null argument$_i$ ...

(31) Chinese (Huang 1984, p. 533)

Speaker A: Zhangsan kanjian Lisi le ma?
Zhangsan see Lisi ASP Q
'Did Zhangsan see Lisi?'

Speaker B:

a. *e* kanjian ta le.
[He] see he ASP
'(He) saw him.'

b. ta kanjian *e* le.
He see [he] ASP
'He saw (him).'

c. *e* kanjian *e* le.
[He] see [he] ASP
'(He) saw (him).'

Because of the definitions of distinct empty categories assumed, an empty category bound by the topic is not considered a pronoun, but a variable. Thus, it is expected to show the behavior of a variable rather than that of a pronoun. This leads to an important part of the analysis of null arguments in languages like Chinese: do they behave more like pronouns or variables? On Huang's analysis, they are expected to behave like variables, in all cases except one. The exception is a case where, on

[16] Although Huang does not mention the possibility that the discourse topic itself would be null (that is, implied from the situation), it is necessary to allow for such cases.

[17] Huang uses the notation "e" for empty category to represent the null arguments in Chinese. We have italicized his *e*'s to make them stand out. Variables, as a type of trace, are usually represented by *t*, and we use this notation when not citing Huang.

Huang's theory, the null argument in Chinese can be a pronominal. We turn now to this case.

In order to account for the distribution of null and overt pronouns, Huang proposes the two universal principles in (32). These rules are intended to capture (part of) Huang's version of binding, which incorporates "control," the theory involved in the distribution and interpretation of PRO.[18] Huang makes no distinction between PRO and other pronouns, subjecting them all to Disjoint Reference and the Generalized Control Rule.

(32) a. Disjoint Reference (DJR)
A Pronoun must be free in its governing category
b. Generalized Control Rule (GCR)
Coindex an empty pronominal with the closest nominal element.
(Huang 1984, p. 552)

Given the DJR and the GCR, empty pronouns must be coindexed with the closest nominal element, but still free in their governing category. This means that a null matrix subject or object, or a null embedded object, could not be a pronoun. In these positions, bound empty pronominals will be ruled out by (32a), and unbound ones by (32b). Therefore, only the variable analysis is available for null arguments in these positions. Under these rules, there is only one syntactic position in which null pronominal arguments would be permitted in Chinese. A null pronoun in the embedded subject position, when coreferential with the matrix subject, satisfies both the DJR and the GCR, and is therefore licit. An example is given in (33).

(33) Chinese (Huang 1984, p. 533)
Zhangsan shuo *e* kanjian ta le.
Zhangsan say [he] see him ASP
'Zhangsan said (he) saw him.'

To sum up, there are two important aspects to Huang's account. One is his proposal that null arguments in discourse-oriented languages are licensed by null topics. The second is his proposal that in most cases, these null elements should be analyzed as variables rather than pronouns.

Other researchers dispute the division of null arguments into the *pro* type and the variable type. In particular, some argue that null arguments in languages like Japanese and Chinese are *pro*, because they do have pronominal characteristics (Saito 1985). There seem to be disagreements regarding the empirical status of crucial examples, such as examples with an embedded null object interpreted as coreferential with the matrix

[18] PRO is the null pronoun generally used as the subject of an infinitive and taking its reference from a matrix subject, as in 'John wants (PRO) to win.'

subject. According to Huang's proposal, this should not be permitted, but according to the *pro* hypothesis, this should be completely acceptable. Most discussions attribute a mixed status to such examples – they seem to be less than perfect, but not completely ungrammatical. Thus, we can ask, how different are the null arguments associated with agreement and those associated with discourse orientation?

Sign languages provide an excellent testing ground for this discussion. They have a rich agreement system, but only some verbs mark agreement. They are also discourse-oriented, in the same way that Chinese is (this property will be discussed further in Chapter 22). Thus, the behavior of sign languages with respect to null arguments might be extremely revealing about the nature of null arguments and the relationship between them, discourse orientation, and rich agreement.

21.2.3 Null arguments in ASL

Lillo-Martin (1986a, 1991) observes that in ASL, null arguments can occur with both plain verbs, as shown in (34)–(35), and with agreeing verbs, as in (36)–(37).

(34) ASL (Lillo-Martin 1986a, p. 421)
$_{a}$JOHN $_{a}$FLY$_{b}$ $_{b}$CALIFORNIA LAST-WEEK. ENJOY SUNBATHE[dur.].
'John flew to California last week. (He's) enjoying a lot of sunbathing.'

(35) ASL (Lillo-Martin 1986a, p. 421)
A. Did you eat my candy?
B. YES, EAT-UP.
'Yes, (I) ate (it) up.'

(36) ASL (Lillo-Martin 1986a, p. 421)
A. Did John send Mary the letter?
B. YES, $_{a}$SEND$_{b}$.
'Yes, (he-) sent (it) to (-her).'

(37) ASL (Lillo-Martin 1986a, p. 421)
a. $_{a}$JOHN KNOW-WELL PAPER FINISH $_{a}$GIVE$_{b}$.
'John$_{i}$ knows (he$_{i}$-) gave the paper to (-her).'
b. $_{a}$JOHN KNOW-WELL PAPER FINISH $_{b}$GIVE$_{a}$.
'John$_{i}$ knows (she$_{i}$-) gave the paper to (-him).'

Lillo-Martin argues that the empty category associated with null arguments of agreeing verbs, like null arguments in Italian and Irish, is *pro*. However, she claims that null arguments of agreeing verbs are different from null arguments of non-agreeing verbs. With agreeing verbs, *pro* acts as a resumptive pronoun; but this behavior is not seen with non-agreeing verbs. We turn now to examine the facts.

As we have seen in Chapter 18, ASL productively permits topics to appear in the sentence-initial position, as in (38).

(38) ASL (Liddell 1980, p. 84)

t n
CAT DOG CHASE.
'As for the cat, the dog didn't chase it.'

There are two possible sources for examples such as (38). Either the topic is moved to the sentence-initial position, or it is base-generated there. These two cases can be compared to the English versions given in (39).

(39) a. The cat, the dog chased.
b. As for the cat, the dog chased it.

In (39a), *the cat* has arguably moved from its position as the object of the verb. Otherwise, how would this verb's subcategorization requirement for an object be fulfilled? Thus, it is generally assumed that a movement operation known as topicalization is used in deriving (39a). In (39b), on the other hand, the verb's requirement to have an object is met by the pronoun *it*. Not only is there no need to employ a movement derivation, there is no obvious position from which the topic might have moved. Thus, examples such as (39b) are assumed to be base-generated. Such examples are known as left-dislocation structures.

If ASL allows null pronominal arguments, it may be difficult pretheoretically to distinguish between topicalization and left-dislocation structures for any particular example, as there is nothing corresponding to the English *as for* in ASL topic structures. This will be true for a variety of cases, since an object or oblique or even the subject may show up as a topic (see also Chapter 22). Therefore, we will refer to all such structures as "topics," in order to be neutral about the analysis until a particular treatment can be spelled out.[19]

Padden (1988 [1983]) observes that topics can be associated with positions in an embedded clause, as discussed in Chapter 18 and illustrated in (40), where the topic EXERCISE CLASS is understood as the object of the deeply embedded verb TAKE-UP.

(40) ASL (Padden 1988 [1983], p. 92)

t
$_a$EXERCISE CLASS, $_1$INDEX HOPE $_b$SISTER SUCCEED $_b$PERSUADE$_c$ $_c$MOTHER $_a$TAKE-UP.
'The exercise class$_i$, I hope my sister manages to persuade my mother to take (-it$_i$).'

[19] Lillo-Martin (1986a) uses "topicalization" rather than "topic," stressing that the term is being used in its non-technical sense. This seems to have led to some confusion in the literature, which the present discussion should clarify.

However, Lillo-Martin (1986a) finds that Padden's observation holds just in case the verb is marked for agreement.[20] When the embedded verb is not marked for agreement, topics associated with an embedded clause argument require an overt resumptive pronoun, as shown by the contrast between (41a) and (41b).[21] (41a) has the resumptive pronoun $_a$INDEX, while the ungrammatical (41b) lacks it.

(41) ASL (Lillo-Martin 1986a, p. 423)

a. $\overline{\text{}_a\text{THAT }_a\text{COOKIE,}}^{t}$ $_1$INDEX HOPE $_a$SISTER SUCCEED $_b$PERSUADE$_c$ $_c$MOTHER EAT $_a$INDEX.

b. *$\overline{\text{}_a\text{THAT }_a\text{COOKIE,}}^{t}$ $_1$INDEX HOPE $_a$SISTER SUCCEED $_b$PERSUADE$_c$ $_c$MOTHER EAT.

'That cookie$_i$, I hope my sister manages to persuade my mother to eat it$_i$.'

The distribution of facts illustrated in (40)–(41) indicates that a movement operation (topicalization) must not be involved in deriving these examples. Apparently, such long-distance movement is not permitted in ASL, as shown by the ungrammaticality of (41b). On the other hand, there is no constraint against a base-generated topic occurring with a distant coreferential pronoun, as in (41a) (as long as the topic satisfies the "aboutness" requirement placed on all base-generated topics; see Chapter 22). This pattern indicates that movement is also not involved in the derivation of (40). Instead, the topic must be base-generated, and there must be a null pronoun in the embedded object position. The null argument associated with agreeing verbs must therefore be pronominal, or *pro*.[22]

In traditional island contexts as well, Lillo-Martin claims that *pro* acts as an island-saving resumptive pronoun. That is, where movement would

[20] Padden's example in (40) uses the verb TAKE-UP, which Padden marks for agreement. Given the more recent understanding of agreement presented in Chapter 3, TAKE-UP would not be considered an agreeing verb, since its object is not human or a potential possessor. TAKE-UP may be like WANT, in that it can be signed in a location but is not, strictly speaking, agreeing. The morphosyntactic behavior of verbs signed in a location as opposed to agreeing verbs has yet to be studied. It seems that verbs signed in a location behave similarly to agreeing verbs with respect to the licensing of null arguments. Note, however, that the formationally identical sign, when used with human objects, is glossed ADOPT, and is considered agreeing.

[21] Why ASL seems to prohibit long-distance topicalization without resumptive pronouns (overt or null) is a matter for future research. Lillo-Martin (1990, 1992) claims that sentences (clauses) are islands in ASL, based on similar apparent restrictions for leftward movement in WH-questions and topics. Neidle et al. (2000) dispute the claim that extraction out of embedded clauses is not permitted in WH-questions, based on their analysis of WH-movement as rightward. Petronio and Lillo-Martin (1997) claim that extraction out of embedded clauses is acceptable only for some speakers; and that it is not commonly used. See Chapters 22 and 23 for extensive discussion.

[22] We refer to the pronoun in such structures as a resumptive pronoun, following McCloskey and Hale (1984). This does not imply a movement analysis (c.f. Shlonsky 1992), but simply a relationship between the left-dislocated topic and the sentence-internal coreferential pronoun.

be ruled out due to universal constraints, a left-dislocated topic can be associated with a pronoun in the island. This pronoun can be null, so long as the verb it is an argument of is marked for agreement.

For example, while overt resumptive pronouns are required when topics are associated with arguments of non-agreeing verbs in WH-islands, as in (42a), a null (or overt) resumptive pronoun with an agreeing verb is permitted, as in (42b).

(42) ASL (Lillo-Martin 1986a, pp. 424–425)

________t
a. $_a$MOTHER, $_1$PRONOUN DON'T-KNOW "WHAT" *($_a$PRONOUN) LIKE.
'Mother$_j$, I don't know what$_k$ (she$_j$) likes t$_k$.'

________t
b. $_a$MOTHER, $_b$PRONOUN DON'T-KNOW WHAT ($_a$PRONOUN) $_a$SEND$_1$.
'Mother$_i$, I don't know what$_k$ (she$_i$-) sent me t$_k$.'

A similar contrast is found in coordinate structures. As Padden (1988 [1983]) shows, ASL respects the Coordinate Structure Constraint by disallowing extraction from one conjunct of a coordinate structure, as shown in (43). However, ASL does permit across-the-board extraction of elements out of both conjuncts, as shown in (44).

(43) ASL (Padden 1988 [1983], p. 93)

________t
*FLOWER, $_2$GIVE$_1$ MONEY, $_j$GIVE$_1$.
'Flowers, he gave me money but she gave me.'

(44) ASL (Lillo-Martin 1991, p. 60)

____________t
$_a$THAT $_a$MOVIE$_i$, $_b$STEVE LIKE e$_i$ BUT $_c$JULIE DISLIKE e$_i$.
'That movie$_I$, Steve likes e$_i$ but Julie dislikes e$_i$.'

Lillo-Martin provides evidence that such across-the-board examples may include a topic associated with resumptive pronouns in both conjuncts. As long as agreement is present, either of the resumptive pronouns can be null, as seen in (45).

(45) ASL (Lillo-Martin 1991, p. 60)

___________t
$_a$THAT MOVIE, $_a$JULIE LIKE $_b$PRONOUN (BUT) $_c$STEVE $_c$HATE$_a$.
'That movie$_i$, Julie likes it$_i$ but Steve hates (-it$_i$).'

Finally, Lillo-Martin also claims that *pro* behaves as a crossover-evading resumptive pronoun, as in (46). Without the overt resumptive pronoun, (46b) violates another universal constraint, the Crossover Constraint. As in the earlier cases, the example with an agreeing verb, (46c), is grammatical with the proposed null resumptive pronoun.

(46) ASL (Lillo-Martin 1991, pp. 61, 62)

a. $\overline{\text{}_a\text{STEVE}}^{t}$, $_b$PRONOUN EXPECT $_1$PRONOUN LOVE.
'Steve$_i$, he$_j$ expects me to love e$_i$.'

b. $\overline{\text{}_a\text{STEVE}}^{t}$, $_a$PRONOUN EXPECT $_1$PRONOUN LOVE *($_a$PRONOUN).
'Steve$_i$, he$_i$ expects me to love *(him$_i$).'

c. $\overline{\text{}_a\text{STEVE}}^{t}$, $_a$PRONOUN EXPECT $_1$PRONOUN $_1$FALL-FOR$_a$ ($_a$PRONOUN).
'Steve$_i$, he$_i$ expects me to fall for (-him$_i$).'

Given the behavior of null arguments with agreeing verbs, Lillo-Martin argues that they are instances of the category *pro*, a null pronominal with characteristics of overt pronouns. She argues that *pro* must be licensed and identified in ASL by agreement (with one exception, to be discussed below).

We have seen that null arguments of agreeing and plain verbs behave differently with respect to constraints on movement. However, we have also seen that null arguments are (sometimes) permitted with plain verbs (as in (34)–(35) above). If null arguments with plain verbs are not *pro*, what are they? Lillo-Martin compares them to null arguments in languages like Chinese, as discussed by Huang (1984).[23]

Following Huang's line of reasoning, Lillo-Martin proposes that ASL permits null arguments which are variables licensed by null topics. She shows evidence similar to Huang's for Chinese that ASL is a discourse-oriented language (cf. Rosenstein 2001 for ISL). Although this will be discussed in greater detail in Chapter 22, of most relevance here is the possibility for a null sentential topic coindexed with a previous discourse topic, as in (47). In this example, extracted from a signed narrative, null arguments appear with spatially marked predicates (indicated by hyphens in the translation). However, there is also a sequence of null subjects with verbs not showing agreement, all referring to the daughter, the topic introduced by the initial sentence.

(47) ASL (Lillo-Martin 1991, p. 81)
ONE DAY, $_a$DAUGHTER NOTHING #D-O, DECIDE WALK $_{b\text{-}c}$WOODS. $_b$WALK$_c$, $_d$PRONOUN SEE$_d$ $_d$FLOWER, PICK-UP$_d$, SEE$_e$ $_e$WATERFALL, $_c$WALK$_e$, FASCINATED$_e$, LOST$^{\text{[resultative]}}$.
'One day, the daughter had nothing to do, so (she) decided to take a walk in the woods. (She) walked around, and saw there some flowers, and picked (-them) up; (she) saw a waterfall, and walked (-near it); and (she) was so fascinated (-by it) that (she) became lost.'

[23] Independently, Shepard-Kegl (1985) makes a similar comparison (although she adopts a different view in more recent work with the ASLLRP, discussed below). We believe the two authors first became aware of each other's proposals at the 1984 NELS conference, at which Lillo-Martin presented her work (Lillo-Martin 1985).

As a discourse-oriented language, then, ASL is expected to permit null sentential topics to bind null arguments of the variable type. The analysis for a null argument such as seen in (48a) is as in (48b).

(48) a. (discourse sets up John as topic ...)
ENJOY SUNBATHE[dur].
'He's enjoying a lot of sunbathing.'
b. [Null topic]$_i$, t_i ENJOY SUNBATHE[dur]

This implies that null arguments of non-agreeing verbs are somewhat less productive, in that they must be topics. Generally, they will not be allowed in island contexts – with one exception. As in Chinese, null subjects of embedded clauses which are coreferential with the matrix subject can be analyzed as empty pronominals (recall the Chinese example in (33)). Thus, an example very similar to (42a) is grammatical even without the overt pronoun in the embedded clause, just when the topic, matrix subject, and embedded subject are all coindexed, as in (49).

(49) ASL (Lillo-Martin 1986a)
________t
$_a$MOTHER, $_a$PRONOUN DON'T-KNOW "WHAT" ($_a$PRONOUN) LIKE.
'Mother$_j$, she$_j$ doesn't know what$_k$ (she$_j$) likes t_k.'

This is strong evidence that the two kinds of null arguments found in ASL are of distinct categories, and that only one is pronominal. A similar conclusion has been reached for Brazilian Sign Language by Quadros (1995).

21.2.4 *Are null arguments in ASL uniformly licensed by agreement?*

The hybrid analysis of null arguments in ASL has been disputed by Bahan et al. (2000).[24] Their alternative depends on their proposal that there are non-manual markers of agreement, namely head tilt and eye gaze, as discussed in Chapters 3 and 18. According to their analysis, both verbs which show manual agreement and those which do not show manual agreement may optionally be accompanied by non-manual markers of agreement. Examples are given in (50).

(50) ASL (Bahan et al. 2000, p. 11)
__________________head tilt$_i$
__________eye gaze$_j$
a. JOHN$_i$ [+agr$_i$]$_{AgrS}$ [+agr$_j$]$_{AgrO}$ $_i$SHOOT$_j$ FRANK$_j$.
'John shoots Frank.'
__________________head tilt$_i$
__________eye gaze$_j$
b. IX$_i$ [+agr$_i$]$_{AgrS}$ [+agr$_j$]$_{AgrO}$ LOVE MOTHER$_j$.
'He/She loves mother.'

[24] Also Neidle et al. (1998a, 2000).

On the analysis of such non-manual markers proposed by Bahan (1996), head tilt toward the locus associated with the subject in the examples in (50) is a realization of AgrS, and eye gaze toward the location of the object in these examples is a realization of AgrO. Thus, according to this analysis, overt agreement may be present with all verb types, both "agreeing" and "non-agreeing."

In this case, it is not surprising that a uniform analysis of the licensing of null arguments can be offered. In particular, Bahan et al. (2000) argue that null arguments are uniformly licensed by agreement, which must be expressed manually and/or non-manually. Without some such marking, they find, null arguments are not acceptable. So, according to them, verbs with manual agreement will always license null arguments. Plain verbs, on the other hand, will allow null arguments only when the non-manual marker of agreement is present.

The examples in (51) show that whether or not the non-manual markers are present, a null subject of an agreeing verb is possible. However, the examples in (52) show that for a non-agreeing verb, non-manual marking of agreement is necessary for the subject to be null. The same contrast is shown for null objects in (53)–(54).

(51) ASL (Bahan et al. 2000, p. 15)

$\overline{\hspace{8em}\text{head tilt}_i}$

$\overline{\hspace{6em}\text{eye gaze}_j}$

a. pro_i $[+agr_i]_{AgrS}$ $[+agr_j]_{AgrO}$ $_i$SHOOT$_j$ FRANK$_j$.
'(He/She) shoots Frank.'

b. pro_i $[+agr_i]_{AgrS}$ $[+agr_j]_{AgrO}$ $_i$SHOOT$_j$ FRANK$_j$.
'(He/She) shoots Frank.'

(52) ASL (Bahan et al. p. 17)

$\overline{\hspace{6em}\text{head tilt}_i}$

a. pro_i $[+agr_i]_{AgrS}$ LOVE MOTHER$_j$.
'(He/She) loves mother.'

b. *pro_i $[+agr_i]_{AgrS}$ $[+agr_j]_{AgrO}$ LOVE MOTHER$_j$.

(53) ASL (Bahan et al. p. 17)

$\overline{\hspace{6em}\text{head tilt}_i}$

$\overline{\hspace{3em}\text{eye gaze}_j}$

a. JOHN$_i$ $_i$BLAME$_j$ pro_j.
'John blames (him/her).'

b. JOHN$_i$ $_i$BLAME$_j$ pro_j.
'John blames (him/her).'

(54) ASL (Bahan et al. p. 17)

$\overline{\hspace{8em}\text{eye gaze}_j}$

a. JOHN$_i$ $[+agr_j]_{AgrO}$ LOVE pro_j.
'John loves (him/her).'

b. *JOHN$_i$ LOVE pro_j.

Empirical counterevidence to the proposal by Bahan et al. that non-manual markers of agreement can license null elements in the absence of manual agreement comes from a study by Thompson and Emmorey (2003). They used a head-mounted eyetracker to determine the direction of eyegaze used by signers while signing narratives and verb lists. They found no spontaneously produced null objects with plain verbs, and, more importantly, they found that eyegaze with plain verbs was "random," directed in most cases at the addressee or toward some "other" location (non-subject, non-object).

Recall from Chapter 3 that Bahan and colleagues (Bahan et al. 2000) propose that there is a neutral form of manual and non-manual subject agreement (although not object agreement). In fact, for manual agreement, there seems to be no clear difference between the neutral form, the first-person form, and the absence of agreement, at least in the singular. Neidle et al. (2000) argue that this is not a case of optional subject agreement, as in Padden's analysis, but a neutral marking whose form is identical to the first-person form. Thus, it should be recognized that according to their analysis it is possible to have a null subject with an agreeing verb which takes the neutral form, as in (55) – a form which is indistinguishable from the first-person form or a form not marked for subject agreement at all. This renders their claim that null arguments must be licensed by agreement unverifiable in this type of case.

(55) ASL (Bahan et al. 2000, p. 15)
pro_i $[+\text{agr}_{neu}]_{AgrS}$ $[+\text{agr}_j]_{AgrO}$ $_{neu}\text{SHOOT}_j$ FRANK_j.
'(He/She) shoots Frank.'

Bahan et al. describe differences between the neutral non-manual form and no agreement at all, but they also indicate that the differences are very subtle. The different forms can be observed on the Quick-Time movie clips available at the ASLLRP website. The neutral form involves a slight head tilt and body lean toward the object. In fact, the subject is not marked at all, just as with the neutral manual form. The head tilt and body lean only indicate the object, which is not predicted by their analysis. Nevertheless, Bahan et al. allege with no further explanation that this form of agreement licenses null subjects, as shown in (56).

(56) ASL (Bahan et al. 2000, p. 15)
$\overline{\hspace{8em}\text{head tilt}_{neu}}$
pro_i $[+\text{agr}_{neu}]_{AgrS}$ LOVE MOTHER_j.
'(He/She) loves mother.'

Notice that the analysis of Bahan et al., like Lillo-Martin's, captures an essential difference between agreeing verbs and non-agreeing verbs. Since agreeing verbs, on Bahan et al.'s account, can have a neutral form of subject agreement, but non-agreeing verbs cannot, there are more contexts in which agreeing verbs can be found with null arguments. Non-agreeing verbs need some additional mechanism to permit null subjects. Of course, the mechanisms proposed by the two analyses are quite different: the one by Bahan et al. employs the purported non-manual marking of agreement, while Lillo-Martin's involves a hypothesized null topic.

We have already seen some reasons to question whether head tilt and eye gaze are expressions of agreement (Chapters 3 and 18). Since the data presented by Lillo-Martin (1986a) do not indicate the presence or absence of such markers, both those data and the examples from Bahan et al. cited here need to be reconsidered with possible alternative analyses of these non-manuals in mind.

Bahan et al. also argue against Lillo-Martin's application of Huang's null-topic analysis of null arguments to ASL. They claim that Huang's proposal is based on the idea that the relationship between the topic and the null argument does not obey subjacency, and thus the null argument must have been base-generated. However, this is not an accurate interpretation of his proposal. His proposal clearly differentiates between null arguments in different positions – and those which can only be analyzed as variables on his account *do* obey subjacency (see especially Huang 1984, pp. 560–562).

Huang makes a clear contrast between null embedded subjects, which when coreferential with the matrix subject can be *pro* (and thus can violate subjacency), as opposed to other null elements, which must be variables. Only the null embedded subjects can escape the island constraints, because only they can be *pro* on his account. (See also Shi 2000 for evidence that the relationship between a topic and its gap is subject to locality constraints in Mandarin.)

Lillo-Martin shows that with plain verbs, ASL behaves the same way as Chinese does. This is why the argument about subjacency is important: all null arguments of agreeing verbs, and (embedded) null subjects of plain verbs, can be base-generated within islands – because these can all be *pro*. Null objects of plain verbs, however, cannot. The only way they can be licensed is as variables bound by a (possibly null) topic; as variables, they are subject to constraints on movement.[25]

In addition to these theoretical issues, Neidle et al. (2000), and Aarons et al. (1992, 1994) claim that there are numerous empirical differences

[25] Bahan et al. criticize Lillo-Martin's use of the term "movement" in describing structures with a topic binding a variable. Since Huang is working within a representational approach which uses a functional definition of empty categories, the difference between movement and base-generation is, in his words, "trivialized" (Huang 1984, p. 542). Using this approach, the nature of an empty category is determined by its configuration, not whether it was produced by binding or base-generation. More current research generally makes the distinction more relevant: traces (including variables) are formed by movement, pronouns are base-generated. In the cases under discussion, the issues are the same whether a derivational approach using movement, or a representational approach without movement is employed.

between null arguments in ASL and Chinese which make Lillo-Martin's proposal untenable. For example, they claim that ASL allows multiple null arguments, but Chinese does not. However, as we have already seen, Huang cites Chinese examples with more than one null argument, as in (31c). They also claim that Chinese does not permit more than one topic, unlike ASL. However, Huang (1984) cites Chinese examples with more than one topic, as in (56), concluding "that a sentence can have multiple topics" (p. 555).

(57) Chinese (Huang 1984, p. 555)
Zhangsan, neiben shu, ta hen xihuan
Zhangsan, that book, he very like
'(As for Zhangsan), that book, he likes very much.'

Aarons et al. also claim that Chinese does not permit null arguments in sentences with (distinct) overt topics, such as (58a), but that ASL does, as in (58b). Huang (1984) does not mention structures of this type.

(58) Chinese and ASL (Aarons et al. 1992)
a. *Shu cài, *e* xihuan bocaì
Vegetables *e* like spinach
'As for vegetables, he likes spinach.'
top________
b. VEGETABLE, e LIKE CORN

Aarons et al. suggest that the difference illustrated in (58) could be related to a difference in the number of topics allowed per sentence between the two languages. They refer to the claim by Aarons (1994) that ASL allows a maximum of two topics per clause (see also Chapter 22). According to this claim, ASL might allow one overt topic plus one null topic, thus accounting for the example in (58b). Since they are under the impression that Chinese has an upper limit of one topic, this would prohibit overt topics from co-occurring with distinct null arguments in this language, as in (57a). However, we have already seen counterevidence to the idea that Chinese allows a maximum of one topic. If the contrast between (58a) in Chinese and (58b) in ASL can be verified, another explanation for it is required.

To make their case even stronger, Neidle et al. say that given the appropriate context, it is possible to have null arguments of non-agreeing verbs in sentences with two overt topics, as in (59). Their view of the null-topic account would fail to generate such examples, since the maximum number of topic positions has been reached with the overt topics.

(59) ASL (Neidle et al. 2000, p. 73)
t2-bg ____t2-bg ________head tilt$_k$
MARY$_i$, VEGETABLE$_j$, e_k KNOW IX$_i$ LIKE CORN.
'As for Mary, as for vegetables, (he = John) knows she likes corn.'

If there is a real difference between ASL and Chinese with respect to the data in (58)–(59), this would need to be accounted for. However, it is not likely that the account would be in terms of the maximum number of topic positions allowed, since we have seen that Chinese does permit multiple topics. Hence, the difference may or may not be related to the null-topic analysis of null arguments in ASL.

To sum up, null arguments are found both with agreeing verbs and plain verbs in ASL. According to Bahan et al. (2000), all null arguments in ASL are *pro*, licensed by overt agreement, either manual or non-manual. A simple account for the licensing of null arguments is all that is required. If correct, this analysis would mean that the more complex hybrid theory of null argument licensing proposed by Lillo-Martin (1985, 1986a, 1986b, 1991) and Shepard-Kegl (1985) (and also by Quadros 1995 for LSB) is not necessary.

However, Lillo-Martin observed systematic differences between null arguments of agreeing and plain verbs which are not accounted for under the uniform analysis. According to her, null arguments with agreeing verbs systematically behave like pronominals, and are therefore licensed and identified by agreement. Null arguments with plain verbs, on the other hand, do not generally show the characteristics of pronouns. Since ASL has other characteristics of discourse-oriented languages, applying the analysis of null arguments in this type of language to ASL has appeal.

An important implication of this analysis is the conclusion that one language can have two kinds of null arguments. If Lillo-Martin is correct, the two kinds of null arguments in ASL follow from the fact that verbs fall into different classes, depending on whether or not they can be marked for agreement. Proposals that would wipe out the distinction between null arguments in Italian-type languages versus Chinese-type languages would not be able to capture the fact that the distinction needs to be made even within one language. Previously, only the work on ASL showed this case so clearly. Recently, however, Legate (2003) observes a similar phenomenon in Warlpiri, where both arguments associated with agreement and those not associated with agreement can be null. Legate finds that a hybrid analysis accounts best for the facts of Warlpiri. The study of ASL paved the way for consideration of such hybrid accounts.

We have seen in this section that ASL has the characteristics of a discourse-oriented language (even apart from null arguments). These characteristics underlie much of what is discussed in the following chapter. There, we turn to examine the nature of topic and focus in sign languages, and how these (and other) discourse notions play a role in syntax.

22 Topic and focus

Languages vary in the ways that they organize sentences to convey different kinds of discourse information. The term *information packaging* is used to refer to the ways that discourse-relevant notions such as topic and focus are conveyed in a language. Typically, languages use both sentence structure and prosodic markers for such information, but some languages rely more on one or the other mechanism. For example, English allows stress to shift in a sentence so that focus can be conveyed primarily through prosodic means (although even English has certain structures, such as topicalization and clefting, to rearrange information). On the other hand, Catalan keeps stress in a constant position in the sentence. This means that syntactic movement operations must apply to rearrange constituents so that the focused element is in the correct position to receive stress. In such languages, analyzing even common syntactic structures requires a deeper understanding of the ways in which truth-conditionally identical content may be conveyed.

Sign languages, like spoken Hungarian, Mayan languages, and Catalan, widely exploit syntactic variations as well as prosody for purposes of information packaging. Thus, we are interested in investigating the extent to which the discourse-based sentence structure variation in sign languages falls within the range of possibilities observed in spoken language universals. Here, we overview some of the basic primitives of theories of information packaging. In the following subsections we then take advantage of these primitives in understanding some of the alternative word orders used in ASL and other sign languages.

22.1 Information packaging

Theories of information structure propose two main ways of dividing sentences (for a helpful overview, see de Swart and de Hoop 1995). According to the first, sentences may offer a *topic*, or what the sentence is about, and then present a *comment* on that topic. Topics generally present old information, although new information (for example, in contrastive topics) can be in a topic position and not all old information is a topic. Most researchers note the strong predominance of sentence-initial position for topics. This is particularly true for shifted topics, i.e., those which change the topic (and may constitute separate intonational phrases), as compared with continuing topics. Sentence topics (which correspond to an overt expression in the sentence) can be distinguished from discourse topics, which may be inferred from the context but unspoken. Finally, not all sentences will have a topic; so-called presentational sentences (or "all focus" sentences in which all the information is new) have no topic.

The second way of dividing sentences is that of *ground–focus*. An element in focus in the informational sense provides new information. Note that the use of "focus" in its informational sense only partially overlaps with phonological focus, or intonational prominence. Although the informational focus may well contain intonational prominence, other linguistic entities may also have phonological focus. The ground (or presupposition, frame, background, or open proposition) contains the already established information, assumed to be shared.

Topic and focus are both relational terms, that is, they are determined relative to a particular context. Although they are often seen as picking out opposite sides (old information vs. new information), the two primitive dimensions of topic–comment and ground–focus cannot be completely collapsed. This can be seen in the following examples, from Vallduví and Engdahl (1996, p. 467), in which topics are indicated by italics and phonological focus by all caps.

(1) What about *Mary*? What did *she* give to Harry?
She [C gave [F a SHIRT] to Harry.]

(2) What about *Mary*? What did *she* do?
She [C gave a shirt to HARRY.]

(3) What about *Harry*? What did Mary give to *him*?
To Harry she gave [F a SHIRT]

The answers in (1)–(3) have the same content, but differ in informational packaging. The topic–comment structure is the same in (1) and (2), but the focus (and phonological prominence) is different. The focus is the same in (1) and (3), but the topics (and syntactic structure) are different.

Vallduví (1992) therefore proposes a tripartite hierarchical articulation of information-packaging primitives. In particular, he proposes that sentences are composed of a focus and a ground. The ground, in turn, may be composed of a link (the topic) and a tail. This proposal can be summarized as in (4).

(4) S = {focus, ground}
ground = {link, tail}

A typical ordering of these three elements would be link–focus–tail. However, in many instances not all three would be overt in a single sentence. Languages may use prosody and/or word order to mark these three functions.

In some languages (known as [+plastic]), intonational contours and stress patterns may be varied to indicate which elements have prominence. For example, English permits the same word order to convey different information packaging, via prosody, as seen in (1) and (2) above. However, other languages (those which are [–plastic]) do not permit such stress shift. Instead, they use syntactic means to place information-relevant elements in particular structural positions. For example, Catalan uses a variety of syntactic processes to place focused information in position so that the ordering link–focus–tail will be achieved. This process is discussed in detail by Vallduví (1992).

We now turn to various aspects of information packaging in sign languages. We begin with topics, which have been noticed and discussed in the sign language literature for many years. We then bring up several different approaches to other aspects of information packaging, particularly focus, a more recently discussed phenomenon in sign language research.

22.2 Topics in sign languages

In languages in general, topics are found in sentence-initial position (de Swart and de Hoop 1995); however, they may be in their regular sentence-internal position. If in initial position, they may have moved to a position outside the clause (via a movement operation of *topicalization*), or be base-generated in such a position.

It has already been noted (see Chapter 18) that even in the 1970s researchers claimed that ASL productively uses topics, either through a process of topicalization or by base generating topic–comment structures (Fischer 1975, Friedman 1976). Liddell (1980) argues that topics are Chomsky-adjoined to the rest of the sentence, using evidence from the scope of the negative marker, as in example (8a) from Chapter 18, repeated here as (5). (See discussion in Chapter 18, Section 18.1 for details of Liddell's proposal.)

(5) ASL (Liddell 1980, p. 84)

___t __________n
CAT DOG CHASE
'As for the cat, the dog didn't chase it.'

As discussed in Chapter 21, Lillo-Martin (1986a, 1986b) notes that the existence of null pronouns in ASL obscures the distinction between moved and base-generated topics (or topicalization and left dislocation). Compare the English examples in (6a,b).

(6) a. Beans, I like.
b. As for beans, I like them.

Since the obligatorily transitive verb *like* is apparently missing its object in (6a), it is generally assumed that the object *beans* has moved to the sentence-initial position. In (6b), however, the presence of a pronominal object means that the topic must have been base-generated in its position (this kind of structure is also known as left dislocation). In ASL, when a null pronoun is possible it may seem impossible to tell the difference between moved and base-generated topics. However, Aarons (1994) finds that these two kinds of topics are associated with distinct non-manual markers.

Aarons (1994, p. 156) identifies three distinct topic markers in ASL, described as follows and illustrated using our own model's version of her images in Figure 22.1.

- tm1 (labeled t1-mv by Neidle et al. 2000): raised brows; head tilted slightly back and to the side; eyes widened; head moves down and forward
- tm2 (labeled t2-bg by Neidle et al. 2000): large movement of head back and to the side; eyes very wide, head moves down and forward
- tm3 (labeled t3-bg by Neidle et al. 2000): head forward, jerked slightly up and down; mouth open; upper lip raised; eyebrows raised; eyes wide open, fixed gaze, slight rapid headnods.

On Aarons' classification, tm3 topics are used with known referents, and introduce a major change in discourse topic. Tm3 topics are easily distinguished by their non-manual markings. The rapid headnods, raised lip, and fixed gaze invite the addressee to concur in recognizing the new topic. Such examples are parsimoniously translated with 'you know X' or "uptalk" (McLemore 1991), as shown in (7). They are the type of topic known as "shifted topics" (de Swart and de Hoop 1995). According to Aarons' analysis, tm3 topics are base-generated.

(7) ASL (Aarons 1994, p. 164)
__tm3
MARY$_i$, JOHN LOVE IX-3rd$_i$
'(You know) Mary, John loves her.'

The difference between tm1 topics and tm2 topics is more subtle. Topics marked with tm1 are used to identify a particular member of the universe of discourse; or for emphasis or contrastive focus. On Aarons' analysis they are necessarily moved topics; hence, there will be a gap in the sentence-internal position. Examples are given in (8).

(8) ASL (Aarons 1994, pp. 158, 159)
a. FOUR WOMEN LIVE IN HOUSE IX.

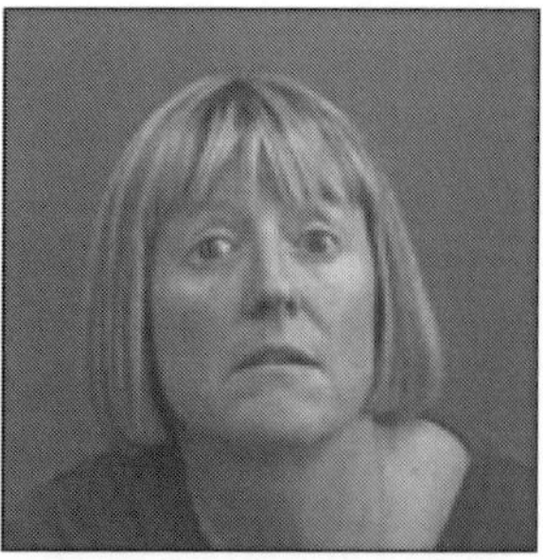

a. tm1

b. tm2

alternate version

c. tm3

Figure 22.1 Three types of topic marking in ASL

tm1

MARY$_i$, JOHN LOVE t_i

'Four women live in that house over there. *Mary*, John loves.'

b. JOHN NOT-LIKE JANE.

tm1

MARY, IX-3rd LOVE

'John doesn't like Jane. *Mary*, he loves.'

Tm2 topics are used to introduce new information which changes the discourse topic. They are necessarily associated with an argument in the following clause, and are therefore base-generated. The topic and clause-internal argument may be in a class:member relation, as in (9).

(9) ASL (Aarons 1994, p. 160)

______tm2
VEGETABLE, JOHN LIKE CORN
'As for vegetables, John likes corn.'

However, the clause-internal argument may be a pronominal, as in the English example in (6b), and the ASL example in (10a). In ASL, as noted, the pronominal may be null, as in (10b). Since the *as for* which distinguishes the English examples in (6a,b) is not expressed in ASL, the only surface difference between a sentence with a moved (tm1) and base-generated (tm2) topic may be the non-manual marker. Hence, the systematicity and reliability of the non-manual marker is crucial to the claim that these base-generated and moved topics can be distinguished on the surface.

(10) ASL (Aarons 1994, pp. 162, 163)

__tm2
a. JOHN_i, IX-3rd_i LOVE MARY
'As for John, he loves Mary.'

__tm2
b. JOHN_i, e LOVE MARY
'As for John, he loves Mary.'

Aarons makes some further interesting but unexplained observations about topics in ASL. They are mentioned here in the interests of future research.

She notes that in embedded structures, it is possible to have a topic at the beginning of the embedded clause. It is also possible, she claims, to have a topic associated with a gap inside an embedded clause, but only if the clause is infinitival (cf. Lillo-Martin's observation that extraction out of some embedded clauses is ungrammatical, mentioned in Chapter 21). Some examples are given in (11)–(12). (11a) shows an embedded clause which Aarons claims is ambiguous between a tensed and non-tensed version. (12a) shows an embedded clause that is unambiguously tensed, due to the presence of the modal MUST, which is assumed to occupy the position of T. As the contrast between (11b, c) and (12b, c) shows, the tensed embedded clause does not allow a topic to be associated with it.

(11) ASL (Aarons 1994, p. 168)

a. TEACHER REQUIRE JOHN LIPREAD MOTHER
'The teacher requires John to lipread Mother.'

__tm1
b. JOHN, TEACHER REQUIRE LIPREAD MOTHER
'*John*, the teacher requires to lipread Mother.'

____tm1
c. MOTHER, TEACHER REQUIRE JOHN LIPREAD
'*Mother*, the teacher requires John to lipread.'

(12) ASL (Aarons 1994, p. 169)

a. TEACHER REQUIRE JOHN MUST LIPREAD MOTHER
'The teacher requires that John must lipread Mother.'

tm1
b. *JOHN, TEACHER REQUIRE MUST LIPREAD MOTHER
'*John*, the teacher requires that must lipread Mother.'

tm1
c. *MOTHER, TEACHER REQUIRE MUST JOHN LIPREAD
'*Mother*, the teacher requires John to lipread.'

Finally, Aarons claims that there is a maximum of two topics per sentence in ASL. (13) is provided as a sample rejected string with more than two topics.

(13) ASL (Aarons 1994, p. 175)

tm2 tm2 tm1
*JOHN$_i$, GIRL-group, MARY, IX-3rd$_i$ LIKE
'As for John, as for girls, Mary, he likes.'

Not only is there a limit to the number of topics, according to Aarons, there are also restrictions on the types and orders of topics. If both topics are base-generated tm2 topics, they can appear in either order, as long as both are in a class:member relationship to an element in the clause, or both are related to coreferential pronouns in the clause, as illustrated in (14a, b, c). However, when one topic is related to a coreferential pronoun in the clause, this tm2 topic should precede a second topic in a class:member relationship, as in (14d).

(14) ASL (Aarons 1994, pp. 175, 176)

tm2 tm2
a. JOHN$_i$, GIRL-group, IX-3rd$_i$ LIKE MARY
'As for John, as for girls, he likes Mary.'

tm2 tm2
b. CHINA IX, vegetable, PEOPLE PREFER BROCCOLI
'In China, as far as vegetables are concerned, people prefer broccoli.'

tm2 tm2
c. JOHN IX$_i$, MARY IX$_j$, IX-3rd$_i$ LOVE IX-3rd$_j$
'John (there), Mary (there), he loves her.'

tm2 tm2
d. JOHN$_i$, VEGETABLE, IX-3rd$_i$ PREFER ARTICHOKE
'As for John, as far as vegetables are concerned, he prefers artichokes.'

If the two topics are a combination of tm1 and tm2, they must be in the order tm2, tm1, as shown in (15).

(15) ASL (Aarons 1994, pp. 177, 178)

tm2 tm1
a. ??JOHN$_i$, MARY$_j$, IX-3rd$_i$ LOVE t_j
'As for John, Mary he loves.'

tm1 tm2

b. **MARY$_j$, JOHN$_i$, IX-3rd$_i$ LOVE t_j
'Mary, as for John, he loves.'

Two tm1 topics are not allowed. A tm3 topic may co-occur with either tm1 or tm2, so long as the tm3 topic is first.

Aarons suggests that the reason for these ordering restrictions is that a moved topic argument occupies the position nearest CP to properly govern the trace. In addition, Aarons states, "When tm2 marks a class, the proposition that follows it must be a comment about a specific element of the generic class expressed by the topic ... Semantically, items marked with tm3 function to bring to the forefront of the discourse information that is specific enough for the audience to conceptualize. Once this information is established, other topics ... may be introduced" (Aarons 1994, p. 183). Further investigation of the properties of moved, base-generated, and multiple topics is needed for a fully explanatory account of their distribution.

Wilbur (1997) claims that the information packaging model of Vallduví (1992), discussed in the introduction to this chapter, can distinguish two ASL structures with apparently identical syntax. One of these structures is what she calls topicalization for contrastive focus purposes, illustrated in (16). Wilbur points out that in example (16), MARY should receive primary stress; and it should be marked with the tm1 (moved topic) marker.

(16) ASL (Wilbur 1997, p. 97)
(Link) Focus Tail
br
MARY, JIM LOVE TEASE [*t*]
(Jim doesn't like to tease Jane.) 'It's *Mary* who Jim loves to tease.'

The second structure is topic followed by traditional comment/assertion, as in (17). In this example, Wilbur points out that primary stress should appear in the clause JIM LOVE TEASE; and MARY should be marked tm2 (change of discourse topic).

(17) ASL (Wilbur 1997, p. 97)
Link Focus (Tail)
br
MARY, JIM LOVE TEASE
'As for Mary, Jim loves to tease her.'

The prevalence of sentences with special topic structures in sign languages has led some to characterize them as "topic prominent" (Friedman 1976, Rosenstein 2001). This characterization is intended to put topic–comment structures as the basic organizing principle of the language, as opposed to the word-order principles of languages with subject prominence. In languages with "high topic prominence," word order always encodes topic–comment structures, and topics are left adjoined to complete sentences (which may themselves have subject–predicate order). Importantly, on this approach topic–comment structures are not considered derived in topic-prominent languages, but basic. In contrast, "low topic-prominent" languages or subject-prominent languages follow a rigid basic word order, only allowing limited use of order-changing operations.

As we saw in Chapter 18, early in the study of ASL, Friedman (1976) claims that topic–comment structures are basic in this language, and that no basic arrangement in terms of subject, verb, and object can be maintained. However, Liddell (1980) argues against Friedman's view, showing that sentences with orders other than Subject–Verb–Object can be derived by a rule of topicalization, with the topics marked using the characteristic non-manual (raised brows, head tilted back, pause between topic and rest of sentence).

Rosenstein (2001) revives the idea of topic prominence using data from Israeli Sign Language. She argues that topic–comment structures are pervasive in the language, not restricted to marked contexts, and basic, not derived. In particular, she argues that because some topics need not be arguments of the verbs in the comments, they cannot be seen as derived from a simpler structure by movement (these are topics such as the type Aarons analyzed as base-generated). Some examples are given in (18).

(18) ISL (Rosenstein 2001)

a. LIST, NEED EXAMPLE SENTENCES
'I had to give examples (sentences) for the words on the list.'

neg (over I NOT-YET FILL-IN PETROL NOT-YET)

b. PETROL X, I NOT-YET FILL-IN PETROL NOT-YET
'As for petrol, I haven't filled the car with petrol yet.'

The contention that topic–comment structures in ISL cannot be derived from other structures follows similar claims made for Chinese by Li and Thompson (1976, 1981) and others. However, Shi (2000) presents evidence that all six types of so-called Chinese topics, that is, "dangling" topics supposedly not associated with positions in the clause, instead are associated with some clause-internal position and can be considered syntactically derived. Shi defines topic and comment as in (19).

(19) A TOPIC is an unmarked NP (or its equivalent) that precedes a clause and is related to a position inside the clause; a topic represents an entity that has been mentioned in the previous discourse and is being discussed again in the current sentence, namely, topic is what the current sentence is set up to add new information to. The clause related to the topic in such a way is the comment.

(Shi 2000, p. 386)

Whether this definition can be extended to cover all the cases in Israeli Sign Language and other sign languages will be a matter for future research.

One apparent important difference between ISL and ASL concerns the topic non-manual marker. Texts on ASL uniformly describe topics as marked by a specific non-manual marker, including raised brows and head tilt, followed by a pause.[1] Rosenstein did not find that topics were consistently marked by any particular non-manual component in ISL. She did find that topics tended to be followed by an intonational phrase break (such as a blink or change in head or body position), as are topics in ASL.[2]

Rosenstein's data are compatible with the type of proposal made by Aarons, that some topics are base-generated while others are moved. No data have been presented for ISL which require some topics to be moved, however. Furthermore, the syntactic structure of ISL is much less studied than that of ASL, so even issues of basic word order (within the comment) are not clear.

Rosenstein's findings with respect to the variability in non-manual marking of topics in ISL suggest that the non-manual marker is not playing a syntactic role, but perhaps a pragmatic role, as does intonation. In a study of focus in ISL, individually elicited sentences usually have brow raise on topics, similar to reports on ASL. Rosenstein's data were from spontaneous discourse and narrative. The fact that she did not find systematic brow raise on topics in the same language reinforces the idea that non-manual marking is related to pragmatics and discourse structure rather than to syntax alone. This possibility will be pursued with respect to the WH-question non-manual marker in Chapter 23, where we discuss prosody and non-manual markers in more depth.

22.3 Information packaging in ASL

In a series of papers, Wilbur has looked at aspects of information packaging in ASL (Wilbur 1991, 1994a, 1996, 1997). One overarching claim has been that in ASL, "topic/given information is sentence initial" and "focus/new information is final" (Wilbur 1991, p. 325). She discusses a number of issues connected with these claims. We have already seen that there is general agreement that the sentence-initial position is used in ASL for topic and given information. Wilbur's emphasis in these papers is on the latter claim, that the final position is used for focus/new information.

This proposal is placed in the context of claims that in ASL, surface word order is determined primarily by discourse factors. Wilbur argues that like Catalan, ASL adjusts the order of words to put a focused item in a position of syntactic prominence; that is, the final position, which is also the position

[1] We have not, however, found any explicit claim that topics without such markings are ungrammatical.

[2] In her data 78 percent of topics were followed by an intonational phrase break.

for prosodic prominence. She argues "that an information packaging model provides a natural explanation for ASL word order permutations in terms of the identification of information as *focus* and the prosodic requirement that focus must receive prominence" (Wilbur 1997, p. 89).

Wilbur lists three types of constructions by which focused/prominent material will be in final position in ASL. One of these is the so-called rhetorical question construction, which takes the surface form of a WH-question followed by an "answer." One major contribution of Wilbur's works is the discussion of this construction in ASL, which Wilbur (1996, 1997) analyzes as WH-clefting. We will hold off on discussion of this construction until Section 22.5, where we discuss it in depth.

Another construction is known as "doubling," in which a focused or prominent element appears in the sentence-final position as well as its usual sentence-internal position.

The third construction is one in which a prominent item simply appears in the sentence-final position. Wilbur (1997, fn. 3, p. 101) suggests that such constructions may have one of three derivations. The focused item may move rightward to the end of the sentence. The focused item may be in a double construction in which the sentence-internal copy is omitted. Or the non-focused material may be preposed to end up preceding the focused element.[3]

The second and third constructions (doubling and sentence-final focus) are related in several proposed analyses of these structures. According to Petronio (1993), doubling involves a focus construction in which the sentence-final element is base-generated in this position. When the sentence-internal copy is null, the sentence-final focus construction results. Quadros (1999) also links the double and final focus constructions in LSB, but she uses the preposing technique – that is, material following the focus is fronted in order to achieve sentence-final focus.

In order to understand in more detail how sign languages use the sentence-final position for focus and prominence, we will shortly turn to a more thorough discussion of the so-called "doubling" constructions, first in ASL and then in LSB. But first, we will summarize another point made by Wilbur's studies of information packaging in ASL, concerning the non-manual marking "brow raise."

Wilbur (1995a, 1999b) and Patschke (Wilbur and Patschke 1999) examine a number of structures which occur with raised brows, and attempt to find a unified explanation for the distribution of brow raises. Coulter (1979) had observed that topics, relative clauses, conditionals, *when*-clauses, and other structures share raised brows in their non-manual markings. He proposes that the structures with raised brows describe background information, and that all the structures can be analyzed as various types of topics.

[3] An alternative proposal by Neidle (2002) places certain elements in the left periphery.

Wilbur and Patschke argue against Coulter's view, pointing out that brow raise is not present with some kinds of old, given, or presupposed information, such as ordinary subjects. Furthermore, there are cases of brow raise used with new information, such as conditionals, contrastive topicalization, and focus constructions with THAT and focus particles (ONLY-ONE). An example with contrastive topicalization is given in (20).

(20) ASL (Wilbur and Patschke 1999, p. 13)

br

JOHN$_i$ NOT-LIKE JANE. **MARY**$_j$, HE$_i$ LOVES t_j.
'John doesn't like Jane. It's *Mary* he loves.'

In spite of their failure to find a unified pragmatic account of brow raise, Wilbur and Patschke argue that there is a common thread to all cases with brow raise. The analysis they advocate is strictly syntactic rather than pragmatic. In particular, they note that all constituents with brow raise occupy A′-positions (either by being generated in these positions or by moving to them), and are associated with non-WH operators. In most cases, this means that sentence-initial constituents other than simple subjects would be included. Since, as we have seen, the sentence-final position is used for focus and prominence, it might frequently be the case that non-focused or presupposed elements would appear in the sentence-initial position – in the structural position where the brow raise marking is expected to appear.

Although it claims to be a syntactic account, Wilbur and Patschke's analysis does not identify any syntactic effect of the presence of the "br." More problematic is that some of the syntactic analyses assumed in order to maintain the [-wh] operator analysis are not justified. For example, Wilbur and Patschke assume that the IP of a yes/no question moves to [Spec, CP] (so that the whole question will have "br" marking). They also assume that a P feature triggers preposing in examples with what they consider focused negatives and modals. The preposing is important to their analysis because it is the preposed part which is marked by "br" (it is within the "checking domain" of the "[-wh] operator"), but there is no evidence that preposing has occurred. All in all, there is no strong evidence for their syntactic account.

Erteschik-Shir (1999) observes that the list of elements which are marked with brow raise, according to Wilbur, is coherent from the point of view of her Focus Structure Theory (Erteschik-Shir 1997). In particular, the list of structures which take brow raise "comprises possibly all nonconstrastive subordinate f-structures" (p. 225). It remains to be seen whether a syntactic or pragmatic account better handles brow raise in ASL. We will consider a very related issue in Chapter 23, where we raise the possibility of analyzing the furrowed brow and other non-manual markings that accompany WH-questions as intonation.

We now return to constructions with sentence-final prominence.

22.4 Double constructions

It has been observed in several sign languages that elements may be repeated in sentence-final position in order to receive prominence. Such repetition of elements within a sentence is not a common feature across spoken languages. However, some researchers have recently examined various ways in which spoken languages do realize two copies of a particular element for various reasons (e.g. Nunes 1999). It is therefore of renewed interest to see whether the syntactic mechanisms needed to generate doubled elements are unique to sign languages, or follow from independently motivated principles.

Several proposals have been presented regarding the analysis of such doubling constructions in sign languages. These proposals relate to issues of information packaging, as they include consideration of syntactic and prosodic focusing. They are also relevant to the discussion of WH-questions in Chapter 23, since WH-questions can appear in the same constructions.

22.4.1 Focus doubling in ASL

Petronio (1993) and Petronio and Lillo-Martin (1997) observe certain cases in which a sign may be repeated at the end of a sentence (such as the cases observed by Wilbur mentioned above). Restricting her attention to those cases in which there is no significant pause or hold between the sentence-final "double" and the preceding sign, since these cases are plausibly analyzed as single sentences, Petronio calls them "double constructions," and investigates their derivation. A further indication that the doubled element is in the same sentence as the preceding signs is that non-manual markers associated with the sentence may extend over the doubled element as well (we will discuss this further below).

Petronio notices that the doubled sign is frequently articulated with more muscle tension than when there is no doubling. She interprets the doubling operation as one of emphasis, or focus, one which "calls attention to [the] doubled sign and makes that particular sign the focus of the sentence"; or "more interesting." There may also be an emphatic facial expression accompanying the doubled element. An example of this is pictured in Figure 22.2.

The use of emphasis or focus to describe the nature of the final doubled element is not completely equivalent to information focus in the sense described above, since the latter is limited to new information. Just how the two notions are related remains to be determined. As Wilbur (1994a) points out, however, the sentence-final doubled element is prosodically prominent. Thus, we retain the term focus, using it in the sense of prosodic focus.

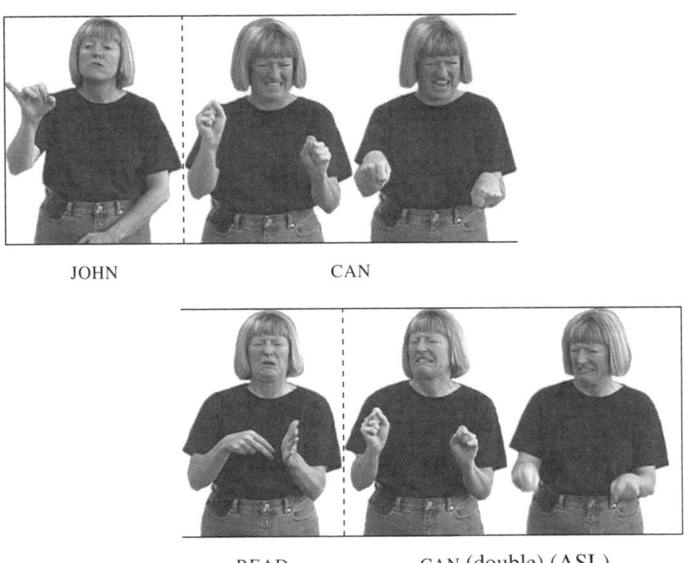

Figure 22.2 Emphatic nature of doubled elements

Petronio notices that modals, verbs, WH-signs, quantifiers, and negatives are among the elements which can double. Some examples are given in (21)–(24).[4]

(21) ASL (Petronio 1993, pp. 134, 135)

____________________neg
a. ANN CAN'T READ CAN'T
'Ann CAN'T read.'

____________________q
b. ANN WILL LEAVE WILL
'Will Ann go?'

(22) ASL (Petronio 1993, pp. 129, 133)

______________________hn
a. ANN LIKE ICE-CREAM LIKE
'Ann LIKES ice cream.'

____t ________________________hn
b. BOOK $_{a}$ANN WANT READ WANT $_{a}$INDEX[5]
'As for the book, Ann really wants to read it.'

[4] In some cases Petronio capitalizes the focused element in the gloss, to indicate its prominence. As we do throughout when we cite others' examples, we maintain her notation.

[5] The INDEX following the doubled WANT is a subject pronoun copy (cf. Chapter 18). Apparently, subject pronoun copy can follow doubles even though other material cannot (see following discussion).

(23) ASL (Petronio 1993, p. 134)

____________ whq
a. WHO BUY C-A-R WHO
'Who bought the car?'

____________________________ whq
b. HOW-MANY BROTHER SISTER $_2$INDEX HAVE HOW-MANY
'How many brothers and sisters do you have?'

(24) ASL (Wood 1999, pp. 63, 64)[6]

a. JOHN NOTHING FIND PAPER NOTHING.
'John did not find any paper.'
b. JOHN NEVER EAT FISH NEVER.
'John won't eat fish.'

Petronio observes that the double construction is characterized by the following properties:

(25) Syntactic properties of doubles:
i. the double occurs at the end of the sentence
ii. the double is an X^0, not an XP
iii. there is only one double per sentence
iv. the twin[7] cannot be within a syntactic island
v. only a WH-double can occur in direct WH-questions (not a modal or verb double) (Petronio 1993, p. 135)

We have already seen evidence for property (25i). The sentences in (26)–(29) exemplify properties (25ii–v).

ii. the double is an X^0, not an XP

Only a single sign, a head, can occur in the doubling construction. Full phrases, as in (26), are not allowed.

(26) ASL (Petronio 1993, p. 135)

_____________________ neg
a. *$_1$INDEX LIKE ICE-CREAM LIKE ICE-CREAM
'I *like* ice cream.'

________________ hn
b. *ANN WANT LEAVE WANT LEAVE
'Ann *wants* to go.'

iii. there is only one double per sentence (embedded or matrix)

As the examples in (27a, b) show, the double can be an element from either the matrix clause or the embedded clause. However, in ASL it is not

[6] These examples of negative doubling are from Wood (1999), although she does not commit to an analysis of negative doubles parallel to other doubles discussed here (cf. Chapter 20, Section 20.4). Wood does not provide an indication of non-manual markers in these examples.

[7] "Twin" is the name Petronio gives to the sentence-internal element which has been doubled.

possible to have more than one double, as shown by the ungrammaticality of (27c).

(27) ASL (Petronio 1993, p. 136)

　　______________________________ hn
　a. ${}_{1}$INDEX FEEL ${}_{a}$INDEX WILL WIN WILL
　　_________________________ hn
　b. ${}_{1}$INDEX FEEL ${}_{a}$INDEX WIN FEEL
　　______________________________________ hn
　c. *${}_{1}$INDEX FEEL ${}_{a}$INDEX WILL WIN WILL FEEL
　　'I feel he will win.'

iv. the twin cannot be within a syntactic island

The examples in (28) indicate that an element inside a relative clause cannot be doubled, either within the relative clause or outside it. Petronio attributes this to the Complex NP island constraint, according to which a relative clause is an island for syntactic operations.

(28) ASL (Petronio 1993, p. 136)

　　______________________________ r
　a. *WOMAN WILL COME TOMORROW WILL NAME S-U-E
　　____________________________ r
　b. *WOMAN WILL COME TOMORROW NAME S-U-E WILL
　　['The woman who will come tomorrow is named Sue.' WS/DLM]

v. only a WH-double can occur in direct WH-questions

Although an element such as WILL can be doubled in other contexts, in a (direct) WH-question only the WH-word can be doubled, as shown in (29).

(29) ASL (Petronio 1993, p. 137)

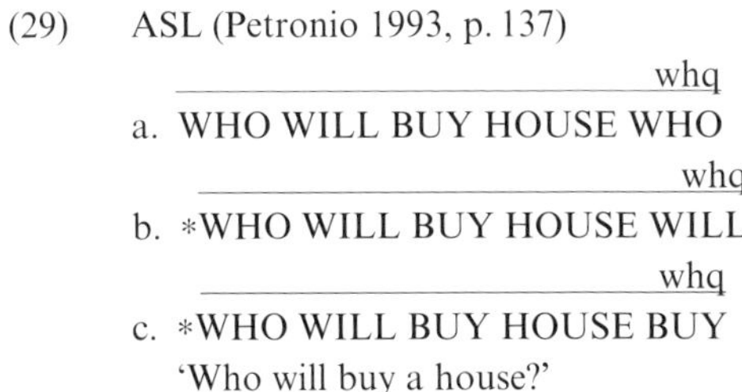

Given these observations, Petronio analyzes double constructions in the following way. First, she assumes the phrase structure given in (30). The structure from TP down was discussed in Chapter 18, where Petronio's arguments from the distributions of modals and agreement were presented (as well as independent arguments for the same structure presented by Aarons et al. 1992 ff.). Petronio's motivation for the head-final CP comes from the double construction itself, as well as WH-movement, to be discussed in Chapter 23.

Under Petronio's analysis the sentence-final double is not the result of movement, but it is base-generated in the C head position. Since there is no gap in the sentence, she assumes there is no place for the double to have moved from. Furthermore, movement from the sentence-internal position of the twin to the C head would violate well-established constraints on the movement of heads (captured by Relativized Minimality (Rizzi 1990), under the assumptions made at the time). Hence, Petronio concludes that the double is base-generated in its position.

(30) (Petronio 1993, p. 140)[8]

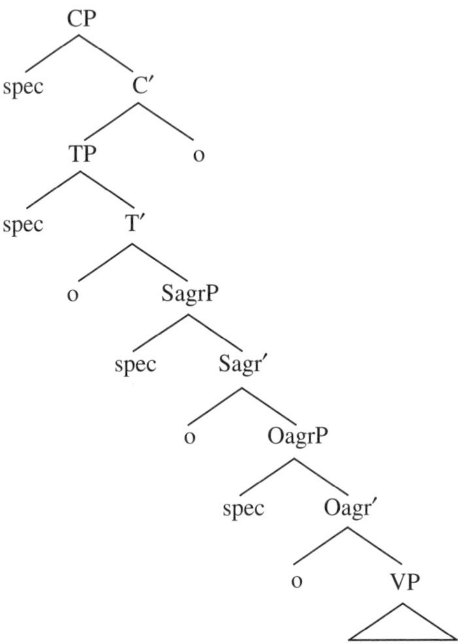

Petronio makes use of some theoretical assumptions about operators to account for the distribution of focused elements. Operators are involved in a particular type of semantic interpretation process, variable binding. In certain syntactic constructions, an operator (which may be overt or null) must bind a variable in order for the correct interpretation to be made. The binding of the variable is commonly taken to be implemented through movement of the operator, which will then bind its trace. This variable-binding relationship must be established by the level of LF, so either overt or covert movement may be involved.[9]

WH-elements and negative elements both involve operator-variable binding. In order to ensure that a WH-element is in the proper position

[8] In this structure and elsewhere, Petronio uses "o" to indicate the head.

[9] On some approaches, variable binding can take place through the semantic process of "unselective binding," which does not require movement.

for operator-variable binding by LF, Rizzi (1991) proposes the WH-Criterion in (31). This criterion begins with the common assumption that the head of CP is marked [+WH] in WH-questions (and other structures with WH-movement). It requires that by LF the specifier of a [+WH] C must itself be an element which has the [+WH] feature, and furthermore that a [+WH] phrase must be in the position of the specifier of a [+WH] C head.

(31) *WH-Criterion* (Rizzi 1991)
If X^0 has a feature [+WH] and XP is an WH-operator, then:
– An X^0 [+WH] must be in a spec-head configuration with a WH-operator
– A WH-operator must be in a spec-head configuration with an X^0 [+WH]

Since the same operator-variable binding relationship is found with negatives, Haegemann and Zanuttini (1991) propose the Neg-Criterion, which also requires negative operators and heads to be in a spec–head relationship by LF.

Rochemont (1986) proposes for English that a focused element must undergo LF raising in order to create the proper operator-variable binding relationship for focus interpretation. Thus, on this analysis focused elements are subject to a similar requirement as WH-elements and negative elements, that is, there must be a spec–head relationship between two [+F] elements.

Petronio proposes that the "twin" of a double construction in ASL, the sentence-internal element which is the target of doubling, is a focus operator. This means that the element is marked [+focus], and undergoes focus raising, parallel to the proposal by Rochemont (1986) for LF focus raising in English. The focus operator raises in the derivation in order to show its scope, as other operators do. In ASL, she assumes, the landing site for movement of the focus operator is [Spec, CP].[10,11] Petronio further proposes that the double occupies the head of CP, which is on the right in ASL, as (30) shows. The head must be marked [+focus] in agreement with its specifier.

Petronio's proposal treats focused elements in ASL in a way parallel to WH-elements and negative elements. The doubled element is licensed by being in a spec–head configuration with its twin, at the level of LF.

In order to capture the requirement that the focus operator must be in the [Spec, CP] position by LF, Petronio generalizes Rizzi's (1991) WH-Criterion to an "Operator Criterion," given in (32). Petronio's version is simply a

[10] On this analysis, the X^0 focus operator moves to an XP position. Although this is not commonly permitted, some authors have argued for its necessity (Koopman 1984, Ortiz de Urbina 1989).

[11] In other languages there might be a special projection known as a Focus Phrase for this element. Petronio makes use of CP instead of FP because she finds no evidence that distinct projections are necessary in ASL. Whether or not this conclusion should be modified is an area for future research.

generalization of the WH-Criterion proposed by Rizzi and the Neg-Criterion proposed by Haegemann and Zanuttini (1991). On Petronio's version, the same requirement applies to all operators, including focus operators.

(32) *Operator Criterion* (Petronio 1993, p. 145)
If X^0 has a feature $[+\alpha]$ and β is an α -operator, then:
– An X^0 $[+\alpha]$ must be in a spec-head configuration with an α -operator
– An α -operator must be in a spec-head configuration with an X^0 $[+\alpha]$

These characteristics account for the properties of doubles observed above. Under Petronio's structure for ASL, the C^0 head is on the right. If the double occupies the root C^0, this accounts for its position on the right of the sentence, the fact that it must be a head, and the observation that only one double can appear in each sentence.

What explains why the twin cannot be in an island? Petronio assumes that the relevant island constraints apply at LF. The requirement that the twin must raise at LF ensures that it will be subject to those constraints which apply at this level.

Finally, why is it that only a WH-double (not a modal or verb double) can occur in direct WH-questions? Petronio proposes that unlike other potential twins, interrogative WH-elements are inherently focused, and must always move to [Spec, CP]. If another element is focused there would be a mismatch of features between the specifier of CP and its head. The only resolution of this conflict permits WH-elements uniquely to be focused in direct questions. This solution may be too strong, however, in that WH-elements are not necessarily doubled (cf. Chapter 23). Petronio also observed other constraints on which potential elements may be doubled, but left detailing and accounting for this as a task for future research.

Petronio notices that sometimes an apparent double construction appears without a twin. She finds that judgments vary across speakers, but at least under certain discourse circumstances sentences like (33) can be accepted.

(33) ASL (Petronio 1993, p. 153)

______________________neg
a. %NANCY BUY COMPUTER CAN'T
'Nancy *can't* buy a computer.'

________whq
b. %BUY CAR WHO
'Who bought a car?'

Petronio analyzes examples like (33) as doubles with a null twin. Noting that ASL permits various null elements in the correct discourse contexts (see Chapter 21), she argues that it is such discourse contexts which also permit null twins. We will discuss examples like (33b) in much more detail in Chapter 23, where we compare competing analyses of WH-movement in ASL.

Petronio's analysis of double constructions accounts for her observations about their distribution, but requires certain stipulations, and makes extensive use of theoretical mechanisms which have since been abandoned. She also hints at some areas for future empirical research. For example, she notes that some verbs double, though not all. Psych verbs and verbs of emotion and feeling are frequent doubles, but she says other verb types are not. What is the proper characterization of verbs which can double – and why would only certain verb types double? What are the proper restrictions on doubling? In what ways is the double construction like – or unlike – typical patterns of focus constructions found across languages? Many empirical and theoretical questions remain to be addressed regarding this construction.

Some insight might be gained by examining the structure of double constructions in Brazilian Sign Language (LSB). This language has a double construction which has many similarities to the one in ASL. Quadros (1999) proposes an analysis which shares some conceptual components with Petronio's analysis of ASL, but is grounded in a less stipulative framework. We turn now to examine her proposal.

22.4.2 Focus doubling in LSB

Quadros (1999) observes that LSB has double constructions of modals, quantifiers, verbs, negation, adverbs, and WH-elements much like those in ASL, though with some important differences. As in ASL, doubles in LSB occur at the end of the sentence, are restricted to heads, and cannot have a twin within syntactic islands. However, as we have seen in Chapter 19, Quadros adopts Kayne's (1994) proposal that all phrase structure is right branching. Under this approach, the focused element would not appear in sentence-final position merely by being generated in C^0, since the rest of the sentence follows C. Everything else must move to the left. In keeping with her Kaynian all-right-branching phrase structure, Quadros proposes the structure in (34) for focus doubling in LSB.[12]

(34) Supra-IP structure (Quadros)

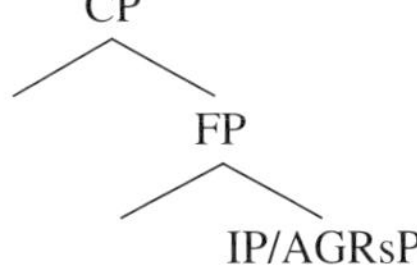

Quadros' proposal makes use of a special projection for focused element, Focus Phrase (FP). According to Quadros' proposal, the focus head F^0 is

[12] Recall from Chapter 19 that Quadros analyzes plain verbs as appearing in structures headed with IP, while agreeing (non-plain) verbs project TP and AGRsP.

base-generated with a [+F] feature, and IP/AgrsP must raise to [Spec, FP]. Following theoretical developments, Quadros uses the notion of feature checking rather than the stipulated Operator Criterion to motivate the movement to [Spec, FP]. On the assumption that spec–head agreement is a means of checking for matching features, the [+F] feature of the head F requires the movement of IP/AgrsP to check this feature. Because the whole clause moves in front of the focused element, it is realized at the end of the sentence. In other respects, her analysis mirrors Petronio's.

However, Quadros notes some empirical differences between double constructions in LSB and ASL. First, LSB requires a non-manual to occur with the focused element (cf. emphasis of focused element in ASL). This is illustrated in (35).

(35) LSB (Quadros 1999, pp. 212–213)

                                          __hn
a. IX<1>CAN GO PARTY CAN

                                   __hn
b. IX<1>LOSE BOOK LOSE

More striking, while Petronio observes only one focus per sentence in ASL, Quadros finds one per clause in LSB. This difference, illustrated in (36), has several consequences.

(36) LSB (Quadros 1999, pp. 212–213)

____hn
a. IX<1>WOULD-LIKE PAY HOUSE WOULD-LIKE

____________________________________hn
b. IX<1>WOULD-LIKE PAY HOUSE PAY

____________________________________hn ________hn
c. IX<1>WOULD-LIKE PAY HOUSE PAY WOULD-LIKE
['I would like to pay for the house.' WS/DLM]

One consequence is that LSB permits doubles within relative clauses, unlike ASL (37).

(37) LSB (Quadros 1999, p. 222)

__________________r
GIRL BICYCLE FALL BICYCLE IS HOSPITAL
'The girl that fell off the bicycle is in the hospital.'

However, like ASL, LSB still disallows doubling across an island, as shown in (38).

(38) LSB (Quadros 1999)

___________r __hn
*GIRL BICYCLE FALL IS HOSPITAL FALL
'The girl who fell off the bicycle is in the hospital.'

Although both Petronio and Quadros use the term "focus" in describing double constructions, it is clear that they refer to prosodic prominence and not necessarily focus in the information-packaging sense. The discourse/pragmatic or semantic import of double constructions should be investigated more closely in both languages. In addition, other constraints on this operation and language-particular differences should be pursued.

Despite these areas requiring further study, it is notable that the mechanisms employed by both analyses are well within the range made available by the frameworks they work within. Once languages which employ syntactic movement rather than stress shift alone to indicate prominence are examined, it is clear that the operations of sign languages are not unique. Quadros is pursuing this issue, comparing sign language double constructions with other spoken language constructions which result in multiple copies of syntactic elements.

22.4.3 Doubles versus tags

Petronio's proposal that double constructions form a special type is based on the lack of a pause before the repeated material. A pause there might motivate a different type of repeated constituent, such as a tag or right dislocation. Neidle et al. (2000) take the position that repeated material should indeed be analyzed as a "tag" construction, whether there is a prosodic break or not. According to them, "In ASL, as in many other languages, sentence-final tags (consisting of a repeated but reduced version of basic material from the main clause) occur productively" (p. 56). They note that affirmative declarative tags with null verbal material are marked by a head nod, of the type Liddell observed in clauses with null verbal material such as null copular constructions, gapping, and verb phrase deletion. They also note that "a pronoun coreferential with the main-clause subject is also commonly found in the tag" (ibid.).

Neidle et al. distinguish between tags and right dislocations. According to them, "pronominal right dislocation of both subjects and objects occurs quite frequently in ASL" (p. 55). Right-dislocated pronouns are not limited to subjects, are normally not preceded by a pause, and do not have the head nod characterizing tags. Note that the transcription they use is sometimes incompatible with their description. They transcribe right-dislocated pronouns following a comma, which is not meant to indicate a pause. Similarly, tags are transcribed with a comma, although they state, "the tag in ASL may or may not be preceded by a pause" (p. 172, n. 11).

Neidle et al. (2000) do not offer any structural analysis of the tag or right-dislocation constructions. However, in Aarons et al. (1992) and Neidle et al. (1997), the position for the tag is indicated as right-adjoined to CP, with positions for right-dislocated elements both above and below the tag position. Neidle et al. define a tag as "structurally a full copy of the basic clausal structure with only a few items overtly instantiated" (p. 259). How this is structurally realized is not stated. Some examples of what Neidle et al. consider tags are given in (40); examples of right dislocation are in (39).

(39) Right dislocation
ASL (Neidle et al. 2000, p. 55)
JOHN_i LEAVE, IX_i
'John left, him.'

(40) Tag
ASL (Neidle et al. 2000, p. 57)
$\overline{\text{JOHN FUTURE}_{tns}\text{ GO, FUTURE}_{tns}}^{\text{hn}}$
a. JOHN FUTURE_{tns} GO, FUTURE_{tns}
'John will go, (he) will.'
b. JOHN_i FUTURE_{tns} GO, IX_i (hn)
'John will go, he (will).'

(41) Tag and right dislocation
ASL (Neidle et al. 2000, p. 57)
JOHN_i FUTURE_{tns} GO, FUTURE_{tns}, IX_i (hn)
John will go, (he) will, him.'

Neidle et al. do not attribute any particular semantic or discourse function or prosodic prominence to tags and right dislocations. They state, "Although further research on the discourse conditions associated with pronominal right dislocation in ASL is needed, preliminary investigation suggests that essentially the same discourse factors are relevant to the use of pronominal right dislocation in languages such as French, Norwegian, and ASL" (p. 55).

Because Neidle et al. do not distinguish between different types of sentence-final constructions, it would be expected that any type of element can appear there, with no particular semantic or discourse effect. In contrast, Petronio and Quadros claim that double constructions are used in particular discourse contexts, and have rather stringent restrictions. For example, double constructions are restricted to a single head; there is a hierarchical restriction on which elements may be doubled; and the "twin" may not appear in a syntactic island. By separating out constructions with and without a pause, Petronio and Quadros are able to capture significant generalizations which the Neidle et al. approach misses.

But how do Petronio and Quadros account for examples with a pause? No explicit proposal is given. Petronio and Lillo-Martin point out that in examples with a pause, "the construction has different syntactic properties." Their proposals are compatible with the possibility that with a pause, the "tag" structure of Neidle et al. is employed. Although this would mean two distinct analyses are used, one for cases with a pause and the second for cases without a pause, this contrast is justified by the different syntactic behaviors Petronio and Lillo-Martin and Quadros observe between such examples.

22.5 Clefting: so-called rhetorical questions

Wilbur (1994a, 1995b, 1996) argues that one of the ways ASL places elements in sentence-final position in focus is through an operation equivalent to WH-clefts, such as *What Bob likes to play is dominoes*. The ASL construction she considers a WH-cleft has been labeled previously as a "rhetorical question" construction (Baker-Shenk 1983). However, Wilbur argues that this construction does not consist of a true rhetorical question plus an answer, as previously claimed (see also Neidle et al. 2000), but rather that it consists of a single clause with the structure of a WH-cleft, including a WH-clause and a focused phrase. (In this context, the term "focus" is being used in its information-packaging sense as well as prominence.) The examples in (42) display the construction. (The traditional rhetorical question analysis is indicated by the 'rhq' non-manual marker in (42a); (42b) uses 'br' for brow raise, reflecting the alternative analysis.)

(42) ASL (Wilbur 1994a, pp. 650, 653)

 ______________rhq ____hn
a. LEE(fs) PAINT WHAT? CHAIR
'What Lee painted was the chair.'
 ______________br ____hn
b. CHAIR PAINT WHO, LEE(fs)
'The one who painted the chair was Lee.'

First, Wilbur notes that there are prosodic differences between true WH rhetorical questions and the construction in (42). Normally, WH-questions have a non-manual marker containing furrowed brow, and Wilbur claims that true rhetorical questions also have a furrowed brow (see also Chapter 23 on the non-manual marking of WH-questions). The constructions in (42) have a non-manual marker with raised brows. Furthermore, Wilbur argues that the WH-clause and its "answer" (the focused phrase) form a single prosodic sentence (although the WH-clause is followed by a blink, head nod, and/or short pause, markers of some kind of prosodic boundary), and that other signs cannot interrupt the WH-clause and the focused phrase. True question–answer pairs do not have the prosody of a single sentence or a restriction against intervening signs.

A further difference between the WH-clefts and question–answer pairs concerns the structure of the WH-clause. As will be demonstrated in Chapter 23, regular WH-questions can have a WH-element in initial position, final position, or doubled, in both positions. Wilbur finds, however, that doubled WH-elements are not permitted in WH-clefts; and there is a preference for the WH-element to be on the right in these structures.

Wilbur (1994a) argues that a WH-cleft analysis is appropriate for these constructions because they display the typical properties of WH-clefts, as discussed by Foley and Van Valin (1985).

- First, WH-clefting, as a foregrounding operation, brings focused phrases outside of the main clause. As the "answer" corresponding to the WH-word must appear after the WH-clause, Wilbur argues that the so-called "rhetorical question" construction has this property.
- Second, the focused phrase of a WH-cleft must contain primary stress. Wilbur (1999a) finds prosodic evidence that the sentence-final position (excluding extrametrical pronouns) has primary stress in ASL. In addition, the fact that extra-stressed "doubled" elements appear in the final position also supports the idea that the sentence-final position is one of special prosodic prominence (see Section 22.4).
- Third, the WH-cleft contains a presupposition, analyzed as an "open proposition" (OP) containing a variable (after Prince 1986). Wilbur argues that since so-called rhetorical questions have the syntactic structure of a question, the WH-clause has an open variable.
- Fourth, the focused phrase of a WH-cleft provides the information missing in the open proposition. The "answer" to the rhetorical question does just that. The relationship between true question–answer pairs is broader: it is not necessary for such a response to be a literal answer to the question, as it is in WH-clefts.

With these observations to support the general notion that the so-called rhetorical question construction should be analyzed as a WH-cleft, Wilbur (1996) proposes the following structural analysis, illustrated in (43). The first aspect of Wilbur's analysis is the generation of the construction as a small clause with the focused phrase as a subject and the WH-clause as its predicate.[13] The focus phrase then moves to a structural focus position. In Wilbur's analysis, this position is Spec, IP, which is marked [+F], in agreement with the head I^0. The non-focused material (WH-clause) moves to Spec, CP. In this position, the WH-clause will be marked with brow raise, according to Wilbur's general treatment of brow raise (see Section 22.3). Within the WH-clause, the WH-element

[13] It is a small clause because it involves a subject and a predicate but not a main verb.

moves to C^0, which is on the right (cf. Chapter 23 on WH-question formation).

(43) (Wilbur 1996, p. 247)

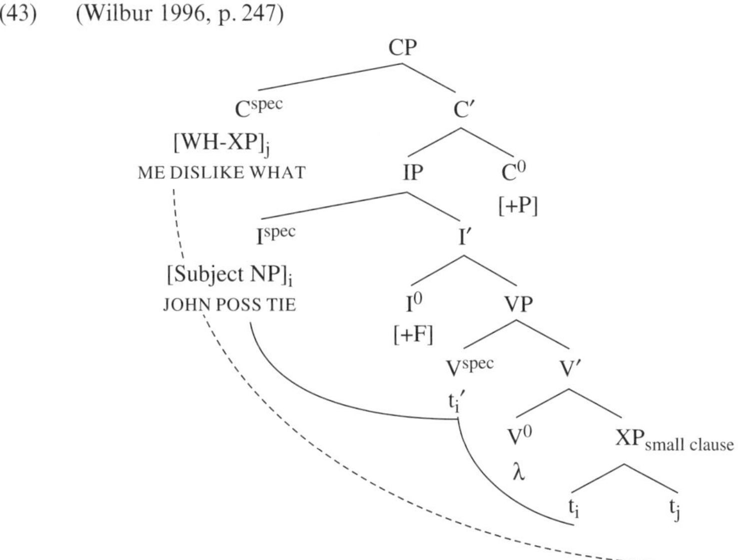

Wilbur's (1996) analysis of WH-clefts bears some resemblance to the analysis we have seen in Section 22.4.2 of doubling constructions in LSB proposed by Quadros (1999; of course, Wilbur's proposal for WH-clefts predates Quadros' proposal for LSB). In particular, the analysis employs the preposing of material following the focused element in order to leave the focused element in sentence-final position. Wilbur draws on the work of Heggie (1988) and Heycock (1991) on WH-clefts in English in developing the model for her account.

Wilbur's arguments that the so-called rhetorical question construction is analogous to WH-clefts is persuasive. However, some questions can be raised about the details of her analysis, and its consequences. For example, Wilbur points out that the full range of options available in true WH-questions is not possible in the WH-clause of a WH-cleft. This observation is not fully explained.[14] She also cites additional structures with WH-clefts in embedded clauses which need to be explained.

Importantly, Wilbur (1994a) points out that those elements which can be doubled (WH-words, modals, verbs, and pronouns) cannot be focused by the WH-cleft. She therefore argues that the WH-clefting operation is the true focuser in ASL. We observe that the WH-cleft focuses phrases, while the doubling construction affects heads. In fact, as Wilbur claims, it is the WH-clefting structure which accomplishes true informational

[14] Although there are some differences between WH-clefts in ASL and English pseudoclefts, it is also true of English that not all types of WH-questions can form clefts (Bošković 1997).

focus. As we have already noted, the doubling construction is used for prosodic prominence, in situations of emphasis and contrastive focus.

To sum up, we have seen that sign languages fall into the category of languages which use extensive syntactic movement operations to achieve discourse and pragmatic effects. While some would characterize the structure of sign language using just such notions, others would derive these structures from a more uniformly rigid structure. In either case, no analysis exceeds the boundaries established by spoken languages – no special mechanisms are required to account for the sign language data. Instead, they fall within the realm of universals regarding the ways in which sentences achieve different informational goals.

We turn next to a structure which has received considerable attention in the ASL literature: WH-questions. We will see that in this domain, questions have been raised regarding whether or not the universal organizing characterizations found on the basis of spoken languages will suffice for sign languages.

23 WH-questions

The study of WH-questions in ASL has generated a fair amount of attention. This is because of the diversity of question types available, leading to debate regarding the proper analysis of questions in general. The issue has importance for syntactic theory, because at the heart is a dispute as to the possible range of phrase structures available across languages. Since Chomsky (1986), it has generally been assumed that WH-movement brings WH-phrases to the specifier of CP ([Spec, CP]). Cross-linguistic generalizations about WH-movement to [Spec, CP] have been challenged by analyses of WH-questions in ASL, and the issue is not settled. Whatever its outcome, it is highly relevant for syntactic theories attempting to account for universal properties of language.

A further reason for interest in sign language WH-questions comes from the increasing attention being paid to the role of intonation in grammatical structure. Although intonation has been considered from the phonological side for some time, recently, more and more generative linguists have recognized that intonational properties have relevance to syntactic structure, whether they adopt an analysis which represents aspects of intonation in the syntax or not (e.g. Zec and Inkelas 1990, Truckenbrodt 1999, Cheng and Rooryck 2000, Bošković 2001, 2002). Recall from Chapter 15 that sign language non-manuals can be fruitfully analyzed as intonation on the phonological side. Some sign language syntacticians are beginning to take note of this analysis as well. The sign language analysis of non-manual markers and the spoken language analysis of intonation may just now be in a position to learn from each other.

We begin this chapter with a brief overview of WH-question formation in spoken languages. Then, we turn to a rather detailed discussion of the debate regarding the position of [Spec, CP] in ASL. We present the proposal that [Spec, CP] in ASL is on the left, and WH-movement brings WH-phrases to the sentence-initial position (as argued for or assumed by, among others, Lillo-Martin 1990, Lillo-Martin and Fischer 1992, Petronio 1993, Wilbur 1995a, 1996, Petronio and Lillo-Martin 1997, Wilbur and Patschke 1999). We also review an alternative proposal, which is that [Spec, CP] in ASL is on the right, and WH-movement brings WH-phrases to the sentence-final position (especially Aarons et al. 1992, Neidle et al. 1997, and other works by the ASLLRP group, as summarized in Neidle et al. 2000). We go over the gist of each analysis, and show how they account for the range of data observed. Along the way, we indicate areas of possible problems for each hypothesis. Then, we turn to evidence from LSB supporting the leftward analysis for that language.

All sign language linguists, regardless of the theories they propound or the approach to analysis they take, are necessarily field linguists. No complete reference grammar of any sign language has yet been written, and the data are usually gathered for these young languages by the linguists who analyze them. The data judgments of native signers working with investigators of WH-questions do not always agree, and the different judgments are responsible for some of the differences in the analyses, though certainly not all of them. We will point out those data judgment differences in the course of the discussion. In some cases, investigators attribute variability in judgments to poor data-collection methodology, and certainly the judgments obtained by one research group should be replicable. In other cases, investigators attempt to account for variability in judgments by describing differences in dialects or idiolects which would lead to such variability. Where possible, we seek explanation for data differences, although in some cases we must leave full solutions on specific issues for future research.

We close this chapter with a new look at WH-questions, taking into consideration the growing body of evidence that the WH-question non-manual marker, like other non-manual markers in sign languages, is more closely analogous to an intonation pattern than previously thought (cf. Chapter 15). The implications this has for the analysis of WH-questions in ASL are raised, and areas for further research are outlined.

23.1 A cross-linguistic look at WH-questions

In some languages, such as Japanese and Chinese, WH-phrases stay in their *in situ* position. This is the position where a corresponding non-WH-phrase would be located in basic sentences. Some languages allow both *in situ* and moved WH-phrases (e.g., French). Examples from Japanese (an SOV language) and Chinese (an SVO language) are given in (1)–(2).[1]

(1) Japanese (Watanabe 2001, p. 207)

a. John-ga dare-ni sono hon-o age-ta no
John-NOM who-DAT that book-ACC give-PST Q
'Who did John give that book to?'

[1] Takahashi (1993) argues that true overt WH-movement is also an option in Japanese.

b. Boku-wa John-ga nani-o katta ka shiritai
I-top John-nom what-Acc bought Q want-to-know
'I want to know what John bought.'

(2) Chinese (Watanabe 2001, pp. 212, 203)
a. ni xiang mai shenme (ne)
You want buy what Q
'What do you want to buy?'
b. Zhangsan xiang-zhidao Lisi mai-le shenme
Zhangsan wonder Lisi bought what
'Zhangsan wonders what Lisi bought.'

In other languages, including English, a WH-question always has an overtly moved WH-phrase, which lands in the sentence-initial position analyzed as [Spec, CP] (3).[2]

(3) a. Who did John give that book to?
b. * John gave that book to who?

Across the world's spoken languages, it has been observed that when WH-phrases move, WH-movement is virtually always to the left, to the sentence-initial position, as in the English example (Baker 1970, Bresnan 1970, Bach 1971). This is true even for languages which generally have their specifiers on the right, such as Palauan (Georgopoulos 1991).

There is one more option, observed in some languages which have overt focus movement, such as Hungarian. Here, the WH-phrase may move to the position associated with focus, which may be something other than sentence-initial position. In Hungarian, for example, focused elements move to the immediate preverbal position, as shown in (4). WH-phrases move to the same position, as shown in (5).

(4) Hungarian (Horvath 1980, p. 4)
a. Mari [$_{VP}$ [$_{V'}$ AZ ÉDÉNYEKET$_i$ rakta az asztalra] t$_i$]
Mary THE DISHES-acc put the table-onto
'Mary put THE DISHES on the table.'
b. János [$_{VP}$ [$_{V'}$ A KÉRTBÖL$_i$ jött be] t$_i$]
John THE GARDEN-FROM came in
'John came in FROM THE GARDEN'

(5) a. Mari [$_{VP}$ [$_{V'}$ mit$_i$ rakott az asztalra] t$_i$]
Mary what-acc put the table-onto
'What did Mary put on the table?'
b. János [$_{VP}$ [$_{V'}$ honnan$_i$ jött be] t$_i$]
John where came in
'Where did John come in from?'

[2] (3b) is acceptable as an echo question. In general, we put aside echo questions here.

WH-phrases are considered focused, for both syntactic and semantic reasons. Semantically, the interpretation of WH-questions involves a presupposition (the known information) and a gap (the question). Thus, it is not surprising that WH-phrases should occur in structures used for focus. Syntactically, in languages such as Hungarian it is clear that the WH-phrase behaves like other focused constituents. In such cases, WH-phrases do not appear in [Spec, CP]. Sometimes this conclusion is clear from the surface order, as in the Hungarian case, since the position of the moved WH-phrase is too low to be [Spec, CP]. In other cases (such as Kikuyu, Bergvall 1987, and Tangale, Kenstowicz 1985, Tuller 1992), tests such as movement restrictions indicate that a WH-phrase in a focus position is not in [Spec, CP].

In addition to the question of whether WH-phrases move overtly or not, there are cross-linguistic differences with respect to the movement of multiple WH-phrases within a single clause (Richards 1997). In English, only one WH-phrase may move per clause, as shown in (6).

(6) a. Who bought what where when?
b. *Who what where when bought?

However, in many Slavic languages, multiple WH-phrases will all move to the sentence-initial position (with language-particular differences with respect to the landing site of the various WH-phrases; see Rudin 1988, Grewendorf 2001, Bošković 2002). Some examples are given in (7)–(8).

(7) Serbo-Croatian (Bošković 2002, p. 353)
a. Ko koga voli?
who whom loves
b. Koga ko voli?
whom who loves
'Who loves whom?'

(8) Bulgarian (Bošković 2002, p. 352)
Na kogo kakvo dade Ivan?
to who what gave Ivan
'What did Ivan give to who?'

While these surface differences exist, many syntacticians have argued that in all languages all WH-phrases must be in [Spec, CP] position by LF, to ensure the correct interpretation of their scope. Huang (1982) famously made this argument for Chinese, pointing out that although the WH-elements in (9a) and (9b) are both in the embedded clause, they take different scope, depending on the matrix verb. In the corresponding English examples, the scope of the WH-phrase is determined by its surface position. Thus, covert WH-movement to [Spec, CP] is often assumed to front any WH-phrases not in this position at the surface level.

(9) Chinese (Huang 1982, pp. 371, 382)

a. Zhangsan xiangxin shei mai-le shu?
Z believe who bought books
'Who does Zhangsan believe bought books?'

b. wo xiang-zhidao Lisi mai-le sheme
I wonder L bought what
'I wonder what Lisi bought.'

This overview of the differences found across languages in the form of WH-questions serves to highlight one similarity. What appears to be without exception is that [Spec, CP] is on the left. Only one recent theoretical approach captures this generalization without stipulation: Kayne (1994). On Kayne's proposal (described in Chapter 19), *all* specifiers are uniformly on the left. Thus, it immediately follows that [Spec, CP] is on the left. In other theories, the generalization must be stipulated. Whether or not Kayne's approach can be upheld, the cross-linguistic generalization about the position of [Spec, CP] is striking, and it would be a surprise indeed to hear that some newly discovered language violates it. But it is this generalization that is being challenged by work on ASL.

23.2 Is WH-movement to left or right?

All ASL researchers seem to agree that WH-elements may remain *in situ*, as illustrated in (10) and Figure 23.1, where the questioned element is in the ordinary position for a subject (a) or object (b). Such straightforward examples have not been extensively discussed, so no proposals have been made concerning the licensing of such cases (cf. Bošković 1998, Cheng and Rooryck 2000, for spoken languages). However, unlike some other languages allowing both moved and *in situ* WH-elements (such as French), no restrictions against leaving WH-elements *in situ* have emerged for ASL. This, of course, makes it impossible to determine whether a WH-element has moved or not in some cases.

(10) a. ASL (Neidle et al. 2000, p. 110)

wh
WHO LOVE JOHN
'Who loves John?'

b. ASL (Petronio and Lillo-Martin 1997, p. 26)

whq
JOHN BUY WHAT
'What did John buy?'

Both the proponents of a leftward [Spec, CP] analysis and the proponents of a rightward [Spec, CP] analysis also agree that WH-elements can be repeated, or doubled, in both sentence-initial and sentence-final

Figure 23.1 *In situ* WH-questions

position, as illustrated in (11) and Figure 23.2.[3] The structural positions of these sentence-initial and sentence-final WH-elements differ for the two proposals, however.

(11) a. ASL (Neidle et al. 2000, p. 115)

______________________________ wh
"WHAT", JOHN BUY "WHAT"
'What, what did John buy?'

b. ASL (Petronio and Lillo-Martin 1997, p. 27)

______________________________ whq
WHAT NANCY BUY YESTERDAY WHAT
'What did Nancy buy yesterday?'

We have already seen in Chapter 22 that Petronio and Lillo-Martin (1997; Petronio 1993) and Quadros (1999) have argued that WH-elements may be "doubled" in the same manner as non-WH focused elements. Let

[3] The sign Neidle et al. gloss "WHAT" is used without the quotation marks by Petronio and Lillo-Martin. It is used in a broader range of circumstances than English *what* would be. Neidle et al. call it a "generic" WH-phrase. See Wood (in progress) for an account of the distribution of this sign in comparison with three other signs for *what*. Neidle et al. include a comma after the first "WHAT" in accordance with their analysis of it as a topic, but state explicitly that this WH-element is not followed by a pause.

Figure 23.2 Doubled WH-question

us review and expand their analyses of WH-questions, and compare their approach to that of Neidle et al. (1997, 1998b, 2000). We begin with the analysis of questions with two WH-words, one at the beginning and one at the end, like those in (11), because we believe it helps to clarify issues concerning the derivation of questions with a single WH-element. We also find that the doubled WH-questions are very commonly used, another reason for tackling them first.

23.2.1 WH-questions with more than one WH-phrase

Petronio (1993), Petronio and Lillo-Martin (1997), and Quadros (1999) argue that the position to which WH-elements move, the specifier of CP, is on the left in ASL and LSB.[4] Neidle et al. (2000) argue instead that in ASL it is on the right.[5] The phrase markers in (12) illustrate the structures associated with doubled WH-questions under Petronio and Lillo-Martin's Leftward Analysis, and Neidle et al.'s Rightward Analysis, respectively.[6]

4 This view is also presented by Lillo-Martin (1990, 1992), Lillo-Martin and Fischer (1992), Wilbur and Patschke (1999). Citations will mainly be to Petronio and Lillo-Martin (1997) for ASL, and Quadros (1999) for LSB.

5 The ASLLRP group has presented this view in virtually all of their published works, including Aarons et al. (1992), Aarons (1994), Neidle et al. (1997, 1998b, 2000). For rhetorical purposes, citations will mainly be to Neidle et al. (2000), which summarizes the previous work.

6 Recall from Chapter 22 that Petronio distinguishes doubled constituents with a preceding pause from those without a pause (or hold). In general, when we discuss doubled elements we follow Petronio in referring only to those with no pause/hold preceding them, unless specified otherwise.

(12) Two proposed phrase structures of WH-questions

A. Leftward Analysis (Petronio and Lillo-Martin 1997)

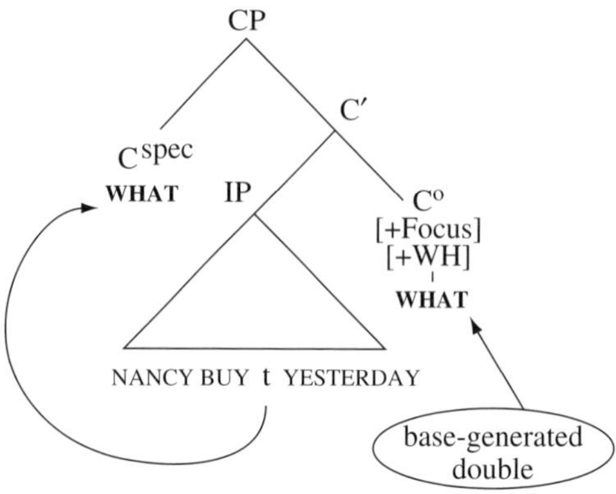

B. Rightward Analysis (Petronio and Lillo-Martin's 1997 diagram of the ASLLRP proposal)

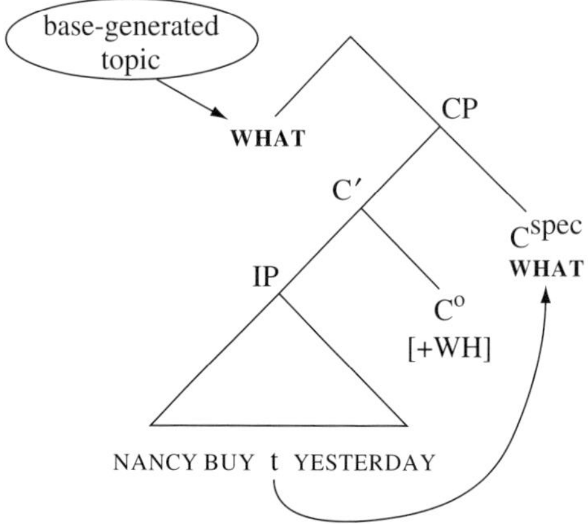

Under Petronio and Lillo-Martin's account, sentences with two WH-elements are derived in the same way as Petronio (1993) analyzed "focus doubles" (see Chapter 22). The right-hand WH-element is base-generated in the head of CP, which has the features [+Focus, +WH]. Its "twin" (the sentence-internal WH-element, also marked [+Focus, +WH]), overtly raises to [Spec, CP], on the left. This analysis leads to the expectation that WH-doubles will have the same characteristics as (other) focus doubles, as repeated in (13) below.

(13) Syntactic properties of doubles:

i. the double occurs at the end of the sentence
ii. the double is an X^0, not an XP

iii. there is only one double per sentence
iv. the twin cannot be within a syntactic island
v. only a WH-double can occur in direct WH-questions (not a modal or verb double) (Petronio 1993, p. 135)

That WH-doubles have these characteristics is illustrated in (14)–(18).

i. the double occurs at the end of the sentence

(14) ASL (Petronio and Lillo-Martin 1997, pp. 26, 27, 32)

a. ______________whq
WHO LIKE NANCY WHO
'Who likes Nancy?'

b. ______________whq
WHAT NANCY BUY WHAT
'What did Nancy buy?'

c. __________________________whq
WHAT NANCY BUY YESTERDAY WHAT
'What did Nancy buy yesterday?'

d. ____________________whq
WHY STUDY LINGUISTICS WHY
'Why do you study linguistics?'

ii. the double is an X^0, not an XP[7,8]

(15) ASL (Petronio and Lillo-Martin 1997, p. 33)

a. ____________________whq
WHO CAR BREAK-DOWN WHO
'Whose car broke down?'

b. ________________________whq
* WHO CAR BREAK-DOWN WHO CAR

c. __________________________whq
WHICH COMPUTER JOHN BUY WHICH
'Which computer did John buy?'

d. __________________________________whq
* WHICH COMPUTER JOHN BUY WHICH COMPUTER

[7] According to Petronio's analysis, examples like those in (15b, d, f) may be grammatical with a pause or hold preceding the doubled element, as in (i).

(i) ______________________________wh
HOW-MANY BROTHER SISTER YOU HAVE [hold],
______________________wh
HOW-MANY BROTHER SISTER

[8] An alternative explanation for the failure of WH-phrases such as WHICH COMPUTER to be doubled may be the observation that so-called "D-linked" WH-phrases cannot be focused. D-linked WH-phrases (Pesetsky 1987) are used when the range of felicitous answers is established in the discourse or context. In this case, the WH-phrase is related to given information, so cannot be focused. Bošković (2002) shows that D-linked WH-phrases are not focused in Slavic. We thank Željko Bošković for pointing out this alternative to us. Further investigation of the effect of D-linking in ASL WH-questions is needed.

whq
e. HOW-MANY BROTHER SISTER YOU HAVE HOW-MANY
'How many brothers and sisters do you have?'

f. * HOW-MANY BROTHER SISTER YOU HAVE
whq
HOW-MANY BROTHER SISTER

iii. there is only one double per sentence

(16) ASL

whq
* WHO BUY WHAT WHO WHAT
'Who bought what?'

iv. the twin cannot be within a syntactic island

(17) ASL (Petronio 1993, p. 137)

hn
a. * MOTHER CURIOUS WHO WILL SHOW-UP WILL
'(My) mother is curious who will show up.'

b. * ANN WANT KNOW WHO CAN'T READ CAN'T
'Ann wants to know who can't read.'

v. only a WH-double can occur in direct WH-questions

(18) ASL (Petronio 1993, p. 137)

whq
a. WHO WILL BUY HOUSE WHO

whq
b. * WHO WILL BUY HOUSE WILL

whq
c. * WHO WILL BUY HOUSE BUY
'Who will buy a house?'

As summarized in Chapter 22, Petronio and Lillo-Martin's analysis accounts for the characteristics in (14)–(18). According to this analysis, [Spec, CP] is on the left, but the C^0 head is final. The WH-phrase moves to the [Spec, CP] position, and island conditions apply to this movement. A focused element which is a head may be base-generated in the C^0 head position. Thus, a single-sign WH-word may be base-generated on the right. Since this WH-word is focused, it receives phonological prominence (this will be discussed in more detail shortly). By stipulation, only the matrix CP can be [+focus] in ASL, so only one focused element may appear per sentence. The Operator Criterion (given in Chapter 22) requires the WH-phrase and the [+WH] head to be in a spec–head relation with each other. Thus, if a WH-phrase is in [Spec, CP], a non-WH-element cannot be in C^0.

Neidle et al. (2000) argue that [Spec, CP] is on the right in ASL, and they dispute the claim that there is a special double construction for WH-questions or other elements. Instead, they account for WH-questions with more than one WH-element in two ways. In one, the sentence-initial

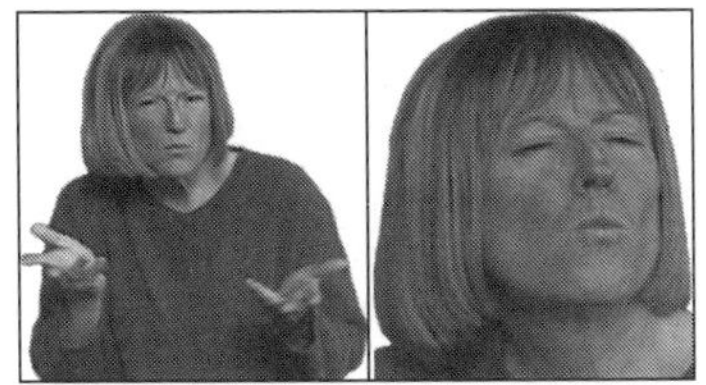

JOHN BUY WHAT YESTERDAY

Figure 23.3 *In situ* WH-element

WH-element is a topic, and the WH-element on the right is in [Spec, CP]. In the other, the sentence-initial WH-element is *in situ*, and the right-hand WH-element is a tag. We now describe their proposals in more detail.

According to Neidle et al., with a WH-element in the sentence-final [Spec, CP] position, a second WH-element can occur as a base-generated topic. This is the analysis shown in the phrase marker in (12). Neidle et al. claim that the non-manual marker used with WH-topics is distinct from the regular WH-question non-manual. In particular, they claim that WH-topics may display "a combination of *wh*-marking and topic marking" (Aarons 1994, p. 124). They say, however, that the non-manual marking associated with WH-topics "exhibits some variability and does not always distinguish *wh*-topics from nontopic *wh*-phrases" (Neidle et al. 2000, p. 115). They also note that WH-topics are not followed by a pause (unlike other topics), although they are notated with a comma. There is no other indication in their notation that the initial WH-phrase has the non-manual marking of a WH-topic.

In order to explore these claims, we present our own video grabs of the non-manual markings accompanying WH-elements in various positions, as well as (non-WH) topics and focused elements, in Figure 23.3 through Figure 23.7. The figure captions provide the contexts from which the grabs were taken, but the illustrations only capture the non-manual markings during the underlined sign.

The *in situ* WH-element (shown in Figure 23.3) and WH-element in initial position (shown in Figure 23.4) share the essential elements of WH-question non-manual marking, including furrowed brows, squinted eyes, head tilted to the side, and a slight side-to-side headshake (Baker-Shenk 1983). The initial WH-element has a backward tilt of the head, while the final WH-elements have a forward tilt. The non-WH topic (in Figure 23.6), on the other hand, is marked by raised brows, wide-open eyes, head tilted back, and a hold or pause following the sign. This indicates to us that the proposal by Neidle et al. analyzing the sentence-initial WH-element as a topic is not fully supported by the behavior of the accompanying non-manual markers.

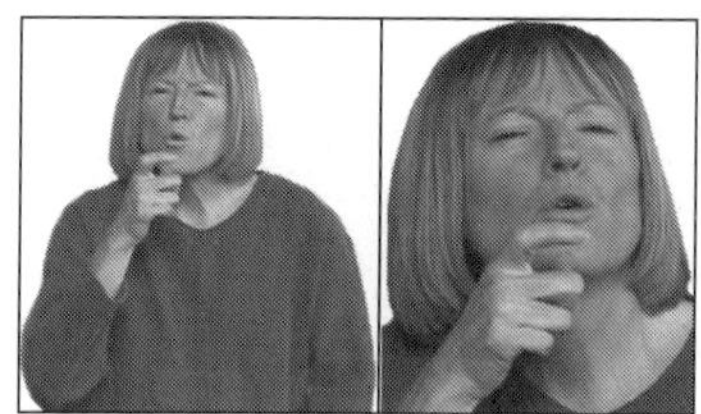

WHO YOU LIKE

Figure 23.4 WH-element in initial position (not *in situ*)

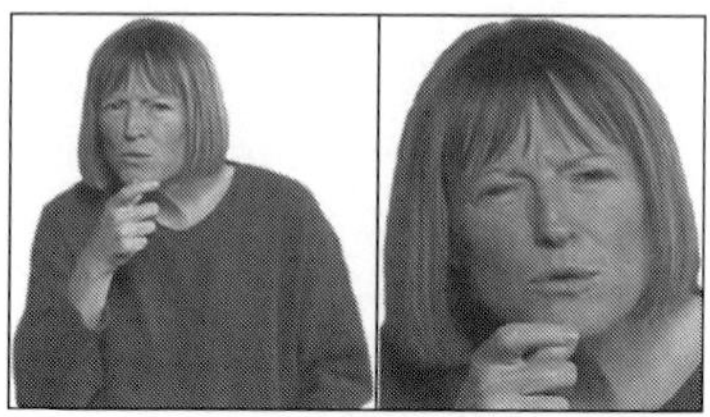

BUY CAR WHO

Figure 23.5 WH-element in final position (not *in situ*)

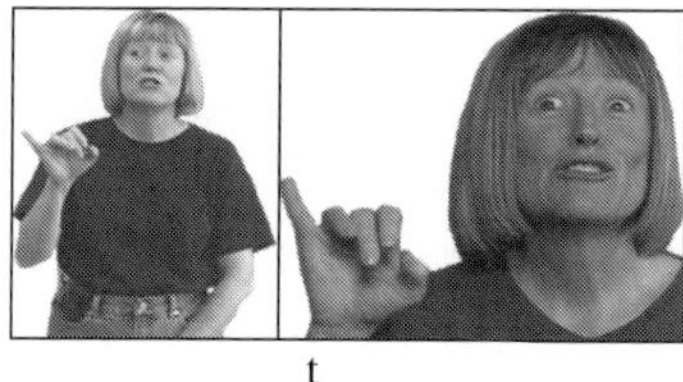

t
JOHN, I LIKE

Figure 23.6 Topic (non-WH)

It is notable that although the facial expressions for the WH-element in final position (Figure 23.5) and focused non-WH-element in final position (Figure 23.7) are distinct, they share some features, including some brow furrowing and eye squinting on the non-WH sign. Eye gaze toward the addressee and forward head position mark the questions only, with the final WH-element having a more intense brow furrow and a more forward head thrust than non-final ones.

The two kinds of final signs share characteristics of phonological prominence (Wilbur 1999a). According to Wilbur, stressed signs are produced with increased muscle tension, obtaining increased peak velocity, and achieving greater displacement. Neidle et al. explain the prominence of sentence-final WH-phrases by claiming of the non-manual marking that "the intensity is greatest nearest the source of the +wh feature with which the marking is associated, and it diminishes as distance from that node increases" (Neidle et al. 2000, p. 114). Any differences between sentence-initial and sentence-final WH non-manuals may then be attributed to the

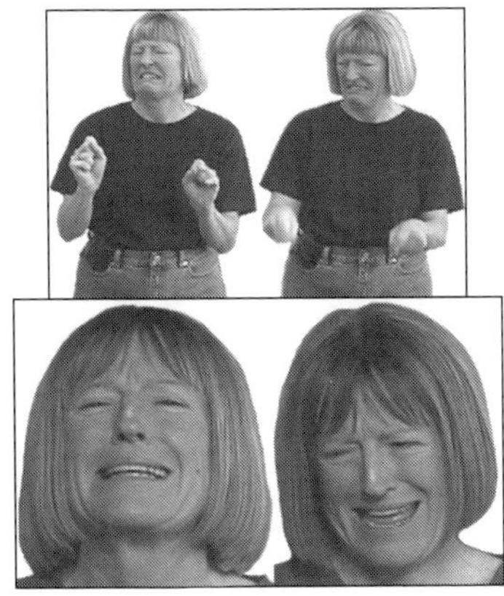

JOHN CAN READ CAN

Figure 23.7 Focus (non-WH)

added prominence or intensity of final WH-elements rather than to topic-like non-manual marking on initial WH-elements. The latter explanation stems from the assumption on which much of their theory is based: that non-manual markers are a direct manifestation of syntactic structure. We will return to this issue and present a different account of non-manuals in Section 23.5, at the end of the chapter.

Neidle et al. also claim that WH-topics behave like base-generated topics in two respects. First, they have the same distributional properties as other base-generated topics, in that (a) at most one other topic can be used with a WH-topic; (b) the WH-topic must precede any moved topics; and (c) the WH-topic may either precede or follow other base-generated topics (cf. Chapter 22 on topics). Their examples of the last claim are given in (19), in which both WHO and VEGETABLE are analyzed as base-generated topics and as such may freely occur in either order.

(19) ASL (Neidle et al. 2000, p. 116)

    ___wh___ ____t2-bg____ __________________wh

a. WHO, VEGETABLE, PREFER POTATO WHO

   'Who, as for vegetables, who prefers potatoes?'

    _______t2-bg_______ ____________________wh

b. VEGETABLE, WHO, PREFER POTATO WHO

   'As for vegetables, who, who prefers potatoes?'

According to Neidle et al., the second way in which WH-topics behave like base-generated topics has to do with ordering of specific and more general elements. They observe that a more specific NP may occur in a topic, followed by a coreferential pronoun in the sentence-internal position, but it is ungrammatical for the pronoun to occur in topic position, followed by the specific NP, as shown in (20). Similarly, the generic WH-element

"WHAT," which can be used to indicate any WH-sign, is often used as the second WH-phrase to a more specific one, but never is the order "WHAT" followed by a more specific WH-phrase, as shown in (21).

(20) ASL (Neidle et al. 2000, p. 117)

 t2-bg
a. JOHN_i, IX_i LIKE MARY
'As for John, he likes Mary.'

 t2-bg
b. * IX_i, JOHN_i LIKE MARY
'As for him, John likes Mary.'

(21) ASL (Neidle et al. 2000, p. 117)

 wh
a. WHO, LOVE JOHN "WHAT"
'Who, who [generic *wh*-phrase] loves John?'

 wh
b. * "WHAT", LOVE JOHN WHO
'Who [generic *wh*-phrase], who loves John?'

We point out that there are important differences between the two types, however. The pronominal restriction can be related to a more general prohibition against using a pronoun indicating a specific referential locus before the referent associated with that locus has been established (see Neidle et al. 2000, p. 56). Thus, even across sentences use of the pronoun first is infelicitous, as seen in our own (22). On the other hand, the generic WH-sign can precede a more specific WH-sign across sentences, as in our own (23). An alternative explanation for the distinction in (21) is that the generic WH-sign can be base-generated in the focus position. The WH-phrase which most clearly satisfies the requirements of the position in which it is generated (the "true" WH-phrase) moves to Spec, CP – on the left. The focused form may be specific or generic.

(22) ASL

 hn neg
* I LIKE a-IX(him), BUT 1-TRUST-a a-JOHN
'I like him, but I don't trust John.'

(23) ASL

 wh wh
"WHAT"? WHO LOVE JOHN "WHAT"?
'What's up? Who, who [generic *wh*-phrase] loves John?'

As mentioned, the second way in which a sentence may have more than one WH-phrase according to Neidle et al. is with one WH-element within the main CP (*in situ*), and the second in a tag. This is illustrated in (24).

(24) ASL (Neidle et al. 2000, p. 114)

    ____hs
    ________________wh
    WHO LIKE JOHN, WHO
    'Who likes John, who (does)?'

According to Neidle et al., such constructions have the properties of other tags: a head movement during the tag (it is a headshake, not a nod); and an optional prosodic break before the WH-element.[9]

To sum up, both the leftward and rightward analyses of WH-movement in ASL can account for cases of two WH-signs within one sentence, but they do so in different ways. According to the leftward analysis, the WH-phrase in sentence-initial position is in [Spec, CP], and the one on the right is in the position for focus. According to the rightward analysis, the position of [Spec, CP] is on the right, and the initial WH-phrase may be a topic. The two approaches have differing predictions about the nature of a sentence-final WH-element. According to Petronio and Lillo-Martin, the sentence-final position is a focus position. It should be expected, then, that WH-elements in this position receive a special, focused interpretation. According to Neidle et al., the sentence-final position is simply the regular position into which a WH-element is moved, so any kind of WH-phrase can appear there, without any special kind of interpretation. In this regard, it is interesting to note that Neidle et al. do observe some semantic effects of WH-elements on the right. They say, "Cases that involve overt movement seem to convey a presupposition of the TP proposition and (additional) focus on the *wh*-phrase" (p. 186, fn. 4).

We will return to the interpretation of rightward WH-elements momentarily. First, however, we demonstrate that the two frameworks lead to differing predictions about sentences with only one WH-element.

23.2.2 Sentence-initial WH-objects

We begin by considering examples with sentence-initial WH-objects such as (25)–(26), illustrated in Figure 23.8. As the distribution of starred and unstarred examples reveals, there is a lack of agreement on the grammaticality of such sentences.

(25) ASL (Petronio and Lillo-Martin 1997, p. 50)

    ___________whq
    a. WHAT JOHN BUY
    'What did John buy?'

[9] The difference between tags and doubles was discussed with respect to non-WH-elements in Chapter 22. There, as here, the analysis of final elements preceded by a pause as tags is non-controversial.

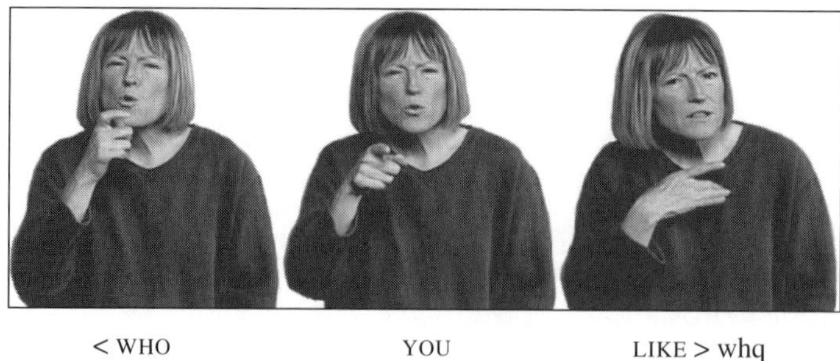

Figure 23.8 Sentence-initial object WH-question

b. ______whq
WHO YOU LIKE
'Who do you like?'

(26) ASL (Neidle et al. 2000, p. 127)

______wh
* WHO JOHN HATE
'Who does John hate?'

Neidle et al. uniformly report that this type of sentence is ungrammatical as glossed.[10] They report, however, that their consultants will accept similar utterances under two conditions. Under one, the non-dominant hand of the generic WH-sign "WHAT" is held while the dominant hand continues with the rest of the sentence. In such cases, they believe that the non-dominant hand perseverates between two articulations of the sign "WHAT." The second situation in which sentences similar to those in (25) are accepted according to Neidle et al. is when there is an intense non-manual WH-marking at the end of the sentence, which they suggest substitutes for the expected sentence-final manual WH-sign.

The sentences in (25) are not starred, indicating that these sentences are grammatical according to Petronio and Lillo-Martin. However, they also report that grammaticality judgments are not uniform. If, as they claim, such sentences exemplify typical leftward WH-movement like that found in English, for example, then why should such examples ever be unacceptable, even for some speakers? Petronio and Lillo-Martin speculate on two possibilities. Perhaps some speakers, but not all, require (or prefer) a [+F, +WH] C to be associated with overt lexical material. In other words, when the C head is marked [+F], some overt lexical material should fill this head to bear the [+F] marking. An alternative explanation for this variation suggests that speakers may differ with respect to whether WH-elements are treated as inherently focused.

[10] Although they add the qualifier "normally," p. 118, or "generally," p. 128.

It is worth noting that in two slightly more complex conditions, a clause-initial non-subject WH-element is widely accepted. The first is adjunct questions. Sentence-initial adjuncts are relatively common (as in (27)), and not subject to as much variation in judgments as sentence-initial objects.

(27) a. ASL (Lillo-Martin 1990, p. 215)

_______________whq

WHY$_i$ $_a$BILL $_a$LEAVE t_i?

'Why$_i$ did Bill leave t_i?'

b. ASL (Aarons et al. 1992, p. 126)

_ _ _ _ _ _ _ _ _ wh

WHERE JOHN LIVE

The second context is indirect questions. Even many signers who reject sentence-initial WH-objects in simple sentences like those in (25) accept clause-initial WH-objects (and adjuncts) as indirect questions. In fact, Lillo-Martin and Fischer (1992) found a strong preference for clause-initial WH-elements in indirect questions for their consultants. Some examples are given in (28). We will return to indirect questions in more detail in Section 23.2.5 below, where we discuss the distribution of WH-phrases in indirect questions together with their lack of WH-question non-manual marking.

(28) ASL (Petronio and Lillo-Martin 1997, p. 41)

_____________________hn

a. ANN CURIOUS WHO YOU LIKE

'Ann is curious who you like.'

_______________hn

b. I KNOW HOW SWIM

'I know how to swim.'

To sum up, sentence-initial WH-elements (not *in situ*) have a variable status. Some signers accept them readily; others accept them only in certain contexts. Adjuncts are more freely accepted in sentence-initial position; and WH-elements are very commonly found clause-initially in indirect questions. The rightward movement analysis claims that sentence-initial WH-elements (not *in situ*) are simply ungrammatical, and therefore the fact that the analysis cannot derive them is not presented as a problem. It would follow from the leftward movement analysis that sentence-initial WH-elements should be completely grammatical, and indeed some consultants accept them as such. Since some signers do not uniformly accept them, however, the leftward movement analysis proposes that these signers require an overt WH-element in focus position. This proposal accounts for the difference found for some signers between matrix and indirect clause-initial WH-elements, since only matrix WH-elements are focused.

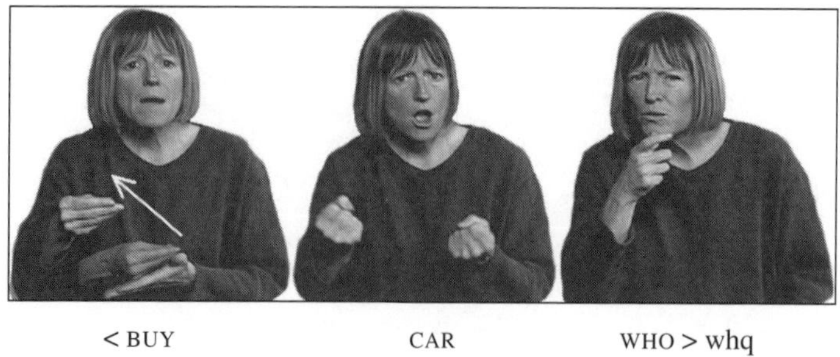

< BUY CAR WHO > whq

Figure 23.9 Sentence-final subject WH-question

23.2.3 Sentence-final WH-subjects

Now we turn to another type of question which involves a single WH-phrase, i.e., where the WH-subject is in the sentence-final position. According to the rightward movement analysis, such examples should be straightforwardly acceptable. According to the leftward movement approach, something special would be needed to derive them. Examples are given in (29) and Figure 23.9.[11]

(29) a. ASL (Neidle et al. 2000, p. 110)

        ______________wh
        t_i LOVE JOHN WHO$_i$

        'Who loves John?'

b. ASL (Petronio and Lillo-Martin 1997, p. 36)

        __________whq
        BUY CAR WHO

        'Who bought the car?'

Neidle et al. consistently report the type of question found in (29) to be grammatical. However, Petronio and Lillo-Martin again find variation in the acceptability of such questions. Their proposal is an attempt to account for this variability.

To begin with, Petronio and Lillo-Martin observe that WH-questions may be formed in ASL with no overt WH-element. Like Aarons (1994, p. 113) and Lillo-Martin and Fischer (1992), they postulate that such questions contain a null WH-element. Examples of questions with null WH-words are given in (30).

[11] Note that our model, like the female model in the videos on the ASLLRP website (but unlike their male model), has different non-manuals for the signs BUY CAR and WHO. This could indicate an alternative structure, perhaps with topicalization of BUY CAR. Since our model and the female ASLLRP model have similar non-manuals, we will consider the example comparable to theirs.

(30) ASL (Aarons 1994, p. 111)

    wh
a. SAY
What did she say?'

    wh
b. JOHN BUY YESTERDAY
What did John buy yesterday?

Such questions are only licensed in appropriate discourse contexts, in which the content of the null WH-element can be recovered. This is also the context found for acceptability of sentence-final WH-subjects. On the analysis of Petronio and Lillo-Martin, questions with a sentence-final WH-subject can be analyzed as double questions with a null twin, as shown in (31).[12]

(31) ASL (Petronio and Lillo-Martin 1997, p. 37)
Possible context: the speaker and addressee are discussing the addressee's car, which was just sold.

    whq
e BUY CAR WHO
Who bought the car?

For Neidle et al., of course, such sentences are expected to be fully grammatical, and no special mechanisms are needed to account for the acceptance of examples like (31). However, here too they do not address variability in acceptability. Given this variation, an approach which accounts both for situations in which such examples are accepted, and those in which they are rejected, is preferred.

23.2.4 Spread of WH-question non-manual marker

The notion that non-manual markers directly manifest syntactic structure is an axiom of the Neidle et al. theory of ASL syntax, as already presented. In keeping with this premise, they base much of the argument for their analysis of WH-questions on the occurrence and spread of the WH-question non-manual marker. On their account, the non-manual marker is associated with the [+wh] feature. WH-words with the [+wh] feature will have this non-manual marker, as will a [+wh] C. The behavior of the WH-question non-manual marker is then expected to be determined by the syntactic positions marked [+wh], in the same way that other non-manual markers are related to other specific syntactic features.

Neidle et al. propose several generalizations about the spread of non-manual syntactic markers, summarized in Chapter 18. We will see now how

[12] As noted in Chapter 22, Petronio also found that other doubled elements could have a null twin.

the generalizations apply to WH-questions. For reference, the phrase markers given in (32) show schematically the basics of their proposal.

(32) Neidle et al. account for spread of WH-question non-manual marker

a. Rightward-moved WH-element

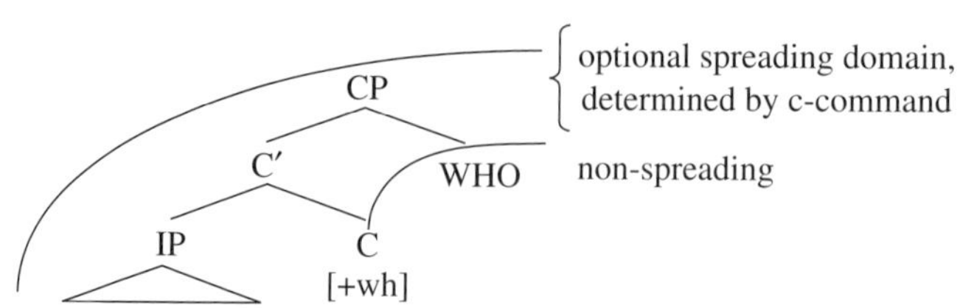

b. *In situ* WH-element

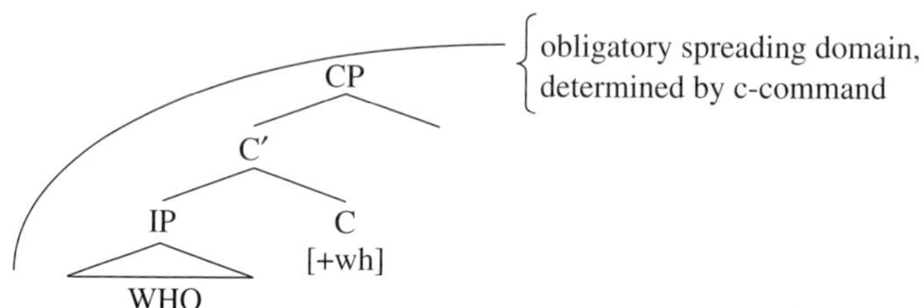

When a [+wh] sign is in Spec of a [+wh] C (as in (32a)), spreading of the [+wh] non-manual marker is optional. This is illustrated in (33).

(33) ASL (Neidle et al. 2000, pp. 110, 113)

a. t_i LOVE JOHN WHO$_i$ (wh over the whole sentence)

b. [t_i LOVE JOHN]$_{TP}$ WHO$_i$ (wh over WHO$_i$)

'Who loves John?'

When no lexical material is in a [+wh] C or its specifier (as in (32b)), spreading of the [+wh] non-manual marker is obligatory. This is illustrated in (34).

(34) ASL (Neidle et al. 2000, pp. 110, 113)

a. WHO LOVE JOHN (wh over the whole sentence)

'Who loves John?'

b. * WHO LOVE JOHN [+wh]$_C$ (wh over WHO)

c. * WHO LOVE JOHN [+wh]$_C$ (wh over the whole sentence)

Neidle et al. notice that the intensity of [+wh] marking is greatest at the end of the sentence in examples like (33a). They explain this by asserting that the intensity of [+wh] marking is greatest at the source, and decreases as distance from the source increases. The source is the syntactic [+ wh] feature, which is found on both the WH-phrase itself and the C head.

Petronio and Lillo-Martin also consider the behavior of non-manual markers to reflect syntactic structure. Their account for the spread of the non-manual marker in WH-questions differs from that of Neidle et al., however. They specify that the WH-question non-manual marker is a realization of the [+ F, + WH] features of the head C of an interrogative (shared with [Spec, CP] by spec–head agreement). Under their account, spread is uniformly obligatory. The phrase marker in (35) illustrates Petronio and Lillo-Martin's account of the spread of non-manual markers.

(35) Petronio and Lillo-Martin account of spread of WH-question non-manual marker

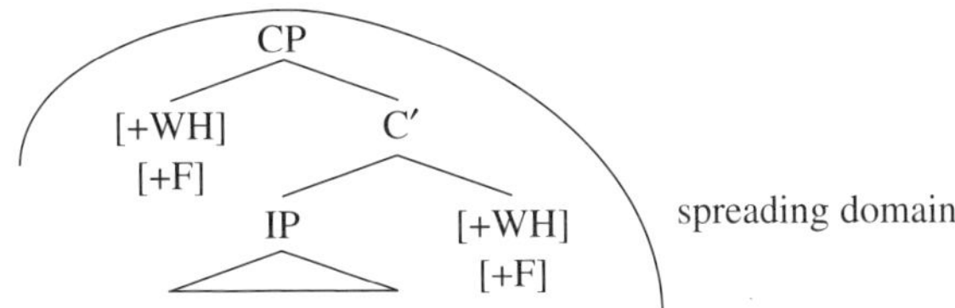

What then, of examples like (33b), which show a non-manual marker only over the WH-sign? Petronio and Lillo-Martin do not dispute the data, but consider such examples two-sentence discourses, similar to the examples in (36), but with a null element rather than the overt SOMEONE/SOMETHING. As would be expected if these sentences contain a discourse-licensed null element, they find again variability in acceptability: the examples show greater acceptability in clear discourse contexts, where the presupposition that there is a felicitous answer to the question is satisfied.

(36) ASL (Petronio and Lillo-Martin 1997, p. 48)

a. SOMEONE BUY CAR $\overline{\text{WHO}}^{\text{whq}}$
'Someone bought a car. Who?'

b. JOHN BUY SOMETHING $\overline{\text{WHAT}}^{\text{whq}}$
'John bought something. What?'

Neidle et al. claim that the spread of non-manual markings, together with the surface word order, provides strong support for their analysis of WH-questions. They state, "An important source of evidence for the analysis proposed . . . is the distribution of non-manual marking associated with the +wh feature" (Neidle et al. 2000, p. 148). However, this argument is circular, as their proposal uses the spread of non-manual markers to determine syntactic structure in the first place. No independent empirical evidence for their particular syntactic structure has yet been proposed.

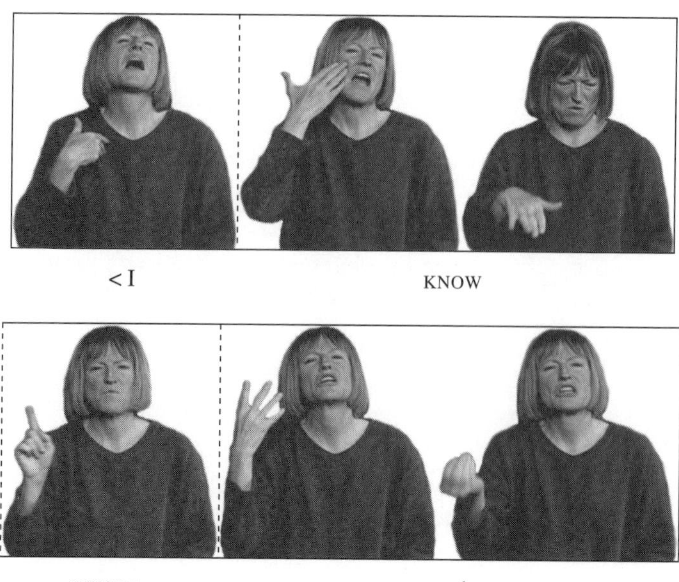

Figure 23.10 Indirect question

Both the rightward and the leftward proposals can account for the distribution of non-manual markers found. Each needs certain stipulations and special mechanisms. In Section 23.5 we will take a new look at the non-manual markers of WH-questions and their relationship to syntactic structure, without the circularity this type of approach has engendered. First, however, we will consider additional data bearing on the issues both from ASL and from LSB. The additional data will bear on the central question of this chapter: do WH-questions in sign languages require the postulation of syntactic mechanisms distinct from those needed for spoken languages?

23.2.5 Indirect questions

Petronio and Lillo-Martin claim that the WH-question non-manual marker is associated with a C which is [+F, +WH]. They require both features rather than simply [+wh], as in Neidle et al., because of the difference they observe between direct questions and indirect questions. Examples like (37), which contain indirect questions, do not display the WH-question non-manual marker, as can be seen in Figure 23.10. Although the brows are furrowed and the eyes are squinting, the head does not come forward as in a direct question. Furthermore, in a direct question the head shakes from side to side, whereas in indirect questions embedded under verbs such as KNOW, the head shakes up and down. Finally, the same non-manual markers characterize the matrix and embedded clauses.

(37) ASL (Petronio and Lillo-Martin 1997, pp. 42–43)

 hn

a. MOTHER CURIOUS WHO YOU LIKE

'My mother is curious who you like.'

 hs/ponder

b. I DON'T-KNOW WHAT HE BUY

'I don't know what he bought.'

 hn

c. I KNOW HOW SWIM

'I know how to swim.'

 ponder

d. I WONDER WHY JOHN FAIL

'I wonder why John failed?'

Indirect questions embedded under matrix verbs like WONDER do show a quizzical or pondering facial expression, but they are different from direct questions in two ways: the form of the expression is different (although similar), and the scope is different (the whole sentence may be included). Indirect questions embedded under verbs like CURIOUS, KNOW, and DON'T-KNOW clearly employ non-manual markings which are distinct from the WH-question non-manual marker.

According to Petronio and Lillo-Martin, embedded clauses cannot be marked [+F]. This stipulation expresses the idea that there is one focus per sentence, and it is a root phenomenon. Two things follow from this stipulation: first, indirect questions will not have the WH-question non-manual marker; and second, indirect questions will not allow doubled WH-elements. That indirect questions do not display the WH-question marker has already been shown. In the following examples, we see that indirect questions do not allow doubles (38). Likewise, they do not allow sentence-final WH-elements (39). This is exactly as expected under Petronio and Lillo-Martin's analysis, since sentence-final WH-elements (which are not *in situ*) are generated through focus doubling.[13]

(38) ASL (Petronio and Lillo-Martin 1997, p. 43)

 hn

*I KNOW WHO WIN WHO

(39) ASL (Petronio and Lillo-Martin 1997, pp. 43, 44)

 hn

a. *ANN CURIOUS LIKE JOHN WHO

'Ann is curious who likes John.'

 ponder

b. *MOTHER WONDER INSULT SON WHO

'[My] mother wonders who insulted [her] son.'

[13] These remarks apply to true indirect questions. Sometimes, a direct question can follow a verb like WONDER or CURIOUS, in which case the verb simply sets the stage for asking the question. An analogous example in English would be, *I wonder. Who did John see?* In these cases the non-manual marking and word order follows that of true questions.

hn (over BOB KNOW WON WHO)

c. * BOB KNOW WON WHO
'Bob knows who won.'

Neidle et al. leave indirect questions for further investigation. In a footnote, however, they say, "Embedded complement clauses of verbs like KNOW in ASL do not exhibit non-manual *wh*-marking, nor do they exhibit the word order typical of *wh*-questions. Thus, the embedded clause in such constructions in ASL does not appear to be a normal + wh clause" (Neidle et al. 2000, p. 190). This conclusion is necessary given their analysis of "normal" + wh clauses. However, the behavior of indirect questions is perfectly normal under Petronio and Lillo-Martin's account.

23.3 Interim summary

Overall, the study of WH-questions in ASL has been full of controversy. There have been disagreements about data, and about how to interpret very similar strings. There have been even deeper disagreements about how to analyze the basic WH-question types. One view stays rather close to the surface – since WH-words are very often found in sentence-final position, this must be the position of [Spec, CP], to which WH-words move. The other view takes into consideration several additional factors: the fact that the sentence-final position is very often used for focus (by both syntactic and prosodic means) in ASL (cf. Chapter 22); and the fact that universally, [Spec, CP] appears on the left in other languages. This second view maintains that [Spec, CP] appears on the left in ASL, and proposes that WH-elements are often focused, as they are in many other languages of the world, explaining their frequent appearance on the right.

This controversy is of general linguistic interest, since it connects to a well-known putative linguistic universal: that the position of [Spec, CP] is on the left side of the phrase marker. This structural universal accounts for the fact that WH-movement in spoken languages is universally leftward. If it were the case that sign languages, unlike spoken languages, used a rightward [Spec, CP], we would be interested in looking for a modality-based explanation for this difference. But none is apparent. Nothing about the manual–visual modality seems relevant to this phenomenon. Is it the case, then, that linguistic theory has got it wrong – or that we are mistaken in applying linguistic theory to the analysis of sign languages? We think not. Fortunately, there is a highly credible alternative to the rightward movement analysis and the theoretical problems it raises, a solution that is completely consistent with linguistic theory and can account for the range of data observed in ASL. The alternative is the leftward analysis, which finds additional support from an analysis of Brazilian Sign Language, to which we now turn.

< WHAT JOHN BUY > whq (LSB)

Figure 23.11 Sentence-initial object WH-question (illustrations provided by Ronice Müller de Quadros, p.c.)

23.4 LSB WH-movement

WH-questions in Brazilian Sign Language confirm many of the qualities of WH-questions in ASL observed by Petronio and Lillo-Martin (Quadros 1999). Like ASL, LSB allows focus doubling (see Chapter 22). As we have seen, some characteristics of focus doubling in LSB differ from ASL, accurately predicting differences between the languages with respect to WH-questions as well.

First, LSB allows WH-*in situ* (40a–b), and also allows a questioned object to appear in sentence-initial position (40c), as in ASL. An LSB example of the latter is shown in Figure 23.11.

(40) LSB (Quadros 1999, pp. 192, 193)[14]

    ______________________wh
a. WHO LIKE IX <the> MARY
    'Who likes Mary?'

    ______________________wh
b. IX<the> JOHN LIKE WHO
    'Who does John like?'

    ______________________wh
c. WHO IX<the>JOHN LIKE
    'Who does John like?'

A WH-element can appear in the sentence-final position on the right in the appropriate contexts, but the non-manual marker must obligatorily spread over the whole sentence (41).

(41) LSB (Quadros 1999, p. 196)

    ______________wh
a. LIKE MARY WHO
    'Who likes Mary?'

[14] As noted in Chapter 19, Quadros glosses some pointing signs as IX< the >, highlighting their determiner usage (cf. Chapter 20, Section 20.1).

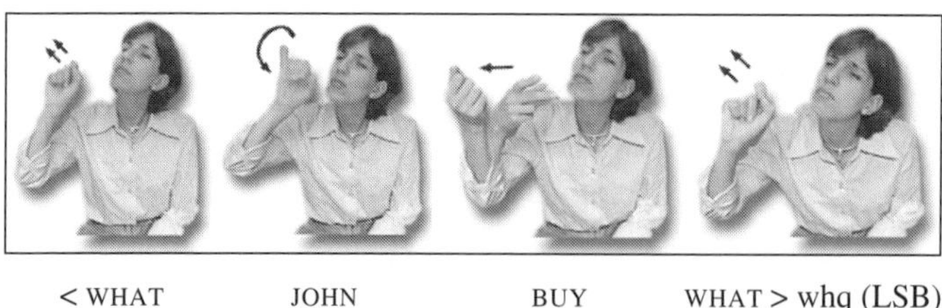

< WHAT JOHN BUY WHAT > whq (LSB)

Figure 23.12 Doubled WH-question (illustrations provided by Ronice Müller de Quadros, p.c.)

wh

b. * LIKE MARY WHO
'Who likes Mary?'

As we have seen in Chapter 22, LSB has double constructions much like ASL, though with some differences. In LSB, elements that can double include modals, quantifiers, verbs, negation, adverbs, and WH-elements. As expected, given the similarities between the languages with respect to focus doubling and WH-questions, WH-elements can be doubled, receiving an emphatic interpretation, as shown in (42) and Figure 23.12.

(42) LSB (Quadros 1999, pp. 197, 202)

wh

a. WHO LIKE MARY WHO
'Who likes Mary?'

wh

b. WHAT JOHN BUY (YESTERDAY) WHAT
'What did John buy (yesterday)?'

wh

c. IX<the> JOHN BUY WHAT YESTERDAY WHAT
'What did John buy yesterday?'

As in ASL, the double must be a single word (43).

(43) LSB (Quadros 1999, p. 220)

wh

a. WHAT MAN IX<2> LIKE WHAT
'Which man do you like?'

wh

b. * WHAT MAN OF-THEM IX<2> LIKE WHAT MAN OF-THEM
'Which man do you like?'

Quadros' analysis of WH-questions in LSB basically follows that of Petronio and Lillo-Martin for ASL, but with some differences to follow. The main points common to both are given in (44).

(44) a. WH-elements can remain *in situ*
b. WH-movement is leftward to Spec of CP
c. spread of non-manual marker is obligatory

d. WH-elements in final position are focused elements
e. focus licenses a null "twin"

The main difference between Quadros' analysis for LSB and that of Petronio and Lillo-Martin for ASL is that Quadros pursues a Kaynian all right-branching structure (Kayne 1994), as shown in (45) (cf. also Chapter 19).[15]

(45)

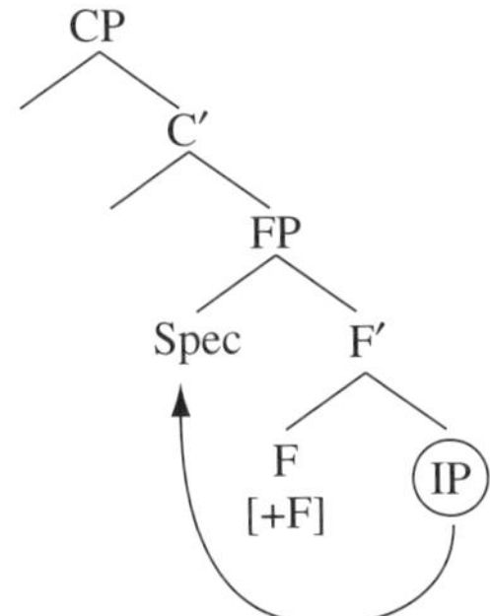

The focus head is base-generated with a [+F] feature, and the IP (or AgrsP) raises to Spec, FP to check this feature. Thus, it is not necessary to use a left-branching category (resulting in C or F being head final) in order to obtain the sentence-final position for focused elements. The same effect is achieved by having everything following the focused element move to the left (cf. Wilbur 1997, for a similar idea with different implementation in ASL).

An important difference between the kind of analysis illustrated here, where material generated to the right of a focused element moves to a position preceding it (the view of Quadros and Wilbur), and the Petronio and Lillo-Martin account which generates the focused element on the right side of the sentence (similarly, the Neidle et al. account with [Spec, CP] on the right) is whether the sentence-final WH- or focus material is structurally higher or lower than the preceding material. It will be necessary to investigate further to determine which approach has greater support (cf. Stjepanović 1999, Zubizarreta 1998).

There are some empirical differences between WH-questions in LSB and ASL. LSB (but not ASL) embedded clauses have different WH-signs and non-manual markers than matrix clauses. The examples in (46) illustrate the use of the special embedded clause manual and non-manual markers, where the embedded WH-sign and non-manual marker are indicated by -E and -e. Two different kinds of embedded question signs, with the appropriate non-manual markers, are illustrated in Figure 23.13

[15] In Nunes and Quadros (2004), focus duplication follows from linearization (Nunes 2004).

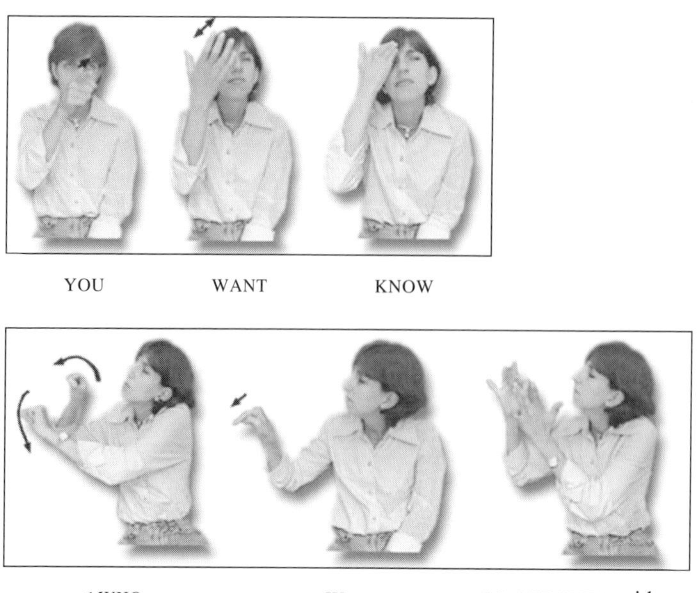

Figure 23.13 LSB embedded clause WH-sign (illustrations provided by Ronice Müller de Quadros, p.c.)

(46) LSB (Quadros 1999, p. 204–205)

a.
　　　　wonder　　　　　　　　wh-e
IX<1> WANT KNOW WHO-E IX<the> JOHN MEET

b.
　　　　wonder　　　　　wh-e
IX<1> WANT KNOW JOHN MEET WHO-E

c.
　　　　wonder　　　　　　　　wh-e
IX<1> WANT KNOW WHO-E JOHN MEET WHO-E

'I want to know who John met.'

cf.

d.
　　　　　　　　　　　　　　　　wh
IX<the> JOHN ASK WHO IX<the> MARY LIKE

'John asked: "Who does Mary like?".'

As (46a, b) show, indirect questions in LSB, as in ASL, permit clause-initial or *in situ* WH-elements – but unlike ASL, the WH-form in LSB is formationally distinct. However, as seen in (46c), the indirect question also allows a WH-double in LSB, unlike ASL. That this example involves a true indirect question is confirmed by the use of WHO-E. In contrast, (46d) involves direct quotation, and uses the main clause manual and non-manual WH-elements.

The explanation for LSB allowing a double in the indirect question is straightforward. While Petronio observes only one focus per sentence in ASL, Quadros finds one per clause in LSB. This difference, which was illustrated in Chapter 22, correctly predicts that LSB should allow doubles in indirect questions, unlike ASL. This prediction is correct, as shown in (46c) above.

23.4.1 Discussion

The fact that LSB WH-questions behave very similarly to those in ASL is not surprising, since the languages behave similarly in other related respects. Of special importance are the differences between the languages, and particularly how the languages have consistent differences with respect to focus and WH-questions. Where ASL and LSB differ in terms of focus (e.g., that LSB, but not ASL, allows a focus position in embedded clauses), they also differ in terms of WH-questions. This generalization is captured by the leftward-movement account, in which focus plays an important role.

The pattern of WH-questions and other focused elements in LSB and ASL strongly supports the analysis that relates WH-questions to focus, the leftward-movement analysis. This analysis handles a broader range of data than the rightward-movement approach does. It handles both WH-questions and other focused elements. It also provides an account of interspeaker variability. On this approach, an explanation is sought for systematically different judgments between signers.

Finally, the leftward-movement analysis refrains from postulating structures unique to sign languages. It places an emphasis on cross-modality universals, and finds that there is not sufficient evidence that sign languages require a different structure. This is an advantage, since there is no obvious motivation for distinct structures between signed and spoken languages in this regard. Clearly, the modalities differ and there are expected to be modality-specific effects for certain kinds of structures (cf. Unit 5). However, with respect to WH-question formation we can find nothing about the modality which should lead to differences in the direction of WH-movement for signed versus spoken languages. Thus, the leftward analysis is preferred.

All analyses discussed so far take the non-manual markers associated with questions to be of direct syntactic relevance. We now turn to a view that puts non-manual markers in a different light.

23.5 WH-questions and intonation

The widespread assumption that the non-manual marker typically accompanying WH-questions is a realization of something present in the syntax must be reconsidered in light of the evidence that this marker has the characteristics of a prosodic element, intonation. For example, as discussed in Chapter 15, the non-manual marker involves the "superarticulators," spreading over domains of varying length that are prosodic in nature.

What consequences would it have for our analyses if we suppose that the WH-question non-manual marker is analogous to an intonational tune? Does this mean it is not represented in the syntax? Not necessarily. Although researchers in the generative tradition have generally excluded information about intonation from the syntactic analysis, there are some reasons to believe that intonation might be represented syntactically.

First, let us consider the assumed architecture of the grammar. Generative models typically involve at least three components. One is the level at which the grammar connects with the articulatory/perceptual mechanisms. Another is the level at which the grammar connects with the conceptual component. The third is the mechanism which connects these components, the computation. Prosodic information is clearly present at the articulatory interface, since it is pronounced. Insofar as intonational and other prosodic elements contribute to the interpretation, they are also present at the conceptual interface. If there is no other component connecting these two interfaces, then prosodic information must be represented in the computational component – the syntax – so that it can be spelled out and interpreted.

On an alternative view, there might be some other means of connecting the pronunciation and interpretation of prosodic elements. For example, intonation and other (potentially cross-sentence) discourse phenomena might be represented at a separate level. If there is no need for this information to be represented syntactically, perhaps it should be excluded from the syntax.

Each approach has points in its favor. Let us consider further the question of whether and how to represent prosodic information in the syntax. First we will take a look at some phenomena in spoken languages which may indicate that there is a closer relationship between intonation and syntax than many researchers have previously noted. Then we will return to the sign language situation, and address two points about the WH-question non-manual markers: how closely is the presence of the WH-question non-manual marker tied to WH-question syntax, and how well does the spread of the non-manual marker mirror the syntax?

The grammatical role of intonational patterns may vary from one language to the next, and possibly from one construction to the next. Lillo-Martin (1999b) observes an intriguing contrast between English and Russian in this regard.[16] This contrast involves the distribution of "polarity items," words such as *ever* and *any* which are only permitted in certain contexts. For both English and Russian, this context includes negatives and yes/no questions. Russian examples with yes/no questions are given in (47).

[16] We thank Arthur Stepanov for bringing these Russian data to Lillo-Martin's attention. He also provided Romanization and translations for the examples which come from Bryzgunova (1975), and additional examples.

(47) Russian
a. * on byl kagda-libo v Moskve
he was when-ever in Moscow
* 'He was ever in Moscow.'
b. byl li on kadga-libo v Moskve?
was Q he when-ever in Moscow
'Was he ever in Moscow?'

Both English and Russian also permit yes/no questions to be formed either with inversion (as in the examples cited already), or without inversion, together with a specific yes/no question intonation (roughly rising in both languages), as illustrated in (48) for Russian. Although this type of yes/no question is marked in English, it is the typical way to form such questions in Russian.

(48) Russian
a. byl li on v Moskve?
was Q he in Moscow
'Was he in Moscow?'
b. on byl v Moskve?
he was in Moscow
'He was in Moscow?'

Now we can see where the languages differ. While a question marked with rising intonation alone (without inversion) is not sufficient to license the polarity item in English (49), it is in Russian (50).

(49) * You have (/you've) ever been to Moscow?

(50) Russian
on byl kogda-nibud' v Moskve?
he was when-ever in Moscow
'Was he ever in Moscow?'

There are various possible differences between English and Russian which might account for the difference between (49) and (50). However, on the surface at least it would appear that the status of yes/no questions indicated by rising intonation alone is different for the two languages: it has consequences in Russian but not in English. A full treatment of this phenomenon requires an understanding of how polarity items are licensed in Russian and in English. But these examples are one indication among a growing number that syntacticians can no longer afford to ignore intonation, but must consider cases when prosody interacts with syntactic phenomena.

Given a need for (some instances of) intonation to be considered syntactically, what form would this take? A proposal for French is instructive. Cheng and Rooryck (2000) propose that there is a morpheme which is realized as (rising) yes/no question intonation, present syntactically in French. This morpheme is used like a question particle, but it is underspecified for yes/no or WH-questions. This means that it may appear with yes/no questions or with WH-*in situ* questions, such as those in (51). French allows WH-*in situ* in non-multiple direct questions (unlike English), and, according to Cheng and Rooryck, such questions have the rising intonation of yes/no questions rather than the typical WH-question intonation. Furthermore, both yes/no questions without inversion and WH-*in situ* questions are associated with a "strongly presupposed context" (Cheng and Rooryck 2000, p. 4, quoting Chang 1997). These similarities can be explained by the proposal that the underspecified question particle [Q:] is associated with both rising intonation and the presuppositional context. This question particle is involved in the licensing of both non-inverted yes/no questions and WH-*in situ*.

(51) French (Cheng and Rooryck 2000, pp. 3, 4)
 a. Jean a acheté un livre?
  'Jean has bought a book?'
 b. Jean a acheté quoi?
  Jean has bought what
  'What has Jean bought?'

Note that French and English are completely different in these examples. In French, the WH-*in situ* strategy is used for true questions (not only echo questions), and the distribution of WH-*in situ* questions is restricted syntactically in a way very unlike echo questions (Bošković 2000). In English, WH-*in situ* is very restricted.

According to the type of approach advocated by Cheng and Rooryck, the "intonational morphemes" are present syntactically, and occupy positions according to their syntactic role. However, the extent of intonational melodies should follow from prosodic structure. Since prosodic constituent structure is built up from syntactic structure, and intonational melodies are linked to prosodic constituents, it is expected that there will be a close relationship between the spreading of the intonational melodies and syntactic structure, but not necessarily a direct one.

As explained in Chapter 15, intonational melodies spread across domains known as Intonational Phrases. Intonational Phrases are defined according to certain syntactic types: for example, parentheticals, non-restrictive relative clauses, topicalizations and other extrapositions, vocatives, expletives, and tag questions. Thus, there is a very close relationship between syntactic structure and intonational structure. However, this relationship is not perfect. It is well-known that there are cases in which the syntactic and prosodic structure do not match up completely – cases of non-isomorphism, like the example from the children's story, "The House that Jack Built," illustrated in Chapter 15, Section 15.5, example (8).

This non-isomorphism is reflected in the intonation as well, which is aligned with the prosodic and not the syntactic constituent in the case of a mismatch. Such intonational non-isomorphism can be seen in an example taken from Pierrehumbert and Hirschberg (1990). In the notation used in this example, H and L stand for high and low tones, the asterisk means that the tone is accented, and the percent symbol indicates the end of an intonational phrase. The interpretation of the question in (52) is that a piece of fruit and a piece of cake are being offered: *Do you want an apple(?) – or banana cake?*

(52) Do you want an apple or banana cake? (fruit or cake)
H* H H* L L%

On the other hand, a different pattern leads to a different interpretation. In (53), the choices being offered are two kinds of ice cream. The difference is signalled by the intonation.

(53) Do you like vanilla ice cream or chocolate?
L* H* L L%

A similar pattern is found in alternative questions in ISL, illustrated in (54). The non-manual marking shows behavior comparable to that of the English example in (53). The yes/no question non-manual marking may spread over the first conjunct and not the second, akin to the rising intonation found only over the first conjunct in (53). A possible interpretation is one in which the part of the sentence with a question marker has the illocutionary intent of a real question, while the second part is declaratively offering another option.

(54) ISL (Meir and Sandler 2004)
______________________________y/n
Index2 LIKE ICE CREAM VANILLA OR CHOCOLATE?
'Do you like vanilla ice cream or chocolate ice cream?'

If the examples in (52)–(54) are treated as single sentences, they would show clear distinctions between sentence structure and prosodic domains. In the ISL example the question non-manual ends where the pitch accent is placed in the comparable English sentence, rather than at the end of the question. The ISL and English examples have much in common. Both are questions syntactically, and both are characterized by a rising intonation pattern. But in both, the rising intonation identifiable with a yes/no question does not characterize the whole question. Instead, the second choice is outside the scope of the yes/no intonation pattern. The point we wish to make is that the intonational tune is not coextensive with the syntactic constituent in either language; the intonation and the syntax are non-isomorphic. In the next section, we expand on the observation that intonational tunes may vary with pragmatic intent.

Table 23.1 *Differences between three constructions with WH-elements in ASL*

	non-manual marker	Position of WH-element
Direct questions	furrowed brows, squinted eyes, head tilted back, slight side-to-side headshake	√doubled √left (%) √right (%) √*in situ*
Indirect questions	various: ponder, or head nod, or headshake, etc.	*doubled √left *right √*in situ*
WH-clefts	raised brows	*doubled ?left √right √*in situ*

23.5.1 Sentence structure and presence of WH-question non-manual marker

These ideas may lead us to reconsider the status of the WH-question non-manual marker in ASL and other sign languages. Both the leftward and rightward analyses of WH-questions in ASL assume that the distribution of the WH-question non-manual marker is determined solely by syntactic factors. However, there are a number of indications that this marker behaves intonationally. As we have seen, the WH-question non-manual marker is not realized on all structures which employ WH-phrases and/or WH-movement. For example, we have already seen that indirect questions and WH-clefts have WH-elements but not the same non-manual marker as direct WH-questions (we assume here the characteristics of WH-clefts provided by Wilbur 1996, discussed in Chapter 22). These two constructions also display differences from direct WH-questions with respect to the range of word orders allowed, as summarized in Table 23.1.

Each of the analyses reviewed can account for a portion of the data summarized in Table 23.1, but none captures all. Petronio and Lillo-Martin (1997) attempted to account for the structural and non-manual differences between direct questions and indirect questions using the same syntactic feature, [+F]. If successful, this account would be good evidence for the syntactic representation of the non-manual marker. However, this proposal does not extend to account for the distribution of WH-elements and non-manual markers in WH-clefts. Furthermore, there are additional sentence types with WH-elements but without the WH-question non-manual marker, including echo questions, true rhetorical

Figure 23.14 Typical WH-question facial expression (ISL)

Figure 23.15 Facial expression in WH-question in non-interrogative context (ISL)

questions, exclamatives, and polite questions, calling further into question a proposal which captures these phenomena uniformly.

The same is true for Israeli Sign Language. Meir and Sandler (2004) demonstrate that the facial expressions associated with questions are dissociable from the syntax of questions. Figure 23.14 shows the facial expression that typically accompanies a WH-question in ISL. However, in non-interrogative contexts, a different facial expression occurs. An example is a WH-question involving reproach, as would be used in the ISL version of, *Why did you just walk out of my store with that shirt without paying*? The facial expression for such a context is illustrated in Figure 23.15.

The evidence just reviewed indicates that it is not the use of a WH-phrase or a [+WH] feature which uniquely determines whether or not the WH-question non-manual marker is used. What is crucial is the pragmatic condition of a content question. When the speaker desires an answer involving content, the WH-question non-manual marker is typically used, but when the information being questioned is already known (for example, when the addressee intended to steal the item), the furrowed brow is replaced with a different expression.

Also like intonation in spoken languages, even when an answer is desired, the expression may be modified. True WH-questions in ISL may be asked with a non-canonical facial expression, depending on factors such as overriding affect. Assume a group of friends are at a party and, early on, one of them makes a bee-line for the door. The host might ask others who had been sitting with the person who left, *Why did he leave like that*? with a facial expression denoting amazement, as shown in Figure 23.16.

In both examples shown in Figures 23.15 and 23.16, the furrowed brow typically associated with WH questions is absent.

Reilly and McIntire (1991) also note that WH-questions in (ASL) Motherese are not marked with the usual WH-question non-manual marker, but are instead marked with wide open eyes and a side-to-side

Figure 23.16 WH-question with atypical superarticulation (ISL)

headshake. They postulate that the furrowed brow of the typical WH-question non-manual marker might be taken as disapproval, so caregivers substitute a different non-manual marker with young children.

The behavior of facial expression in these examples is directly analogous to the behavior of intonation in spoken language. The use of the non-manual marker is dependent on factors other than syntactic structure: pragmatic force and sociolinguistic contextual information.

In addition to use of a facial expression other than the WH-question marker in the presence of WH-structures, the inverse can also be found; viz., the use of the WH-question non-manual marker with questions that do not have an overt WH-element. Baker-Shenk (1983), Lillo-Martin and Fischer (1992), Aarons (1994), and Petronio and Lillo-Martin (1997) all observed that ASL allows WH-questions without overt manual WH-elements, such as those in (30) above, repeated as (55), and those in (56). Meir and Sandler (2004) make the same observation for ISL, illustrated in (57).

(55) ASL (Aarons 1994, p. 111)

a. <u>wh</u>
SAY
'What did she say?'

b. <u>　　　　　　　　wh</u>
JOHN BUY YESTERDAY
'What did John buy yesterday?'

(56) ASL (Petronio and Lillo-Martin 1997, p. 53)

a. <u>whq</u>
TIME
'What time is it?'

b. <u>　　　　t</u> <u>whq</u>
EARRINGS, GIVE
'Who gave you those earrings?'

(57) ISL (Meir and Sandler 2004)

a. TIME?
'What time is it?'

b. MONEY?
'How much does it cost?'

c. AGE index-2?
'How old are you?'

d. HEALTH index-2?
'How are you?'

These authors have assumed that the presence of the WH-question non-manual marker in (15a–d) is related to the acceptability of these examples as questions without an overt WH-element. This might then indicate that some representation of the non-manual marker is required in the syntax. However, we will see that even in such cases it is their pragmatic force as content questions which leads to the presence of the WH-question non-manual marker.

It has been proposed (by Lillo-Martin and Fischer 1992, Aarons 1994, and Petronio and Lillo-Martin 1997) that examples such as (55)–(56) involve a null WH-element.[17] With a null element, they require appropriate contexts. Such contexts are readily obtained for simple questions, like those in (55a), (56a), and (57), but more support is required for examples like (55b) and (56b).

An alternative to the null WH-element analysis might have it that such examples are comparable to English questions without WH-words such as those in (58) (see Ausín 1999 for discussion of such examples in English and Spanish).

(58) (Do you) want something?
= What do you want?

Such an analogy would only require that ASL allows a null counterpart of SOMETHING – a proposal which has already been made (see Section 23.2.4). However, there is a further difference between the English and ASL examples. The English use of *something* in a pseudo-WH-question does not satisfy the [+WH] complement requirement of matrix verbs like *wonder*, *ask*, as shown in (59).

(59) a. * I wonder want something.
b. * I wonder do you want something.
c. I wonder what you want.

In ASL, however, a null WH-question can be used in a [+WH] complement context, as shown in (60) (Lillo-Martin and Fischer 1992).

[17] Neidle et al. (2000, p. 194, fn. 54) argue against this proposal by claiming instead that examples like (56a) are simply sentence fragments. Neidle et al. do not make it clear how the WH-question non-manual marker is generated in such fragments on their analysis, and it is not clear how to extend such a proposal to examples like (55b), (56b), and others.

(60) ASL

a. I KNOW TIME SHOW-UP (hn)

'I know what time to show up.'

b. I CURIOUS JOHN BUY YESTERDAY (squint)

'I'm curious what John bought yesterday.'

Importantly, as with other indirect questions, the WH-question non-manual marker is not used in the examples in (60). Hence, the presence of the WH-question non-manual marker is more closely related to the pragmatic force of an interrogative than it is to the presence of a WH-element (overt or null).

23.5.2 Sentence structure and spread of WH-question non-manual marker

We have seen many reasons to believe that the presence of the WH-question non-manual marker is determined by discourse/pragmatic factors rather than syntactic factors. If the relevant factors should be represented in the syntax, an approach like the one used by Cheng and Rooryck (2000) could be used. To account for the presence of the WH-question non-manual marker, a [WHQ] morpheme can be hypothesized. This morpheme would not be the same as the [+wh] feature which is involved in the syntactic operation of WH-movement, since we have seen that the syntactic operation is independent of the WH-question non-manual marker. The morpheme would be used only in those pragmatic contexts which involve a true WH-interrogative, and it would be spelled out as intonation by the prosodic component.

We have so far been concentrating on what signals the presence of the non-manual marker. In the case of the ASL WH-question non-manual marker, not only has the previous view been that the presence of the marker is signaled by a syntactic feature, but it has also been claimed that the spreading of the marker is determined by hierarchical structure. On the analysis of the non-manual marker as intonation, it would be expected that the spread of the marker is determined by Intonational Phrasing. Is there any way to separate these two proposals? Since, as we have seen, intonational phrasing is often – but crucially, not always – related to syntactic structures, the intonation analysis, but not the purely syntactic analysis, is consistent with the possibility of non-isomorphism. Let us consider how WH-questions interact with phrases known to influence prosodic structure.

One pattern occurs in the interaction of topics and WH-questions. Topics are outside the domain of the WH-question non-manual marker, as (61) shows.

(61) ASL (Petronio and Lillo-Martin 1997, p. 49)

COFFEE (t), WHERE BUY WHERE (whq)?

'As for the coffee, where did (you) buy it?'

The intonational phrasing of such an example would separate the topic from the rest of the sentence, as (62) shows. Thus, it is not surprising that the non-manual marker does not extend over the topic.

(62) [COFFEE]$_I$ [WHERE BUY WHERE]$_I$

Syntactically, an example like this one should have a structure in which the topic is attached higher in the tree than the position of the WH-phrase. Then, if the question non-manual marker spreads according to the structural hierarchy, it won't spread over the topic. This structure, schematized here, is very similar to the example of topics outside the domain of negation discussed by Liddell, which was presented in Chapter 18.

(63)

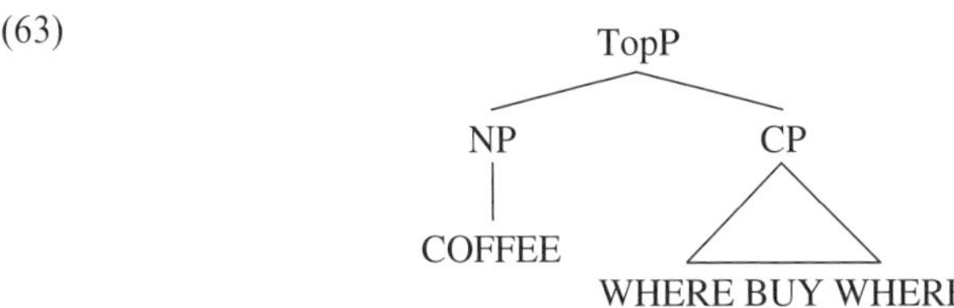

In this case, the syntactic structure and the intonational structure produce the same result. However, whether the spread of the WH-question non-manual marker should be determined by Intonational Phrasing, or just by syntactic structure, can be seen by examining examples with parentheticals or non-restrictive relative clauses inside WH-questions.

Adjunct parentheticals are generally placed at the edge of a sentence if possible. However, some parentheticals are found interrupting sentences, including WH-questions. When such an element is used, it is clear that the non-manual markings must change. If the parenthetical indicates a temporal adjunct, the non-manual marking of the adverb will break up the WH-question non-manual marking, as shown in (64). If the parenthetical indicates the speaker's viewpoint, there will be a body shift as well as a change in facial expression to the signer's opinion, with a return to the original position and WH-question expression following the parenthetical, as shown in (65).

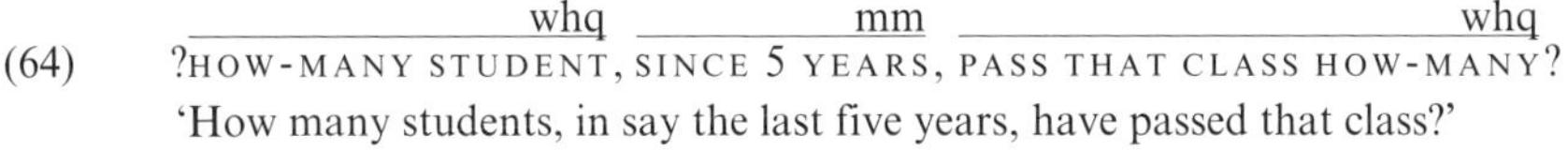

(64)
whq mm whq
?HOW-MANY STUDENT, SINCE 5 YEARS, PASS THAT CLASS HOW-MANY?
'How many students, in say the last five years, have passed that class?'

(65)
whq shift whq
WHY IX-a STUDENT –STUDENT TRUE^BUSINESS HUH – FAIL CLASS (WHY)
'Why did that student – if he can be called a student – fail the class?'

A similar situation arises with some adverbials expressing speaker's viewpoint. These may have specific accompanying facial expressions. When embedded in WH-questions, the non-manual markings change. The WH-marking is not combined with the adverbial marking; rather, it is dropped while the adverbial is signed. Examples are given in (66) (in these examples, the abbreviations 'obv' and 'acc' are used to indicate the adverbial non-manual markers for 'obviously' and 'accidentally').

(66)
a. ___whq (WHO YOU FEEL) ___obv (OBVIOUSLY SMART) ___whq (WHO IX)
WHO YOU FEEL OBVIOUSLY SMART (WHO IX)
'Who do you think is obviously smart?'

b. ___whq (IX-a ARRIVE) ___acc (ACCIDENTALLY) ___whq (WHERE)
IX-a ARRIVE ACCIDENTALLY WHERE
'Where did he accidentally go?'

Neidle et al. also claimed that a topic can intervene between a sentence-initial WH-phrase (in base-generated topic position on their account) and the rest of the clause, as shown in (67) (repeated from (19a)). In their example, the non-manual marking changes.

(67) ASL (Neidle et al. 2000, p. 116)
___wh (WHO) ___t2-bg (VEGETABLE) ___wh (PREFER POTATO WHO)
WHO, VEGETABLE, PREFER POTATO WHO
'Who, as for vegetables, who prefers potatoes?'

If these interrupting elements are under the scope of the WH-element in the syntactic structure, then the non-manual marker would be expected to spread over them. The interruption of the non-manual marking is thus unexpected under the syntax-only account. An Intonational Phrase, however, will be interrupted by the presence of another Intonational Phrase boundary, and thus the interruption of the non-manual marker is expected under the prosodic account.

Since the Intonational Phrase divisions are often isomorphic with the syntactic structure, it is usually difficult to determine which level controls the spread of the non-manual marking. However, the examples just provided demonstrate that the two can be teased apart, and that when they are, the intonational analysis has the advantage.

Future research should follow up on this by determining just where the syntactic and intonational phrasing differ. This will require a more detailed explanation of how intonational structure is determined. It also requires justification of particular syntactic structures which is independent from the spread of the non-manual markers. Until now, most proposals have started by assuming that the distribution of the non-manual markers reveals aspects of the syntactic structure. As we have seen, this should not be assumed.

23.6 Conclusions

In this chapter, we have reviewed in some detail a current debate regarding the structure of WH-questions in ASL. The detail is warranted because the issues involved are very important. Do sign languages require a structure different from that employed by spoken languages to account for WH-questions? Does the theory of syntax need to be expanded to include the data from sign languages, or are the current concepts sufficient? Along the way, we have encountered several places where disagreements about data have impeded the formation of a widely accepted analysis. This is a concern which future research must continue to address.

Our general conclusion is that no, grammatical theory need not introduce radically different concepts to account for the formation of WH-questions in sign languages. The same kinds of structures and operations are found in both modalities. Further research must be undertaken to discover whether sign languages and spoken languages fall under the same set of constraints on movement, multiple questions, and conditions on WH-*in situ* – and where spoken languages allow diversity, it remains to be seen how particular sign languages behave.

However, the investigation of sign languages highlights the need for syntactic investigation to consider in much more detail the potential interaction of intonational information with the syntax. Syntacticians have, in large part, ignored intonation, making considerable progress in the investigation of sentence structure by abstracting away from influences of prosody. However, in various domains, including question formation and the representation of information packaging, the role of intonation in syntactic structure is becoming more apparent, and it cannot be ignored much longer. Indeed, some recent analyses of WH-questions in spoken languages have crucially relied on aspects of intonation (e.g. Cheng and Rooryck 2000, Bošković 2002, Deguchi and Kitagawa 2002).

The parallels between non-manual marking and intonational melodies are firmly established. What remains to be done is to fine-tune our understanding of the interaction of syntax and prosody in WH-question formation in both language modalities.

24 Syntax: summary and directions

In this unit, we have explored a wide range of phenomena. We have discovered some facts, made some observations, and learned some things about the syntactic structure of sign languages. As in many areas, once we know a bit about something, we have a much greater understanding of what we don't know, and that is certainly the case here. Much more research is needed to make new and more refined generalizations about data, in the service of addressing theoretical questions.

This book focuses on the ways in which sign languages display the universal properties of all languages. Certainly when it comes to syntax, we have seen many similarities between what has been found for sign languages and what is known from the much longer study of spoken languages. But we have argued that studying sign languages contributes more to linguistic theory than studying any other exotic language. This is because where we find similarities across modalities, we can be more certain that we have discovered true universals. Even more important, where we find differences we can begin to understand the contribution of modality to language.

In this chapter we expand on the points just made. We summarize the findings from the chapters on syntax. We outline the need for further research. And we look at the unique position of sign languages for enhanced understanding of the relation between language and modality.

24.1 Summary

As a relatively young field, it should not be surprising that there is much controversy regarding sign language syntax. Linguists are just beginning to crack this nut, and each one may observe something slightly different from the others. As we've mentioned earlier, even gathering the data can be more of a challenge than in more well-studied languages. A greater level of variability across speakers may also be found (perhaps for reasons of language youth, to be discussed in Unit 5).

Still, there are some observations which most will agree with. The field has gone through some debate regarding basic sentence structure, but most see sign languages as having the kind of basic structure found across spoken languages. ASL (like a number of other sign languages) has the characteristics of an SVO language. German Sign Language and Japanese Sign Language have the characteristics of SOV languages. Even if constituents frequently move out of this order, embedded clauses typically do not, and are more likely to reveal aspects of a language's canonical structure.

And sign language constituents do tend to move around a lot. From what we can see, sign languages are generally discourse oriented: they place a high priority on organizing sentences around discourse concepts such as old/given versus new information. ASL, ISL, and other sign languages clearly place topics in sentence-initial position. ASL also seems to have operations for displacing other elements, getting prominent or heavy elements to the sentence-final position. The analyses of these constructions vary, but the structures have been frequently observed.

We already know that sign languages also have productive verbal morphology, and this will have some interaction with syntactic structure. Many researchers have observed more flexibility in word order with agreeing verbs, with those marked for aspect, and with classifiers. Again, the analyses vary, but clearly there are productive mechanisms for reordering constituents in sign languages.

ASL and other sign languages are among the languages which permit null arguments. The relationship between nulls and agreement – and between nulls and discourse – has been studied and debated.

Finally, sign languages make much use of non-manual markers to accompany specific syntactic structures. It is clear that sign linguists must pay careful attention to non-manuals in order to fully understand sentence structure.

24.2 Future research

More information is needed in all of the areas mentioned. Future research has a large number of possible topics to pursue. Many empirical and theoretical questions remain. Ideally, future research on sign languages will help us to better understand the nature of sentences in signed and spoken languages, testing the predictions of linguistic theory, contributing to its refinement and development.

Since a great deal of generative research in spoken languages has concentrated on constraints on movement, this domain is especially ripe. Is syntactic movement in sign languages restricted in the same ways as in spoken languages? What triggers are there for movement in sign languages – and do these differ across the modalities? How are sign languages different from one another with respect to syntactic movement?

There are many other aspects of syntax which have received only initial attention in sign languages. One additional area for exploration is the interface between syntax and semantics. Very little research has examined aspects of the logical form or semantics of sign languages, an area of great potential interest.

We would like to focus on an over-arching point: more *cross-sign language* research is crucial. It is especially useful when a particular research group, or a team of researchers using similar methodology and framework, look at similar or related phenomena across sign languages. This approach is beneficial because of the increased comparability it brings. All too often, different researchers use different terms, different methods, and different tools, making comparison across results more complicated.

Finally, the field will make the greatest advances with more native signer researchers. Given the real difficulties of obtaining replicable data on subtle distinctions, an increase in native signer linguists will contribute much to the development of the field.

24.3 Modality effects

We have reserved Unit 5 for discussion of the ways that sign languages and spoken languages are different. There we will discuss aspects of the modality which contribute to such differences, as well as aspects of the history of signed languages.

But first, we take a moment to consider what kind of modality effects would be expected in syntax specifically (cf. Lillo-Martin 2002). Aspects of the modality such as the use of the hands, body, and space around the signer will surely have some effects on the phonology. At the very least, the kinds of meaningless elements which combine in sign languages are physically different from the kinds which combine in spoken languages. But whether such aspects will have much of an effect on syntax depends on how separated syntax is from other components of grammar.

A relatively isolated view of syntax is quite possible: syntax could be the level of computation which manipulates symbolic elements without any concern for the pronunciation of these elements. In this case, few modality effects would be found.

On the other hand, syntax can be seen as the level which mediates between meaning and articulation. Aspects of pronunciation would necessarily connect with syntax. When pronunciation is manual/corporeal rather than vocal, something will be different.

In the end, the issue is empirical – what kind of modality effects will be revealed in the investigation of syntax in sign language? As this unit has shown in detail, the theoretical questions are important as well, for they tell us where to look.

With these points in mind, we move now to the last part of the book. Here we look at the ways that sign languages and spoken languages are different, and seek explanations.

Unit 5
Modality

25 The effects of modality: linguistic universals and sign language universals

25.1 Signed languages and linguistic universals

As the preceding twenty-four chapters of this book have demonstrated, languages produced by the hands and body and perceived by the eyes bear striking resemblance to the languages that are used more widely, those that are spoken and heard. A body of research that is quite large compared to its relative recency clearly proves that this is so.

The resemblances are far from trivial. While it might not be remarkable to discover that sign languages convey propositions as spoken languages do, the finding that sign languages distinguish between coordinated and recursively embedded sentences is certainly important (Chapter 18). That they allow arguments of a verb to be covert provided they are properly licensed is of similar significance (Chapter 21). That syntactic movement exists and is subject to the same constraints found in spoken languages (Chapters 20, 22, 23) provides strong evidence for the universality of such linguistic properties. Aspects of syntactic structure such as these are quite abstract, and they are fundamental to human language.

The combination of meaningful words with word partials to form more complex words may not be a particularly surprising discovery at first glance. But given that the words of sign language are often iconically motivated, this discovery becomes more interesting. And it is clearly significant that the two different types of morphology commonly found in spoken languages exist in sign languages as well (Chapters 3, 4): the morphology of syntax (inflection) and the morphology of lexeme formation (derivation). An abstract property of morphology is allomorphy – systematic alternation of different forms for the same word partial – and this too is found in sign languages (Chapter 4).

Similarities at the level of the meaningless units that combine to form words – the level of phonology – may be the most striking of all, given the absence of any similarity in the physical production and perception systems to which this level is bound. Signs are comprised of organized categories of distinctive features, and there are constraints on the ways in which these features and feature categories may combine (Unit 3). A syllable-like unit has even been identified (Chapter 14). When words and word partials are combined, phonological alternations occur that go beyond mere phonetic coarticulation and result in surface forms that are systematically different from those that underlie them (see especially Chapters 10, 12, 14, 15). The phonology segments and interprets utterances through a prosodic system with characteristics that are comparable to those of spoken languages (Chapter 15).

A universal property of both spoken and signed languages that is found at all three levels of analysis is hierarchical organization. In phonology, feature classes are organized in this way (Chapter 10), as are prosodic constituents (Chapter 15). In morphology, complex words such as compounds have hierarchical organization (Chapter 4). The existence of embedded clauses, island constraints, and binding relations reveals that the syntax too is hierarchically structured (Unit 4). Chomsky's earliest work (Chomsky 1957) showed that key aspects of linguistic patterning could only be explained if hierarchical structure is assumed, a demonstration which dealt the death blow to flat, linear models of language. In so doing, Chomsky established hierarchical organization as fundamental to human language. The pervasive existence of the same types of hierarchies in sign languages seals the case for this property as a true language universal.

Significant similarities such as these, and many others that have also been presented in detail in earlier chapters, may reliably be considered universals of human language. We argue, in fact, that the claim for the universality of such properties is made conclusive where the properties are shared by natural languages in two different modalities.

Yet each chapter also contains areas in which sign languages as a group differ from spoken languages. Certain structures and types of organization are shared by all sign languages we know of, but are absent from spoken language, or, more often, found only in some spoken languages but not in others. Such differences are usually referred to as modality effects, and are all too frequently swept under the carpet in the study halls of linguistic investigation.

We wish to roll up the rugs and take a look at these differences here, to cull explanations for them that have been offered, and to suggest new ones where possible. We address the issue of modality effects from four different perspectives. The first three are straightforwardly related to differences in physical modality. These are the use of space (Section 25.2,), simultaneity (Section 25.3), and iconicity or motivatedness in the lexicon and the grammar (Section 25.4). These three modality effects are closely intertwined, as will become apparent. But as they are conceptually distinct, we believe that considering them independently will enable us to assess the contribution of each with greater clarity. The fourth aspect

a. BOOK (citation form) b. a-BOOK (sign produced in another neutral location)

Figure 25.1 Non-contrastive spatial locations

concerns the sociolinguistic situation in which sign languages are found and the way in which they develop over time. This is the aspect of language age (Section 25.5). The chapter is organized accordingly, dealing with each of these perspectives in turn, at the levels of linguistic organization laid out in Units 2–4. After weighing the forces of modality effects, we conclude this treatise by considering some implications of the similarities and differences between spoken and signed languages for the study of language generally.

25.2 The use of space

As discussed in Unit 3, on phonology, the location of a sign must be included in its lexical representation. Such locations may include the head, torso, non-dominant hand or arm, or the "neutral space" immediately in front of the signer (cf. Chapter 1). Particular locations within the "neutral space" are not contrastive for the lexical stems of sign languages. So, for example, a sign like BOOK may be signed in the center of the neutral space. If it is signed on the right or left side, it is still the sign BOOK – different locations within neutral space, such as those illustrated in Figure 25.1, are not contrastive.

However, producing a sign like BOOK in some location other than directly in front of the signer is usually not simply a free variant of the citation form. Instead, producing a sign in a specific location serves to set up a relationship which can be used in various ways when other signs are produced relative to that location. This relationship can also be made by producing a sign followed by a point to a location, or even by producing a sign with eye gaze to a location, as shown in Figure 25.2.

The relationship between a sign and a location is exploited by the grammar in several ways. For example, it was shown in Chapter 3 that both verb agreement and pronouns make use of locations associated with referents. Once a referent (say, Kim) has been associated with a location

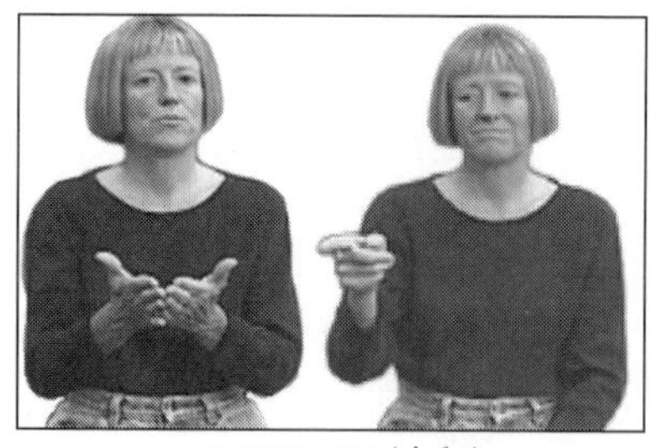

a. BOOK a-IX (right)

<e.g. R>
b. BOOK

Figure 25.2 Associating a sign with a location

in space (say, on the right), then this location will be used when a pronoun picks out the referent – in this case, by pointing towards the location associated with Kim on the right. Similarly, agreeing verbs taking Kim as an argument will move with respect to this location.

We also saw in Chapter 3 that non-agreeing verbs and adjectives may be articulated in spatial locations associated with their arguments, and we reviewed Padden's (1988 [1983]) claim that in these cases, the spatial locations are a kind of spatial clitic rather than agreement markers. No further analysis of the use of spatial locations in this way has been offered, but it clearly bears some similarity with the way in which space is used in the verb agreement system.

The "neutral space" is also used to represent spatial relations, in spatial verbs and classifier constructions. In such constructions, the locations of particular signs might represent the relative locations of different objects, or the movements of referents through physical space. Such constructions were discussed in some detail in Chapter 5.

The various uses of space we have just summarized comprise a subsystem of the sign language grammar which some have called "spatial syntax." While we presented reasons (Chapter 24) to believe that the formal properties of syntax are not affected by space, their spatial realization is an important part of the syntax of sign languages, critical to a full understanding of the system.

Another way that space is used in sign languages shows up at the discourse level. Space can be used metaphorically at this level, for example by establishing oppositions in space to convey oppositions in point of view. A signer might convey a person's views on one side of an argument on the right side of space, opposing it with other views on the left side of space. Different physical spaces might also be used to convey different time periods, or hypothetical situations (van Hoek 1992).

Clearly, the fact that sign languages make use of space is a modality effect. We want to explore whether this effect is relevant only at the surface level, or whether it has greater significance to the organization of sign languages. This question has been asked in one way or another about all the uses of space just summarized. In the next subsections, we look in some detail at how this question has affected analyses of pronominal reference and verb agreement, considering the possibility that gestural elements may systematically interact with linguistic elements in sign language.

25.2.1 *Pronouns and the use of space*

Sign language pronouns point to locations in space which are associated with referents in order to pick out those referents. However, unlike locations used in lexical items (e.g., head, trunk), the locations used in the pronominal reference system cannot be listed. Frequently, referents are associated with locations in space so as to be maximally distinct: e.g., one on the right side and one on the left side. However, *any* location in neutral signing space can be associated with a referent, and a pronoun picking out that referent will use that location. A diagram of some of these options is provided in (1).

(1) Possible locations associated with referents

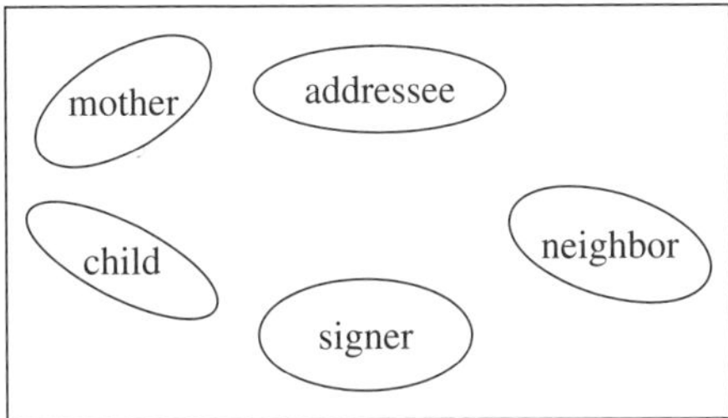

This means that between any two points in the signing space, another point can be identified as a potential location with which to associate a referent. Thus, the locations are not listable. Furthermore, since locations are associated with particular referents, pronoun signs are generally unambiguous – they pick out the particular referent associated with a location, not a class of potential antecedents.

Concerned with this issue, in Chapter 21 we raised the question of what features characterize sign language pronouns. There we saw Meier's (1990) argument that pronoun signs are marked only for a first versus non-first person distinction. If singular pronouns only distinguish first versus non-first person, it would seem that there are exactly two singular pronouns in the ASL lexicon. Why, then, can pronouns point, virtually unambiguously, anywhere?

As discussed in Chapter 21, to answer this question, Lillo-Martin and Klima (1990) propose that ASL pronouns receive a referential index during the course of deriving a sentence. Within and across sentences of a discourse, elements with the same referential index will be interpreted as coreferential. So far, this is no different from what has been proposed for spoken languages (Kamp and Reyle 1993). However, in signed but not spoken languages, the referential index is realized overtly, in that all signs within a discourse with a particular referential index will be produced with respect to the same referential locus.

Thus, the Lillo-Martin and Klima analysis attempts to keep the modality effect strictly at the surface: in sign languages only there is an overt realization of the referential index on pronouns. This is a modality effect – spoken languages do not overtly realize referential indices, but sign languages can do this because the spatial modality affords it. As spatial locations are unlimited, and referential indices are expressed using spatial locations, there is an explanation, in the modality, for why there is an unlimited number of referential indices overtly expressed in sign languages. Furthermore, this is the extent of the modality effect, since otherwise the pronominal system adheres to the same syntactic universals that are observed in spoken languages, such as the Binding Conditions.

The discussion of this issue in Chapter 21 stopped with pronouns. Can the same account be extended to verb agreement and other uses of space? In the next subsection, we go beyond the straightforward linguistic analysis of verb agreement presented in Chapter 3 by taking into consideration certain criticisms that have been raised, especially those of Liddell. We will argue that a range of properties of verb agreement in sign languages can only be explained with a linguistic analysis, but we will also isolate particular characteristics that are modality driven and apparently extralinguistic.

25.2.2 *Verb agreement and the use of space: linguistic and extralinguistic aspects*

Since the same referential loci are used in verb agreement as in pronouns, an analysis of verb agreement using referential indices has some validity. Under such an analysis, verbs are seen as agreeing with their subject and object (or source and goal, as in Meir's 1998a analysis) by virtue of sharing referential indices. Such an analysis has been proposed by Aronoff et al. (2000, 2005). As they point out, agreement morphology for languages in general is "the realization of the universally copied syntactic indices, but mediated by the partly arbitrary referential and classificatory morphosyntactic categories of the individual language." For sign languages the morphological form of the element that agrees between the noun and the verb is the referential locus.

A similar analysis, within the terminology of Head-driven Phrase Structure Grammar (Pollard and Sag 1994) is offered by Cormier, Wechsler, and Meier (1998). They describe agreement in general as "structure-sharing of the index value of one expression with the index value of another expression" (p. 222). The values for indices specify locations used by verbs and noun phrases.

Cognizant of the boundless instantiations of loci, other sign language researchers have made different claims about what it is that verbs agree with. The ASLLRP group make a direct comparison between the components of agreement in signed and spoken languages. They say, "spatial locations constitute an overt instantiation of ϕ–features (specifically, person features)" (Neidle et al. 2000, p. 31). Since the spatial locations are theoretically unbounded, they elaborate: "although … there is a primary distinction between first and nonfirst persons, nonfirst person can be further subclassified into many distinct person values" (ibid., pp. 166–167). Thus, they seem to allow for an unlimited number of person values in the grammar of sign languages, an unexplained anomaly under their analysis.

By contrast, the index copying/sharing analysis of sign language agreement highlights the similarity between sign and spoken language agreement, keeping the modality effect outside of the syntax. The features employed by sign language agreement systems are distinct from those of spoken languages, but the mechanism is the same.

In fact, intriguing evidence of referential index copying can even be found in spoken languages. Aronoff et al. (2000, 2005) describe spoken languages which employ the mechanism of literal alliterative agreement. One example comes from the Niger-Congo language Bainouk (Sauvageot 1967). For some nouns in this language, agreement between a noun and its target takes the form of an affix copy of the first CV of the noun stem, in certain agreement environments. An example is given in (2).

Bainouk (Aronoff et al. 2000; data from Sauvageot 1967)

(2) a. kata:ma
river (sg)

b. kata:ma-ŋɔ in-ka
river-DEF this-CV

c. kata:ma-ã
river-PL

d. kata:ma-ã ka-nak-ã
river-PL CV-two-PL

In (2a), the singular form of the word for 'river' is given. In (2b), the singular form is used with a demonstrative, in an agreement environment. The demonstrative takes as its agreement suffix a copy of the first CV of the noun stem (*-ka*). Similarly, in (2c) the plural form is given, and in (2d) the plural form is used with a numeral, which takes a prefix copy of the first CV of the noun stem (*ka-*). Dobrin (1997) argues that the alliterative copy agreement forms are the default forms which appear where grammatically specified agreement markers (the more frequent type in Bainouk) do not.

Although literal alliterative agreement systems are rare across the world's languages, Aronoff et al. (2005) consider them to be a paradigm example of the emergence of the unmarked, a concept developed within Optimality Theory (McCarthy and Prince 1994). Aronoff et al. explain: "Literal alliterative agreement, like sign-language agreement, reflects the universal syntactic nature of agreement as copying, but this universal normally does not surface in spoken languages, because of the principle of lexical integrity" which prevents the syntax from looking inside a word's phonology (Zwicky and Pullum 1983). The authors further explain that lexical integrity can be violated in extreme circumstances – where the language requires morphological agreement but it meets a gap in the agreement system. When that happens, they argue, the unmarked state of language, in this case, of verb agreement, is revealed. In sign languages this unmarked default is the norm.

There are two noticeable similarities between alliterative copy agreement and sign language agreement: the open-endedness of the system and the non-arbitrariness of the agreeing element. The system is unlike agreement in more familiar languages in which the form of the agreement marker is arbitrary, productive, and independent of the form of the nominal that controls the agreement. In Bainouk-type languages, as in sign languages, the agreement marker may get its form from the particular coindexed element with which it agrees. The two systems are not identical, however: Bainouk-type agreement makes use of phonological structures of the agreeing element's lexical entry, while sign language agreement makes use of a location in space associated with a referent, a location which is not part of the lexical form of the referent itself. This difference between signed and spoken languages is a true modality effect, and we will discuss it below. But be that as it may, we now see that the open-endedness and non-arbitrariness of the sign language agreement system is found in spoken languages as well. This finding will play a role in arguing against the non-linguistic analysis of the phenomenon in sign language proposed by Liddell, to which we now turn.

Liddell (1995) argues that the failure to delimit the specific morphological elements used in sign language agreement is unacceptable in a linguistic system. He also rejects the idea that the morphological element of agreement might completely lack phonological content, as in the case of spatial loci. Working within the theory of Mental Spaces (Fauconnier 1985), he defines Real Space as a mental object which is "an individual's conception of what is physically real in their current, directly perceivable physical environment" (Liddell 1995, p. 23). He argues:

> There appears to be an unlimited number of possible locations for referents in Real Space and, correspondingly, an unlimited number of possible locations toward which the hand may be directed. Attempting a morphemic solution to the problem

> of directing signs toward any of an unlimited number of possible locations in Real Space would either require an unlimited number of location and direction morphemes or it would require postulating a single morpheme whose form was indeterminate ... The concept of a lexically fixed, meaningful element with indeterminate form is inconsistent with our conception of what morphemes are.
>
> (Liddell 1995, pp. 24–25)

In addition to the listability problem, Liddell points out that the traditional analysis oversimplifies the (so-called) agreement phenomenon by describing it in terms of points in neutral space (Liddell 1990a). It is not accurate to say that a single geometric point is associated with each referent, and that verbs agree with these points. Some verbs are specified as being produced at a higher or lower location, such as forehead height, chin height, or chest height. These verbs are directed at the appropriate heights, so that a single referent might be picked out by different verbs at three (or more) different points, depending on the verb. Furthermore, the verbs may indicate the relative heights of the referents, so that a verb might move to a lower location (indicating a relatively shorter person) or to a higher location (indicating a relatively taller person).

In view of these difficulties with the traditional analysis, Liddell (1994) proposes that referents are not equal to points in space, but that referents are thought of as being located in space. The located referents are either "surrogates" – imaginary referents of full size (used in the cases where verbs indicate relative height of referents) – or "tokens" – schematic referents with some depth, but equivalent and parallel to the signer.

Furthermore, he concludes that there is no linguistic process of verb agreement in ASL. Instead, he proposes that "the handshapes, certain aspects of the orientations of the hand, and types of movement are lexically specified through phonological features, but ... there are no linguistic features identifying the location the hands are directed toward. Instead, the hands are directed ... by non-discrete gestural means" (Liddell 1994, p. 26). In other words, he employs a mixture of linguistic and gestural elements to analyze what he calls "indicating verbs," and specifically argues that the process employed is *not* agreement (see also Liddell 2000).[1]

Liddell's arguments have been the object of considerable attention and controversy. The debate has served to increase our understanding of the process known as verb agreement, and has led many researchers to consider more seriously the nature of the use of space in sign languages, and how that aspect of sign languages affects their structure. Some have responded by incorporating certain aspects of Liddell's proposal into

[1] McBurney (2002) argues that traditional analyses of sign language pronouns are faced with the same problems, leading her to conclude that there are no grammatical elements which should be characterized as pronouns in sign languages.

their models, while still arguing that verb agreement has linguistic characteristics that must be maintained as well.

Aronoff et al. (2000, 2005), Lillo-Martin (2002), Meir (2002), Meier (2002a), and Rathmann and Mathur (2002) have each presented arguments to maintain the linguistic status of verb agreement in sign languages. One is the argument made above, that determining the form of the agreement marker by some aspect of an element with which it is coindexed, is not so anomalous as previously believed. It may even be thought of as the universal unmarked case, although it rarely emerges in spoken languages. There are several other ways in which constraints on the process of verb agreement are clearly linguistic. For example, only certain linguistically defined verbs participate in agreement, and they do so only in linguistically specified ways.

As we have seen, the class of verbs which participates in agreement is linguistically defined. If what we call verb agreement is purely non-linguistic, why would the class of agreeing verbs be linguistically restricted? Why would a verb like BUY, for example, not show agreement, while a verb like PAY does? Why would verbs which do not actually convey spatial notions, such as TEACH, be agreeing verbs? Why is it the indirect object of ditransitive verbs which participates in agreement and not the direct object or both the direct and indirect object in an analogic sequence? As explained in Chapter 3, linguistic analyses account for these phenomena. Furthermore, morphophonological constraints block the application of the agreement process for some verbs or for some arguments. These rules are not simply reflexes of articulatory possibilities (i.e., where the arm can or cannot reach), but are determined at a more abstract level of linguistic structure (Mathur and Rathmann 2001).

In addition, agreement must be represented in the syntax, because syntactic processes such as null argument licensing and even word order variations may be correlated with agreement, as we have seen in Unit 4. As discussed there, different sign languages, while employing virtually identical systems of verb agreement, may have different consequences in the way that agreement interacts with syntactic phenomena, such as word order and the use of an AUX sign (Chapter 19). Even evidence from language acquisition supports the postulation of a linguistic system of verb agreement (Meier 2002a), as children sometimes err in the direction of linguistic overgeneralization instead of mime-like analogy. It is not clear how a model which entirely divorces agreement from the linguistic system could capture this range of generalizations. It seems instead that the evidence for a linguistic analysis is strong, and that attributing a role to linguistic structure in verb agreement is unavoidable.

Yet how can a linguistic analysis be reconciled with the observations Liddell makes about the form of agreement? In order to address this question, we first point out that Liddell's arguments stem from a single observation: that the form of the putative agreement marker cannot be lexically specified. This challenge can be met by assuming a more abstract notion of morpheme, so that no concrete, specifiable form is required. We do not have to go far to find abstraction of this kind in the morphology of spoken language. For example, in English, zero morphemes are postulated for cases such as noun/verb conversion (e.g., *license*), and the zero plural allomorph for some forms (e.g., *sheep*). The prosodic templates of Semitic languages are also abstract, employing both specific consonantal and vocalic segments and abstract prosodic patterns in a complex morphological system (see Chapter 3, Section 3.4). Reduplicative morphology employs similarly abstract morphemes. Still, the sign language case is not exactly like any of these, since it involves forms which can only be described by reference to the world, not the linguistic system.

We suggest that the solution is a proposal that follows Liddell in taking the non-analyzable out of the linguistic system, but maintains a linguistic agreement analysis for the rest. Under such a proposal, verb agreement and pronouns would be seen as combining linguistic elements with gestural specification of location. An analogy can be made to the pointing gestures which frequently accompany spoken pronouns.

Suppose a speaker utters an English sentence like (3) and points to distinct locations along with each pronoun.

(3) Larry voted for her, not her.

The pronouns in (3) are ambiguous, in that they may pick out any of the (relevant) third-person female referents in the discourse. If the speaker points while using the pronouns, they become disambiguated. The locations the points will be directed towards are determined by the actual or imagined locations of the referents. The present proposal is that the abstract non-first-singular sign language pronoun is lexically and syntactically ambiguous, just as *her* is in the English example – but when it combines with a concrete gesture, it may be directed at any location, and its reference is disambiguated. Similarly, verb agreement combines linguistic elements with gesture. In this view, we acknowledge the influence of gesture on the system, like Liddell, but contrary to his model, we demonstrate how gestural elements combine with aspects of the system that are linguistic. To begin with, an important difference between the pronouns and verb agreement loci of sign language and the gestures that accompany speech is that spoken language gestures are optional, but pronouns and loci in sign languages must obligatorily be articulated in some spatial location. Signers are also consistent in their use of space within a discourse, presumably more so than speakers are. Apart from obligatoriness and consistency, the system bears properties that are explicitly linguistic, described in Chapter 3.

Proposals that sign language verb agreement combines linguistic aspects (i.e., that agreement is linguistic) with gestural aspects (to account for locations) have been made by Lillo-Martin (2002) and Rathmann and Mathur (2002), and are compatible with treatments by Aronoff et al. (2000, 2005) and Meier (2002a). These proposals stress the importance of the linguistic aspects of sign language agreement and pronouns, while acknowledging that the use of space brings in a component unique to sign languages. There is no denying that language universals which apply to verb agreement and pronouns also apply in sign languages. But, while spoken languages implement agreement systems using "the partly arbitrary referential and classificatory morphosyntactic categories of the individual language" (Aronoff et al. 2005), sign languages employ the gestural–spatial medium in the manifestation of their agreement systems.

25.2.3 Other uses of space

Spatial contrasts are meaningful not only in the pronominal and verb agreement systems, but in "spatial" verbs and classifier constructions as well (see Chapter 5). In these forms, in contrast with the "frozen" words of the lexicon, the spatial layout of signs is used to convey spatial information. For example, the spatial verb PUT is produced so as to show by its use of space the spatial arrangement between its direct and indirect objects. Similarly, a signer conveys the physical relationship between two chairs (or small animals or two-legged upright beings, etc.) by manipulating the physical relationship between the two hands representing these objects with entity (or SASS) classifiers.

The same problem we have seen with verb agreement comes up in specifying the spatial relations between elements in this use of sign language as well. Again, an approach which combines linguistic elements described in earlier chapters with a gestural component may be required. When it comes to describing the layout of furniture in a room, mapping directions from one location to another, or showing the precise components of a spatially complex action, like a picture (or movie), a sign may be worth 1,000 words (see Emmorey 1996 for psycholinguistic evidence of this, based on the time it takes subjects to describe room layouts in ASL and English).

In addition to the morphosyntactic uses of space in pronouns and verbs, are there other influences of the signing space on higher levels of linguistic structure, such as the arrangement of words and sentences, and making reference to or connections among elements of a discourse? As for the former, we have seen a proposal in Chapter 18 that the option of using spatial relationships to indicate the grammatical relationships between elements in a sentence makes word order and even structured hierarchies unnecessary in sign languages (Bouchard and Dubuisson

1995, Bouchard 1996). However, we argued strongly against this view, showing that hierarchy and word order are just as crucial in sign languages as they are in spoken languages.

In any case, the encoding of grammatical relations does not exhaust all conceivable uses of space in sign language structure. We have already noted that spatial contrasts may be used metaphorically, to indicate contrasting opinions, time periods, situations, or possible worlds. There is a gestural analogue to this in spoken languages: speakers may point or lean to one side to contrast one point with another, indicated on the other side. As with the previous examples, such combinations of language and gesture are decidedly more systematic and conventionalized for signers than for speakers.

Sign languages are articulated in three-dimensional space, and it is crucial to understand this aspect of the modality in order to find both the similarities and differences between sign and spoken languages. There is another feature of the modality which has the potential to have a strong impact on linguistic structure of sign languages as opposed to spoken languages: simultaneity. Because of the articulatory–perceptual characteristics of signs, the two independent articulators (the two hands), and the use of non-manual markings together with manual signs, sign languages have the possibility of articulating more than one thing at the same time. In the next section we show some of the ways in which sign languages do and do not encode linguistic information simultaneously, at every level of structure.

25.3 Simultaneity

Simultaneity has been evident throughout the descriptions and analyses in Units 2–4, though not consistently pointed out there. We begin our discussion of simultaneity by highlighting its contribution to morphology, phonology, syntax, and discourse, and then we seek to explain it.

In morphology, even the very earliest explorations noted the simultaneous layering of information (Bellugi and Fischer 1972, Fischer and Gough 1978). Models of morphology that had been developed to explain non-linear structure in spoken language were exploited to demonstrate formally how the morphological elements combine systematically in sign language (Liddell 1984b, Sandler 1989, 1990). It has also often been observed that signs tend overwhelmingly to be monosyllabic (Coulter 1982), even when they have complex morphological structure. It is simultaneous juxtaposition of morphological elements that allows morphologically complex signs to remain monosyllabic. In Unit 2, several such morphological processes were analyzed. The tendency of morphologically complex signs and host-clitic complexes to reduce to one syllable was suggested to result from pressure within the phonology to encode elements simultaneously, described in detail in Chapter 14 (Sandler 1993d, 1999b).

Early views of the phonological structure of sign languages (Stokoe 1960, Klima and Bellugi 1979) actually held that all phonological elements within a sign are produced simultaneously. Even as researchers discovered sequentiality within the sign (e.g., Liddell 1984b), the impression of simultaneity still had to be accounted for. The Hand Tier account proposed essentially simultaneous representation of hand configuration and major place of articulation through autosegmental association with the specific locations and movements that are sequenced (Sandler 1989; see Chapter 9). In fact, as Chapter 16 shows, it is only a very small number of features in any sign that differ across sequential segments – very often only one – and the rest are constant throughout the sign. In other words, the morphology and the phonology together encode information simultaneously.

At higher levels of structure, simultaneity also plays a role. For example, whole prosodic constituents are simultaneously characterized by superarticulatory arrays, analogous to intonation in spoken language. Intonation is instantiated simultaneously with sequential units in both modalities – reflected in the traditional term, suprasegmental. But the superarticulatory arrays of sign language differ from spoken language intonational tunes in that they too are simultaneous. Spoken language high and low tones associate suprasegmentally with accented syllables and prosodic constituent boundaries, but they select elements which are sequenced with respect to each other, and the tones themselves are also sequenced, both within and across intonational tunes. Sign language superarticulations, such as furrowed brow and eye squint, are simultaneously layered in arrays, and the arrays are in turn simultaneously superimposed on whole prosodic constituents (Nespor and Sandler 1999, Sandler 1999a; Chapter 15 here).

Other non-manual actions are also simultaneously articulated with signs. For example, headshakes and nods, eye movements, and body shifts usually occur together with a sign or sign sequence. These non-manual behaviors do not behave entirely like intonational tunes, but do have a role to play in sign language grammars (see, for example, Chapters 20 and 21). Furthermore, a linguistic superarticulatory array, a particular head/body position, and a manual sign may all occur simultaneously.

At the syntactic and discourse level, classifiers articulated on one hand can persist simultaneously throughout an entire chunk, backgrounding the information while keeping it in the signal. An excellent example of this from Emmorey (2002) was shown in Chapter 5, Figure 5.6, in which the VEHICLE classifier handshape, representing the fancy car of the person in the story, stays in the mind of its owner – and in the view of the interlocutor – from the time she disembarks to do her errands until she hops back in and zooms home.

Miller (1994) discusses several "simultaneous constructions" in LSQ and ASL. His examples include classifier constructions, and lexical signs which are decomposed as classifiers – these result in simultaneity at the syntactic and discourse levels. He also brings up discourse-regulation devices such as holding a pointing sign on one hand while the other hand expands on the point being made; holding a sign (such as a point or a classifier) to mark a location and directing a non-classifier sign with respect to it; and plays on signs, which might involve simultaneous constructions not otherwise allowed. See also footnote 12 in Chapter 12 for references to additional simultaneous uses of the non-dominant hand.

The linguistic functions expressed through simultaneous structure in sign languages find expression in spoken languages too, but in a much more sequential fashion (see Chapter 16). Normally, both phonemes and morphemes follow each other sequentially. Even where there is simultaneity – in non-concatenative morphology, for example, or in the superimposition of tones onto vowels and other sonorants – the superimposed material is itself both sequentially organized and sequentially associated. These generalizations are expressed in theoretical constructs such as association conventions and the no-crossing constraint for autosegments and for tiered morphology (Goldsmith 1976, McCarthy 1979, 1981). In contrast, the types of simultaneous structure described in the preceding paragraphs are found universally in sign languages, and, though there is also sequential structure, there is comparatively little of it.

Why is there so much simultaneity in sign language? The answer has three prongs: (1) motivatedness; (2) the nature of the production and perception systems; (3) processing constraints.

25.3.1 *Motivatedness and simultaneity*

In Section 25.4 we will show that motivatedness pervades sign language structure. But we wish to stress that this motivatedness in itself results in simultaneity of structure. The objects, events, qualities, and relations represented at the level of lexemes are usually holistic concepts with no inherent sequential structure. Instead, the propositions formed by these words involve events in which objects and events, with their concomitant qualities, aspects, etc., often coincide simultaneously in the real world. If Mabel gives Rupert a book, the act of giving, the giver, the receiver, and the presence of the book are all simultaneously involved. Similarly, if a person approaches a car, the person, the car, and the approach are simultaneously present in the event. Sign languages universally express these two types of simultaneous event through morphemes that are themselves simultaneously occurring – in the verb agreement system and in the classifier system, respectively. The reason that sign languages express simultaneous events through simultaneous form may be simple: they do so because they can.

25.3.2 Production/perception and simultaneity

The main articulators of sign language, the hands, are big and slow compared to the vocal organs. Typically, spoken language is produced at a rate of ten to fifteen segments per second (Liberman 1996) while an informal study conducted by Emmorey (2002) indicates that signs are produced at a rate of seven to eleven segments per second (where segments correspond to the Ls and Ms of the HT model described in Chapter 9). The average number of words per second in running speech is about four to five, while only two to three signs are produced per second under similar conditions (Bellugi and Fischer 1972).

Yet the manual articulators have certain advantages. First, the hand is capable of articulating a wide range of configurations by combining different finger selections, finger positions, and hand orientations. These configurations can visually replicate properties of objects in the world. They also have the ability to move while instantiating these configurations, providing a second building block in the resulting simultaneous grammatical structures. In verb agreement and classifier constructions, then, we have now described two elements conspiring toward simultaneity: motivatedness and production capabilities.

Another advantage of the manual articulatory system is the existence of two hands which can articulate independently, creating structure in which each hand may simultaneously articulate a different meaningful element. Interestingly, within lexical items, the two hands do not take advantage of this capability (see Chapter 12), and we have suggested an explicitly linguistic explanation for this: the requirement that there be independent, identifiable constraints on the central grammatical building block of language, the word. But in the marking of prosodic constituents (Chapter 15), in creating morphological complexity, (classifier constructions, Chapter 5), and at the level of discourse (e.g., backgrounding, Chapter 5) the simultaneity option presented by the existence of two relatively independent articulators is productively exploited.

25.3.3 Processing and simultaneity

In an early and intriguing study (Bellugi and Fischer 1972), hearing native signers were asked to tell the same story twice – once in ASL and once in English. The researchers found that, although it takes significantly longer to produce a sign than to speak a word, the length of the sentences (the propositions) was about the same in the two versions. They attribute this apparent paradox to the tendency for linguistic complexity to be expressed simultaneously in signs and linearly in spoken language.

They further suggest that there are memory constraints on the processing of propositions in any language, which may require the overall duration of propositions in spoken and signed language to be the same. More recent research, cited in Emmorey (2002), has demonstrated that signers have a shorter working memory span for signs than hearing subjects do for words (Krakow and Hanson 1985, Wilson and Emmorey 1997). Emmorey suggests that this may be because signs take longer to articulate. These findings suggest that simultaneity of structure within the sign, and the resulting proposition duration, may be partly mandated by processing constraints. If a sign takes longer to articulate and consequently is retained for a shorter time in working memory, then, in order to transmit the same amount of information in the same time as spoken language, it is essential that more grammatical information be heaped simultaneously upon the sign than upon the spoken word.

Further experimental investigation is needed to explain how motivatedness and constraints on production and perception actually work in sign language, individually and together, and we hope that such studies will ensue. Psycholinguistic work of this kind will provide a basis for comparison with spoken language that will surely lead to a better understanding of the relation between modality and language form in both cases. Yet even in advance of such research, it is reasonable to deduce that these factors together provide overwhelming pressure for simultaneous structure to arise in sign languages.

Space and simultaneity are two aspects of the articulatory–perceptual apparatus of signing which enable the modality to have an effect on language. Similarly, because the manual–visual modality is more suitable for iconic representation of visual elements, iconicity or motivatedness is more prevalent in sign language than in its oral counterpart. We now turn to a discussion of this modality effect. In the following discussion, we use the terms "iconic" and "iconicity" broadly. In fact, the linguistic element, whether spoken or signed, is not a precise icon of what it is representing, but rather is motivated by some aspect of it – appearance, sound, sensation, spatial or temporal position, etc. Let us tackle this issue by taking a closer look at iconicity in spoken and signed languages.

25.4 Iconicity/motivatedness

The term "iconicity" in language refers to a direct or transparent relation between form and meaning. In the heady early years of sign language research, when investigators were in the business of demonstrating to a skeptical public that sign languages are real languages, the role of iconicity in these languages was portrayed as negligible. One reason for this emphasis in sign language research is the claim, made by the influential Swiss linguist Ferdinand de Saussure, that arbitrariness is a fundamental property of language. That a tree is called *tree* in English, *arbre* in French, *ets* in Hebrew, etc., shows that there is an arbitrary relationship between sound and meaning in language. To show that sign languages are languages like any other, researchers sought to underscore their arbitrariness rather than their motivatedness or iconicity.

On closer inspection, however, we find more iconicity in language than one might think. Let's have a look at some examples in spoken language before tackling the issue in sign language. First, there is onomatopoeia. For example, words for the sounds animals make which resemble those sounds, such as *cockadoodledo*, *tweet-tweet*, *bow-wow*, etc., can probably be found in all languages. So too can other words, like *splash*, that evoke the sound of the events they represent. Sometimes, certain sounds or combinations of sounds come to represent a sensation, whether or not the origin of the link is motivated in any obvious way – like *gl* in *glow*, *glare*, *glint*, *glimmer*, *glisten*. The sound *gl* is not an affix because it does not attach to any discernible stem. It is a sound that represents a sensation directly, a phenomenon sometimes referred to as sound symbolism.

Some languages have sets of word-like units, called ideophones or mimetics, that mimic a sound or other sensation, or reflect a judgment or attitude of the speaker (see Diffloth 1972). These forms are unlike ordinary words because they have different lexical, morphological, and phonological structure, and because the relation between form (sound) and meaning is often far less arbitrary.

Japanese is an example of a language with a rich system of mimetic forms. Kita (1997) demonstrates that Japanese adverbial and nominal mimetics constitute a separate semantic dimension from that of ordinary words. It is clear that mimetics represent a separate dimension, as they co-occur without redundancy with words which convey similar meaning, and they behave differently from other words at every level of structure: semantic, morphological, syntactic, and phonological. Example (4) illustrates the non-redundancy of the mimetic *sutasuta*, 'hurried walk of a human.'

(4) Japanese (Kita 1997, p. 388)

[Taro	wa]	[sutasuta to]	[haya-aruki	o]	si	-ta
Taro	Topic	Mimetic	haste-walk	Acc	do	Past

'Taro walked hurriedly.'

The attitude of the speaker is also represented through mimetics, expressing such impressions as vulgarity, appropriateness, reliability, and tastefulness. Such effects may even be represented with a single phonological feature, in a particular kind of sound symbolism. For example, Kita cites Hamano's (1986) demonstration that phonological features of the first consonant of an adverbial mimetic make a predictable semantic contribution, as shown in (5).

(5) Japanese mimetics (from Hamano 1986)
[−voice] = small/light/fine
[+voice] = big/heavy/coarse

palatalization = childishness, excessive energy
[−continuant] = abrupt movement, surface
[+continuant] = continuous movement, shapelessness

We see in these tendencies a system that does not observe duality of patterning: the smallest formational atoms are meaningful. This brings us back to sign language. Stokoe launched the field of sign language linguistics by demonstrating that, contrary to popular impression, sign languages do have duality: handshapes, locations, and movements are generally meaningless in the lexemes of the language, just as sounds are generally meaningless in the lexemes of spoken languages. Yet we have seen that sign languages also have subsystems such as the classifier subsystem in which each element is meaningful. The example from Japanese mimetics shown in (5) demonstrates that duality is not absolute in spoken language either – language may universally avail itself of iconic form-meaning atoms.

Another example of the iconicity of the Japanese mimetics system is in the use of reduplication to indicate iteration, and of repetition to indicate the actual number of times of occurrence. This distinction between temporal aspect (iterative) and iconic representation of a temporal event (once, twice, etc.) is reminiscent of the distinction drawn in Chapter 5 between the interpretation of reduplication in ASL ordinary verbs and in classifier constructions, respectively. In Japanese, both interpretations are available with different forms within the mimetic system, while in ASL, the literal interpretation of repetition is only available in the classifier system, while reduplication is interpreted more abstractly (e.g., as duration) in the grammaticalized system of verbal aspect.

The mimetics of Japanese are also characterized by affective (and apparently gradient) intonation and, interestingly, by co-speech gesture. The latter is argued by McNeill (1992) and Kita (1997) to represent an imagistic level of representation in language, and Kita sees the co-occurrence of mimetics with gesture as further evidence that mimetics require their own dimension of semantic representation.[2] It should be stressed that Japanese mimetics are fully conventionalized and rule governed, and, at the same time, iconic.

At higher levels of linguistic structure, form–meaning isomorphism is referred to as diagrammatic iconicity.[3] Haiman explains that "linguistic forms are frequently the way they are because, like diagrams, they resemble the conceptual structures they are used to convey" (Haiman 1985, p. 1).

[2] Sandler (2003) argues that sign languages have an equivalent system to co-speech gesture. She brings examples of co-sign mouth gestures which are distinct from grammaticalized facial adverbials such as those discussed in Chapter 4, and shows that they fit McNeill's (1992) definition of iconic gestures. Emmorey (1999) also discusses gesture in sign languages.

[3] Parts of this discussion draw from an overview of iconicity in Meir (1998a).

In diagrammatic iconicity, unlike lexical iconicity, the form of each sign – "sign" in the semiotic sense – need not resemble its referent at all (Haiman 1980, p. 515). Instead, it is the arrangement of the linguistic signs that mirrors the relation of their referents, creating a kind of diagram. For example, the order of clauses or sentences in a narrative may mirror the actual sequence of the events they describe.

Given that even spoken languages display a certain amount of motivatedness, is there a genuine contrast between signed and spoken languages? We examine this question by returning to the earliest studies of iconicity in sign language, most of which focused on the lexical level. We then take a deeper look at the phenomenon, one that is informed by subsequent research, at other levels of linguistic structure.

25.4.1 Iconic motivation at the lexical level

At the level of lexical iconicity, at least, Saussure clearly had a point: spoken languages are rather poor in motivated form. Even in Japanese mimetics, which involve a direct mapping of form and meaning, the particular sounds chosen are arguably more arbitrary than are the formational properties of signs. Sign languages are indeed different. They have gestural origins and are perceived visually, both of which contribute to pervasive motivatedness in form at the level of the sign.

The relation between motivated gesture and sign language has been both overemphasized and underemphasized by many who have written about it. In his important book, the American structuralist linguist Leonard Bloomfield wrote that sign languages are "merely developments of ordinary gestures and . . . any and all complicated or not immediately intelligible gestures are . . . derivative of (spoken) language" (Bloomfield 1933, p. 144). The implication is that all indigenous signs are immediately intelligible because they are iconic.

The early sign language literature tackled Bloomfield's claim head-on, and succeeded in showing that abstract, discrete, and componential properties of language often win out over holistic and analogic characteristics that might be expected if signs were completely iconic. This work was squarely at the opposite extreme, vigorously playing down the role of iconicity, and emphasizing the abstract, formal linguistic structure of sign languages.[4] During the period when researchers bore the onus of proving that sign languages are real languages, some may have feared that if the form of the sign for TREE is motivated on the basis of the form of a tree, and maybe even similar across sign languages because of this iconicity,

[4] Actually, some iconoclasts in the early years of sign language research did focus on iconicity (e.g., DeMateo 1977, Mandel 1977, Boyes-Braem 1981). In fact, in later years William Stokoe himself took an interest in iconicity (Armstrong et al. 1995).

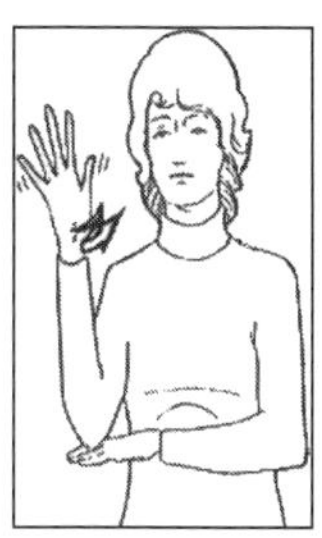

a. TREE (ASL)

b. TREE (Danish SL)

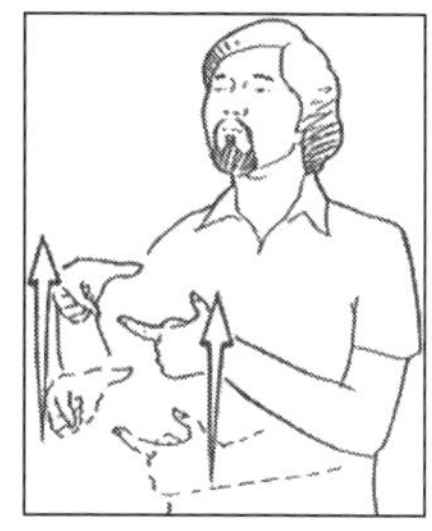

c. TREE (Chinese SL)

Figure 25.3 Lexical motivatedness (© Ursula Bellugi, the Salk Institute)

then sign languages might be thought of as less arbitrary and by extension less language-like. Klima and Bellugi (1979) observe that although the sign for tree is iconically based in many sign languages, the signs may be distinct both in the aspects of trees which are represented and in the form of the signs. They provide examples from ASL, Danish Sign Language, and Chinese Sign Language, reproduced in Figure 25.3.

The attention that was paid to iconicity yielded interesting results, demonstrating that iconicity plays a far less important role in the system than might be expected. Experiments showed that naïve non-signers could not perform above chance when asked to guess the meanings of signs, even clearly iconic ones. Sign-recall tasks revealed that deaf signers made phonological substitutions like hearing people do on word-recall tasks. They do not make meaning substitutions, which is what would be expected if signs were encoded iconically (Klima and Bellugi 1979). A comparison between ASL of the 1970s with ASL in films from around 1913 showed diachronic changes in signs away from the iconic and toward the arbitrary (Frishberg 1975). For example, the shape and movement of the two hands tends to become symmetrical, even when they lose iconicity in the process. Similar diachronic changes have been traced in Israeli Sign Language (Meir and Sandler 2004).

Even aspects of the system described as "mimetic depiction" by Klima and Bellugi were soon shown to be far more discrete and orderly in the classifier analysis of Supalla (1982, 1986) (see Chapter 5). While highly motivated, this system is still distinct from mime in the degree to which it is rule-governed and consequently in its interpretability and acquisition path. The type of discourse that requires a high proportion of classifier constructions can be the most difficult for later learners to master. Native acquisition studies have demonstrated that deaf signing children, like hearing, speaking children, make mistakes that reveal the regularity and componentiality of the system. In fact, the mistakes made by deaf children sometimes even result in forms that are countericonic – that are less like the real world objects or events being expressed than the correct forms are (e.g., Meier 1982).

All of this together led many researchers to the following conclusion: the iconic origins of sign languages take a back seat to the pervasive organizing principles found in language in general. These findings are critical to the development of sign language research. They demonstrate that the role of iconicity in sign language is neither simple nor obvious. Also, by focusing on general linguistic properties of sign languages, a weighty body of data and analysis has been amassed, achieving finer and finer levels of descriptive detail, and demonstrating convincingly that sign languages exhibit defining properties of language.

Nevertheless, the fact that there is much more iconicity in signs than in words should not be dismissed. In the subsections that follow, we raise some interesting issues that are concerned with iconicity in sign language lexicons as directions for future research: (1) the influence of iconicity in lexicons across related and unrelated sign languages, and (2) the distinction between the iconic and the symbolic. After that, we explore iconicity at other levels of sign language structure.

Differences across sign language lexicons

The majority of the widely published research in the first decades of sign language investigation was conducted on American Sign Language. A significant change in the field has been the addition of other sign languages to the body of research. In the process, many similarities across barely related or unrelated sign languages have been revealed. Interestingly, the most striking of these similarities are not at the level of the lexical item; in fact, the overlap of vocabulary items across sign languages is not nearly as broad as one might expect.

In a study comparing the lexicons of the sign languages of Spain, Mexico, France, and Japan, Currie, Meier and Walters (2002) found a 38 percent overlap between two sign languages known to have historical ties (those of Mexico and France) and 23 percent between the unrelated sign languages of Japan and Mexico. Nearly all of the signs that are articulated similarly across the unrelated sign languages studied are reported to have shared symbolism, i.e., to rely on the same iconic motivation. Of the two related sign languages, Spanish and French, 31 out of 43 of the similar signs had shared symbolism, and the rest were the result of borrowing. It is noteworthy that even for sign languages that are unrelated and in which the similar signs are traceable to iconicity alone, the percentage of similar signs is not far above the percentage of similar words in unrelated spoken languages. Currie et al. cite Greenberg's (1957, p. 37) assessment that borrowing or a genetic relationship between spoken languages must be assumed if the percentage of lexical resemblance is about 20 percent or more. This means that the sign languages of Japan and Mexico, with 23 percent similar lexical items, all of them iconically motivated, are barely above the threshold for *unrelated* languages, according to measures applied to spoken language. Compare these figures with sign languages that are so closely related as to be considered co-dialects. British and Australian sign languages are reported to have an 80 percent overlap in lexicon (Kyle and Woll 1985, p. 168, McKee and Kennedy 2000).

Arbitrary, iconic, and symbolic

The Dutch scholar Teervort, one of the first to maintain that sign languages are real languages, expressed the role of iconicity in them this way:

> The manual sign not only functions as a global whole, it also can and does derive great expressive force, directness, and unambiguousness from representing what it stands for through indication of its shape or movement, outline, or any other typical visual characteristic. This is at least how signs usually are born . . . and no matter how much they mature into arbitrary and conventional signs thereafter, they retain a dormant relation to this force that can be reawakened at any time . . . 'Iconicity' is not a more or less *accidental* feature because it comes to the surface once in a while, but a basically *concomitant* characteristic that is potentially present all the time.
>
> (Teervort 1973)

Distinguishing the arbitrary from the iconic should not obscure the fact that both kinds of signs/words are symbolic. This leads us to the conclusion that symbolism – and not arbitrariness – is the real defining property of words in human language.

The cognitive expanse that must be traversed in order to translate a concept into a motivated symbol made by the hands is far from trivial. Taub (2001) develops a model of the way in which iconic signs arise, consisting of four parts: conceptualizing, image selection, schematizing, and encoding. To create the ASL sign TREE, illustrated in Figure 25.3a, Taub hypothesizes that the first stage is having the concept of a tree; the second involves selecting a representative (often visual) image; the third is schematization or extracting the important details to represent the image; and the fourth is encoding it in linguistic form, conforming to the conventions of the language.

The ability to select the salient aspect, to make iconically motivated representations of it with parts of our own bodies (the hands), and to understand and conventionalize these representations, is abstract in the sense that it is symbolic. Our ability to symbolize at will in this way appears to be uniquely human. It is therefore not in the degree to which signs are symbolic that spoken and sign languages differ, but in the degree to which they are arbitrary.

While sign language lexicons are surprisingly different from one another, it is likely that general principles can be identified that will predict which aspects of a concept are likely to find iconic expression in a sign language, and what constrains the possible forms of that iconic expression. Future research in this area across different sign languages is likely to reveal much about the way human cognition experiences and categorizes the world.

This section has demonstrated, among other things, that the lexicons of sign languages are not as similar as one might think, given the iconicity with which they are imbued. Even the iconic signs for TREE differ in the three sign languages shown in Figure 25.3. However, when we look at other levels of analysis, a different picture emerges. Central aspects of grammatical structure seem clearly to repeat themselves in sign language after sign language. It has recently been suggested that many of these similarities are due to motivatedness of a more sophisticated kind (Aronoff et al. 2000, 2003). In the next section, we focus on the role that motivatedness plays in the morphology of sign language.

25.4.2 Iconic motivation in morphological processes of all sign languages

As visual languages, sign languages take advantage of their modality for conveying visually perceived aspects of objects and events in the world. As we explained in Chapter 5, most of the handshapes in the classifier system either represent directly the size and shape of something or the shape of the hand as it handles an object. The shape or dimensions of some referent, its spatial relation to other referents, the path and manner in which it moves – all of these are expressly visual experiences, and all are conventionally encoded in classifier systems across sign languages, apparently all established sign languages (see Emmorey 2003). Classifiers are found in spoken languages, to be sure, but sign languages are unique in two ways. First, apparently all established sign languages have such systems, while only scattered spoken languages do. Second, all sign languages use classifiers for the same functions: to depict shape or dimensions of a referent, its spatial relation to other referents, and its path and manner of movement. This contrasts with spoken languages, whose classifiers encode a variety of generic properties of their referents in different ways, and for which the use of classifiers is not necessarily selected for expression of spatial relations and motion.

It is not only in their classifier systems that sign languages share common morphological patterns. Basic features of verb agreement also appear to be common to sign language after sign language. In particular, all well-studied sign languages have three classes of verbs: plain, agreeing, and spatial. As discussed in Chapter 3, the class to which a verb belongs is determined in part by its semantic properties – on Meir's (1998a) proposal, whether or not it is a verb of transfer (literally or metaphorically). Similarly, "backwards verbs" exist in all sign languages, and they too are determined by inherent properties – namely, the matching of the source of the activity with the syntactic object rather than the subject of the sentence (Friedman 1976, Meir 1998a). As in the case of classifiers, the grammatical properties that determine verb agreement patterns are common to all sign languages but different from spoken languages – and they are motivated by spatial relations among referents (or metaphorical extensions of such relations).

Other properties of sign language morphology are motivated by temporal rather than spatial structure. For example, sign language after sign language uses morphological reduplication of verbal signs for representing iteration and duration. This occurs in spoken languages too, sometimes even involving direct iconicity, as in the case of Japanese mimetics described above. But here too, such iconicity occurs randomly across spoken languages, while in sign languages this motivated use of reduplication is widespread and possibly universal. As is to be expected in language, differences in the grammatical marking of temporal aspect have arisen across sign languages, in both the movement trajectory and the rhythmic patterns that accompany reduplication (Sandler 1996b), as well as in the range of temporal aspects described. But the use of reduplicational morphology for repeated or persisting activity is everywhere.

In the theory of sign language morphology developed by Aronoff et al. (2000, 2005), these sign-language-universal tendencies are contrasted with sign-language-specific processes (that is, processes specific to individual sign languages). Their theory incorporates the observation that sign languages are young languages, to be taken up in Section 25.5. We postpone further discussion of these interacting elements until then.

25.4.3 Motivatedness can penetrate phonology

By establishing that ASL has phonology, William Stokoe showed that there is a level of structure below the sign that is *not* iconic, that has no meaning associated with it. Indeed, without that discovery, this book and all the research reported in it would probably never have been written. Yet even phonology interacts with iconicity. Although the handshapes, movements, and locations of lexical words normally do not function synchronically as if they are meaningful, their iconic origins may sometimes be retrieved to shape a discourse, in the service of metaphor, or for other reasons.

Iconic influences on the phonology are a focus of attention for van der Kooij (2002) in her work on Sign Language of the Netherlands (SLN). For example, the position of the unselected fingers, normally determined by a phonological redundancy rule, may also be determined on iconic grounds (van der Kooij 1998). The position of the unselected fingers is normally predicted by a constraint, stating that these fingers will have the opposite value for openness from that of the selected fingers (Chapter 10). But van der Kooij shows that the specification may vary in ways that contribute nuances of meaning which sometimes override the purely phonological constraint. For example, the handshape, in which the index fingertip and thumbtip meet, ought to have extended selected fingers, according to the constraint. Yet, in many signs, this position may vary depending on the physical characteristics of the object referred to by the sign. For example, the SLN sign CALENDAR may be signed with the same selected fingers (index and redundantly the thumb) but with closed unselected fingers, if the pages of the calendar under discussion are thin, or with open unselected fingers, if the pages are thick. The SLN sign APPLY-LIPSTICK is signed with extended unselected fingers if the lipstick is applied in a thick layer, while a more demure toilette is implied when the same sign is pronounced with closed unselected fingers.

These are good examples of lexical signs that originated as classifier constructions which may in part explain their flexibility of form in response to nuances. As we showed in Chapter 6, signs like WRITE, that were lexicalized from classifier constructions, may be decomposed back into their classifier components in a discourse, in what we characterized as a sign-language-particular type of backformation. In examples like WRITE, this is possible because of the iconic nature of the classifiers for 'flat object' and 'handle a thin object' from which the sign is likely to have evolved. In this way, phonological elements that diachronically have lost their iconicity may be coaxed into revealing it synchronically.

Iconicity may also constrain the phonological rule of Weak Drop (WD) (Chapter 12). The Weak Drop process optionally omits the non-dominant hand from certain signs in which the two hands are symmetrical (h2-S signs), and to some signs in which h2 is a place of articulation (h2-P signs) as well (Padden and Perlmutter 1987, Brentari 1998). In her analysis of Weak Drop in SLN, van der Kooij (2002) argues that the amount of semantic information expressed in the non-dominant hand may constrain WD. Even symmetrical signs like SLN FIGHT, SAME, TOGETHER, can resist WD, as each hand is interpreted as standing for a meaningful element, according to the claim. Semantic constraints on WD have been found in Israeli Sign Language as well. Levy (2001) claims that READ, for example, a sign in which the non-dominant hand is a place of articulation, is resistant to WD because h2 is interpreted as the object being read from. In both languages, more semantically opaque signs with similar phonetic form allow WD. The significance of these suggestions lies in the fact that the signs in question otherwise function as monomorphemic signs, in which the non-dominant hand is just a phonological element, a place of articulation. Yet, the retrievability of its meaningful iconic origin apparently blocks the application of a phonological rule.

Finally, van der Kooij (2002) also argues that motivatedness creeps into phonology in the form of anomalous handshapes and places of articulation. The side of the back is the location for KIDNEYS in SLN, a location that is otherwise non-existent in the language. Though van der Kooij's claims are limited to SLN, it is easy to find similar examples in other sign languages. For example, in ASL the handshape is used for the airplane classifier, and the back of the head is a place of articulation (together with the forehead) for the sign HAT, all elements otherwise rare or non-existent in the language. In order to provide a parsimonious model of phonological primitives in Sign Language of the Netherlands, van der Kooij proposes that such semantically motivated but anomalous elements should be lexically specified, rather than included in the phonological feature inventory.

In sum, iconicity or motivatedness not only underlies numerous lexical items in sign languages, it is also behind certain morphological and phonological processes. Some of these motivated processes are prevalent across all languages employing the visual modality, as far as is known.

Up to this point, we've examined modality-specific factors that result in properties that are universal across sign languages, and that distinguish them from spoken languages. We now turn to the last factor responsible for molding sign languages generally, but one that is shared (with somewhat different effects) by spoken languages as well: language age.

25.5 Language age and language structure

Human language as an evolutionary phenomenon arose many millennia ago. Yet individual new languages still arise. Populations speaking different languages are sometimes put into contact, as in trade situations or, some centuries ago, on plantations where there were slaves. Under these circumstances, contact languages or pidgins form. As the situation stabilizes and children are born whose input is the pidgin, a more conventionalized language develops in the first generation of native speakers – a creole.

Sign languages have sometimes been compared to creoles (Fischer 1978, Gee and Goodhart 1985, Kegl, Senghas, and Coppola 1999, Aronoff et al. 2000, 2005, Newport and Supalla 2000). The comparison may seem surprising at first, since signers do not have the same social history as creole speakers. But the analogy becomes more compelling in consideration of the fact that the parents of most signers are not signers themselves. In the United States, for example, only about 8.5 percent of deaf children grow up in a home in which even one parent or sibling uses sign language (Gallaudet Research Institute 2001). And in households that do have adult signers, those signers are usually not native – in most cases, their parents did not sign. Thus, like children forming a creole from pidgin input, most children acquire sign language without a consistent, stable linguistic model. Furthermore, like spoken creoles, all known sign languages are also chronologically young, none of them exceeding an age of about 250–300 years, and many of them far younger than that. Given these sociolinguistic similarities between sign languages and creoles, we may expect similarities in form as well.

And in fact, some researchers have shown that there are similarities between sign languages and creoles. For example, Fischer (1978) draws the following correspondences between ASL and creoles: use of particular content words for grammatical purposes (e.g., FINISH as a perfective marker); reliance on word order rather than bound morphemes to indicate case relations; frequent use of topicalization and intonation for organizing information in a sentence. In addition, iconic use of reduplication to mark various kinds of intensification, iteration, and distribution is present universally in creoles (Kouwenberg 2003), and in sign languages as well (Aronoff et al. 2005).

But this is where the analogy seems to end – at first glance at least. Young spoken creole languages are reported to have very limited morphological complexity (McWhorter 1998). As young languages, they have not accrued much inflectional or derivational morphology with the arbitrariness and quirkiness that such systems often entail.[5] But sign languages, as we have seen, do have quite a bit of complex morphology: verb agreement with certain classes of verbs, polymorphemic classifier constructions, and temporal aspect morphology. What's more, this morphological profile characterizes all mature sign languages we know of. How can these generalizations, and the apparent discrepancy between sign languages and other young languages (i.e., young creoles), be explained?

25.5.1 *Resolving the contradiction*

The puzzle we are faced with is the discrepancy between the relative youth of all sign languages and the complex morphology attributed to them. Aronoff et al. (2000, 2005) suggest a solution through contrasting the prototypical sign language morphology – that includes verb agreement and complex classifier constructions – with a different type that they have also occasionally encountered in their research on ASL and ISL. The second type is sequential affixal morphology (see Chapter 4).

Aronoff et al. argue that affixes like the ASL –ZERO suffix and the ISL sense prefixes are precisely the type of sequential morphology that one

[5] This is not to say that creoles have no morphology or that all older languages have complex morphology. Older creoles have accumulated varying degrees of morphological complexity, while Vietnamese has none (Thompson 1965). Our point is only that, typically, young creoles have very little morphological complexity.

a. MAN-DRAGS-DOG (ASL)

b. SEE # SHARP (ISL)

Figure 25.4 Simultaneous vs. sequential sign language morphology: classifier construction and prefixed form

would expect in a young language. It tends to arise through grammaticization of free words; it is arbitrary; it is of limited productivity; there is variation in its patterning and use across the community; and there are very few such processes. There is another aspect to the dichotomy of morphological types that Aronoff et al. observe. The prototypical, productive, simultaneous morphology of sign language is iconically motivated, while the more limited affixal kind is not.

To get a sense of the contrast, consider Figure 25.4a and b. The first example shows a typical complex sign language form, a classifier construction meaning 'human walk; dragged legged-being trails behind,' interpreted as 'A man pulls a dog, which trails behind.' In this case, the example comes from ASL, but a similar classifier construction could be used in any other sign language. The second example shows the affixed form SEE-SHARP, which means to discern by seeing. This example is specific to ISL.

In Figure 25.4a, two classifiers are simultaneously combined, one for a human and the other for a legged being, referring to a dog in this instance. Their spatial relation is made explicit by the relation of the two hands: the man is taller, and they progress at the same rate, indicating that the dog is being pulled along by the man. The manner of motion of the dog is conveyed by a repeated sideways rotation at the wrist of the 'legs' hand as it moves forward. This construction is typical of classifier constructions, in which each hand may convey a different classifier, and may combine very productively with each other and with a range of locations, movement manners, paths and shapes, as explained in Chapter 5. While the event depicted may continue and change in detail, the combination of handshape, location, and movement morphemes at any point in the string is simultaneous.

The second example, Figure 25.4b, shows the word meaning 'to discern by seeing,' formed from a base, glossed SHARP, and a sequentially combined prefix, glossed SEE. As is commonly the case with grammaticalization from free words to affixes, the meaning of the complex word is not transparently predicted by the meanings of each of the contributing forms. In the sign language case this is especially interesting because the individual words from which the base and affix arise are iconically motivated, but their combination is not. As explained in Chapter 4, the prefix belongs to a set of such forms, which create verbs when affixed to a base. They are relatively productive, but do not approach the degree of productivity with which classifier handshapes, locations, and types and shapes of movement can combine with each other. There is individual variation in the use of the affixes (see especially the discussion of the ASL –ZERO suffix in Chapter 4), again, typical of the idiosyncrasy so familiar in derivational affixation.

By contrasting these two types of morphology, the explanation for the use of morphologically complex forms in languages with little diachronic depth emerges. Sign languages naturally exploit the manual–visual medium by generating motivated and simultaneous morphology early in their developmental histories. Spoken languages use motivated structure where they can also, but the oral–aural medium is not well suited to it, so there is little of it. As corporal–visual languages, sign languages can make extensive use of motivated structure. In certain respects, then, morphology is modality driven.

In this light, neither the extent nor the type of sign language morphology is surprising, despite the youth of the languages. The joint forces of iconic motivation and simultaneity of structure make it possible to encode linguistically concepts that are present in all human cognition, within a relatively short span in the age of the language.

By the same reasoning, the youth of sign languages explains the dearth and relative unproductiveness of arbitrary sequential affixation. Aronoff et al. review an example from Modern French *chanterai*, 'I will sing,' which was grammaticalized from the Latin *cantare habeo*, 'I have (something) to sing,' via a sequence of intervening processes over a period of several hundred years (Fleischmann 1982, Hopper and Traugott 1993, Campbell and Janda 2001). Given the opacity, idiosyncrasy, and individual variation that characterize this type of morphology, it is not surprising that such affixation is a long time coming, and that there is consequently little of it in any sign language.

All known established sign languages take advantage of the modality to create complex morphology that is motivated and simultaneous. In this way, sign languages have an advantage over other young languages. And as a sign language "ages," it begins to develop the kind of morphology more typically found in spoken languages: morphology that is both arbitrary and sequential. These two properties, according to Aronoff et al., arise as a result of grammaticalization of free words that are sequentially adjacent because they are related grammatically – but not necessarily iconically. The relation of ASL –ZERO to its base is one of negation of the base word, and ISL SEE- or SMELL- has a modifying relation with respect to its base (by seeing, by smelling or intuiting, etc.).

Sign languages, then, behave morphologically like any young language when it comes to arbitrary affixal morphology. Over time, such morphology is predicted to increase. It is also quite possible that such sequential morphology will ultimately erode by reducing to monosyllabic form, becoming even more opaque, a phenomenon we see already in compound reduction in ASL and ISL, and in so-called negative incorporation in ASL (see Chapter 14).

25.5.2 *Diachronic development of sign-language-typical morphology*

We've said that the morphological profile which includes simultaneous, motivated morphology for verb agreement, aspect, and classifier constructions characterizes all established sign languages we know of. For reasons outlined in Sections 25.3 and 25.4, it is likely that this type of morphology will persist even as the sequential, arbitrary type increases – the sign modality is so well suited to it. However, it would be a mistake to think that this morphology, modality driven though it may be, arises in a sign language full-blown and overnight. Instead, like other grammatical systems, it takes time to develop. Evidence for gradual development is beginning to accrue through comparison across sign languages which, though all young, are not all equally young.

In Nicaragua, a new sign language has grown up over the past thirty years, sparked by the creation of a community of deaf people at a new school. Nicaraguan Sign Language reflects a time course for the development of morphology (Senghas 1995, Kegl et al. 1999, Senghas 2000). Significant differences were found in the signing of the first and second cohorts of signers at the school. The first had arrived at the school with only simple and idiosyncratic home signs, but, by the time the research was conducted, they had already been signing together for some years. The second cohort arrived at the school before the age of ten, and had the first cohort as their language model. The first cohort used more referent projections than the second cohort, who showed greater use of handshape classifiers. As referent projections use the body to represent animate beings (Chapter 5), they are more mimetic and less abstract than handshape classifiers. In addition, the first cohort's use of space in constructions that would be conveyed through verb agreement and classifier constructions in established sign languages is much less systematic than that of the second cohort.

New work on an isolated Bedouin sign language in a small village in Israel, Al-Sayyid Bedouin Sign Language (ABSL) (Aronoff et al. 2004, Sandler et al. 2005) provides evidence from a natural language community that the sign language type of morphology does not arise overnight. The first deaf people in the community were born about seventy years ago, and today about 150 of the 3,500 villagers are deaf (Kisch 2000). Interestingly, researchers have found systematic word-order patterns in this new language (Sandler et al. 2005). However, the research team has uncovered only the kernels of verb agreement and classifier systems across two generations of signers in this language (Aronoff et al. 2004).

As ABSL is about the same age as Israeli Sign Language, which does have developed, systematic verb agreement and classifier systems (Meir and Sandler 2004), it is clear that chronological age is not the only factor involved in language development; size of the community, language contact, and other social factors must also play a role. Thus, we must distinguish between early sign languages, like ABSL and NSL, and young established sign languages, like ISL. Nevertheless, in the two early language communities, NSL and ABSL, the kernels of modality-driven morphology are there, and they are predicted to grow much more quickly than arbitrary affixation through grammaticalization.

It is not only early sign languages that show the effects of language age in their modality-driven morphology. Differences in this type of morphology found in more established sign languages have also been attributed to relative age. For example, a comparison of classifiers in ASL and ISL suggests that the older language has more abstractness in the system (Aronoff et al. 2003). ASL makes more extensive and frequent use of entity classifiers like VEHICLE and UPRIGHT-OBJECT than ISL. The researchers also found that ISL signers often used referent projections – the whole body to represent an animate being (see Chapter 5) – in contexts where ASL signers would be likely to use handshape classifiers in morphologically complex constructions. ASL signers use referent projections too, but usually in special contexts like story-telling, whereas ISL signers use them in a wider range of contexts. Entity classifiers are less iconic and more abstract than other types of classifiers, and using the hands to represent the body is less iconic than using the body itself. The fact that ASL is older than ISL on all measures, chronological, social, and cultural, may explain a higher degree of abstractness in the ASL system.

The moral of the story is this: once modality-driven advantages and language age are taken into account, the morphological profile of sign languages is not mysterious.

25.6 Conclusion, implications, and directions for future research

Our exploration has guided us through a rich landscape of human language transmitted in the manual/corporal–visual medium. The map we have followed is one whose major landmarks were established over the centuries by explorations of a different (and predominant) kind of human language, the kind that is transmitted in the oral–aural medium. We chose that map, here as in our previous research, because of our expectation that fundamental principles of structure and organization will be the same in any language produced by the human brain, regardless of modality. And, as before, we were rewarded with the discovery of key properties that are common to all human language.

In the course of this study, we have elaborated the landscape as well, creating a new map that charts details about the structure of sign languages, and posts new landmarks that belong to sign language alone. Holding the two maps side by side reveals the differences that must be attributed to modality. We expect these differences to be at least as instructive as the similarities.

The cross-sign-language characteristics that are due to modality are largely attributable to the fact that sign languages are capable of encoding experience in a way that is iconically motivated and that they are constrained by a variety of factors to use simultaneous structuring. This results in certain universals of structure across sign languages. The relative transparency in the way that some types of objects or events in the world are linguistically encoded – in languages that are too new to have acquired a great deal of purely arbitrary and opaque apparatus – may provide a unique window into the way in which the mind categorizes, represents, and transmits information.

The differences between spoken and signed languages that emerge from the comparison must not be interpreted as modality effects that mold sign languages alone. Such an interpretation would miss the point. Instead, we think that these differences should prompt scientists to look anew at spoken languages as well. If simultaneity is a modality effect of sign language, for example, then linearity is a modality effect of spoken language. Therefore, it would be a mistake, in our view, to attribute the sequentiality of sounds in a word or of tones in an intonational tune to an arbitrarily predetermined pool of language universals. Instead, these are effects of the oral–aural modality (see Chapter 16).

The direction for future research is illuminated by such an approach. In order to account for these effects, more abstract theories are needed, theories that are not modality-bound. At the same time, and from the other side of the issue, more thoughtful and penetrating investigation of what it is about each modality that results in the particular structures it manifests is likely to reveal important results. These two roads originate at different points, but it is at their convergence that most will be learned about language.

Much more sign language research is required, at ever more detailed and rigorous levels. This work will explain in a more unified and comprehensive way those structures and properties that have been uncovered so far. More sign languages ought to be studied and compared, with an eye to language age as a factor in language structure. Overall, the weight of this investigation leads us to the following conclusion: we stand to advance our understanding of the phenomenon of human language by continuing to elaborate the description and analysis of languages in each modality, without ever losing sight of the properties of mind that correspond between the two.

References

Aarons, Debra. 1994. Aspects of the syntax of American Sign Language. PhD dissertation, Boston University.

Aarons, Debra, Bahan, Benjamin, Kegl, Judy, and Neidle, Carol. 1992. Clausal structure and a tier for grammatical marking in American Sign Language. *Nordic Journal of Linguistics* 15: 103–142.

1994. Subjects and agreement in American Sign Language. In *Perspectives on Sign Language Structure: Papers from the Fifth International Symposium on Sign Language Research*, eds. Inger Ahlgren, Brita Bergman, and Mary Brennan, 13–28. Durham: International Sign Language Association.

1995. Lexical tense markers in American Sign Language. In *Language, Gesture, and Space*, eds. Karen Emmorey and Judy Reilly, 225–253. Hillsdale, NJ: Lawrence Erlbaum.

Ablorh-Odjidja, J. R. 1968. *Ga for Beginners*. Accra: Waterville Publishing.

Abney, S. P. 1987. The English Noun Phrase in its sentential aspect. PhD dissertation, MIT.

Ahlgren, Inger. 1990. Deictic pronouns in Swedish and Swedish Sign Language. In *Theoretical Issues in Sign Language Research*, Volume 1: *Linguistics*, eds. Susan Fischer and Patricia Siple, 167–174. University of Chicago Press.

Ahn, Sung-Ho. 1990. A structured-tiers model for ASL phonology. In *Sign Language Research: Theoretical Issues*, ed. Ceil Lucas, 11–26. Washington, DC: Gallaudet University Press.

Allan, K. 1977. Classifiers. *Language* 53: 285–311.

Anderson, D. E., and Reilly, Judy. 1998. PAH! The acquisition of adverbials in ASL. *Sign Language & Linguistics* 1: 3–28.

Anderson, John, and Ewen, Colin. 1987. *Principles of Dependency Phonology*. Cambridge: Cambridge University Press.

Anderson, Stephen R. 1992. *A-morphous Morphology*. Cambridge: Cambridge University Press.

Ann, Jean. 1992. Physiological constraints in Taiwan Sign Language handshape change. *Nordic Journal of Linguistics* 15: 143–157.

1993. A linguistic investigation of the relationship between physiology and handshape. PhD dissertation, University of Arizona.

1996. On the relation between ease of articulation and frequency of occurrence of handshapes in two sign languages. *Lingua* 98: 19–42.

Armstrong, D. F., Stokoe, W. C., and Wilcox, S. E. 1995. *Gesture and the Nature of Language*. Cambridge: Cambridge University Press.

Aronoff, Mark. 1976. *Word Formation in Generative Grammar*. Linguistic Inquiry Monograph Series 1. Cambridge, MA: MIT Press.

1994. *Morphology by Itself*. Cambridge, MA: MIT Press.

Aronoff, Mark, Meir, Irit, Padden, Carol, and Sandler, Wendy. 2003. Classifier complexes and morphology in two sign languages. In *Perspectives on Classifier Constructions in Sign Languages*, ed. K. Emmorey. Mahwah, NJ: Lawrence Erlbaum Associates.

2004. Morphological universals and the sign language type. In *Yearbook of Morphology 2004*, eds. Geert Booij and Jaap van Marle. Dordrecht/Boston: Kluwer, 19–39.

Aronoff, Mark, Meir, Irit, and Sandler, Wendy. 2000. Universal and particular aspects of sign language morphology. In *University of Maryland Working Papers in Linguistics*, eds. K. K. Grohmann and C. Struijke, 1–34.

2005. The paradox of sign language morphology. *Language* 81.2: 301–334.

Aronoff, Mark, and Sridhar, S. N. 1987. Morphological levels in English and Kannada: or Atarizing Reagan. In *Phonomorphology*, ed. E. Gussman. Lublin: Redakcja Wydawnictw Katolickiego Uniwersytetu Luelskiego.

Ausín, Adolfo. 1999. Chinese-type questions in English. In *Proceedings of The Seventeenth West Coast Conference on Formal Linguistics*, eds. Kimary Shahin, Susan Blake, and Eun-Sook Kim, 30–43. Stanford, CA: CSLI.

Bach, Emmon. 1971. Questions. *Linguistic Inquiry* 2: 153–166.

Bahan, Benjamin. 1996. Non-manual realization of agreement in American Sign Language. PhD dissertation, Boston University.

Bahan, Benjamin, Kegl, Judy, Lee, Robert G., MacLaughlin, Dawn, and Neidle, Carol. 2000. The licensing of null arguments in American Sign Language. *Linguistic Inquiry* 31:1–27.

Bahan, Benjamin, and Petitto, Laura. 1980. Aspects of rules for character establishment and reference in ASL storytelling. Unpublished ms.; Salk Institute for Biological Studies, La Jolla, CA.

Baker, C. L. 1970. Notes on the description of English questions: the role of an abstract question morpheme. *Foundations of Language* 6: 197–219.

Baker, Charlotte. 1977. Regulators and turn-taking in American Sign Language discourse. In *On the Other Hand: New Perspectives on American Sign Language*, ed. Lynn A. Friedman, 215–236. New York: Academic Press.

Baker, Charlotte, and Cokely, Dennis. 1980. *American Sign Language: A Teacher's Resource Text on Grammar and Culture*. Silver Spring, MD: TJ Publishers.

Baker, Charlotte, and Padden, Carol A. 1978. Focusing on the non-manual components of ASL. In *Understanding Language through Sign Language Research*, ed. Patricia Siple, 27–57. New York: Academic Press.

Baker-Shenk, Charlotte. 1983. A micro-analysis of the non-manual components of questions in American Sign Language. PhD dissertation, University of California.

Baltin, Mark, and Collins, Chris. 2001. *The Handbook of Contemporary Syntactic Theory*. Malden, MA: Blackwell.

Banfield, Ann. 1973. Narrative style and the grammar of direct and indirect speech. *Foundations of Language* 10:1–39.

Barlow, Michael, and Ferguson, Charles A. eds. 1988. *Agreement in Natural Language: Approaches, Theories, Descriptions*. Stanford, CA: Center for the Study of Language and Literature.

Battison, Robbin. 1974. Phonological deletion in American Sign Language. *Sign Language Studies* 5: 1–19.

1978. *Lexical Borrowing in American Sign Language*. Silver Spring: Linstok Press.

Beckman, Mary, and Pierrehumbert, Janet. 1986. Intonational structure in English and Japanese. *Phonology Yearbook* 3: 255–310.

Bellugi, Ursula, and Fischer, Susan. 1972. A comparison of signed and spoken language. *Cognition* 1: 173–200.

Bellugi, Ursula, and Newkirk, Don. 1981. Formal devices for creating new signs in ASL. *Sign Language Studies* 10: 1–35.

Benedicto, Elena, and Brentari, Diane. 2004. Where did all the arguments go? Argument-changing properties of classifiers in ASL. *Natural Language and Linguistic Theory* 22.4: 743–810.

Berenz, Norine, and Ferreira-Brito, Lucinda. 1990. Pronouns in BCSL and ASL. In *SLR '87: Papers from the Fourth International Symposium on Sign Language Research*, eds. William H. Edmondson and Fred Karlsson. Hamburg: Signum.

Bergman, Brita. 1983. Verbs and adjectives: morphological processes in Swedish Sign Language. In *Language in Sign: An International Perspective on Sign Language*, eds. J. Kyle and B. Woll, 3–9. London: Croom Helm.

Bergvall, Victoria. 1987. The position and properties of in situ and right-moved questions in Kikuyu. In *Current Approaches to African Linguistics*, ed. David Odden, 37–54. Dordrecht: Foris.

Blevins, Juliette. 1993. The nature of constraints on the non-dominant hand in ASL. In *Current Issues in ASL Phonology*, ed. Geoffrey R. Coulter, 43–62. New York, San Francisco, London: Academic Press.

1995. The syllable in phonological theory. In *A Handbook of Phonological Theory* ed. John Goldsmith, 206–244. New York: Basil Blackwell.

Blondel, Marion, and Miller, Christopher. 2000. Rhythmic structures in French Sign Language (LSF) nursery rhymes. *Sign Language & Linguistics* 3: 59–78.

Bloomfield, Leonard. 1933. *Language*. New York: Holt.

Bobaljik, Jonathan. 1995. The syntax of verbal inflection. PhD dissertation, MIT.

Bolinger, Dwight. 1986. *Intonation and its Parts*. Palo Alto, CA: Stanford University Press.

1989. *Intonation and its Uses*. Palo Alto, CA: Stanford University Press.

Borer, Hagit. 1983. *Parametric Syntax: Case Studies in Semitic and Romance Languages*. Dordrecht: Foris.

Bos, Heleen. 1990. Person and location marking in SLN: some implications of a spatially expressed syntactic system. In *Sign Language Research and Application: Proceedings of the International Congress on Sign Language Research and Application, March 23–25, 1990, Hamburg*, eds. S. Prillwitz and T. Vollhaber, 231–246. Hamburg: Signum.

1994. An auxiliary in Sign Language of the Netherlands. In *Perspectives on Sign Language Structure: Papers from the Fifth International Symposium on Sign Language Research*, eds. Inger Ahlgren, Brita Bergman, and Mary Brennan, 37–53. University of Durham: International Sign Linguistics Association.

1995. Pronoun copy in Sign Language of the Netherlands. In *Sign Language Research 1994: Proceedings of the Fourth European Congress on Sign Language Research*, eds. Heleen Bos and Trude Schermer, 121–147. Hamburg: Signum.

Bošković, Željko. 1997. Pseudoclefts. *Studia Linguistica* 51: 235–277.

1998. LF movement and the Minimalist Program. In *NELS 28*, eds. Pius N. Tamanji and Kiyomi Kusumoto, 43–57. Amherst, MA: GLSA.

2001. *On the Nature of the Syntax-Phonology Interface*. Amsterdam: Elsevier.

2000. Sometimes in [Spec, CP], sometimes in situ. In *Step by Step: Essays on Minimalist Syntax in Honor of Howard Lasnik*, eds. Roger Martin, David Michaels, and Juan Uriagareka, 53–87. Cambridge, MA: MIT Press.

2002. On multiple Wh-fronting. *Linguistic Inquiry* 33: 351–383.

Boster, Carole T. 1996. On the quantifier-NP split in American Sign Language and the structure of quantified noun phrases. In *International Review of Sign Linguistics*, eds. William H. Edmondson and Ronnie B. Wilbur, 159–208. Mahwah, NJ: Lawrence Erlbaum Associates.

Bouchard, Denis. 1996. Sign language and language universals: the status of order and position in grammar. *Sign Language Studies* 91: 101–160.

Bouchard, Denis, and Dubuisson, Colette. 1995. Grammar, order and position of wh-signs in Quebec Sign Language. *Sign Language Studies* 87: 99–139.

Boyes-Braem, Penny. 1981. Distinctive features of the handshapes of American Sign Language. PhD dissertation, University of California.

1999. Rhythmic temporal patterns in the signing of deaf early and late learners of Swiss German Sign Language. *Language & Speech* 42: 177–208.

Boyes-Braem, Penny, and Sutton-Spence, Rachel, eds. 2001. *The Hands are the Head of the Mouth: The Mouth as Articulator in Sign Languages*. International Studies on Sign Language and Communication of the Deaf 39. Hamburg: Signum.

Braze, F. David. 2004. Aspectual inflection, verb raising, and object fronting in American Sign Language. *Lingua* 114.1: 29–58.

Brennan, Mary. 1981. Grammatical processes in British Sign Language. In *Perspectives on British Sign Language*, eds. Bencie Woll, Jim Kyle, and Margaret Deuchar, 120–135. London: Croom Helm.

1983. Marking time in British Sign Language. In *Language in Sign: An International Perspective on Sign Language*, eds. Jim Kyle and Bencie Woll, 10–31. London: Croom Helm.

1990. *Word Formation in British Sign Language*. Stockholm: University of Stockholm.

Brennan, Mary, and Turner, Graham H. eds. 1994. *Word-Order Issues in Sign Language: Working Papers (presented at a workshop held in Durham, 18–22 September 1991)*. Durham: International Sign Linguistics Association.

Brentari, Diane. 1990. Theoretical foundations of American Sign Language phonology. PhD dissertation, University of Chicago.

1993. Establishing a sonority hierarchy in American Sign Language: the use of simultaneous structure in phonology. *Phonology* 10: 281–308.

1995. Sign language phonology: ASL. In *A Handbook of Phonological Theory*, ed. John Goldsmith, 615–639. New York: Basil Blackwell.

1998. *A Prosodic Model of Sign Language Phonology*. Cambridge, MA: MIT Press.

Brentari, Diane, and Goldsmith, John A. 1993. Secondary licensing and the non-dominant hand in ASL phonology. In *Current Issues in ASL Phonology*, ed. Geoffrey R. Coulter, 19–41. New York, San Francisco, London: Academic Press.

Brentari, Diane, Hulst, Harry van der, Kooij, Els van der, and Sandler, Wendy. 1996. [one] over [all]; [all] over [one]: a dependency phonology analysis of handshape in sign languages. Ms.

Brentari, Diane, and Padden, Carol A. 2001. Native and foreign vocabulary in American Sign Language: a lexicon with multiple origins. In *Foreign Vocabulary in Sign Languages: A Cross-Linguistic Investigation of Word Formation*, ed. Diane Brentari, 87–119. Mahwah, NJ: Erlbaum.

Brentari, Diane, and Poizner, Howard. 1994. A phonological analysis of a deaf Parkinsonian signer. *Language and Cognitive Processes* 9: 69–99.

Brentari, Diane, Poizner, Howard, and Kegl, Judy. 1995. Aphasic and Parkinsonian signing: differences in phonological disruption. *Brain and Language* 48: 69–105.

Bresnan, Joan. 1970. On complementizers: toward a syntactic theory of complement types. *Foundations of Language* 6: 197–260.

Bricker, Victoria. 1978. Antipassive constructions in Yucatec Maya. In *Papers in Mayan Linguistics*, ed. Nora C. England, 3–24: Columbia University of Missouri.

Browman, Catherine, and Goldstein, Louis. 1989. Articulatory gestures as phonological units. *Phonology* 6: 201–251.

Bryzgunova, E. 1975. The declarative-interrogative opposition in Russian. *Slavic and East European Journal* 19: 155–161.

Campbell, Lyle, and Janda, Richard. 2001. Introduction: conceptions of grammaticalization and their problems. *Language Sciences* 23.2–3: 93–112.

Campbell, Ruth, Woll, Bencie, Benson, P., and Wallace, S. 1999. Categorical perception of face actions: their role in sign language and in communicative facial displays. *Quarterly Journal of Experimental Psychology* 52A: 67–96.

Cardinaletti, A. 1994. On the internal structure of pronominal DPs. *The Linguistic Review* 11: 195–219.

Chang, L. 1997. Wh-in-situ phenomena in French. Master's thesis, University of British Columbia.

Channon, Rachel. 2002a. Beads on a string? Representations of repetition in spoken and signed languages. In *Modality and Structure in Signed and Spoken Language*, eds. R. Meier, K. Cormier and D. Quinto-Pozos, 65–87. Cambridge: Cambridge University Press.

2002b. Signs are single segments: phonological representations and temporal sequencing in ASL and other sign languages. PhD dissertation, University of Maryland.

Chen Pichler, Deborah. 2001. Word order variability and acquisition in American Sign Language. PhD dissertation, University of Connecticut.

Cheng, Lisa Lai-Shen, and Rooryck, Johan. 2000. Licensing *wh*-in-situ. *Syntax* 3: 1–19.

Chinchor, Nancy. 1978. The syllable in American Sign Language: sequential and simultaneous phonology. Ms.

Chomsky, Noam. 1957. *Syntactic Structures*. The Hague: Mouton.

1965. *Aspects of the Theory of Syntax*. Cambridge, MA: MIT Press.

1970. Remarks on nominalization. In *Readings in English Transformational Grammar*, eds. R. Jacobs and P. Rosenbaum, 184–221. Waltham, MA: Ginn.

1981. *Lectures on Government and Binding*. Dordrecht: Foris.

1982. *Some Concepts and Consequences of the Theory of Government and Binding*. Cambridge, MA: MIT Press.

1986. *Barriers*. Cambridge, MA: MIT Press.

1991. Some notes on economy of derivation and representation. In *Principles and Parameters in Comparative Grammar*, ed. Robert Freidin. Cambridge, MA: MIT Press.

1993. A minimalist program for linguistic theory. In *The View from Building 20*, eds. Ken Hale and Samuel J. Keyser, 1–52. Cambridge, MA: MIT Press.

1995. *The Minimalist Program*. Cambridge, MA: MIT Press.

Chomsky, Noam, and Halle, Morris. 1968. *The Sound Pattern of English*. New York: Harper and Row.

Chomsky, Noam, and Lasnik, Howard. 1993. The theory of principles and parameters. In *Syntax: An International Handbook of Contemporary Research*, ed. J. Jacobs et al., 506–569. Berlin: Walter de Gruyter.

Cinque, G. 1994. On the evidence for partial N-Movement in the Romance DP. In *Paths Towards Universal Grammar: Studies in Honor of Richard S. Kayne*, eds. G. Cinque, J. Koster, J.-Y. Pollock, L. Rizzi, and R. Zanuttini, 85–110. Georgetown: Georgetown University Press.

1999. *Adverbs and Functional Heads*. Oxford: Oxford University Press.

Clark, Eve L., and Grosjean, F. 1982. Sign recognition processes in American Sign Language: the effect of context. *Language and Speech* 25: 325–340.

Clements, George N. 1975. The logophoric pronoun in Ewe: its role in discourse. *Journal of West African Languages* 2: 141–177.

1985. The geometry of phonological features. *Phonology Yearbook* 2: 225–252.

1990. The role of the sonority cycle in core syllabification. In *Papers in Laboratory Phonology 1: Between the grammar and Physics of Speech*, eds. J. Kingston and M. Beckman, 288–333. Cambridge: Cambridge University Press.

Clements, George N., and Keyser, Samuel. 1983. *CV Phonology: A Generative Theory of the Syllable*. Cambridge, MA: MIT Press.

Coerts, Jane. 1992. Non-manual grammatical markers: an analysis of interrogatives, negations, and topicalizations in Sign Language of the Netherlands. PhD dissertation, University of Amsterdam.

1994. Constituent order in Sign Language of the Netherlands and the functions of orientations. In *Perspectives on Sign Language Structure: Papers from the Fifth International Symposium on Sign Language Research*, Volume 1, eds. Inger Ahlgren, Brita Bergman, and Mary Brennan, 69–88. Durham: International Sign Linguistics Association.

Coerts, Jane, and Mills, Anne. 1992. Early sign combinations of deaf children in Sign Language of the Netherlands. Paper presented at *The Fifth International Symposium on Sign Language Research*, Salamanca, Spain.

Cogill-Koez, Dorothea. 2002a. Signed language classifier predicates: linguistic structures or schematic visual representation? *Sign Language & Linguistics* 3: 153–207.

2002b. A model of signed language "classifier predicates" as templated visual representation. *Sign Language & Linguistics* 3: 209–236.

Collins-Ahlgren, M. 1989. New Zealand Sign Language. PhD dissertation, Victoria University.

Corina, David. 1990a. Handshape assimilations in hierarchical phonological representations. In *Sign Language Research: Theoretical Issues*, ed. C. Lucas, 27–49. Washington, DC: Gallaudet Press.

1990b. Reassessing the role of sonority in syllable structure: evidence from visual-gestural language. In *Papers from the Chicago Linguistic Society*, 33–44. Chicago: Chicago Linguistic Society.

1993. To branch or not to branch: underspecification in ASL handshape contours. In *Current Issues in ASL Phonology*, ed. G. Coulter, 63–95. New York, San Francisco, London: Academic Press.

1996. ASL syllables and prosodic constraints. *Lingua* 98: 73–102.

Corina, David, Bellugi, Ursula, and Reilly, Judy. 1999. Neuropsychological studies of linguistic and affective facial expressions in deaf signers. *Language and Speech* 42: 307–331.

Corina, David, and Hildebrandt, Ursula C. 2002. Psycholinguistic investigations of phonological structure in American Sign Language. In *Modality and Structure in Signed Language and Spoken Language*, eds. Richard Meier, Kearsy Cormier, and David Quinto-Pozos, 88–111. Cambridge: Cambridge University Press.

Corina, David, and Sagey, Elizabeth. 1989. Are phonological hierarchies universal? Evidence from American Sign Language. Paper presented at *ESCOL*.

Corina, David, and Sandler, Wendy. 1993. On the nature of phonological structure in sign language. *Phonology* 10: 165–208.

Cormier, Kearsy, Wechsler, Stephen, and Meier, Richard. 1998. Locus agreement in American Sign Language. In *Lexical and Constructional Aspects of Linguistic Explanation*, eds. Gert Webelhuth, Jean-Pierre Koenig, and Andreas Kathol, 215–229. Stanford, CA: CSLI.

Coulter, Geoffrey. 1979. American Sign Language typology. PhD dissertation, University of California, San Diego.

1982. On the nature of ASL as a monosyllabic language. Paper presented at the Annual Meeting of the Linguistic Society of America, San Diego, CA.

1990. Emphatic stress in ASL. In *Theoretical Issues in Sign Language Research, Volume 1: Linguistics*, eds. Susan D. Fischer and Patricia Siple, 109–126. Chicago: University of Chicago Press.

Crasborn, Onno. 2001. Phonetic implementation of phonological categories in Sign Language of the Netherlands. PhD dissertation, Leiden University.

Crasborn, Onno, and Kooij, Els van der. 1997. Relative orientation in sign language phonology. In *Linguistics in the Netherlands 1997*, eds. J. Coerts and H. de Hoop, 37–48. Amsterdam: John Benjamins.

Currie, Anne-Marie, Meier, Richard, and Walters, Keith. 2002. A crosslinguistic examination of the lexicons of four signed languages. In *Modality and Structure in Signed Language and Spoken Language*, eds. Richard Meier, Kearsy Cormier, and David Quinto-Pozos, 224–236. Cambridge: Cambridge University Press.

Dachkovsky, Svetlana. 2004. Neutral and counterfactual conditionals in Israeli Sign Language. MA thesis, University of Haifa.

Davies, D. 1985. The tongue is quicker than the eye. In *SLR '83: Proceedings of the III International Symposium on Sign Language Research*, eds. William Stokoe, and Virginia Volterra, 185–193. Silver Spring, MD: Linstok Press.

Davis, Barbara, and MacNeilage, Peter. 1995. The articulatory basis of babbling. *Journal of Speech and Hearing Research* 38: 1199–1211.

Deguchi, Masanori, and Kitagawa, Yoshihisa. 2002. Prosody and wh-questions. In *Proceedings of the Thirty-second Annual Meeting of the North Eastern Linguistic Society*, ed. Masako Hirotani, 73–92.

DeMateo, Asa. 1977. Visual imagery and visual analogues in American Sign Language. In *On the Other Hand: New Perspectives on American Sign Language*, ed. Lynn Friedman, 109–136. New York: Academic Press.

Deuchar, Margaret. 1983. Is BSL an SVO language? In *Language in Sign*, eds. Jim Kyle and Bencie Woll, 69–76. London: Croom Helm.

Diffloth, Gérard. 1972. Notes on expressive meaning. In *Papers from the Eighth Regional Meeting of the Chicago Linguistic Society*, eds. Paul M. Peranteau, Judith N. Levi, and Gloria C. Phares, 440–447. Chicago: Chicago Linguistic Society.

Dively, V. 2001. Signs without hands: nonhanded signs in ASL. In *Signed Languages: Discoveries from International Research*, eds. V. Dively, M. Metzger, S. Taub, and A. Baer, 62–73. Washington, DC: Gallaudet University Press.

Dobrin, L. 1997. The morphosyntactic reality of phonological form. *Yearbook of Morphology*: 59–81.

Dresher, Elan, and Hulst, Harry van der. 1998. Head-dependent asymmetries in phonology: complexity and visibility. *Phonology* 15: 317–352.

Durand, Jacques. 1986. *Dependency and Non-Linear Phonology*. London: Croom Helm.

Edge, VickiLee, and Hermann, Leora. 1977. Verbs and the determination of subject. In *On the Other Hand*, ed. Lynn Friedman, 137–179. New York: Academic Press.

Ekman, Paul, and Friesen, Wallace V. 1975. *Unmasking the Face: A Guide to Recognizing Emotions from Facial Clues*. New Jersey: Prentice Hall.

1978. *Facial Action Coding System: A Technique for the Measurement of Facial Movement. Investigator's Guide*. Palo Alto: Consulting Psychologists Press.

Emmorey, Karen. 1995. Processing the dynamic visual-spatial morphology of signed languages. In *Morphological Aspects of Language Processing: Crosslinguistic Perspectives*, ed. L. B. Feldman, 29–54. Hillsdale, NJ: Lawrence Erlbaum Associates.

1996. The confluence of space and language in signed languages. In *Language and Space*, eds. P. Bloom, M. Peterson, L. Nade, and M. Garrett, 171–209. Cambridge, MA: MIT Press.

1999. Do signers gesture? In *Gesture, Speech, and Sign*, eds. L. S. Messing and Ruth Campbell, 133–159. New York: Oxford University Press.

2002. *Language, Cognition, and the Brain: Insights from Sign Language Research.* Mahwah, NJ: Lawrence Erlbaum Associates.

ed. 2003. *Perspectives on Classifier Constructions in Sign Languages.* Mahwah, NJ: Lawrence Erlbaum Associates.

Emmorey, Karen, and Corina, David. 1990. Lexical recognition in sign language: effects of phonetic structure and morphology. *Perceptual and Motor Skills* 71: 1227–1252.

Emmorey, Karen, and Falgier, B. 1999. Processing continuous and simultaneous reference in ASL. Ms. Los Angeles, CA.

Engberg-Pedersen, Elisabeth. 1990. Pragmatics of non-manual behaviour in Danish Sign Language. In *SLR '87: Papers from the Fourth International Symposium on Sign Language Research*, eds. William H. Edmondson and Fred Karlsson, 121–128. Hamburg: Signum.

1993. *Space in Danish Sign Language.* Hamburg: Signum.

1994. Some simultaneous constructions in Danish Sign Language. In *Word-order Issues in Sign Language: Working Papers (presented at a workshop held in Durham, 18–22 September 1991)*, eds. Mary Brennan and Graham H. Turner, 73–87. Durham: International Sign Linguistics Association.

1995. Point of view expressed through shifters. In *Language, Gesture, and Space*, eds. Karen Emmorey and Judy Reilly, 133–154. Hillsdale, NJ: Lawrence Erlbaum Associates.

Erteschik-Shir, Nomi. 1997. *The Dynamics of Focus Structure.* Cambridge: Cambridge University Press.

1999. Focus structure theory and intonation. *Language & Speech* 42: 209–227.

Fauconnier, Giles. 1985. *Mental Spaces: Aspects of Meaning Construction in Natural Language.* Cambridge, MA: MIT Press.

Fischer, Susan. 1974. Sign language and linguistic universals. Paper presented at *Actes du Colloque Franco-Allemand de grammaire Transformationnelle*, Tübingen.

1975. Influences on word order change in American Sign Language. In *Word Order and Word Order Change*, ed. Charles Li, 1–25. Austin: University of Texas Press.

1978. Sign language and creoles. In *Understanding Language through Sign Language Research*, ed. Patricia Siple, 309–331. New York: Academic Press.

1990. The head parameter in ASL. In *SLR '87: Papers from the Fourth International Symposium on Sign Language Research*, eds. W. H. Edmondson and F. Karlsson, 75–85. Hamburg: Signum.

1996. The role of agreement and auxiliaries in sign language. *Lingua* 98: 103–120.

Fischer, Susan, Delhorne, Lorraine A., and Reed, Charlotte M. 1999. Effects of rate of presentation on the reception of American Sign Language. *Journal of Speech, Hearing and Language Research* 42: 568–582.

Fischer, Susan, and Gough, Bonnie. 1978. Verbs in American Sign Language. *Sign Language Studies* 7: 17–48.

Fischer, Susan, and Janis, Wynne. 1990. Verb sandwiches in American Sign Language. In *Current Trends in European Sign Language Research: Proceedings of the Third European Congress on Sign Language Research*, eds. Siegmund Prillwitz and Tomas Vollhaber, 279–294. Hamburg: Signum.

Fleischmann, Suzan. 1982. *The Future in Thought and Language: Diachronic Evidence from Romance*. Cambridge: Cambridge University Press.

Foley, W., and Van Valin, R. 1985. Information packaging in the clause. In *Language Typology and Syntactic Description*, ed. T. Shopen, 282–364. Cambridge: Cambridge University Press.

Friedman, Lynn. 1975. Space, time, and person reference in American Sign Language. *Language* 51: 940–961.

1976. The manifestation of subject, object, and topic in American Sign Language. In *Subject and Topic*, ed. Charles Li. New York: Academic Press.

1977. Formational properties of American Sign Language. In *On the Other Hand*, ed. L. Friedman, 13–56. New York: Academic Press.

Frishberg, Nancy. 1975. Arbitrariness and iconicity: historical change in American Sign Language. *Language* 51: 696–719.

1985. Dominance relations and discourse structures. In *SLR '83: Sign Language Research*, eds. W. Stokoe and V. Volterra, 79–90. Rome: Linstok Press and CNR.

Fromkin, Victoria. 1973. *Speech Errors as Linguistic Evidence*. The Hague: Mouton.

Gallaudet Research Institute. 2001. *Regional and National Summary Report of data from the 1999–2000 Annual Survey of Deaf and Hard of Hearing Children and Youth*. Washington, DC: Gallaudet Research Institute, Gallaudet University.

Gee, James Paul, and Goodhart, Wendy. 1985. Nativization, linguistic theory, and deaf language acquisition. *Sign Language Studies* 49: 291–342.

Georgopoulos, Carol. 1991. Canonical government and the specifier parameter: an ECP account of weak crossover. *Natural Language and Linguistic Theory* 9: 1–46.

Gijn, Ingeborg Van, Kita, Sotaro, and Hulst, Harry van der. In press. How phonetic is the Symmetry Condition in sign language? In *Phonetics and Phonology – Selected Papers of the Fourth HIL Phonology Conference*, eds. Vincent J. van Heuven, Harry G. van der Hulst, and Jeroen M. van de Weijer. Amsterdam, Philadelphia: John Benjamins.

Givón, Talmy. 1976. Topic, pronoun and grammatical agreement. In *Subject and Topic*, ed. C. N. Li, 149–188. New York: Academic Press.

Glück, Susanne, and Pfau, Roland. 1998. On classifying classification as a class of inflection in German Sign Language. In *ConSole VI Proceedings*, eds. Tina Cambier-Langeveld, Anikó Lipták, and Michael Redford, 59–74. Leiden: SOLE.

1999. A distributed morphology account of verbal inflection in German Sign Language. In *ConSole VII Proceedings*, eds. Tina Cambier-Langeveld, Anikó Lipták, Michael Redford and Erik Jan van der Torre, 65–80. Leiden: SOLE.

Goldin-Meadow, Susan. 2003. *The Resilience of Language: What Gesture Creation in Deaf Children Can Tell Us about How All Children Learn Language*. New York: Psychology Press.

Goldsmith, John. 1976. Autosegmental phonology. PhD dissertation, MIT.

1990. *Autosegmental and Metrical Phonology: a New Synthesis*. Oxford: Blackwell.

Greenberg, Joseph. 1957. *Essays in Linguistics*. Chicago: University of Chicago Press.

Greftegreff, Irene. 1993. Anatomy and features in sign language handshapes. Ms. University of Trondheim.

Grewendorf, Günther. 2001. Multiple wh-fronting. *Linguistic Inquiry* 32: 87–122.

Grinevald, Colette. 2000. A morphosyntactic typology of classifiers. In *Systems of Nominal Classification*, ed. Gunter Senft, 50–92. Cambridge: Cambridge University Press.

Grosjean, F. 1981. Sign and word recognition: a first comparison. *Sign Language Studies* 32: 195–219.

Gruber, J. 1976. *Lexical Structures in Syntax and Semantics*. North Holland, New York.

Gussenhoven, Carlos, ed. 1984. *On the Grammar and Semantics of Sentence Accents*. Dordrecht: Foris.

1999. Discreteness and gradience in intonational contrasts. *Language & Speech* 42: 283–306.

Haegeman, Liliane. 1991. *Introduction to Government and Binding Theory*. Cambridge, MA: Basil Blackwell.

Haegeman, Liliane, and Zanuttini, Rafaella. 1991. Negative heads and the neg criterion. *The Linguistic Review* 8: 233–251.

Haiman, J. 1980. The iconicity of grammar: isomorphism and motivation. *Language* 56: 515–540.

ed. 1985. *Iconicity in Syntax*. Amsterdam: John Benjamins.

Hale, Ken. 1980. Remarks on Japanese phrase structure: comments on the papers on Japanese syntax. In *MIT Working Papers in Linguistics 2: Theoretical Issues in Japanese Linguistics*, eds. Yukio Otsu and Ann Farmer, 185–203. Cambridge, MA: MIT.

1983. Warlpiri and the grammar of non-configurational languages. *Natural Language & Linguistic Theory* 1.

Hall, T. Alan, and Kleinhenz, U. eds. 1999. *Studies on the Phonological Word*. Amsterdam: John Benjamins.

Halle, Morris. 1992. Phonological features. In *International Encyclopedia of Linguistics*, Volume 3, ed. W. Bright, 207–212. New York: Oxford University Press.

Halle, Morris, and Marantz, Alec. 1993. Distributed morphology and the pieces of inflection. In *The View from Building 20: Essays in Linguistics in Honor of Sylvain Bromberger*, eds. Ken Hale and Samuel J. Keyser, 111–176. Cambridge, MA: MIT Press.

1994. Some key features of Distributed Morphology. In *MIT Working Papers in Linguistics*, 275–288. Cambridge, MA: MIT Department of Linguistics and Philosophy.

Halle, Morris, and Stevens, Kenneth. 1971. A note on laryngeal features. In *Research Laboratory of Electronics Quarterly Progress Report*, 198–212. Cambridge, MA: MIT.

Hamano, Shoko Saito. 1986. The sound-symbolic system of Japanese. PhD dissertation, University of Florida.

Hanks, William F. 1992. The indexical ground of deictic reference. In *Rethinking Context: Language as an Interactive Phenomenon*, eds. Alessandro Duranti and Charles Goodwin, 43–76. Cambridge: Cambridge University Press.

Harder, R., and Schermer, T. 1986. A first phonological analysis of handshapes in SLN. In *Signs of Life: Proceedings of the Second European Congress on Sign Language Research*, ed. B. T. M. Tervoort, 47–51: Institute of General Linguistics.

Hayes, Bruce. 1993. Against movement. In *Current Issues in ASL Phonology*, ed. G. Coulter, 213–226. San Diego: Academic Press.

1999. Phonetically driven phonology: the role of optimality theory and inductive grounding. In *Functionalism and Formalism in Linguistics*, eds. Michael Darnell, Edith Moravscik, Michael Noonan, Frederick Newmeyer, and Kathleen Wheatley, 243–285. Amsterdam: John Benjamins.

Hayes, Bruce, and Lahiri, Aditi. 1991. Bengali intonational phonology. *Natural Language & Linguistic Theory* 9: 47–96.

Heggie, L. 1988. The syntax of copular structures. PhD dissertation, University of Southern California.

Heycock, C. 1991. Layers of predication: The non-lexical syntax of clauses. PhD dissertation, University of Pennsylvania.

Hoji, Hajime. 1985. Logical Form Constraints and Syntactic Configurations in Japanese. PhD dissertation, University of Washington.

Holmberg, A. 1986. Word Order and Syntactic Features in the Scandinavian Languages and English. PhD dissertation, University of Stockholm.

Hopper, P. J., and Traugott, E. C. 1993. *Grammaticalization*. Cambridge: Cambridge University Press.

Horvath, Julia. 1980. Movement in "Logical Form": evidence from Hungarian. Ms. UCLA.

Huang, C. T. James. 1982. Move wh in a language without wh movement. *The Linguistic Review* 1: 369–416.

1984. On the distribution and reference of empty pronouns. *Linguistic Inquiry* 15: 531–574.

Hulst, Harry van der. 1989. Atoms of segmental structure: components, gestures and dependency. *Phonology* 6: 253–284.

1993. Units in the analysis of signs. *Phonology* 10: 209–242.

1995. The composition of handshapes. *University of Trondheim Working Papers in Linguistics* 23: 1–17.

1996. On the other hand. *Lingua* 98: 121–143.

Hulst, Harry van der, and Sandler, Wendy. 1994. Phonological theories meet sign language: two theories of the two hands. *Toronto Working Papers in Linguistics* 13: 43–73.

Hyman, L., and Comrie, B. 1981. Logophoric reference in Gokana. *Journal of African Languages and Linguistics* 3: 19–37.

Jackendoff, Ray. 1977. *X′ Syntax: A Study of Phrase Structure*. Cambridge, MA: MIT Press.

1990. *Semantic Structures*. Cambridge, MA: MIT Press.

Jaeggli, Osvaldo, and Safir, Kenneth eds. 1989. *The Null Subject Parameter*. Dordrecht: Kluwer.

Jakobson, Roman. 1968 [1941]. *Child Language, Aphasia, and Phonological Universals*. The Hague: Mouton. (Original publication: *Kindersprache, Aphasie und allgemeine Lautgesetze*.)

Jakobson, Roman, Fant, Gunnar, and Halle, Morris. 1951. *Preliminaries to Speech Analysis*. Cambridge, MA: MIT Press.

Janis, Wynne. 1992. Morphosyntax of the ASL Verb Phrase. PhD dissertation, SUNY Buffalo.

1995. A Crosslinguistic Perspective on ASL Verb Agreement. In *Language, Gesture, and Space*, eds. Karen Emmorey and Judy Reilly, 195–223. Hillsdale, NJ: Lawrence Erlbaum Associates.

Janzen, Terry. 1998. Topicality in ASL: Information ordering, constituent structure, and the function of topic marking. PhD dissertation, University of New Mexico.

1999. The grammaticization of topics in American Sign Language. *Studies in Language* 23: 271–306.

Janzen, Terry, and Shaffer, Barbara. 2002. Gesture as the substrate in the process of ASL grammaticization. In *Modality and Structure in Signed and Spoken Languages*, eds. Richard P. Meier, Kearsy Cormier, and David Quinto-Pozos, 199–223. Cambridge: Cambridge University Press.

Johnston, Trevor, and Schembri, Adam. 1999. On defining lexeme in a signed language. *Sign Language & Linguistics* 2: 115–185.

Kahn, Daniel. 1976. Syllable-based generalizations in English phonology. PhD dissertation, MIT.

Kamp, Hans, and Reyle, Uwe. 1993. *From Discourse to Logic: Introduction to Model Theoretic Semantics of Natural Language, Formal Logic and Discourse Representation Theory*. Dordrecht: Kluwer.

Kayne, Richard. 1994. *The Antisymmetry of Syntax*. Cambridge, MA: MIT Press.

Kegl, Judy. 1976. Relational grammar and American Sign Language. Ms.

1986. Clitics in American Sign Language. In *Syntax and Semantics*, Volume 19: *The Syntax of Pronominal Clitics*, ed. Hagit Borer. New York: Academic Press.

1990. Predicate argument structure and verb-class organization in the ASL lexicon. In *Sign Language Research: Theoretical Issues*, ed. Ceil Lucas, 149–175. Washington, DC: Gallaudet University Press.

2003 [1976]. Pronominalization in American Sign Language. *Sign Language and Linguistics* 6.2: 245–265. (Originally distributed as ms.).

Kegl, Judy, Neidle, Carol, MacLaughlin, Dawn, Hoza, Jack, and Bahan, Benjamin. 1996. The case for grammar, order and position in ASL: a reply to Bouchard and Dubuisson. *Sign Language Studies* 90: 1–23.

Kegl, Judy, Senghas, Ann, and Coppola, Marie. 1999. Creation through contact: sign language emergence and sign language change in Nicaragua. In *Language Creation and Language Change: Creolization, Diachrony, and Development*, ed. Michel DeGraff, 197–237. Cambridge, MA: MIT Press.

Kegl, Judy, and Wilbur, Ronnie B. 1976. When does structure stop and style begin? Syntax, morphology, and phonology vs. stylistic variation in ASL. Paper presented at the 12th Regional Meeting, Chicago Linguistic Society, Chicago.

Kenstowicz, Michael. 1985. The phonology and syntax of wh-expressions in Tangale. *Studies in Linguistic Science* 15: 79–91.

1994. *Phonology in Generative Grammar*. Cambridge, MA: Blackwell.

Kingston, John. 1999. Extrapolating from spoken to signed prosody. *Language & Speech* 7: 251–282.

Kiparsky, Paul. 1982. Lexical phonology and morphology. In *Linguistics in the Morning Calm*, ed. I. S. Yang, 3–91. Seoul: Hanshin.

2002. Paradigm effects and opacity. Ms. Stanford University.

Kisch, Shifra. 2000. Deaf Discourse: social construction of deafness in a Bedouin community in the Negev. MA thesis. Tel Aviv University.

Kita, Sotaro. 1997. Two-dimensional semantic analysis of Japanese mimetics. *Linguistics* 35: 379–415.

Klima, Edward S. 1964. Negation in English. In *The Structure of Language: Readings in the Philosophy of Language*, eds. J. A. Fodor and J. J. Katz, 246–323. Englewood Cliffs, NJ: Prentice-Hall.

Klima, Edward S., and Bellugi, Ursula. 1979. *The Signs of Language*. Cambridge, MA: Harvard University Press.

Kooij, Els van der. 1998. The position of unselected fingers. In *Linguistics in the Netherlands 1998*, ed. R. van Bezooijen and R. Kager, 149–162. Amsterdam: John Benjamins.

2002. Phonological categories in Sign Language of the Netherlands: the role of phonetic implementation and iconicity. PhD dissertation, Leiden University.

Koopman, Hilda. 1984. *The Syntax of Verbs: From Movement Rules in the Kru Languages to Universal Grammar*. Dordrecht: Foris.

Koopman, Hilda, and Sportiche, Dominique. 1989. Pronouns, logical variables, and logophoricity in Abe. *Linguistic Inquiry* 20: 555–588.

1991. The position of subjects. *Lingua* 85: 211–258.

Koster, J., and Reuland, Eric J. eds. 1991. *Long Distance Anaphora*. Cambridge: Cambridge University Press.

Kouwenberg, Silvia. 2003. *Twice as Meaningful: Reduplication in Pidgins, Creoles, and other Contact Languages*. London: Battlebridge.

Krakow, Rena, and Hanson, Vicki. 1985. Deaf signers and serial recall in the visual modality: memory for signs, fingerspelling and print. *Memory and Cognition* 13: 265–272.

Kuroda, S.-Y. 1983. What can Japanese say about government and binding? In *Proceedings of the West Coast Conference on Formal Linguistics*, eds. Michael Barlow, Daniel P. Flickinger and Michael T. Wescoat, 153–164. Stanford: Stanford Linguistics Association.

1988. Whether we agree or not: a comparative syntax of English and Japanese. In *Papers from the Second International Workshop on Japanese Syntax*, ed. W. J. Poser, 103–143. Stanford, CA: CSLI.

Kyle, J. G., and Woll, B. 1985. *Sign Language: The Study of Deaf People and Their Language*. Cambridge: Cambridge University Press.

Ladd, Robert. 1996. *Intonational Phonology*. Cambridge: Cambridge University Press.

Laka Mugarza, Miren Itziar. 1990. Negation in Syntax: On the Nature of Functional Categories and Projections. PhD Dissertation, MIT.

Lane, Harlan, and Philip, F. eds. 1984. *The Deaf Experience: Classics in Language and Education*. Cambridge, MA: Harvard University Press.

Langacker, Ronald. 1969. Pronominalization and the chain of command. In *Modern Studies in English*, eds. D. A. Reibel and S. C. Schane, 160–186. Englewood Cliffs, NJ: Prentice-Hall.

Langdon, M. 1970. *A Grammar of The Mesa Grande Dialect*. Berkeley and Los Angeles: University of California Press.

Lasnik, Howard. 1995. Verbal morphology: syntactic structures meets the Minimalist Program. In *Evolution and Revolution in Linguistic Theory: Essays in Honor of Carlos Otero*, eds. H. Campos and P. Kempchinsky, 251–275. Georgetown: Georgetown University Press.

Lasnik, Howard, and Uriagereka, Juan. 1988. *A Course in GB Syntax*. Cambridge, MA: MIT Press.

Lee, Robert G., Neidle, Carol, MacLaughlin, Dawn, Bahan, Benjamin, and Kegl, Judy. 1997. Role shift in ASL: A syntactic look at direct speech. In *Syntactic Structure and Discourse Function: An Examination of Two Constructions in American Sign Language*, eds. C. Neidle, D. MacLaughlin and R. G. Lee, 24–45. Boston, MA: American Sign Language Linguistic Research Project, Boston University.

Legate, Julie Anne. 2003. Arguments and adjuncts in Warlpiri. Paper presented at the University of Connecticut, February 2003.

Lehmann, Christian. 1988. On the function of agreement. In *Agreement in Natural Language*, eds. Michael Barlow and Charles A. Ferguson, 55–66. Stanford: CSLI.

Lentz, Ella Mae. 1986. Teaching role shifting. In *Proceedings of the Fourth National Symposium on Sign Language Research and Teaching*, ed. Carol Padden. Silver Spring, MD: National Association of the Deaf.

Levy, Doron. 2001. Weak drop in Israeli Sign Language. Ms. Tel Aviv.

Li, Charles, and Thompson, Sandra. 1976. Subject and topic: a new typology of language. In *Subject and Topic*, ed. Charles Li, 457–489. New York: Academic Press.

1981. *Mandarin Chinese: A Functional Reference Grammar*. Berkeley: University of California Press.

Liberman, Alvin. 1996. *Speech: A Special Code*. Cambridge, MA: MIT Press.

Liddell, Scott K. 1978. Non-manual signs and relative clauses in American Sign Language. In *Understanding Language through Sign Language Research*, ed. P. Siple, 59–90. New York: Academic Press.

1980. *American Sign Language Syntax*. The Hague: Mouton.

1984a. Unrealized-inceptive aspect in American Sign Language: feature insertion in syllabic frames. *Papers from the Chicago Linguistic Society*, 257–270.

1984b. THINK and BELIEVE: sequentiality in American Sign Language. *Language* 60: 372–392.

1986. Head thrust in ASL conditional marking. *Sign Language Studies* 15.52: 243–262.

1990a. Four functions of a locus: reexamining the structure of Space in ASL. In *Sign Language Research: Theoretical Issues*, ed. Ceil Lucas, 176–198. Washington, DC: Gallaudet University Press.

1990b. Structures for representing handshape and local movement at the phonemic level. In *Theoretical Issues in Sign Language Research*, eds. Susan Fischer and Patricia Siple, 37–65. Chicago: Chicago University Press.

1994. Tokens and surrogates. In *Perspectives on Sign Language Structure: Papers from the Fifth International Symposium on Sign Language Research*, eds. Inger Ahlgren, Brita Bergman, and Mary Brennan, 105–119. Durham: International Sign Linguistics Association.

1995. Real, surrogate, and token space: grammatical consequences in ASL. In *Language, Gesture, and Space*, eds. Karen Emmorey and Judy Reilly, 19–41. Hillsdale, NJ: Lawrence Erlbaum Associates.

2000. Indicating verbs and pronouns: pointing away from agreement. In *The Signs of Language Revisited: An Anthology to Honor Ursula Bellugi and*

Edward Klima, eds. Karen Emmorey and Harlan Lane, 303–320. Mahwah, NJ: Lawrence Erlbaum Associates.

2003. Sources of meaning in ASL classifier predicates. In *Perspectives on Classifier Constructions in Sign Language*, ed. Karen Emmorey. Mahwah, NJ: Lawrence Erlbaum Associates.

Liddell, Scott K., and Johnson, Robert E. 1986. American Sign Language compound formation processes, lexicalization, and phonological remnants. *Natural Language and Linguistic Theory* 8: 445–513.

1989 [1985]. American Sign Language: the phonological base. *Sign Language Studies* 64: 197–277. (Originally distributed as ms.).

Lillo-Martin, Diane. 1985. Null pronouns and verb agreement in American Sign Language. In *Proceedings of NELS 15*, eds. S. Berman, J.-W. Choe, and J. McDonough, 302–318. Amherst: GLSA.

1986a. Two kinds of null arguments in American Sign Language. *Natural Language and Linguistic Theory* 4: 415–444.

1986b. Parameter setting: evidence from use, acquisition, and breakdown in American Sign Language. PhD dissertation, University of California, San Diego.

1990. Parameters for questions: evidence from WH-movement in American Sign Language. In *Sign Language Research: Theoretical Issues*, ed. C. Lucas, 211–222. Washington, DC: Gallaudet University Press.

1991. *Universal Grammar and American Sign Language: Setting the Null Argument Parameters*. Studies in Theoretical Psycholinguistics. Dordrecht: Kluwer.

Lillo-Martin, Diane. 1992. Sentences as islands: on the boundedness of A′-movement in American Sign Language. In *Island Constraints*, eds. Helen Goodluck and M. Rochemont, 259–274. Dordrecht: Kluwer.

1995. The point of view predicate in American Sign Language. In *Language, Gesture, and Space*, eds. Karen Emmorey and Judy Reilly, 155–170. Hillsdale, NJ: Lawrence Erlbaum Associates.

1997. The modular effects of sign language acquisition. In *Relations of Language and Thought: The View from Sign Language and Deaf Children*, eds. Marc Marschark, Patricia Siple, Diane Lillo-Martin, Ruth Campbell, and Victoria Everhart, 62–109. New York: Oxford University Press.

1999a. Modality effects and modularity in language acquisition: the acquisition of American Sign Language. In *Handbook of Language Acquisition*, eds. William C. Ritchie and Tej K. Bhatia, 531–567. San Diego, CA: Academic Press.

1999b. Syntactic aspects of intonation. Paper presented at the Linguistic Society of America Annual Meeting.

2002. Where are all the modality effects? In *Modality and Structure in Signed Language and Spoken Language*, eds. Richard Meier, Kearsy Cormier, and David Quinto-Pozos, 241–262. Cambridge: Cambridge University Press.

Lillo-Martin, Diane, and Fischer, Susan. 1992. Overt and covert wh-questions in American Sign Language. Paper presented at the Fifth International Symposium on Sign Language Research, Salamanca, Spain.

Lillo-Martin, Diane, and Klima, Edward S. 1990. Pointing out differences: ASL pronouns in syntactic theory. In *Theoretical Issues in Sign Language Research*,

Volume 1: *Linguistics*, eds. Susan D. Fischer and Patricia Siple, 191–210. Chicago: University of Chicago Press.

Lobeck, Anne. 1986. VP Ellipsis in infinitives: INFL as a proper governor. *NELS* 17: 425– 442.

1990. Functional heads as proper governors. Paper presented at *NELS 20*.

Loew, Ruth. 1984. Roles and reference in American Sign Language: a developmental perspective. PhD dissertation, University of Minnesota.

Lucas, Ceil. 1995. Sociolinguistic variation in ASL: the case of DEAF. In *Sign Language Research 1994*, eds. H. Bos and T. Schermer, 189–210. Hamburg: Signum.

Lucas, Ceil, and Valli, Clayton. 1992. *Linguistics of American Sign Language: A Resource Text for ASL Users*. Washington, DC: Gallaudet University Press.

MacLaughlin, Dawn. 1997. The structure of determiner phrases: evidence from American Sign Language. PhD dissertation, Boston University.

MacNeilage, Peter. 1998. Evolution of the mechanism of language output: comparative neurobiology of vocal and manual communication. In *Approaches to the Evolution of Language: Social and Cognitive Bases*, eds. James R. Hurford, Michael Studdert-Kennedy, and Chris Knight, 222–241. Cambridge: Cambridge University Press.

Mandel, Mark. 1977. Iconic devices in American Sign Language. In *On the Other Hand: New Perspectives on American Sign Language*, ed. Lynn A. Friedman. New York: Academic Press.

1981. Phonotactics and morphophonology in American Sign Language. PhD dissertation, University of California.

Marantz, Alec. 1982. Re reduplication. *Linguistic Inquiry* 13: 435–482.

Mathur, Gaurav. 2000. Verb agreement as alignment in signed languages. PhD dissertation, MIT.

Mathur, Gaurav, and Rathmann, Christian. 2001. Why not GIVE-US: an articulatory constraint in signed languages. In *Signed Languages: Discoveries from International Research*, eds. V. Dively, M. Metzger, S. Taub, and A. Baer, 1–25. Washington, DC: Gallaudet University Press.

Matsuoka, Kazumi. 1997. Verb raising in American Sign Language. *Lingua* 103: 127–149.

2000. The lexical verb sandwich in American Sign Language and the hybrid feature. Ms.

Matthews, P. H. (Peter Hugoe). 1974. *Morphology: An Introduction to the Theory of Word Structure*. Cambridge: Cambridge University Press.

McBurney, Susan. 2002. Pronominal reference in signed and spoken language: are grammatical categories modality-dependent? In *Modality and Structure in Signed and Spoken Languages*, eds. Richard Meier, Kearsy Cormier, and David Quinto-Pozos, 329–369. Cambridge: Cambridge University Press.

McCarthy, John. 1979. Formal Problems in Semitic Phonology and Morphology. PhD dissertation, MIT.

1981. A prosodic theory of nonconcatenative morphology. *Linguistic Inquiry* 12: 373–418.

1988. Feature geometry and dependency: a review. *Phonetica* 43: 84–108.

McCarthy, John, and Prince, Alan. 1986. Prosodic morphology. Ms. University of Massachusetts, Amherst, and Brandeis University.

1993. Prosodic morphology I: constraint interaction and satisfaction. Ms. University of Massachusetts, Amherst, and Rutgers University.

1994. The emergence of the unmarked: optimality in prosodic morphology. In *Proceedings of the North Eastern Linguistic Society 24*, ed. M. González, 333–379.

1995. Prosodic morphology. In *The Handbook of Phonological Theory*, ed. John Goldsmith, 318–366. Oxford: Blackwell.

McCloskey, James, and Hale, Ken. 1984. The syntax of person-number inflection in Modern Irish. *Natural Language and Linguistic Theory* 1: 487–533.

McDonald, B. 1982. Aspects of the American Sign Language predicate system. PhD dissertation, University of Buffalo.

McIntire, Marina. 1977. The acquisition of ASL hand configurations. *Sign Language Studies* 16: 247–260.

McKee, David, and Kennedy, Graeme. 2000. Lexical comparison of signs from American, Australian, British, and New Zealand Sign Languages. In *The Signs of Language Revisited: An Anthology in Honor of Ursula Bellugi and Edward Klima*, eds. Karen Emmorey and Harlan Lane, 49–76. Mahwah, NJ: Lawrence Erlbaum Associates.

McLemore, Cynthia. 1991. The pragmatic interpretation of English intonation: sorority speech. PhD dissertation, University of Texas.

McNeill, David. 1992. *Hand and Mind: What Gesture Reveals about Thought*. Chicago: University of Chicago Press.

McWhorter, John. 1998. Identifying the creole prototype: vindicating a typological class. *Language* 74: 788–818.

Mehler, Jacques, Jusczyk, R., Lamberz, G., Halsted, G., Bertoncini, J., and Amiel-Tison, C. 1988. A precursor of language acquisition in young infants. *Cognition* 29.2: 143–178.

Meier, Richard P. 1981. Icons and morphemes: models of the acquisition of verb agreement in ASL. *Papers and Reports on Child Language Development* 20: 92–99.

1982. Icons, analogues, and morphemes: the acquisition of verb agreement in ASL. PhD dissertation, University of California, San Diego.

1987. Elicited imitation of verb agreement in American Sign Language: iconically or morphologically determined? *Journal of Memory and Language* 26: 362–376.

1990. Person deixis in American Sign Language. In *Theoretical Issues in Sign Language Research*, eds. Susan D. Fischer and Patricia Siple, 175–190. Chicago: University of Chicago Press.

1993. A psychologinguistic perspective on phonological segmentation in sign and speech. In *Current Issues in ASL Phonology*, ed. G. Coulter, 169–188. San Diego, CA: Academic Press.

2002a. The acquisition of verb agreement: pointing out arguments for the linguistic status of agreement in signed languages. In *Current Developments in the Study of Signed Language Acquisition*, eds. Gary Morgan and Bencie Woll, 115–141. Amsterdam: John Benjamins.

2002b. Why different, why the same? Explaining effects and non-effects of modality upon linguistic structure in sign and speech. In *Modality and*

Structure in Signed Language and Spoken Language, eds. Richard Meier, Kearsy Cormier, and David Quinto-Pozos, 1–25. Cambridge: Cambridge University Press.

Meier, Richard P., and Willerman, Raquel. 1995. Prelinguistic gesture in deaf and hearing infants. In *Language, Gesture, and Space*, eds. Karen Emmorey and Judy Reilly, 391–410. Hillsdale, NJ: Lawrence Erlbaum Associates.

Meir, Irit. 1998a. Thematic structure and verb agreement in Israeli Sign Language. PhD dissertation, Hebrew University of Jerusalem.

1998b. Syntactic-semantic interaction of Israeli Sign Language verbs: the case of backwards verbs. *Sign Language & Linguistics* 1: 3–37.

1999. Verb classifiers as noun incorporation in Israeli Sign Language. *Yearbook of Morphology 1999*: 299–319.

2002. A cross-modality perspective on verb agreement. *Natural Language and Linguistic Theory* 20.2: 413–450.

2003. Grammaticalization and modality: the emergence of a case marked pronoun in Israeli Sign Language. *Journal of Linguistics* 39.1: 109–140.

Meir, Irit, and Sandler, Wendy. 2004. *Language in Space: A Window on Israeli Sign Language (Hebrew)*. Haifa: University of Haifa Press.

Miller, Christopher. 1991. Une théorie prosodique de la phonologie des langues des signes. *Revue Québecoise de Linguistique Théoretique et Appliquée* 10: 21–55.

1994. Simultaneous constructions in Quebec Sign Language. In *Perspectives on Sign Language Structure: Papers from the Fifth International Symposium on Sign Language Research*, Volume 1, eds. Inger Ahlgren, Brita Bergman, and Mary Brennan, 131–147. Durham: ISLA.

1996. Phonologie de la langue des signes Québequois: structure simultanée et axe temporal. PhD dissertation, Université du Québec à Montréal.

Mithun, Marianne. 1984. The evolution of noun incorporation. *Language* 60: 847–895.

1986a. The convergence of noun classification systems. In *Noun Classes and Categorization* (Typological Studies in Language 7), ed. Colette Craig, 379–397. Amsterdam: John Benjamins.

1986b. On the nature of noun incorporation. *Language* 62: 32–38.

Moravcsik, Edith. 1988. Agreement and markedness. In *Agreement in Natural Language*, eds. M. Barlow and Charles A. Ferguson, 89–106. Stanford, CA: CSLI.

Murasugi, Keiko. 1991. Noun Phrases in Japanese and English: A Study in Syntax, Learnability, and Acquisition. PhD dissertation, University of Connecticut.

Nadeau, Marie, and Desouvrey, Louis. 1994. Word order in sentences with directional verbs in Quebec Sign Language. In *Perspectives on sign language structure: Papers from the Fifth International Symposium on Sign Language Research*, Volume 1, eds. Inger Ahlgren, Brita Bergman, and Mary Brennan, 149–158. Durham: International Sign Linguistics Association.

Nagahara, Hiroyki. 1988. Towards an explicit phonological representation for American Sign Language. MA thesis, University of California.

Neidle, Carol. 2002. Language across modalities: ASL focus and question constructions. *Linguistic Variation Yearbook* 2: 71–98.

Neidle, Carol, Bahan, Benjamin, MacLaughlin, Dawn, Lee, Robert G., and Kegl, Judy. 1998a. Realizations of syntactic agreement in American Sign Language: similarities between the clause and the noun phrase. *Studia Linguistica* 52: 191–226.

Neidle, Carol, Kegl, Judy, Bahan, Ben, Aarons, Debra, and MacLaughlin, Dawn. 1997. Rightward WH-movement in American Sign Language. In *Rightward Movement*, eds. D. Beerman, D. LeBlanc, and H. vanRiemsdijk, 247–278. Amsterdam: John Benjamins.

Neidle, Carol, Kegl, Judy, MacLaughlin, Dawn, Bahan, Benjamin, and Lee, Robert G. 2000. *The Syntax of American Sign Language: Functional Categories and Hierarchical Structure*. Cambridge, MA: MIT Press.

Neidle, Carol, MacLaughlin, Dawn, Lee, Robert G., Bahan, Benjamin, and Kegl, Judy. 1998b. The right(ward) analysis of *wh*-movement in ASL. *Language* 74: 819–831.

Nespor, Marina, and Vogel, Irene. 1986. *Prosodic Phonology*. Dordrecht: Foris.

Nespor, Marina, and Sandler, Wendy. 1999. Prosody in Israeli Sign Language. *Language and Speech* 42: 143–176.

Nettle, Daniel. 1995. Segmental inventory size, word length, and communicative efficiency. *Linguistics* 33: 359–367.

Newkirk, Don. 1978. The form of multiples and exhaustives in ASL. Ms.

1979. The form of continuative aspect inflection on ASL verbs. Ms.

1981. Rhythmic features of inflections in American Sign Language. Ms.

1998 [1981]. On the temporal segmentation of movement in American Sign Language. *Sign Language & Linguistics* 1: 173–212. (Originally distributed as ms.).

Newkirk, Don, Klima, Ed, Pedersen, Carlene Canady, and Bellugi, Ursula. 1980. Linguistic evidence from slips of the hand. In *Errors in Linguistic Performance: Slips of the Tongue and Hand*, ed. V. Fromkin. New York: Academic Press.

Newport, Elissa L. 1981. Constraints on structure: evidence from American Sign Language and language learning. In *Aspects of the Development of Competence. Minnesota Symposia on Child Psychology*, ed. W. A. Collins. Hillsdale, NJ: Lawrence Erlbaum Associates.

Newport, Elissa L., and Meier, Richard P. 1985. The acquisition of American Sign Language. In *The Cross-Linguistic Study of Language Acquisition*, ed. Dan I. Slobin, 881–938. Hillsdale, NJ: Lawrence Erlbaum Associates.

Newport, Elissa L., and Supalla, Ted. 2000. Sign language research at the millennium. In *The Signs of Language Revisited: An Anthology to Honor Ursula Bellugi and Edward Klima*, eds. Karen Emmorey and Harlan Lane, 103–114. Mahway, NJ: Lawrence Erlbaum Associates.

Nunes, Jairo. 1999. Linearization of chains and phonetic realization of chain links. In *Working Minimalism*, eds. Samuel David Epstein and Norbert Hornstein, 217–249. Cambridge, MA: MIT Press.

2004. *Linearization of Chains and Sideward Movement*. Cambridge, MA: MIT Press.

Nunes, Jairo and Quadros, Ronice. 2004. Phonetic realization of multiple copies in Brazilian Sign Language. Presented at Theoretical Issues in Sign Language Research (TISLR VIII), Barcelona.

Odden, David. 1980. Associative tone in Shona. *Journal of Linguistic Research* 1.2: 37–51.

Ohala, John. 1984. An ethological perspective on common cross-language utilization of F0 of voice. *Phonetica* 41: 1–16.

Ortiz de Urbina, J. 1989. *Parameters in the Grammar of Basque*. Dordrecht, Holland: Foris Publications.

Osugi, Yutaka. 1997. In search of the phonological representation of ASL. PhD dissertation, University of Rochester.

Ouhalla, J. 1990. Sentential negation, Relativized Minimality, and the aspectual status of auxiliaries. *The Linguistic Review* 7: 183–231.

Padden, Carol A. 1986. Verbs and role-shifting in American Sign Language. In *Proceedings of the Fourth National Symposium on Sign Language Research and Teaching*, ed. Carol Padden. Silver Spring, MD: National Association of the Deaf.

1988 [1983]. *Interaction of Morphology and Syntax in American Sign Language*: Outstanding Dissertations in Linguistics. New York: Garland. (Originally distributed as: PhD dissertation, University of California, San Diego.)

1990. The relation between space and grammar in ASL verb morphology. In *Sign Language Research: Theoretical Issues*, ed. Ceil Lucas, 118–132. Washington, DC: Gallaudet University Press.

1998. The ASL lexicon. *Sign Language & Linguistics* 1: 39–64.

Padden, Carol A., and Humphries, Tom. 1988. *Deaf in America: Voices from a Culture*. Cambridge, MA: Harvard University Press.

2005. *Inside Deaf Culture*. Cambridge, MA: Harvard University Press.

Padden, Carol A., and Perlmutter, David. 1987. American Sign Language and the architecture of phonological theory. *Natural Language and Linguistic Theory* 5: 335–375.

Parisot, Anne-Marie. 2000. Do plain verbs agree in Quebec Sign Language? Ms. Amsterdam.

Perlmutter, David. ed 1983. *Studies in Relational Grammar I*. Chicago: University of Chicago Press.

1991. Feature geometry in a language with two active articulators. Ms. Santa Cruz.

1992. Sonority and syllable structure in American Sign Language. *Linguistic Inquiry* 23: 407–442. Reprinted as: Sonority and syllable structure in American Sign Language. In *Phonetics and Phonology*, Volume 3: *Current Issues in ASL Phonology*, ed. G. Coulter. San Diego, CA: Academic Press (1993).

1996. Compounds and lexemes in American Sign Language. Ms.

Perlmutter, David, and Rosen, Carol eds. 1984. *Studies in Relational Grammar II*. Chicago: Chicago University Press.

Pesetsky, David. 1987. Wh-in situ: movement and unselective binding. In *The Representation of (in)Definiteness*, eds. Eric Reuland and Alice ter Meulen, 98–129. Cambridge, MA: MIT Press.

Petronio, Karen. 1991. A focus position in ASL. In *Papers from the Third Student Conference in Linguistics, 1991*, eds. Jonathan D. Bobaljik and Tony Bures, 211–225. Cambridge, MA: MIT Working Papers in Linguistics.

1993. Clause structure in American Sign Language. PhD Dissertation, University of Washington.

Petronio, Karen, and Lillo-Martin, Diane. 1997. Wh-Movement and the position of Spec CP: evidence from American Sign Language. *Language* 73: 18–57.

Pfau, Roland. 2002. Applying morphosyntactic and phonological readjustment rules in natural language negation. In *Modality and Structure in Signed and Spoken Languages*, eds. Richard Meier, Kearsy Cormier, and David Quinto-Pozos, 263–295. Cambridge: Cambridge University Press.

Pfau, Roland, and Quer, Josep. 2003. V-to-Neg raising and negative concord in three sign languages. Paper presented at the XXIX Incontro di Grammatica Generativa, Urbino, February 2003.

Pierrehumbert, Janet. 1980. The phonology and phonetics of English intonation. PhD dissertation, MIT.

Pierrehumbert, Janet, and Hirschberg, Julia. 1990. The meaning of intonational contours in the interpretation of discourse. In *Intentions in communication*, eds. P. Cohen, J. Morgan, and M. Pollack. Cambridge, MA: MIT Press.

Pizzuto, Elena, and Corazza, Serena. 1996. Noun morphology in Italian Sign Language. *Lingua* 98: 169–196.

Pizzuto, Elena, Giuranna, Enza, and Gambino, Giuseppe. 1990. Manual and non-manual morphology in Italian Sign Language: grammatical constraints and discourse processes. In *Sign Language Research. Theoretical Issues*, ed. Ceil Lucas, 83–102. Washington, DC: Gallaudet University Press.

Poizner, Howard, Klima, Edward S., and Bellugi, Ursula. 1987. *What the Hands Reveal about the Brain*. Cambridge, MA: MIT Press.

Pollard, Carl, and Sag, Ivan. 1994. *Head-Driven Phrase Structure Grammar*. Chicago: University of Chicago Press.

Pollock, J.-Y. 1989. Verb movement, UG, and the structure of IP. *Linguistic Inquiry* 20: 365–424.

Poulin, Christine, and Miller, Christopher. 1995. On narrative discourse and point of view in Quebec Sign Language. In *Language, Gesture, and Space*, eds. Karen Emmorey and Judy Reilly, 117–131. Hillsdale, NJ: Lawrence Erlbaum Associates.

Prillwitz, Sigmund. 1989. *HamNoSys: Version 2.0; Hamburg Notational System for Sign Languages. An Introductory Guide*. International Studies on Sign Language and Communication of the deaf 5. Hamburg: Signum.

Prince, Alan, and Smolensky, Paul. 1993. Optimality theory: constraint interaction in generative grammar. Ms. New Brunswick and Boulder.

Prince, E. 1986. On the syntactic marking of presupposed open propositions. *Chicago Linguistic Society* 22: 208–222.

Quadros, Ronice Müller de. 1995. As categorias vazias pronominais: uma análise alternativa com base na língua de sinais brasileira e reflexos no processo de aquisição. MA thesis, Pontifícia Universidade Católica do Rio Grande do Sul.

1999. Phrase structure of Brazilian Sign Language. PhD dissertation, Pontifícia Universidade Católica do Rio Grande do Sul.

Quadros, Ronice Müller de, and Karnopp, Lodenir B. 2004. *Língua de sinais brasileira: estudos lingüísticos*. Porto Alegre: Artes Médicas.

Quadros, Ronice Müller de, Lillo-Martin, Diane, and Chen Pichler, Deborah. 2000. A little change goes a long way: capturing structural differences between Brazilian Sign Language and American Sign Language. Paper presented at the Seventh International Conference on Theoretical Issues in Sign Language Research, Amsterdam.

2004. Clause structure in LSB and ASL. Paper presented at the 26. Jahrestagung der Deutschen Gesellschaft für Sprachwissenschaft, Mainz, Germany.

Quer, Josep. 2003. Operadores negativos en Lengua de Signos Catalana (LSC) (Negative operators in LSC): Presented at the Jornadas del Comahue de

Lingüística de Lenguas de Señas, San Martin de los Andes, Argentina, March 2003.

Rathmann, Christian. 2000. The optionality of agreement phrase: evidence from signed languages. MA report, University of Texas.

Rathmann, Christian, and Mathur, Gaurav. 1999. The linguistic status of joint-based constraints in signed languages. Paper presented at The 35th Annual Chicago Linguistics Society Meeting.

2002. Is verb agreement the same cross-modally? In *Modality and Structure in Signed and Spoken Languages*, eds. Richard P. Meier, Kersy Cormier, and David Quinto-Pozos, 370–404. Cambridge: Cambridge University Press.

Reilly, Judy S., and Bellugi, Ursula. 1996. Competition on the face: affect and language in ASL motherese. *Journal of Child Language* 23.

Reilly, Judy S., and McIntire, Marina L. 1991. WHERE SHOE: the acquisition of wh-questions in American Sign Language. *Papers and Reports in Child Language Development* 30: 104–111.

Reilly, Judy S., McIntire, Marina L., and Bellugi, Ursula. 1990a. The acquisition of conditionals in American Sign Language: grammaticized facial expressions. *Applied Psycholinguistics* 11: 369–392.

1990b. Faces: the relationship between language and affect. In *From Gesture to Language in Hearing and Deaf Children*, eds. Virginia Volterra and Carol J. Erting, 128–141. Berlin: Springer-Verlag.

Reinhart, Tanya. 1976. The syntactic domain of anaphora. PhD dissertation, MIT.

Reinhart, Tanya. 1983. *Anaphora and Semantic Interpretation*. London: Croom Helm.

Reinhart, Tanya, and Reuland, Eric J. 1993. Reflexivity. *Linguistic Inquiry* 24: 657–720.

Reuland, Eric J., and Everaert, Martin. 2001. Deconstructing binding. In *The Handbook of Contemporary Syntactic Theory*, eds. Mark Baltin and Chris Collins, 634–669. Malden, MA: Blackwell.

Richards, Norvin. 1997. What moves where when in which language? PhD dissertation, MIT.

Riemsdijk, Henk van, and Williams, Edwin. 1986. *Introduction to the Theory of Grammar*. Cambridge, MA: MIT Press.

Rizzi, Luigi. 1986. Null objects in Italian and the theory of *pro*. *Linguistic Inquiry* 17: 501–557.

1990. *Relativized Minimality*. Cambridge, MA: MIT Press.

1991. Residual verb second and the WH-criterion. Ms., Technical Reports in Formal and Computational Linguistics. Faculté des Lettres, University of Geneva.

1997. The fine structure of the left periphery. In *Elements of Grammar*, ed. L. Haegeman, 281–337. Dordrecht: Kluwer.

Rochemont, M. 1986. *Focus in Generative Grammar*. Philadelphia: John Benjamins.

Romano, Christine. 1991. Mixed headedness in American Sign Language: evidence from functional categories. In *Papers from the Third Student Conference in Linguistics, 1991*, eds. Jonathan D. Bobaljik and Tony Bures, 241–254. Cambridge, MA: MIT Working Papers in Linguistics.

Rosen, Sara Thomas. 1989. Two types of noun incorporation: a lexical analysis. *Language* 65: 294–317.

Rosenstein, Ofra. 2001. ISL as a topic prominent language. MA thesis, University of Haifa.

Ross, J. R. 1967. Constraints on variables in syntax. PhD dissertation, MIT.

Rudin, Catherine. 1988. On multiple questions and multiple WH fronting. *Natural Language and Linguistic Theory* 6: 445–501.

Sagey, Elizabeth. 1986. The representation of features and relations in non-linear phonology. PhD dissertation, MIT.

Saito, Mamoru. 1985. Some asymmetries in Japanese and their theoretical implications. PhD dissertation, MIT.

Sandler, Wendy. 1986. The spreading hand autosegment of American Sign Language. *Sign Language Studies* 50: 1–28.

1987a. Assimilation and feature hierarchy in American Sign Language. In *Papers from the Chicago Linguistic Society, Parasession on Autosegmental and Metrical Phonology*, 266–278. Chicago: Chicago Linguistic Society.

1987b. Sequentiality and simultaneity in American Sign Language. PhD dissertation, University of Texas.

1989. *Phonological Representation of the Sign: Linearity and Non-linearity in American Sign Language*. Dordrecht: Foris.

1990. Temporal aspect and American Sign Language. In *Theoretical Issues in Sign Language Research*, eds. S. Fischer and P. Siple, 103–129. Chicago: University of Chicago Press.

1993a. Hand in hand: the roles of the non-dominant hand in sign language phonology. *The Linguistic Review* 10: 337–390.

1993b. Linearization of phonological tiers in American Sign Language. In *Phonetics and Phonology*, Volume 3: *Current Issues in ASL Phonology*, ed. G. Coulter. San Diego, CA: Academic Press.

1993c. Sign language and modularity. *Lingua* 89: 315–351.

1993d. A sonority cycle in American Sign Language. *Phonology* 10: 243–279.

1995a. One phonology or two? Sign language and phonological theory. *GLOT International* 1. Reprinted in *The GLOT International State-of-the-Article Book*, eds. L. Cheng and R. Sybesma, 349–384. Berlin: Mouton de Gruyter (2000).

1995b. Phonological characteristics of sign languages: Similarities and differences. *Trondheim Working Papers in Linguistics* 23: 18–37.

1995c. Markedness in the handshapes of signs: a componential analysis. In *Leiden in Last: Holland Institute of Linguistics Phonology Papers*, eds. Jeroen van der Weijer and Harry van der Hulst, 369–399. The Hague: Holland Academie Graphics.

1996a. Representing handshapes. *International Review of Sign Linguistics* 1: 115–158.

1996b. Phonological features and feature classes: the case of movements in sign language. *Lingua* 98: 197–220.

1996c. A negative suffix in ASL. Ms.

1999a. Prosody in two natural language modalities. *Language and Speech* 42: 127–142.

1999b. Cliticization and prosodic words in a sign language. In *Studies on the Phonological Word*, eds. T. Hall and U. Kleinhenz, 223–254. Amsterdam: Benjamins.

1999c. The medium and the message: prosodic interpretation of linguistic content in Israeli Sign Language. *Sign Language & Linguistics* 2: 187–216.

2003. On the complementarity of signed and spoken languages. In *Language Competence across Populations*, eds. Y. Levy and J. Schaeffer, 383–409. Mahwah, NJ: Lawrence Erlbaum Associates.

In press. Phonology, phonetics, and the non-dominant hand. In *Papers in Laboratory Phonology: Varieties of Phonological Competence*, eds. Louis Goldstein, Douglas Whalen, and Catherine Best. Berlin: Mouton-deGruyter.

Sandler, Wendy, and Dachkovsky, Svetlana. 2004. Superarticulation in Israeli Sign Language: the grammar of the face. Ms.

Sandler, Wendy, and Lillo-Martin, Diane. 2001. Natural sign languages. In *The Handbook of Linguistics*, eds. Mark Aronoff and Jamie Rees-Miller, 533–562. Malden, MA: Blackwell.

Sandler, Wendy, Meir, Irit, Padden, Carol, and Aronoff, Mark. 2005. The emergence of grammar: systematic structure in a new language. *Proceedings of the National Academy of Sciences*. 102.7: 2661–2665.

Sauvageot, S. 1967. Note sur la classification nominale en Bainouk. In *La classification nominales dans les langues Négro-Africaines*, 225–236. Paris: CNRS.

Schembri, Adam. 2003. Rethinking "classifiers" in signed languages. In *Perspectives on Classifier Constructions in Sign Languages*, ed. Karen, Emmorey, 3–34. Mahwah, NJ: Lawrence Erlbaum Associates.

Schick, Brenda S. 1987. The acquisition of classifier predicates in American Sign Language. PhD dissertation, Purdue University.

1990. Classifier predicates in American Sign Language. *International Journal of Sign Linguistics* 1: 15–40.

Selkirk, Elizabeth. 1984. *Phonology and Syntax: The Relation Between Sound and Structure*. Cambridge, MA: MIT Press.

Sells, Peter. 1987. Aspects of logophoricity. *Linguistic Inquiry* 18: 445–479.

Senft, Gunter, ed. 2000a. *Systems of Nominal Classification: Language, Culture, and Cognition*. Cambridge: Cambridge University Press.

2000b. What do we really know about nominal classification systems? In *Systems of Nominal Classification*, ed. Gunter Senft. Cambridge: Cambridge University Press.

Senghas, Ann. 1995. Children's contribution to the birth of Nicaraguan Sign Language. PhD dissertation, MIT.

2000. The development of early spatial morphology in Nicaraguan Sign Language. In *Proceedings of the Boston University Conference on Language Development*, eds. S. C. Howell, S. A. Fish and T. Keith-Lucas, 696–707. Boston: Cascadilla Press.

Shepard-Kegl, Judy. 1985. Locative relations in ASL word formation, syntax and discourse. PhD dissertation, MIT.

Shi, Dingxu. 2000. Topic and topic-comment constructions in Mandarin Chinese. *Language* 76: 383–408.

Shlonsky, Ur. 1992. Resumptive pronouns as a last resort. *Linguistic Inquiry* 23: 443–468.

Siedlecki, Theodore, and Bonvillian, John D. 1993. Phonological deletion revisited: errors in young children's two-handed signs. *Sign Language Studies* 80: 223–242.

1997. Young children's acquisition of the handshape aspect of American Sign Language signs: parental report findings. *Applied Psycholinguistics* 18: 17–39.

Siple, Patricia. 1978. Visual constraints for sign language communication. *Sign Language Studies* 7: 95–110.

Skorik, I. P. 1977. *Grammatike Cukotskogo Jazyka. Tom 2* [A Grammar of Chukchee Volume 2, Russian]. Moscow: Izdatel'stro Akademii Nauk.

Slobin, Dan, Hoiting, Nini, Kuntze, Marlon, Lindert, Reyna B., Weinberg, Amy M., Pyers, Jennie E., Thumann, Helen, and Biederman, Yael. 2003. A cognitive/functional perspective on the acquisition of "classifiers." In *Perspectives on Classifier Constructions in Sign Language*, ed. Karen Emmorey, 271–296. Mahwah, NJ: Lawrence Erlbaum Associates.

Smith, Wayne. 1990. Evidence for auxiliaries in Taiwan Sign Language. In *Theoretical Issues in Sign Language Research*, Volume 1: *Linguistics*, eds. Susan D. Fischer and Patricia Siple, 211–228. Chicago: University of Chicago Press.

Snyder, William. 2001. On the nature of syntactic variation: evidence from complex predicates and complex word-formation. *Language* 77: 324–342.

Spencer, Andrew. 1991. *Morphological Theory: An Introduction to Word Structure in Generative Grammar*. Oxford: Basil Blackwell.

Stack, Kelly. 1988. Tiers and syllable structure: evidence from phonotactics. MA thesis, University of California.

Stevens, Kenneth, and Keyser, Samuel. 1989. Primary features and their enhancement in consonants. *Language* 65: 81–106.

Stjepanović, Sandra. 1999. What do second position cliticization, scrambling, and multiple wh-fronting have in common? PhD dissertation, University of Connecticut.

Stokoe, William C. 1960. Sign language structure: an outline of the visual communication systems of the American deaf. In *Studies in Linguistics: Occasional Papers*. Buffalo: University of Buffalo.

Stokoe, William C., Casterline, Dorethy, and Croneberg, Carl. 1965. *A Dictionary of American Sign Language on Linguistic Principles*. Washington, DC: Gallaudet College Press. [Reprinted in 1976 by Linstok Press.]

Stowell, Timothy. 1991. Determiners in NP and DP. In *Views on Phrase Structure*, eds. K. Leffel and D. Bouchard, 37–56. Dordrecht: Kluwer.

Supalla, Ted. 1982. Structure and acquisition of verbs of motion and location in American Sign Language. PhD dissertation, University of California, San Diego.

1986. The classifier system in American Sign Language. In *Noun Classes and Categorization*, ed. Collette Craig, 181–214. Philadelphia: John Benjamins.

1998. Reconstructing early ASL grammar through historic films. Ms.

Supalla, Ted, and Newport, Elissa. 1978. How many seats in a chair? The derivation of nouns and verbs in American Sign Language. In *Understanding Language Through Sign Language Research*, ed. P. Siple, 91–132. New York: Academic Press.

Supalla, Ted, and Webb, Rebecca. 1995. The grammar of international sign: a new look at pidgin languages. In *Language, Gesture, and Space (International Conference on Theoretical Issues in Sign Language Research)*, eds. Karen Emmorey and Judy S. Reilly, 333–352. Hillsdale, NJ: Erlbaum.

Sutton-Spence, Rachel. 2000. Aspects of BSL poetry: a social and linguistic analysis of the poetry of Dorothy Miles. *Sign Language & Linguistics* 3: 79–100.

Sutton-Spence, Rachel, and Woll, Bencie. 1999. *The Linguistics of British Sign Language*. Cambridge: Cambridge University Press.

Swart, Henriette de. 1995. Topic and focus. *Glot International* 1. Reprinted in *The First Glot International State-of-the-Article Book*, eds. L. Cheng and R. Sybesma, 105–130. Berlin: Mouton de Gruyter. 2000.

Szabolcsi, A. 1994. The noun phrase. In *Syntax and Semantics*, Volume 27: *The Syntactic Structure of Hungarian*, eds. F. Kiefer and K. É. Kiss, 179–274. San Diego, CA: Academic Press.

Takahashi, Daiko. 1993. Movement of wh-phrase in Japanese. *Natural Language & Linguistic Theory* 11: 655–678.

Talmy, Leonard. 2003. The representation of spatial structure in spoken and signed language: a neural model. *Language & Linguistics* 4.2: 207–250.

Taub, Sarah F. 2001. *Language from the Body: Iconicity and Metaphor in American Sign Language*. Cambridge: Cambridge University Press.

Teervort, B. 1973. Could there be a human sign language? *Semiotica* 9: 347–382.

Thompson, Henry. 1977. The lack of subordination in American Sign Language. In *On the Other Hand: New Perspectives on American Sign Language*, ed. Lynn Friedman, 181–195. New York: Academic Press.

Thompson, Lawrence C. 1965. *A Vietnamese Reference Grammar*. Previously published as Mon-Khymer studies XIII–XIV [1965]. Honolulu: University of Hawai'i Press.

Thompson, Robin, and Emmorey, Karen. 2003. The relationship between eye gaze and verb agreement in American Sign Language: an eye-tracking study. Paper presented at the Linguistic Society of America Annual Meeting.

Thráinsson, Höskuldur. 1994. On the (non-)universality of functional categories. Ms. Harvard University / University of Iceland.

2001. Object shift and scrambling. In *The Handbook of Contemporary Syntactic Theory*, eds. Mark Baltin and Chris Collins, 148–202. Malden, MA: Blackwell.

Torigoe, Takashi. 1994. Resumptive X structures in Japanese Sign Language. In *Perspectives on Sign Language Structure: Papers from the Fifth International Symposium on Sign Language Research*, Volume 1, eds. Inger Ahlgren, Brita Bergman, and Mary Brennan, 187–198. Durham: International Sign Linguistics Association.

Truckenbrodt, Hubert. 1999. Syntactic phrases and phonological phrases. *Linguistic Inquiry* 30: 219–255.

Tuller, Laurice. 1992. The syntax of postverbal focus constructions in Chadic. *Natural Language & Linguistic Theory* 10: 303–334.

Uyechi, Linda. 1996 [1994]. *The Geometry of Visual Phonology*. Stanford, CA: CSLI Publications. (Originally distributed as PhD dissertation, Stanford University.)

Vallduví, Enric. 1992. *The Informational Component*. New York: Garland.

Vallduví, Enric, and Engdahl, Elisabet. 1996. The linguistic realization of information packaging. *Linguistics* 34: 459–519.

Valli, Clayton, and Lucas, Ceil. 1992. *Linguistics of American Sign Language*. Washington, DC: Gallaudet University Press.

van Hoek, Karen. 1992. Conceptual spaces and pronominal reference in American Sign Language. *Nordic Journal of Linguistics* 15: 183–200.

Veinberg, Silvana C., and Wilbur, Ronnie B. 1990. A linguistic analysis of the negative headshake in American Sign Language. *Sign Language Studies* 68: 217–244.

Wallin, Lars. 1983. Compounds in Swedish Sign Language in historical perspective. In *Language in Sign: An International Perspective on Sign Language. Proceedings of the Second International Symposium of Sign Language Research in Bristol, UK in July 1981*, eds. Jim Kyle and Bencie Woll, 56–68. London: Croom Helm.

1994. Polysyntetiska tecken i svenska teckenspråket. [Polysynthetic signs in Swedish Sign Language]. Doctoral dissertation, Stockholms Universitet.

1996. *Polysynthetic signs in Swedish Sign Language* (English edition). Stockholm: University of Stockholm.

Watanabe, Akira. 2001. Wh-in-situ languages. In *The Handbook of Contemporary Syntactic Theory*, eds. Mark Baltin and Chris Collins, 203–225. Malden, MA: Blackwell.

Webelhuth, Gert. 1995. *Government and Binding Theory and the Minimalist Program: Principles and Parameters in Syntactic Theory*. Oxford: Blackwell.

Whittemore, Greg. 1986. The production of ASL signs. PhD dissertation, the University of Texas at Austin.

Wilbur, Ronnie B. 1979. *American Sign Language and Sign Systems: Research and Application*. Baltimore: University Park Press.

1982. A multi-tiered theory of syllable structure for American Sign language. Ms.

1987. *American Sign Language: Linguistic and Applied Dimensions*. Boston, MA: College-Hill Press.

1991. Intonation and focus in American Sign Language. Paper presented at ESCOL '90: the Seventh Eastern States Conference on Linguistics.

1993. Syllables and segments: hold the movement and move the holds! In *Current Issues in ASL Phonology*, ed. Geoffrey R. Coulter, 135–168. New York, San Francisco, London: Academic Press.

1994a. Foregrounding structures in American Sign Language. *Journal of Pragmatics* 22: 647–672.

1994b. Eyeblinks and ASL phrase structure. *Sign Language Studies* 84: 221–240.

1995a. What the morphology of operators looks like: a formal analysis of ASL brow-raise. In *FLSM VI: Proceedings of the Sixth Annual Meeting of the Formal Linguistics Society of Mid-America*, Volume 2: *Syntax II and Semantics/Pragmatics*, eds. L. Gabriele, D. Hardison and R. Westmoreland. Bloomington: Indiana University Linguistics Club.

1995b. Why so-called "rhetorical questions" (RHQs) are neither rhetorical nor questions. In *Sign Language Research 1994: Proceedings of the Fourth European Congress on Sign Language Research*, eds. Heleen Bos and Trude Schermer, 149–169. Hamburg: Signum.

1996. Evidence for the function and structure of wh-clefts in American Sign Language. In *International Review of Sign Linguistics*, eds. William H. Edmondson and Ronnie B. Wilbur, 209–256. Mahwah, NJ: Lawrence Erlbaum Associates.

1997. A prosodic/pragmatic explanation for word order variation in ASL with typological implications. In *Lexical and Syntactical Constructions and the Constructions of Meaning*, eds. Marjolijn Vespoor, Kee Dong Lee, and Eve Sweetser, 89–104. Amsterdam, Philadelphia: Benjamins.

1999a. Stress in ASL: empirical evidence and linguistic issues. *Language and Speech* 42: 229–250.

1999b. A functional journey with a formal ending: what do brow raises do in American Sign Language? In *Functionalism and Formalism in Linguistics*, Volume 2: *Case Studies*, eds. E. Moravcsik, F. Newmeyer, M. Noonan, and K. Wheatley, 295–313. Amsterdam: John Benjamins.

2000. Phonological and prosodic layering of non-manuals in American Sign Language. In *The Signs of Language Revisited*, eds. K. Emmorey and H. Lane, 215–244. Mahwah, NJ: Lawrence Erlbaum Associates.

2002. Phrase structure in ASL and ÖGS. In *Progress In Sign Language Research: in Honor of Sigmund Prillwitz*, eds. Rolf Schulmeister and Honour Reinitzer, 235–247 Signum.

Wilbur, Ronnie B., Klima, Ed, and Bellugi, Ursula. 1983. Roots: on the search for the origins of signs in ASL. In *Proceedings of CLS 19: The Chicago Linguistic Society Parasession on the Interplay of Phonology, Morphology, and Syntax*, eds. J. Richardson, M. Marks, and A. Chukerman, 314–336: Chicago Linguistic Society.

Wilbur, Ronnie B. and Patschke, Cynthia. 1998. Body leans and marking contrast in ASL. *Journal of Pragmatics* 30: 275–303.

1999. Syntactic correlates of brow raise in ASL. *Sign Language & Linguistics* 2: 3–30.

Wilbur, Ronnie B., and Schick, Brenda. 1987. The effects of linguistic stress on sign movement in ASL. *Language and Speech* 30: 301–323.

Wilbur, Ronnie B., and Zelaznik, H. N. 1997. Kinematic correlates of stress and position in ASL. Paper presented at the Annual Meeting of the Linguistic Society of America, Chicago, IL.

Wilcox, Phyllis. 2000. *Metaphor in American Sign Language*. Washington, DC: Gallaudet University Press.

Wilson, M., and Emmorey, Karen. 1997. A visual-spatial "phonological loop" in working memory: evidence from American Sign Language. *Memory and Cognition* 25: 313–320.

Woll, Bencie. 1990. International perspectives on sign language communication. *International Journal of Sign Linguistics* 1.2: 107–120.

2002. The sign that dares to speak its name: echo phonology in British Sign Language (BSL). In *The Hands Are the Head of the Mouth: The Mouth as Articulator in Sign Languages*, eds. P. Boyes-Braem and R. Sutton-Spence, 87–98. Hamburg: Signum.

Wood, Sandra K. 1999. Semantic and syntactic aspects of negation in ASL. MA thesis, Purdue University.

Woodward, James. 1974. Implicational variation in American Sign Language: negative incorporation. *Sign Language Studies* 3: 20–30.

1978. All in the family: kinship lexicalization across sign languages. *Sign Language Studies* 7: 121–138.

Woodward, James C. Jr. and Erting, Carol. 1975. Synchronic variation and historical change in American Sign Language. *Language Sciences* 37: 9–12.

Zanuttini, R. 1997. *Negation and Clausal Structure*. Oxford: Oxford University Press.

Zec, Draga, and Inkelas, Sharon. 1990. Prosodically constrained syntax. In *Phonology-Syntax Connection*, eds. Sharon Inkelas and Draga Zec, 365–378. Chicago: University of Chicago Press.

Zeshan, Ulrike. 2004. Interrogative constructions in signed languages: crosslinguistic perspectives. *Language* 80: 7–39.

Zimmer, June, and Patschke, Cynthia. 1990. A class of determiners in ASL. In *Sign Language Research: Theoretical Issues*, ed. Ceil Lucas, 201–210. Washington, DC: Gallaudet University Press.

Zubizarreta, Maria Luisa. 1998. *Prosody, Focus, and Word Order*. Cambridge, MA: MIT Press.

Zwicky, A. M., and Pullum, G. K. 1983. Cliticization vs. inflection: English n't. *Language* 59: 502–513.

Zwitserlood, Inge. 2003. Classifying hand configurations in Nederlandse Gebarentaal (Sign Language of the Netherlands). PhD dissertation, University of Utrecht.

Index